Praise for Bruno Morchio and
The German Client

"The novel smoothly transitions between events that occurred in 1944 and those in the present day, providing readers with a sobering view of the dangers faced by members of the Italian Resistance movement as well as giving a visceral feel of Italy then and now. Morchio skillfully unfurls a poignant story of survival and betrayal." *Publishers Weekly*

"For mystery fans, Bacci Pagano is one of Italy's most beloved characters." *Vanity Fair*

"In the able intertwining of the past and present, historical events in Nazi occupied Italy come to life . . . The ultimate truth, revealed in the very last pages, will stun the reader." *L'Indice*

"Bacci Pagano is a fixture in the Italian imagination. One grows fond of Bacci. After reading a few of these novels, you find you can no longer do without him." *Il Secolo XIX*

"The plot, the twists, the suspense, the emotions and, above all, the grand finale work together to make this the best novel Morchio has written so far." *Il Giornale di Brescia*

"Bacci Pagano, the noir detective with the heart of gold, always fighting for the underdog." *Il Secolo XIX*

"A masterful tale." *La Repubblica*

"Morchio interweaves the novel's two temporal planes with great narrative mastery. You can taste the places and feel the drama and the emotions." *Bresciaoggi*

"This is the beauty and the distinctive trait of Italian noir. There is more than just crime: history, politics, society, love, friendship." *Telegraph Avenue*

The German Client

Bruno Morchio

Originally Published as *Rossoamaro*

Kazabo Publishing

Translation © 2020 Kazabo Publishing
© 2008 First published in Italy by Garzanti Libri S.p.A.
This edition published in arrangement with Grandi & Associati.

Garamond MT Std 12/16/22

ISBN: 978-1-948104-18-0

Kazabo books are available at special
discounts when purchased in bulk or by
book clubs. Special editions of many of
our books can also be created for
promotional and educational use. Please
visit us at kazabo.com for more
information.

Dedicated to the women and men
who fought on the right side

1.
TILDE

Sestri Ponente, January 1944

She pants and thinks about her woolen stocking. She mended it quickly and now, pushing the pedals of the heavy bicycle and struggling along Sant'Alberto's dirt road, the patch hurts her foot. With these old shoes, it has happened before; when she pulls them off, there will be a blister ready to burst. Clouds escape from her mouth and float in the freezing air to be swallowed by the solid darkness of the night broken only by the stain of yellowish light in front of the wheel. The regular squeak of the chain breaks the silence and sometimes, under the patched tires, the gravel crackles.

Even Sestri, in the distance, is drowned in the dark of the anti-aircraft blackout. As if it were enough to protect it from the apocalypse, when the flying fortresses decide to rain death on a tank factory or a railroad bridge. Sestri is full of factories and railway bridges. Nothing is spared; explosives and incendiaries rain from the sky and houses collapse like card castles. Castles without kings and princesses, but crammed with women, old people, and children. One of her cousins in Genoa died like this, just over a year ago. She was sleeping in her flat in Piazza Bandiera, near the church of Nunziata, and the next morning, she and the house were just gone.

Her thoughts go to Fulvio, *il signorino,* the "little gentleman." He was shot two days ago in Cairo Montenotte along with three other recruits just like him. The newspapers have said nothing, but rumors run faster than ink. She had known him when they were children and since then they had remained friends. Son of a wealthy family, he was one of the few boys she could talk to and trust without the awkwardness of adolescent desire. Perhaps he was shy, or perhaps he was intimidated by Biscia, the tall, blond young man she began dating when she was fifteen.

They had decided to get married right after the war ended. But would this damn war ever end? The scratchy voice of Candidus from Radio Londra says that Americans and Brits are moving up to Rome without finding resistance. But is this true? Italian radio, instead, glorifies the brave Italian soldiers, allies of the German army, victorious in their fight to save the country's honor from the invaders.

She feels burning under her feet. The shoes, with their patched soles made of cardboard, are dry and hard. The effort makes her sweat and the frosty sweat that goes down her back makes her shiver. It's a calm, clear night, with no moon and no wind. Fortunately, the old coat that her mother had turned inside out to hide the signs of wear protects her and it was unnecessary to use an old newspaper to keep out the cold. But the temperature is close to freezing and the cold air slides under her skirt, between her thighs, where the stockings tighten and leave her bare skin uncovered.

She thinks about Biscia waiting for her on Mount Gazzo with his comrades. Commander Grandi was clear. Bombing the fascist headquarters in Sampierdarena hadn't been enough. More guerrilla action was required to restore the confidence of the workers. After the lockout imposed by Basile, the prefect, they had all returned out of fear of losing their jobs. Three men must go to Sestri with their weapons, hide them, and be ready to use them. The partisans of the GAP, the patriotic action groups, must execute Commander Buranello's orders. Although, this time, Olindo didn't seem convinced himself.

She's now pedaling along the cemetery wall. In her shoulder bag are a loaf of black bread and a bag of dried beans. If they were to stop her, that would become her safe-conduct.

She turns a corner and hell opens up in front of her. A dazzling light explodes and shouts in German order her to stop. Two, three, four headlights shatter the darkness and strike her like a hail of bullets. Blinded, she can't see either men or equipment. She stops the bicycle and puts her feet on the ground. She still feels pain under her left foot and realizes that she is trembling, with her heart in her throat. From the light emerge two figures, a green-gray uniform and a man in civilian clothes. The German is young and thin. He barely looks at her and asks a question, only one. Somehow, he makes it seem an insult: *"Sprechen sie*

2

She shakes her head no, and the German turns and starts talking to the man in plainclothes, who remains a few steps behind. He comes closer and she recognizes him. It's Maestri, the political officer called Tearnails by his victims, famous for his infallible method of making partisans talk. Tearnails had a busy schedule, dividing his time between the police station and the old Casa dello Studente which had become Gestapo headquarters. The few he eventually let go would return with stories of seeing people die under Maestri's bloodstained hands. The German seems to be almost a boy but he treats Tearnails with complete disregard. He orders him to speak and Maestri blindly obeys.

"What are you doing out on this isolated road?" he asks. "Don't you know there's a curfew?"

Meanwhile, the German points at the now-extinguished bicycle light and screams something, as if he is cursing, pulls out the gun from the holster, and with the barrel cracks the glass open, and the bulb too. Maestri comments, like a diligent schoolboy, "It's dangerous to use lights." And he adds, "Those are enough," pointing to the whitewashed stripes on the bicycle's black frame.

Shaking, she slowly puts her hand into her purse and displays its contents. "I'm bringing these to my aunt. She is old and sick, and cannot move."

Telling the truth, even though it is neatly packaged to conceal a lie, gives her courage.

Maestri translates and the German mumbles something.

"We'll check," says Tearnails bluntly. "Now show us your papers."

From the coat's pocket she takes out an old leather wallet and gives him her factory card. She has begun to get used to the light. She hears the noise of the engines. Now she can see German soldiers and rifles pointed at her. There are two motorcycles with sidecars and, behind them, a truck and a big dark car.

"Do you work at the Fossati factory?" asks Maestri, eyes on the document.

"At the canteen."

"What time did you finish your shift?"

"At three."

"Couldn't you come in the afternoon?"

She feels anger growing under her fear.

"If I could I would have come, wouldn't I?"

"Who knows what you had to do that was so important."

He checks her out with an indecent look, full of threats. He keeps the document and turns to the German again. The two talk briefly, then the policeman concludes tersely, "Now you will come with us."

The young German gives orders. A soldier rips the bicycle out from under her and brings it to the truck where he throws it into the back with a crash. Tilde is escorted to the black car and is seated in the back, near Maestri. The young German sits in front with the driver. The car starts and she feels the policeman's hand go between her legs and trace the thick woolen stockings up to her bare thighs. She tightens her legs, feeling the vomit in her throat. She thinks about Sandra, the young relay captured a month earlier while carrying a dispatch to a partisan of the Mingo division that was hiding in Coronata at the time. They sent her to German headquarters and she was never heard of again. The rumor was she had been deported to Germany, but who knows? Maybe she was dead. She also thinks about Mariù, the madam who gave refuge to several wounded partisans. A few days ago she disappeared, and even though no one has the courage to say it, everyone is convinced that she had been murdered by the fascist paramilitary Black Brigades.

The car, the truck, and the motorcycles continue down the dirt road to Via Merano and head towards the center of Genoa like a funeral parade. They pass in front of the tobacco factory, the shipyard, and the railway station. She knows that it is useless to hope for rescue by her comrades. She remembers the assault on a stagecoach seen in an American movie a few years ago when she went to the Splendor Cinema with her friends. But not even the heroic lunatics of the *Leggeroni* could assault this convoy without being shot down like dogs.

4

They pass through the neighborhoods Cornigliano and Sampierdarena, dark and deserted, littered with the remains left by the American's bombs. "What kind of life is this?" she asks herself in desperation. "If Germans and fascists don't shoot us, Americans bomb us."

She remembers her father's parable about the fate of anchovies. As a boy, he would make a bit of money helping fishermen on their boats. He explained to her that when the tuna attacks them from below, the anchovies defend themselves by going to the surface and forming a spherical cluster. Then, seagulls coming down from the sky have a go at them, not to mention the fishermen and their nets.

Breaking from her reverie, she screams at Maestri to stop. The young German turns and gives him a severe look. The swine ceases to molest her but says, "Wait until they give you to me, wild kitten. I'll know how to tame you."

She now realizes where they are taking her: the *Militar-Kommandantur* on Via Pagano Doria. She enters the big hall of what used to be the Grand Hotel Miramare, as bright as daylight, and she's overwhelmed by the warmth and glamour enjoyed by Italy's new masters. Thoughts of Sandra and Mariù come again like a punch in the gut. Even though the car's interior had been warm and comfortable, she has icy hands and she shivers, whether from cold or fear, she doesn't know.

The young German takes them to the second floor, goes through a long corridor and stops at a closed door. He knocks, enters, and shuts the door behind him, leaving Tilde alone with Maestri. He continues to consume her with his eyes, and his obscene leer leaves her feeling naked. "You're lucky, bitch," he whispers. "The sergeant is Captain Hessen's orderly. Wehrmacht soldiers. Do you understand what that means?"

She shakes her head no. He laughs again, more and more lascivious. "You are to be spared from the SS."

Meanwhile he stretches out a hand and touches her breast through her coat. She steps back abruptly and replies, "What will happen to my bicycle?"

"Now is the time to think about your skin," Tearnails replies, lighting a cigarette. He smokes Aurora, women's tobacco. "Want one?"

She shakes her head no again and insists, "How can I bring food to my aunt without a bicycle?"

"I'm sure your bandit friends will think of something," he sneers. "Trust me, if she has to rely on you, your poor aunt will starve."

The door opens and the sergeant ushers them into a large office that, until a few months ago, was a luxurious hotel room. Exquisite oriental carpets cover the floor, creamy curtains veil the wide windows opening on the dark and silent harbor. Tilde is seated on a velvet padded chair, in front of the desk, and for a moment she forgets about the pain in her foot. Maestri sits next to her and the young sergeant leaves the room and closes the door.

The captain is about forty years old. He wears his uniform with the collar unbuttoned and has a few days' beard. He looks tired and sad. Light complexion, thin lips, blond hair, and two deep blue eyes. Tilde is struck by them and looks into them without fear. They remind her of Biscia's. He is also blond and has eyes as blue as the sea. What a couple they make, the pair of them! She is so dark, almost Moorish, with black hair and black eyes like coal, and he is washed out, tall and thin. When they walk along Via Garibaldi holding hands, everybody stares with envy and admiration.

The officer scans Tilde silently. His gaze slips along the girl's body like a caress. But it's different from Maestri's. It almost seems as if the beauty of the young woman makes him even sadder. The silence seems never-ending. Now, her fear is back. After an eternity, the officer speaks.

"How old are you?"

"Nineteen."

Maestri barks, "You reply: nineteen, *sir.*"

Captain Hessen quiets him with a waive of his hand, his eyes fixed on Tilde's.

"What's your name?"

She answers, reciting her first and last name and, holding back a smile, she adds, *"Sir."*

The officer's lips compress slightly in what might have been a smile. "What were you doing on that road at midnight?"

She shows him the bag, pulling out the black piece of bread, the beans, and gives him the aunt story. She is struck by how good this German's Italian is. Where did he learn it? If it weren't for his pronunciation, no one would know he's a *crucco*. There's no need for an interpreter. Why doesn't that kiss-ass Maestri leave? Go and torture some partisans, you swine.

"You were not afraid of having a bad encounter, at that time?" the captain asks.

"Only with a bomb, *sir.*"

"She did have a bad encounter, *Herr Hauptmann,* with us," intervenes Maestri. "This is a partisan relay."

"Hold her and check the aunt's story. If it is true we must let her go."

"But our sources. . ."

Hessen replies scornfully, "Your sources are despicable scum who would sell their mother for a kilo of bread."

He calls the sergeant, who appears instantly as if he had been eavesdropping, and gives him some precise orders in German. Then he points at Tilde and gestures for her to rise. She obeys and again feels the knot in her stocking that is plaguing her foot.

"Désolé, mademoiselle, but you must stay here, locked in a room," he says gently. "Provide Sergeant Walden with the name and address of your aunt. If everything checks out, tomorrow morning you can go to work."

"With my bicycle?" She dares to ask, pausing on the threshold.

"Naturally."

As the sergeant closes the door behind her, she catches a brief exchange between Hessen and Maestri.

"The woman is a reliable source," the policeman growls. "The bitch is lying."

"We'll see," the officer replies.

Tilde spends the night alone, in a small, locked room on the second floor. She sits on the wooden bench, pulls the shoe and the stocking off, and puts her foot on her knee to check the blister. It's as big as a coin and, brushing it with her fingers, it's hard, on the point of bursting. She puts stocking and shoe back on and looks at the little wristwatch her mother gave her for her First Communion. She realizes she forgot to wind it because it says a quarter after eleven. She feels the cold rising from inside her again and she wraps her coat around herself more tightly. She puts her bag under her head and lies on her side on the hard wooden bench. She's tired, her body shakes, but she knows she won't sleep. Thoughts buzz through her mind like demented bees. She can hear voices in German and the noise of boots squeaking on the marble floor.

The hours pass slowly, and when she hears the key turning in the lock, the sky is still black outside the big window. Captain Hessen is alone and closes the door behind him. He looks less tired and sad than before.

"It's all right, *mademoiselle,*" he says with a smile which shows an unexpected satisfaction. "My men talked to your aunt. You can go home." Before opening the door, he stares straight into her eyes and whispers, "But don't go out after the curfew. And, above all, don't mix with bad company."

He leads her down the large staircase to the atrium, where he entrusts her to a sleepy soldier who takes her out into the cold air. Her bicycle is leaning against the wall next to a motorcycle. Tilde leaves the soldier with a wave of her hand, raises the collar of her coat, takes the bike, and pedals toward Sestri. It will be dawn soon, and when she gets home, her blister will have started bleeding.

2.
JASMÌNE

I had been sitting in the corridor for over fifteen hours, but the chair was hard, too hard to allow me to sleep. And still, that damned door remained closed. No nurse, no doctor to give me the news.

Who was I to ask for news, after all? The police, sure, they were public officials. They had the right to ask for news, if the patient was still alive, if there was still hope. But the guards posted by Deputy Police Superintendent Pertusiello changed every six hours and they didn't even know her. They hadn't had her living in their house. They hadn't been her lover, as I had, even if it was for money. And they weren't falling in love with her, as I seemed to be.

For them she was only a prostitute from the Ivory Coast on her deathbed because of a sadistic killer who had bought her from a criminal organization like you buy a blow-up doll in a porn shop. Only the price had been exorbitant in exchange for the guarantee that she was returnable. When the toy was broken, *they* would take care of everything. They would erase every trace of her. They'd make her corpse disappear and no one would ask any questions.

After fifteen hours I didn't know any more than I did when we started. Guarded prognosis, probability of survival less than fifty percent, non-quantifiable brain damage. I had eaten a disgusting sandwich with ham and plastic cheese, drank a bottle of mineral water, ingested four coffees from the vending machine, and visited the hospital bathroom three times.

The police guard, black boots and regular blue uniform, sat in front of me reading *La Gazzetta dello Sport* and, from time to time, he lowered the newspaper to give me a look of compassion. Pertusiello was afraid there were other members of the gang at large. Jasmine could identify them and therefore had to be protected.

Among the gang members who already been rounded up there was a certain Antonio, a loser who convinced me he was her pimp. From beneath the table, I had shoved the barrel of my Beretta into his testicles. He had gone pale like the plaster of the hospital wall. I had been staring at it for hours, the wall of that damned corridor, and as in the cinema, I could see the memories of the events of these recent months go by. It had been October, in a club called Lap Dance in Sampierdarena. I couldn't forgive myself for leaving her there that night. If I had taken her with me, I would have spared her torture, fear, and horrible suffering, and now, I wouldn't find myself in front of the closed door of an intensive care unit.

I looked at the time. Two in the afternoon. The hospital was deserted and silent. From the big windows, the sun of a cold February day glittered on the metal chairs and showed the dirty stains on the floor.

Suddenly, at the end of the corridor, a man appeared. He looked old, even though he was trying to maintain a proud and erect posture. He started to move toward us and the policeman was immediately on alert. He brought his hand to his gun, loosened the strap on the holster, and flicked off the safety. As he drew closer, it became increasingly clear that he was an old man. He was wearing a dark coat with a fur lining, and in his hands he was holding a wide-spread felt hat. The coat was too big and danced on him making him look even skinnier. When he walked, he dragged his feet a little, even though his stride revealed a determined, almost military bearing. He had white hair, slightly wavy, and light blue eyes where an iron will flickered. He seemed disinterested in the guard and stared in my direction.

He stopped a few feet away and, catching my eye, asked, "Good morning. Mr. Pagano?"

He had an unmistakable German accent.

"That's me," I said, passing my hand over my face.

"Can we talk for a few minutes?"

"Sure," I said, gesturing to the chair to my left. The one on the right was occupied by my sheepskin jacket.

"Is it too much to ask to speak alone?" he asked without moving.

"Don't ask me to leave this door."

"I understand," he said, nodding. "It would be enough to move over there." He pointed to the last chairs in the row, at the beginning of the corridor.

I sighed and shot a look at the policeman, who smiled and reassured me. "Don't worry. I'm not moving for the next four hours."

I got up and moved to the end of the row. We sat on two adjacent chairs, so that in order to speak we had to sit at an angle and keep our heads to the side.

"You are distressed," said the man, continuing to look in my eyes. "So I'll try to be quick. My name is Kurt Hessen and I come from Köln." He put his hat on a chair, and immediately picked it up again. "Cologne," he added.

I nodded.

"I speak your language well because before I retired I taught Italian at the university. I called your office and a lady told me I would find you here."

Zainab, as usual, was being my secretary.

"I'm looking for you because I'd like to give you a job. . ."

"Not now," I stopped him. "There's a woman in there who is important to me."

"I understand," he repeated, nodding again. "But please let me speak. I assure you I will be very brief."

I glanced at the door to the ward, sadly closed, and I nodded again.

"It's about finding my brother. I don't know his first or last name. I don't know where he lives. I have never seen him, and I don't have a photograph of him."

"Wonderful," I said.

"I only know that he is the son of an Italian woman named Nicla, who died thirty years ago, and that he could live in the neighborhood of Sestri Ponente, where his mother lived."

"What kind of brother would that be?"

He smiled slightly and nodded for the third time. "You're right, I have neglected an important detail. I am also Nicla's son. My father's name was Helmut Hessen and during the war he was a Wehrmacht officer assigned to the German headquarters in Genoa. He died on May 15th, 1944, killed by a bomb in a downtown cinema. . ."

"The Odeon Cinema on Via Vernazza."

"Precisely. I never met him. I was born in late 1944 in Gargnano, on Lake Garda, where Nicla had joined my father's sister and her husband. In November, we left for Cologne, but my mother wouldn't come and abandoned me. According to my aunt, she was a member of the Resistance, but perhaps my aunt was just jealous. I was raised by my aunt and uncle, who had no other children, and I've always had everything I needed—except for the truth."

"What does that mean?"

"They had always told me my mother died during childbirth and they claimed they never met her. According to their version, they came to pick me up a few days after my birth. Two months ago, before she died, my aunt told me the truth."

"And what truth was that?"

"My father had had a relationship with Nicla and had gotten her pregnant. He made plans to get her to someplace safe before the birth but he was killed before he could carry them out. His orderly, a young sergeant, fulfilled my father's wishes and accompanied my mother to Gargnano where she gave birth assisted by my aunt and uncle from Germany."

"According to my aunt, after the war, my mother got married to an Italian and had a son that should be a few years younger than me. If he is still alive, I would like you to find him."

"Why?"

"Because I'm very sick and, before I die, I would like to meet him."

"Who kept your aunt informed?"

"I believe it was my father's orderly. He lived in Mannheim and came to visit us at least once a year. He died about ten years ago and he never spoke to me of this."

"I imagine on your aunt's orders."

"Of course."

"Your mother's name was Nicla. And. . .?"

"I don't know, my aunt told me nothing else. Believe me, I did some research, talked to friends and acquaintances of my family as well as the orderly's, but I discovered nothing."

I turned to the ward door and sighed deeply.

"By the smell of it," I said concisely, "it seems like an impossible job. I think I wouldn't accept it anyway."

"Why?"

"The only way would be to ask the survivors of that period. Do you realize what kind of investigation you are offering to me? The youngest will be over ninety by now."

"If you know the story well, *Herr* Pagano," he replied, annoyed, "you should know they were all very young, many under twenty. Nowadays, the ones who are not as ill as I am are very likely to make it to eighty-five and still be in good shape."

He might be right. My father had been a partisan, too, and was born

13

in 1925. He hadn't been in very good shape at 85 but a lot of things, including his job at the factory, the war and his wife's death had taken a toll on his heart. Unfortunately, I, too, had done my part. If I hadn't ended up in jail, Guido Pagano would probably still be alive.

"I'm sorry, Professor Hessen," I said, blinking, my eyes burning with fatigue. "Your offer comes at the wrong time. You'll have to go to someone else."

"No one is asking you to start right away," he insisted firmly.

"Didn't you say you have little time?"

He remained silent, his gaze fixed on the hat in his hands. What could he say to that? Some time passed and each of us were lost in our own thoughts. I was hoping I had been discouraging enough to make him give up. Instead, point-blank, he said, "I have no children or grandchildren. I was the only heir to a substantial inheritance. Between shares, and movable and immovable assets, it should be about three million Euros. If you find my brother, he will be able to live without working for the rest of his life. And for you there will be a very substantial check."

"May I ask you a question?"

"You want to know why I chose you."

I nodded.

"A fair question, *Herr* Pagano. I've researched investigative agencies, something I've never needed, until now. It seems they are usually run by ex-police officers or *carabinieri*. In the circles you'd have to investigate in the hunt for my brother, that would raise more suspicion than sympathy. You, on the other hand, have a past that will open many hearts and doors. I'm almost certain that there is someone you already know, some contact you have, that could take you straight to him."

"I'm starting to think you know more than you say."

"What do you mean?"

"My father was a worker at the Fossati factory in Sestri Ponente. He

14

was a partisan and in 1945 he was injured in a firefight with the Germans. Did you know?"

"Of course not."

"My mother was born and raised in Sestri. She worked at the cigar factory and her father, Grandfather Baciccia, was a worker at Vaccari Ceramics in Borzoli. You didn't know this?"

"I didn't know that your ties with Sestri Ponente were so strong. I only know you through the newspapers. But isn't your nickname, *La Pantegana dei Caruggi*?

"Yeah." I said with a half-smile. "I guess I *am* the rat of the *caruggi*. I grew up in them, the alleys and byways in the heart of the city, the *centro storico*. My father's family lived for generations in Madre di Dio, a neighborhood that no longer exists. In its place they've built a formidable pile of crap now. I was born there, in a large building on Via dei Servi that I barely remember, and I grew up in Sarzano, Ravecca, and San Bernardo. It was just like in that movie, *The Walls of Malapaga*. But in the *centro storico* there were no factories. They've always been in the west and in the Polcevera valley. For over fifty years, Sestri was the center of industry and had more workers than anywhere else. That's what made it the heart of the Genoese Resistance."

"Very well, this will make it all easier."

"Not for me. I have no easy relationship with my past, and if I decide to go down memory lane, I'm not doing it for money."

"Not even for a figure like this?" He pulled out a check from the breast pocket of his coat and waved it under my nose. I could get a glimpse of a number with four zeros. "Of course, this only covers your initial expenses," he added.

At that moment, that damn door finally opened. Without a word, I got up and rushed to the doctor who was leaving the ward. He was wearing green surgical scrubs. He was a short, chubby little man with a dark face and a tired expression. My police friend put down the newspaper, got up, and went to him. The doctor closed the door behind him and the three of us formed our own little crowd where the tension could be cut with a knife.

"Surgery was successful," the doctor said. Unfortunately I knew this didn't mean much. "We put the patient in a therapeutic coma to ease her recovery."

"Will she live?" I asked anxiously.

The man looked at me like I was begging for charity. "At the moment, if there are no complications, there is no danger. But we'll have to wait for at least forty-eight hours to be sure."

"No prognosis?" I insisted.

He raised his eyebrows and took a deep breath. "It will take a long time, very long. My advice is to go home and go back to your normal life. Anyway, we won't know anything for at least a week."

"Is she allowed visitors?"

He raised the palms of his hands, as if to push back my requests. "In forty-eight hours. Not sooner."

I thanked him, shaking his hand, and I saw him disappear behind the door as it inexorably closed again.

When I finally turned away, the German was gone. I felt relief. I didn't know whether it was because of the doctor's words or the fact that the old man was gone. The only thing that was clear to me was that I needed to sleep. Sleep and forget. The idea that a loved one might die is wearing. You can't bear it for long without defending yourself and catching your breath.

I waved goodbye to the policeman, grabbed my jacket, and started down the stairs. When I hit the crowded lobby of the massive hospital complex, I realized that I didn't remember where I had parked my Vespa. I went outside and the sun dazzled me. But it was a dull sun that didn't warm me up. The old man was there at the curb now, waiting for me, a cigarette dangling from his lips. He had put his hat on and he kept his hands in the coat's pockets.

"Good news?"

He grabbed the cigarette between his fingers and smiled. "Is there a difference? Aren't we in the same boat?"

I quietly pulled out my pipe, packed it, and lit it. I hadn't smoked for sixteen hours. I told myself that for the second time, this damned *crucco* had hit the mark. If there was no immediate danger and one had to wait, it was worth filling the time with an activity that would distract me from thinking about Jasmìne.

"Do you want to show me the check?" I asked.

"The one for the initial expenses?"

"That one."

He put his hand into his breast pocket and, as if by magic, the check reappeared between his fingers. This time he didn't wave it in the air but gave it to me so I could contemplate it calmly. I was right, forty thousand Euros. As an advance payment for expenses, it was too much, much too much.

"I would like you to write me another one," I said. "Three thousand is enough."

He frowned and looked at me suspiciously.

"It's my rate," I explained. "Five hundred a day."

With a slightly shaking hand, he put the cigarette in his mouth and pulled out his checkbook, wrote out a new check and passed it to me. I tried to hand him back his forty thousand euro check but he stopped me. "Keep it. You are not obliged to collect it. Keep it as a pledge."

Then he lifted his hat, wished me luck, and started off toward a nearby taxi.

17

3.
BIANCOAMARO

Sestri Ponente, January 1944

Tilde rushes into the bar on the Pontinetto. She had to give an injection to her mother, prepare her father's lunchbox, and treat the blister on her foot, and she is fifteen minutes late. Outside, the four o'clock sun projects long shadows on the sidewalks and announces another night of curfew.

The bar is full of smoke. Cheap tobacco, which goes out constantly and stinks of the stable. Voucher number 65 in the ration book allows thirty *Nazionali* brand cigarettes a week, too few for serious smokers. After that, you smoke whatever you can find.

She closes the door and, without looking around, makes a beeline to the table where the man is waiting for her with *Il Secolo XIX* wide open in front of him. Some customers at the counter follow her movements with eyes filled with admiration and desire. She sits with her back to the eyes and with her heart beating fast because she has so much to tell and fears what she will be asked to do.

The man is between twenty-five and thirty years old, but he looks older. Maybe it's the responsibilities weighing on his shoulders. His eyes are large and watery, mouse grey. Whatever thoughts and feelings lurk in them are invisible behind an imperturbable veil. His face is yellowish and pockmarked. His hairless cheeks make him look oddly juvenile. He works as a baker at the Gaggero's bakery and his shift ends at eleven in the morning.

"They stopped me at the curve near the cemetery. I spent the night

"What do you want to drink?" he abruptly interrupts.

She is upset. She doesn't like being treated that way, not even by the comrades who give the orders. He looks over her head and whispers, "It's raining." Startled, she realizes that there are police among them. It isn't a good time to talk.

The man points to a newspaper article. A knife in the belly would have hurt less. It blandly reports the shooting at Cairo Montenotte of Fulvio and three other partisans of Savona. Though she already knew, Tilde's eyes flood with tears. But that's not good; she can't draw attention to herself.

"What are you drinking?" he repeats.

"I don't know," she replies, floundering.

He turns to the bartender, calling him by name: "Hey, Giovanni! Bring us two *bianchiamari*," he says in Genoese, the dialect of Genoa.

The police must have left, because the man has relaxed.

"Do you think they followed me?" she asks, frightened.

He shakes his head. "Don't worry, when I came in, they were already here. They couldn't have followed either of us." Glasses of white wine with tonic are brought to the table. He folds the newspaper and starts to sip.

"So you spent the night at the Miramare," he mumbles, smiling. "Did they offer you a luxury suite?"

"How do you know they didn't torture me?"

"Biscia told me everything."

Tilde takes the glass to her lips and lowers her eyes. "Not everything."

"There's more?"

"It was the German captain who snatched me from the hands of Maestri."

"Captain of the SS?"

"Wehrmacht officer. His name is Hessen, and the young sergeant, the one who was with Maestri, Walter or Walden."

There is an ambiguous smile on the man's lips. She understands the thought behind it and she is frightened.

"Are you sure the informant is a woman?"

"As the door was closing, Maestri said, '*The woman is a reliable source.*' I heard it perfectly."

"It adds up. First Sandra, then Mariù, and now you. Only a tip-off could have brought them to that deserted road at midnight. Someone is passing information to the fascists. Do you have any ideas?"

"What do you mean?"

"Friends, neighbors, canteen colleagues. Who knew you were going up to Gazzo's pit?"

That insinuating tone begins to get on her nerves.

"Are you out of your mind? Do you think I talk to people. . ."

"So how did they know?"

"It must be because of my aunt."

"So someone knows you go to see her every two days and got suspicious?"

"It must be so."

"Who knows about your aunt?"

"Everyone. Neighbors, friends, work colleagues."

He has finished his drink and asks for another. Tilde's is still in her glass. He scratches his head and looks at her sideways. "Biscia can't believe they let you go like that. When there's a bastard like Toernaile around. . ."

"When it comes to the Germans, he rolls on his back and wags his tail like a lovesick puppy," she interrupts him.

For no apparent reason, the words came out aggressively. The man has noticed it, and he stares at her for a long time, in silence. That look gets inside her and leaves no escape. She feels she's blushing all over.

"Tell me, Olindo, what idea have you gotten into that head of yours?"

He remains silent, waiting for his drink. "You tell me," he finally replies.

"You don't think that. . ."

The phrase is suspended in the smoky air of the bar. Olindo understands and stretches out a hand to her.

"That you have betrayed us? Don't worry, no one thinks that."

"So. . .?"

"You haven't answered me yet, Tilde."

"I think the captain was interested in me."

"I think that, too," he replies.

Meanwhile, the second drink arrives, and the two men exchange banter. The bartender avoids looking at her, as if she doesn't exist. It doesn't seem to matter to him that Olindo is accompanied by a young woman with coal-colored eyes and black hair that falls on her shoulders and back. A still-ripening beauty with a touch of the wild. This means he knows Olindo well and knows not to ask questions. She avoids raising her eyes and keeps them glued to the pink liquid in her glass.

When they are alone again, Olindo studies her and begins to talk. He must have had his speech ready, like the revolver that he always keeps in the pocket of his coat. "At the moment, Maestri is too well protected," he begins. "We have no way to get at him. But that

21

informant is likely to destroy us all, do you understand?"

Her worst predictions were coming true. There was nothing left for her but surrender.

"What do you want me to do?"

"Nothing, for now. We will limit ourselves to protecting you. Maestri won't put his hands on you again."

"Biscia told you that in the car. . ."

The man nods and goes back to smiling, with the look of someone who knows more than he says. Telling her boyfriend that Tearnails put a hand between her thighs was easier than. . .

"You will go to work and bring food to your aunt before the curfew. We'll look for another girl to be our relay." Then, suddenly, he changes subject. "Do you know that Biscia is like a son to me?"

Now she is the one who remains silent, waiting. Sooner or later, Olindo will have to show his cards.

"Did you decide when you'll be getting married?" he asks, looking away and touching the rim of the glass with his index finger.

"No date yet. We are waiting for the war to end."

He nods and takes a sip. It seems that his proverbial frankness has melted in his *biancoamaro*. "I understand I'm asking you a lot," he adds.

"You haven't asked me anything yet, Olindo."

Blunt words, which finally push him to get to the point: "This Captain Hessen is the only one who can unmask the informant. . ."

". . .and I'm the only one who might be able to get him to speak. Are you asking me to do it?"

Olindo shakes his head. His face is drawn and pained, as if he had a stomachache.

"I must first discuss it with brigade command. Tomorrow, I will see

Duranello."

"And I have to talk to Biscia."

"Only if you feel like it. . ." he adds, grabbing her hand over the table. "Think well about the consequences."

"I'll talk to him and I'll decide."

She frees her hand, takes a sip of *biancoamaro* and gets up. Only when she's outside, on the crowded sidewalk, walking fast with her eyes fixed on the ground, does she realize she doesn't know what the barman looks like.

4.

SAND CASTLES IN THE WATER

The apartment was in a working class building in the Borzoli neighborhood, on Via Ottava Società. I arrived on my Vespa at ten o'clock in the morning and the old road, named after the co-operative that in the early twentieth century had built the apartments, welcomed me with bright but cold sunshine. I hadn't been here for many years and seeing the old balconies with the iron banisters made all the memories come flooding back.

From one of those balconies, on the fourth floor, my grandmother used to wave goodbye to me, and each time I read in my mother's eyes her fear that it might be the last. I used to walk with my nose in the air, waving one hand furiously with the other tightly clenched in my mother's. Together, we set off towards the Chiaravagna, a watercourse the color of coffee, and we crossed a wobbly wooden bridge that was inevitably wiped out by the floods. Then we went down the stairs to Via Ramiro Ginocchio to reach our bus stop.

Unfortunately, my mother's fears came true and my grandmother died. It was then that Grandfather Baciccia, who remained alone, decided to come and live with us in Via dei Servi and take full-time care of his only grandson. That choice was a real godsend, not just for me, but also for our precarious family finances. My mother went back to the cigar factory, and my father worked at an auto-repair shop. With their salaries and Grandpa's pension - and the help of a small loan from the bank - the first refrigerator appeared in our home. After a few years, we also indulged in the luxury of a brand new Fiat Seicento. It was the early Sixties, the years of the Italian Economic Miracle, and even the Pagano family was able to keep up with the times. I think this was down to my mother, because my father, always a good communist, had a deep distrust of consumerism and never gave up the hope of building something resembling socialism in Italy.

The man I had come to see lived in the apartment next door to my grandmother's. He welcomed me with distrust, like any elderly person who sees a six-foot-tall stranger at his door. But I knew two names that not only opened the door but his mouth as well.

The apartment was clean and tidy and the old man cared for it with meticulous, almost maniacal dedication. It seemed that the effort of keeping everything in its place absorbed all his energies and I wondered about his motivation. Was it the illusion of stopping time? The fear of death? Or was it the fear of loss of identity, of memory, or of some bygone affection embodied now only in the objects that surrounded him?

We went into the sunlit kitchen. I sat at the Formica table and, without asking, he filled the Neapolitan coffee maker and put it on the stove. Hanging on the wall, near the window, I noticed a calendar of the Cassa di Risparmio bank for the year 1998. On the cupboard there was a color photograph of a woman, beautiful but not so young, with white hair in a bun and a perplexed, almost sorry, smile.

"That's my Amelia," he said as soon as he realized I was looking at her. "You don't remember her, do you?"

I tried to recall that face, but nothing came.

"In March it will be ten years since she died. Yet when I wake up and don't feel her next to me," his big, gray eyes, veiled in cataracts, had become moist, "it's still like the first morning. I think it will be so until the end."

"I'm sorry. . ." I stammered.

"She and Anna, your mother, were friends. They worked together at the cigar factory until '65, when it was automated and the last cigar girls were fired. Then they lost track of each other, as often happens in life. We didn't even live in two different cities. . ." He shook his head and said, "Sometimes we forget that, without friends, we are nothing."

I thought he was right. What really separates the outskirts of town from its center is more than just a few miles.. Once the factories were closed and the suburbs became just places to sleep, people had less reason to meet and relationships gradually loosened until they became lost altogether. Everyone became walled into increasingly solitary lives made up of markets and shops, and everyday habits. Old age makes it worse. It widens the distance and condemns people to a loneliness that, all too often, becomes the antechamber of death.

"We did get back in contact with your parents when they arrested and tried you," he continued as he turned off the gas and inverted the coffee-maker. "Now that I've gotten a better look at you, I do remember you. There was a lot of agitation among your parent's old companions. Ricci, the lawyer, moved heaven and earth, but they were difficult times and the judges wouldn't listen. But I like to think all the pressure did accomplish something. . ."

"I believe it too," I confirmed. "They gave me ten years and I served only five."

"You know, Bacci," he said awkwardly, "there were some people in the party who didn't want to back you because they didn't believe in your innocence. We were not tender-hearted with terrorists. I remember a federal committee in which several people balked when asked to sign an appeal for your release. But in the end, the vote was unanimous, because Guido Pagano trusted you and they trusted him and that was more important than any political calculation."

He was moving slowly and cautiously around the kitchen, but his voice had an energy that sadness and old age hadn't touched. Standing bent over the table, he poured coffee into the cups, and put the coffee-maker back on the stove. His hands were barely shaking. When I told him I didn't want sugar, he was thrilled.

"Me neither," he said. "The doctor has forbidden me sugar because of diabetes."

Then he sat down and began to blow on the hot coffee. I watched him carefully. His sparse, white hair was carefully combed, leaving a glimpse of a long-ago parting on the side. He had thick tortoiseshell glasses that magnified his already large eyes. His face was round, almost bloated with wrinkles that widened and formed a net of grooves on his

26

forehead and neck. His cheeks were clean shaven and pockmarked, and his hands resembled the gnarled, winter branches of an ancient olive tree. His legs were crossed, and I noticed the swelling of his ankles, wrapped in thick, checkered socks. Seeing him so old now, with his slippers on his feet, and a wool sweater, nearly worn through at the elbows, awoke great tenderness in me. I vaguely remembered his face. I had seen it at my mother's funeral and then at my father's. On both occasions, it was under the Flag of the Partisan Association, black-edged for the funeral. But it was Grandfather Baciccia who had told me about him, recounting what he had done as an active member of the partisan Resistance. He was a true hero. He'd even earned a commendation from the President of the Republic. I also knew that after the liberation, he hadn't quit the movement, occupying various minor positions: secretary of the local branch of the communist party, a member of the party's federal committee, and, finally, one of the officers of the Partisan Association. There had been no brilliant political career for Olindo Grandi, the man who had led one of the most deadly patriotic action groups of the entire Resistance.

Together, we sipped coffee until the cups were empty. In no hurry, he was silent, waiting. The sun lit him from the side and seemed to give him comfort and energy, as if he were an ancient, rugged reptile. There was a big radio on the cupboard in a wooden case. I wondered if it still worked.

"Did you listen to Radio London with that?" I asked. He smiled and shook his head. "Amelia gave it to me in 1957, when I turned forty."

"Congratulations, Sig. Grandi," I commented. "So you must be over ninety now."

"I turned ninety in December, surrounded by children and grandchildren," he said with satisfaction. "But if you don't mind, no, "Sig. Grandi." I would prefer if we spoke informally and candidly. That's always the way it was among comrades and, in any case, it will make me feel younger."

I took the hint. It was time to come clean and get to the point. I asked Olindo if I could smoke my pipe and he said that was fine, as long as I opened the window a bit. He had read about my work as a private investigator in the papers and he was curious. While packing and lighting my pipe, I began to talk to him about my assignment and the story reported by Professor Hessen. He listened to me carefully, not missing a word. I realized that, as I went through the story, his expression changed. He began to shake his head, furrowing his thick eyebrows, and showing impatience. When I was finished, he gave a long sigh and said, "It sounds like a hoax to me."

I was surprised and he noticed. "I commanded a PAG," he explained abruptly, allowing a glimpse of his old steel. "I met fighters, organizers and any number of men and women who helped the Resistance, both formally and informally. But I assure you that I've never heard of this Nicla."

"What about an officer named Hessen?"

"Maybe, but it's been so long. . . Why don't you just check the names of the Germans that were killed in the Odeon bombing?"

"I did that. They're reported in the proceedings on the Turchino pass massacre. Among them is a captain of the Wehrmacht named Helmut Hessen."

"So?"

"Couldn't he have had a relationship with an Italian girl who gave him a son?"

"It seems an unlikely story."

"Why?"

He waived his hand, almost annoyed. "Because partisans didn't sleep with Germans!"

"My client isn't absolutely sure Nicla was a partisan."

"I bet he's not sure of a lot of things," he replied insolently. "Your client claims she abandoned her son. Normal mothers don't do that voluntarily."

"Do you think they might have forced her?"

He seemed sorry for his reaction. "Do you want more coffee?" he

I stopped him, putting my hand on his arm, "Do you?"

"Another sip, thank you," he said, relaxing. "That's not what's going to keep me awake at night."

I got up, took the coffee-maker, and poured the contents into the cups. I went back to sip with him. He seemed calmer now.

"The Third Reich," he resumed in a friendly tone, "had fired the Germans with a true obsession for the future. The plans they had in mind required a growing number of Aryan citizens, but their young people and children were dying like flies under the bombs of the Allies and Soviets."

"So my client might have been stolen as a baby."

"That's right," he said, satisfied. "Stolen."

"So you don't rule out that this Nicla might have existed and might have given birth to another son."

He shook his head again. "Who can rule it out? But even if it's true, you'll never find him."

"Maybe you underestimate me, Olindo."

"No way!" he replied, trying to infuse cheer in his voice. "I've followed your investigations in the newspapers and I know that, if your father were alive, he would be proud of you. But since Nicla is dead and you don't know her or her husband's last name, how do you think you'll find her son?"

"As usual, by asking questions, lots of questions. My client says she lived in Sestri. Someone would have known her."

He kept shaking his head with obstinacy. "If I were you I would let it go. It sounds like building sand castles in the water to me."

That expression brought back a wave of bittersweet memory. When she was happy, my mother said that all the time. She used it with me, with my father and with my Grandfather Baciccia every time we started

29

one of those lively, pointless discussions that never resolved anything but that made the house we lived in into a home. I remember one evening, all four of us sitting in front of the TV watching an Inspector Maigret mini-series. The episode featured a poor old man who was utterly terrified of something. It made him seem oddly sympathetic and likeable. There were also two women, mother and daughter—real harpies—who seemed to be the cause of the old man's fear. My grandfather started trying to guess why they frightened him so much. My father started to contradict him, and I, having read the book and knowing the story, began to drop clues without saying too much. My mother didn't take part in the discussion and, at the end of the episode, stood up and, with a distracted smile, said, "It's all sand castles in the water."

My grandfather laughed. I blurted out the ending, ruining the rest of the series. But, on my father's face, I saw a deep resentment that came from humiliation.

My mother was as beautiful as she was superior. The cigar factory, where the work was hard and the wages low, hadn't diminished her expectations. She had a way of making all of us feel as if we didn't quite measure up. This bothered me for years and I'm afraid my father never recovered from her unspoken disappointment. However, at some point in my life I realized it wasn't me, it was her. This helped me come to terms both with her and myself.

Olindo looked at me curiously. He seemed to realize that I was lost in my memories, but he had no idea why. At that moment, the bell rang.

"It's my daughter. She comes to make sure I eat," he said.

I got up and opened the door to a sixty-year-old woman, elegant and looking younger than her age. She was surprised and almost afraid to see me. She wore a warm astrakhan coat. She took care of herself. She had an expensive head of blond hair, probably bleached. Before I could introduce myself, Olindo appeared in the corridor and reassured her.

She took off her coat and headed straight into the kitchen. It was clear she had little time to waste and many things to do. The old man explained to her who I was and she seemed to recall my family

30

perfectly, my father, my mother, and even my grandfather. A veritable maven of memory, her. She talked to me kindly, but with no warmth. Perhaps the smoke of the pipe bothered her. Or perhaps the fact that I plagued her father with questions upset her. Our conversation was short and didn't go beyond social niceties.

Olindo wanted to accompany me to the door and, before saying goodbye, he suggested that I see Balletta, the partisan nickname for a man named Enrico Parodi who had gone to fight in the mountains when he was sixteen.

"He's still young," he explained, "so I'm sure he'll remember everything. For thirty years he's had a hardware store and knows half of Sestri."

He told me that Balletta lived on Viale Canepa, an old road that used to lead to a monastery, and that he would make a phone call to let him know I was coming. After our conversation, so much enthusiasm surprised me. So it was no surprise that, as we shook hands goodbye, he said, "I do this because you ask it and because you are the son of Anna and Guido, but it's still a waste of time."

5.
A ROMANTIC WALK

Sestri Ponente, January 1944

Another cold, sunny day. When she had entered the factory, at six in the morning, it was still dark and she was too sleepy to check if the stars were shining. These days, nobody looks up at the stars. The only time you look up is when there's an air-raid siren. And then you run, as fast as you can, faster, to the nearest shelter.

At the exit, standing by the factory gates, Tilde greets some of her friends as her shift ends. They are all tired and sore, after nine hours on their feet serving hot meals to the workers. A few head to the tram stop. The lucky ones grab the handlebars of the bicycle that will take them home. She takes a few steps, holding the old, heavy bike, and looks around at the workers who, after their shift, swarm the road. The first thing she sees makes her wince. About a hundred feet from the factory gates, there's a military truck full of Germans carrying glittering, new Mauser rifles. That's new. It hasn't happened before. It must be a dozen men, too few for a round-up. Does Prefect Basile just want to send a warning to the "Reds" of the Fossati factory? Or are they waiting for someone particular?

Then, finally, she sees him and her pulse races. She feels short of breath and her legs tremble, almost unable to support her. It happens every time. But, this time, there's also something else. An uncomfortable feeling, almost nausea. He's there, leaning against the factory wall and he's waiting for her, wrapped in a raincoat over his gray overalls. He works in the shipyard and the heart murmur he's had since he was a child saved him from military service. She hasn't seen him for several weeks and he looks even thinner and ganglier. That's why they call him *Biscia*, "snake." His hair is longer than when she saw him last, blond and thin, and he wears it combed to the back and shiny with grease. Between his fingers he holds a cigarette that he probably rolled himself to make the wait less nerve-wracking. They both know that this meeting isn't just an ordinary date.

Seeing him after such a long time comforts her and at the same time frightens her. Are the *crucchi* there because of him? After all, Biscia belongs to a PAG, a patriotic action group, and had come down from Mount Gazzo, bringing his gun with him. Although he's her age, he's proven himself a determined and courageous fighter. Tilde heard Grandi saying he could use others like him on his team. Biscia is quick and relentless. He doesn't freelance or have fits of temper. Biscia always follows orders. This thought chills her and makes her want to vomit the watery soup she ate at eleven, before serving in the canteen.

Biscia always follows orders.

She walks towards him slowly, making her way through the crowd. The workers, especially the younger ones, are looking at her. It's hard not to notice that thick, midnight hair. He, too, saw her, but today he has no smile to give her. When she reaches him, he throws away the cigarette and lightly kisses her cheek. His face is tired and his eyes dark and elusive. Tilde hugs him and feels the gun under the raincoat. Biscia's eyes are on the truck.

"What do they want?" she asks, trying, and failing, to look into his eyes.

"To frighten people," he replies, still facing the Germans. "They feed on our fear. It makes them feel strong."

They start walking, side by side, in the direction of Sestri, the bicycle a barrier between them. The silence makes them wary, almost hostile.

It's Biscia who speaks first. "It would have been so easy to roll a grenade under the truck," he says, beginning to make a cigarette. "They wouldn't even notice and. . . *boom!*"

"The road was full of workers," she replies. "It would have been a massacre."

"Hm? Yeah, innocent blood. . ." he replies, distractedly. Then he adds, "But earlier, before everyone came out. . . The *Leggeroni* wouldn't

33

have thought about it twice."

"And you?" she challenges as she feels her unnamed anxiety growing.

Biscia smiles, still looking at nothing: "I haven't got any grenades with me."

"But otherwise, would you have done it?"

"Well, well. Aren't you full of questions today." And finally, he decides to meet her eyes. But the words that follow sting. "I hear you're spending a lot of time with your friend Maestri."

"I was expecting you to say 'I wouldn't do it because no one ordered me to.'"

"Maybe I wouldn't. But you never know what you'll do in a situation like that. You may surprise yourself."

"I suppose so. Have you talked to Olindo?"

He nods and takes a drag off the cigarette. The light breeze blowing from the mountains dispels the smoke behind him. Despite the north wind, the air is heavy with the smell of iron and coal from the smokestacks of the foundries. They are on Via Merano and are walking past the Ansaldo factories. A tram goes clanging by in the direction of Pegli. The enamel-blue sky extends to caress the green line of the mountains. The sun shines on the gray walls of the houses that shimmer in the vivid light. It's the perfect day for a romantic walk. They continue on for a good quarter of an hour at a steady pace. Their thoughts are frenetic but between them there is only a deafening silence.

This time it is Tilde who breaks the silence. "What are the orders?"

"We need to find out who the spy is, or they'll pick us all off, one by one."

"And they are asking me to do it."

"Only if you feel up to it."

34

A flare of anger blinds her. She flings the bicycle away. Biscia yelps in pain.

"Are you crazy?" he yells, face going red. But in his words there is no anger or jealousy. Only surprise. Where the rest should be, there is only duty. No emotions, only duty and the struggle. It is a cold place "where the sun of the future rises."

Fuck you, Biscia!

"And if I don't?" she asks defiantly, barely holding back her fury.

"Nothing's happening, then," he answers, as he picks up the heavy bicycle.

But she isn't finished, and her words tumble out sharp and poisonous: "Oh no? So instead, they'll hunt us down one by one and Tearnails will take by force what you're asking me to give to Hessen."

"It's not our fault if its come to this."

"Oh, no. It's not *our* fault. Is it yours?"

Biscia stares at their shadows on the sidewalk and answers in a hard, metallic voice. "Perhaps I shouldn't have been the one to tell you."

"So why did you?"

"We were not raised by Jesuits. Hypocrisy isn't for us."

"Are you so sure?"

"Besides, you asked me to come and talk to you."

Her nails bite into her palms and she's afraid to speak, not because of him, but for fear of what she might say. She wants to ask if he's stupid or just pretending to be. Instead, after a long silence, she says, "How can you not understand? I was hoping that they would send me someone else, anyone else, to give me *this* order. But I *had to* talk with *you* because you're the man I want to marry."

Finally, she has moved him. He no longer knows what to do with his hands, so he rolls another cigarette. His face freezes in a grim rictus that was meant to be a half-smile. When the cigarette is finally finished and the first puff of smoke rolls out into the cold air, he asks, "Tilde, do you need my permission?"

They are now at the end of Via Merano. Tilde looks across the road to Piazza Gattini. Beyond the gate of Villa Rossi, there is a park with holm oaks, palms, and magnolias. In that park, her little brother and his friends run, play, and pretend to be children again in the middle of all this hell. Somehow, they manage, despite the bombings and the fear and the debris. Despite the round-ups and deportations that make fathers and brothers disappear. Despite the shoes repaired with cardboard, the cold schools with no oil to heat them, and the cold houses with no wood to burn. Despite their too-short and too-worn coats and their thin woolen shirts, unable to protect them from the north wind. Despite the bellies filled only with watery polenta and black cabbage.

From this side of the road, she can see the tobacco factory, the shipyards and the railroad. Nothing but cement, walls, and other factories, wrapped by the gray effluence of smoking chimneys.

Silent tears fill her eyes and roll down her cheeks, reddened by the cold. Whether her tears are for the hopelessness that surrounds her or for Biscia's brutality, she doesn't know. She thinks about her mother's bad lungs, about her father, an anti-fascist worker who risks arrest and deportation every day. She thinks about how her youth is being wasted, lost to misery, air-raid sirens, and ambushes. If this hell is to be her life, it isn't worth living.

She feels pain under her left foot, like a pin prick. Angrily, she rubs the back of her hand on her face to dry her tears. She turns suddenly, seeking Biscia's eyes without finding them. Taking a deep breath, she speaks slowly and clearly, as if she were a judge pronouncing a death sentence. "Tell Commander Grandi that I accept the assignment. I'll be waiting for instructions on how to approach Captain Hessen."

Biscia nods. Without another word, he crosses the road and Tilde watches him enter Via Garibaldi and turn onto the Pontinetto. She's too upset to wonder if she will see him again, but the silent tears, that have begun again, are a scream of anger that no one can hear.

6.
THE CLOSED DOOR

Back in the corridor of the hospital again, I came across Totò Pertusiello. His face was a thundercloud. His hands were stuffed in his coat pockets, and he walked back and forth like a caged lion. The guard, a young policeman who didn't look like he'd been chosen for this job because of his keen intelligence, watched him, uneasy and bewildered. Perhaps he feared that his discontent was somehow his fault. He apparently didn't realize that someone like Deputy Police Commissioner Pertusiello wasn't in the habit of cooling his heels outside a closed door.

The second he saw me, Pertusiello asked about Jasmìne. If I'd been just a bit quicker, I would have asked him the same. I told him what I'd heard from the doctor a few days ago, and disappointment mingled with the thunder on the dark, almost Moorish face of this descendant of Amalfian olive pickers and fishermen. None of this was news to him. He explained that the head of neurology had painted a more optimistic but less comforting picture. Oxymorons have always been a passion of the Deputy Commissioner, like stockfish Genoese, French tobacco, or arias from *Rigoletto*. According to the neurosurgeon, the risk of permanent disability was more remote than death. Put that way, the prognosis frightened me. But Pertusiello hastened to explain: if she survived, Jasmìne probably wouldn't end up as a vegetable and would make a full recovery. A CAT scan and an MRI didn't show any injuries that might compromise her higher brain functions. If her heart and lungs kept working, she'd be able to talk, read, and reflect on her shitty life.

We sat next to each other, his chair barely containing his three hundred pounds. He nervously checked the time and then glued his eyes to the floor. Then silence. I've known him for more than twenty years, otherwise I would have thought, like the bovine guard, that he was angry with me.

I wondered if the new prognosis ought to be considered good news. My continued anxiety gave me the answer by reminding me that what had kept me awake for sixteen hours before this very door was the fear that Jasmìne would die. The risk of disability, even though it was important, seemed like a minor problem.

I recalled the long nightmare that had led to her release but still might end in tragedy. It took three months of patient stakeouts and wiretaps by the Homicide Division to discover where the girls were held and arrest the bastards. They were all young foreigners, *extracomunitarie*, Africans and Slavs without residence permits, waiting to be sold to their executioners. When they broke into the farmhouse between the villages of Voltaggio and Gavi, the police managed to release eight of them, four of whom were minors. The operation, carried out on a cold January night, had gone exactly according to plan, and if the newspapers had found out about it, it would have been remembered as one of the most dramatic successes of the decade. No bloodshed, five merciless thugs arrested and eight girls saved from the slaughterhouse. Unfortunately none of the eight was an Ivorian prostitute named Jasmìne Kilamba. According to the girls, two of their number were missing, but only their captors knew where they were. So there would be no press conference. We couldn't risk having the butchers they'd been sold to panicking and getting rid of them. In addition, some members of the gang were still free. Tipping them off that the ring had been broken wouldn't make them any easier to catch.

Pertusiello had directed the operation in person, along with Inspectors Fois and Levrero. The actual assault was entrusted to a SWAT team armed with submachine guns and protected by bulletproof vests. Getting back to the police station at six in the morning, he called me to tell me that Jasmìne wasn't in the farmhouse. But he kept repeating, "We'll find her, we'll make them talk."

I had rushed to his office to find out exactly what had happened. The organization itself was made up of Italians and Eastern Europeans and they all had rap sheets as long as my arm. The leaders were two brothers, Celso and Gustavo Trevisan, originally from Vicenza and already wanted for murder and pimping. Pertusiello explained that his officers were questioning them while they waited for Dr. Ferlito, the lead prosecutor for the investigation.

"Celso is a tough one," he said as he sipped coffee delivered from the bar next door. "But I'm sure Gustavo will crack in less than twenty-four hours."

Twenty-four hours was twenty-four too many as far as I was concerned, but saying so wouldn't change anything.

"Have you talked to the girls?" I asked.

"I was on the bus with them."

"Did anyone know Jasmìne?"

"Two of them remembered her."

"Did you ask when was she sold?"

He nodded and, shrugging wearily, took out a cigarette and lit it. "A week ago yesterday."

"Can you live through eight days of torture?" I asked with a shudder.

"They didn't know what was in store for them. To keep them quiet, they told them they were going to be marrying rich men."

"And they told Jasmìne that as well?"

"How would I know?" he snapped.

That wasn't going to be enough for me. "Where did you take the girls?"

"To a safe place."

I admit, I lost it. "Knock it off, Totò!" I started screaming, "Don't give me that bullshit. I'm not a journalist looking for a scoop."

He turned red and roared, "Yeah, Bacci. That's the problem. Who the hell *are* you and why are you here?"

"You know damn well why I'm here. And you call yourself a friend."

"You ungrateful bastard," he shouted. "Do you know where I was last night, while you were tucked up in your bed? And do you have any idea what kind of day I'm facing or when I'll get any sleep myself? You were the first person I called after the SWAT team had carried out a *covert* operation—does that word mean anything to you?—I called you before I called the prosecutor! Even though we're friends, you are still a private citizen. What more do you want from me?"

"Fine, fine," I said, getting up to leave. "But without the help of a *private citizen,* there wouldn't have been any operation at all, covert or otherwise."

That was only the truth. It had all started with a letter from Chérie, Jasmìne's transsexual friend, which landed in my mailbox just before he was killed. In those few lines Chérie outlined the chilling commerce of which Jasmìne was now a victim. Young illegal aliens sold for money to sadistic killers who then tortured them to death. Once they disappeared, it was as if they had never existed. I remembered Olindo Grandi's words: "Sometimes we forget that without friends, we are nothing."

I was on my way out the door when Totò Pertusiello stopped me.

"Wait," he said. "We're both tired and it's too easy to say things we'll regret. The girls are at the Belvedere Boarding School in Sampierdarena, guarded by ten men, all armed to the teeth."

We decided to have breakfast at the coffee bar next door. Even though it was seven o'clock in the morning, there was a lot of activity in the police station and Dr. Ferlito had not yet arrived. Pertusiello told me that he would also question a Russian crime boss that one of the girls had fingered. He had helped her enter Italy secretly and then sold her to the Trevisan brothers. The man, fat and looking like a caricature from the Brezhnev era, apart from the missing bearskin hat, showed up around eight-thirty accompanied by his lawyer. At nine o'clock the prosecutor rushed in, a fifty-year-old lady, tall and thin, strong-willed, and dressed as if she were twenty years older. After Pertusiello had introduced us, she shook my hand and threw me out, shutting herself in the office with him for a full briefing. I decided to prowl the hallways. I eavesdropped behind a door where they were questioning one of the men they had captured and I recognized the metallic voice of Levrero. There must have been a couple of other officers with him. It sounded like the usual: make him believe that one of the others was cooperating and then accuse him of being the mastermind. The dialogue was punctuated by loud, wet sounds followed by yelps and groans.

I went back to the crowded waiting room, and there was the Russian, sitting next to his lawyer, a man of sixty with a pleasant appearance, a subtly-dyed mustache, dressed as a dandy, and so pleased with himself he might burst. The Russian was nervous, constantly fidgeting. He seemed impatient to tell his side of the story. At that moment, an officer arrived and invited them to follow him. They slunk into the office and left half an hour later, the lawyer as fresh when he went in and the Russian with a red face and glassy eyes. Meanwhile two officers brought in the man questioned by Levrero. He had a swollen eye and was swabbing his bloody nose with a tissue. A third officer came into the waiting room and called: " Gustavo Trevisan's lawyer!"

As soon as he was inside, the lawyer began shouting and threatening to sue. I heard Pertusiello grumbling, Dr. Ferlito shrieking—so loudly it made my skin crawl—and Levrero repeating, "Come on, Trevisan, tell them how it went. You tried to escape and you fell down the stairs. If you hadn't had to be handcuffed, none of this would have happened."

Two hours passed, and Trevisan was still inside. This made me very hopeful, because I was beginning to smell a deal. Perhaps, to save the girls, the prosecutor had promised a reduced sentence in return for cooperation.

I ran into Inspector Fois at the coffee vending machine. He was very tired and told me he had turned the screw on Celso, but that you can't get blood out of a stone. I asked him to tell Pertusiello I was leaving and that I'd call him that afternoon.

Outside my head, the phone rang and I returned to the present. The number on the display indicated that the call came from a landline in the western part of Genoa. As soon as I answered, a woman's voice, cracking with emotion, asked, "Mr. Pagano?"

"Speaking."

"I'm sorry to bother you," she said. "I'm Enrico Parodi's daughter. I'm calling you on behalf of my father. I went to visit him, as I do every day, and I found him upset, almost hysterical. It took half an hour to calm him enough to find out what had happened."

"Did Olindo Grandi call him?"

"Yes, to tell him you'd be visiting."

"That's odd. Some people find me slightly annoying but . . . "

"The fact is, Dad has a delicate nervous system. The war marked him. He joined the partisans and went to fight in the mountains when he was still almost a child."

"Look, I'm sorry," I cut her short. "But it was Grandi who suggested I visit him."

"You know how these old men are. They remember things as they were, but they forget things like how frail their friends are now."

"So a visit isn't a good idea."

"Don't be offended," she added. "My parents knew yours well and they were very fond of them. I don't want you to think I'm being rude, but I'm worried about my father's health. . ."

"Don't worry, ma'am. I'll ask Grandi for someone else I can talk to."

"Really?" she asked, surprised, as if we had been talking about the weather.

"I don't want to be responsible for giving one of the last living partisan heroes a nervous breakdown."

A laugh came over the line, a sort of giggle that had something hysterical in it.

"It wasn't easy," she explained. "I looked you up in the phone book and I called your office. A very kind lady answered me, who, after some convincing, understood the urgency of the situation and gave me your number."

Once again Zainab had exceeded her duties and become my secretary.

"OK," I said. "Can I take advantage of your courtesy and ask you something else?"

"Of course," she replied.

"How old are you?"

She froze. That was no question to ask a lady, even an unknown lady you'd only spoken with on the phone.

"Fifty-eight," she replied slowly. "Why do you ask?"

"Have you ever met a woman, a little older than your father, named Nicla?"

She remained silent for a few seconds, and from her hesitant answer, I realized that she had been trying to remember. "I met a Nicla who lived in Panigaro and had a stand in the market of Piazza dei Micone. She died twenty years ago."

"Married, with children?"

"She was crippled and never married. She certainly didn't have children, because she left the stand to her niece, her brother's daughter, who still runs it today."

"You don't remember a Nicla from Sestri, married, the mother of a man who could be about your age?"

Another silence, another flight over a past that had opened up behind her like a sinkhole.

"No," she said eventually, very sure of herself.

"Since you are so kind, let me ask you one last thing."

"OK," she said, embarrassed. "But please make it quick, I'm calling you from my father's home phone so this is costing him a fortune."

"Forgive me," I replied. "I'm a real jerk. Can I call you back at the number you called me from?"

"Certainly," she said, very pleased.

When I called her back she answered immediately. I could hear a raspy voice—her father, no doubt—grumbling in the background.

"Of course, you have no obligation to answer me," I said, "but your father's reaction intrigues me. What could have shaken him so much?"

"I really don't know," she said, and she seemed sincere. "I tried to find out myself but he was too agitated to explain."

"I have a proposition for you," I said. "When he calms down, talk to him and then call me back. This might be a huge help and you can talk to him without disturbing his peace of mind."

"Sure. I'm happy to do that," she said warmly.

We said goodbye and hung up.

Pertusiello had followed the conversation, puffing and moving nervously in his chair.

"What the hell are you doing?" he asked. "Why are you harassing old partisans?"

"I have a new client who's forcing me to reopen my family album."

"You're having quite a week, aren't you?" he said sympathetically. "I hope you can let your sleeping dragons lie."

"After all these years I've already had to return to Sestri Ponente. Did I ever tell you that my mother was born and raised there, and that she even met my father there?"

"I guess not. If you did, I'd remember. How did it go?"

"I talked with a commander of a RAG. And that seems to have uncovered an entire world that had been safely buried."

"So it's true! You really don't have anything better to do than to bother poor old men!"

"My client doesn't have much time left to live and has asked me to find the brother he never met. And do you know why? To leave him his fortune."

"Fortune as in capital F?"

"About three million Euros."

"Son of a!" he gasped. "Tell him the brother he's looking for is me. For that kind of money I'll quit the police and counterfeit documents."

"Feh. The minute you open your mouth even a German will know you're not from Sestri."

"I'll practice, I'll take an accelerated pronunciation course. For three million Euros, I'll throw in Polish and Chinese, too."

"Well, if I can't find this brother, I'll consider your offer."

"Why wait? Let's share! 50-50."

Pertusiello liked to joke like this, pretending an amorality and cynicism that only existed in his imagination. In fact, he was a stand-up guy, a straight arrow who took things like Truth and Justice seriously. I knew this dark side helped him to get into the heads of the criminals he hunted, but this time it all had a different purpose. He was concerned about me and he was trying to make our impotence bearable.

After all, we were both men cooling our heels outside a closed door.

7.
COFFEE WITH IOLANDA

Sestri Ponente, February 1944

Iolanda is waiting for Tilde at four o'clock in her home on Via Cavagnaro, an old road that once led to a monastery but now goes to a hospital. Olindo Grandi had said she would arrange for her to meet Captain Hessen. The woman speaks German very well and at the cigar factory she was promoted from the production line to office worker. Everyone knows that she's friendly with the new masters; she had been seen leaving the *Kommandantur* on Via Pagano Doria arm in arm with officers sporting swastikas. Several people had made certain that the Resistance knew about this, but they did nothing. Iolanda, it seems, is playing both sides. She works in the offices where you don't breathe the terrible air of the factory and, in exchange for her "friendliness" with the *crucchi*, brings home all sorts of exotic things like meat, pasta, eggs, and cheese. She also had a sideline in passing valuable information to the partisans.

She's a venal woman who's chosen to play a dangerous game, betting that her good looks will be a trump in the rigged game of an occupied country. Just thirty years old, green eyes, slim waistline, and wide hips. Breasts overflow the neckline of the silky blouses that a tailor's shop on Via Ramiro Ginocchio makes just for her, along with her elegant suits and coats. She wears high-heeled shoes and sheer stockings with a seam on the back. Her brown hair is cut in the latest style by a hairdresser from Via Garibaldi who never tires of telling her she looks like various movie stars. She uses creams and lipsticks and wears makeup on her eyes, but does it tastefully and without vulgarity. Those lucky enough to get close to her realize that she wears a refined perfume, probably French. Iolanda arouses desire and forbidden thoughts as well as hatred more careful, she answers that she feels safe because she has something good to offer to everyone.

"As long as this war lasts," she tells Tilde while she's still at the door, "no one has the luxury of shame." She speaks to her woman-to-woman, with a frankness that suggests genuine solidarity. She wears a chenille dressing gown that protects her from the cold. She's not wearing makeup but even so, to Tilde, she seems very beautiful. She invites her in as if they've been friends for years. "Come on, let's go to the kitchen."

The kitchen is warmer than the rest of the house, but not enough to make her want to take off her coat. Iolanda scoops some wood up off the floor and throws it into the tiled stove. Then she picks up a jute bag and adds coal to the fire.

"So you have to meet the captain," she says, taking a tin can out of the cupboard. When she takes off the lid, Tilde realizes that it's full of coffee. Real coffee. Not the barley surrogate she drinks at home. While Iolanda prepares the coffee-maker and puts it on the stove, Tilde picks up the tin left on the table and sniffs it. She always liked the smell of coffee.

"So good," she sighs, enjoying the noise of the fire that's now beginning to crackle.

"It tastes even better," her hostess replies with a smile.

Then she sits and says, "Sunday evening there will be a party. We'll go together. I'll introduce you as a friend. Will you have problems at home?"

"I'll say I'm sleeping at my aunt's."

"Good girl. At seven p.m., we'll take the tram to Genoa. We have to be there before curfew."

In the coffee-maker, the water is boiling. Iolanda flips it upside down and puts it on the marble table-top. From the cupboard, she takes a second tin and hands it to Tilde who opens it and stares, enchanted. It's full of sugar. Completely full. At her house, what sugar there is comes courtesy of the ration book. Her mother is sick and needs care, her brother goes to school, and the black market is beyond what little they earn.

"Do you have something to wear?" the woman asks without preamble.

Tilde was expecting this question. Obviously she doesn't have stylish clothes or sheer stockings and shoes with heels. It's hard for her to imagine herself being dressed like that and she's sure she would feel uncomfortable. But it's not just that. She wonders if that's what Captain Hessen would expect from her. When he met her, she was wearing an old coat and mended woolen stockings. She tries to explain it to Iolanda, who listens to her carefully.

"Good thinking, Tilde," she finally says. "We're going to need to find you a convincing look."

She puts two chipped cups and two teaspoons on the table and starts pouring coffee. In a time of war, saucers would be a luxury even for someone like her. "After all," she adds, "your youth does more for you than any dress. Hessen has good taste, makeup adds little to beauty like yours."

Tilde hesitantly pours a teaspoon of sugar into the coffee and seeks out Iolanda's eyes. She smiles. "Don't be shy. It's all free."

She adds two more and stirs the spoon in the cup. She sips it slowly, her eyes almost closed. The blessed coffee. It goes down hot and sweet and gives her a feeling of languor she hasn't felt in ages. In those moments, which she tries to make last as long as possible, the pain of Biscia's memory fades. She doesn't forget him, she couldn't even if she wanted to, but she manages to think of him without agony. The heat invades her and she feels a comfortable sense of well-being. The kitchen is warm now and she can take off her coat.

Iolanda has also finished her coffee. From a pocket she pulls out a pack of Eva cigarettes and lights up with a kitchen match.

"Do you smoke?"

Tilde shakes her head no, even though she's tempted to start. Then

48

she remembers the last time she met him, those cigarettes consumed one after the other to show himself a man while avoiding acting like one.

Stupid little boy, you think you're a tough guy, now, huh?

The pain comes cascading back, taking revenge for that brief moment of coffee-induced happiness.

"The problem is the shoes," says Iolanda, glancing under the table. "Have you got a decent pair?"

She realizes that the ones she's wearing, with their cardboard soles, aren't going to work. Her last stylish shoes were given to her by her mother before the war. They were sequined and she had worn them at Elisabetta's wedding, her cousin who was killed during an Anglo-American bombing.

Despair overwhelms her. Will this hell will never end? She remembers the nights when the air-raid siren jarred her awake. Still half asleep, she listens to the dark rumble of the aircraft getting closer and closer. Then her mother barges into the room where she sleeps with her brother. "Get up! We've got to get out of here now!"

"You go," she mutters, turning her face to the wall. "Leave me here."

"Are you crazy, Tilde?" her mother replies, pulling her blankets off and shaking her hard. Her assault gives Tilde the strength to get up, throw something on, and run out into the night that begins to light up with the glowing trails of tracer bullets. The once-black sky comes to life with colorful fireworks and the muffled thump of the first bomb arrives. Yet they are still alive. They enter the shelter knowing that their number isn't up yet.

Why do you ask us to risk our lives by fighting the Germans and then bomb us?

Her brother isn't like her. As soon as the siren sounds, he is already up, standing in the middle of the room, shaking. But her mother's violence has given her the strength to continue living and struggling for another day. In her exhausted voice, weakened by illness, she heard the dismay and disbelief of a parent watching a child slip away. Tilde didn't want to disappoint her and add her pain to her mother's, blaming her for her unhappiness as if it was her fault. Her mother has no faults, neither her father. They work so hard to survive and provide for her and her brother.

"Where are you, Miss?" Iolanda asks gently, shaking her loose from her memories.

"Do you know the captain?" she answers, blushing. She isn't ashamed of what is waiting for her, but that her memories, ruthless and relentless as hunger, throw her weakness into glaring relief.

Of course, Iolanda understands none of this, and looking at her, with large green eyes full of tenderness, she whispers, "Tilde, can I ask you something?"

She nods, lost and surprised by this unfamiliar display of interest and concern.

"Is it your first time?"

She's about to say no, but she is seized with an irresistible desire, as sweet and warm as the coffee she just drank, to trust in someone. The truth comes out. "Yes," she confesses, blushing again.

Iolanda leans forward and stretches a hand across the table, taking hers. It is cold and Iolanda smiles. "It might sound blasphemous," she murmurs in a deep voice, "but you are lucky. Hessen is different from the others. A kind man, who has found himself in a uniform because of a twist of fate."

Her words infuse Tilde with courage. "Have you slept with him?" she asks.

The woman shakes her head. "Unfortunately, no. I'm not doing the choosing."

"It's war," Tilde blurts out, and then silently asks herself what those words mean.

Iolanda inhales cigarette smoke and lets it out in small puffs, her gaze far away. "War," she repeats. "Maybe it just shows us what we really are."

"Nothing," she says. "Let's get back to shoes. What's your size?"

"Maybe size eight?"

"Let me see."

Tilde gets up and stands in front of her. The woman puts out the cigarette in the cup, bends over, and, with a gentle gesture, takes off Tilde's shoe and slips her foot into it. She moves it to the sides, right and left.

"They fit," she says. "I'd say size eight is fine. I'll get you a pair."

She gives the shoe back to Tilde and slips her foot back into her slipper. Tilde wants to hug her, but she holds back.

"Iolanda," she asks with a lump in her throat, "Why do you do it?"

The other hesitates for a moment, then, shrugging, she replies, "I do like the easy life, but this is my country. I won't stand against my own people."

Throughout the week, Iolanda occupies her thoughts. She believes she understands why Iolanda gets along so well with both Germans and partisans. It isn't just because she gives her body to the former and her soul to the latter. It's the generosity of her spirit that makes her untouchable. When she offered Tilde warmth, clothes, and coffee, she hadn't done it to flaunt her privileged condition. Iolanda had been moved by her being so young, only nineteen, and had only wanted to share the best she had with her. That is why knowing her had been a source of comfort and gratitude instead of humiliation. As the days go by, she realizes that thinking of Iolanda makes the prospect of the German party less distressing, even exciting.

So when, during the lunch break at the factory, Dolores, who had limped badly as long as Tilde could remember, predicts that sooner or later "we'll find that whore dead on a sidewalk," she angrily replies, "What do you know about it? You've never even met her!"

"Why," replies the other, "have you?"

Tilde knows she can say nothing because of the mission they have given her. But Iolanda deserves to be defended.

"They say she's a generous woman."

"Oh yes, really generous!" Dolores mocks, laughing loudly and clapping her hands. Then she becomes serious and adds, "Generous with the *crucchi* and a bastard with our own men."

"What do you mean?"

"Oh, nothing, nothing," she winks, with an air of someone who knows more than she says.

"No," she insists, "you're not getting away with that. What do you know?"

"Why are you getting so upset, Tilde? What's it to you?"

Tilde realizes that this is getting out of hand and that she may have said too much. "You have to be careful what you say. These days casual gossip like that can get someone killed."

But Dolores isn't backing down. "It's not casual gossip. Everyone knows she's a source for the *crucchi*."

"Sleeping with Germans is one thing. Being a spy is another."

The lame woman lowers her voice and returns to the attack. "And who do you think it was that reported Sandra and had her deported?"

"You're saying it was Iolanda?"

"Who else? Didn't they both work here, at the factory?"

"So? You work at the factory."

"From her perch in the office—where they put her on purpose— that bitch finds out everything about everyone and passes her information to German headquarters."

Sunday is still two days away and Dolores's words have alarmed her. She can't wait to finish her shift and, as soon as she leaves the factory, she takes her bicycle and searches for the commander. A gray blanket of *maccaia*, typical Genoese weather, humid and oppressive, covers the streets, and chimney smoke poisons the air. She tries his house on Via Paglia, without finding him. Then the Gaggero bakery, hoping he's still at work. Eventually, she decides to try the Becca, the Green Cross Center of Sestri. She enters and sees him with three young men, crouched down to repair the wheel of a stretcher. She marches up to him and, under the astonished eyes of the others, says, "I need to talk to you."

Olindo realizes something must have happened. He gets up, grabs her by the arm and pushes her into an office. He closes the door and, when they are alone, orders her to explain.

Her words rush out, explaining her conversation with Dolores, but also the impression Iolanda made on her. She seems to implore him for reassurance. She wants to hear that the woman is trustworthy. But he can't provide guarantees he doesn't have.

"I don't know this Dolores," he tells her stiffly. "Who knows? She might be right. If you don't feel up to it, it's still not too late to change your mind."

"I don't care about Dolores," she replies, her voice breaking with emotion. "I want to know about Iolanda from you."

Olindo realizes that it wasn't just fear that made her seek him out. Perhaps, at nineteen, trusting someone is more important than risking your life. He can't provide guarantees he doesn't have. But he can lie. He replies, "Tilde, if I had any suspicions, do you think I would have sent you to her?"

8.
FIRST TRUTHS

T Just outside the hospital I said goodbye to Pertusiello and I started making phone calls on my cell phone. Finally, we had been able to see Jasmìne, bandaged like a mummy and sunk into the black hole of the medically-induced coma, a tangle of wires and tubes without which she wouldn't have survived two minutes. We talked to the head of the department who, with both kindness and fatalism, reiterated that everything had been done that could be done and that it was now in the hands of time and fate.

From the small square in front of the hospital complex, I called Olindo Grandi to let him know that his friend Balletta didn't want to meet me. He knew it already, because Balletta's daughter had called him first.

"What's he afraid of?" I asked.

"Everything," he grinned. "Including his own shadow."

"Did he know Nicla?" I asked point-blank.

"He says no," he replied. Then he added, "I suppose you'll be needing another address."

I admitted it would have been helpful and, just to twist his tail, I begged him to choose an informant who wouldn't have a nervous breakdown when he heard my name.

"Balletta is unique," he said, playing along. "Anything unexpected that breaks his daily routine and he ends up under the bed, shaking like a leaf." Then he added, "Old age is a curse. But if you really want my advice, talk to Longo. He's maybe not the friendliest guy you'll ever meet, but we fought together and maybe he can help."

"Where can I find him?"

He asked me to wait and went to retrieve his address book. When he came back, he began to apologize. "It's been so long since I've heard from him, that I'd forgotten his number. My memory isn't what it used to be. I'll make a phone call to introduce you."

I thanked him and entered the number on my phone. Once on the street, I started my Vespa and headed toward Sestri. It was almost noon. The sky was gray and the wind had shifted. It was coming from the sea bringing warmth, humidity, and rain. Against the western mountains, the clouds thickened and covered their snowy peaks. The air was full of the unmistakable smell of Cornigliano's steel mills. The smell wasn't as bad as it used to be when they worked at full speed, spreading a thin red dust on balconies and windows. In Sestri, back in the day, that smell used to invade the streets like a poisonous gas, spread by the wind out of Africa, the sirocco.

Fifteen minutes later, I parked my Vespa on Via Biancheri. I walked toward Piazza Baracca, looking for somewhere for a quick bite. Passing the square, I found myself on the corner between Via Cavalli and Piazza Oriani. My eye was drawn to the Cinema Verdi and what had been the fascist headquarters, where, according to my grandfather, on that night in '44 the partisans had hoisted the red flag and the tricolor. After eating a sandwich at the counter of a café, I began walking aimlessly. As I wandered down a side street, and past a small, half-closed door, something I had seen slowly surfaced from my subconscious and I retraced my steps. It was the plaque of the Italian Partisan Association of Sestri. How many times I had passed it without noticing it?

I decided to try my luck. I went in and took the steep staircase that led me to a cramped office with two clean desks. Through the glass door, which opened onto a large terrace, an opaque, almost timid, light entered. On the walls were flags, billboards, and yellowed photographs—portraits of fallen partisans and pictures depicting groups of Sestri's Garibaldi brigades: Longhi, Alpron, and Sordi. The office was completely deserted so I called out, "Is there anyone here?"

55

From an adjacent room, an old man emerged. "Good morning," he said politely. "Can I do something for you?"

"If you have a minute, I'd like to ask you a few questions."

He smiled and said, "I'm eighty-nine. Better make it quick!"

His voice was rough, almost scratchy. He wore a dark beret and had a well-groomed white mustache. He was a big man and dressed in stylish simplicity, corduroy trousers, a checked shirt and a wool vest the same color as the beret.

I laughed and sat in front of one of the desks. "I'm looking for a person," I said. "The son of a woman who lived here in Sestri."

"What's his name?" he asked.

"That's the problem. I don't know."

He looked at me with an eloquent expression, a mixture of amazement and mirth, and dropped his hand on the desktop.

"So you've got your work cut out for you," he said. "Why are you looking for him?"

"Because I have to tell him he's going to inherit a lot of money."

"Lucky him," he said, holding back a laugh. Then, with a bit of mistrust, he asked, "Are you a notary?"

"Let's say I'm helping a notary out. The brother of the man I'm looking for is very sick and asked me to find him."

"Well, if he's his brother," he said, leaning his elbows on the desk, "doesn't your client know?"

"They're actually half-brothers. They have different fathers," I explained. "The only thing he knows is that their mother was called Nicla."

"So you don't even know the mother's last name?"

"It's complicated."

"He was born during the war. His father was a German officer who died in '44. . ."

"Did we kill him?" he interrupted.

"Yup. In the attack at the Odeon Cinema. Remember?"

"How could I forget? They remind me of it every day." he said, waiving his arm at a frame on the wall behind me filled with photographs of the Turchino Pass martyrs. "One of them was from Sestri. I knew him well; his name was Sandro."

I stared at the photograph of Sandro Fallabrino, killed in retaliation by the Germans when he was just nineteen, the same age my daughter is now. I thought Hessen was right. The Resistance was made up of kids like this, boys who had killed before they had had their first woman. It was a time when picking up a rifle was just what you did. The only decision they really made was who to shoot.

"Before dying," I went on, "this German's father had a relationship with a partisan girl and got her pregnant. At birth, the child was taken to Cologne by his German aunt and uncle. He was never told anything about his mother and he thought she had died in childbirth. He just recently discovered that she had actually died several years ago and that she had another son with an Italian man after he was born."

"A partisan girl named Nicla?" he asked, frowning. He was lost in his thoughts for some time, then he sighed, "I don't trust my memory, especially with names. Many have fallen into oblivion. But the memories of those days are still fresh and I think I would remember her."

"I'm sure of it," I said.

"Didn't you tell me you work for a German notary?" he asked abruptly.

"More or less," I said.

"*More* or *less?* Which is it?"

Mistrust and suspicion showed on his face. I couldn't really blame him. I hadn't even introduced myself.

"My client is called Hessen," I said. "He lives in Cologne and his father was the captain of the Wehrmacht."

"The name doesn't ring a bell," he observed. "But you didn't answer me."

"I did explain that I'm working to make a stranger rich."

"And are you paid for that?"

"Naturally."

The atmosphere was becoming tense and I feared he was about to kick me out. It was for moments just such as this that I kept an ace up my sleeve: my father's name. You could bet that any man who worked in this shrine to the memory of the Partisans had heard of him. Before I could speak, the old man became animated and raising his head and looking me square in the eye, asked, "Do you know why I'm asking you this?"

"I'm sure you've got questions about my job."

"No. Something's not quite right," he said, shaking his head. "When did this Hessen find out he has a brother?"

"A few weeks ago."

"Bullshit," It wasn't an exclamation. It was a verdict.

"Bullshit?"

"He has known for at least twenty years."

I began to think that time had taken its toll on him. At that age it happens, even though he spoke and moved with enviable ease.

"I'm sure I'm not wrong," he continued, frowning. "It must have been in the early 1990s. Some German guy came in here asking questions, a blond man with blue eyes, about forty. He spoke perfect Italian and asked me about a woman, just like you are doing now."

"I told you. I don't remember names, but the story he told me was identical to yours. It stuck with me."

"Nicla and Hessen mean nothing to you?"

"Nothing at all, and maybe it's not even important. I know that he questioned other comrades as well; it's a pity so many of them are gone." He paused, then asked, "By the way, what's your name?"

"Bacci Pagano."

His face lit up and he pointed his index finger.

"Would you be Pagano, the private investigator?"

"I would."

"But then," he said, bursting into a booming laugh and pounding his fist on the desk, "you're the son of Guido and Anna! Your father worked with my brother at the Fossati factory. Then he went to the auto-repair shop in Sampierdarena. Your mother worked at the cigar factory. I knew them well, both of them!"

"When?"

"After the war. We used to go to Borzoli, to the Vacca Morta restaurant, to celebrate, and any excuse would do. I still remember the white wine from Coronata and how we usually ended up under the table. If I'm honest, it tasted like sulfur and we'd probably hate it today, but then it seemed like champagne. We all had a lot of living to catch up on, after the war."

"Did you fight?"

"Of course!" he said proudly. "I started here in town, right after September 8th, the day the Germans took over. By the end of '43, the Germans had me on the list of wanted partisans and I had to move up to the mountains. I joined Miro's men in the Borbera Valley, in the sixth operational zone, and came back to town on April 24th, the day before the liberation. For two years I survived eating chestnuts. Your

59

father, if I'm not mistaken, was in Urbe with the Mingo division."

"That's right, he left town in '44."

"I've also met your grandfather, your mother's father. During the war he worked for Vaccari Ceramics."

"Yes, Grandfather Baciccia. . ."

"A good man, an anti-fascist from the start."

"You know everything about my family. What's your name?"

"Luigi Bavastro, but everyone calls me Gino. It was my battle name. Surely your parents must have spoken of me."

Of course they had. Grandfather Baciccia had told me about him. He was one of the *Leggeroni*, a famously daring group of partisans from Sestri who had worked in the city. The anarchist spirit that animated them had earned them their reputation but the name seemed ungenerous to me—*Leggeroni*: The Wild Boys—a small injustice of history. I always thought that if I had found myself living in those times, I would have been one of them.

"Absolutely," I said. "Grandfather Baciccia gave me an earful about you."

"And your father?"

"He never spoke much."

"True, Guido was always one of few words. Your grandfather must have told you that we were known as the *Leggeroni*. Maybe they were right. At the end of '43 I had to escape from Sestri because I screwed up big time. I worked as a bricklayer and I always went armed. One morning, I was repairing the roof of a house in Calcinara, when a Black Brigade truck passed, filled with men belting out that horrible fascist song, *Giovinezza*. Even with all that practicing, they were as out of tune as a pack of braying donkeys. It was an actual war crime. I had in my pocket a brand new Mauser, stolen from the shipyard. I couldn't resist and I started shooting. I'm sure I hit someone. Anyway, I ran for it but one of them recognized me so they came to my house to pick me up. I saved myself because I liked women. That evening, to celebrate my feat, I went to Mariù's brothel. My brother came to warn me and I took refuge at the Becca hospital. Eventually, they smuggled me out lying on a stretcher."

His tale fascinated me, and, for a moment, I forgot Hessen, my assignment, and even the bandages, wires, and tubes wrapping Jasmìne's body. I had a glimpse of how the path I thought I had chosen myself had been laid out for me.

So many times I had wondered what had induced me to do this job, which alternated between filth and absurdity, the way that I had chosen to do it. Why did I risk, not just my skin, but the dreams and aspirations that make a normal life worth living for the uncertainty that comes with living on the edge of catastrophe. I always thought that there were two ways to kill. You had to either believe you were saving your own life or not care if you lived or died. In that moment, I understood the boys like Gino and my father who had gone off to war. We were the same, with the same motivations, the same outlook on life. For the first time I realized I was the son of my father, a man who, during the Resistance, fought and killed other men. Was my chronic inability to plan for the future a direct consequence of my twenty-year-old father's inability to believe a future might exist? It's true that they were twenty and I am fifty; that between their present and their future stood a wall of history and war, occupation, starvation and death while the only thing that stood between my present and future were the obstacles of my own making. But then why did I feel such an affinity for them?

I wondered why none of this had occurred to me before, and the answer was easy. My father never talked about his experiences. Gino was right, Guido Pagano was a man of few words. Everything I knew about the war I heard from my grandfather. He was a worker and a communist, he had survived prison, had been beaten by the Fascists, had suffered the humiliation of walking home covered in his own shit after being forced to drink castor oil in the center of town. But Grandfather Baciccia had never killed anyone. I don't think he ever even picked up a gun. The enthralling stories he told me with such care had shown me much of the world that had shaped me. But they didn't, they couldn't, reveal certain hard truths. Grandpa was made of different, better stuff.

I lifted my eyes and saw Gino staring at me silently. He smiled gently, an affectionate and sympathetic smile, almost as if he had read my mind.

"Look," he said, distracting me from my gloomy thoughts, "I'd like to help you, but I'm not sure how I can."

"You've done it already," I said.

"Have you tried asking around?"

"I talked to Olindo Grandi."

"To Olindo?" he asked, surprised.

"The commander of the PAG. . ."

"*You* are going to explain to *me* who Olindo Grandi is?" he interrupted with a snort. "And he told you nothing?"

"About what?"

"About the German, twenty years ago."

"Maybe he forgot."

He waved his arm in a theatrical gesture of dissent. "Are you kidding? He never forgets anything. The memory of an elephant, that one."

"Did Hessen talk to him too, then?"

He shook his head, but not in answer my question. I think he was wondering why Grandi had kept silent.

"I'll call him, when I get a minute," he said. "How can I find you?"

I left him a business card and thanked him. He walked me to the door and took leave of me with an energetic handshake. I had the impression that, saying goodbye to me, he was remembering my family, one by one, and saying goodbye to all those who were now gone. A surge of self-pity welled up out of my past: I was a survivor of a time lost forever. Perhaps he read my mind again because, as I made my way down the stairs, I heard his hoarse voice echo behind me, "Hey, Pagano! Remember to shut the door behind you!"

9.
MISSION ACCOMPLISHED

Genoa, February 1944

The car, driven by Sergeant Walden, enters the gate and makes its way through the park surrounding a hillside villa in the Albaro neighborhood. She can hear the gravel crackling under the tires as the headlights flicker through the night. From the shadows, silhouettes of giant trees take shape, sunk in humidity and silence.

They turn off the road over the Terralba railway line just after Gestapo headquarters and Tilde feels a shiver run up her spine. At the party, she had drunk three glasses of champagne, but even her unaccustomed inebriation doesn't prevent a feeling in the pit of her stomach that makes her feel as if she is suddenly suspended over a void. She'd never tried French champagne before and she had expected something similar to the moscato that her father used to buy at Christmas near Acqui Terme, before the war. Tonight, she had learned that champagne is something quite different and that, in another life, its bubbles would have given the world, at least for a while, a rosy glow.

Iolanda, elegant in a long, black dress, had introduced her to some officers who eyed her hungrily in the dim light of the candles. There had been an air-raid alarm and all the electric lights were off. In the semi-darkness, Tilde watched the room fill with shadowy figures, minions of hell celebrating a dark Sabbath, incomprehensible incantations and cruel laughter echoing. Men displayed their uniforms adorned with eagles, skulls, and swastikas as if they were magical talismans that made them invulnerable. There were many women, some blondes who spoke German, and others with dark hair who spoke a universal language. They needed no interpreter to understand what singer with long platinum hair. She sang songs so melancholy that, listening to them, Tilde found herself moved even by the harsh language of the *crucchi*.

Iolanda had found a light colored overcoat for her, barely frayed on the sleeves, which fit her perfectly. Like a caring mother, she had worked to create an *ensemble* suited for her debut in society. Silk blouse buttoned to the neck, a suit with a tube skirt, and a pair of black shoes with low heels made her look like an innocent young Italian girl out with her friends for a pleasant evening.

Tilde searched for Captain Hessen's pale face among the other officers without finding him. However, she identified Sergeant Walden and pointed him out to her friend. Iolanda wasted no time and soon, they were amiably chatting, without Tilde understanding a word. There was a long conversation that seemed to retelling the story of her first meeting with Captain Hessen: the ambush on Via Sant'Alberto, the interrogation at headquarters, the brief detention and Sergeant Walden's checking her story by visiting her aunt's house. They had awakened her in the middle of the night, that poor old woman, and she had been utterly terrified. When they got to that part, the sergeant and Iolanda laughed hard and long, filling Tilde with anger. She wondered just how long ago it had been. Maybe two weeks? She didn't remember, exactly, but it seemed like a lifetime to her.

She was terrified of the idea that Tearnails might appear at the party, although Iolanda had reassured her on the tram: "Don't worry," she had said, "the Germans don't socialize with their servants."

Sergeant Walden was very kind to her and served her the first glass of champagne. Using gestures, interspersed with a few words in Italian, he apologized for breaking her bicycle lamp. Then he disappeared and, within half an hour, among hugs and hand kissing with an endless stream of officers, Iolanda had taught her to distinguish the gray Wehrmacht uniforms from the black ones of the SS. She also pointed out the Gestapo.

The champagne was starting to kick in. Biscia's words came to her and she was overcome by a fit of laughter. "It would be so easy to roll a grenade and. . . *boom!*" If she had had a grenade with her, she would have rolled it, alright. Right under the table where the waiters had arranged delicacies that she had only read about in books. Iolanda told her about salmon, caviar, and *foie gras,* but it was the large platter of roast pork that consumed her. She asked a waiter for a plate full and it was quickly devoured, along with a slice of black bread.

She had just emptied the second glass of champagne when she saw Hessen entering the salon with an uncertain step. It appeared that Walden had warned him of Tilde's presence and that he was looking for her in the crowd. Without hesitation, she set down the glass and went to meet him. He recognized her from afar and gave her a warm smile that seemed almost grateful. This time the officer had a spotless appearance, a shaved beard and buttoned collar.

"Good evening, Captain," Tilde said, with a playful air that was new to her. "I'm happy to see you again."

"Bonsoir, mademoiselle," he replied, with a hint of a bow. "What are you doing here?"

"A friend invited me," she replied. "Iolanda. Do you know her?" She glanced around, seeking her in the crowd, without success. "I told her what happened the night I got stopped. I would have liked to thank you for what you did for me but I never had the chance. So she invited me to this party."

"Excellent!" he replied, and offered her the third glass of champagne.

Hessen didn't touch the food, but began to smoke thin filtered cigarettes and drink in large quantities, giving the impression of doing it more to stun himself than for pleasure. Tilde tasted the salmon and the *foie gras,* convincing herself that the pork was much better, then she wolfed down a slice of a rich chocolate cake. Regretfully, she turned down another glass of champagne, so she wouldn't risk losing control. She spent the whole evening glued to the captain. They danced and chatted, recounting their lives as if they were the plot of a movie. She learned that Hessen spoke Italian so well because, during his youth, he had spent the summers in Chianti where his paternal grandparents owned a farmhouse and fields with vineyards and olive groves. He remembered those vacations, the sunny Tuscan sunshine, the games with the tenants' children, and the first kisses he had stolen with the local girls, as the happiest experiences of his life. Around ten o'clock, the captain began to get nervous. Alcohol apparently didn't agree with him. Without warning, he looked into her eyes and said, "This party is boring. Do you want to come to my house?"

She tried to ignore her flushing face, telling herself the champagne was to blame. "All right," she replied, looking away.

While Sergeant Walden remains in the car with the lights aimed at the villa, Hessen opens the heavy door and invites her to enter and they are immersed in darkness. They can still hear the roar of the car's engine outside, then it's off and a door is slammed.

"There's no electricity," the captain says. "We'll have to settle for candlelight."

Tilde sighs; her heart beats in her throat and her legs tremble. She takes comfort thinking that in the dark it will be easier.

A candelabra flares to life. Little by little, emerge ancient, precious objects that the darkness had guarded jealously, protecting them from a shabby present that cannot appreciate them, but can only use them. There are couches and armchairs covered with damask, a crystal display case, books, carpets, and a grand piano. Symbols of wealth and elegance, accumulated over the centuries, that leave Tilde with an ancient, almost religious, awe. She knows she's in a patrician home that has been commandeered by their new overlords. Perhaps it had belonged to a wealthy Jewish family that had been deported to Germany, or perhaps to a bourgeois family who had fled to the security of a comfortable country residence.

She hears Sergeant Walden come in, close the door, and walk into the corridor. His boots advance with a staccato click along the marble floor but then fall silent as he crosses a carpet.

Now she is alone with Hessen she knows it's too late for a change of heart. He approaches the crystal display case, opens it, and removes a bottle and two glasses. "Cognac?" he asks, putting everything on the table.

Tilde hesitates. Getting drunk might help. It is tempting to lose consciousness and awaken in the morning, with everything over. But she is unpleasantly aware that mere surrender isn't enough. She is here to extract the informant's name from the German and she will. The cold is suddenly biting and she wraps herself more tightly in her overcoat.

"Are you cold?" the captain asks.

"A little," she answers, swallowing.

"Have a sip," the man insists, and in his voice she senses tenderness. "It'll warm you."

He hands her the glass, which she grips like a lifeline. The liquor is strong and burns in her throat and stomach. She stifles a gag and sits on the couch, her arms folded and her knees held tightly together.

"Walden went to light a fire in the room," Hessen says brusquely. "We'll be warm soon enough."

His frankness startles her. To hide her trembling, she clenches her fists and presses her thighs tighter against each other. Even her teeth start to chatter. She fears the man can hear the noise and keeps her jaw clenched so tightly it hurts.

The silence that follows freezes every fiber of her being. The longer it lasts, the more terrifying it becomes. She can stand it no longer. Tilde takes a deep breath and, with her eyes closed, blurts out, "Is Walden your chamber maid?" with a tinge of hysteria and an uncontrollable snort of laughter.

"He's my attendant," the captain replies calmly. He approaches the sofa from behind, and smells her hair, freshly washed. He complements her and adds, "The French perfume you have on, did your friend give it to you?"

Tilde nods and, at that moment, something happens that she had not expected. Maybe because of the champagne, or perhaps the cognac, but her fear is gone. In its place there is a sensation of warmth and power she has never experienced before. The man is standing behind the sofa, bent over her, and his breath caresses her neck. She can feel it, warm and smelling of alcohol and smoke, but she doesn't find it unpleasant. She wonders if there is something monstrous in her. Then she thinks about Iolanda. How many times she has experienced this? *As long as this war lasts, no one has the right to be ashamed.*

She turns slowly and offers him her lips. It's an instinctive gesture that comes naturally. He whispers something in German that she doesn't understand. In his blue eyes, barely lit by the wavering candlelight, she can read a desperate need . . . and the same sadness as in their first encounter.

"What. . .?" she asks with a whisper.

"You are so young," he murmurs, caressing her face. Then he draws her to him and kisses her. A long, delicate kiss that seems to hold more pain than desire.

When they finally separate, he surprises her saying, "All of this will soon be over."

Tilde looks at him, confused. It's what she wants, with her whole being, for all this to be over. But why does hearing it from a *crucco* upset her?

"On one side and the other," continues the man, "we continue to kill and die, but it's useless."

"I don't understand," she says with a shudder.

Hessen moves away, pulls out his cigarettes and lights one. Tilde, still puzzled, senses his annoyance. In the semi-darkness of the room, the red tip of the cigarette gesticulates nervously. "Don't lie to me," he says harshly. "I have shown you that you don't need to."

It is time to begin. She's aware of the risk she's taking, but she must have the name. "Do you really think that I was going to meet the partisans that night?"

The answer is clear, almost annoyed: "Yes."

"So why didn't you leave me to the Italian, Helmut?"

He laughs with contempt: "Maestri? What would be the point?" he say, pretending not to notice they were now on a first-name basis. "You have your whole life ahead of you, and in a few months the war will be over."

"How can you say that?"

"For me it was over long ago. Since an English bomb destroyed my family."

Tilde is silent. So this is the secret hiding behind his forlorn desperation. Why didn't he say anything to her at the party? She knew many victims of the war and none of them wore a gray uniform and a shiny badge with a swastika.

"Poor captain," she's surprised to think, *"even though you're my enemy, the war has taken everything from you too."*

"Your family." she repeats flatly.

"My wife and my three little girls. Everyone died two years ago, during a RAF incursion in Cologne. The Third Reich owes me a lot."

She says nothing, but her expression speaks volumes.

The man pours another cognac and empties the glass in a single swallow.

"Don't be sorry, *Fräulein,*" he mutters, lightening his tone and clicking his tongue. "The Americans will soon arrive and you'll celebrate."

"If your comrades could hear you. . ."

"They'd shoot me, as if I were one of the bandits you are working for."

"That pig really convinced you, didn't he?"

He shrugs and takes a deep drag off his cigarette. Then he blows away the smoke and throws the butt on the marble floor, crushing it

"If you don't mind," she says, getting up and placing her hand on her chest, "*I* care. You won't always be around to protect me."

"Then learn to protect yourself," he replies, making his tone playful. He pours another cognac and approaches her, glass in hand, his eyes half-closed and a fatuous smile on his face. "How about a dash of Armagnac, *Fräulein?*" he asks, raising his glass. "There is so little time left. Only this can save us."

His words are beginning to slur and his balance is wobbly, his feet set wide apart. He comes closer and tries to hug her. She pushes him away and he staggers clumsily.

"I don't have a uniform to hide under," she murmurs. "And there is someone who wants to hurt me."

"I saved you once. What else do you want from this poor soldier?"

She bursts into laughter. "You're drunk," she says, grinning.

"Of course I'm drunk. So?"

"So, let's play."

"What game?" he asks, leaning against her.

"Truth or Dare."

"All right," he replies, grabbing her arm. "But in the bedroom."

She fights down an impulse to run and hears herself saying, "Bring the cognac; I want a drink."

"Good idea. You take the candle."

They start along the marble staircase leading to the second floor. Hessen can barely stand, and he has to use the balustrade to climb the stairs. The room is comfortable and warm. A fire burns in a large fireplace that occupies half of one wall. Its reddish glow fills the room making everything dance, the large mirror, the frescoes on the ceiling, and the thick velvet curtains that hide the large windows, beyond which

71

lay an impenetrable wall of darkness and silence. In the flickering light, the canopy bed is an arena where wild beasts will fight to please a crowd who isn't there. Life or death. Tilde pours herself a glass of Armagnac and drinks it without tasting it. Hessen tries to grab her, but she's agile, jumps on the mattress and settles on the opposite side.

"So, let's start the game!" she challenges him. Her face is flushed and her eyes are smiling.

"Let's start. How does it work?"

Her head is spinning and her stomach churning, but there is also a frenzy that goads her on.

"I'll ask you a question and you'll have to answer truthfully. Then you give me a dare."

"What should I dare you to do?"

"I'll take off my clothes, one piece at a time."

"And then?" the man asks.

"Then we'll make love, if you still can!"

Hessen shakes his head and begins to unbutton his jacket. "Will your friends kill her?"

Tilde is momentarily taken aback but responds, "Do really care for that pig's confidants?"

"That pig will be asking a lot of questions and demanding an explanation from my superiors."

"You're no coward, Captain Hessen."

"It isn't a question of . . ."

"Then have courage. Where shall I start?"

"With the overcoat."

"She's a woman, isn't she?"

The man nods and Tilde takes off her overcoat and throws it at him. Hessen grabs it and tosses it onto a padded armchair behind him.

"Do I know her?" Tilde asks, sensing victory.

Hessen nods again. Tilde pulls off her shoes and throws them violently at him, forcing him to protect himself with his arm. With difficulty, the man takes off his jacket.

"Is she a colleague from work?"

Hessen shakes his head and Tilde takes off her suit jacket.

"The blouse next," he murmurs, pointing his finger.

"Is she a friend of mine?"

Hessen confirms it.

"Are you toying with me? How do you know who my friends are?"

"She's a friend," he confirms seriously.

Tilde starts unbuttoning her blouse. First in front, from top to bottom, then the cuffs. She drops it on the floor. Her white bra struggles to hold breasts that are too large. Hessen looks at her and, for the first time, his eyes are filled with desire.

"Do you know her name?" Tilde asks.

"Of course I know it," he replies, removing his shirt and remaining in his undershirt and trousers, the suspenders hanging on his hips.

"Then tell me the first letter."

"The I of *Italy*," he says firmly. "Now take off your skirt."

She unbuttons it from behind and lets it fall on the floor. She remains in her bra, panties, and rayon stockings that cling to her thighs. She's cold, and not just because she's almost naked.

"The second letter," she asks urgently, praying that it isn't her. She struggles desperately to remember the names of all the women she knows: Ida, Ines, Iride as well as those of women she has never met: Isotta, Ilaria, Ingrid. . .

But the verdict is merciless: *"O like Ovid."*

"Iolanda," she says, blankly.

Hessen looks at her and remains motionless like a statue. With compassion heightened by his drunkenness, he sees Tilde's eyes fill with tears. He turns his back to her and sits on the edge of the bed to pull off his boots. "I'm sorry," he whispers. "Yes. It's her."

The game which had begun as a playful skirmish has ended in tragedy. Tilde once again asks herself if he's mocking her. She kneels on the bed and grabs his hair. "You're not deceiving me, are you, you damned *crucco*?" she hisses in his ear.

He surrenders himself and falls back. He lets her arms hold him and in that embrace he feels the despair of a little girl who refuses to believe in a harsh truth that will steal her childhood from her.

The night is still young. The light from the fireplace dances along their entwined bodies. Outside the silence and the darkness seal their one night of intimacy away from the world. But there is no velvet curtain or darkness that can seal away the disappointment that burns more than the loss of her virginity. It was not how she had imagined her first time would be, even though the cognac and the champagne have worked their magic and she been ready. Rather, it was Hessen's words that hurt her, hurt her more than his manhood.

Now that she has discovered the truth, she no longer knows what to do with it.

But it isn't for her to decide. She will return to her comrades and say: "Mission accomplished."

10.
HIGH PRESSURE

Unlike Olindo Grandi and Gino Bavastro, Lanza welcomed me coldly but with a distant courtesy. He lived in a stately building on Via Molfino. His wife's name was Ada, and she was a tiny, solicitous woman who, after taking my jacket, began to fuss and ask a series of questions. Would I like a coffee or a tea, had I had lunch, would I care for an orange juice or a glass of cognac, instead. Her husband was visibly annoyed by such zeal, but refrained from commenting. After I surrendered and accepted a glass of red wine, we went to the living room and sat on two comfortable dark brown leather armchairs. He lit an American cigarette, so I could take the liberty of smoking my pipe.

The old man wore a heavy dressing gown and underneath he was dressed to the nines. White shirt and dark tie, gray jersey and woolen trousers with a crease. On his feet, he wore a pair of suede shoes with a rubber sole, identical to mine. I don't know if he had dressed for the occasion, or if that was his ordinary domestic attire.

The apartment was immersed in a soft semi-darkness, like a sacristy, and you could smell camphor and naphthalene in the air. The decor was luxurious, almost excessive. Antique wooden furniture, crystal chandeliers, large carpets stretched over the glossy parquet, and paintings on the walls, mostly by 19th century artists, which seemed authentic and of some value. I could see that the young man who had served under Olindo Grandi had come a long way, certainly a much longer way than his commander.

"So, Mr. Pagano," he said, puffing a cloud of bluish smoke. "What can I do for you?"

His formality marked another difference. I wondered if he had known my family or whether he had lived on the moon after the war.

"About twenty years ago," I started, "a German came to Sestri and began asking questions of the old partisans. Did he also speak with you?"

A barely perceptible shadow passed over his face. In the foyer, he had told me that Olindo had called to announce my visit. I would have bet my three thousand Euros in expense money that he was prepared to be asked a lot of questions, but not that one. He reminded me of someone who suddenly realizes that they've back into the wrong theater at the multiplex.

"A German?" he asked slowly, as if playing for time.

"The son of a Wehrmacht officer."

"I don't remember. . . I don't think so," he said cautiously.

"Not even Olindo seems to remember him," I said.

"So?"

"I found out accidentally that they actually did speak."

He tried for a smile on his face, but it looked forced, nervous.

"Olindo is old," he said with condescension. "Like all of us, we few that are left."

"He certainly has no problem remembering other things from his past." I replied.

"What are you implying?"

"I wonder why he would keep silent about something so important and, since I'm here, I'm asking you."

"Why the hell do you think I would know?" he shouted, his face red with anger. "I don't even know why you think it's important."

"Don't tell me Grandi didn't tell you the reason for this visit."

"No more than two hours ago," he said slowly, "he warned me that you'd be coming. He didn't specify when; frankly, I didn't expect you so soon. All he did was ask me to help you."

"So you knew I'm looking for someone."

"Yes, but nothing more."

Now I was sure he was lying. I could read it in his face. It was dark, perhaps tanned, and his wrinkled skin was turning a mottled red, revealing his growing irritation. I wondered if he was angry with me or if he was angry with his former commander, who had put him in this embarrassing situation.

Ada returned, slightly bent, carrying a tray with a dusty bottle and two long-stemmed glasses. "Sorry to have kept you waiting," she said, "but the best wines are in the cellar."

The bottle had already been opened and, placing the tray on the table, the woman filled the glasses. Judging by the inviting ruby color, it had to be a vintage wine. Lanza took the bottle and turned it to read the label. He couldn't see well and asked his wife for help: "What did you choose?"

"The '98 Amarone ," she replied. "The same you opened on Sunday."

"We had my son at lunch, with the grandchildren," he explained. "They live in Milan and they rarely honor us with their presence."

"I understand," I said. "I'm afraid it will happen to me, too, with my daughter."

"You have a daughter, Mr. Pagano?" he asked, handing me a glass. He raised his and we mimed a toast.

"Won't you have something?" I asked his wife, who stood with her hands clasped, as if she was praying.

"The doctor has forbidden me," she replied in apology. "I have high blood pressure."

I took a sip. The Amarone was really excellent. Full-bodied, solid, and with a delicious finish of cherry and tar. Pouring that nectar on the disreputable hot dog I had eaten for lunch was a true blasphemy. One of those absurd juxtapositions that my friend Pertusiello so thoroughly enjoyed.

"A nineteen-year-old daughter just finishing high school," I said.

"Our son is a bit older," he said smiling. "He has been working in Milan since 1975 and in a few years he'll retire. We had him a little late and he followed our example. He married a much younger woman and finds himself with two children attending elementary school. We don't see them enough, unfortunately. A few weeks in the summer, when they come to Celle Ligure, where we have a house."

"They are our reason for living," the wife added with a sad smile. She was standing next to her husband, leaning on the armchair. She had to be younger than him, even though, with her resigned air and slightly bent posture, she didn't really look it.

I looked around and, turning to both of them, I said, "Congratulations, you have a beautiful home."

"Thank you," said Ada quickly.

"Do you like it?" he asked. "We decorated it over the years, piece by piece. When you become old, the house gains an importance that you wouldn't have imagined when you were younger. Having a comfortable home helps you age well."

"As long as you have health," she added, smiling.

"Even more so once your health is gone," the old man contradicted. "It's the only place you spend your time, unless you end up in the hospital." No one laughed, except him. An embarrassed silence followed that prompted him to refill his wine glass, and mine, too. He raised his glass again. "So, to your daughter."

"To your grandchildren," I replied. I took a sip and added, "Tell me something, Mr. Lanza. What did you do before you retired?"

"When the war ended, I took a job on a boat as a sailor, and for five long years, I sailed. But that life was not for me. I had put aside some money and bought a share in a servicing company based at the port. I also resumed my studies and graduated. I've always worked like a dog and if I'm honest, even though I'm over eighty, sometimes I miss my office."

"You came a long way."

"In the 1950s and 1960s, if you worked hard, you could make something of yourself. Then my old comrades turned up and ruined everything."

"Your comrades?"

"All the businesses were nationalized and placed under public management. The ships stopped coming and the port experienced one of the worst crises in its history. I'm sad to have to say this, but my old friends have a lot to answer for. Ideology is a dangerous toy. It can cause you to make horrible mistakes."

"For example?"

"You can't ignore the fact that a business does better with an owner who cares instead of a committee of employees. Nationalized companies never work."

"Well," I said, disappointed, "you're biting the hand that fed a lot of people. If nothing else, that ideology had the merit of sharing the cake so that everyone got to have some. Today, workers have to settle for mere crumbs. But I'm curious to know why you joined up with Commander Grandi."

"They were different times," he said, staring at nothing. "Perhaps we were wrong, but we were eighteen and we believed in something."

"And now you don't believe in anything?"

"I haven't believed in those ideas for a long time. And I was right. They've been a disaster for mankind. But don't forget. We were all in a partisan brigade run by Communists."

"Grandi still believes," I replied.

"Perhaps, but only out of nostalgia."

I studied him, with his dignified aplomb. An old man who had preserved intelligence and elegance through a lifetime spent observing the principle that a healthy personal detachment preserves one, if not from mistakes, at least from their most devastating consequences. This was the exact opposite of what I had done.

"Do you regret believing in them?" I asked.

"Regret?" he said, energetically shaking his head. "Absolutely not. The Resistance was a demonstration of how one can do the right thing, even if inspired by misguided ideas."

The wine had restored his tranquility and self assurance. During all this, Ada hadn't moved from her spot. She was still standing behind him, leaning on the back of his chair, looking for all the world like a parrot perched on a pirate's shoulder.

I looked at my watch; it was four o'clock. Beyond the curtain of the glass door, a dull light filtered into the room. The days were getting longer, but, with the gloomy weather, no one realized it.

"I'll have to go shortly," I said. "If you don't mind, I'd like to ask you some questions."

"That's why you're here," he replied, encouraging me.

I told him of my assignment and, for the third time, I repeated the same unlikely story. As I expected, the names of Nicla and Hessen didn't ring any bells, nor had he ever heard of a relationship between an Italian girl and a German officer that resulted in a child. He answered casually, perfectly at ease, following a script so predictable, it was boring. He confirmed that he had never met my client and had no idea why his friend Olindo, if he had met him, had hidden that fact from me. Lastly, with an almost comical disingenuousness, he even suggested, "Why don't you ask Grandi and the German? Surely, they must know."

"I'll do just that," I said.

I took another sip of the Amarone, then got up to leave. Ada left us and went to retrieve my jacket. Before she returned, Lanza approached me and whispered in my ear, "She's a wonderful woman, but she has a fear of being useless. Her high blood pressure comes from that."

When she reappeared on the threshold of the foyer, I smiled and said, "You were very kind, ma'am. I haven't had such good wine in years."

"Really?" she replied, incredulously.

"It is a rare pleasure for me to encounter such an excellent hostess."

"Thank you, thank you," she said, blushing.

I could hear her continuing to repeat it as I walked down the stairs, until the door closed and an austere silence descended. But then, there came the muffled notes of a piano. They filtered through the door of the second floor apartment in a haunting, delicate melody.

It was the *Clair de Lune* by Claude Debussy.

11.
THE MEETING

Sestri Ponente, February 1944

The appointment is scheduled for Sunday at Dria's home, at ten o'clock in the morning. His isolated, rustic home in Borzoli, amid market gardens and not far from the Acqui railway, is often chosen for group meetings. It's out of the way and it's easier to avoid surveillance. Besides, Dria lives alone so no one else gets put at risk.

"You'll have to be there, too." said Grandi, when they met in front of the factory gates. Then he explained to her how to get there.

This is the first time she is attending a group meeting. If she didn't know why she was there, she would feel proud. She has always been just a messenger, doing nothing more important than bringing news, dispatches, and orders. No one ever asked her opinion of them before. But this time is different. She was given an important mission and she made the best of it, performing her duty to the letter. Just like Biscia does. The thought fills her with a fury full of despair. She wonders if she's still able to look him in the eye.

She reaches the cottage by bicycle, pedaling down a dirt road that climbs among the market gardens ravaged both by winter and war. Even the yellow patches of mimosas are too pale to convey any cheer. The sky is dark and threatens rain, the weather has shifted and is now coming from the south and the cold is less intense. When she reaches the top of the hill and sees the smoke rising from the chimney, she realizes that sweat has soaked the woolen undershirt, that now clings to her skin. Dria waits for her on the threshold and jerks his thumb at a wooden hut next to the house: "Put it in there so nobody can see it."

She hides her bicycle and walks through the door, entering directly into the kitchen, a small room where the heat and smoke choke her and make her eyes burn. The floor and the ceiling are made of rustic wood beams and the plaster covering the stone walls is peeling and yellow. The furniture is also somewhat shabby. A cherry wood table, many chairs, some upholstered but in bad condition, a chipped, white cabinet and a shelf on which sit jars, a coffee grinder, a copper pail with a blackened bottom, and a stuffed hare. A shotgun hangs on a nail on the wall. In the corner, a small cast-iron stove is lit. Judging by the amount of smoke leaking into the room, it's burning green wood. The little window facing the farmyard is wide open, and Dria leaves the door open as well, hoping to cause a draft. "Damn *maccaia*," he swears.

They are waiting for her. Including Dria, there are five of them and Tilde has the clear impression that they have been there for some time for a meeting to which she hasn't been invited.

Dria is a big man who speaks little. Tilde has seen him in front of the church a few times and knows he works at Vaccari Ceramics, but they barely know each other. He must be about twenty-five but he looks older. He has already lost some teeth, he's dirty, and he doesn't take care of himself. This annoys her. She's sure the war is just an excuse and that he'd still live like a pig even if things were normal. Then she remembers that he lives alone and wonders what has happened to his parents.

Olindo is leaning against the wall, near the window, with his ankles crossed and his arms folded. She can see gratitude in his eyes.

A young stranger with brown curly hair and wearing an old brown jacket is sitting at the table and watches her admiringly through his round metal spectacles. He looks like a student and she is struck by the paleness of his thin face.

Near him sits another boy, who looks younger, with a shaved head and teenage fuzz where, someday, he'll have a mustache and beard. He wears a knitted woolen sweater two sizes too big for him, and looks at his hands, nervously rubbing them on the tabletop. Tilde notices that he has red knuckles and dirty nails.

Opposite the stove, his eyes glued to the floor, sits Biscia. He's smoking one of his damn cigarettes and when she enters, he doesn't look at her. Tilde doesn't know what to do. Her repeated glances are ignored. Desperate, her eyes beseech Olindo for help. He smiles at her sympathetically and begins to make introductions.

"Dria and Biscia you know. This is Lanza," he says, pointing at the man with the shaved head. "He was in the Navy and after September 8th, he deserted and joined us. Curly, here, goes by Calcagno. He's our intellectual. He studies law; he's a little behind with his exams but has read almost all the texts of Marx and Lenin."

"Hello," she says awkwardly, embarrassed.

"This is Tilde, everyone, a German's worse nightmare."

They smile at her, all except Biscia, who continues to look away and smoke in silence.

"We can start now," Grandi says. "Tell us what you've discovered, Tilde."

Her face burns and her stomach cramps. She feels like a little girl suddenly thrust on stage—and she has forgotten her lines. She isn't used to putting herself forward and being the center of attention. She's always preferred to listen in the background. She's also convinced that nothing of what has happened should ever be acknowledged. Hiding, forgetting, letting time heal the wounds—this is what her heart demands. She thinks of her mother and the pain she would feel listening to her explain what had happened. Her father's face. . . she can't even imagine. It would be useless to remind him that he's a card-carrying party member, to shout at him that she was following orders, just as he would have done. He wouldn't want to hear it, not when it was *his* daughter. Certain sacrifices must be made. Certain things must be done. But let others do them.

She immediately regrets her anger, remembering how badly Biscia's hypocritical assent had hurt her. She hears herself begin to speak. Sparse details and the essential truths create a story, some might call it a lie, that she can bring herself to relate in the presence of the man who has asked her to marry him. She says that at the party the Wehrmacht captain drank a lot, made her dance. . . and blurted out the name of the spy. It was Iolanda who reported Sandra and Mariù to the Germans. They were loaded onto a cattle car and taken to a labor camp in

Germany. She doesn't say that Hessen confided this to her in the morning, between sheets that were still wet. A cold blade of sunlight filters through the heavy, dark curtains and cuts the room in two.

With relief, she hears Olindo objecting, "What if it's a trick?"

"A trick?" she repeats, stunned.

"Why would the German blow such a valuable informant's cover?"

"That's true," Calcagno agrees. "She wouldn't be easy to replace."

"I don't understand," Dria intervenes. "Everyone already knows she's involved with the Germans. What would make her so special?"

Calcagno smirks at him. "Oh, she's something special alright. . ."

Dria bursts into laughter. "Well, as for that. . ."

Grandi remains serious, almost melancholy. "It isn't that simple," he says. "That would make sense if she hadn't taken Tilde to the party. Hessen apparently knows that Tilde is one of us." He turns to her and his eyes are merciless, just as they had been when she had met him in the bar. "Isn't that right?"

Again she flushes, but she's also happy to say something that could save Iolanda. "Yes," she confirms, struggling to hold his gaze.

"So," Olindo continues, "he also knows that we trust Iolanda. Why deprive himself of a spy that his enemy trusts?"

"We need to know," says Calcagno sharply, "exactly what the Captain told you."

"Though he is a soldier," she replies, weighing her words carefully, "he no longer believes in this war. His family was wiped out a year ago during a bombing in Cologne."

"And that's the reason he saved you after they took you to headquarters?"

"He said that it wasn't worth it. The war will be over soon. Why kill young people with the whole lives ahead of them. He thought it was all pointless."

"He could be court-martialled for that," Olindo murmurs.

"I wish he was right," adds Dria, shaking his head.

Suddenly, Lanza, who had not yet spoken, snaps, "You know what? This is all bullshit! How many comrades will she destroy before we decide to act?"

"I've talked to Buranello and Scano," Olindo says. "No one says they can absolutely guarantee that Iolanda is trustworthy. But, at least until now, we've had no reason to suspect her. The information she's provided to us has always been accurate."

"Maybe she was found out and they forced her to betray us," says the young student.

"It's true," Dria says, "One can act out of fear as easily as duty."

"Especially a woman who is accustomed to living a good life," adds Lanza.

Biscia rouses himself from his morose silence. "Have none of you considered that this might be a trap?" he grunts, raising his eyes for the first time.

Everyone stares at him blankly, even Tilde, who is relieved just to hear him talk.

"She's nothing. A small fish," he continues, pointing at Tilde, without looking at her. "They aren't interested in her."

His words ooze disdain. She feels pain, as if he had slapped her, then a wave of rage she can barely contain. She has a sudden urge to spit in his face. He knew her mission but he didn't even try to stop her. He didn't even try. And now he throws all of this in her face, treating her like some kind of a slut?

It's so easy, isn't it, Comrade Biscia, to preserve your own conscience at the expense of others?

"If they had tortured her," objects Olindo, "she could have taken

"But they didn't know that," he insists. "But now that they know who and what she is, they can pick her up whenever they want. So they let her go. She carries on like before. But now, they are watching her. They see where she goes, who she hangs out with. Hessen makes her believe he doesn't care and is letting her move freely. Who knows where she might lead them? In the meantime they've already scored a point: Iolanda is finished. If we don't kill her, they will."

Olindo leaves his spot against the wall and approaches Tilde, who, for the entire time, has stood in the middle of the kitchen like a student being examined in front of the class. Gently, he puts his hands on her arms and, almost imploring, whispers, "You are the only one who can judge, Tilde. Do you think Hessen is playing both sides?"

Olindo's words slide over her like a poisoned mantle. They have been spoken to cover her and, in a way, protect her from the others. The sacrifice that had been requested from her deserved respect and discretion. But Olindo's well-meant words won't protect her from herself. Instead, they are an invitation to take on a new and terrible responsibility.

She doesn't answer immediately. She thinks back to the two meetings with the German and her impressions and feelings. Finally, her words drop into the waiting silence. "Hessen is sincere."

"Then," Olindo concludes, "that's it. We'll check on Hessen's story and then take action."

Tilde feels her heart bursting. *And what about Iolanda? Will you hear nothing from her?*

"If it's true that the captain has lost his family in a bombing," he continues, "we must eliminate the informant."

"And how do we check?" Dria asks.

"We have our sources," Grandi answers. "A story like that won't be a state secret."

"Let's put it to a vote," demands Lanza.

Tilde forces herself to speak up. She will not do to Iolanda what Biscia did to her.

"She's a good woman!" she cries out. "She isn't a spy for the Germans!" Her damp eyes and broken voice convey a terrible despair. She knows she won't sway them, that they won't believe her.

They all look at her in shock. Even Biscia looks up from the floor with a silent question in his anguished eyes.

"That isn't possible," says Calcagno harshly. "One of them is lying."

"But it's true." she insists.

Now it's Olindo's turn to stare at the dirty wooden floor. It should be up to him to speak, but he remains silent, immersed in his thoughts.

"Well, Olindo," Dria urges him, "what's it to be?"

"It's not so easy," he mutters. "It's a woman."

"So were Sandra and Mariù," replies Lanza. Everyone notices the "were."

"When I asked her to introduce Tilde to the German command officers," Grandi continues, almost as if talking to himself, "she asked me how old she was."

"So?"

"So she was worried about her. She seemed sincere."

In the room, the silence is thicker than the smoke that still clogs the air. Everyone stares silently, waiting for an easy answer that will never come. Only Lanza is sure of himself. Off in the distance there's a whistle and an endless clacking as the train goes over the rough tracks. A dog barks.

Finally, Calcagno takes the floor. "Sometimes informants are victims, too. They must be eliminated not because they are bad people, but because of the losses they cause."

"He's right," Dria says. "We're at war. There's always going to be some collateral damage. It's not like Fascists and Germans have pity for us."

"Yet," Olindo insists, "I, too, like Tilde, am not convinced."

"We'll never be sure," Calcagno says again, "either way."

Tilde rebels. "And what does that mean? 'Better safe than sorry?' Is that it? You're ready to kill someone just because?"

"If it might save the lives of our comrades," he answers dryly, "yes."

She wants to reply, but she can't find the words. "Our intellectual" is a master of the coldly rational argument. He can tie her in knots with his logic and could best her in an argument a thousand times. But this isn't about logic. Tilde *knows*.

"All right," Grandi says, shaking himself, "then we vote." and Tilde hears the voice of death.

"Finally," Lanza echoes. "Who's in favor?"

Dria, Calcagno, Lanza, and Olindo raise their hands.

"Against?"

Biscia doesn't move. He has lit another cigarette and is staring at the floor again.

"Well, Biscia?" Lanza says laconically, "abstaining are you?"

"Fuck you," he replies, exasperated.

Tilde, too, hasn't raised her hand; she doesn't even know if she should vote. Olindo notices. "Tilde, no comments?"

She shrugs. There is no embarrassment in her gesture. She's done her part; it isn't up to her to decide on the execution of Iolanda. Grandi understands and hastens to add, "Maybe you're right."

Let them both stay out of it, he thinks. As if abstaining from the vote could accomplish that.

Tilde looks nervously at the clock and, in her heart, hopes that she'll never attend another partisan meeting for the rest of her life. At home, they are waiting for her for the traditional Sunday lunch. Even if they leave the table still hungry, every Sunday the family gathers and everyone talks about the joys and successes of the previous week . . . but not about the sorrows. Her father insists on that.

She is waiting for the meeting to break up, for someone to take their leave, but nobody moves.

"There is. . . one other thing," says Olindo, gravely.

Tilde hopes that tone is because of the horrible decision they have just made. She can tell that he has suffered more than the others. But she fears that something worse is waiting and she quails. *Worse than that?*

"If we execute Iolanda," Olindo says—she knows they will, and he knows it too. Why this act? Is it just to make Biscia happy, to make him believe his arguments are being taken seriously? 'Biscia is like a son to me,' he had said. . . Dear God!—"you must disappear."

Perhaps it's the smoky air, perhaps it's that she's had nothing but a persimmon and some of that fake barley coffee since early this morning, but her head is spinning and she feels like fainting. The sense of nausea, like hunger and anxiety, her constant companion, blossoms into an impulse to vomit.

"Disappear? Why. . . where?" she stammers.

Olindo sees her face suddenly drained of color. "Tilde, are you alright?"

"I'm fine. . . fine," she manages to croak, betrayed by her own voice.

Biscia moves for the first time since Tilde arrived. He strides across the room, gently takes her hand and makes her sit. She finally is able to look into his eyes but meets the same confusion that lies in her own. With an effort she says, "Explain."

"You must go to the mountains."

"The mountains? Why?"

90

hunt you down and you'll be a danger to us all."

So these were the *consequences* she had to think about before accepting the mission. Not only to forfeit Biscia, but also abandon her family. Her beloved, needy, difficult family. What would they do without her? Life is already so harsh, even with her miserable pay added to that of her father.

Why didn't Olindo make this clear from the beginning?

"They need me. They won't make it on their own," she whispers, talking to herself. She doesn't realize she has been shaking her head "no" over and over.

"We'll try to help them."

An avalanche of thoughts and feelings cascade through her mind in a hopeless tangle.

"Who will bring food to my aunt?"

"We will," Grandi insists. "We want you alive, Tilde, can't you understand that?"

She thinks how Hessen, before she left, asked to meet her again and said, "Don't worry, nothing will happen to you." She's sure he will protect her from bastards like Tearnails and his minions. But now she can't say that. Not with Biscia here. So she masters herself and, somehow, answers in a steady voice. "We'll see. Everything at the right time."

Biscia, standing next to her, can't read her thoughts and keeps holding her hand.

12.
THE SLAUGHTERHOUSE

I should have known better. Whenever a customer promises easy money and a simple job with no complications, it's a scam. This job was no exception.

Professor Hessen had lied to me and Olindo Grandi, my father's best friend, had done the same. As I made my way home, I wondered why. I came up empty. Maybe they had both lied for the same reason. Maybe they had different, even contradictory motives. But they had both lied. I could face down the old partisan and demand answers. But somehow, that didn't seem like a good idea. It all started with the German client so that's where I had to begin. But Professor Hessen hadn't given me either his address or his phone number. My bad. Nothing kept me from trying to find him on-line, but I decided it wasn't worth the trouble. I had two checks in my pocket, for a total of forty-three thousand Euros; sooner or later he would find me.

I had intended to prepare myself an excellent dinner. I kept thinking of Jasmìne. Trying to think of something else by drowning myself in work just wasn't going to get me very far. I parked my Vespa right in front of my door—lucky me—and went off towards Via Canneto il Lungo for some grocery shopping. It was already happy hour, and the Caffè degli Specchi was packed. The alley was crowded, too. As I went from shop to shop, the butcher, the baker, the greengrocer, I began to feel depressed and out of sorts. I just wasn't that into it anymore. I had intended to go home and cook a particularly nice veal roast with broccoli and potatoes, which I would have accompanied with an amusing little Refosco that I'd recently rediscovered in my pantry. But the idea of eating alone was killing off any pleasure at the prospect. I thought about calling my ex, Mara or my friend, Gina Aliprandi. I hadn't seen Gina since my daughter Aglaja's eighteenth birthday. Come to think of it, I hadn't seen much of the Captain, either. It had been a long time since we'd been on one of our fishing trips. I promised myself that, on my way home, I'd drop by his crêperie and catch up.

I found myself in front of the Roger Café. Tony was standing in the doorway smoking. I was practically staggering under the weight of my shopping and he said I looked like I needed a break. He was right. More right than he knew. He prepared me a Negroni on the rocks accompanied by a cutting board with the works: French cheese, pizza, salami, you name it. I drank the first Negroni and I realized that my mood was slightly improving. The thought of dining alone was still unappealing, but the idea of finding some company was growing on me. So I ordered another drink and then a third. By now, I had given up on the idea of cooking and had conceived of a new project: go home, put on some Mozart, lie on the couch and drink scotch, Lagavulin if there was any left. But now the alcohol was catching up with me and the world seemed colored in melancholy pastels. I was at the counter, perched on a stool, and my thoughts, fueled by the three Negronis, were running loose. I hadn't seen Aglaja for fifteen days and I somehow felt I had betrayed her. After we had found each other again, she had taken to having lunch at my house every couple of days. Why didn't she do that anymore? Because she would have found nobody at home. In the weeks before the arrest of the Trevisan brothers, my life had been frantic, I'd hardly found the time to eat or sleep. Even so, I was ashamed to realize that I hadn't even had time for my daughter.

I tried, once again, to analyze the events of that terrible last day but I drifted off into reverie instead. Too drunk, I guess.

When I had left the police station, leaving Pertusiello and the prosecutor in conference in Pertusiello's office, a cold drizzle blown by the north wind was polishing the asphalt. I retrieved my Vespa and, without putting on my rain gear, I drove straight to the Belvedere Boarding School where the girls were lodged. I arrived wet to the bone and called Pertusiello so that he could tell the guards to let me in rather than shoot me. He wasn't happy about it, but in the end he agreed. I asked him how his interrogation of the Russian *mafioso* had gone. He replied things had gone as expected. The man had admitted that he had "directed" the young Nadjezna Ivanovna to the Trevisan brothers, but he swore on holy mother Russia that he had no idea about the nature of their business. He only knew that the two men were running a lap dance club. Yes, he got paid to procure them, he admitted, but for dancing. Normal business, in short. He had actually broken down in tears when they had explained what had happened to all the Natashas, Irinas, and Svetlanas he had unwittingly condemned to slaughter.

Deputy Commissioner Totò Pertusiello, a man of the world, had listened patiently to him, wondering if this ruthless gang leader was telling the truth and, in his heart, he couldn't exclude the possibility. Perhaps the mafia organization providing the "goods" didn't know or didn't want to know what eventually happened to them, just as the banks insuring and reinvesting the profits of criminal activities do so without asking too many questions about their origin. The deputy commissioner had learned that finance and crime were the first to seize the opportunities of the globalized economy, finding its unwritten laws and turning them to their own advantage. Pertusiello had consulted with Dr. Ferlito, then with the head of Public Prosecutions, and they had all concluded that, since the Russian women were adults, this particular mobster couldn't be prosecuted, and his sworn statement had to be accepted as true. Pertusiello also had some bad news about the Trevisan interrogation.

"Didn't you say that he'd crack within a day?" I asked.

"I was wrong," he said in a voice numb with exhaustion and discouragement.

"Why?"

"There is no evidence against them, and those bastards know it. It seems they had been treating the girls with kid gloves. The girls don't know what was waiting for them and won't press charges. We can't base our case on the word of your dead transsexual, Chérie. If we can't find at least one of the victims who will testify, we'll have to release them."

The nun was called Caterina and was of indefinite age, probably somewhere between forty and sixty. She was a bony and energetic woman who welcomed me with the distrust due to a man who, with no official position, neither a magistrate, a lawyer, or a social worker, insisted on visiting eight young prostitutes in a safe house who had just been taken off the street. She accompanied me along an endless hallway illuminated by tiny windows that reminded me of prison. There was a vague smell of incense mixed with odors coming from the kitchen. The ceilings were high and in the deep silence of the building the screeching of my wet soles echoed ominously. The nun, on the other hand, glided over the floor, moving with short and quick steps in the manner of a geisha.

Two recently remodeled apartments on the second floor were reserved for the girls. I tried to follow sister Caterina in but she closed the door in my face. After a few minutes, she returned with the two young women who had met Jasmìne. One was a minor, from somewhere in West Africa. She called herself Hoogy. The other, a barely clad, tall Ukrainian, said her name was Lara, like Doctor Zhivago's wife. They spoke broken Italian, but we could communicate well enough. And Pertusiello was right, they had no idea they had escaped being sold and butchered like animals. When I said I was a private investigator, they stared at me with dismay mixed with distrust. All they were worried about was being sent back home. After the introductions, Sister Caterina accompanied us to a small room that she called "the parlor" containing a table and four chairs. She closed the door behind her and moved to sit in a corner while we gathered around the table.

"Do you remember Jasmìne?" I asked.

They looked at each other and then nodded.

"How long had you been with her before she left?"

"I was for fifteen days there," Lara said, putting her hand on her chest. "She, two or three, because she came after."

"Three," Hoogy confirmed.

"The deputy commissioner has told me that Jasmìne left eight days ago."

The young Ukrainian, with emphatic gestures, rolled her eyes to the ceiling, opened one hand, and with the other began counting on her fingers. She confirmed that eight days had passed.

"Did you often talk to her?" I asked.

"Often? Normal," she replied. "We stayed there all the time. She talk, cook, play with cards. She very sweet."

"Have you seen her worried or frightened?"

"Not scared. Quiet."

"Not even before she left?"

"No," Hoogy confirmed.

I was sure that if she had known something, Jasmìne would have told her friends. So she, too, was unaware of the fate that awaited her. When she had kicked me out of the lap dance bar, she didn't do it to protect me, but because she was convinced that a better destiny was waiting for her. This meant that her friend Chérie had found out later, perhaps from her Ivorian pimp.

"I must find her," I said, exasperated.

"You said your name *Bashi?*" Lara asked point blank.

I nodded silently.

"Jasmìne talked about you. She love you. She told me that you tried to take her away."

"What else?"

She lowered her eyes and shook her head. "I don't know if I can tell."

"Lara," I begged, "it's very important. . ."

"Important for who?" she replied harshly.

"What do you mean?"

"Her feelings are as important as yours. If she doesn't say, she has

96

It made complete sense. I wondered if she would have thought this way even knowing that Jasmine was in the hands of a sadistic killer. Probably not. So I decided to lay it on the table.

"The man to whom she was sold is killing her little by little. If I don't get there in time, she will die."

The look on their faces and their instant acceptance filled me with a chilling realization. Their captors might have treated them well and told them that they would provide them with a man too timid to find a wife and rich enough to make them ladies. Like little girls, they had wanted to believe in a fairytale Prince Charming because it helped them to survive. But they were not little girls and they *knew*. The truth was there, festering in their brains, and it didn't take much to get it to rise to the surface. A jolt of fear went through their eyes, leaving them both astonished and resigned. They didn't cry, they didn't ask questions. After a few seconds, Hoogy said, tonelessly, "I saw the car."

"What car?" I raised my voice. "What car are you talking about?"

"The car that took Jasmine away. I was afraid; at night I was awake at the window."

"What did the car look like? Did you recognize the license plate?"

"It was dark. Didn't see the license plate, but a large, white station wagon with drawing and writing on the door."

I felt the impulse to hug her, but I held back. "What kind of writing? What design?"

"Sorry," she said, blushing. "I can't read."

"And the drawing?"

"Oh, yes," she said with a smile. "A cartoon animal. . ."

"Mickey Mouse? Donald Duck?" I asked.

"No, like a dog, but. . . a very, very smart dog."

"A fox!" I shouted.

She confirmed that it was a fox and mimicked its expression, squeezing an eye and smiling. After this revelation, the horror disappeared from her face. Helping me had filled her with satisfaction. I thanked both of them and saw that Sister Caterina was pleased.

I was already standing, along with the nun, who was looking at me quite a lot differently than when we had met, almost with . . . gratitude? But Lara's next words made me shiver: "You're really good," she said, shaking her head. "You should know the truth. Jasmine didn't follow you because she thinks that she's a whore and that she isn't good enough for you."

". . . she thinks that she's a whore and that she isn't good enough for you," I repeated in a whisper. Sister Caterina responded in a surprisingly gravely voice, "Are you okay, Bacci?"

Now Tony's face swam into view and I realized I was back in the bar just finishing a fourth Negroni. From his concerned expression, between being sloppy drunk and the pain I felt every time I remembered those words, I must have looked terrible.

"All right, all right," I repeated, like an idiot. I slurred my words. I half-fell off the stool, made sure that my legs were still under me, and paid for the four drinks. The bar was filling up with people. Someone knew me and greeted me with the exaggerated care you give drunk people. As I was leaving, Tony popped out from behind the counter and whispered, "I think you're wrong."

I looked at him blankly.

"Sometimes," he said, "the whores are the good people."

I smiled and agreed without commenting. I struggled with the shopping bags and, with an uncertain step, I weaved my way home. I was exhausted and I was no longer in the mood to visit the Captain. I made it into the house, dumped the groceries in the fridge, and went into my study. The light on my answering machine blinked red, warning me that there were new messages. I sat in my desk chair and let my finger slide over my pipes, lined up in a beautiful display, looking for the lucky one that would complete the victory of those four stupid cocktails over my will to live. God, I felt awful.

I opted for an elegant Meerschaum pipe, a gift from my parents. They had come to visit me in jail in Novara on my twenty-first birthday, with a box of books and that wonderful pipe. "Meerschaum pipes," my father had said, "are made to be smoked in the house. Your mother and I have chosen it hoping you'll be home soon." My sentence was halved, but I didn't come back in time. When I finally got out of prison, they were both gone.

As I packed my pipe with the Dunhill, I began to smile at the thought that I had never had the satisfaction of becoming an adult. Italian law had stolen that from me as well. When I had turned eighteen, adulthood was legally set at twenty-one. A few months after I had been sent to prison, they had dropped it to eighteen, so turning twenty-one became meaningless. I started to laugh at myself. When I turned twenty-one, I was in a maximum security prison. What difference would it have made anyway?

I lit the tobacco and pressed the "play" key on the answering machine. I closed my eyes and began to suck at the dry smoke of the English tobacco.

The first message was from Mara, wondering where I had been and inviting me for dinner at her home on Saturday night.

The second one was from Olindo Grandi, who, in a worried voice, asked me to call him.

On the third, I heard the harsh voice of my German client, "Good morning, *Herr* Pagano, this is Professor Hessen. I hope everything is okay with your friend. When you have news, call at this number. . ."

A phone number followed, a string of figures as long as the amounts on his damned checks. I guessed he must have returned to Germany.

I smoked for a while, gazing into the void, my mind crowded with anxieties. Like hunting sharks, they glided silently under the surface of consciousness and then struck without warning. I felt on my skin the same frost I had felt back in the parlor when I told the girls about

Jasmine's fate. With an effort, I put the pipe in the ashtray and then surrendered to sleep. I knew that, between the uncomfortable chair and the upcoming horrible hangover I was going to have, life wasn't going to be worth living. But at least it gave me one good reason not to go to Tony's every night.

As soon as I fell asleep I began to dream.

I was with my Grandfather Baciccia in a small clearing. Around us, ruins and rubble, perhaps the legacy of war. We stood in front of a wall and a closed gate. A large truck was waiting for the gate to open. My grandfather picked me up to let me see better. The back of the truck had a series of openings protected by bars. From the smell, I realized it was a cattle car. Looking inside, I could see it was crowded with young women covered in filth and crawling on hands and knees over a straw-covered floor. They moved incessantly, restlessly, and it seemed to me that they must have caught the scent of the slaughterhouse that awaited them. It was then that I realized I was standing in front of the *Ca' de Pitta*, the old municipal slaughterhouse on the outskirts of Genoa. In the crowd, I recognized Lara and Hoogy. I also saw Jasmine, whose eyes were wide with terror. The crowd parted, and I could see a young woman with an olive complexion and curly black hair, beautiful, yet sad and hopeless. She saw us and moved up to the bars. "Hello, Baciccia," she said.

"Are you in there as well?" he replied from far away.

"I belong here. I'm a whore. I'm not good enough for you," she replied.

The truck turned on its engine. The gates were opening. I felt my grandfather surge forward. "No!" he shouted, clinging to the bars and slamming me against them. "I'll save you, Nicla, I swear it!"

13.
THE EXECUTION

Sestri Ponente, March 1944

A frosty and colorless dawn announced that terrible day. Tilde hadn't know when it would happen, nor to whom Grandi would give the assignment, but anxiety had never left her because any day could be *the* day. For more than two weeks, her nights were endless. She lie awake at night, thinking about Iolanda and wondering whether she should warn her. Should she betray her comrades or the kind woman who, for once, had made her feel that she belonged, that she wasn't alone? Warning Iolanda meant betraying her father and the man who had asked her to marry him. Not warning her meant betraying the demands of her heart. But perhaps that was merely weakness.

She wondered why they were waiting so long. She knew that the PAGs had tried to encourage Genoa to back the general strike yesterday. They had all seen Tram Number 16 motionless in the center of the city, blocked by TNT on the tracks. Someone had told her that, on a late February night, Commander Grandi's men had surrounded a German patrol, taking all their weapons and hiding them in a safe place outside the city. Two fascist officers, members of the Republican Guard, had been gunned down in full daylight as they left the barbershop on Via Mazzini. They had been shot by a blond, gangly young man and a teenager. The two had calmly walked away and, by the time the Germans arrived, had seemingly vanished into thin air. But the strike in Genoa had been a disaster due to German threats of deportation and concentration camps. As far as Tilde could tell, only a handful of people had stopped working and the failure could be read in the sullen faces of the workers.

Then something happened that crushed any lingering hope of

reprieve. The news arrived at ten o'clock in the morning. It moved fast, mouth-to-mouth, whispered among the canteen workers. She was cutting cabbages, onions, and beets, preparing the usual noon meal when she heard. During the night, the Black Brigades, the paramilitary arm of the Black Shirts, had stopped Liliana on the road to Mount Gazzo. This time the fascists had acted alone, without warning the German command. They had taken her to police headquarters and no one had heard from her since. Liliana had been Tilde's replacement as a courier for the partisans.

The next morning, she came to work with a dread certainty. It would be soon. The verdict would come, not as a whisper, as in Liliana case, but in a shout of liberation and exultation. She wasn't sure if she could bear that.

The big black car had left the woman in Piazza Oriani and then made its way back to headquarters. The long night was dying; a dim, bluish light was flooding the sky and spreading over the roofs along Viale Canepa, an old road that once lead to a monastery. It would be a cold and sunless day. The air already stank and tasted of rust. She had drank a lot and this had made it easier for her to spend the night with a fat SS officer who had had his eyes on her for a long time. She felt tired and empty, worse than she had felt in years. She wondered whether it was all worth it, if food, luxury, and clothing were really a fair exchange for her soul. But she was tired and it was another day. Finding a way out of all this would have to wait. Yes, she could abandon everything and run off, go to the mountains with the partisans. But at the moment she had only two hours to get cleaned up and make it to the office. The road was deserted and the sound of her heels echoed rhythmically on the pavement.

About twenty feet from her door, she heard the heavy breathing and rapid footfalls of someone half-running. Thinking it might be a thief, she instinctively clutched her purse to her chest and turned. She saw a tall, slim young man with light eyes and blond, combed-back hair cutting towards her across the street. In his right hand, he carried a gun like those of the German officers. He looked like a little boy, and although he was armed, she wasn't frightened. He stopped a few feet from her and fixed her with a pitiless stare. It was only then she understood that it was all over. The young man's gaze was cold and inexorably determined.

"Iolanda Danzi?" he asked, in a raspy, tense voice, sounding like a child who smoked too many cigarettes.

"That's me," she said, without thinking.

"You are accused of reporting Sandra Traverso, Mariù Pavarotti, and Liliana Stanchi to the Germans," he intoned in an oddly formal voice, like a judge about to pronounce sentence.

"You're wrong," she answered firmly, but without hope. "Ask Commander Grandi, he'll vouch for me."

"For your crimes, you are condemned to death."

His detached, formal façade had cracked and the words came out loudly, quavering with emotion. Iolanda smiled. At least she'd be spared the trouble of escaping a life she could no longer live. "Long Live Freedom! Long Live Italy!"

As he aimed at her heart and pulled the trigger, the young man saw a profound regret in her eyes. It was impossible for him to imagine the reason. He assumed it was because death had torn her from the good life: the parties, the social life, the elegant clothes, and all the comforts that she earned with German money and German favors. He couldn't know that Iolanda's most profound regret was that she was going to die with the stench of an SS officer still on her skin.

The blond boy fled and left her there, sprawled lifeless on the road in a puddle of blood. As he ran toward the hospital, some fascists, attracted by the sound of gunfire, came running out of the Fascist Party Headquarters and saw him. They did not shoot him, perhaps they were too far away, but one of them recognized him and shouted his name, urging him to stop. Biscia ran all the faster. As he disappeared into a side street, he thought that now he would have to go to the mountains, too. The idea held no terror for him. Finally, he would be with Tilde.

From the kitchen she hears a growing murmur and shouts of triumph. It has happened. "The informant got hers today," Wanda tells her with satisfaction. Wanda is a friend of her mother. She has three daughters who are about Tilde's age. When Tilde was a child, she used to go play at their house on Salita Campasso di San Nicola, and at five o'clock, they would have *merenda* and everyone would sit down to tea and cookies.

"What informant?" she replies, already knowing the answer.

"That woman who works in the office at the cigar factory. The *crucchi's* bitch."

Tilde excuses herself, quickly making her way to the bathroom. She passes Dolores, who says something but Tilde runs on. She locks the door behind her and abandons herself to silent tears, tears she has been holding in for two weeks now. It was really over. There would be no more doubt or hesitation. All that remained of Iolanda was the memory of a generous woman and a dark sense of guilt. But she was used to that, and she knew it would be a part of her for the rest of her life.

"We executed her this morning at dawn."

Olindo is waiting for her outside her house and these are the first words he says. He says them in a tone of grim resignation that makes her even angrier.

They go into the entrance hall and, as she locks the bicycle to a chain attached to the wall, she asks, "Who did it?"

"Why do you want to know?"

"Because," she says, shrugging. That gesture makes her look vulnerable, like a little girl. Olindo is moved and he's sorry that he can't answer her.

"No one wanted to do it. It's hard to kill a woman in cold blood."

"What about a man?" she asks sarcastically.

"A man, too," he admits. "Unless he's like Maestri."

She would like to ask why they didn't try to kill Maestri, but she knows it would be useless.

"Why did you wait so long?"

He's slow to answer. So she urges him: "Was it difficult to find out if Hessen was a widower?"

"That's not it."

"So, what?"

"I told you, no one wanted to do it."

"That young man with the dirty nails," she replied fiercely, "he couldn't wait to do it. You know what, Commander? You should keep your dogs muzzled."

"He's eighteen," Olindo replies.

"Exactly!" she interrupts, raising her voice. "He's reckless, like that student wearing glasses, who pretends to be intellectual. People like them shouldn't be deciding who dies and who lives."

"People like them," replies Olindo, "die every day to free Italy."

"But they're afraid to kill a defenseless woman."

"Yes. Because she's a defenseless woman. If they hadn't rounded up Liliana, nothing would have been done."

"And instead?"

Grandi shakes his head. He will never tell her that the night of the meeting at Ca' Bianca, Lanza had provoked Biscia, accusing him of causing Liliana's capture.

"If you hadn't decided to kiss up to your girlfriend," he had grumbled. "Anyone who sleeps with the Germans. . ."

Biscia had immediately jumped him and knocked him to the floor. Three of them had to hold him back, otherwise Biscia would have killed him.

"I'll do it," he had shouted. "I'll show you who's nothing but mouth and who has balls!"

This was wrong and Olindo didn't like it. It was no way to take on a mission like this. But this time he had decided to make an exception. Lanza had been unfair with his comrade and deserved what he had gotten. But he had a point. Choosing Biscia seemed to Olindo the only way to redeem him in the eyes of the others. So, when peace had been restored and everyone had calmed down, he said, "All right, Biscia. It's you. Start preparing yourself."

They had been following her for weeks and knew that Iolanda had gone to German headquarters that night. On these occasions, a car always took her home at dawn.

Olindo had been worried. He feared that the situation with Biscia was unsustainable. But, above all, he feared the first to realize it would be Biscia himself. When Biscia left with a furious scowl on his face and without saying goodbye to anyone, he had shuddered at the thought he wouldn't take the necessary precautions.

"It was Biscia, wasn't it?" Tilde asks.

Olindo shrugs, feeling trapped. He won't be the one to reveal the name, but the story is already on everyone's lips and Tilde will hear it soon enough. Biscia had been recognized and is now wanted for murder. At noon, with his backpack, he set out to reach the partisans on Mount Tobbio. Tilde clenches her fists and stares at Olindo with hatred.

Why him?

"Now you need to leave," Grandi orders.

"Why?"

"You know why." he says. "You put us all in danger."

"Relax," she replies calmly. "I've seen the captain again, and he assured me. . ."

"You have seen Hessen?" he interrupts with surprise.

106

"He wanted to see me. When he came looking for me. I couldn't tell him no," she answers dryly. "We have a relationship and he'll protect me." She's about to add "I trust in your discretion," when Olindo's pock-marked and hairless face tightens into a look of disgust. His large, protruding eyes close tightly and, when they open, they frighten her. They have lost their usual dullness and are blazing with rage.

"By what authority?" he hisses.

"What authorizes me, *Commander?*" she says haughtily. "Love for my family? The fact that I will pass you precious information? Or do you want to hear me say I like to sleep with him?"

He grabs her and covers her mouth to silence her. "What are you saying, you fool?"

She pulls his hand away and points her finger at his face, all fear and deference forgotten. She spits, "You have ruined my life. I've done what you asked but I'm not your puppet any longer. Enough! I'll do what I think best, now. And if you think I'm a danger, you can murder me just like you did Iolanda!"

Olindo remains silent, looking at her—he doesn't recognize her. He knows he has lost her but he's still worried about her safety.

"Maestri will hunt you down. . ." he insists.

"I know, and Hessen knows it too," she answers boldly. "That's why he wants to help you kill him."

Olindo is stunned. He'd like nothing more than to get rid of a bastard like Tearnails who is both a powerful Fascist and a ruthless killer. But he's troubled. Things have gone too far between Tilde and the German. Olindo isn't a man to flee from the consequences of his decisions. For better or worse, he knows that everything that's happened is his responsibility. His thoughts turn to Biscia, who, unaware, is probably just reaching the partisans in the mountains. Thank God he doesn't know about this!

He's silent for a while, listening to Tilde's angry panting. Then he lowers his eyes and says, "I will speak with the command."

"Yeah. Have a chat with your friend Buranello," says Tilde, who now knows she has him under her thumb. "Try to convince him not to miss a chance like this."

"It's a dangerous game," he replies without conviction.

"Like everything else, Olindo."

They say goodbye. The man opens the heavy door and goes out. Tilde starts to go up the stairs when she an indistinct shout and the sound of running footsteps. Frightened, she goes back and puts her ear to the door. She hears a panting voice she doesn't recognize: "*Belin!* I finally found you. I've been looking everywhere!"

"What's wrong, bad news?"

"They got Buranello coming out of a bar."

14.
LIFTING THE VEIL

"I don't understand why you're so upset, *Herr* Pagano. If I didn't tell you that twenty years ago I did some investigating myself, I have my reasons."

"They had better be damn good reasons, my dear professor. Otherwise, you can find yourself another sucker."

"It's not that much of a mystery. The truth is that my uncle's and aunt's explanations never really convinced me. So I tried to check into it on my own, but I didn't manage to discover anything useful."

"Bullshit."

"Bullshit?"

"Your aunt didn't tell you that you had a brother."

"Really? Who did?"

"An old partisan from Sestri."

"I must admit that you have a nose for these things."

"Tell me the name."

"It will not be very useful to you, unfortunately. His name was Adriano Ratto and everyone called him Dria, but he died fifteen years ago."

"Did you talk to Commander Grandi?"

"Yes. With him and with his men, at least those who were still alive."

"Do you remember names?"

"How could I forget them? Enrico Parodi and Giovanni Lanza. None of them told me anything, either about Nicla or about a son born after the war. I did get the impression they were hiding something."

"And what about Ratto?"

"Ratto fought under Grandi, like the others. He was the first I talked to. He was suffering from Alzheimer's disease by then so I guess the others couldn't silence him. What I learned of the story, I learned from him."

"And he didn't tell you the last name of Nicla and her husband?"

"He didn't remember it, or perhaps he never knew it. He had only heard that she'd had a son. As far as I could tell, he hadn't seen her in person since the war. His account was very confused. As I said, he was ill."

"Why did you keep this from me?"

"Because talking with Grandi and his comrades would be a waste of time. Who knows if they're even still alive? If they've decided not to talk, they aren't going to talk. Not even the SS could open their mouths. I think you have to follow other leads."

"Grandi was one of my father's best friends."

"I'm sorry, *Herr* Pagano. I didn't mean to hurt your feelings."

"It doesn't matter. . ."

"You said he *was?* Is the commander dead?"

"No, *Herr* Hessen, he's alive and well. It's my father who is dead."

The phone call finished with a string of apologies that left me cold. *Herr* Professor hadn't convinced me.

The hangover was just as bad as I'd expected. My head pulsed and felt as if someone had hammered a nail into it. I tried taking a long hot shower and drinking an entire pot of coffee but all it did was leave me more fully awake to contemplate my misery. In the condition I was in, the prospect of working was exhausting, but the prospect of staying at home, awaiting an improbable phone call from Pertusiello, was far worse.

I was starting to suspect that "Nicla" was a pseudonym. If it had been a *nom de guerre* that the woman had abandoned once the war was over, Bavastro would have recalled it. Instead, that name hadn't rung any bells for him.

I telephoned Olindo Grandi, who answered immediately, almost as if he was waiting for my call.

"I owe you an explanation," he said seriously and without preamble.

"I think so too, Commander," I replied, trying to lighten the tone.

"I talked to Lanza and Gino. They told me what you said."

"Can I disturb you again?" I asked. And I added, "There's no hurry—whenever's convenient."

"This story is dear to my heart," he replied firmly. "The sooner we clear it up, the better."

We agreed to meet in the afternoon. "My daughter leaves at two o'clock and we can talk privately," he said conspiratorially.

I had a few hours of free time and decided to use them to complete my plan of the previous day. With my bathrobe on, I went to the kitchen and started cooking the roast I had bought and dumped in the fridge to await better times. Cooking helped me relax, and after lunch even my headache had receded a little.

At two-thirty I was sitting in the Commander's kitchen. The *Cassa di Risparmio* calendar kept time stopped in March, 1998, and Amelia's portrait kept staring back at me sheepishly, as if apologizing for the trick her husband had played. From the window, a faint light spattered the floor. There was no smell of food, and the sink and the stove were shiny and empty, as if they didn't cook in that house and never had dishes or pots to wash. Olindo was wearing the usual brown cardigan with worn elbows, a pair of moleskin pants, and cloth slippers. From

111

behind the thick glasses, he studied me with his enormous opaque eyes.

"It wasn't easy," he began, "but I had no choice."

"Lying?" I asked.

"Yes, I always avoided doing so when I could, even when I was a partisan."

"You lied to my client," I said.

"With you it's different. I owed nothing to the German."

"Nor to me, if we're being honest."

"You are the son of Guido and Anna, and it has cost me to feed you all that bullshit."

"But you wanted to keep me away from the truth."

"It's true, but nothing personal. I made a promise and I have to keep it."

"To Nicla?"

He nodded and bent his head. His hands, twisted and wrinkled, had lain motionless on the table. Now he clasped and unclasped them almost convulsively. Grandi was nervous.

"So you knew her."

"Of course I knew her. She was the one who swore me to secrecy."

"About what? The existence of my client?"

"That she had a relationship with the captain of the Wehrmacht. That she had a son that the Germans took away from her."

"So it's true that after the war she married and had another child."

"She had a little girl who recently became a grandmother. She never knew anything about this, and her mother, on her death bed, made me swear, again, I would do whatever was necessary to make sure she never did."

"Not even for all the gold in the world, Bacci. It's not a matter of money."

"Is her father dead too?"

"I don't know. I never met him. When she was a few years old, he emigrated to South America and no one has heard from him since. Nicla raised her daughter alone. . ."

"Nicla," I interrupted, ". . . is that a fictitious name?"

"It's the name you told me."

"Hessen told me that's what she was called."

"So let's call her that."

"You talked to him twenty years ago. Even then he used the name Nicla?"

"Your client is lying. He doesn't know anything about this story, except some confused information that poor Dria passed on to him before he died. Dria was one of my men. A big boy full of courage, but not the sharpest knife in the drawer. By the time he was fifty, Dria was already suffering from Alzheimer's and told Hessen a tangled story full of wrong names, half-truths and outright fantasies."

"You didn't answer me, Olindo. Did Hessen mention Nicla's name?"

"No, he mentioned another name, but not one that had anything to do with this. Dria confused Hessen's mother with another woman."

"Was Nicla a partisan?"

"Yes, one of our bravest couriers. She was captured by a Wehrmacht patrol on the Sant'Alberto road and brought to German headquarters for questioning. It was there she met Captain Hessen. She was only nineteen and was special."

He could tell from my face that I had no idea what he was talking about.

113

"An unusual, naïve, beauty with an almost animal attraction. She caught Hessen's eye and volunteered to approach him to get useful information for the Resistance. She was extremely successful until he died in the blast at the Odeon Cinema. Then she disappeared. We all thought she had been deported. I saw her again after the Liberation and she told me that she had been a prisoner of the Germans near Lake Garda and that, after she gave birth, they took the child away and forced her to work in a nearby factory. She thought I had a right to know but she made me promise I'd take her story to the grave."

"So even Lanza and Balletta knew her."

"Balletta was in the mountains and never met her."

"My client claims he was one of your men."

He shook his head and smiled. "He was sixteen," he said. "He joined the group in May of '44, and, by that time, she'd already disappeared. During his first engagement, he managed to get himself both recognized and wounded. We sent him straight to Urbe, where your father was, and there he remained until the Liberation."

"And Lanza?"

"The couriers didn't know the comrades. They only knew me. An elementary safety measure."

"And Dria, then?"

"I've known Dria since before the war."

"So," I said, changing direction, "Nicla had a daughter."

"She did indeed. She's nearly sixty and, as I told you, she's been a grandmother for a few months now."

"Don't you think she might like to meet her brother?"

"It doesn't concern me. I promised her mother."

"Do you have the right to decide for others?"

"This decision was made long ago, and not just by me."

"This Hessen fellow would be like discovering a rich uncle from America."

He smiled. "Historically speaking, it might not be an exact comparison. And what if he's just lying about the money? Are you sure your German client is so rich?"

"For my initial expenses he gave me a check for forty thousand euros, which of course, I refused to cash."

"Believe me, Bacci, that man isn't out to do someone a good deed. Get rid of him. He's looking for vengeance."

"How can you say that?"

"I don't know. But I know. Call it the instincts of an old partisan."

15.
THE TWO FLAGS

Genoa, March 1944

The big alarm clock ticking on the bedside table won't let her sleep. Dawn is still far away and it's too dark to read the time. The embers in the fireplace are dying and the air in the room has become frosty. She hears the man snoring at her side and she suppresses an urge to run home to her family. She wonders if they suspect something. She begged her aunt for help: "I work for the partisans and I don't want them to worry at home." The old woman accepted, though reluctantly, and asked her mother to let Tilde sleep at her place twice a week. Her mother didn't object, and now she wonders if she wouldn't have preferred that she had objected and stopped all this. How odd that she was more willing to risk her life than defy her mother!

This has gone on for almost a month and she is beginning to feel tired. She's beginning to look tired, too. At work, a friend asked her, "Are you all right, Tilde? You look terrible!" Is it possible no one's noticed anything at home? Perhaps they have too many other things to think about. And she does feel terrible. She's even been nauseous for a few days and unable to eat.

Twice a week, before curfew, she pedals her bicycle up the short stretch of road to the cemetery. She hides it among the shrubs and waits. The car, driven by Sergeant Walden, always arrives right on time and takes her to the villa. At five o'clock in the morning, after breakfast, he returns her to the exact spot that he picked her up and Tilde gets back on the bicycle and rushes to work. Those who see her pedaling down Via Sant'Alberto and along Via Merano must think she's such a good and dutiful daughter! They'll assume that she's been taking care of her aunt as well as the rest of her family.

116

Walden's Italian is improving. She wonders if he's making the effort for her sake. The trip from Sestri to Albaro is so long.

Hessen drinks and smokes every night just as he did on their first night together. Alcohol is what keeps him alive. It stuns his mind and anesthetizes his invisible wounds. She also fears that she, too, has become a drug and she is irritated by that, without knowing why. Perhaps it's that everyone wants something from her, without ever asking what she would like for herself. Sometimes, she feels as if the real Tilde were invisible, dissolved in so many small pieces ready to meet someone else's needs and expectations. Tilde the worker, Tilde the spy, Tilde the nurse, Tilde the lover. . . There's only one person who didn't make her feel this way and, in return, she arranged to have her killed by her boyfriend. Perhaps Hessen feels he is living up to his half of the bargain by saving her from torture and death. But what is it that she really wants from him?

Her conversations with the German, at the table and in bed, transform the dark man's mood into a vacuous fatalism. Listening to his esoteric pontifications about how the war would end while the Fascists and the SS were killing dozens of people every day makes her angry. So angry that she can only conceal her rage with cognac and sex. Some nights, she imagines she can hear the screams of the tortured partisans coming from the basement of Gestapo headquarters. She knows it isn't far from the villa where the captain lives. Sometimes, telling herself that this is all a dream is the only way she can stop herself from grabbing a knife and planting it in his heart. Other times, she repents and would like to show him her gratitude. Thanks to him, four partisans escaped arrest and a courier changed her route to avoid a checkpoint. For Hessen, these pieces of information are precious offerings that confirm the power of her femininity. For the PAG command, these are good reasons to accept things as they are.

She feels her stomach turn and her anxiety becomes unbearable. Then she starts shaking him. "Helmut, Helmut, wake up!"

When they went to bed he was dead drunk; he's a heavy sleeper and he slowly struggles his way to consciousness. *"Was passiert, Fräulein?"*

"Couldn't you hear that?"

"Hear what?"

"Screams, screams of pain."

"What are you saying? You must be dreaming. . ." he mumbles, his eyes still closed.

"They're coming from Gestapo headquarters. Your comrades are torturing partisans."

"It's impossible, Tilde. It's too far away."

"But I've heard them. . ." She pretends to cry, but she's ashamed because she hasn't actually heard anything and doesn't cry for the partisans but for herself. Her anguish and the impulse to vomit are demanding she find a distraction. "Let's talk a little bit, please?"

Hessen continues to fight his way back to full consciousness. "But tomorrow you have to get up before five."

"I don't care, I want to talk!"

Hessen is now resigned. His own little girls acted like this when they woke up from a bad dream and called him in the middle of the night. So he says: "Shall I tell you a story, *meine kleine Prinzessin?*"

"You have already told me a fable." she says spitefully. "You promised that you'd free me from the nightmare Tearnails. Have you forgotten?"

"Is this what keeps you awake?"

"I'm afraid," she whimpers, getting closer to him. The strong smell of alcohol on his breath almost makes her gag.

"There is no reason to be afraid."

"Oh yes, there is! After the partisans killed your informant, he must know I'm the one who denounced her. You promised to take care of him but you've done nothing."

"He's smart and he always travels with an escort."

"I'm sure there is. But it's not as easy as you think," he murmurs with a sigh. Then, surprisingly, he gives her a sly smile and adds, "Even though I think I've discovered his weakness."

"Really?" she asks, brightening. For a moment her nausea has disappeared.

"He's a gambler. He spends all his nights at the table and loses a lot."

"How did you learn that?"

"He borrows money and this makes him unreliable."

Tilde whistles, in admiration. "Congratulations on you efficiency, *mein Hauptmann!*"

"It's a rumor at headquarters. I'm not sure where it started. Maybe he asked for a loan from some officer, or maybe it was the Gestapo who found out. They have a low opinion of the Italian political police."

Gestapo. The word fills her with fright. She clings to him and presses her ruffled black hair against his chest. She suddenly becomes serious and asks, "Are you sure they don't suspect you?"

The man smells her hair, catching its animal scent, and smiles. "With them, you can't be sure of anything."

"You have to find out where he gambles."

"And what will you do?"

Tilde thinks about the morning before, at the gates of the Fossati factory. As the workers were arriving there was much giggling and slapping of backs. It had been a long time since she had felt such a carefree atmosphere at the factory. She approached a group with some people she knew, including and old friend of her father. He was a Communist in his thirties who was originally from Ovada and who worked with the trip hammers. He'd been married for a few months to the daughter of Maria, their neighbor.

"What's going on?" she asked. For a moment she imagined the war was over.

The man, a handsome young man with olive skin, curly hair, and a solid, strong physique, looked at her and winked. "On the tower of the Fascist Party Headquarters, this morning they were flying two flags."

"Two?" she asked, mystified.

"The Tricolor and the Red."

That memory gives her new energy and drives away her fear. She looks at the captain and, teasingly answers, "What will I do? I'll wait for him in the car to console him, right?"

He grunts something in German and grabs her forcefully. Roughness excites him. She has managed to awaken him from his alcohol-induced torpor and this please her. It makes her feel strong. He tries kissing her, but she twists her head away and avoids his mouth. One smell of his still-alcohol-laden breath and she will vomit instantly. She turns her back on him and moves against his already erect manhood, offering herself with a complicity disguised as submission. He needs no further encouragement and takes her from behind. He's so excited that in a matter of seconds he gives a dull moan and a wave of hot liquid fills her.

It's always like this. Nobody asks questions, takes precautions, considers the consequences. Those are things you do when you have a future. But Tilde and Hessen see no future. They don't know that the future is already written in those waves of nausea she strives to hold back.

Now she bites the pillow and cries in silence, thinking of what she felt when he reached orgasm. She has never felt so alone.

16.
THE PROMISE

I got home around four. The conversation with Olindo Grandi had put me in a bad mood. I felt guilty about continuing the investigation, though I realized that made no sense. After all, Grandi was the one with the problem, not me. I hadn't promised anyone anything. Refusing to tell Nicla's daughter, or whatever the hell her name was, that she had a rich brother ready to die and leave her a fortune didn't seem like much of a good deed to me. In fact, I thought it was a pretty shitty thing to do.

According to Olindo, the sixty-year-old woman had been abandoned by her father and her mother had raised her all on her own. They couldn't have had it easy. Now she found herself with a grandson, and common sense suggested that a substantial inheritance would be a godsend. The astonishment at learning the existence of a half-brother, the result of her mother's clandestine relationship with a German officer, seemed a pretty small price to pay for spending the rest of her life on easy street.

And yet, I was obsessed by a nagging doubt: *Would she really want to know?*

More than sixty years had passed since the war, and nowadays no one, not even Commander Grandi, saw the Germans as enemies. And, of course, now just as it was then, Italy's worst enemies are the Italians themselves. During my trips to Germany I had the impression that the effort to turn the page on the past without forgetting it has been more serious and deeper for Germans than for us Italians. The sins they committed were monstrous, apocalyptic. However, we too, even if in smaller measure, promulgated racial laws and had concentration camps, like the one established in the rice factory of San Sabba. We, too, exiled dissidents and beat, tortured, and assassinated opponents of the regime. The fact is that we've failed at the only task that humanizes a nation: learning from our defeats. Although we've been losers since the fall of Rome, pretending to be victors has been our way of deluding ourselves that we could cheat history.

My musings were interrupted by the ringing of the phone and a metallic voice brought me back to the present.

"Mr. Pagano?"

"Yes."

"Do you remember me?" she asked with a bit of apprehension. "I'm Elsa Parodi."

I recognized the voice of Balletta's daughter, the old partisan who had refused to meet me.

"Of course I remember," I replied, striving to express a warmth that, at the moment, didn't come naturally. "I'm glad to hear from you. To what do I owe. . .?"

"You asked me to talk to my father, once he had calmed down. Remember?"

She was convinced that I had forgotten about her. Perhaps she feared I hadn't taken her seriously or that I had underestimated her regard for my family.

"Of course," I said. "I hope I didn't re-open any old wounds or put you to any trouble."

"Let's just say I had to apply a little pressure. Dad didn't want to talk about it. But I made it a matter of honor because I feel a debt of gratitude towards your parents. Whenever we came to Genoa, my mother always took me to see her friend Anna, on Via dei Servi. I was young and you weren't born yet. But I remember Anna well. She would always hold me in her arms, go to the kitchen, and prepare my favorite snack, bread with oil and tomato. It sounds strange, but I still remember the smell of her clothes. When I was in her arms, I'd close my eyes and breathe it in deeply, and the scent lingered for the entire day. She was such a beautiful woman, Anna. I confess I would have liked my mother to be more like her." She paused, then added, "You must think I'm silly to tell you these things. . ."

"Oh no, Elsa," I interrupted. "May I call you Elsa?"

"Of course! There's no need to be formal with me. After all, we're of an age. We could've played together when we were children. We missed each other by just a few years."

"It's really a pity," I said, and I meant it.

The memory of my mother had changed my mood. It seemed to me that I, too, could still smell her perfume. A spicy fragrance that my father gave her at every wedding anniversary and that must have been very expensive. Grandfather Baciccia himself had once told me, "Your mother is a lucky woman. Your father knows how much she wants that perfume and, to give it to her, he saves all year. He must love her very much."

That was the truth. I had never seen the moment when he offered his gift. Probably it happened in the intimacy of their bedroom. But I remembered the tiny, elegant package, and the amber glass bottle. She kept it on her vanity in the bedroom and cared for it as if it were a sacred relic. One day, she caught me sniffing it and made a scene I never forgot. I had the impression that the flask was somehow more than just a perfume for her. Her femininity blossomed in its exotic aroma. A drop on her neck and wrists transformed her. Her beauty, so compelling as to make men turn in the street, causing my father and me an acute jealousy, was not enough for her. The perfume was a symbol, a concrete pledge of my father's unconditional love. Perhaps it reassured her, helped convince her that she had chosen wisely in life. After all, she had married a workman, an honest man who would do anything for her, but one who had nothing else to offer her other than his dedication and his salary.

"Well, anyway," Elsa resumed, "it wasn't easy to get Balletta to talk." She laughed. It was shrill and not particularly pleasant. "Did you know they used to call him that?"

123

"Olindo explained to me that he entered the Resistance very young."

"It wasn't easy to get him to talk about her."

"Nicla?" I asked, daring.

"I don't know if she was called Nicla. He told me he didn't remember, even though that seems a little suspicious. By the way," she interrupted herself again, "Olindo and my father had a meeting, just like the old days."

"They had a meeting?"

"Yes, at Olindo's house. After sixty years, they had another PAG meeting!" She laughed her shrill laugh again.

"Really? Who was there?"

"In addition to the commander, there were Lanza, my father, and one of the *Leggeroni*, Gino Bavastro."

I had to admit that Professor Hessen was right. Asking questions of the old members of the PAG was a waste of time. Once a partisan, always a partisan.

"I tried to catch him off-guard," Elsa continued, "and I was able to wheedle two pieces of information. But please," she interrupted again, "he must not know we talked."

"Don't worry," I reassured her, "He won't hear it from me."

"The woman did exist. She was a partisan courier. But, in the spring of 1944, she disappeared. According to my father, she had been deported to Germany. After the Liberation she returned to Sestri and married her boyfriend, a PAG member who had fought in Grandi's group with Lanza and my father. He was tall and thin as a pole. They called him Biscia. According to Dad, he was one of the best members of the Resistance. The Germans and the Fascists were hunting him for killing an informant, a young woman named Iolanda, who worked at the cigar factory. Biscia and his wife had a daughter and went to live in another town. It seems everyone lost touch with them after the war."

"So you heard about the promise? That seems to be what's behind all this. According to my father, Grandi made the woman some sort of promise on her deathbed. I gather the point of the meeting was to come to an agreement about it."

Here was another piece added to the puzzle. The father of the woman I was looking for was a PAG member, a tall, thin young man named Biscia. Olindo had lied to me again, but poor Balletta was less disciplined and had let the name slip. I mused that it was fortunate these men had been on top of their game in the old days and hadn't made this kind of mistake during the war. Dropping the wrong name back then could have gotten someone killed.

I thanked Elsa Parodi and I was about to say goodbye when she said, "Now *you* have to promise *me* something."

I agreed. She couldn't want much.

"If you find out what really happened, will you tell me?"

"I will," I promised, and ended the call.

I went to my study and started a Mozart CD. I chose *The Magic Flute,* foolishly thinking that listening to an opera in German would somehow help me piece this mess together.

I wondered why Olindo had "forgotten" to mention that Nicla's husband, the father of the woman I was looking for, was a partisan in his group. Stupid question. He wanted to do everything possible to make sure I didn't find her. Instead of being mad at Grandi, I was almost euphoric. Now, I was motivated. If Grandi was so intent on lying, she must be close, so close I could almost smell her.

My German client, that sly old bastard, had seen right when he suggested I start in Sestri. I decided to call him and let him know about the latest developments while keeping in mind the possibility suggested by the commander. Maybe he was motivated by revenge rather than a cozy family feeling.

I tried calling his home number in Cologne and he answered almost immediately.

"*Herr* Pagano," he said emphatically. "What a pleasure to hear your voice." He noticed the background music. "And the overture of Mozart's *Die Zauberflöte* as well. Even better!"

"There's been a development," I said, before he could go on. "Your brother is a woman."

"What? A woman?" he asked, shocked.

"It turns out your lost sibling is actually a sister who has just become a grandmother."

"Did you find her?"

"Not yet."

"May I ask you," he said with a meticulous, professorial tone—and not without a certain irony—"Who gave you this scoop?"

"My sources are entitled to anonymity."

"Certainly," he said, annoyed. His tone had become hard and bitter. "But they don't have the right to make a fool out of you. That's bad enough. But since you are working under me, they're making a fool out of me, too."

I didn't care for the idea of working *under him*, much less for the tone with which he'd expressed it.

"Listen, Professor," I said, with a deep sigh, "why don't you tell me your brother's name and we finish it here?"

"Because I don't know it," he replied thoroughly unconvincingly.

"So how can you exclude. . ."

"That my brother is a woman?" he interrupted. "Because Dria Ratto told me about a man."

"Dria Ratto suffered from Alzheimer's disease."

"And you, my dear detective," he said, returning to a sort of bitter joviality, "suffer from too much awe for your father's old comrades. You ignored me completely, didn't you? I bet you kept trying to get the story from Commander Grandi's men."

"It is not my habit to let clients decide on the method of my inquiries." I said formally.

"I'm afraid you're wasting your time and my money, but do as you wish," he said, trying to wrap up the conversation. "After all, you're the detective."

Thanks for nothing, I thought, but I said, "I have to ask myself what it is you're really after. . ."

"My brother's name," he said dryly.

"And what else?"

Hessen remained silent. Maybe I was imagining things, but I was sure my question had touched a nerve. I decided to pile on the pressure and see what happened. "Your father died in an attack by a PAG squad."

"A *PAG* squad?" he asked, as if confused.

"Partisans operating in the city were called Patriotic Act Groups, PAGs."

"So your father was in this PAG group?" he asked abruptly.

"No, my father fought in a mountain division," I said. "Why do you ask?"

"To avoid giving offense," he said in a tense voice. "Do you know what your 'PAGs' would be called today?"

I began to guess where he was going with this and I let him run.

"Terrorists." He said the word with emphatic harshness, stressing each syllable as if he was striking it with a hammer. "The man who put the bomb in the Odeon Cinema was nothing but a terrorist."

"Is that why your boys took fifty-nine political prisoners waiting for trial and shot them in a ditch at Turchino Pass?"

"War is a serious business, *Herr* Pagano, even if you Italians have always considered it a game, switching sides as it suits you and refusing to pay the price when you lose."

"So the lives of fifty-nine young men don't seem like a high enough price to you? I'm curious, just how many innocent people should have been killed, in your opinion?"

I heard a grunt mixed with anger and annoyance. Hessen wasn't stupid. This useless debate had convinced me I was right. Hessen had gone on the attack to defend himself. I went back to where I started, to the same observation that had set him off in the first place. "So your father was killed in an attack."

"I know. I'm the one that told you," he said irritably, but also cautiously.

"And your mother was a partisan."

"Perhaps. I don't know for sure."

"Who do you think you're kidding? You know she was."

He laughed, but it was a weak, tired laugh. "Somehow I doubt she, too, was a PAG member."

"Let's suppose she was. History is full of female terrorists. You Germans know all about that. Remember Ulrike Meinhof?"

"What are you saying?" he snarled, exasperated. "It wasn't a woman who put the bomb in that cinema."

"I read the proceedings from the Butcher of Genoa's trial. Friedrich Engel was a Nazi officer who thought about the war the same way you do. It's known that the perpetrator of the attack was a young blond partisan with blue eyes."

"And so?"

"If your mother had been in a PAG, she would have known."

"Isn't that why you hired me, Professor Hessen?"

A silence charged with tension crackled between us interrupted only by his labored breathing. I could almost hear the buzz of his thoughts, a confused tumult of emotions barely contained. For the first time, under the surface of his affable veneer of the cultured gentleman, I sensed something more primal: hatred, an elementary, sharp, absolutely human feeling.

He made a real effort and his next words were light, almost playful and tinged with irony. "I fear that you have a vivid imagination, *Herr* Pagano. If things were as you say, I'd be wrong about everything."

"Explain."

"Suppose what you say is true, that I knew from the beginning. When you discovered the horrible truth, would you have come to tell me?"

His argument was dead on target and I had nothing to say. I would have ended up finding myself in an impossible conflict. If Nicla really had known about the attack, how could I have told her son that she had helped to kill his father?

I thought at least one of us had done something terrible and that it was too late to fix it now.

"You should not have come looking for me," I said in a flat, colorless voice, "and I should have refused to take the job."

"You think?" he asked with a mocking laugh that had something devilish in it.

Suddenly, Olindo's concerns about the Professor became clear to me. I felt an urge to protect this Nicla, as if it were me who had made that deathbed promise.

"It's not difficult to get out of this, *Herr* Pagano," taunted Hessen.

"How?"

"Just stick to your job. Find my brother and make him rich."

17.
TILDE ALONE

Sestri Ponente, March 1944

Tonight she is at home, in her bed. She hears the rhythmic, light breathing of her brother sleeping on the other side of the room. Her parents, too, are asleep after another typically long and busy day: work at the factory, the elaborate therapies to relieve her mother's suffering, toiling in the kitchen which smells of cabbage, and the long wait in the ration line in the hope of exchanging coupons for half a pound of bread and four ounces of dried fava beans. Alberto Rabagliati's swing music and the songs of the Trio Lescano still come from the old radio, but they're no longer capable of reminding people of better times. People still go through the motions, reading old copies of *La Domenica del Corriere* over and over until they are worn out just as her brother spends his evenings reading year-old copies of comic books like the *L'Intrepido* in the pale light of a single candle. But none of it helps.

Darkness and silence have taken over the apartment, as well as every bit of her life. In that spectral calm, the ticking of the great alarm clock set on the bedside table expands and becomes the beating of a remorseless, merciless metal heart. It beats out the seconds and marks her thoughts.

Now she *knows*. She's pregnant. A boy? Or maybe a girl? Maybe she'll be blonde, like Tilde's father and brother. Perhaps even Biscia's daughter would have been blonde. But what she is expecting is not Biscia's daughter. She's not even Hessen's daughter. She's the daughter of this damn war.

How long will she be able to hide the truth from the world? She seems to feel her belly swelling day-by-day, although it's still too soon to show. Maybe it's just her imagination. But at the factory, after eight hours on her feet peeling beets and potatoes, and serving the workers their meals, her ankles swell and her legs are lead. Her breasts are bigger and harder. But instead of being pleased and proud, she's ashamed like when she was a little girl. She turns to stare at the wall, and curses the fate that made her hate the only wealth and power she possesses, her body and her femininity.

She wonders how she got to this point. Should she ask Commander Grandi, who pushed her into the arms of the German officer? Biscia, who stood by and watched him do it? Her mother, who thought her daughter was visiting a sick aunt and had no idea her little girl had become a whore? Can a good cause absolve a bad conscience? Is the child growing inside her redeemed by the lives saved by Hessen's information or can it be sacrificed without remorse?

Without remorse? She smiled bitterly. When did she ever manage to do anything without remorse?

She tells herself that the blame and the responsibility are hers. How many times was she told, "If you're not up to it, don't do it!" But something always pushed her to persevere, to show that she was willing to make the sacrifice. It was the price of acceptance.

But she was wrong. If she had chosen differently, no one would have blamed her. She knows that now just from the way Olindo looks at her. He gave her the same look on the day Iolanda was killed and Giacomo Buranello was captured. Back in the dim light of the entrance way, when she told him that Hessen was ready to give them Maestri, she saw a lightning bolt of despair flash through his eyes before the reserved calculation of a partisan commander took over. She would see that same despair in the eyes of her parents when they knew what she had done just as she had seen it on Biscia's face that day at Dria's house.

Who can she trust? Who can she tell that an enemy's child is growing inside her?

This is her cross. The deep wound that poisons her soul. Being alone, not having a friend, a person with whom to share her fears. It has always been thus, ever since she was a child. Her mother let her want for nothing, squeezing from their poverty everything she could for her a wall of silence built of disillusion and rancor grew between them. She couldn't acknowledge it, so she masked it by tirelessly busying herself, working incessantly. As she grew older, her father began to distance himself from her. He lost the spontaneity with which he once communicated warmth and tenderness. Then came her brother, her mother's illness, the war. . . No one made the effort to look inside the others' hearts, to read their intimate thoughts. Surviving was already a daily act of heroism. Who could have the strength for more?

She realizes that the pillow is wet. She is weeping bitter tears of loneliness without remedy or consolation. She knows she can expect nothing now from the people she loves.

She could talk to Hessen, tell him the truth. She wonders how he would react to the news of a child born to a woman who offered him her body in exchange for his betrayal. Could he ever find a place for another child in a heart dulled by alcohol and sex? A son of no one, the bastard of war. She feared it would take more than that to drag him away from the memory of his dead wife and his precious girls.

The image of a blond baby with heavenly blue eyes is the last thing imprinted in her memory before the air-raid alarm starts.

Her mother barges into the room shouting. Her brother leaps to his feet, puts on his pants and shoes and wraps himself in his coat as if he were sleepwalking. Tilde is slow to move; if she could, she would remain there, under the blankets. After all, she's already done her part to serve her country, and the prospect of being buried under the debris with her secret seems a better way to go than the needle of the abortionist, madness, or suicide.

Instead, her father enters and grabs her by the arm, forcing her to stand up and put her feet on the frozen floor. She wears a short flannel nightshirt and it's a matter of a moment, the prominent breasts, her father being forced to look at her, the look in her eyes. Can he tell? Has he read her secret on her face? He says nothing but rips the old blanket from the bed, wraps her in it, and drags her down the stairs and out of the house. In the crowded street, the night air is cold but already smelling of spring. The black surface of the sky is covered by the silver trails of the parachute flares. They explode and fall in flashes of light.

The anti-aircraft artillery crackles uselessly. It won't be able to stop them. Like thunder, the planes' rumble echoes ominously, until the earth begins to shake as the first bombs find their mark. The glow illuminates the roofs of Sestri and explosions follow linear and ruthless trajectories. The red flames of the first fires begin to flicker on the horizon, and soon, smoke in the air burns the eyes and makes breathing difficult. They must be quick, they must reach the shelter before her mother suffers a crisis.

Tilde sees all three of them slip into the air raid shelter, like terrorized mice hiding in a sewer. But she remains standing there, in the middle of Via Chiaravagna, still wearing the old blanket her father had wrapped her in. A young woman comes running up, her brown hair tangled with sleep and partially covering a refined profile of ancient beauty. She recognizes her immediately. This is the daughter of Maria, their neighbor. Her brother was a member of the city's marching band but had been deported to Germany. Tilde had played with her youngest sister when they were little girls. She has come looking for her family, anguish burning in her eyes.

"Tilde," she says, panting. "Have you seen them?"

"They were just ahead of us. They're already inside," she reassures her. It comes to her that this is the wife of the worker who, at the gates of the Fossati factory, told about the two flags that had been hoisted by the partisans over the Fascist Party Headquarters.

The woman hugs her with gratitude, and asks "What are you waiting for? Why aren't you inside?"

Tilde looks at the sky, now silent. It's over. She wonders whether it wouldn't have been better if the Allies had mercifully saved the last bomb for her and her child.

18.
THE HUNT

The next morning at eleven o'clock I went to the San Martino Hospital. The *buriana*, a cold wind out of the northeast, had risen, and its gusts made my Vespa sway like a runaway horse. I went down Via Rivoli to Corso Aurelio Saffi, where the blinding panorama of the gulf opened before me. The sea was a flickering turquoise and the buildings of the city seemed to shiver in the gusts.

I entered the building in a fevered anticipation. I had convinced myself that Jasmìne was about to regain consciousness. That I knew this was based on nothing at all left me in a state of agitation. Curiously, though it was two hours before visiting hours, I found the door of the ward open. The same policeman was on duty in the corridor as on the day I had met the German client. Just as before, he was reading a sports newspaper, from which he looked up, greeted me with a smile tinged with a touch of pity, and then looked down again.

I went in and found two nurses so focused on their work that they didn't notice my presence. Seizing my opportunity, I slipped into Jasmìne's room and closed the door behind me. There were two beds, but the second was empty and perfectly made. The dazzling light flooded her face but she did not stir. With a shiver, I thought of how deep the darkness in which her mind was immersed must be. I grabbed a metal chair and sat next to the bed, silently watching her.

She was intubated and I couldn't hear her breathing, but I could almost imagine that she was sleeping quietly. Her head and neck were wrapped in a white bandage and the uncovered part of her face was pitifully stretched. I lowered the sheet covering her up to her chest and I realized that, under the sterile gown, her skin had lost its once-vibrant glow. Her arms were thin, and so were her long, once-muscular legs. Jasmìne had once reminded me of a jungle cat. No more.

She had an IV drip in her right arm and on her wrists, deep scars left by the steel wire with which she had been bound. The massive bruise that deformed the features of her face, causing a noticeable swelling of her left cheek and eye, was slowly fading. Her captor had beaten her savagely, just for the fun of it. He had bound her hands behind her back, leaving her free to walk the squalid, windowless basement where she had been held. All so he could beat and rape her at his convenience. The doctors had told me that her belly and back showed the marks of a lash and, in the house, the police had found a whip.

I kept staring at her, silently. Perhaps, somehow, I was hoping to reach her in whatever silent realm she wandered. Of course, I found nothing and my thoughts returned to the day she was rescued. It seemed so long ago. . .

When I had left the Belvedere Boarding School, I was euphoric. Although I didn't quite know what, I knew I had something important on my hands. The young Hoogy had told me that Jasmìne had been taken in a white car, a station wagon, that had writing and a drawing of a fox winking on the door. I rushed home and started franticly scanning the phonebook, first the white and then the yellow pages. I tried *volpe, fox, renard,* but found nothing. I wasted almost an hour before I was convinced this was going nowhere. But why? First of all because my research was limited to the province of Genoa and Jasmìne could be captive in another city. Secondly, knowing nothing about the writing on the car made my search desperately difficult.

I decided to call Pertusiello, and get the resources of the police behind the search. I repeated Hoogy's words to him and he assured me he would immediately put his men on it. But I couldn't stand around waiting and doing nothing. So I called Essam, the son of my maid and self-appointed secretary, and made an appointment to meet him at his home behind the Coro delle Vigne. He was all about technology and the Internet. Perhaps his computer skills could help.

The kid was alone; his mother Zainab had gone to visit her oldest again using the words with which I had started, with no appreciable results. We'd hoped to find a site that reproduced the company's logo, a fox that smiled and winked. We worked for fifteen minutes, then thirty, using all the keywords linked to foxes we could think of. Nothing.

All of a sudden, Essam looked at me and said, "Did you say it could be a cartoon?"

"So she said."

"And what animated film features a fox as a protagonist?"

His dark eyes had taken on a look of cunning. It was clear that he was enjoying the thrill of the investigation. Maybe too much.

"You're asking me?" I answered. "How the hell should I know? I haven't watched a cartoon since Aglaja was a little girl."

"That's right. You haven't." he replied.

I tried to think back to all the movies my daughter had forced me to watch which, though I'd never admit it, I had enjoyed immensely. From *Snow White* to *Cinderella*, from *Beauty and the Beast* to *Lion King*. There was *The Sword in the Stone, Dumbo,* and. . .

"Son of a bitch! *Robin Hood!* It's goddamn *Robin Hood!*"

"That's it!" he said smiling, proud to have beaten me to the answer.

We started searching; the list was gigantic, but nothing seemed quite right. After an hour of the boy pounding the keyboard like a madman, we'd written down three addresses. A moving company in Merano, a plumber in Gioia del Colle, and an electronic components company in Piazza Armerina, Sicily. All three of them had a logo similar to the fox in Disney's *Robin Hood* but they were all hundreds of kilometers away. Essam kept up the hunt, banging on the keys and running endless lists of sites, which he opened and immediately closed, all the while thinking furiously.

Suddenly, he sat back and said, "And what if it's not Robin Hood?"

"Then we're screwed. We'd be back to square one," I said.

"Not necessarily," he replied, convinced.

"What do you mean?

"Bacci, there were *two* foxes in *Robin Hood*."

"You mean it could be. . ."

"Yes, go on." he encouraged me, as if I were a schoolboy.

". . . Lady Marian?"

"Why not?"

He launched the new keyword, and almost instantly, a link appeared for a commercial page that made us say in unison: "That's it!"

It was a cleaning company, "Lady Marian - Bright Houses and Offices," whose logo consisted of the affable fox we were looking for. It was hard to see the connection between a cleaning service and a medieval noblewoman, but whatever. We were sure we were on the right track. The company was right here in Genoa, on Corso de Stefanis, the busy road that runs behind the stadium and the Marassi prison. I decided to go there immediately and Essam offered to come with me.

How could I say no? If this was the place, the credit was all his. We ran out the door and made our way to Piazza Sarzano, where I had parked my Vespa. The rain had stopped, and the last pale rays of the afternoon sun were starting to push through the thick clouds in the western sky. I tried to read this as a sign, a hope of finding Jasmìne alive. But you know what they say about hope. I thought I might take out a little insurance so, before leaving, I ran around the corner and up the stairs, took off my jacket, and put on my shoulder holster. From the desk drawer I pulled out the Beretta Cougar 8000, inserted the magazine, and put the gun in the holster. I put my jacket back on, grabbed a box of bullets shoved them in my right pocket.

The roads were busy with rush hour traffic, but, on the Vespa, it didn't take us more than ten minutes to reach the location of the cleaning company. I took advantage of a free parking lot for motorbikes and put the Vespa on its stand. After locking the helmets to the seat, Essam and I began to walk casually, pretending to look in shop windows until we found ourselves in front of the one we were interested in. Inside, sitting at the desk, there was a young woman about thirty, who was working on the computer. She had straw-colored hair and a sloppy demeanor that suited the dull furniture of the small office. I wondered if she was the Lady Marian who had given the company its name or whether she was just a secretary. We looked around, but saw no sign of a white station wagon. We had no choice but to wait, hoping we hadn't hit a dead end.

Essam was as focused as a hunting dog and remained silent and intent. There was a bar next door so I suggested a drink while we waited. He ordered a tomato juice and I drank a glass of Dolcetto. I didn't know how long it would be; I was ready to stay there all night. But the thought we might be at the wrong place gnawed at me. When we finally left the bar, the traffic had become a mess and the air was unbreathable. The cars headed toward the Val Bisagno were motionless and someone who'd had enough began to honk furiously. It was almost dark, and the streetlights came on, bathing the sidewalks with a cold, white light. We continued to haunt the window of the cleaning business. Suddenly, across the street, where traffic flowed smoothly, we saw a light-colored station wagon approaching. But it passed us and headed downtown without slowing. And the doors were blank. No writing. No drawings.

I decided to risk it. We couldn't stand here all night. In any case, if we had the wrong address, there was no danger of compromising the investigation. Having ordered Essam not to move and to keep his eyes open, I entered the business with a confidence I didn't feel.

The young woman with the bad hair barely lifted her eyes from the computer and said mechanically, "Good evening, can I help you?"

"I'm looking for mister. . ." I said, pretending to be disoriented and confused. "The guy who drives the company's white station wagon."

"Mr. Randazzo?"

"Maybe that's his name. Isn't he the owner?"

"Oh, no," replied the woman with a patronizing smile. "The owner is Mrs. Mariani. Otherwise, we would call ourselves 'Lady Randazzo,' don't you think?"

Despite the horrible color of her hair, she seemed intelligent and helpful. Maybe she wasn't so bad after all.

"But who drives the car. . ."

"It's Mr. Randazzo. He's just an employee, like me. He's the one who provides the supplies, brooms and detergents, and sometimes drives workers to the jobs. Anyway," she added, "he will be here any moment. Do you want to wait for him?"

"I have an urgent errand to run," I said, trying for a captivating smile. "I'll be back in five minutes."

"Could I give him a message for you, Mr. . .?"

"De Prà," I said, ready. "It doesn't matter, I'll talk to him personally."

"As you wish," she replied, almost annoyed. "But do it soon, because he has to leave again right away."

I walked triumphantly out of the office and found Essam. We moved behind a van parked across the street where we could see into the window without being seen. As we settled in to wait, I told him what I'd discovered. Essam was pleased. He, too, had gotten to know Jasmìne while she had been living with me. Because of her profession, his mother wasn't too happy about him hanging out with her. No one ever said I was a good influence.

A lady entered the office. She was wearing a light coat, was fairly corpulent, and had short blond hair. It had gotten easier to see inside the office because my new friend had turned on the light. The two women began talking to each other; the older one seemed impatient, as if waiting for something or someone. Twenty minutes had passed when the secretary turned off the computer and lifted the phone. A brief conversation followed and the secretary nodded. She hung up and said something to the fat woman, who replied by throwing her arms wide as if to say "Finally!"

And, sure enough, after about five minutes, a large white vehicle pulled out of traffic. It was a station wagon and on the door was a winking fox and the words, "LADY MARIAN - CLEANING COMPANY." A man about forty years old got out. He was fat, too, on the short side and sporting a red mustache and goatee. He had on a white and red windbreaker, jeans, reddish-tan boots with rounded toes and a dark woolen cap. As soon as she saw him pull up, the older woman came to the door and appeared impatient, even agitated. He went into the office, and began talking to the secretary. His mood changed immediately. He pulled out his wallet and hurriedly dismissed the fat lady, giving her some cash in an apparent invitation to take a taxi. Then he turned and said something to the secretary before he came barreling back onto the sidewalk and began scanning the street with a worried, hunted look. Was he searching for the stranger who had asked for him? He rushed to the bar where we had had our drink so I sent my young Egyptian friend after him. Essam returned after a few minutes and reported that the man had made a phone call.

"It's show time." I said to the boy. "Run to the police station and ask for Deputy Police Superintendent Pertusiello. Tell him everything that's happened and that he should assemble another SWAT team. I'll call in as soon as I know where they need to go."

I gave him a hundred euro banknote. He'd earned it. Despite the cash, he looked at me with disappointment in his big eyes. He was going to miss the most exciting part of the investigation. This was the scene in American movies where there's a big, final confrontation, the mysteries get resolved, Truth and Justice win out, the bad guy gets punished and the good guy gets the girl. There's usually an explosion or two and maybe a car chase. But this was Italy and we weren't in a movie. We were huddled in the shelter of an old Ford Transit, in front of a cleaning company in the Marassi district, where the neighborhood market is held twice a week, and old housewives buy cheap underwear and socks for their husbands who live on their small retirement checks and spend their Sundays rooting for the local soccer team. There were plenty of good guys and bad guys, but Truth and Justice were in short supply.

I had no doubts whatsoever that Randazzo had phoned the organization. The situation was becoming dangerous and I wouldn't put Essam in the middle of it.

The man came out of the bar and went straight to the station wagon, turning constantly to check if someone was following him. When he reached the car, he already had the keys in his hand. It was parked down the street, in an angled space about ten feet from my van.

Abandoning my post, I pretended to cross the road, weaving my way through the near-stationary traffic. At the median, I crouched down, made my way back up the street and then crossed back over so I could come up behind him.

I unbuttoned my sheepskin jacket, and, as he was getting into the driver's seat, I blocked the door with my body. I pulled my Beretta from its holster and shoved the barrel against his temple. "If you so much as squeak, you're a dead man." I promised.

He stared at me sideways with terror in his eyes. I closed his door and slid into the backseat. I shove my hand between the seat and the door so I could jab the barrel in his left kidney. I couldn't miss and it couldn't be seen from outside.

"Let's go." I ordered calmly.

Finally, I heard his voice. He swallowed and quavered, "Where?"

"To Jasmine."

I was bolstered by the idea that I was dealing with a loser and a sick one at that. Any man who would buy a woman and torture her is no fucking hero. Sure enough, like an obedient little boy, he started the car, backed it up, and, forgetting to use his turn signal, merged with the traffic and headed towards Staglieno.

But I wasn't fooling myself. I knew I was playing a weak hand. I didn't know where the girl was and I was sure he had phoned the organization and told them the game had been blown. If Randazzo was cunning, he could drive me around in circles while his buddies erased every trace of their crimes. Maybe I could deal myself another card. "Listen, friend, let me explain two things to you."

I saw him nodding, but he didn't speak.

"You need to know that this is personal. I love Jasmine and I'm willing to do anything to save her."

Silence. He continued to drive, motionless, focused on the road, even though traffic was at a snail's pace.

"So, if I don't find her *alive,* you're going to join her. We'll go to a secluded place and I'll blow your brains out."

He swallowed and nodded again, his arms stretched straight and his hands tight on the steering wheel.

"On the other hand, if we do arrive in time, before your butcher friends finish the killing and dispose of the corpses, well, this is your lucky day." I continued. "I promise you I'll drop you off somewhere and I won't turn you in to the police. What do you think of my offer?"

In a strained voice, tense as a violin string, he replied, "I'm afraid it's too late."

"Not necessarily," I replied. "Try to stop them with a phone call. Say it was a false alarm."

"If I call with my mobile phone, they'll know the jig's up without even answering it."

I realized he was cooperating. The fear of death had pushed everything else to the side.

"Call them using mine and say you stole it in a bar."

He thought for a few seconds, then said, "If I do that, they'll be the ones to kill me."

"You're a worthless bastard, who deserves to fry in Hell. And I couldn't care less. All I'm interested in is Jasmine. So I promise you, I'll find a place to hide you. We'll get an airplane ticket and you'll disappear."

"Would you really do that?" he asked in an unbelieving, almost childish voice.

"I *will*," I said convincingly. I handed him my mobile. Then I added, "Speak normally and try to be believable."

Randazzo grabbed the phone with his right hand but he was shaking convulsively. Despite the tension, I almost laughed. He wouldn't even be able to dial the number.

"Calm down," I said, "everything will be fine. Give me the phone. Tell me the number and I'll dial it."

He gave me the phone back and like an obedient dog, did as I asked. He gave me the number and when I handed it back, he tried to play his part as best he could. By then, we had passed the Staglieno cemetery and taken the Lungobisagno road in the direction of Molassana. The road was still busy, but traffic was moving more quickly.

His side of the conversation was telegraphic: "It's me again." Pause. "False alarm, it was a customer." Second pause. "I stole the phone in a bar, but don't worry, I'm destroying the card now." Third pause. "Where are you?" After the fourth pause, he even started to get angry: "Look, I've paid a lot of money and I don't want to give her up because of a stupid misunderstanding!" On the other side of the conversation, they must have put him in his place. "All right, fine, you're right, I've been hasty. It won't happen again."

He stopped talking and returned the phone to me.

"They fell for it," he said. "Your Jasmine is safe."

19.
APRIL

Genoa, April 1944

Twice she tries to speak and can't. The Armagnac seems to make her more talkative, but not about anything important. It only allows her to tease the Captain and mock his rituals and habits. He, in turn, pretends to have lost the war and behaves as if peace has already broken out by wallowing in vacant compassion for all the boys that have died.

"An officer who doesn't believe in the war he's fighting," she tells him with a fierce yet gratuitous laugh, "should either resign his commission or be shot." She's become brave now, and can flaunt her helpless rage without fear. Hessen told her that he and his fellow soldiers had been sent to the movie theater to watch one of those newsreels where the little man with the mustache flails his arm like a spastic marionette.

"You'll see, *Herr Hauptmann,*" she teased him, "sooner or later, you'll find yourself watching an Amedeo Nazzari movie, because your fucking newsreel will have been stolen by the partisans."

She had told him about the episode a few days before when the PAG "attacked" the screening room at Cinema Vittoria on Via Merano. No one in the theater had been hurt but a fascist propaganda film had been "executed." He had laughed his usual joyless, drunken laugh. But it was, nonetheless a laugh and, without her, Hessen would have been even darker and more desolate.

Tilde has become ever more adept at managing her captain. But she hasn't yet been able to tell him that she is pregnant. What stops her isn't the fear of an answer she already knows—that he doesn't want her bastard. She expects nothing from a Wehrmacht officer. When he repudiates her, he won't make her feel any more worthless or more insignificant than she already does just from continuing to see him. But it will force her to leave this room once and for all. Here, everything is unreal and grotesque, another world. Every gesture, word, and act is sealed away by the darkness of the park that makes it seem like the bottom of the ocean where even the echoes of storms don't reach. But no longer. Soon, she will have to confess her humiliation to her family and beg forgiveness from her mother, her father, and even Biscia. That her pregnancy will put an end to her mission, so critical for the Resistance, doesn't touch her.

She remembers Hessen's look the very first night they met, when he saved her from Tearnails. There was a melancholy gentleness in it, just overshadowed by a decidedly unmilitary carelessness. Still, those pale eyes had lit with emotion when confronted by her fear and beauty. Is there something left of that, in these meetings drowned in Armagnac and the sweat of the sheets? Did the illusion that their relationship could become something more lurk inside her without her noticing it?

She can't believe that his feelings have been destroyed by the turn of fate that made her a spy and him a traitor. Tilde knows she is on the right side and knows that even the captain doesn't despise her for her choice. But she is not naïve and understands that saving lives isn't enough for Hessen to soothe his conscience as a German soldier. Even what he claims the Third Reich owes him for his annihilated family might not be enough on the day he stops drinking. After all, those bombs on Cologne were unleashed by the British, not the Luftwaffe.

She is not afraid of Hessen, not really. Instead, she's sorry for him. It pains her that his arrogance is a bluff, an ostentation born of his powerlessness. The real reason for her silence is the fear of losing control. As long as she keeps the secret, it is she who decides whether to continue to see him or not to see him. Whether to love Biscia, a partisan hero, or Hessen, a German traitor. Whether to keep the child or have an abortion. As long as she keeps the secret, she can pretend to be the master of her fate. She is aware Hessen might get tired of her, or decide to pay for his treason by selling her to Maestri. But that would exert a power over her life, not her soul.

Tilde smiles bitterly that even he, who knows every line of her nakedness, has noticed nothing. Maybe it's just because, when they finally do end up in bed, he's already drunk and the fear of allied bombers allows only flickering firelight.

"Helmut," she says abruptly, her knees against her chest and her gaze fixed on nothing. "I have to tell you something."

"Speak, *Fräulein,*" he says with a slight slur in his voice. They are both sitting on the bed, still dressed.

"I'm with child."

Silence. Tilde continues to stare at nothing; she lacks the courage to turn her head and look him in the eye. Not because of what she fears she might see, but because of what she knows she will not. Hessen says nothing. Slowly, almost against her will, she turns to look at the man beside her. Hessen, too, is staring at nothing, but his eyes glisten. Her senses are oddly heightened and the wood crackling in the fireplace sounds like gunfire.

"A child?" he repeats, confused.

"Yes, a child." she confirms. "Your child."

Silence again, a long silence broken only by the sounds of the night. The fire crackling, the shriek of a night bird in the depths of the park. She wonders if these were the cries of tortured partisans she had heard.

Finally, Hessen hides his face in his hands and begins to cry, like a child, with short sobs that shake his chest and shoulders. Only now does she notice that he's still wearing a wedding band. When he finally lowers his hands and looks at her, tears are running down his face.

"A child. . . a child," he repeats.

Tilde carefully studies him as an entomologist studies a bug, coldly, clinically. She is slightly surprised and a little disturbed that his weeping doesn't move her. She cannot tell if he is more thankful than desperate but it is obvious that those two emotions are at war inside that blond

147

head.

It has been a few days since she heard the news that made her fear for Biscia. On Mount Tobbio, where he had fled, there was a massive raid by the Germans with the support of the Republican National Guard, the Black Brigades, and even the *Bersaglieri*. They surrounded the partisans and dozens were killed. Olindo was also worried about Biscia and had been pushing his superiors for news.

This morning, Tilde was at work at the factory when word came that he was alive. The news was brought to her by Dolores, who had gotten it in turn from a young man riding a bicycle passed the gates.

"Do you work at the canteen?" he had asked. Dolores confirmed it.

"Do you know Tilde?"

"Of course I know her, we work together."

"Perfect. Tell her that her lover is fine and sends her his greetings." he said before pedaling off.

Dolores tried to stop him, to ask where Biscia was, but he was already gone, slaloming through the groups of arriving workers.

"What do you care where Biscia is?" Tilde asked, resentful and suspicious—everyone in Sestri knows he is wanted for the murder of a young employee of the cigar factory.

"I don't," replied Dolores, throwing up her hands. "I thought you cared, honey. Have you broken the engagement?"

She shrugged, disgruntled. After a moment, she apologized; after all, none of this was Dolores's fault and she had relieved her of a terrible fear.

"You have to go away," says Hessen peremptorily. "Now."

The same, old story, she sighed to herself. Men get her in trouble and then their only solution is to get rid of her.

"Are you crazy?" she answers firmly. "My family needs me."

"We'll help them," he replies. Tilde doesn't like that tone. She doesn't like it from a partisan commander and she likes it even less from a German officer.

"Help them do what? If they're being looked after by the German army, the partisans will treat them as collaborators, *mein Hauptmann*."

"Tilde," he says, firmly, but with both concern and warmth, "I don't know how much longer I can protect you. After Iolanda's assassination, Maestri wants your head."

She flushes, a blind fury invades her. She pushes her head forward, her jaw clenched, and pokes her index finger against his chest as if it were the barrel of a gun.

"You son of a bitch, didn't you say that I would always be safe?" she snarls.

"And you have been, so far. I have done everything possible to ensure your safety."

"Of course! You wanted to have your toy on hand, the little girl who would warm your bed and help you forget your wounds for a while. After all, if something went wrong, what could happen? I would end up in Gestapo headquarters, tortured and raped by that swine Maestri. It wouldn't be difficult for you to replace me. Oh no! A compliant young woman is easy to find in a country of starving people like mine." She takes a breath and sees him searching his uniform pockets, looking for cigarettes. Then she adds: "But now it's different, isn't it? Now that your child is involved, my safety really is important to you and you tell me I have to leave."

He doesn't even look at her. He pulls out a cigarette from the package and lights it with a gold lighter, perhaps a gift from his wife. "Don't be stupid," he answers calmly. "If they made you talk, I'd be the first person up against the wall."

"Bullshit," she replies with an angry hiss. "You're untouchable, one of the bosses. I saw how Maestri crawls at your feet."

"You know nothing," he says with a slight irritation in his voice that, for a moment, reminds her he is still a German officer. "Maestri spoke with my superiors; he did everything possible to ruin me at headquarters. If it hadn't been for a highly-ranked SS officer in Cologne who vouched for me, I'd already be in prison myself on charges of treason. But even that wasn't enough. Do you know what saved me in the end?" he asks with a strange intensity.

"No."

"My wife and my little girls. The German command considers me a proxy hero. Their death is my salvation." he replies bitterly.

Tilde looks at him as if he were a big jungle cat stretched out on the bed. He looks calm and affectionate, but he is dangerous. One wrong move, and he can destroy her with a casual swipe of his paw. She has never seen him like this. She realizes that confessing her secret to him might have been a mistake.

"Have you told anyone else?" he asks, crushing the cigarette stub in the crystal ashtray on the bedside table.

"No. I don't want my family to know."

"Your family?" a sardonic grin on his face.

"My family and my comrades," she admits in one breath.

"No one needs to know. We'll spread the rumor you were deported."

An icy chill runs down her back "Deported. . . where?"

"My sister lives in Cologne; I'm sure she'll take care of you until the baby is born."

"In Germany?" she replies in a voice in which terror lurks. "Never. I'd rather have an abortion."

"You'll be safe there until the war is over. They aren't involved."

"Who is *they?*"

"My sister and her husband. They are young and have no children."

"I will not leave my country!" Tilde screams, her eyes full of tears.

"To a safe place. Here, in Italy."

He stops looking at her and begins to think. Tilde is panicking now. She had seen it one night in October at the Borzoli railway crossing, one of those dreadful trains heading to the German labor camps. It had stopped at a signal light and she approached and looked through the cracks between the wagon's doors. Beyond the barbed wire that ran along the slit, twisted like a poisonous snake, she met empty eyes staring from the bottom of hell. A moment later, the convoy started again. The image of an endless line of freight cars crammed with hungry and thirsty men and women, living in their own shit like animals passes in front of her eyes.

But something more immediate intrudes on her terror. It is less intense and less chilling but all the more important for all that: She must find shelter for herself and her baby. She hadn't expected Hessen to care, certainly not to the point of sending a partisan rebel to live with his sister in Germany.

"Yes! I will ask Greta to come to Italy," Hessen says, breaking the silence and joyously hitting the mattress with his hand. "I'm sure she will."

"Then look for a farmhouse in the lower Piedmont," she suggests, thinking of the farms where her father was supplying his family with wine, potatoes, and flour.

"Slow down. I won't send you to Germany, but don't ask me to send you someplace that might fall under the control of the partisans."

"Where, then?"

"I'll ask Walden," he concludes in a tone that strives to instill confidence and optimism. "He's very resourceful."

20.
THE LIBERATION

As I watched Jasmìne, lying in the sun-drenched room, I thought of the dream I'd had a few days before, where Grandfather Baciccia had seen my mythical Nicla in a cattle car full of young, naked women, dirty and terrified. The dream had been set in Piazzale Bligny in Molassana. In the dream, it had been a mess, full of debris from the war. I now realized I had passed that very spot with Jasmìne's jailer as we drove to the house where she was held prisoner.

After we passed the supermarket and the municipal slaughterhouses, the car turned and climbed toward the village of Sant'Eusebio. As we crept along the curves of Via Mogadiscio, I said, "Tell me, Randazzo, where'd you get the money to buy the girl? You don't look like you're swimming in it to me."

"I sold some land, a family inheritance," he replied. "My parents are from Bavari."

After passing the church of Sant'Eusebio, we continued along Via Montelungo and I realized we were, in fact, heading towards that mountain village between the valleys of the rivers Bisagno and Sturla.

There are a lot of ways to waste an inheritance that's been built by generations of sweat and hard work in the fields, but buying a random woman to torture to death was a new one on me. Maybe, I thought, he ought to get into the Guinness Book of World Records. Randazzo was an evil piece of shit, but credit where credit is due.

Once we'd passed the houses, the street became less illuminated. The road became a tunnel through an almost-primeval forest, our headlights flashing along the branches overhead. After about two kilometers, the road began to climb and, after a sharp turn, the car slowed down. Randazzo was about to turn left into a small clearing beyond which lay a climbing lane blocked by a chain, when I ordered him to pull over and turn off the headlights.

"How far is the house?" I asked.

"Thirty, forty meters maybe," he said in a state of agitation that made his voice tremble. "Just beyond the hill."

There were no street lamps and, once the headlights were off, it was pitch black. On the left, the ground sloped upwards.

"We'll continue on foot," I said.

"You don't trust me?" he asked without turning, still facing the darkness beyond the windshield. Since we'd left, I'd seen nothing of him except for the back of his head covered by the woolen cap. From time to time I had tried to catch his eye by looking in the rearview mirror, but each time I'd found them fixed on the road.

"I don't trust *them*," I said. "Maybe they didn't fall for it."

"They seemed pretty convinced to me," he replied.

I ordered him to get out of the car and warned him not to make any noise. I did the same. We began moving along the lane. I held him by one arm and, in my other hand, I held my Beretta. I couldn't see him but I could hear him breathing hard. He was cold and stiff, about as lively as a frozen cod.

We advanced in silence through a darkness that smelled of manure and death. At the end, we found a country cottage. In the cold air, I caught a whiff of gasoline. Our footsteps echoed like an invading army and I feared all our caution was useless. If the gang were nearby, we weren't going to surprise them. I still could see nothing. No doors, no windows. Nothing. I was forced to rely on my hostage to guide us by touch.

Stumbling through the darkness, Randazzo eventually found the front door. "We're here," he said.

I heard a metallic jingling and after a few attempts he managed to get the key in the hole. The lock turned with a *click* and the door opened. My worst suspicions were realized: He had not unlocked the deadbolt. Only an idiot would leave a house, any house, without locking it completely, and certainly not one that held a prisoner you were torturing to death. Randazzo said nothing. He knew. Someone else had keys and was definitely inside. I was ready to bet that the smell of gas in the air came from their car, parked somewhere in the darkness. My new friend was setting me up. Well, we'd see about that.

Holding him close by the arm, I pointed the gun against his jaw and felt his whole body tremble. Taking shelter against the wall, I shoved him into the open doorway. "Where's the light switch?" I growled between my teeth.

"Here on the right, next to. . ."

He never finished. From inside the house came a blast of gunfire. Randazzo gave a faint groan, I felt the muscles of his arm stiffen and he slumped over the threshold.

I crouched down and stuck the Beretta around the door jamb. I'd seen where the muzzle flashes had come from and began shooting blindly in that direction. I had fired six rounds when I finally heard a cry of pain and the sound of a body falling heavily against the furniture.

I didn't dare turn on the light but the darkness presented a problem. I didn't know the place, I didn't know how many more were inside or where I could take cover. I only knew that Jasmine was inside somewhere and that they had come to kill her and make her disappear. I retreated a few meters into the yard, popped the magazine out of the Beretta and loaded six more rounds. Then I pulled out my phone. Time to call the cavalry.

"Where the fuck are you?" Pertusiello asked angrily.

"On the road to Bavari," I whispered. "Outside the house where Jasmine's being held prisoner. It's a couple of kilometers past Sant'Eusebio. You'll find a white station wagon parked on the road.

"Bacci, don't. . ." I hung up and switched off the phone. From inside came a shrill voice, "Mario, can you hear me. Mario, are you OK?" Whoever it was sounded like he was little more than a boy. He sounded scared, too.

There was nothing for it. I needed to get inside. Every second lost could cost Jasmìne her life. I crawled over Randazzo's body, and began making my way into the house on my belly.

"Mario!" the voice shrieked louder. "Are you still alive?"

I heard a groan. Mario was still alive, for the moment, but he didn't sound too happy about it. The kid did exactly what I hoped he'd do. Panicking, he began to shout. "Where are you, bastards? Come out!" Now I knew generally where he was but I didn't feel like shooting a boy blindly, in the dark, not yet. Anyway, I was still counting on my young friend and he came through for me once again. Like his pal, Mario, he had a submachine gun and he began firing it blindly at the open doorway. The muzzle flashes illuminated the room like a strobe light. I caught a glimpse of a table in the middle of the room and Mario slouched against a sideboard. Of course, I could also see the guy shooting at me so I was able to wing him in the shoulder with my Beretta. The kid fell to his hands and knees with a sob and I heard the metallic sound of a gun striking the tile floor. I began crawling in the direction of the first man, who still held a submachine gun. I was ready to fire at the first sound of movement but there was nothing. By now, I could dimly make out my surroundings so I stood up and, keeping my gun trained on him, cautiously approached. When I reached him, I kicked the weapon out of his hands but he didn't react.

All my adrenalin drained away. I felt like retching and began to shake. I was in a room with a dead man, maybe two, and I was responsible for it. It had been twenty-four hours since I had eaten. I suddenly decided to get rid of the drink I'd had with Essam in the bar on Corso de Stefanis. I felt cold, as if the frost of death were clinging to me. But now wasn't the time. I couldn't stop. I had to find Jasmìne.

I tried to make my brain work. If there was someone else in the house, he had to be busy with her. Otherwise, he'd have been in on the battle I'd just had. I tried to listen very carefully. Except for the muffled groans of the wounded guy in the corner, there was nothing, absolute silence. I decided there was nothing to do but turn on the light so I started looking for the switch bearing in mind Randazzo's last words. After a minute or so of fumbling around, I found it.

I was almost sorry I had. There was blood and red vomit everywhere. Mario was motionless, leaning against the sideboard with his head bent forward. I had been right. The wounded guy in the corner was just a kid and as thin as a rail. He moaned again and wriggled on the floor, his hand, red with blood, pressed against his shoulder. Randazzo lay supine, with his arms and legs spread wide and head just outside the door, staring up at a starless sky. The room smelled of gunpowder and acid wine. I noticed a marble sink and realized this was a kitchen. The kid's gun and Mario's Uzi were on the floor. On the far wall, a sturdy wooden door opened on a second room at the back.

Holding the Beretta, I moved to the door. I was trembling, I felt feverish and stinging cramps in my stomach gave me a cold sweat. It was then that I heard a voice and recognized her unmistakable French accent: "You are screwed, my friend. Police is here."

I had gotten here in time. Jasmine was still alive.

"Shut up, bitch!" said a voice with a strong foreign accent. Then the sound of a blow and a choked cry. A dull thud.

I peeked through the door from which a slight glow came. It was a storeroom with wooden walls and a crude concrete floor, full of tools and old furniture, including a dusty sofa, an armchair covered with a white sheet, and a dirty rug that had been rolled up to uncover a heavy iron trapdoor that had been thrown open. Light came from below. I lay on the floor and crawled like a worm toward the entrance. I peered over the edge and was confronted with the eyes of a man climbing the stairs, gun in hand. He saw me and began to shoot. I just had time to roll to my left and take cover. A fusillade of shots flew through the air ripping into the walls and ceiling and showering me with debris. I stuck the Beretta through the trapdoor and fired blindly. The first shot missed, but after the second, I heard a cry of pain and the noise of a body falling down the stairs. When I peered over the edge again, he was lying face down, and his gun lay on the floor, well out of reach. He wasn't dead, though, as I could hear him swearing in a language I couldn't understand.

I jumped up and went down the stairs. I wasn't taking any chances, though, so I kept the Beretta trained on him. I saw Jasmine lying in the middle of the room, her face crushed against the gray stone and her hands bound behind her back. I went around the man, picked up the gun and rushed to her. She was unconscious but still breathing. At the base of her skull was a cut that bled profusely, her black curly hair stained red. The man had struck her hard with his gun and, with her hands bound, she couldn't break her fall and had fractured her skull on the hard floor. If he hadn't decided to toy with her first, she would have been dead already. Her wrists were bound with wire, causing deep wounds. It must have been my old buddy Randazzo who'd done that as the blood was dry and black. She wore a grotesque, sheer pink baby doll, no panties or bra. Her back was scored with long, red streaks. Her arms, legs, and bottom were covered with bruises. I gently freed her wrists but avoided moving her for fear of causing even more serious injuries. I covered her with my jacket and, kneeling down on the floor, caressed her shoulders and back while I waited for Pertusiello and his cavalry.

The cellar was filthy and squalid, with no windows, and weakly lit by a dusty bulb hanging from the ceiling. It smelled of sweat and humidity. The walls and the floor were bare stone and the shaky wooden shelves were empty. The furniture consisted of a cot on which lay a mattress, a pillow, and an old wool blanket. There were also two chairs and a table on which sat a small bowl of water. On the ground, near the bed, a pitcher, a metal basin, and a chamber pot were lined up. The back of one of the chairs was covered by a large terrycloth towel.

After an age, I thought I could hear the sound of an approaching siren. I ran upstairs and into the kitchen where the blue flashes of police cars and ambulances finally broke the darkness and the deadly silence.

The man who had hit Jasmine was a Croatian who had recently joined the Trevisan organization. I was right about the kid. The guy I had shot in the kitchen was a minor from Vicenza named Lando. I had gotten both of them in the shoulder. As I'd suspected, Randazzo and

Mario had both permanently checked out by the time the police arrived. Lando and the Croatian helped Pertusiello and his people reconstruct the sequence of events. Randazzo did know the gang would be waiting for me and that I'd walk into an ambush. When he had called them from the car with my phone, he'd purposely omitted using the agreed password. He had decided that his best bet was screwing me over. He probably lost money on the horses, too.

The door opened suddenly.

Snapping out of my reverie, I turned and saw a man about forty, blond, distinguished, almost handsome. He wore a white lab coat, open to show a custom-made shirt, striped tie and dark designer slacks, maybe Armani or Valentino, but expensive, anyway. Even if he hadn't been wearing a lab coat, everything about him said "doctor." The light pouring through the window lent his coat an aura as if he were a sort of Hippocratic angel.

He looked down on me, and not just because he was standing and I was sitting. "What are you doing here?" he snapped.

For a moment, I was at a loss for words. I was slumped over in the chair and my mind was still in that filthy, damp cellar. In the presence of that bright seraph, I felt like a burrowing creature of the night. No more or less than what I have always been, *La Pantegana dei Caruggi*.

"I'm talking to her," I said.

I was hoping to elicit a smile, but he gasped and looked at me with a growing contempt. "You're talking to her."

"Yup."

"Who authorized you?"

"I've heard it can help people come out of a coma."

"Not from a drug-induced coma."

I shrugged and smiled. "If it doesn't do any good," I said, "it can't hurt, either."

He turned red with anger and stretching out his arm, pointed to the exit. "Out! Get out of this room now!"

"She's alone all day long. . ." I objected.

"Alone or not, it makes no difference to her."

"Are you sure?"

"I said out!" he shouted.

Maybe it was time to go. With a last look at Jasmine, I stood up. Without taking my eyes from the doctor, I made my way slowly to the exit while, in a low voice, I recited my mantra, a kind of superstitious bargain: "If I don't rearrange your face, she'll come back to me." I don't know if he was impressed, but it seemed like a fair bargain to me.

21.
THE TRAP IS SPRUNG

Genoa, May 1944

The road goes straight down the hill, on which Albaro sits, to Corso Italia. It's enveloped in an unnatural silence that reminds you of a cemetery. Many of the apartments in the buildings along the road are empty, the owners having taken themselves off to less luxurious but greener pastures. Places where you can be fairly sure when you go to bed at night that you'll wake up to the see the sun and not the Pearly Gates. The blackout is total and swallows everything: buildings, windows, doors, and gardens. Only from a single balcony on the third floor, through closed shutters, does the weak light of a candle filter out. There is no moon tonight to make the roofs of the houses glisten like quicksilver, and, down the road, the sea opens out, infinite and invisible. In the clean air, which already carries the scents of summer, twinkling stars celebrate a celestial party to which men have not been invited.

The darkness surrounds and reassures the six young men, armed and waiting. Commander Grandi's entire PAG has turned out for this operation. If it does end badly, this group of comrades will be no more than a memory. An old car, engine and lights off, waits on the corner of Corso Italia. At the wheel sits the student, Calcagno, ready to block Maestri's car at the critical moment. The rest of the squad is crouching in the garden of an uninhabited house, near where their man will come out. Once they knew exactly where Tearnails gambles, they'd had to reconnoiter the site only twice to finalize the plan.

According to Hessen's information, Maestri's car comes from Forte San Giuliano and goes down along the sea, with a driver and a plain clothes officer. When he thinks he's lost enough money, Maestri phones them to pick him up, usually around three o'clock in the morning. Once they've determined that everything is secure, they honk the horn and Maestri comes out.

There was no time for a stakeout to double-check the Captain's information. At three o'clock in that afternoon, Tilde had gone to Olindo's house to let him know that tonight was the night. The PAG was at full strength, now. A week ago Grandi had called Biscia back from the mountains and a new person joined the group, a sixteen-year-old nicknamed Balletta.

No talking and no cigarettes make the hours pass with maddening slowness. Crouching like geckos attached to the garden wall, the smell of Jasmine fills the warm night air.

The plan has been thoroughly discussed in all its details. The goal is to capture Maestri alive and make him talk. Alternatively, if something unexpected happens, to kill him. To do that, they must exploit the darkness of the blackout and the element of surprise. When he leaves the casino, they must wait for him to get in the car and for the car to move away. Then they will leave the garden and follow the car without being seen, up to the waterfront promenade, where Calcagno will cut off Maestri's escape route by blocking the road. When the car stops, they'll take out the driver and the plain-clothes officer and capture Maestri.

It is just after three o'clock when they hear the approaching roar of an engine. Headlights flick on and a beam of light strikes the street, and suddenly the walls of the building, the garden, and the windows of the ground floor emerge from the darkness, revealing their now-tattered bourgeois elegance. The car arrives at full speed and stops with a screech of tires, exposing the crude arrogance of its occupants. A car door is heard opening and the engine continues to idle. The horn blows. Then an endless wait. The five men in the garden are motionless as statues. They know the headlights are pointed directly at the garden in which they hide and that even the rustle of a bush will attract unwanted attention. They hear the door of the casino open, voices. . . Two or three people must have come out. This could complicate things. Other car doors open and then slam in unison. The car begins to move, passing in front of the garden and plunging it back into darkness. Phase one has gone well.

It's time to move out, weapons at the ready. Balletta and Dria carry German MP 40 submachine guns, Olindo, Biscia, and Lanza have Walther P38s with full clips. They silently chase the car, and as it reaches the outlet at the end of the street, the old car driven by Calcagno, with its headlights off, pulls across the road and stops. Maestri's car slams on its brakes while its occupants curse. The five partisans are just meters away when headlights suddenly illuminate Calcagno's car. In the darkness, you have to be careful who you shoot. Capturing Maestri instead of killing him won't be easy.

Dria and Balletta have the honor of opening the dance. They manage to take out the rear tires and tongues of fire tear the darkness. The noise is deafening. Bullets spark off the body of the car and red taillights explode into the night. From inside the car, they hear screaming: "Down, stay down!" Grandi moves up to the driver's side and fires. Glass explodes and he hears a sob, a sort of choked groan. Olindo fires again and from the passenger side comes a muzzle flash. But the shot goes wide as Biscia is firing through the passenger window. The car is surrounded now. Dria and Balletta point the Schmeisser barrels at the back window of the car, and the other three, with guns at the ready, order those sitting in the back seat to get out. Biscia opens the rear door and recognizes Maestri, sitting on the passenger side. There are two other men, strangers. One cries, terrified, "Please, we have nothing to do with this!"

In that instant, the sound of a gunshot comes from Corso Italia. Grandi winces in despair. "Calcagno. . ." he curses.

Biscia grabs Maestri by his lapels and drags him out of the rear seat. The headlights still illuminate the car blocking the road. Calcagno's head is resting on the steering wheel, motionless. There are three fascists crouching behind Calcagno's car, armed with pistols and a rifle. They aren't shooting yet because they're blinded by the headlights and are afraid of hitting Maestri. But the partisans can see them and only the possibility that Calcagno is alive keeps Olindo from giving the order. Lanza aims at one, his head clearly visible over the hood, and fires. He misses, and the man throws himself on the ground and disappears.

Biscia remains standing at the side of the car, holding Maestri by his neck and shielding himself with his body. "Careful!" he tells the fascists without raising his voice. They are close and there is no need to shout. "I've got Maestri here. Do you want to let us go or would you like us to kill him?" As he grips him tightly, he can feel Maestri shivering, terrified.

Olindo has drifted to the side, near the wall, and has one of the three in his sights, the one with the rifle. He carefully takes aim and pulls the trigger. Then he throws himself to the ground and rolls behind the car as the fascists return fire in unison. He feels stone and plaster fragments striking him and can't see the man with the rifle drop. Finally seeing sense, one of the fascists pops up and tries to shoot one of the headlights through the window. It takes him three tries.

Olindo makes a decision. "Calcagno!" he shouts. "Calcagno, can you hear me?"

Calcagno doesn't answer. He remains completely motionless, his face glued to the steering wheel. Grandi feels a sudden sickness and his throat closes up. But only for a moment. Then he turns to Dria and Balletta and gives the order: "Let's go, boys; light them up."

One functioning headlight is more than enough for the job they must do. The two submachine guns begin spitting hellfire against Calcagno's car. The survivors have dropped flat on their faces and Olindo and Lanza come at them from both sides. There comes the staccato crack of four pistol rounds being fired and then Grandi's voice. "Enough, it's over!"

Everyone has ignored Maestri's companions. They are still in the car, utterly rigid. Lanza approaches, opens the door and bows sardonically. "You may go home now, gentlemen. The danger has passed." Then the triumphant shout, "Long Live Italy! Long Live Freedom!"

The two stretched out in the rear seat remain terrified and motionless. One of them manages to choke out, "Thank you!" but his good manners probably owe more to fear than gratitude.

Dria grabs Maestri by one arm. He and Biscia drag him to Corso Italia and push him into the car his henchmen had left on the street.

Lanza collects the fascists' weapons, shoving the pistols in his belt and picking up the rifle.

Grandi approaches Calcagno's car, the car that should have taken them all home. Even though he is brightly lit by the remaining headlight, no one can see the tears in his eyes. He opens the door and sees that his face has been reduced to a bloody mask. He must have been attacked from behind and shot in the temple. On impulse, he takes Calcagno's glasses off, and notices that a lens is broken. He feels a pang in his heart, thinking that when he gives them to his mother, it will be even more painful for her. He puts them into the pocket of his jacket and before he closes the door, he passes a hand over the boy's brown curls in a last farewell.

They all get into the third car, which fate has left there for them, with the engine running. Lanza is driving, Balletta in the front seat between Olindo's legs, like a child. In the back seat, between Dria and Biscia, Maestri is pale as death and says nothing.

The car heads west. Afraid of coming to a roadblock, they take a circuitous route through the hills. They go up to Corso Firenze, Montegalletto, Lagaccio, Granarolo, then descend to Sampierdarena on their way back to Sestri and the Gazzo quarry, where Maestri will be questioned.

22.
"THERE IS NO BROTHER"

When I left the hospital, I wasn't in the best mood. I felt like a starving man who'd just been kicked out of the only restaurant in town. In a situation like that, you wonder why. Is it because you're not dressed right? Because you smell bad? Because you look like someone with a fake credit card? And that's pretty much what I felt like, someone who didn't belong. A homeless man, a stranger, a refugee with hunger in his eyes and misery tattooed on his skin.

It was drizzling; the sky was a dirty, greasy color and weighed on the buildings of San Martino like a stifling blanket, swollen with humidity and saturated with car exhaust. I had a hard night behind me, spent spinning thoughts and conjectures that led nowhere. Jasmìne was dying, maybe, and I could do nothing to help her. My father's dearest friends kept lying to me and doing everything possible to stymie my investigation.

I came home drenched, took off my clothes, and threw myself under the shower, hoping to find a moment's peace. It was almost noon, maybe Saturday, but I wouldn't swear to it. I had not bought a newspaper lately and, for someone like me, this was a very bad sign. I didn't feel like cooking and the fridge was empty anyway. In the pantry, all I could find was an old box of crackers. Still wearing the wet bathrobe, I lay down on the couch and started eating a pack of them. They were damp and stale and fit my mood perfectly. Fortunately, the bottle of Lagavulin was still almost full and I started sipping directly from it. I felt a rising desire to call Olindo and tell him what I thought about him. I wanted to ask him why he'd lied to me about Nicla's husband, the tall, blond man, nicknamed Biscia, who'd executed the informant who worked in the cigar factory.

Nonetheless, I'd finally arrived at some conclusions. Nicla was a fake name, a smokescreen, but Biscia had to be a real name, at least a nickname. If I had asked about "Biscia", someone in Sestri would have remembered. Some names are not forgotten. Surely the name of Iolanda, too, would have gotten a response from someone.

If only I could go back in time, when my parents were still alive, and ask them. Actually, that probably wouldn't have gotten me anywhere. My father probably wouldn't have told me much; he was like that. Maybe Grandpa Baciccia would have been more forthcoming. My mother probably didn't know anything about the partisans. Her memories of the war were filled with film titles and actresses' names, such as Alida Valli and Isa Miranda, whom she admired and imitated, copying their hairstyles and dressing like them. When I was a child, she would tell me about them, in the evening, sitting on my bed before turning off the light. They were not interesting to me, and made me fall asleep within a few minutes. I remembered some old photographs, kept in a shoebox, of her mimicking the poses in old film posters.

I got up and went to search the wardrobe, looking for that white box. I searched through several drawers before finding it. Finally successful, I returned to the living room, sat down on the couch, and began to look through what was left of my family album.

First I came across a black and white photo taken on the day of their wedding. On the back, in pencil, the date was marked: August 6, 1945, the day of the Hiroshima bombing. My parents stared into the camera with eyes that lacked the expected enthusiasm. My mother's lips were curved in their usual detached smile. She always smiled like that, as if nothing really touched her. Her distracted air of constant disappointment kept my father in a state of emotional pain and left me in a morass of self-doubt. But it made her apparently immune to both pain and doubt. I say "apparently" because her attitude must have been a way to shield herself from her own issues. But it also closed the door to happiness.

My dad was solemn that day, as usual. He must have turned toward the camera after trying to catch his wife's eye, and the expression on his face immortalized that failure to connect. Had he known that was their destiny? My mother had a sultry, Mediterranean beauty that turned heads. My father was a handsome man in his own right, tall and almost ethereally thin. The wedding suit hung on his body as if hanging on a hanger.

Ever since I was a child, their friends had said I looked like both of them. I had my mother's eyes, hair, and complexion, and my father's stature and physique. An enviable mix, if only it hadn't meant growing up watching them tormented by demons only they could see.

Now I held a second photograph in my hands, one that had also been taken at the wedding. There were my parents together with Grandfather Baciccia and his wife, Grandma Celeste. Even so long ago, his naïve face, the slightly crooked tie and the cigar in his mouth, conjured his usual reassuring air. When I was growing up, his good-tempered smile always made me feel better.

I rummaged through the box, in search of a picture from the war years, and found it at the bottom. The old photo depicted a group of partisans, armed with old Carcano M91 rifles, leaning against a rock with a sloping meadow in the background. The oldest was probably twenty-five. They all smiled, including my father. They wore lightweight shirts and shorts. It must have been taken in the summer, before he was injured in combat. I wondered if any of them were still alive. He could have known Nicla, or fought with Biscia. Then I remembered that Biscia was a PAG member and, probably, hadn't fought in the mountains.

I was taken by a sudden urge to do something, anything. I hurriedly dressed and had the phone in my hand to call Olindo when a thought struck me. Olindo was not inclined to be helpful. So why not call someone else? Someone who had promised to help me and hadn't, at least not yet.

I searched the phone book for Luigi Bavastro, the partisan known as Gino. He had also been a great friend of my parents, and he, too had apparently decided to screw me like everyone else. I wondered why. He didn't know Nicla and had promised nothing to no one. According to Elsa, Balletta's daughter, he had attended the meeting at Olindo's home and Grandi had apparently convinced him of something. What terrible secret could there be that kept all these old comrades silent after so many years? Was it something to do with the death of the informant,

Iolanda? The one that had been executed by Nicla's husband Biscia?

I did know one thing, though. It was time to stop pussy-footing around and do the job for which I had been paid. My client was right, it was time to find his brother.

The phone rang for quite a while before someone answered.

"Hello?" Over the phone, the voice was even more raspy and scratchy than I remembered.

"Good morning," I answered. "It's Bacci Pagano."

"Oh, Bacci," he said, with unconvincing casualness. "I'm glad you called. I would have called you, but. . ."

". . .your PAG meeting ran late."

Dead silence. Eventually, he said. "Olindo asked me to come." His resentment was almost a physical thing. But there was something else . . . fear?

I'd pressed him hard enough, for the moment. "Yes, I know, Gino." I said in a conciliatory voice. "After all these years, he's still Commander Grandi."

"No. You're wrong," he replied, and this time he really was upset. "Olindo was never my commander. I was in the *Leggeroni*.

"I know." I replied. "But now I need to talk to you."

I was expecting him to object but all he said was. "If you need to talk, we'll talk. Do you want to come to the Partisans' Association, where we met before? I was about to go to the office."

"Fine by me. I'll be there in an hour."

All this left me with a grudging respect, Unlike a lot of his old comrades, he wasn't living in the past. The Partisans' Association wasn't just a shrine for him. He considered it a job, an activity like any other, free of rhetoric and trappings and, above all, relevant and valuable. I couldn't say he was wrong.

when I left the hospital had become a pouring rain, lashing the pavement of Stradone Sant'Agostino, collecting along the sidewalks in the deep gutters and rushing down towards San Donato. I decided that it was not the best time to be riding a Vespa, especially all the way to Sestri. Instead, I went around the corner—getting plenty wet in the process—to Piazza Sarzano and opened the garage, resigned to making the long drive in my old VW Beetle.

There was a fair amount of traffic and it took me almost an hour to get there, triple the time it would have taken on my Vespa. When I arrived in Sestri, I got lucky and found a free parking spot next to the Church of the Assunta. When I entered the Partisans' Association, I found Bavastro with two elderly people, a man and a woman, who were working in the office.

"We are compiling the list of new members," he explained before he introduced them. The two were sitting at a table, facing each other. The man, with glasses resting on his nose, read the names on the membership cards and the woman transcribed them on a register. She was called Elide, had short, white hair, was dressed simply, and greeted me with an energetic handshake. The other claimed to be her husband and said his name was Berto. He was very tall and this made his poor posture seem even worse. They both must have been over eighty. Gino told me they had been with him in the sixth operating zone. Then he told them that I was the son of Guido and Anna Pagano, but he didn't mention my job or my current investigation. They knew my parents by name but had never met them. In fact, they didn't know they were both dead and didn't seem to remember anything about my trial.

As we talked, I looked at them carefully and, for a moment, I got the strange notion that they must be the parents of the man I was looking for. Unfortunately, the Commander's version and that of my client agreed on one point: that Nicla had died about thirty years ago. However, after the barrage of bullshit they had all fed me, nothing would surprise me. Not even meeting a woman who had been dead for thirty years.

Gino excused us and we went into a small office, closing the door so we could talk freely. He was dressed differently today, a light blue

169

jersey, a blue woolen scarf, and flannel trousers. Only the beret remained unchanged. He went behind the small desk and invited me to sit.

"So then," he said firmly, "what do you want to know?"

"Bavastro," I said sardonically, "you know exactly why I'm here. How did Olindo persuade you to screw me over?"

For the first time since I had met him, he removed his beret and placed it on the desktop. His hair, which was fine and flowing, became disarranged.

"Olindo has his reasons," he murmured, scrutinizing me and passing a hand over his head. His eyes had a cloudy look, perhaps caused by cataracts, which I hadn't noticed at our first encounter. "The woman was a courier for his group and he has always tried to protect her, even during the war. They entrusted her with a delicate mission, approaching a German officer who had fallen for her. The girl was very young, the officer about forty. You have to understand . . . it wasn't like now. What they asked of her . . . And she was also already engaged."

"With a man from Olindo's group," I interrupted him. "A PAG member called Biscia."

That silence again. He stiffened and his jaw tensed. "Who told you about Biscia?" he almost snarled.

"As you can see," I continued calmly, "I'm good at my job, despite your efforts to prevent me from doing it."

"Do you know who Biscia was?"

"The man who executed Iolanda, the informant who worked at the cigar factory."

"A bad story," he said, turning his gaze away. Somehow, my answer seemed to reassure him. "It was the German captain who gave her name to the girl, Nicla. Iolanda was a friend of hers and she didn't want to believe it. She did her best to save her, but in war, mercy can be expensive. Back then, the fascist police were ruthless. They had already arrested and tortured three partisans, all women. The comrades were fingered Iolanda, they didn't hesitate."

"Fascinating story," I said insolently. "But I want the name."

"What name?" he responded, alarmed.

"Biscia's name."

"Biscia is dead and buried," he replied, struggling to maintain his smile under the white mustache that he had not stopped caressing since we sat down. With a tell like that, he must be a lousy poker player.

"So what's the problem then? I need to know what his name was, so I can contact his son."

He grabbed the beret and jammed it back on his head as if it were part of a military uniform. He sat up straighter, too. I knew, then, that he was still a member of the resistance and he would never reveal the secrets with which he'd been entrusted. "You might as well relax, Bacci." His solemnity was pompous, almost ridiculous. "You're wasting your time here. I'm not going to tell you. Ever."

The direct approach was proving to be a dead end. Time to shake the tree and see what came out. "I'm starting to think," I said, as nastily as possible, "that there's something really dirty behind all this and you're terrified that it will come out, even after all these years."

His face became a dramatic shade of puce. His lips tightened and he clenched his fists. "How do you . . . what are you suggesting, you . . . " he spluttered.

"Olindo and his men did something. Something bad. Something very bad. Something so bad that they'll do anything to keep it buried, even now."

He shrugged and took a deep breath. His unhealthy color gradually faded. Shaking his head, he sighed with disappointment, "It's not worth getting angry over. Some things don't deserve an answer."

"Do you know why I accepted this assignment?" I went on, pressing him. "There is a friend of mine in San Martino hospital who is likely to die. She is not yet twenty-seven. She was a prisoner of a sadist who beat, raped, and tortured her for eight days. Her name is Jasmìne Kilamba and she's from the Ivory Coast."

"I'm sorry," he muttered.

"I accepted this job for two reasons," I went on. "Waiting in the hospital corridor for news was driving me crazy. But it wasn't just that. A wealthy German professor wants to leave his fortune to a poor man. The son of two partisans who were probably factory workers, just like my parents. It's a lot of money, and it would certainly make him more comfortable. It might even change his life. Do you want to give me one good reason why I should turn my back on this guy?"

He opened his mouth to reply, but I stopped him. "Is this about Olindo's promise to his mother?" I continued. "Let's assume knowing that she was sleeping with a Wehrmacht officer isn't going to make his day. I'm sure that knowing she gave birth to a son and then left him to a stranger will make him even more upset. But eventually, he'll understand. There was a war on. What his mother had to do. . . well, she was a hero of the Resistance. And for God's sake, it was over sixty years ago! Who would want to give up a big inheritance over that?"

"Olindo promised. . ."

"See, that's what doesn't convince me. Yeah, *he* promised, but none of the rest of you did. What does he have over you?"

He pulled the beret off again and put it on the desk. He sighed deeply, and then said, "You're forgetting one thing."

"What?"

"The captain died in a PAG attack."

"Do you mean that the woman knew?"

He shrugged and let his lower lip protrude from his carefully trimmed mustache. He was staring at something above my head, his eyes half-closed.

"Gino," I repeated, "I asked you a question."

He started. And then, waving his hands, he almost shouted, "I don't know! Nobody knows!"

"Not even Olindo?"

"Olindo says that she left *before* May 15th."

"But did she know? Did he ever tell her they were planning the attack?"

He kept fidgeting in his chair, "I don't think so," he said without conviction. Then suddenly he froze, lowered his head, and looked up at me through half-lidded eyes. "Why does it matter, anyway? She was already far away. Even if she had known about the attack, how could she have known the captain would go to the Odeon Cinema that day?"

He shook his head again. I sensed he was near cracking. The temptation to rid himself of this demon, whatever it was, was growing.

"Is it possible," he asked, "that you still don't get it?" He stared at his clasped hands on the desk, hands gripping so tightly that his knuckles were white against the tanned skin.

"And what, exactly, do I not understand?"

He sighed and lifted his eyes from the desk and looked at me sternly. His tone was a reprimand, softened by a hint of compassion. "There is no brother, Bacci. There never was."

"Explain."

"Your client has always known there is no brother. It's twenty years he's been obsessed by Biscia and his wife, but not because he wants to find his family."

"Why, then?"

"Because . . . because poor, senile Ratto told him about Iolanda," he said, finally surrendering. "That was enough to convince him that Tilde was responsible for the death of his father."

"Tilde?"

173

He lowered his gaze and his face became a flaming red as he suddenly realized what he had said. I could see that he felt he had betrayed his old comrades.

When I could catch his eye again, I gave him a smile of gratitude. But I knew he would never forgive himself. After all, he was still a partisan, and he hadn't been tortured in a cell at Gestapo headquarters. Instead, he'd been broken by a two-bit detective who'd questioned him at the Sestri Ponente Partisans' Association.

23.
THE WAR CONTINUES

Sestri Ponente, May 1944

The news is repeated on every corner. There is no café, factory, office, or door where it isn't whispered with a sense of liberation and joy by a people who have had enough of war and fear. The name of Maestri has always evoked feelings of panic and terror. Behind the nauseous fear of having said a word too much to a stranger, a colleague, or even a friend, loomed the image of one man, a man about fifty, with cold, empty eyes, slightly stocky, a perfect shave and a crew cut . . . and blood on his hands. He seemed untouchable, unreachable, sheltered in his fortress, protected by guards and his informants. But somehow, a small group of ordinary men, their friends and neighbors, had captured him alive and taken him to some hidden place for questioning. Now the tables were turned and it was Tearnails answering the questions.

The Germans, the Republican Guard, the Black Brigades, and the Italian political police have launched a formidable manhunt to find him alive or dead, but after four days the search has gotten nowhere. Rumor has it that, after a lengthy interrogation which had yielded a very interesting list of names, he had been moved away from the city and beyond the reach of the forces assembled to find him.

It doesn't take long for the dismantling of his network of informants to begin.

Over the next few days, four people thought to be above suspicion find justice at the end of the barrel of a PAGist gun. The executions are meticulously organized and planned misdirection allows the PAGs to strike at will. Feigned and rumored attacks have the Germans and Fascists protecting the wrong people and so, the informants continue to fall, one after the other.

Tilde continues to go to work. Captain Hessen sees her once a week and is organizing her relocation. In a few weeks, his sister Margaretha and her husband will arrive at Gargnano, on Lake Garda, where Sergeant Walden has set up an elegant apartment with a lake view.

For Tilde, coming home becomes more painful every day. Her parents' care and concern merely emphasize her ultimate degradation. She thinks of the pain and horror they will feel when the Germans tell them she has been taken and deported to a forced-labor camp. Some nights, the fear that her mother could actually die from the stress of all this makes her resolve to give up the whole plan and have an abortion instead. The captain calms her, and assures her that she'll be able to write and tell them that she's has been transferred to an Italian factory near Salò and that she's fine. Tilde doesn't know if she believes him or not. Does it matter?

She wonders how they'll survive without her miserable salary, and even on this point Hessen is reassuring. Her mother has submitted a claim for a pension on account of her lung disease and he is working to have it approved quickly. The new masters, it seems, don't just deport, shoot and rob people. They can also extend benefits to the favored few they have decided they want to protect.

She hasn't been in contact with Olindo personally since that day at her apartment and it's just as well. Looking him in the eye now would be truly difficult. Dria, however, did pass her a message from him one evening in the church square. Biscia had gone back to the mountains.

The thought of Biscia never leaves her. His absence makes him that much dearer to her, and when she imagines a future without him, she feels a great sadness. Now that the days have become warmer and the sun begins to shine on the gray walls of houses and factories, the idea of having lost him becomes unbearable and the prospect of a life without him meaningless. She tries to replace the sadness with anger. After all, when hope is gone, anger is better than resignation. But anger is a bitter medicine, a poison that destroys dreams and the capacity to take joy in life. It leaves behind only emptiness and, ultimately, a sense of futility.

imagines she is starting to feel move inside her. "My little bastard," she calls him. She feels trapped and can't imagine a way out of all this that will allow her a return to the love and fellowship of her family and friends. But it's far too late to back out now. And the German captain has proved understanding and has offered her an honorable solution to her immediate problem while asking nothing in return. When he told her of his sister and her husband, pointing out that "they are young and have no children," he, perhaps unintentionally, suggested what she should do: this child of war could live without his mother, cared for and loved by someone who hadn't been steeped in all the evil that touched her. "When the war ends, you'll be safe," he added, "they're not involved." So the child, too, will be safe. *His* baby, *his* little bastard.

She has never felt so confused. She changes her mind every day, every hour, every minute.

But life moves forward, whether we are ready or not. And in times of war, life is nothing but war.

She has not seen Dolores for a week. She hasn't shown up at work; she sent word that she had fallen and broken a leg. Dolores lives alone in a small apartment in the first group of houses you encounter when entering Pegli. She isn't married or engaged. She's just over thirty, but she's had a hard life due to her disability and looks twenty years older which robs her of any attractiveness. Apart from that, no one really knows much about her life. Iolanda was everything Dolores is not and Tilde is convinced that her anger towards Iolanda was down to her bitter envy.

One day, around noon, while handing a bowl filled with cabbage and potato soup to an older worker, one of her father's comrades, he whispers to her "They got Dolores. Apparently, she'd been getting paid by the *crucchi*. Her house looked like a pirate ship full of loot."

Her heart skips a beat and her hands tremble so violently that she spills broth and vegetables on the counter. Wanda turns to her, concerned, "Tilde, what's wrong?"

She has a sudden wave of nausea that isn't from her morning sickness and she begins to sway on her feet. Her fellow workers gather around her, and some are holding her upright by her arms. Across the counter, a buzz of alarm runs through the line of waiting workers. She is taken to the kitchen and made to sit.

"You look like you've seen a ghost," says a coworker she does not recognize. "Are you feeling alright?"

Someone brings her a glass of water and she refuses it. The heat in the kitchen is overwhelming, unbearable. She is desperate for fresh air and staggers to her feet to get herself out in the open. Wanda offers to accompany her into the yard, holding her by her arm and walking by her side in silence.

"Tilde, what's happened?" Wanda asks, as soon as she sees Tilde's face returning to its normal color.

"They shot Dolores," she answers, her eyes full of tears.

A tall, thin foreman, who, behind his back, everyone calls "the asshole," arrives trailed by another of Tilde's coworkers.

"What's going on here?" he barks. "You girls are paid to work, not stand around sunning yourselves. If she's sick, she goes to the infirmary!"

As they make their way back, Wanda whispers something to the coworker and, in minutes, all the women in the canteen are buzzing. They don't understand; no one can think of a plausible explanation. Was Dolores involved in the black market? No one had ever suspected her of that. And those who traffic commodities off the books don't keep it a secret. People know who's got what. A business needs advertising. But, anyway, the partisans don't go around killing people just for dealing in the black market.

Tilde returns to the kitchen, her mind crowded with a whirl of thoughts and questions. Deep inside, though, she knows. But she lacks the courage to admit it to herself. She clings to doubts and disbelief, to anything that will help her avoid confronting the abyss that is the truth. She knows partisans don't execute people for dealing in the black market. But the partisans have captured Tearnails and Tearnails is talking now, telling them everything he knows. . . and how he knows it.

She waits for the end of her shift, consumed with anguish. She keeps looking at the watch her mother gave her; time seems to have stopped. She tries not to listen to the voices around her, madly speculating. With all her body and soul, she throws herself into her work, washing and drying pots and bowls without thinking, until, finally, the siren announces the end of the shift. She changes and rushes into the courtyard. She gets on her old bicycle and pedals forcefully towards Via Paglia until she is gasping. She must find Olindo. It's a warm, humid day. The stench from the factory hangs in the air and breathing is like swallowing coal dust. She leans the bike against the wall and runs through the open entrance. She takes the stairs two at a time and knocks at the door. It's only a few seconds, which still seem eternal, before Olindo says "Who's there?"

"It's Tilde," she answers with her heart in her throat.

He opens the door and pulls her inside, closing it behind her. He says nothing, but waits for her to ask.

"You've executed Dolores, haven't you?"

Olindo nods and in his watery grey eyes, Tilde can read the answers she already knew.

"Maestri told you it was her, that *she* was the informant."

He takes her gently by one arm and pulls her along the dimly lit corridor to the kitchen where the glow of the incipient summer bathes the room in a deceptive warmth. "You were right," Olindo says, almost in an attempt to comfort her. "Maestri is a coward. Once we had him he couldn't answer our questions fast enough. We were ready to give him a taste of his own medicine, but we didn't even have to threaten him."

"It was Dolores. Dolores was the informant." Tilde repeats feebly, staring blankly at the patch of sunshine on the wall.

"She had an entire room full of stuff, different cheeses, oil, flour, expensive wines. Tearnails didn't lie."

179

"Then Hessen did. Iolanda had nothing to do with it. . ."

"Your German fooled us," admits Grandi, his gaze fixed on the floor. His brow is furrowed and his lips set grimly. "We condemned an innocent. I will carry this weight with me for the rest of my life."

"All of us will," she replies, in a flat, almost robotic voice. She blinks. Two tears spill out and begin to descend her tanned cheeks. "We'll all carry it, Olindo."

"We've been deceived, Tilde," Grandi tries to answer. "We do all this to free Italy."

From her throat comes a strangled cry, half mourning and half defiance. She throws herself against him and begins to pound his white, freshly ironed shirt with her fists. "But what about us?" she weeps, "Who will free *us* now?"

Olindo doesn't seem to feel the pain. He hugs her tightly, holding her against his chest, almost as if he is afraid of losing her forever. She abandons herself to his embrace, resigned and desperate, and continues to cry wordlessly. Words are slippery things. They can be used to mislead the speaker just as easily as they can the listener. Words of absolution are stained with blood, just like the supplies Dolores accumulated selling the lives of her people to Maestri and his henchmen. The right words can justify anything, no matter how shameful. Even now, she and Olindo could find the words to absolve themselves and tell themselves that nothing else could have been done. But they both know they will not, because Iolanda's death deserves the silence of acceptance.

"Why did Hessen deceive you?" he asks. He can still smell the acrid odor of the canteen on her hair.

She feels that she knows why, but she can't focus on it. She smells it, a distant stench caught on a gust of wind.

"The information provided by Hessen on Maestri's habits," he explains, letting go of her, "was accurate except for one thing. There was a second fascist car waiting for him at the crossroads by the seafront. They took Calcagno by surprise and killed him."

"The German?" Grandi replied. "He must have known what we were going to do. If he'd wanted us dead, he could just have tipped off the Black Brigades. No, I don't think he knew about the second car. Although. . ."

"Although. . .?" she invites him to continue, spurred by an avid ferocity. If Hessen had intentionally misdirected them to Iolanda, he wasn't what he pretended to be.

"Maestri swore there were always two cars."

"He'll pay for all the things he did," she snarls between her teeth. Then she adds: "Does Biscia know about Iolanda?"

"He was with me when I interrogated Tearnails," Olindo replies tersely.

"Has he really gone back to the mountains?"

Grandi nods. "We had a job that seemed to be made for him. Biscia is tall and blond, anyone would take him for a German. We asked him to visit a *crucchi* cinema dressed as an officer and leave a bomb behind."

"And. . .?"

"He refused. When he heard about Iolanda, he decided that Biscia was dead. He no longer wants us to call him that. From now on, he will fight in the mountains using his own name."

"Like you do."

Olindo shrugs and begins to brood. She knows who he is thinking about. After a brief silence, he replies, "No. Like Calcagno."

A sense of unease comes over her, making her shudder. She can't resist the sudden urge and asks, "Will the attack happen anyway?"

He forces a smile and confirms: "It will. We've found another man who, in uniform, will mix wonderfully among the Wehrmacht. Next week, one of their newsreels is going to have an ending they'll never forget."

24.
ROSSOAMARO

A few days passed with no developments. Rain continued to fall out of a slate sky. All was an endless grey and spring seemed to be on permanent hold. My daily trip to the hospital on my Vespa, wrapped in an old yellow oilskin, had become a religious ritual lacking only faith.

After talking to Gino Bavastro I had decided to sit back and wait. It seemed to me that everything was clear and my search was over. I was tired of being batted back and forth like a ping-pong ball. Now it was up to one of the two players, the German Client and the Partisan Commander, to make their move.

The call arrived on a Saturday morning and dragged me up from a dream about Jasmìne trying to escape her torturer on an old bicycle with a black frame and whitewashed stripes. She was trying to pedal up an ever-steepening hill. Her pursuer was gaining ground and almost within arm's reach when the phone began to ring.

Keeping my eyes closed, I stretched out my arm without having the slightest idea of where I was, what time it was, or what was going on. I put the handset to my ear upside-down, swore silently and turned it over. I realized I was damp with sweat.

"Bacci, it's Olindo," a voice squawked in my ear. "Did I wake you up?"

"Not yet." I opened my eyes and tried to raise myself on one elbow. A golden light filtered through the blinds, and a thick dust filled the air, permeating the semi-darkness with an unexpected cheerfulness. It must have stopped raining.

"Eight-thirty," said the commander. "Old people are herbivores, we only need a little sleep. Carnivores like you who still enjoy the hunt need a few more hours."

I thought of Jasmìne lying in a hospital bed in a coma. I didn't laugh.

"I was waiting for you to call."

"I know," he said slyly. "It's a magnificent, sunny morning. If you have nothing else to do, I'll offer you an aperitif before lunch."

"Where?"

"I'll see you at eleven at Bar Preti on Via Garibaldi." He immediately corrected himself: "I mean Via Sestri, now everybody calls it that."

It was the pedestrian-only street of Sestri Ponente, the one with the historic shops I often heard my mother talk about: Bagnara, Bruzzo, Guano & Dodero. Temples of old-fashioned good taste which she always entered with a sense of awe that she had transmitted to her son. The cobblestone street that teenagers cruise up and down just to watch each other. Where women go shopping and men have serious discussions about things they can never change, like soccer and politics. For people in Sestri over a certain age, it's still Via Garibaldi. That's in spite of the reorganization after the war that made Sestri a part of Genoa and renamed the Strada Nuova—the New Road—which was lined with Renaissance-era palaces, as Via Garibaldi. In Italy, old habits die hard. When they go downtown, people from Sestri, young and old alike, still say they are "going to Genoa."

I arrived early and had thirty minutes to kill before meeting Olindo so I took a stroll. I parked the Vespa in Piazza Poch, the ancient Piazza dei Gattini, and I lingered to look at the stately trees beyond the open gate of Villa Rossi. Holm oaks, palm trees, magnolias, and centuries-old pines, all flooded by air and light. I walked along the restored façade of the ancient cigar factory, where for almost twenty years, my mother had worked. Now nicely restored, the building had taken on a chic look she would have thoroughly appreciated. She would have loved to work there as a clerk or a librarian. Returning to the square, I passed the

Pontinetto and went along Via Sestri, toward the bar where Olindo was waiting for me. The street was crowded with people and, along the walls, Senegalese sold their wares displayed on tarps lining the ground.

I hadn't been here for years and it was an effort to recognize the modern version using what was imprinted on my memory. On both sides of the street, there was an endless succession of commercial businesses, all in a sort of bland postmodern style. It was a triumph of brainless neoconsumerism that might have increased the average GDP but reduced the average intelligence. Shiny phone shops full of hyper-complex technology that people would make use of in utterly useless ways. Yogurt shops, bakeries, bio-herbalists, ice-cream parlors, specialty food shops of ever kind you can imagine—and some you can't. Name brands of all sizes, cookie-cutter monuments to the breeding of capital free from liability and risk. Banks and real estate agencies everywhere. It was no use. Even the proudly communist Sestri, nicknamed "the Red," was now lashed by the winds of the global economy. The working class Sestri of my father and ideals of the "68" student movement that had animated my own youth were gone.

At eleven o'clock, Olindo and I, wrapped in padded jackets and seated at an open-air table, basked in the glow of a bright, sunny day invigorated by the brisk Tramontane wind. As we lazily watched the crowd passing in front of us, we could make out a large number of foreigners, especially South Americans, with dark skin and almond-shaped eyes. It was easy to spot them. They were the people traveling as families and surrounded by swarms of lively, chirruping children.

"My treat," Olindo said in a tone that brooked no refusal. "You are my guest."

When the waitress arrived, I ordered a martini on ice. The young woman, a girl in her twenties with olive skin and dark eyes and hair, turned to the old man and asked, "And you, sir?"

"A *biancoamaro*," replied the Commander.

The waitress looked at him, frowning. He smiled at her fondly and explained, "A glass of white wine with a touch of amaro."

"Averna or Santamaria?" she asked, trying, and failing, to hide her

"Not that kind of amaro," Olindo explained patiently. "I mean a drop of bitters."

"Campari?" the girl asked, her brow clearing. As Olindo nodded, she added professionally, "Have you a preference for the wine, Sir?"

"Any sparkling wine will be fine." He watched her return to the bar, his large grey eyes veiled in melancholy.

"Tilde looked much like her," he said. "I remember it as if it were yesterday, our meeting at Bar 900 on the Pontinetto. We had ordered two *biancoamaros* and she was terrified at the thought of what I would ask her to do. But she was a fighter and, in the end, she was the one who proposed that she should approach the German."

I looked at him affectionately, almost moved by the emotion in his voice. Olindo must have caught some of that because he paused and said "You've really been dragged through it, haven't you? I'm sorry."

"I have a friend in the hospital, halfway between life and death. They sold her, raped her, and beat her. . ."

"Yes, Gino told me," he interrupted. "She comes from Africa, doesn't she?"

I nodded and added, "Her name is Jasmìne."

"I often think of the terrible months that followed September 8th, the day the Germans became our masters." he said, looking away. "When the war was over, we believed that the nightmares we experienced were gone for good. But we were wrong. There are always new nightmares, aren't there?"

"My grandfather always spoke of the war as a terrible experience."

"It was indeed," he replied, becoming animated. "But we had something else. Something to hold onto. Something that people like your Jasmìne can never have."

"What?"

"A purpose. Our suffering had a purpose. The hope of changing everyone's life, not just our own. And it was a well-founded hope. We were not alone. As our ragtag groups fought the Nazis and the Fascists, the most powerful army in the world was working its way up through Italy to fight on our side."

"Do you mean you could have waited for someone else to do your fighting for you?"

"On the contrary, we felt the need to prove that a new nation was emerging. The only way to do it was to fight, and the price we all had to pay was to kill or to die. A nation is not born when one army of occupation replaces another. We did all this to free Italy."

The girl arrived with the martini and the *biancoamaro*, accompanied by trays of chips, little squares of pizza, and small *tartine*. As she placed everything on the blue plastic table, Olindo watched her with an admiration tinged with sadness. When she had left us, he reiterated: "Oh, yes. Just like her."

"What was Tilde like?" I asked, starting to sip my drink.

He took off his glasses and placed them on the table. Then he brought his open hands to his face and rubbed his eyes for a long time. When he finally looked back at me, his big gray eyes were shining. He sighed and seemed to be looking at something off in the distance that only he could see. "Tenacious and generous," he replied, "but also infinitely sad. I don't know how she managed to deal with those horrible months without falling apart. She really lost herself after Iolanda died. She had just met her, but that meeting somehow changed her."

"Iolanda was an informant," I said.

He shook his head and twisted his lips in a grimace. "Iolanda had always been faithful to our cause," he replied sharply. "The only one who genuinely believed that at the time was Tilde and she never forgave herself for her death."

"It was Biscia who executed her, wasn't it?"

He nodded, then grabbed his glass with both hands. They trembled

"He was not to blame," he replied angrily. "It was the German. The German had deceived us. We never understood why. He always provided valid information and many partisans were saved by what he passed on."

"When you saw her again, after the liberation, didn't you ask her?"

He sipped the *biancoamaro*, still holding his glass with both hands. When he put it on the table, he shook his head. "No one had any interest in rehashing what we had had to do during the war, especially not *that* story." he replied. "Who knows? Maybe he wanted to protect Tilde. Maybe he wanted to protect himself."

"A cruel fate, Iolanda's," I said. "To die blamelessly, a patriot, but executed by her own people for being on the wrong side. . ."

Olindo gave a snort of annoyance. "When you die," he said dryly, "there are no right or wrong sides. You just die. It's while you're alive that you have to choose on which side to fight. And Iolanda had chosen to fight on the right side."

"You sound like have no interest in the losers, in justice for those who lost everything in the war."

He shook his head and shrugged. "Justice. Just words. A way to rewrite history. The right words can justify anything." Then he added, "And anyway, I've always struggled to consider myself a winner."

That was enough philosophy for one morning. I decided to return to our story and asked if after the war Tilde had resumed working at the Fossati canteen.

"No. I think even the idea of doing that would have made her gag," he replied, replacing his glasses. "The real informant, the one in whose place Iolanda was killed, was a canteen worker, a lame woman who Tilde trusted, a friend. Biscia, however, did go to work at the Fossati factory as a turner after the war. He left the shipyard because he, too, wanted something different."

"There's one thing I don't understand," I said, emptying my glass.

187

"In our first interview, I was sure Gino Bavastro didn't know about any of this."

"That's right," he confirmed with a smile in which you could see a glint of the old PAG commander. "It was all a secret for 60 years. Gino heard the true story at the meeting we had last week."

I realized that, for him, having kept this secret for so long was an act of valor, just as it would have been in the old days when, in the cellars of Gestapo headquarters, the Black Brigades and the SS tortured partisans to death trying to discover the names of their comrades in the Resistance.

"And yet," I continued, "twenty years ago, he gave at least some information to Professor Hessen."

"Gino met Tilde and Biscia after the war. He didn't know them by those names. As far as Biscia and Tilde were concerned, Biscia and Tilde were dead. They buried those names and the story with them."

"But wouldn't Dria have given Hessen their real names?"

"No. Your client's lying." he replied with contempt. "Dria, though ill, told him nothing. I know that for a fact. And when he began looking us up and asking questions, Hessen knew only one name, the name his aunt had given him."

"Tilde?"

"Tilde!" he confirmed, knocking his fist on the table. Plates and glasses tinkled.

"But then," I asked, more and more confused, "how did Hessen manage. . ."

"To find out their names? There's only one explanation: one of us told him."

"Who might that have been?" I asked, sure he knew the answer.

He gave me a bitter smile and shrugged. "What does it matter now?" He closed his eyes and sighed heavily. "Once, he would have been shot for passing information like that to a German. But that was a long time ago. Whoever it was will have to deal with his own conscience."

I remained silent, contemplating the pockmarked skin of his face. He was again staring at me blindly. Eventually, I gathered my courage and asked him the question that, in the interview with Bavastro, had remained unanswered: "Did Tilde know you were planning the attack at the Odeon Cinema?"

"I told her myself, before she disappeared."

"So she sent him to his death."

"I don't think so," he replied thoughtfully, almost absently. "Tilde left days before the attack. Why would she have expected Hessen to go to that cinema on that day?"

"But she could have warned him of the danger."

"She had to choose between us and them. When she left, the captain had no reason to protect us. If Tilde had warned him, the action would have failed and everyone involved would have been captured and killed."

I remembered reading the record of Engel's trial, the man responsible for the Turchino pass massacre. It included details about how the attack had been carried out.

"The person who placed the explosive was wearing a Wehrmacht uniform and was a young man, blond with blue eyes," I said. "That sounds a lot like Biscia."

Olindo looked at me with a conspiratorial smile, as if he had expected the question. He shook his head and said, "As a German officer he would've been perfect. We offered him the job, but he refused."

"So it wasn't him."

"Some believe that his career in the PAG ended the day he discovered that Iolanda was innocent, but that's not the case. I suppose I could tell you that it was over months before, when the group decided

189

that the woman had to be executed, but that wouldn't be telling the whole truth. Biscia began to resent the PAG from the moment he knew that Tilde would be offering herself to Hessen. I confess to you now that I bear all the responsibility for this and it's a sin for which I'll never forgive myself. A few months later, we learned who the informant really was. As a PAG member, Biscia was ruthless. His hits were clean and efficient, and he could disappear with extraordinary skill. The command asked me to call him back to eliminate the real informant, but I was adamant and, eventually, they chose someone else. Biscia was in the mountains, by then, and I knew he wasn't going by Biscia anymore. He was ashamed of that name and never used it again."

We sat for some time in silence, enjoying the sun and watching the people strolling on Via Sestri. I pulled my pipe from the pocket of my jacket, packed it and lit it. Olindo looked at me with his enormous liquid eyes. But it seemed he wasn't looking at me but at his favorite soldier, the young Biscia.

Eventually, he came back from his reverie and emptied his glass. Then, wiping his lips with the back of his hand, he asked: "Now that you have discovered the truth, what will you do?"

I felt an odd apprehension in his voice, almost a father's concern. I decided he had already suffered enough and deserved an answer that would reassure him.

"What I've always done," I said with a smile. "I'll call my client and collect my fee."

25.

THE INHERITANCE

The policeman was in his forties, athletic and stocky, with the unmistakable face of a veteran brawler. He wore a uniform, well-polished boots, and a cap. His gun and nightstick were proudly displayed on his hip. Periodically, he'd check the time, pushing back his sleeve to display a diver's watch that had to weigh a pound. It was obvious that he had a problem with the assignment and would have preferred to be elsewhere. Sitting with his legs spread apart, he watched me silently with a mixture of mistrust and contempt. If the woman he was guarding was an Ivorian prostitute, the man waiting in the hospital corridor could only be her pimp.

I checked the time myself. Ten-thirty. My client was late. We had spoken on the phone on Saturday afternoon, after I'd met Commander Grandi. I told him that my investigation was over. I had found his brother. After asking about Jasmìne, he had assured me that he would come to Genoa on Tuesday. The appointment was set for ten, in front of the same closed door where we had met two weeks earlier.

I saw him hurrying down the corridor breathless, worried about being late. He was clearly terrified he might miss out on meeting me and the satisfaction it would bring. He was sporting an elegant camel coat, too wide for him, that hung loosely from his shoulders and flapped when he moved, making him look even more emaciated. On his neck, he wore an elegant white wool scarf and he turned the usual felt hat in his hands nervously. I wondered if, perhaps, he always removed his hat because his long illness had caused him to think of hospitals as a sort of sacred place, like a church.

As soon as he saw the new arrival, my chatty friend got nervous. He got up and put his hand on his gun but I stopped him. "Whoa there!

191

Calm down. I'm a private investigator and that's my client. He's no threat to anybody."

I showed him a copy of my license. He turned it over in his hands as if he wasn't quite sure what it was. Then he returned it and told me to keep myself and my client away from the door. I went to sit at the far end of the corridor and Hessen sat on a nearby chair. Unconsciously, we were reenacting our first meeting.

"Good morning, *Herr* Pagano," he said in a very formal tone. An ironic smile fluttered over his face, even though he seemed to be physically suffering. His skin had become yellowish and he appeared to have problems breathing. He didn't look good.

"Good morning, Professor," I replied. "So you've come here for the big payoff?"

"I came to take the last bit of satisfaction I will enjoy in this life." he said quietly. "So you've found my brother."

I looked at him and nodded.

"From a detective of your reputation," he continued flatly, "I would have expected quicker results."

"I was busy. I had things on my mind." I said.

"Yes," he replied, as if thinking aloud. "Your friend. . . have the doctors finally given you a prognosis?"

"Not yet. Have yours?"

"I've had it for a while, now," he said indifferently, smiling without hostility. "Twenty years ago I was given six months to live. I went to America, where they managed to save my life. Unfortunately, my bank account did not survive. As you can see, I've postponed my final appointment and made it here to see you. That's all I care about now. There is nothing else."

I cut him short. I knew that the door of the ward would open any minute and the doctors would give me the daily update on Jasmine's condition. "What do you want to know?"

"I don't know yet. This story has shed light on old pain and mysteries. We'll have to see."

"So you should thank me, *Herr* Pagano."

"Let me decide who to thank, and why."

"I hope you don't mind," he added with a hint of sorrow that I found irritating. "I got information about your *friend.*"

"Jasmìne?"

"She's an African prostitute."

My hands clenched but I restrained myself. Lucky for him, he was an old man with cancer and about to die.

"Who told you?" I asked, raising my voice. My thoughts went to the doctor who had thrown me out of the ward a few days before.

"Why are you getting so upset? I read the newspapers. Her story was in the local section, along with your name."

How long had it been since I'd opened a newspaper? Jasmìne's problems had obliterated my habits and trapped me in a well of isolation and loneliness. But what really hurt was that this mess had made me push away everyone I cared about. I hadn't spoken with my daughter in weeks. She'd even left me messages and I hadn't answered. Now, she no longer called. Aglaja is like that, touchy, like her mother. The Captain and Gina Aliprandi, had also disappeared. Zainab and Essam had probably reassured everyone that I was alive and well, and now, no one bothered to come looking.

"As far as I'm concerned," I grunted, "the death of an African prostitute is as terrible as the death of a German professor."

He put on a forced smile that was as precarious as his health. "I'm aware of how you think," he said, shaking his head. "I guess now she'll be even dearer to you."

"Do you know what I think, Professor?" I replied. "It wasn't just the cancer destroying you. Cancer has consumed your body. But the hatred you accumulated over the years has done worse. . ."

"You're right, *Herr* Pagano," he interrupted me quietly. "It gnawed at my soul. But I would've liked to see you in my place. My father betrayed his country for that woman. He made his sister come down to Italy to take care of her and her son, and that. . ." he could barely hold in the insult, ". . .repaid him by sending him to his death."

His faded blue eyes had taken on a maniacal gleam and his face was grim. Flecks of spittle dotted his lips and he began to pant. His hands trembled, clasped tightly around the hat in his lap.

"That's not what happened!" I said. "Beat yourself up all you want, but you've got the wrong end of the stick."

"Don't tell me. . ."

"Who told you Tilde knew about the attack?"

He made a superhuman effort to regain control. If he wasn't careful, he was going to check out before we finished our conversation. He remained silent, his eyes fixed on the hat he turned compulsively in his hands. When he had mastered himself, he said, "My aunt told me that, from the moment she arrived in Gargnano, my mother treated her and her husband with coldness and detachment. She was absent and distant, probably dreaming of her partisan boyfriend. When news of my father's death arrived, she didn't shed a tear. No pain, no confusion, no surprise. According to my aunt, she was actually pleased. She welcomed his death as her liberation. After giving birth, she didn't even want to see me and asked to return to Genoa immediately. That wasn't possible so, when my aunt and uncle returned to Cologne, she chose to go to work at a factory near Brescia."

"Why didn't the Germans just deport her?"

"My father had asked his aide to ensure that didn't happen. Don't you understand? My father loved her."

I was expecting him to start crying. But this man's capacity for pity had been eaten away by his festering hate and tears would do nothing for his pain. I pitied him and, for a moment, I forgot he had played me.

194

I owed him nothing but I resolved to do him good for evil and share what I had learned from those partisans he hated so much.

"Tilde could not have known that your father would go into that cinema on May 15th."

"Did your PAGist friends tell you that?" he sneered.

"They are certain of it."

"And why should I believe you?"

"Because you do believe them. They have no reason to lie. You believed them, one of them, at least, when he told you the real names of Tilde and her husband."

He gave me a sideways, uncertain look, between surprise and distrust. "It was the truth," he replied.

"Would you be willing to tell me who it was?"

"Why not?" he replied with an evil grin of satisfaction. "It was Lanza. The partisan Lanza. I never understood why he told me. Perhaps he was in love with her and it was somehow revenge for her marrying someone else."

"Perhaps," I said.

He paused and said, "You, however, *Herr* Pagano, are lying through your teeth."

"Think what you like. But Tilde left a few days before the attack. I imagine that in that situation she and the captain would not have been spending what little time they would have had together chatting about cinema."

He clasped his hat to his chest as if it were a child who needed comfort.

"But she knew they were planning it."

Now we had come to it. It was decision time. Should I lie to him? Tell him a lie he would never be able to verify, one way or the other?

"You may not like it," I said firmly, "but your father had helped the partisans. The Resistance never wanted him to die."

"And Iolanda?" he replied with a sigh. "Do you know the story of the false information about an informant that my father passed to the partisans?"

"Yes. I know all about it," I said. "I also know that Dria Ratto told you. I'm convinced that your father did it to protect both Tilde and himself."

"What do you mean?" he asked intently, revealing a desperate, avid curiosity.

"If he had passed along the name of the real informant, the Gestapo would have been all over them."

He stared at me for a long time. In his blue eyes, I could read contradictory feelings passing like clouds in a turquoise sky. Sadness, hate, maybe even regret. He sighed, then dropped his eyes to the hat, which he had not ceased to torment. When he lifted them up again, the fatal question reappeared, popping up like a sniper from a trench: "*But did she know about the attack?*"

I shrugged, and sighed in turn. "I don't think so," I said "Operational details of the attack remained secret until the very last moment."

"You are not convinced," he replied, shaking his head. Then, in the grip of a kind of paroxysm, he asked, "So *Herr* Grandi didn't tell you Iolanda and Tilde were friends?"

"Of course he told me."

"And wouldn't that have been enough of a reason. . ."

He was again lost in his own thoughts. That *idee fixe* had haunted him for twenty years. Should I tell him the unvarnished truth so that he would not have to face the fact that his entire life—a life dedicated to revenge he could never really achieve—had been wasted? It came to me that the idea that his mother had been innocent was not a release. It had made him feel even worse.

"Why didn't she talk to him about Iolanda before she left?" he asked tonelessly.

I shrugged. "You told me why yourself, Professor."

"I did?"

"A few days ago, on the phone. *War is a serious thing.*"

"Yes," he repeated. "War is a serious thing."

He sat there for a moment, lost in confusion and agitation. Then, suddenly, he became animated. "I suppose you'll want to know about the inheritance," he said, almost happily.

I tried to smile, but only managed a grimace of fatigue. "Not really. There is no inheritance, *Herr* Hessen. Just like there is no brother. War and disease have squandered both."

"You're right," he replied, idly trying to reshape the hat he had been mangling. "There was a lot of money, once, but there is nothing left besides an interest-bearing bond and a luxurious home in the center of Cologne."

"I'm still holding a check for forty thousand euros. Is it good?"

"Of course," he said firmly. "That I left you as a pledge. So you have decided to accept it?"

"I don't know," I said. That was the truth.

At that moment, the door of the ward opened. The head of the neurology department and a young doctor appeared in the corridor. The guard jumped out of his seat and hurried to join them. I asked the professor to excuse me and rushed over myself. I didn't want to miss anything. My friend in uniform looked at me suspiciously, but the doctors knew me well by this time and greeted me so he left me in peace. For the first time since I had met them, they were smiling.

"Good news," said the head of neurology, who had personally overseen Jasmine's care. "Our patient's awake now. We've brought her out of the coma and run some tests."

"Is she going to live?" I asked anxiously.

The doctor smiled widely and opened his arms. "Better than just live." he said, "She'll eventually make a full recovery."

"What do you mean, *eventually*?" I pressed him.

"She'll need rehabilitation; it's a process, and it will take time, but she'll fully recover."

"Can I see her?"

"If you wait for about an hour, yes, we'll let you see her," said the younger doctor, clapping me on the shoulder.

"Now, if you'll excuse me. . ." Both doctors turned to the door and, while my ever-chatty friend the policeman grunted in thanks, they closed it behind them and disappeared from sight.

I could barely contain my happiness. Jasmine had made it! I briefly considered hugging the uniformed Mr. Personality who had been there to share the joy of the moment. Well, "shared" is such a strong word. In fact, the doctor's report had done nothing to improve his mood. He sat down again, pulling out his phone to pass the news on to headquarters.

"Are you calling Deputy Commissioner Pertusiello?" I asked.

He didn't answer, just looked at me with a mixture of annoyance and condescension.

"If you're calling him," I insisted, "tell him I'm going to visit Jasmine in an hour."

He answered with another grunt and availed himself of the opportunity to lift his jacket cuff with his little finger again and check the time. On second thought, he might have just been admiring his watch.

I went back to Hessen who remained sitting where I had left him. He sat watching as I approached him radiating happiness.

"So everything's going to be alright, then," he said with a hint of

"She'll make it," I said.

"I'm pleased." I couldn't tell if he was pleased for me or for Jasmine.

I sat down and tried to catch his eye but couldn't. Now, he was disinterested in his hat and had, instead, turned his gaze to the white wall, where, perhaps, he was watching bad memories and painful feelings play out before him. I had been there myself.

"I've come here for vengeance," he said. "But now I don't know why I'm here."

I had trouble following him; I was still replaying my conversation with the two doctors over and over in my head. The emotions I was feeling were just too distant from his.

"You know, I don't think I will tear up that check," I said, pointing at the door of the ward. "Those forty thousand euros will go a long way towards helping her recover and start over."

"I'm pleased," he repeated. And this time there was no doubt about his meaning. "I came," he said, continuing his train of thought, "because that woman left me to grow up without a father. I wanted the only revenge left to me, making her son face the truth about his mother."

"*Our* mother," I corrected him.

"Yes," he replied, looking back at the hat, which he had again begun to torment. "*Our* mother."

In the silence that followed, we slipped into a companionable languor. It was sad, really. He would return to Germany where, very soon, he would end his days with us having never reminisced about what might have been while sharing a bottle of scotch. Because, even though the war lay like a minefield between us, Kurt Hessen and I did have something in common.

He was the son of a captain of the Wehrmacht and I of a communist laborer who had fought in the patriotic action group of Commander

Grandi under the name of Biscia. But we both had been borne by the same woman. Her name was Annamaria Clotilde Canepa, a black-eyed ingénue with raven hair for whom great beauty was a curse that had robbed her of taking real joy in life.

That was the inheritance I would receive from my half-brother.

The brave partisan courier that everyone called Tilde was my mother.

26.
THE TWO WOMEN

The young doctor escorted me to Jasmìne's bedside, treating me as if I were a fragile porcelain vase. I felt the tip of his fingers touching my arm with a gentleness that irritated me. I said nothing and hoped that, once in the room, he would leave us alone.

"Can she talk?" I asked.

"Of course she can talk," he said.

He opened the door and brought me inside. He remained on the threshold, and looking at me sideways, said, "I can give you ten minutes. She needs to conserve her strength." I nodded consent and he closed the door and disappeared. A strong smell of disinfectant filled the air that I hadn't noticed on my previous visits.

Jasmìne, bathed by the light that poured through the wide-open window, had her eyes open and turned slightly to look at me. The whiteness of the sheet, intensified by the brilliance of the noon sun, made her long, lean arms appear even darker. Behind her back, they had placed two pillows that kept her propped up slightly. She stared at me wordlessly, as if wanting to steal my secret.

I dragged over one of the hard metal chairs and settled beside her.

"Hello, Jasmìne," I whispered.

In answer, she blinked her eyes and her lips curved slightly in the hint of a smile. She had recognized me.

"It's all over," I added. "The doctors say you'll be as good as new."

She smiled again, opening her lips to show her teeth, regular and white as snow. Her face expressed both perplexity and happiness, like that of a child who, after an unpleasant experience, finds herself in the

201

arms of her parents. She was an orphan and had little experience of that. But she'd certainly just escaped from an unpleasant experience and she'd raced death and won, although it had been a photo-finish.

"I just wrapped up what's probably my strangest case." I said. "In my pocket, we've got a check for forty thousand euros! You can start over now. You don't have to live in fear anymore."

She smiled for the third time, but remained silent. I was starting to get concerned again. Was talking still too difficult for her?

I stretched out my hand and put it lightly over hers, emulating the pianist's touch of the young doctor who had accompanied me here. Jasmine lowered her eyes to our hands, then raised them to meet my own. Hers, shaded by long black lashes, glittered, revealing a confused tumult of feelings. Was it gratitude and affection, or only disbelief?

"It was really a weird investigation," I continued. "Do you want me to tell you about it?"

She blinked and nodded, barely moving, impeded by the bandage that wrapped her head and neck.

"A German client commissioned me to find his brother," I said. "The father was a Wehrmacht officer who was killed during the war. He had a relationship with a young Italian who got pregnant and, after giving birth, abandoned her son. My client grew up in Cologne, in the home of his father's sister and her husband. After the Liberation, his mother married her boyfriend, a very courageous partisan, and a second child was born. The German gave me forty thousand euros to find out who it was."

"And you?" she asked with an effort.

"I did my job and found him," I said, giggling incongruously from the joy of hearing her voice again.

"As always," she said, smiling again, with a hint of irony.

Her voice was slightly slurred, raspy. She was having difficulty speaking, even though her French accent remained unmistakable. Well, it was still early days yet.

She asked for something to drink. On the bedside table, there was a bottle of mineral water and an empty glass. I poured some and gently brought the glass to her lips. She took a few sips and, with her hand, made a sign that it was enough. After I had wiped her mouth and chin with a handkerchief she asked, "Why did he look for him after so long?"

"He wanted revenge. He's very sick and before he dies he's made it a point of honor to repay his half-brother for the pain he has suffered." I remained silent for a few seconds, then added, "Although I have the impression that now he sees things differently. When he left, he seemed confused and, perhaps, his hate was being replaced by remorse and regret."

She studied me and her expression became worried. "And what about you?" she said.

"And what about me?"

"How are you?"

"I'm fine," I said, tentatively.

"So you're fine with having a brother," she said, abruptly.

That left me speechless. "How. . .?"

She took a deep breath and tried to explain: "You were the one talking about your *strangest* case. On top of that, forty thousand euros is too much. I do have some experience with setting fees, you know."

"Was it really that easy?" I asked, surprised and amused.

"*Bashi,*" she said warmly with a tender smile, "You should see your face."

She closed her eyes and took another deep breath. The doctor was right, talking made her tired. And so we remained for a while, close and still, saying nothing.

Eventually, she broke the silence and asked, "The name?"

"The German client's?"

"Your mother's."

"Tilde," I said, without thinking. My answer surprised me. To me, she had always been Anna.

"Was she also. . ." she could not find the word.

"A prostitute?"

She winced and her mouth bent in a grimace, a mixture of dismay and amusement. "No," she responded quickly, "one like your father."

"A partisan?"

She nodded, batting her eyelashes and, stretching out her hand, invited me to intertwine my fingers with hers. I did so and replied, "Yes, she maintained contact between the armed groups of the Resistance. She was captured and that's when she met the German officer."

"I don't know your history," she said. "I just know who the Nazis were, and I guess the partisans were their enemies."

I confirmed it, but I didn't understand where she was going with this.

"There are wars in Africa, too, but it's different," she continued, starting to breath hard. I wanted to stop her but she didn't let me. "It's hard to understand who fights on the right side."

"They understood," I said. "They were fighting to free Italy."

"Then she didn't do it just to survive," she said.

"I don't think so," I replied, though I knew I would never have a definitive answer. "Why are you asking?"

"Just because," she replied with a bitter smile. Then she gripped my hand more tightly. In a firm voice, she added, *"Bashi,* you should not make that face. You're a lucky man, *they've* left you something."

At that moment, the door opened and the young doctor appeared.

Our time was up, but now I could leave her without a sense of loss and despair. It wasn't "Goodbye," merely "See you soon." I knew that our life would continue and we would be granted the time and the opportunity to heal our wounds.

"*Arrivederci*, Jasmìne."

27.

AUFWIEDERSEHEN, FRÄULEIN

Genoa, May 12, 1944

The black car is parked in the yard in front of the villa's imposing entrance. By now, it has become a familiar presence. She recognizes the smell of the leather and the tobacco smoke that soaks the seats, the deafening noise of the engine as it accelerates through the turn on Via Sant'Alberto, the pleasant rocking feeling that lulls her to sleep like a child. Now, the trunk holds a large suitcase filled with summer clothes for her and a complete set of everything she would need for the baby she's carrying. The ever-faithful and thoroughly-meticulous Sergeant Walden had taken care of everything. He'd now gone up to his room to prepare his own luggage. Soon, they'd be ready to leave.

The air is mild and a breeze gently sways the branches of the great trees in the park. The sky is hazy with mist and the morning sun shines dully on the intense green of the horse chestnuts and sycamores.

Hessen is sitting on the bed, in a white shirt and uniform trousers with elastic suspenders. His boots are shiny and move nervously on the parquet floor. Tilde keeps her back to him and stares out the window at the car that is going to carry her away to an unknown place and an unknown future. A place where *Frau* Greta and her husband are waiting for her.

She wears a light turquoise dress. The light passing through it silhouettes her long, muscular legs. She wears blue shoes, with laces and low heels, which constantly thump against each other, as if she is trying to get them off so she can return them, along with everything else, to the man who gave them to her. The captain looks at the thick cascade of black hair that flows down her back with a mixture of anger and concern.

The silence is becoming heavy. Tilde has just arrived and greeted him peremptorily while avoiding his gaze. But the German has caught something in those eyes he had never seen before. Not the mocking and combative expression she used when challenging him, throwing his cowardice in his face. Nor was it the wild fury with which she used to provoke and arouse him. In the young woman's eyes there is something new, a mixture of hatred and contempt, something which disdains words and seeks only escape and solitude. Even the long journey ahead of her will not reconcile her and restore her mood and he knows why. He knows about Maestri's capture and the execution of Dolores at the hands of the partisans.

Her lips tightened fiercely, Tilde finally breaks the silence. "Just tell me one thing," she says, her voice hollow. "Why? Why did you do it?"

He considers, briefly, pretending not to understand. But he know he would look ridiculous. "You really don't know?"

"Maybe I do," she replies, without turning. "But I want to hear it from you."

"It was all a setup. If I had told you the truth, they would have shot both of us the next day. Maestri had warned Major Engel about me and the SS was only waiting for the trap to close."

Tilde turns abruptly, her fists clenched and her head sunk between her shoulders. "Why give me a name at all? Why not just say you didn't know?"

She searches his face with the ferocity of a wounded animal, determined not to surrender but to fight until the end. She doesn't do it for herself. It's the last thing she can do for Iolanda. Her body is tense, so tense she can feel her belly cramping with her anger. She feels she will never be free of it, not until death . . . yes, the death of the German might be enough to lift at least a part of her burden.

Hessen stands his ground and maintains a preternatural calm. He tries producing an ironic smile and hangs a cigarette on it. "Would you have believed me, *Fräulein?*"

"No."

"So?" While still speaking around the cigarette in his mouth, he begins searching the crowded nightstand for his gold lighter. He radiates a confidence that, in Tilde's eyes, is purely ostentatious.

"So what?"

"Would you have preferred that swine to take you to Gestapo headquarters, where he would have raped you and tortured you until you had given him every one of your comrades' names before watching you die?"

"You might not believe it, *Herr Hauptmann,* but I would have."

"You can say that now, Tilde."

She approaches him slowly while he continues the hunt for the lighter, the unlit cigarette still dangling, his lips still bent in that ironic smile that fills her with murderous fury.

"You're wrong, coward," she hisses. "Now everything is ruined. Why didn't you tell me the truth? Do you think I wouldn't have understood?"

"Of course you would have," he responds with a grin that reminds her of his mindless laughter when he was drunk. "But that wouldn't have been playing by the rules of your game. You demanded a name at any cost."

She grimaces in disgust and responds, without thinking, "I will not become the mother of a murderer's son."

"It's a little late for that, isn't it?"

"Not really, no." she answers coldly, touching her belly. "Oh, don't worry, I'll give birth to this bastard of yours and leave it to your Greta. After that, I don't care what happens to me. Instead of raising your child, I'd rather be deported to Germany, as you've made my family believe."

"I don't know what *I* am saying?" she bursts out with a loud laugh that is as wild as the thoughts crowding her mind. "Oh, very true, *Herr Hauptmann*. I always said just what *you* told me to say and I murdered an innocent woman because of it."

"Enough!" Hessen interrupts her, flushing. His cigarette drops to the floor, but he doesn't notice. He gets up from the bed and tries to grab her by the shoulders. She jumps back to lean against the windowsill.

"Don't touch me!" she cries.

Seeing her on the edge, suspended over the void, he takes a step back. "I'm sorry for your friend, but I had no choice."

"You did have a choice. You wanted me, and you didn't care who you had to sacrifice to get what you wanted."

"You know that's not true. . ."

"Your talk about war, about young people dying uselessly was nothing, just talk. Oh, it was all very noble, but it was just a way of getting me to satisfy your whims. A convenient tool, just like I was."

"And what about those I saved?" he replies vehemently. "Have you forgotten them? There must have been a reason your superiors allowed you to consort with an enemy officer."

"Not all of them, Hessen," she answers. Her voice is suddenly sad. "You didn't save them all."

"What do you mean?"

"During the capture of Maestri, a young student died."

Hessen stretches out his arms. "So?" he asks with consternation.

"There were *two* escort cars," she replies contemptuously. *"There have always been two.* Didn't you know?"

He stamps his boot and points a furious finger at her. "Do you know what you are? A stupid, arrogant little girl." The strong Teutonic accent pounds the three adjectives home like nails in her flesh. "How can you think I wanted to ambush your comrades? If I had wanted to do that, they'd all be dead. *Kaputt,* is that clear?" he adds, sliding his index finger across his throat. "Why would I want that? I had. . ."

"Don't get upset, Captain," she interrupts him with an eerie calm. "I never thought you wanted my comrades dead. You just wanted Maestri dead."

"Are you suggesting that I would. . ."

Again Tilde interrupts him. "Wouldn't that have saved you a lot of trouble?"

"You're crazy," the man whispers without looking at her. He goes back to hunting for his lighter and another cigarette appears between his lips.

"If Maestri had been killed in a shootout instead of captured, you would have been safe. It would have guaranteed you immunity both from the Germans and from us. And maybe a decent mother for your child."

"You *will be* the mother of my child," he replies as if giving an order.

Another macabre and desperate laugh. "No, not a mother. Just a *stupid, arrogant little girl* who will add one more *crucco* to the marching ranks bringing misery to the world. Don't ask any more of me."

"Come on, Tilde," he says, trying to cajole her. "Everything seems bleak to you right now. But when you hold our child in your arms. . ."

"I'm sorry, Captain," she whispers. "That's something I will never do. It would be too painful. If they'll let me, I'll come back home immediately after the birth."

Hessen begins to pace back and forth. He finally finds the damn lighter and holds it to his cigarette. He smokes with a furious hunger, the same with which he empties the cognac glasses and loses himself in Tilde's body, the hunger to forget.

She watches him and an irresistible feeling of triumph takes hold of balm for her. She feels herself relaxing and her anger clearing, replaced by a cold purpose.

"The baby will need to be breastfed," he whispers, trying to catch her eyes. It is a supplication more than a statement. It vibrates in his wavering voice and manifests in his bright blue eyes, which tears and the light have made even brighter. Tilde hardens herself, though she wonders how despair can bring such tenderness.

There is no more fear now. If they lock her in a cattle car and ship her to hell, what does it matter? Hell is now a familiar place for her: the grey courtyard of the Fossati factory, the smoky bar on the Pontinetto, the car driven by the trusty Sergeant Walden.

"Your sister can find a wet nurse," she answers unconcerned. "You are the masters. I'm sure you can force someone to do it."

Hessen closes his eyes, sealing in who knows what violent reaction. Tilde finally feels a sense of satisfaction. She knows that Captain Hessen had seen in her the possibility of escaping his cycle of despair. Perhaps he imagined that, once the war had ended, he would marry her and rebuild the family that war destroyed. Perhaps he imagined fleeing somewhere to start a new life with her, whether in Germany, Italy, or even America. After all, he has a clean conscience. He is a partisan hero, is he not? The enemy German who helped the Liberators free Italy. Except, he wasn't moved by an ideal, only the certainty that, in the end, his dictator's armies would fail. Hessen fought only to save himself, and that's not fighting on the right side.

Unwillingly, Tilde has become the guardian of his dream. She is now *his* master and the dream will die. Is that enough for her? She will leave it to Greta to raise his child, at least until the captain returns to Germany.

There is a knock on the door. It's Sergeant Walden. He is dressed in what she jokingly calls his "chauffeur uniform" and carries a small leather case. Speaking German, Hessen asks him to go downstairs, and tells him that Tilde will join him in a moment. The faithful Walden receives his last instructions, snaps a salute, and withdraws down the corridor leaving the door open behind him. Hessen looks at Tilde imploringly and asks, "Are you really determined to do this?"

From somewhere deep inside herself, Tilde feels an echo of emotion that she ruthlessly suppresses. With a self-control she did not know she possessed, she looks this German officer in the eye and is almost amazed to hear herself say casually, almost intimately, "Good-bye, Captain. What are you going to do these evenings without me? Take in the usual film and a game of cards?"

He smiles and his eyes hold the hope that she is changing her mind, softening. "In a few days they're going to be showing a new German movie at the Odeon."

"And will you go?" she asks, with a casual detachment that makes her feel as if she were watching this conversation play out on a screen.

"Of course," he replies, approaching her and kissing her lightly on the cheek.

"Have fun, then," Tilde says in the doorway, pushing her finger under his suspender and popping it. *"Auf Wiedersehen, mein Hauptmann."*

Hessen watches her walking along the corridor, her turquoise dress floating in the air and her long black hair loose on her back. Then he goes to the window to watch Walden open the back door of the car and the young woman bending to get in. She doesn't look up for a final goodbye, fearing her courage might fail her at the last. Her tanned, muscular calves and her blue shoes are the last things he sees of her as he silently whispers, *"Auf Wiedersehen, Fräulein."*

The End

If you enjoyed this book, please leave us an Amazon review, even if it's just a star rating. Your opinion will influence thousands of readers and we really appreciate your feedback!

Think this would be a good read for your book club? Visit Kazabo.com for The German Client Discussion Guide and special book club discounts!

AUTHOR'S NOTE

This story is a work of fiction, though the historical context, places, and some characters are real. This includes the *Vacca Morta* restaurant— The "Dead Cow"—which was a very popular restaurant in Coronata, near Sestri, that was established in the nineteenth century. The partisan fighters Giacomo Buranello, Andrea "Elio" Scano, Andrea "Fulvio" Bottaro, and Sergio Fallabrino are also real. The so-called *Leggeroni* are an integral part of the history of the Resistance in Sestri.

Maria, Tilde's neighbor, was my grandmother. Her daughter, the young woman "with a refined profile of ancient beauty" that Tilde spoke with in front of the air-raid shelter, was my mother. The worker from Ovada Tilde met at the gate of the Fossati factory was my father. They married in August 1943.

The Anglo-American bombing reported in the novel occurred on March 11, 1944. The episode of film theft at Cinema Vittoria really happened, while the raising of the two flags over the House of the Fascists probably happened between the end of March and the beginning of April 1944. The PAG attack on the Odeon Cinema on Via Vernazza happened on May 15, 1944, and in retaliation the Nazi-Fascists killed, without trial, 59 prisoners who are remembered as the martyrs of the Turchino pass.

The Publisher

Since you are a fan of international mysteries, we've included the prologue of our book, *Death in a Bookstore*, by the father of the Italian mystery novel, Augusto De Angelis. We hope you enjoy it. But first, a word from our sponsor, which is us!

Kazabo Publishing is a new idea in the literary world. Our motto is, "Every Book a Best Seller . . . Guaranteed!" And we mean it. Our mission is to find best-selling books from around the world that, for whatever reason, have not been published in English.

When you visit Kazabo.com (our website!), we hope you will always discover something new, either a book from a favorite author you didn't know existed or a completely new author with a fresh perspective from a country you admire. We promise you that everything you see with the Kazabo name – even authors you have never heard of – will be a best-seller; maybe in Italy, maybe in Japan, maybe in 1902, but a best seller. We hope you enjoy reading these literary gems as much as we enjoy finding them and bringing them to you.

But enough about us. Here is an excerpt from our mystery novel by Augusto De Angelis, *Death in a Bookstore*.

Thanks for reading!

The Kazabo Team

Kazabo.com

Death in a Bookstore

By Augusto De Angelis

Prologue

Please deliver to the police station.

He contemplated the bundle lying on the steps of the church.

The early light of dawn illuminated the deserted square. Under the entrance corridor, which led to an open courtyard, the sunrise lit up the image of the Madonna. A few minutes before, all the streetlights had turned off suddenly. The air was chilly.

A new day was born in the big city, which remained nearly motionless. The noise of trams could be heard in the distance, on Corso Vittorio Emanuele, and on the other side, Via Cavallotti.

The man in the gray uniform looked at the bundle.

It must be rags wrapped up in newspaper, he thought. Yet the parcel appeared too carefully packaged to contain rags.

He hit it with the broom and the bundle rolled down the stairs onto the pavement. It didn't open. It had to be closed with some pin, because it was not tied. From the center of the bundle, below the newspaper's edge, a white envelope appeared.

The sweeper bent to reach the envelope. It was open. It contained a piece of paper folded in fourths. Upon the paper was scrawled a message in large and hurried script in blue ink. *"Please deliver to the police station."*

In his eyes, the parcel had now gained importance. He looked at it with respect , even a little fear. Whatever was wrapped in that newspaper, now that he had found it, he had the irritating responsibility of going to the San Fedele Police station to deliver it. After that would come the even bigger nuisance to be questioned, give explanations, repeat them in court... He knew how it worked! Once he had picked up a bunch of fake tickets, and due to that experience he cursed counterfeiters around the world.

So many things had happened to him! In twenty years as a street sweeper, he had found nothing but rubbish and trouble on the ground.

He looked around. There was nobody.

He kicked the package, which rolled farther. But it was not so light, because it didn't go too far.

Sighing, he passed the back of his hand over his mouth. Finally, he picked up the parcel. There were two pins, in fact, to keep the folds of the newspaper closed around the parcel. He touched the bundle. It was soft; there were certainly garments inside. Still, there was something hard in the middle of the garments, which weighed more.

He approached the empty cart, and placed the package on the closed lid. He secured the broom on the two side hooks and put the letter inside his pocket. He grabbed the rods and pushed the cart. He started slowly down Via Pasquirolo, toward Piazza Beccaria, the iron cart resonated on the pavement.

When he arrived at San Fedele, it was broad daylight.

He took the long way and stopped in front of the Galleria to buy coffee with grappa from a street vendor. The vendor looked him up and down twice before serving him, as he had never seen him before.

"Are you new here? Who are you replacing?"

"Nobody. I was just passing by."

"Are you taking a stroll with your *Isotta Fraschini*?"

He didn't answer. He didn't want to talk. The story of the bundle to be delivered to police headquarters had put him in a bad mood. He grabbed his *Isotta Fraschini* and left.

At the door of San Fedele, he stopped with the bundle in his hands. Who should he deliver it to?

A *carabiniere* was looking at him.

"I don't know anything. There, under the porch, there is an agent."

The sweeper addressed the agent, who was smoking.

"I found this on the steps of the church of San Vito, off Via Pasquirolo."

"And you brought it here?! You should know that City Hall takes care of such things..."

"Lost items, yes I know. And you get a ten percent tip, too, when you bring them in. But please, read this!"

He gave him the envelope containing the note.

The agent read it and laughed.

"It's a joke! Have you looked inside?"

"No. I don't want to get in trouble!"

"Why? Is it heavy? You think there's a woman's head cut into pieces inside?!"

And he kept on laughing.

The street sweeper stared at the bundle in his hands in terror. No! It couldn't be someone's head. It was soft. The heavier part was in the middle, but it was too small to be a head.

"Well! Go over there to the Flying Squad. The Inspector is in. The night shift agent must still be asleep."

The sweeper crossed the yard and knocked on a door on which he read: "Flying Squad- Chief Inspector."

A gentle, courteous voice answered him.

"Come in. What's up?"

Inside, he found a brunette young man elegantly dressed, who looked at him with vague eyes. He was still absorbed in some thought or his reading.

"I found this, Inspector... on the steps of San Vito al Pasquirolo..."

"So?"

"There was this letter too."

The inspector read the letter.

"Ok, give it to me."

He took the bundle, removed the pins, looked at them – they were common pins – and opened the newspaper.

A clean, white coat appeared, like those worn by doctors or nurses. The inspector opened the coat and four surgical instruments fell on the table; they were bright, shiny, and sharp.

Nothing else.

The sweeper stood observing.

The inspector took the instruments and examined them one at a time. He recognized a scalpel and then saw some kind of screwdriver, surgical scissors, and a long caliper.

The scalpel had some brown spots. The other tools seemed new.

The inspector rang the bell and a little later the guard appeared.

"Call Sergeant Cruni," he intoned in his courteous voice.

The guard disappeared.

When Cruni arrived, he was still sleepy. He was short and muscular, and his body was too massive for such short legs.

"I am needed, sir?"

"Draw up a report of found objects and register this man's personal data."

"Yes, *Cavaliere*. Please come with me."

then looked at the surgical instruments. He took up the scalpel and examined it closely.

"Blood stains," he murmured.

He got up and locked everything in the closet.

Then he sat back at his desk and took the book he was reading out of the drawer. It was the last novel by Körmendi. He read all sorts of things.

Almost immediately he looked up from the page and stared at the closet. The piece of paper with the strange request was still on the desk.

Who would abandon four surgical instruments, including a blood-spotted scalpel and a white coat?

He examined the handwritten note. It was written quickly with a fountain pen. It didn't look fake: whoever wrote it was serious. At the very least, they were in a hurry.

He dropped the note on the desk and glanced at the clock: it was almost seven. He began reading aloud, with a bitter smile, the calendar in front of him:

"At 8:30 AM the Sun enters the sign of Aries... and at 2:28 PM Spring begins."

He tore the page from the calendar and March 21 appeared, completely blank.

"Aries..." he murmured again. "If only I believed in horoscopes!"

Then he shrugged. The truth was, he did believe in horoscopes as well as in many more things, including misfortune, telepathy, and premonitions. He was superstitious.

Why did he receive four surgical instruments and a white coat on the very first day of Spring?

What should he do? Nothing, obviously. The letter and the bundle could not force him to do anything, neither as a police inspector nor as a man. But he could think about it, of course.

The newspaper in which they had been wrapped was the *Corriere* of March 20th. He read it and found nothing special. He folded it and put it in the drawer.

In the afternoon, when he came back to his office, he would show the instruments to a doctor to find out more about them. And then he would wait. Nothing else had happened, or maybe something was happening or could have happened already.

Maybe a murder?

No! He closed the book and put it in the drawer, then got up, put on his overcoat, grabbed his hat and, when he reached the door, he turned off the light.

From the arch facing the courtyard, through the dirty railing and the closed, even dirtier windows, a pale daylight came in.

De Vincenzi sighed. He had become accustomed to going to bed when the sun was already high, for he spent most nights at the police station, working or reading. Yet, he sighed every morning. Because every morning, at the sight of the new day, he thought of the country house, in the Ossola, where he was born, and where his mother still lived, with the hens, the dogs and the maid. He would have been so glad to join his mother. He was young, not even thirty-five, yet he felt old. He had fought in the war. And he had a contemplative spirit. Some of his boarding school mates called him a poet to make fun of him. He was so much a poet, that he became a police inspector...

He was about to open the door to leave when the phone rang. He winced. Why now?!

Want to know what happens next?

Get your digital copy of **Death in a Bookstore** *at Kazabo.com, Amazon or Kobo. Order the print edition from your local bookstore or on Amazon.*

Film Junkie's
Guide to
North Carolina

Film Junkie's Guide to North Carolina

Connie Nelson
and
Floyd Harris

John F. Blair, Publisher   Winston-Salem, North Carolina

*The paper in this book meets the guidelines
for permanence and durability of the Committee on
Production Guidelines for Book Longevity
of the Council on Library Resources.*

*Design by Debra Long Hampton
Cover image -
Greensboro's Carolina Theatre © NyghtFalcon Photography*

Library of Congress Cataloging-in-Publication Data
Nelson, Connie, 1959–
Film junkie's guide to North Carolina / by Connie Nelson and Floyd Harris.
p.   cm.
Includes index.
ISBN 0-89587-269-2 (alk. paper)
1. Motion picture locations—North Carolina.   2. Television program
locations—North Carolina. 3. Actors—Homes and haunts—North
Carolina. 4. North Carolina—Description and travel.   I. Harris, Floyd,
1959– II. Title.
PN1995.67.N74N45   2004
384'.8'09756—dc22
2004003914

The authors wish to dedicate
Film Junkie's Guide to North Carolina
to their significant others, families, and friends.

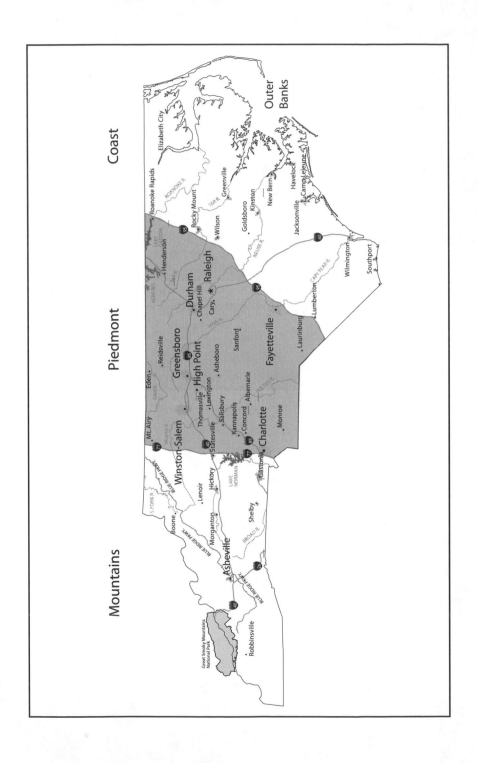

Contents

The Coast

The Piedmont

THE TRIANGLE   153

THE TRIAD   213

The Mountains

Preface

Welcome to *Film Junkie's Guide to North Carolina*, a lively look at some Tar Heel locations through a prism that blends history with pop culture. In writing this book, we believe we have broken new ground. Very few comprehensive resources exist for North Carolina film locations, and none in this format. We believe this to be the first travel guide based on movie locations in our great state.

The subjects herein are touched by Hollywood glamour and independent and indigenous filmmaking spunk. You'll also find a sprinkling of favorite haunts and hangouts frequented by visiting stars and celebrities. It's a guide for movie fans who want to visit particular locations, as well as an entertaining companion for "Hey, isn't that . . . ?" armchair travelers watching a favorite film at the theatre or at home. Maybe we'll even settle a few bets.

Filmmakers have been visiting North Carolina since the dawn of celluloid. The past 25 or so years have brought in many big-time stars and directors. Independent filmmaking and the home-grown industry have blossomed. We've aimed for a nice mix of Oscar® winners and obscure gems, cult classics and documentaries. We've also presented both the prominent locations and a few off the beaten path. You'll discover locations where there's a lot to see and do (downtown Wilmington and Lowe's Motor Speedway) and a few where the circus has definitely left town (the *Sleeping with the Enemy* house, the *Last of the Mohicans* fort, and the *Black Knight* castle). Some locations boast of the movies made there (Buckner Hill Plantation, Lake Lure, and Durham Bulls Athletic Park). Many are wonderful attractions in their own right (Biltmore House, the Battleship *North Carolina*, and Old Salem). There are even movie studios in the mountains (Blue Ridge Motion Pictures) and on the coast (EUE/Screen Gems Studios) that offer guided tours. In the case of those locations that are in neighborhoods or private residences, please honor trespassing laws.

Of course, everyone's interested in how and where the stars tasted the local culture. We've provided a healthy sampling of where a star or two may have eaten, shopped, spent the night, or generally hung out. And we've attempted to do so with tact and respect. It goes without saying that said stars will probably not be there when you visit—and if they are, please be respectful.

North Carolina has an impressive list of film locations. If we've left out your favorite, we'll try to catch it next time. You'll also find a subjective comment or two on the various films. These opinions are ours. We're film junkies who are justifiably proud of North Carolina filmmaking. We'll see you at the movies. In the meantime, here are a few facts to ponder.

•In 2003, Governor Mike Easley announced that for the 18th consecutive year, North Carolina ranked third in the nation (behind California and New York) among filmmaking states, based on direct revenues derived from production.

•Since the North Carolina Film Commission was formed in 1980, the state has attracted over 600 features, nine network television series, and more than $6 billion in production revenue. That's a return of more than $1,000 for every dollar spent by the agency.

•Filmmakers and visitors seek similar qualities in choosing destinations. From the mountains to the coast and across the Piedmont, North Carolina offers an irresistible package: a moderate climate with four distinct seasons; a variety of landscapes and architectural styles; unique attractions and locations; excellent accommodations and restaurants; abundant natural beauty; and good old-fashioned Southern hospitality. Truly, nothing could be finer.

It is our hope that you will enjoy *Film Junkie's Guide to North Carolina* not only as a travel guide but also as an entertaining account of North Carolina pop culture. While we have tried to be as comprehensive as possible, many locations are not included. Given space constraints, we have had to make some very difficult decisions regarding cuts. And please know that we have made every effort to ensure accuracy. However, references were often contradictory. Some research is based on oral history, and memories do fade. We will try to correct any errors in future editions.

If you know of movie locations or star tracks that we have overlooked, or if you notice an error in this guide, please write to the publisher so we can consider it for a future edition.

The entries in this guide should not be considered endorsements or recommendations, but merely as useful information for exploring North Carolina's film connections.

Film Junkie's Guide to North Carolina is divided into three sections: The Coast (east of I-95), The Piedmont (west of I-95 and east of I-77), and The Mountains (west of I-77). Credits in italics indicate a feature film, while credits in quotation marks indicate a television production. *Locations*, of course, are places where filming has occurred; *Star Tracks* indicate places celebrities have frequented; the book's sidebars contain information related to movies or celebrities; *Film Junkie Trivia* includes little-known movie facts.

A film junkie is defined as one who derives inordinate pleasure from, or is dependent upon, contact with or knowledge of motion pictures and people or places associated with the motion-picture industry.

All right, film junkies, prepare for a 432-page fix!

Acknowledgments

Without the assistance of film commissioners and location managers, this book would not have been possible. Throughout our research, we relied heavily on their input. As a result, we have gained a much deeper understanding of and respect for the talents of good location managers. They, along with directors and cinematographers, are largely responsible for the look of a film. It's truly a crime that their names appear buried in the film credits. So, the next time you're watching the credits roll, give a nod to the unsung heroes of the film industry.

We'd like to thank location managers E. Michael Hewett, Geoffrey Ryan, Doug Whitley, Lance Holland, and Vick Griffin; North Carolina film commissioner Bill Arnold; Randy Schumacher and Paula Wyrick of the North Carolina Film Office; the staff of the North Carolina Division of Tourism, Film and Sports Development, especially photographer *extraordinaire* Bill Russ; and film-office directors Johnny Griffin of the Wilmington Regional Film Commission, Mary Nell Webb, formerly of the Western North Carolina Regional Film Commission, Beth Petty of the Charlotte Regional Film Office, and

Rebecca Clark of the Piedmont Triad Film Commission. We also owe special thanks to Zenda Douglas of the Durham Convention and Visitors Bureau; Laura Chase of the Asheville Convention and Visitors Bureau; Judith Grizzel of the Cape Fear Coast Convention and Visitors Bureau; Julie Pharr of the Greater Mount Airy Chamber of Commerce; and Lynn Fuhler of the Winston-Salem Convention and Visitors Bureau. Special thank-yous go to Brad Chappell and Terry Grimes of Buckner Hill Plantation; Sarah Thomas of Biltmore Estate; Marcia Greene of the Chetola Resort; Kim Lyons of Great Smoky Mountains Railroad; Hugh and Catherine Morton of Grandfather Mountain; Elaine "Lainie" Johnston of Wild Bunch Films; Jay Winer of the Grove Park Inn; Karen Moon of the University of North Carolina; Marla Carpenter of the North Carolina School of the Arts; the staff at Old Salem; Bob Cox at New Hanover County Public Library; Rick Gregory; Falcon at NyghtFalcon Photography; and a cast of thousands.

Those who assisted with various aspects of the project include E. Michael Hewett (of Locations . . . +, Inc.), Ann Formy-Duval, Ann J. Harris, William T. Strickland, and intellectual property attorney William J. Mason. We also appreciate the efforts of the staff of John F. Blair, Publisher, especially President Carolyn Sakowski, editor Steve Kirk, Director of Design and Production Debbie Hampton, and Vice President of Sales and Marketing Anne Waters. A word of thanks is also due to film historian Jenny Henderson for writing *The North Carolina Filmography*, the most comprehensive resource on North Carolina film history to date. And most of all, we give our heartfelt thanks to the family and friends whose love and support allowed us to take on and complete this book.

SCENE: *The Coast*

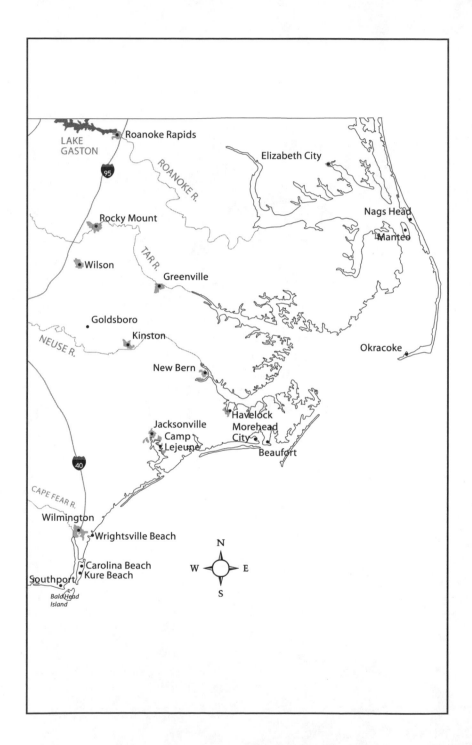

Temporary medieval castle on the EUE/Screen Gems backlot
for the Martin Lawrence comedy *Black Knight*
COURTESY OF CAPE FEAR COAST CONVENTION AND VISITORS BUREAU

*O*ne could say that Hollywood discovered North Carolina's coast by accident, but that its transformation into a movie mecca was by design. Thanks to the coast's urban, rural, beach, and marsh settings, nearly any look is possible. All that's missing is mountains—and they're closer than you think.

Hollywood came calling in the early 1980s, when filmmakers Dino De Laurentiis and Frank Capra, Jr., were scouting locations for Stephen King's *Firestarter*. They wanted a secluded mansion like one Capra saw on a *Southern Accents* magazine cover featuring Orton Plantation, which was constructed around 1725. A five-state search prompted Capra and director Mark L. Lester to meet Orton's owners, and a legacy began. De Laurentiis imported his crew members from Los Angeles, New York, and Italy. He soon built DEG (De Laurentiis Entertainment Group) Studios, a 32-acre moviemaking complex in Wilmington. For four years, DEG produced films including *Blue Velvet, King Kong Lives*, and *Cat's Eye*, among others. Carolco Studios owned the facility from 1989 until 1996, and EUE/Screen Gems Studios has owned it since then, staking its claim as the largest working movie production facility east of Hollywood.

While Dino was discovering Wilmington's charms, a movement to revitalize and preserve downtown was under way, and I-40 was nearing completion. These factors positioned the city for a filmmaking boom. And boom it did.

But it takes more than a sound stage to make a film center. In 1994, the Wilmington Regional Film Commission, Inc., was formed as a liaison organization serving the production industry and the community in an 11-county region. Two additional film commissions formed in other coastal regions—the Global Transpark office serves 13 counties, while the Northeast Regional Film Commission serves 17 northeastern counties. Collectively, these organizations represent 41 of North Carolina's 100 counties.

While this section covers all 350-plus miles of the state's coast, the lion's share of production takes place in the Wilmington region, a.k.a. "Wilmywood." Direct film expenditures in the area since 1983 number in the hundreds of millions of dollars. In 2002, film revenue for Wilmington was $51 million. Impressed? That was actually considered a soft year, especially when compared to 1993's take of $361 million.

Established in 1739, the port city of Wilmington has a population of over 90,000. It offers versatile urban, suburban, and recreational settings, intriguing streetscapes, and a historic river front, as seen in *Domestic Disturbance, Rambling Rose,* "Dawson's Creek," "Matlock," and "One Tree Hill," among other productions. Located just 19 miles south, Carolina Beach has an appealing 1930s Art Moderne coastal retro look that has shown up in *The Bedroom Window, New Best Friend,* and *Black Knight,* among other movies. Kure Beach has colorful contemporary homes that saddle up to older cottages and a nostalgic pier; it boasts credits like "Dawson's Creek" and *To Gillian on Her 37th Birthday.* Wrightsville Beach and Figure Eight Island offer celebrity appeal, thanks to their wide beaches, upscale houses, beach cottages, and resorts; they have hosted *Sleeping With the Enemy* and *Divine Secrets of the Ya-Ya Sisterhood.*

Brunswick County's shining stars include Bald Head Island, a ferry-access island with the state's oldest lighthouse, undeveloped beaches, and lush coastal golf links. Winnabow boasts Brunswick Town and the magnificent Orton Plantation. Southport and its picturesque marina have appeared in *Crimes of*

Pender County is where you'll see cotton fields like those in the independent gem *Once Upon A Time . . . When We Were Colored.* The county's sleepy Southern towns, particularly Burgaw, have provided period locations and outdoor settings in *Rambling Rose, The Angel Doll, Divine Secrets of the Ya-Ya Sisterhood,* "American Gothic," "The Summer of Ben Tyler," and "The Runaway."

Duplin County's biggest claim to movie fame is as the plantation setting for Pecan Grove in *Divine Secrets of the Ya-Ya Sisterhood.* Quaint towns like Kenansville, Wallace, and Rose Hill have lured Hollywood with their turn-of-the-20th-century ambiance. Other local credits include *Fall Time* and *Lolita.*

Mainstream film production is less prominent in the central and northern portions of the coast, due to the expense of transporting equipment and crews. However, documentary credits abound in places like Jacksonville/Camp Lejeune and New Bern/Tryon Palace. Although Beaufort appears briefly in *A Walk to Remember,* Carteret County's credits are primarily documentaries about lighthouses, pirates, and shipwrecks.

One might wonder why the picture-perfect Outer Banks have so few credits. The remote islands pose logistical challenges. For this reason, Outer Banks credits are mainly documentaries tracing Orville and Wilbur Wright's first flight, Blackbeard's adventures, English colonists, and shipwrecks. *Brainstorm* showcases Wright Brothers National Memorial, and an early "Matlock" episode filmed in downtown Manteo.

Hollywood frequently calls on the coast for its star qualities, many of which are detailed in this section. Who knows? A chance film crew or celebrity sighting could occur while you're visiting some of the places described in the pages that follow.

For tourist information, contact the Cape Fear Coast Convention and Visitors Bureau (800-222-4757; www.cape-fear.nc.us), North Carolina's Brunswick Islands (800-795-7263; www.ncbrunswick.com), the Southport-Oak Island Chamber of Commerce (910-457-6964), Pender County Tourism (888-576-4756; www.visitpender.com), North Carolina's Crystal Coast (800-786-6962; www.sunnync.com), or the Outer Banks Convention and Visitors Bureau (800-446-6262; www.outerbanks.org).

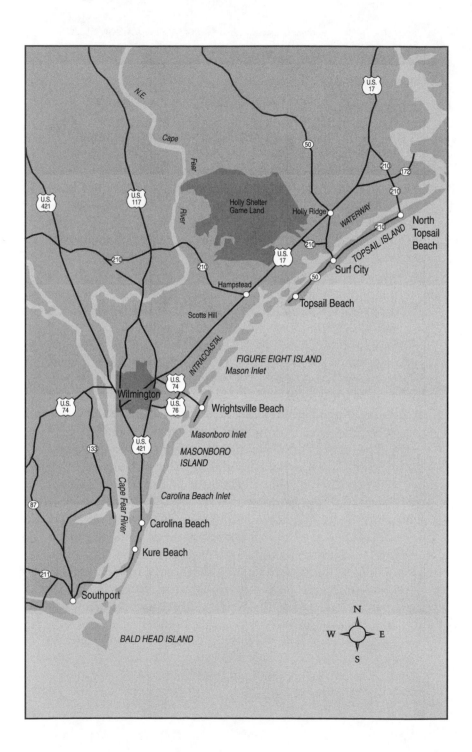

Riverfront Park is a recurring location for
"Dawson's Creek" and other productions.
The Cape Fear Memorial Bridge looms in the background.
PHOTOGRAPH BY C. L. NELSON

Historic Wilmington Locations

Riverfront Park

*The park stretches along Water Street north to Grace Street and
south to Ann Street.*

Since its completion in the early 1990s, Riverfront Park has
appeared in productions such as *New Best Friend, A Walk to Remember, Empire Records,* and "Matlock." It's also where Capeside
teens Pacey (Joshua Jackson) and Andie (Meredith Monroe) first
kiss in the second season of "Dawson's Creek" and where Dawson
(James Van Der Beek) tells Joey (Katie Holmes) that he still
loves her in the show's fifth-season finale. The Capeside Re-
gatta is set here—well, here and at Banks Channel in
Wrightsville Beach. Both camera points of view are matched to
complete the shot.

Located at the foot of Market Street at Water Street, Riverfront Park is a component of Wilmington's Riverwalk. The wooden-plank walkway has benches, a fountain, and a visitor center. The Riverfront Visitor Information Booth appears as a hot dog stand in an early "Dawson's Creek" episode. During the show's fourth season, it appears as a snack bar across from the Capeside Christmas tree. When the show wrapped after six seasons, creator-writer Kevin Williamson and cast members Joshua Jackson, Katie Holmes, Michelle Williams, Kerr Smith, Busy Philipps, Mary-Margaret Humes, and Nina Repeta joined approximately 500 fans, friends, crew members, and community leaders at Riverwalk's Coast Guard dock at Water and Chestnut streets for a community tribute, during which they accepted accolades and keys to the city. In turn, the show's executive producer presented Wilmington's mayor with a Capeside road sign, which was donated to the Cape Fear Museum (see pages 44-45).

Movie sites near Riverfront Park include the Cape Fear Memorial Bridge (see pages 53-54) and the Battleship *North Carolina* (see pages 54-57).

CREDITS

"One Tree Hill" (The WB, 2003-);"Dawson's Creek" (The WB, 1998-2003); *New Best Friend* (2002); *A Walk to Remember* (2002); *Empire Records* (1995); "Matlock" (ABC, 1993-95)

The Icehouse

115 South Water Street. At press time, the venue was closed, but visitors could view its exterior and imagine what a cool juke joint and star track it once was.

Still there in spirit, if not in one of its many incarnations, The Icehouse was one of Wilmington's first icehouses, dating back to the mid-1800s. After refrigeration took its toll on the ice trade, the building housed a variety of other businesses. In 1991, it opened as The Icehouse, an outdoor beer garden along the Cape Fear River. Its rustic no-frills ambiance, magnificent river sunsets, and outdoor stage (the former ice dock) brought in locals, visitors, location managers, and, yes, even celebrities.

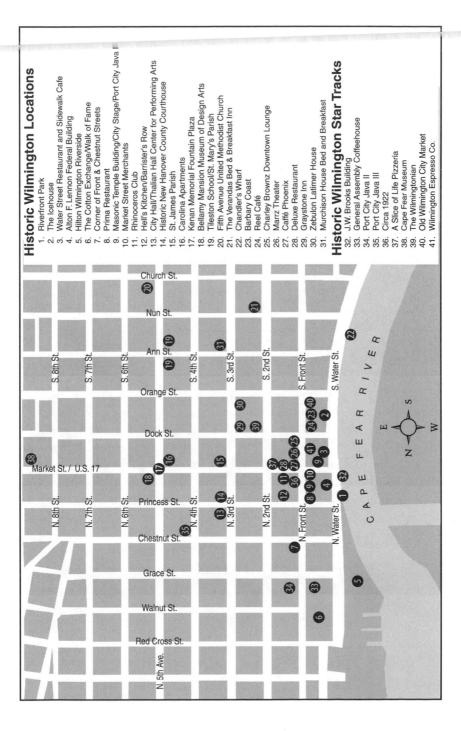

Historic Wilmington Locations

1. Riverfront Park
2. The Icehouse
3. Water Street Restaurant and Sidewalk Cafe
4. Alton F. Lennon Federal Building
5. Hilton Wilmington Riverside
6. The Cotton Exchange/Walk of Fame
7. Corner of Front & Chestnut Streets
8. Prima Restaurant
9. Masonic Temple Building/City Stage/Port City Java
10. Market Street Merchants
11. Rhinoceros Club
12. Hell's Kitchen/Barrister's Row
13. City Hall/Thalian Hall Center for Performing Arts
14. Historic New Hanover County Courthouse
15. St. James Parish
16. Carolina Apartments
17. Kenan Memorial Fountain Plaza
18. Bellamy Mansion Museum of Design Arts
19. Tileston School/St. Mary's Parish
20. Fifth Avenue United Methodist Church
21. The Verandas Bed & Breakfast Inn
22. Chandler's Wharf
23. Barbary Coast
24. Reel Café
25. Charley Brownz Downtown Lounge
26. Marrz Theater
27. Caffé Phoenix
28. Deluxe Restaurant
29. Graystone Inn
30. Zebulon Latimer House
31. Murchison House Bed and Breakfast

Historic Wilmington Star Tracks

32. J.W. Brooks Building
33. General Assembly Coffeehouse
34. Port City Java II
35. Port City Java III
36. Circa 1922
37. A Slice of Life Pizzeria
38. Cape Fear Museum
39. The Wilmingtonian
40. Old Wilmington City Market
41. Wilmington Espresso Co.

Though it has appeared in movies such as *Empire Records* and "Search for Grace," The Icehouse achieved its real screen fame during the first two seasons of "Dawson's Creek." The show retained the actual name of The Icehouse, where Joey Potter (Katie Holmes) worked with her sister, Bessie (Wilmington resident and Shelby native Nina Repeta). Crew members transformed the beer garden into a restaurant, but only from the outside looking in. To maintain the look of Capeside, Massachusetts, Icehouse scenes were matched to scenes filmed at the Dockside Restaurant (see pages 83-84) on the Intracoastal Waterway.

When condos replaced a nearby parking lot and made equipment access a logistical nightmare, scripts were rewritten to burn the show's Icehouse. Shortly thereafter, the legendary venue was up for sale. Given the building's current disrepair, locals lament what once was. Film junkies and Creekheads stop by for photo opportunities.

The Icehouse was a place where locals could sometimes hang out with the stars. Celebrity sightings included media mogul Ted Turner, Jane Fonda, Edward James Olmos (best known for his role on "Miami Vice"), William Baldwin (*Virus*), David Carradine, Dennis Hopper (*Blue Velvet; Super Mario Brothers*), Anthony LaPaglia (*Empire Records*), the late director Leo Penn ("Matlock"), and the cast of "Dawson's Creek." Performer Taj Mahal even joined in on a jam session while filming *Once Upon a Time . . . When We Were Colored*. When The Icehouse served as a base camp for *The Hudsucker Proxy*, passersby were able to catch glimpses of Paul Newman and Tim Robbins.

At press time, the future of The Icehouse was unknown. Regardless of its fate, its legacy lives on in the minds of former Icehouse patrons . . . and film junkies.

CREDITS

"Dawson's Creek" (The WB, 1998-2003); *Empire Records* (1995); "Search for Grace" (CBS, 1994)

Water Street Restaurant doubles as
Leery's Fresh Fish on "Dawson's Creek."
COURTESY OF CAPE FEAR COAST CONVENTION AND VISITORS BUREAU

Water Street Restaurant & Sidewalk Café

5 South Water Street (910-343-0012). The restaurant is open from 11:30 A.M. to 10 P.M. Sunday through Thursday and from 11:30 A.M. to midnight on Friday and Saturday; call for winter hours.

Rustic nautical ambiance makes Water Street Restaurant & Sidewalk Café a premier film location and hangout. Its outdoor waterfront dining area provides an added camera attraction. This popular restaurant and live music venue's biggest claim to fame is as Leery's Fresh Fish on "Dawson's Creek." Pat the good-luck tiger as you enter and take your time admiring the exposed beams, wood floors, and nautical artifacts so you'll recognize them in episodes aired during seasons three through six. Also noteworthy is the wall of fame, where Chuck Liese's paintings of Water Street's musicians hang.

Andie MacDowell (*Shadrach; Muppets From Space*) and her preschool daughter enjoyed dinner and live flamenco guitar here. Other celebrity customers have included Patrick Swayze (*Black Dog*), Kelly McGillis ("In the Best of Families: Marriage, Pride, Madness"), Nina Repeta (Bessie on "Dawson's Creek"), and Jordan Rhodes ("Matlock"). Actor Tom Skerritt bears a striking resemblance to owner Harper Peterson, who has served as Wilmington's mayor. The two actually met during the filming of "What the Deaf Man Heard." Former "Days of Our Lives" star Joe Gallison (Dr. Neil Curtis) now lives in Wilmington and occasionally stops by.

CREDITS

"Dawson's Creek" (The WB, 1998-2003)

Alton F. Lennon Federal Building

The building is at the south corner of Water and Princess streets. You'll have to limit yourself to an exterior view, due to security restrictions.

Constructed around 1916, the stately Alton F. Lennon Federal Building comes as something of a shock to first-timers strolling downtown Wilmington's waterfront walkways and cobblestone streets. The vague Charleston/Savannah feel is suddenly interrupted by an imposing building that would look more at home in Washington, D.C.—or maybe 1939 Chicago, as in George Lucas's comical whodunit *Radioland Murders*, or Albany, New York, as in Shirley MacLaine's directorial debut, *The Dress Code*. This is just one example of the diversity that filmmakers find so appealing about Wilmington.

The three-story Neoclassical Revival stone structure serves as a federal courthouse in real life. Its architectural style has worked especially well in films like the original *Manhunter*. Tight shots from the Princess Street and Market Street entrances were

Shows such as "Matlock" achieve a big-city look when filming outside the Alton F. Lennon Federal Building.
PHOTOGRAPH BY C. L. NELSON

matched with long shots of federal buildings in the nation's capital. *Manhunter*, based on the novel *Red Dragon* by Thomas Harris, was the first of the Hannibal Lecter films. The film's 2002 remake filmed elsewhere. However, the third movie in the series, *Hannibal*, filmed in Asheville.

The prominent courthouse steps are just yards from the Cape Fear River. One of the most striking features is the fountain at the top of the steps, easily recognizable in establishing shots on "Matlock," starring North Carolina native Andy Griffith. The fountain is also the setting for Shannen Doherty's impulsive dance in "A Burning Passion: The Margaret Mitchell Story."

Other productions have used the interior lobby and hallways; however, it took Superman, Commissioner Gordon, and a persuasive location manager to film in a courtroom on a weekday. The climactic courtroom scene in Hallmark's "The Runaway" features Dean Cain of "Lois & Clark" fame, Pat Hingle of *Batman* fame, and North Carolina poet and director Maya Angelou. Another Hallmark production, "The Locket," filmed in the corridors.

CREDITS

New Best Friend (2002); "The Locket" (Hallmark/CBS, 2002); *The Dress Code* (2000); "The Runaway" (Hallmark/CBS, 2000); "Nathan Dixon" (CBS pilot, 1999); "CI5: The New Professionals" (BBC, 1998); "The Perfect Crime" (USA, 1997); "What the Deaf Man Heard" (Hallmark/CBS, 1997); "Matlock" (ABC, 1993-95); *Radioland Murders* (1994); "Simple Justice" (PBS, 1993); "A Burning Passion: The Margaret Mitchell Story" (NBC, 1994); *Everybody Wins* (1990); *Manhunter* (1986)

Hilton Wilmington Riverside

301 North Water Street (*800-HILTONS or 910-763-5900; www.wilmingtonhilton.com*)

The Hilton Wilmington Riverside stars as the city's largest river-front hotel. During the filming of *Domestic Disturbance*, John Travolta rented a suite for relaxing between scenes. Imagine the staff's delight when the Hollywood A-lister interrupted a meeting to thank employees for their hospitality!

Film junkies will recognize the red awning on the north-side entrance from the scene in *Domestic Disturbance* when Frank Morrison's (John Travolta's) son Danny (Matthew O'Leary), ex-wife Susan (Teri Polo), and Rick Barnes (Vince Vaughn) exit to find Frank waiting in his truck. A parking-lot scuffle ensues, producing the wallet that helps Frank nail Rick.

The fifth and sixth seasons of "Dawson's Creek" showcase the hotel's parking lot, ballroom, lobby, bar, lobby bathroom, and third-floor guest suites. The one-season road-trip series "Going to California" used the premises for a bachelor-party scene featuring former MTV host and Playboy Playmate Jenny McCarthy, who makes a guest appearance as Amber Beamis in the episode called "The Big Padoodle."

Celebrity guests at the Hilton have included James Garner (*Divine Secrets of the Ya-Ya Sisterhood*); Paul Newman (*The Hudsucker Proxy*); Sony Pictures television executives; and Coastal Classic Celebrity Golf Tournament guests Jason Gedrick (*Summer Catch*, "Dare to Love"); Howdy Doody's pal, Buffalo Bob Smith; and Richard "Shaft" Roundtree.

CREDITS

"Dawson's Creek" (The WB, 1998-2003); "Going to California" (Showtime, 2001); *Domestic Disturbance* (2001); "Something Borrowed, Something Blue" (CBS, 1997); commercials

The Cotton Exchange/Walk of Fame

308-316 *North Front Street (910-343-9896). The Cotton Exchange is open from* 10 A.M. *to* 5:30 P.M. *Monday through Saturday and from* 1 P.M. *to* 5 P.M. *on Sunday. Restaurant hours vary. Parking is free for customers.*

Visitors to the Cotton Exchange look down—not up—to see stars.

The promenade in the parking lot flaunts brass stars honoring celebrities with ties to Wilmington, including producer and

EUE/Screen Gems Studios president Frank Capra, Jr., journalist and broadcaster David Brinkley, musician Charlie Daniels, author Robert Ruark, football star Roman Gabriel, tennis pioneer Althea Gibson, and artists Minnie Evans and Claude Howell. The parking lot's screen credits include a "Dawson's Creek" fifth-season scene in which Pacey's (Joshua Jackson's) car breaks down and a sixth-season confrontation between Pacey and Audrey (Busy Philipps).

The Cotton Exchange was constructed around 1900. In the mid-1970s, the former cotton warehouse became the state's first downtown shopping complex to effectively adapt and utilize existing buildings. Visiting celebrities like William Baldwin (*Virus*), Dustin Hoffman (*Billy Bathgate*), John Travolta (*Domestic Disturbance*), Nick Nolte (*Weeds*), and Dennis Hopper (*Blue Velvet; Super Mario Brothers*) haven't been able to resist browsing the 30-plus specialty shops and eateries housed in eight restored buildings.

The side entrance facing Grace Street serves as a bus station in a snowy episode of "Matlock." Academy Award® winner Halle Berry appears in a scene with local jazz musicians in Paddy's Hollow, an Irish pub and restaurant, in "Oprah Winfrey Presents: The Wedding."

CREDITS

The Italian Bistro appears in "The Locket" (Hallmark/CBS, 2002). Paddy's Hollow appears in "Oprah Winfrey Presents: The Wedding" (ABC, 1998) and "Windmills of the Gods" (CBS, 1988). The Cotton Exchange has also served as a location for "Dawson's Creek" (The WB, 1998-2003); "Matlock" (ABC, 1993-95); "Stompin' at the Savoy" (CBS, 1992); and *Teenage Mutant Ninja Turtles* (1990).

Corner of Front and Chestnut Streets

Since the advent of Wilmington's film industry, the corner of Front and Chestnut streets has received its share of camera time. Commanding attention are some of the city's most historic and versatile buildings.

The Murchison-First Union Building stands at the north-west corner of the intersection. Constructed around 1913, this 11-story brick-and-stone Neoclassical Revival skyscraper is the tallest in downtown Wilmington. Its tenants include Pender's Café, a 1950s-style diner that appears in an early episode of "Dawson's Creek." The outside of the building is covered with movie snow in Truman Capote's "One Christmas." The ground floor appears in "The Stepford Husbands," "Nathan Dixon," and "The Perfect Crime." Pender's Café is located at 205 North Front Street. It is open from 8 A.M. to 3 P.M. Monday through Friday. For information, call 910-762-4065.

The Murchison National Bank Building/ACME Building is at the northeast corner of Front and Chestnut. Built around 1902, this Neo-Renaissance structure made of blond brick serves as the Chicago Police Department in *Raw Deal*, starring Arnold Schwarzenegger, and as the Southport Police Station in *Domestic Disturbance*. Film junkies will recognize it in the latter film in

Crews set up at the corner of Front and Chestnut streets for the scene at the "Southport Police Station" in *Domestic Disturbance*.
PHOTOGRAPH BY C. L. NELSON

the scene in which Frank Morrison (John Travolta) threatens Rick Barnes (Vince Vaughn) if he harms his son. Another room in the building appears as Sidda Walker's (Sandra Bullock's) New York City apartment in *Divine Secrets of the Ya-Ya Sisterhood*. Among the building's other credits are "The Twilight Zone: Rod Serling's Lost Classics," "Against Her Will: The Carrie Buck Story," *Tune in Tomorrow*, and *Weekend at Bernie's*. You'll have to limit yourself to an exterior view, since the building is privately owned.

The United States Post Office, located at the intersection's southeast corner, is an example of the Neoclassical Revival style favored by the federal government during the 1930s. This building demonstrates how a creative location manager can maximize a location's potential. In "The Locket," its exterior appears as the Wilmington Police Station, the lobby as a hospital pharmacy, the basement as a jail, and the second-floor hallway as a veterans' hospital. It is used as a police station in "Freedom Song" and as a mental ward in "Dare to Love." Other credits include "A Mother's Instinct" and "Terror on Highway 91." The downstairs counter is open from 9 A.M. to 5 P.M. Monday through Friday and from 9 A.M. to noon on Saturday.

CREDITS

"Dawson's Creek" (The WB, 1998-2003); *Divine Secrets of the Ya-Ya Sisterhood* (2002); "The Locket" (Hallmark/CBS, 2002); *Domestic Disturbance* (2001); "Freedom Song" (TNT, 2000); "Nathan Dixon" (CBS pilot, 1999); "The Perfect Crime" (USA, 1997); "A Mother's Instinct" (CBS, 1996); "The Stepford Husbands" (CBS, 1996); "Dare to Love" (ABC/Lifetime, 1995); "One Christmas" (CBS, 1994); "The Twilight Zone: Rod Serling's Lost Classics" (CBS, 1994); "Against Her Will: The Carrie Buck Story" (Lifetime, 1994); *Tune in Tomorrow* (1990); *Weekend at Bernie's* (1989); "Terror on Highway 91" (CBS, 1989); *Raw Deal* (1986)

Prima Restaurant

35 North Front Street (910-762-7700). The restaurant opens daily at 5 P.M.

Prima, one of downtown Wilmington's newest restaurants, is a veteran film location. It appears at least once per season in

"Dawson's Creek," either as an upscale eatery or lounge or as a trendy coffee shop decorated with blue mannequin legs in the fifth season. In the psychological teen thriller *New Best Friend*, it's the restaurant where Alicia (Mia Kirshner) dines with Hadley's father. In *Divine Secrets of the Ya-Ya Sisterhood*, it's the hip and noisy New York bar and restaurant where Siddalee (Sandra Bullock) joins the Ya-Yas for dinner and a rather potent drink.

When it's not a movie location, Prima is an upscale eatery serving creative and innovative American cuisine. The building was originally a bank; the ladies' room is located in an old vault. The structure once housed Paleo Sun Café/Atomic Bar, where recording artists such as The Dirty Dozen Brass Band performed.

CREDITS

The building serves as a medical clinic in "Labor of Love: The Arlette Schweitzer Story" (CBS, 1993). You can also see it in "Dawson's Creek" (The WB, 1998-2003); *New Best Friend* (2002); and *Divine Secrets of the Ya-Ya Sisterhood* (2002).

Masonic Temple Building
17-21 North Front Street. Hours vary for the shops, eateries, theatre, and club.

What do actor Dennis Hopper and President William Howard Taft have in common? Each crossed the threshold of Wilmington's Masonic Temple Building, built around 1898. Hopper purchased the abandoned building 83 years after Taft's visit in 1909. His plan to convert the structure into a visual and performing-arts complex never materialized.

Finely carved Masonic symbols adorn the clay-colored stone exterior of the five-story Romanesque Revival building. Today, a thriving coffeehouse and retail shops occupy the street level.

The fourth-floor ballroom has appeared in productions such as *The Road to Wellville*. The recently renovated fifth-floor Masonic theatre retains its original stage, seating, and proscenium arch. The venerable stage is the setting for the school play in *A Walk to Remember*, in which Jamie (pop singer Mandy Moore)

Over 100 years old, the Masonic Temple Building (once owned by Dennis Hopper) still holds its own in "A Different Kind of Christmas" (pictured here), *A Walk to Remember*, and other films.
COURTESY OF E. MICHAEL HEWETT, LOCATIONS . . . +, INC.

and Landon (Shane West of "Once and Again") enjoy their first kiss. Known as City Stage, the venue hosts theatrical productions, concerts, screenings, and film festivals (see pages 68-69). "Dawson's Creek" stars Michelle Williams (Jen) and Mary Beth Peil (Grams) performed onstage here in a 2002 production of *The Vagina Monologues*. Level Five, a fifth-floor private rooftop club overlooking the river, has hosted parties for *Divine Secrets of the Ya-Ya Sisterhood* and *A Walk to Remember*.

Dennis Hopper also owned the building next door, which has housed several businesses, including a fondly remembered gym favored by *Raw Deal* star and future California governor Arnold Schwarzenegger.

CREDITS

The Chester Story (2003); *A Walk to Remember* (2002); A Different Kind of Christmas" (Lifetime, 1996); "The Twilight Zone: Rod Serling's Lost Classics" (CBS, 1994); *The Road to Wellville* (1994)

Market Street dressed as turn-of-the-century Atlanta for
"A Burning Passion: The Margaret Mitchell Story."
COURTESY OF E. MICHAEL HEWETT, LOCATIONS . . . +, INC.

Market Street Merchants

*This stretch of Market Street is located between Water and Front
streets. Shop hours vary. Walking tours of downtown are
available. For tourist information, call 800-222-4757 or 910-
341-4030 or visit www.cape-fear.nc.us.*

> *"The town of Capeside is as much a part of the story as
> the characters. . . . I fell in love with the look of it—like
> Market Street and Water Street."*
> Paul Stupin, executive producer,
> "Dawson's Creek," *Reel Carolina*,
> October 1997

The shops and restaurants on Market Street between Front
and Water streets lend an urban commercial feel dating back to
the 1800s. Two to four stories in height, the buildings were
intended for mixed retail, wholesale, and residential use. Their
proximity to the river and varying architectural styles make them
attractive to merchants, residents, and filmmakers.

Located at 2 Market Street, Roy's Riverboat Landing has a
colorful, distinctive exterior that livens up the street scene. Andie

MacDowell (*Shadrach*) once dined on the same wrought-iron balcony where *Dream a Little Dream* filmed. The second-floor balconies also appear in an early episode of "Dawson's Creek" as employees brace for a hurricane. During the fifth season, the front window seats pose as a coffeehouse. Other credits include *From the Hip*, starring Judd Nelson. Open for lunch and dinner daily, Roy's has a reputation for excellent food, good service, and Southern hospitality. For information, call 910-763-7227.

Island Passage Elixir, located at 4 Market Street, is a hip specialty shop that offers clothing, accessories, and handmade soaps. It appears in the "Dawson's Creek" first-season episode entitled "Full Moon Rising." For information about Island Passage Elixir, call 910-762-0484.

CD Alley, at 8 Market Street, is referred to as "that funky CD store" by Joey (Katie Holmes) in the fifth-season finale of "Dawson's Creek." This independent music retailer recurs as a Capeside music store. To contact CD Alley, call 910-762-4003.

Located at 1 North Front Street, Tom's Drug Co. has been downtown Wilmington's only pharmacy since 1932. It is a recurring location in episodes of "Dawson's Creek." Tom's friendly longtime employees welcome fans of the show, who stop by almost daily to take pictures of the independently owned drugstore. For information, call 910-762-3391.

CREDITS

"Dawson's Creek" (The WB, 1998-2003); *"A Burning Passion: The Margaret Mitchell Story"* (NBC, 1994); *Dream a Little Dream* (1989); *From the Hip* (1987)

The Rhinoceros Club

125 Market Street (910-763-2582). The club is open to members and guests daily from 4 P.M. to 2 A.M. Membership costs $15 annually.

Watching over patrons at this club is a rhinoceros head that has seen it all, from locals making the scene to stars making movies, from Ashley Judd singing karaoke tunes to John Travolta's character crying the blues after the custody hearing in *Domestic Disturbance*.

One of the city's few remaining Gothic Revival structures, the Rhinoceros Club is located in the St. John's Masonic Hall building, constructed around 1841. The building's celebrity karma began during the 1840s, when it hosted receptions for dignitaries such as Daniel Webster and President James K. Polk.

The club was established in 1996. Its first silver-screen credit was in the *Domestic Disturbance* bar scene. Its original wooden floors, antique bar, and turn-of-the-20th-century ceiling fans give the Rhino its big-city ambiance in fifth-season episodes of "Dawson's Creek."

The Wilmington club's celebrity guests have included William Baldwin (*Virus*), Vince Vaughn (*Domestic Disturbance*), Mitchell Laurance ("Dawson's Creek"; "Matlock"), John O'Hurley (best known as Mr. Peterman in "Seinfeld"), Richard "Shaft" Roundtree, and Joshua Jackson and other "Dawson's Creek" cast and crew.

CREDITS

Stateside (2004); "Dawson's Creek" (The WB, 1998-2003); *Ball of Wax* (2003); *Domestic Disturbance* (2001); *Takedown* (2000)

Hell's Kitchen/Barrister's Row

Located on Princess Street between Front and Third streets. Business hours vary. Hell's Kitchen, at 118 Princess Street, opens Monday through Friday at 11:30 p.m.; Saturday and Sunday at 5 p.m. For information, call 910-763-4133.

Within weeks after the final "Dawson's Creek" episode aired, a savvy restaurateur opened this establishment in the location where the show filmed its Hell's Kitchen scenes in season six. The real deal retains the same rustic look and dive-like atmosphere; about 80 percent of its furnishings and props are from the show. It's so true to the "Dawson's Creek" set that you almost expect Joey (Katie Holmes) to serve you while Audrey (Busy Philipps) and other members of the Hell's Belles band take center stage. The menu items that cost $6.66 include burgers, wings, sandwiches, and burritos. Interestingly, the building also appears in seasons two through four as Mollye's Market, a Capeside hangout named for the business that formerly occupied the space. Film junkies will want to stop in for a dose of pub fare, spirits, and "Dawson's Creek" nostalgia.

Hell's Kitchen is one of several businesses on Princess Street, Wilmington's most scenic "legal" street. Cinematographers needing law and bail bondsmen's offices set up their shots here between Second and Third streets. Dubbed "Barrister's Row" by filmmakers, this stretch has made appearances in television shows like "Matlock." The runaway hula hoop in *The Hudsucker Proxy* rolls merrily along Princess Street.

CREDITS

"Dawson's Creek" (The WB, 1998-2003); "Matlock" (ABC, 1993-95); *The Hudsucker Proxy* (1994); *Everybody Wins* (1990); *Weeds* (1987)

City Hall/Thalian Hall Center for the Performing Arts

310 Chestnut Street (Box office: 800-523-2820 or 910-343-3664; www.thalianhall.com). Guided tours are offered by appointment Monday through Friday from 9 A.M. to 5 P.M.; a fee is charged. Self-guided tours are also available. For tour information, call 910-343-3660.

A grand theatre palace constructed in the 1850s, City Hall/Thalian Hall is an architectural treasure listed on the National Register of Historic Places. Built largely by free and enslaved African-American craftsmen, it is a stunning example of Italianate and Classical Revival architecture.

Long before Hollywood directors discovered Thalian Hall, its ornately framed stage attracted stars of the golden age of theatre. The original drop curtain still hangs in the lobby alongside a photo gallery of famous performers who appeared here many years ago, including Maurice Barrymore (father of Lionel, John, and Ethel), Oscar Wilde, James O'Neill (father of playwright Eugene), and Lillian Russell.

Thalian Hall's interior has served as Capeside's Rialto Theater in "Dawson's Creek," as an Atlanta theatre in episodes of

Watching a movie while making a movie—this scene shot inside
Thalian Hall features young actors Cody Newton (*l*) and
Michael Welch (*r*) in *The Angel Doll.*
PHOTOGRAPH BY JAMES BRIDGES, © ANGEL DOLL PRODUCTIONS, 2000

"Matlock," as a New York theatre in *The Dress Code*, and as the
theatrical setting for Siddalee's (Sandra Bullock's) interview with
a *Time* reporter (Wilmington's Barbara Weetman) in *Divine Secrets of the Ya-Ya Sisterhood.*

Today, Thalian Hall is a showcase venue for traveling and
local troupes such as the Thalian Association; established in
1788, the association is one of the nation's oldest community
theatre companies. Transplanted celebrity residents Pat Hingle
(Commissioner Gordon in *Batman*) and Joe Gallison (Dr. Neil
Curtis in "Days of Our Lives") perform here, and Linda Lavin
(from TV's "Alice") and Screen Gems Studios president Frank
Capra, Jr. (son of the legendary director), have taken an occasional directing turn.

Thalian also serves as Wilmington's premier art-house movie
venue, offering bimonthly cinematique screenings.

CREDITS

You can spot Thalian Hall's outside steps in the fight scenes in
"Freedom Song" (TNT, 2000) and in the ballroom scene for the
Fancy Dress Christmas Gala in *The Hudsucker Proxy* (1994). The
building also appears in *The Angel Doll* (2003); "Dawson's Creek"
(The WB, 1998-2003); *Divine Secrets of the Ya-Ya Sisterhood* (2002);
The Dress Code (2000); *Shadrach* (1998); "The Ditchdigger's Daugh-

ters" (Family Channel, 1997); "A Different Kind of Christmas" (Lifetime, 1996); "The Twilight Zone: Rod Serling's Lost Classics" (CBS, 1994); "A Burning Passion: The Margaret Mitchell Story" (NBC, 1994); "Matlock" (ABC, 1993-95); "The Young Indiana Jones Chronicles" (ABC, 1992-94); *Sleeping With the Enemy* (1991); *Dream a Little Dream* (1989); *From the Hip* (1987); and *Weeds* (1987).

Historic New Hanover County Courthouse

24 North Third Street. The visitor center is open from 8:30 A.M. *to* 5 P.M. *Monday through Friday; from* 9 A.M. *to* 4 P.M. *Saturday; and from* 1 P.M. *to* 4 P.M. *on Sunday. Holiday hours vary.*

> *"To me, fair friend, you never can be old. For as you were when first your eye I eyed, such seems your beauty still."*
>
> William Shakespeare

Time stands still for the historic New Hanover County Courthouse, built around 1892. Its classic beauty far outshines the newer judicial building and the W. Allen Cobb Courthouse Annex next door. Showy and symmetrical, this brick-and-stone architectural treasure in Victorian-Gothic style beckons filmmakers with its marble floors, high ceilings, and imposing vaults. Outside, its clock tower rises more than 100 feet and has a 2,000-pound bell that chimes on the hour.

The second floor's T-shaped breezeway appears as a Boston train station in "Dawson's Creek." John Travolta spent an entire day in this hallway in scenes cut from *Domestic Disturbance*. Other stars who have walked the historic halls include Paula Abdul (visiting John Travolta), Carrie Fisher (*Stateside*), and "Dawson's Creek" cast members.

The third-floor courtroom, which serves as the county commissioners' chambers in real life, appears as a courtroom in "The Locket." In "A Different Kind of Christmas," a second-floor administrative office is used to portray city attorney Elizabeth Gates's (Shelley Long's) office. The large front room on the second floor appears as a 1960s Board of Elections office in "Freedom Song."

The sidewalk facing Princess Street is a recurring location on "Dawson's Creek." For Boston scenes, set dressers placed copies of the *Boston Globe* in temporary newspaper racks on the sidewalks. In an episode in the show's fifth season, flags touting the Boston Arts Festival hang on light posts. "One Tree Hill" fans will recognize the intersection of Third and Princess streets from the intense car-crash scene in the show's inaugural season. To escape the freezing January temperatures between takes, extras and crew members huddled inside the venerable courthouse, which houses a Visitor Information Center.

CREDITS

"One Tree Hill" (The WB, 2003-); *Stateside* (2004); 20 *Funerals* (2003); "Dawson's Creek" (The WB, 1998-2003); "The Locket" (Hallmark/CBS, 2002); Domestic Disturbance (2001); "Freedom Song" (TNT, 2000); "The Almost Perfect Bank Robbery" (CBS, 1999); "CI5: The New Professionals" (BBC, 1998); "Three Lives of Karen" (USA, 1997); "The Perfect Crime" (USA, 1997); "Kiss and Tell" (ABC, 1996); "The Summer of Ben Tyler" (Hallmark/ CBS, 1996); "The Perfect Daughter" (CBS, 1996); "A Different Kind of Christmas" (Lifetime, 1996); "The Sister-in-Law" (USA, 1995); "The Face on the Milk Carton" (CBS, 1995); *The Hudsucker Proxy* (1994); "Labor of Love: The Arlette Schweitzer Story" (CBS, 1993); "In a Child's Name" (CBS, 1991)

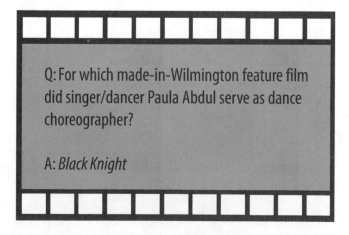

Q: For which made-in-Wilmington feature film did singer/dancer Paula Abdul serve as dance choreographer?

A: *Black Knight*

St. James Parish

~~~Smith Third Street~~~ (910 763-1628, http://www .stjamesp.org/). *Call for hours; the sanctuary is accessible during office hours and church services.*

Renowned architect and historian Tony P. Wrenn, the author of *Wilmington, North Carolina: An Architectural and Historical Portrait*, contends that the corner of Third and Market streets boasts works by more nationally known architects than does any street corner in New York City. On this corner stands the 1840-vintage St. James Parish, a shining example of Gothic Revival church design.

A confessional inside the Great Hall is where young Vivi (Ashley Judd) reveals her desire to become famous in *Divine Secrets of the Ya-Ya Sisterhood*. The parish grounds pose as a 1928 campus in "Oprah Winfrey Presents: The Wedding." The church office in the adjacent brick-and-shingle Donald MacRae House, built around 1901, appears in *Household Saints*, starring Tracey Ullman.

Although filming is not allowed in the sanctuary, it is a must-see showcase of decorative woodwork, stained glass, chandeliers, and frescoes. It also boasts a Cassavant Freres organ. A brochure near the front entrance interprets the handmade banners on display.

CREDITS

"Dawson's Creek" (The WB, 1998-2003); *Divine Secrets of the Ya-Ya Sisterhood* (2002); *The Dress Code* (2000); "Oprah Winfrey Presents: The Wedding" (ABC, 1998); *Household Saints* (1993); "Windmills of the Gods" (CBS, 1988)

Carolina Apartments

420 *Market Street. The interior is open only to residents.*

Will anyone ever look at the Carolina Apartments the same after the shocking 1986 cult classic *Blue Velvet?* Film junkies can get in a noirish mood just being near the six-story brick structure, also

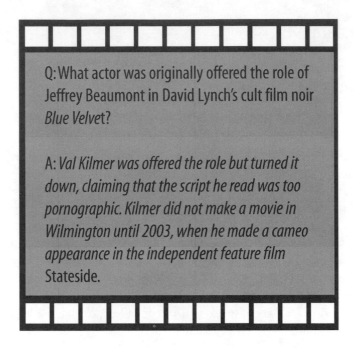

Q: What actor was originally offered the role of Jeffrey Beaumont in David Lynch's cult film noir *Blue Velvet*?

A: *Val Kilmer was offered the role but turned it down, claiming that the script he read was too pornographic. Kilmer did not make a movie in Wilmington until 2003, when he made a cameo appearance in the independent feature film* Stateside.

seen in the would-be Hitchockian thriller *The Bedroom Window* as Denise's (Elizabeth McGovern's) Washington, D.C., apartment building. But it's the building's incarnation as the Deep River Apartments, the home of blue lady Dorothy Vallens (Isabella Rossellini) that attracts fans from around the world. Part of the offbeat atmosphere of *Blue Velvet* is its reality-bending blend of innocence and depravity. Rosellini's apartment calls to mind the 1950s, while the events that take place suggest anything but. Though the interiors were done on a soundstage at nearby DEG Studios (now EUE/Screen Gems Studios), the overall exterior feel of the Carolina Apartments contributes strongly to the film's mood.

One of Wilmington's few brownstones, the Carolina Apartments, built around 1911, provide a New York City high-rise look. Architect Robert Louis Shape, whose credits include the New York Stock Exchange building, used apartments lining New York's Fifth Avenue as his inspiration. The structure's fire escapes are featured in key scenes near the end of *Blue Velvet* and *The Bedroom Window*, as well as in a shootout on "Matlock."

Distinguished tenants have included artist Claude Howell

(1915-97), who was born in the building and lived here most of his life.

The premises are used to portray Thurgood Marshall's apartment in "Simple Justice" (PBS, 1993). You can also spot the Carolina Apartments in *Takedown* (2000); "The Almost Perfect Bank Robbery" (CBS, 1999); "Ambushed" (HBO, 1998); "Bloodmoon" (HBO, 1997); "The Sister-in-Law" (USA, 1995); "Matlock" (ABC, 1993-95); "Stompin' at the Savoy" (CBS, 1992); *Weeds* (1987); *The Bedroom Window* (1987); and *Blue Velvet* (1986).

This dramatic corner at Fifth Avenue and Market Street showcases the Kenan Memorial Fountain and the Carolina Apartments. The apartments were Deep River Apartments in *Blue Velvet*.

COURTESY OF WILMINGTON REGIONAL FILM COMMISSION

Kenan Memorial Fountain Plaza
Fifth Avenue and Market Street

The eye-catching Kenan Memorial Fountain Plaza is a wonderful photo opportunity both on sunny days and when it's dramatically lit at night. Carvings of turtles, fish, and gargoyle-like faces dispense water on all four tiers of the distinctive limestone sculpture.

Perhaps the fountain's most famous appearance is in the foreground of the Deep River Apartments, home to Dorothy Vallens (Isabella Rossellini) in *Blue Velvet*. The Deep River building is actually the Carolina Apartments (see pages 27-29), making this a fine starting point for fans of the David Lynch classic. The fountain also appears in *The Bedroom Window*. It is showcased in the final scene, when Terry (Steve Guttenberg) and Denise (Elizabeth McGovern) tell their story to the police.

Designed by Carrere & Hastings, whose credits include the New York Public Library, the fountain was given to the city in 1921 by Wilmington native William Rand Kenan, Jr., in honor of his parents. Believe it or not, the massive landmark has actually been downsized over the years to accommodate traffic.

CREDITS

"Ambushed" (HBO, 1998); "The Sister-in-Law" (USA, 1995); "A Burning Passion: The Margaret Mitchell Story" (NBC, 1994); *The Bedroom Window* (1987); *Blue Velvet* (1986)

Bellamy Mansion Museum of Design Arts
503 Market Street (910-251-3700). The mansion is open from 10 A.M. to 5 P.M. Monday through Saturday and from 1 P.M. to 5 P.M. on Sunday. An admission fee is charged.

You'll feel like you're on the set of *Gone With the Wind* when you visit the Bellamy Mansion Museum of Design Arts. The four-story, 22-room wooden palace with period gardens appears as an Old South Atlanta mansion in the TV movie "A Burning Passion: The Margaret Mitchell Story," starring

Shannen Doherty in the title role. Built between 1859 and 1861 for Dr. John Dillard Bellamy, the antebellum mansion is a classic example of Greek Revival and Italianate architecture. Its majesty is evident in the craftsmanship of African-American free and enslaved artisans.

In the television movie adaptation of Truman Capote's "One Christmas," the Bellamy Mansion is the setting for the New Orleans society party scene featuring Henry Winkler as a struggling bachelor and Katharine Hepburn as the wealthy Miss Cornelia Beaumont. One of the final scenes in the screen legend's illustrious career was filmed here. On the morning of Hepburn's Bellamy shoot, fans lined the sidewalk. When she stepped out of the limousine, she smiled at the crowd, gave a little bow, and proceeded to the house as fans cheered her every step. Between takes, Hepburn, perhaps deep in character, looked up at a tray-bearing extra and, in her famous sharp lilt, demanded, "Who are you?" The flustered player, a kid of about 65 who, like many retirees, was enjoying a second career in film, could only stammer, "I-I'm a waiter!"

The Bellamy Mansion has hosted special events including wrap parties for productions such as *Divine Secrets of the Ya-Ya Sisterhood*. Although the mansion was scouted for *Ya-Ya*, other spectacular houses—including the Emerson-Kenan House (see pages 62-64), Orton Plantation (see pages 110-13), and Buckner Hill Plantation (see pages 128-30)—were selected for filming.

CREDITS

"The Sister-In-Law" (USA, 1995); "Matlock" (ABC, 1993-95); "One Christmas" (CBS, 1994); "A Burning Passion: The Margaret Mitchell Story" (NBC, 1994); "The Young Indiana Jones Chronicles" (ABC, 1992-94); Stephen King's "The Golden Years" (CBS, 1991); "Lovejoy Mysteries" (BBC, 1993)

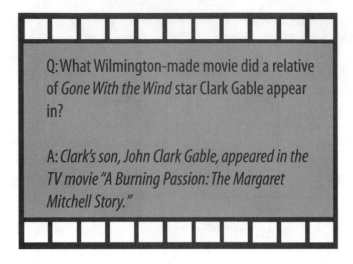

Q: What Wilmington-made movie did a relative of *Gone With the Wind* star Clark Gable appear in?

A: *Clark's son, John Clark Gable, appeared in the TV movie "A Burning Passion: The Margaret Mitchell Story."*

Tileston School/St. Marys Parish

Tileston School is located at 412 Ann Street; visitors are limited to exterior viewing except during games. St. Marys Parish is across the street; services are held Sunday at 11 A.M.

School days. Is any period of life more dramatic? Schoolyards, locker-lined hallways, auditoriums, gymnasiums, and classrooms find their way into most scripts featuring children and teachers. In Wilmington, the path back to the good old days (or the torture chamber) often leads to Tileston School, which opened in 1872. Famous students here have included Woodrow Wilson.

Thanks to renovations begun during the filming of *Hiding Out*, today's Tileston School building provides classrooms and athletic facilities for St. Marys Catholic School. Its red-brick Italianate exterior puts in a vivid performance in *Domestic Disturbance*. Early in the movie, Frank Morrison (John Travolta) meets his son, Danny (Matthew O'Leary), in the gymnasium parking lot. Tileston's main entrance appears in the scene in which Frank and Susan (Teri Polo) argue about custody of their son, Danny.

Across Ann Street is the stunning Spanish Baroque St. Marys Parish, built around 1908. Young Vivi (Ashley Judd) enters its doors to confess her sins in *Divine Secrets of the Ya-Ya Sisterhood*.

The confessional scenes were filmed at St. James Parish (see page 27).

During the fifth season of "Dawson's Creek," a car driven by Alex (Sherilyn Fenn) spins out of control on the corner of South Fifth Avenue and Ann Street. In a curbside scene, Pacey (Joshua Jackson) consoles Alex, who reconsiders her suicidal rampage.

CREDITS

"One Tree Hill" (The WB, 2003-); *Stateside* (2004); "Dawson's Creek" (The WB, 1998-2003); *Divine Secrets of the Ya-Ya Sisterhood* (2002); *Domestic Disturbance* (2001); "The Ditchdigger's Daughters" (Family Channel, 1997); "A Mother's Instinct" (CBS, 1996); "A Step Toward Tomorrow" (CBS, 1996); "The Young Indiana Jones Chronicles" (ABC, 1992-94); *Alan & Naomi* (1992); *Billy Bathgate* (1991); "Too Young the Hero" (CBS, 1988); *Weeds* (1987); *Hiding Out* (1987); commercials

Fifth Avenue United Methodist Church
409 South Fifth Avenue (910-763-2621). Services are held at 9 A.M. and 11 A.M. on Sunday.

The Gothic-style Fifth Avenue United Methodist Church was built around 1889. It stands much as it did over 100 years ago. Scenes for *The Angel Doll*, based on the novella by North Carolina author Jerry Bledsoe, were filmed in the graceful sanctuary, showcasing its impressive pipe organ and stained-glass windows.

Filmmakers like the versatility offered by the fellowship hall's nondescript walls and dark wood trim. Perhaps its most amazing transformation occurred when "Dawson's Creek" turned it into the russet-colored lobby of a Hooksett, Vermont, inn for the town's film festival during season five. After filming, the show donated the elegant tapestry curtains that still grace the hall's windows. In other episodes, the fellowship hall appears as a train station and a library.

The main hallway upstairs appears as a dormitory hall in

the fifth season of "Dawson's Creek." Two upstairs rooms were used in scenes cut from *Divine Secrets of the Ya-Ya Sisterhood;* however the DVD version features the outtakes.

Modern-day stars aren't the only celebrities who've been to this church. In 1880, Charles Soong was baptized here. A ship stowaway, he attended Trinity College (now Duke University) and became a successful businessman in China. Two of his daughters married Chiang Kai-Shek and Sun Yat-sen.

CREDITS

The church appears as a courtroom and jail cell in "Freedom Song" (TNT, 2000). You may be able to spot its exterior in the bonfire scene in "What the Deaf Man Heard" (Hallmark/CBS, 1997). The church also appears in *The Angel Doll* (2003); "Dawson's Creek" (The WB, 1998-2003); "Young Indiana Jones Chronicles" (ABC, 1992-94); and *Billy Bathgate* (1991).

The Verandas Bed & Breakfast Inn

202 Nun Street (910-251-2212; www.verandas.com). The inn is open year-round.

The inviting front-porch entrance at The Verandas makes its film debut at the end of *The Chester Story*, when leading lady Teri Hatcher (Lois Lane in "Lois & Clark") forlornly looks back at The Chester Inn. Other scenes were shot in Room 1 and at the reception desk.

Located at the corner of Second and Nun streets, this 1853 Victorian Italianate house was in post-fire disrepair when innkeepers Dennis Madsen and Chuck Pennington purchased it in 1995 and began transforming it into a showcase bed-and-breakfast. The inn now boasts a AAA Four Diamond rating and an *Arrington's Inn Traveler* "Best of the South" endorsement. Its eight comfortable sleeping rooms have different themes and ample baths. Guests enjoy exquisite antiques, original art, gourmet breakfasts, and four verandas overlooking the landscaped gardens. Celebrity guests have included Billy Zane (*Morgan's Ferry*).

CREDITS

The Chester Story (2003)

Chandler's Wharf

Chandler's Wharf is located at 225 South Water Street. It is open daily; shop and restaurant hours vary. Elijah's (910-343-1448) and the Pilot House (910-343-0200) are open from 11:30 A.M. to 10 P.M. Sunday through Friday and from 11:30 A.M. to 11 P.M. on Saturday. Parking is free for patrons.

One of Wilmington's earliest films, *From the Hip*, starring Judd Nelson and Elizabeth Perkins, features the nostalgic Chandler's Wharf.

An old ship chandler's building constructed around 1884, the vernacular-style brick-and-stucco Calder-Thorpe Warehouse was rehabilitated in 1978 for shops and offices. The adjoining five acres at the foot of Ann Street were developed by relocating 19th-century homes and adapting them into an enclave of shops and restaurants. Elijah's Restaurant, located in a shingle-sided cottage that formerly housed a small maritime museum, has appeared in "Matlock" and "Dare to Love." Much of "Dawson's Creek: The Final Episode" was filmed in Elijah's bar, kitchen, and outside deck, which serves as Pacey Witter's (Joshua Jackson's) and joy—the reincarnated Icehouse Restaurant, where the Capeside friends reunite after five years; you can view the original Icehouse location by visiting 15 South Water Street. Elijah's is a favorite among locals and visitors for its excellent Cape Fear cuisine and river-front setting. While in town shooting *The Road to Wellville*, Matthew Broderick and Bridget Fonda savored Elijah's regional specialties. Other celebrities who have dined here include Al Freeman, Jr. (*Once Upon a Time . . . When We Were Colored*), and Pat Hingle ("The Member of the Wedding").

The historic Craig House, built around 1870, was spared from demolition and moved to Chandler's Wharf in the early 1980s. Major renovations transformed it into the Pilot House Restaurant, where celebrity diners have included Pat Hingle, Linda Lavin, Senator Elizabeth Dole, Vice President Dick Cheney, and the cast of "Dawson's Creek."

In April 2003, "Dawson's Creek" blocked off Chandler's Wharf for a spectacular wrap party at the Pilot House and Elijah's. Approximately 400 principals, crew members, studio executives, community leaders, and invited guests celebrated six successful seasons at an extravaganza that lasted well into the night.

CREDITS

A scene in "Timepiece" (CBS, 1996) was shot in front of A. Scott Rhodes Jewelers. You can also see Chandler's Wharf in "Dawson's Creek: The Final Episode" (The WB, 2003); "Oprah Winfrey Presents: The Wedding" (ABC/Lifetime, 1995); "Buried Alive II" (USA, 1997); "Dare to Love" (ABC, 1995); "Matlock" (ABC, 1993-95); *The Bedroom Window* (1987); and *From the Hip* (1987).

Barbary Coast

116 South Front Street (910-762-8996). Barbary is open daily from 2 P.M. to 2 A.M. Patrons must be at least 21 years of age.

Leave the kids at home (unless they're over 21) when you venture into Barbary Coast. Wilmington's oldest bar—and a real dive—made its film debut in the cult film *Blue Velvet*. The infamous neon "This Is It" sign over Barbary Coast's front door is from the movie. Film junkies will remember it as the sign that hangs over the brothel run by pill-popping pimp Ben (Dean Stockwell). It also signifies the "This is it" line exclaimed by Frank Booth (Dennis Hopper) upon entry. The scene's most memorable moment occurs later when Ben mimes Roy Orbison's "In Dreams."

Once inside, you'll feel as if you've happened upon the *Star Wars* bar scene. Originally a loud and lusty seaman's bar, Barbary carries on that tradition today. Even if you don't stay to enjoy a cold one, let your eyes wander along the left wall, where an unusual movie prop hangs. The life-sized skeletal impression is from another Dennis Hopper vehicle, *Super Mario Brothers*; it makes its appearance when Lena (Fiona Shaw) gets fried by a meteorite. While other curious decorations may look like movie props, they're likely not.

Characters in their own right, Barbary patrons might recognize stars such as Dennis Hopper and Michael Keaton, but

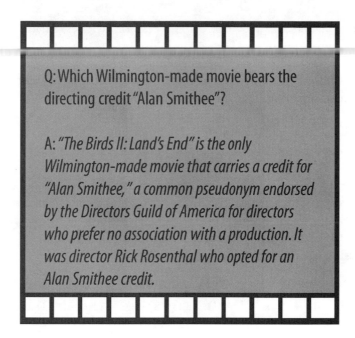

Q: Which Wilmington-made movie bears the directing credit "Alan Smithee"?

A: *"The Birds II: Land's End"* is the only Wilmington-made movie that carries a credit for *"Alan Smithee,"* a common pseudonym endorsed by the Directors Guild of America for directors who prefer no association with a production. It was director Rick Rosenthal who opted for an Alan Smithee credit.

for the most part they care little about social status. What else would you expect from a bar upon which the motto "We've upped our standards—Up yours!" is emblazoned across the entrance?

CREDITS

Barbary Coast appears as the He Just Left Tavern in *New Best Friend* (2002). You can also glimpse it in "The Birds II: Land's End" (Showtime, 1994) and *Blue Velvet* (1986).

The Reel Café

100 South Front Street (910-251-1832). The café is open daily from 4 P.M. to 10 P.M.; it is also open for lunch during the summer. Live entertainment is offered on the weekends from April to October.

Wilmington's answer to Planet Hollywood, The Reel Café offers "reel" appeal for movie buffs and, yes, even movie stars. A display of movie props, costumes, stills, posters, autographed photos, and memorabilia from films decorates the main dining room, where the menu offers entrées, sandwiches, salads, and late-night appetizers. The second floor serves as a dining room, sports bar, and late-night dance club. Live music is featured seasonally on the third-floor rooftop, and an outdoor oyster bar invites sports fans.

Scenes from "Dawson's Creek" were filmed inside the café, and the show's cast members have been among its celebrity customers. Others include Sandra Bullock (28 *Days*), Goldie Hawn, Louis Gossett, Jr. ("To Dance with Olivia"), Danny Glover ("Freedom Song"), Vince Vaughn (*Domestic Disturbance*), and basketball superstar Michael Jordan, who grew up in Wilmington. Private wrap parties have been held upstairs for productions such as *Summer Catch* (starring Freddie Prinze, Jr., Brian Dennehy, and Jessica Biel), "The Locket," and 28 *Days*.

CREDITS

"Dawson's Creek" (The WB, 1998-2003); *Domestic Disturbance* (2001)

Charley Brownz Downtown Lounge

21 South Front Street (910-254-9499). The lounge is open daily from 11 A.M. to 2 A.M.

While most restaurant/lounges find it difficult to be all things to all people, Charley Brownz Downtown Lounge successfully caters to sports fans, music lovers, and film junkies. Its TV debut came during season four of "Dawson's Creek," when set dressers transformed the busy restaurant, sports bar, and live music venue into a strip club. After the cameras left, it was back to business as usual—without the exotic dancers!

Charley Brownz is a great place to meet friends for a big game, a cold beer, and a gourmet sandwich, burger, or plate of buffalo wings. At night, the bar offers a steady flow of libations and TV sports. On the stage, you'll find live blues, jazz, or rock on Wednesday nights and reggae on Sunday nights.

Celebrity diners have included Louis Gossett, Jr. ("To Dance with Olivia"), James Van Der Beek ("Dawson's Creek"), Vince

Vaughn (*Domestic Disturbance*), and Katie Holmes and Joshua Jackson ("Dawson's Creek").

CREDITS

"Dawson's Creek" (The WB, 1998-2003)

Marrz Theater

15 South Front Street (910-772-9045; www.marrz.net). Marrz Theater opens at 9 P.M. nightly. Patrons must be at least 18 years of age and have a valid ID and a membership.

Over the years, this private over-18 nightclub has operated under several banners, including The Palladium and The River Club. Its current incarnation is Marrz Theater, a dance club and concert venue. The brick-and-glass storefront serves as the fiercely independent record store where rising stars Liv Tyler and Renée Zellweger portray Gen-X employees in *Empire Records*. The concert finale was filmed on the rooftop here and atop a taller building overlooking the river several blocks north; the shots were matched in post-production. Actor Jeremy Irons rented The River Club for a *Lolita* crew party. The club's interior appears in "Dawson's Creek" in a high-school dance scene during season one. It reappears in the season-five episode "Highway to Hell" when Joey sings a rendition of Rick Springfield's 1980s hit "Jessie's Girl."

CREDITS

"Dawson's Creek" (The WB, 1998-2003); *Empire Records* (1995)

Caffé Phoenix

9 South Front Street (910-343-1395). The restaurant is open from 11:30 A.M. to 10 P.M. Sunday through Thursday and from 11:30 A.M. to 11 P.M. Friday and Saturday. Sunday brunch is served from 10:30 A.M. to 3 P.M.

Caffé Phoenix could pass for a hip L.A. bistro. Eavesdroppers can always catch good industry buzz at the bar and at tables occupied by film crew and talent. It's a place to see and be seen. The awnings and sidewalk tables appear in an outdoor dining sequence featuring Liv Tyler and Renée Zellweger in *Empire Records*. *Domestic Disturbance* chose Caffé Phoenix for the breakfast scene in which Frank Morrison (John Travolta) runs into Ray Coleman (Steve Buscemi). Later in the film, the cops stop Frank in front of the restaurant after a brief chase. It makes a third appearance when Frank returns for a burger.

While the distinctive atmosphere lures celebrities, it's the talented chef and creative Mediterranean-inspired menu that keeps them. Film junkies should scan the upstairs, where "inconspicuous" stars are sometimes seated. The star-studded guest list has included Sandra Bullock (*Divine Secrets of the Ya-Ya Sisterhood*); Jennifer Jason Leigh (*The Hudsucker Proxy*; "Bastard Out of Carolina"); Peter Coyote (*A Walk to Remember*); Vince Vaughn (*Domestic Disturbance*); John Travolta (*Domestic Disturbance*) and actress-wife Kelly Preston; Katie Holmes ("Dawson's Creek") and boyfriend and *American Pie* hunk Chris Klein; Ashley Judd (*Divine Secrets of the Ya-Ya Sisterhood*); Michelle Pfeiffer (*To Gillian on Her 37th Birthday*); Shirley MacLaine (*The Dress Code*); Nicolas Cage (*Amos & Andrew*); Shane West (*A Walk to Remember*); and Dennis Hopper (*Blue Velvet*; *Super Mario Brothers*).

CREDITS

Domestic Disturbance (2001); *Empire Records* (1995)

Deluxe

114 Market Street (910-251-0333). Deluxe is open from 5 P.M. to 10 P.M. Monday through Saturday; brunch is served from 11 A.M. to 2 P.M. on Sunday.

It's no wonder that stars like John Travolta and Vince Vaughn (*Domestic Disturbance*), Ashley Judd (*Divine Secrets of the Ya-Ya Sisterhood*), Louis Gossett, Jr. (*To Dance with Olivia*), *American Pie* heartthrob Chris Klein, and "Dawson's Creek" sweetie Katie Holmes have dined here. The stylized interior of this renovated century-old building serves as a location in "The Locket" during Alice's (Lori Heuring's) less-than-innocent lunch with Mike (Chad Willett).

When the young cast of "Dawson's Creek" first arrived in 1997, they quickly discovered Deluxe, which was then a trendy coffeehouse. It was also convenient, since James Van Der Beek (Dawson) and Joshua Jackson (Pacey) rented apartments on the second floor. As the show's run ended, Michelle Williams (Jen) told a local reporter that Deluxe was among the places she would miss in Wilmington.

Seasonal menus include creatively prepared seafood, chicken, beef, pasta, and vegetarian selections. Guests enjoy live Spanish guitar music during Sunday brunch.

CREDITS
Ball of Wax (2003); "The Locket" (Hallmark/CBS, 2002); *Takedown* (2000)

The Graystone Inn

100 South Third Street (888-763-4773 or 910-763-2000; www.graystoneinn.com). The inn is open daily for guests and special events.

If the walls of the award-winning Graystone Inn, built around 1905, could talk, they would tell of notable personalities who have attended parties, spent the night, or starred in movies filmed at this seven-room bed-and-breakfast.

"Dawson's Creek" filmed in the reception area, the parlor, and the second-floor Bridgers guest room. The Graystone also appears in "A Burning Passion: The Margaret Mitchell Story," when Shannen Doherty performs a wild Apache dance at 1920s Atlanta society party. The inn also hosts the New Year's Eve party in "The Locket."

Innkeepers Paul and Yolanda Bolda restored the mansion's turn-of-the-20th-century grandeur when they purchased it in 1997. Handsome and elegantly appointed with period furnishings, this Wilmington landmark is now a AAA Four Diamond bed-and-breakfast where all guests receive star treatment. The

Graystone, listed on the National Register of Historic Places, has been cited as one of North America's most romantic inns by American Historic Inns and *Arrington's Bed & Breakfast Journal*. The many couples who marry and honeymoon here can attest to the inn's romantic appeal.

Academy Award® winner Anthony Hopkins (*The Road to Wellville*) enjoyed playing the baby grand piano in the music room before retiring to the Latimer Suite. Alan Alda (*Betsy's Wedding*), Goldie Hawn, and Peter Falk (*Tune in Tomorrow*) also chose that exquisite suite. Tom Cruise (visiting then-fiancée Nicole Kidman), Phyllis Diller, and Billy Zane (*This World, Then the Fireworks*) checked into the roomy Bellevue Suite on the secluded third floor. Other famous guests have included Jay Leno (*Collision Course*) and Dennis Hopper (*Blue Velvet; Super Mario Brothers*).

CREDITS

"Dawson's Creek" (The WB, 1998-2003); *New Best Friend* (2002); "The Locket" (Hallmark/CBS, 2002); "Something Borrowed, Something Blue" (CBS, 1997); "Timepiece" (CBS, 1996); "Matlock" (ABC, 1993-95); "The Young Indiana Jones Chronicles" (ABC, 1992-94); "A Burning Passion: The Margaret Mitchell Story" (NBC, 1994); *Billy Bathgate* (1991); *Rambling Rose* (1991); "Windmills of the Gods" (CBS, 1988)

Zebulon Latimer House

126 South Third Street (910-762-0492; www.latimerhouse.org). The house is open from 10 A.M. to 3:30 P.M. Monday through Friday and from noon to 5 P.M. on Saturday. Walking tours are offered at 10 A.M. on Wednesday and Saturday. An admission fee is charged.

Period carpeting and wallpaper from "Oprah Winfrey Presents: The Wedding" remain in the hallway, the front parlor, and a second-floor bedroom of the Zebulon Latimer House, constructed around 1852. Three generations of Latimers lived in this handsome Italianate Revival house before it was sold in 1963 to the Lower Cape Fear Historical Society. The elegant

Corinthian columns and filigreed cast-iron supports beckon visitors to explore the period gardens and the historical home.

CREDITS
"Oprah Winfrey Presents: The Wedding" (ABC, 1998)

Murchison House Bed and Breakfast
305 South Third Street (910-762-6626; www.murchisonhouse.com)

You've seen this spectacular 1876 inn in the sci-fi series "American Gothic," the action-adventure series "Young Indiana Jones Chronicles," and "Oprah Winfrey Presents: The Wedding." On the silver screen, it has appeared as the abandoned house in Jodie Foster's *Dangerous Lives of Altar Boys*.

Today, film junkies can bunk for the evening in one of five guest rooms at the 6,077-square-foot David Reid Murchison House, built around 1876. Innkeepers Sharon and Ronald Demas have restored the magnificent Neoclassical Revival home from a state of disrepair, after it had gone untouched (except by the movies) for nearly 20 years. The owners enjoy sharing stories about their elegantly appointed bed-and-breakfast, which is now a showcase of period antiques. Beautifully manicured gardens adorn the grounds that surround this grand old dame.

CREDITS
Dangerous Lives of Altar Boys (2002); "Oprah Winfrey Presents: The Wedding" (ABC, 1998); "American Gothic" (CBS, 1995-96); "Young Indiana Jones Chronicles" (ABC, 1992-94)

Historic Wilmington Star Tracks

Cape Fear Museum

814 Market Street (910-341-4350; www.capefearmuseum.com).
The museum is open from 9 A.M. to 5 P.M. Tuesday through
Saturday and from 1 P.M. to 5 P.M. on Sunday. It is open on
Mondays from 9 A.M. to 5 P.M. from Memorial Day through
Labor Day. An admission fee is charged.

When the cast of "Dawson's Creek" graduated from fictitious Capeside High, the show donated props to the Cape Fear
Museum, which displayed them at a one-night sold-out event.
The Capeside icons included Jen's locker, Dawson's crab trap,
and the Capeside High Minuteman mascot.

Founded in 1897, North Carolina's oldest history museum
collects information and artifacts of regional historical and so-
cietal significance, including pop-culture items. Future plans include a 20th-century exhibition. One noteworthy display showcases memorabilia of native Wilmingtonian Michael Jordan, including items that trace his life from elementary school to Laney
High School and the University of North Carolina. It is located next to the Michael Jordan Discovery Gallery, an inter-

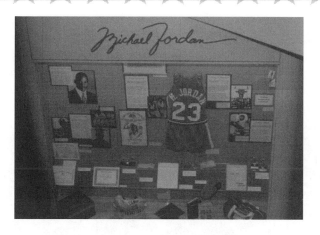

Wilmington native Michael Jordan
is showcased at the Cape Fear Museum.
COURTESY OF THE CAPE FEAR COAST CONVENTION AND VISITORS BUREAU

active exhibit named for its primary benefactor.

Famous museum visitors have included Michael Jordan (of course) and Jamie Lee Curtis (*Virus*), who came with her daughter.

The Wilmingtonian

101 South Second Street (800-525-0909 or 910-343-1800; www.thewilmingtonian.com). The inn is open year-round.

Stars feel right at home in the elegant and comfortable accommodations at The Wilmingtonian (formerly the Inn at St. Thomas Court), especially in the Cinema House. Guests can choose from spacious one- and two-bedroom suites named in honor of legends Charlie Chaplin and Marilyn Monroe and major motion pictures such as *Gone With the Wind, The Music Man, The King & I, South Pacific, Casablanca,* and *Oklahoma.*

Built around 1841, the Greek Revival de Rosset House is

also part of the inn. It houses the City Club's private dining room and bar. Upstairs, six luxurious suites with period furnishings appeal to movie directors, producers, and actors who favor the inn's proximity to downtown shops, restaurants, and nightspots.

Celebrities who have laid their famous heads at The Wilmingtonian include Donald Sutherland (*Virus*), Kris Kristofferson (*A Soldier's Daughter Never Cries;* "Inflammable"), Richard Gere (*The Jackal*), Shelley Long ("A Different Kind of Christmas"), Louis Gossett, Jr. ("To Dance with Olivia"), James Earl Jones ("What the Deaf Man Heard"; "Timepiece"), Tim Robbins (*The Hudsucker Proxy*), Matthew Broderick (*The Road to Wellville*), George Lucas ("Young Indiana Jones Chronicles"), Dana Carvey (*The Road to Wellville*), Tom Berenger (*Chasers*), screenwriter Kevin Williamson, and the cast of "Dawson's Creek." William Shatner, better known as Captain Kirk of "Star Trek" fame, even beamed down from the *Starship Enterprise* to spend a night or two here.

Old Wilmington City Market

120-124 South Front Street and Water Street (Contact Marty K. Hats at 910-762-9977). The market is open from 9 A.M. to 5 P.M. Monday through Saturday and from noon to 5 P.M. on Sunday.

While it's not exactly Hollywood's Mann's Chinese Theater, the stars have left behind visible tracks at the Old Wilmington City Market, built around 1879. Film junkies will recognize the cracked wall hanging at the Front Street entrance from the boardroom scenes in the Coen brothers' *The Hudsucker Proxy*. Just ahead is a wall of fame displaying handwritten messages and autographs from Ally Sheedy (*Betsy's Wedding*), Gena Rowlands, Henry Winkler "One Christmas", Edward Woodward ("CI5: The New Professionals"), Phylicia Rashad (*Once Upon a Time . . . When We Were Colored*), Jamie Lee Curtis (*Virus*), James Earl Jones ("Timepiece"), Rue McClanahan ("A Burning Passion: The Margaret Mitchell Story"), and Mary Tyler Moore ("Stolen Memories: Secrets from the Rose Garden"), and others. Joshua Jackson ("Dawson's Creek") wrote of his delight to sign between Darth Vader and The Fonz.

Formerly a produce market and auditorium, the Old Wilmington City Market currently houses retail shops and vendor booths. James Earl Jones has shopped at Barouke Exotic Woods, Etc. Michelle Williams found some of her trademark hats at Marty K. Hats. Other celebrity shoppers have included Paul Newman (*The Hudsucker Proxy*) and Linda Lavin ("Stolen Memories: Secrets from the Rose Garden"). Shopkeepers will gladly share their brushes with fame.

Q: What actress was the first African-American to be crowned Queen Azalea during Wilmington's annual N. C. Azalea Festival?

A: *Phylicia Rashad was named Queen Azalea in 1985. She later returned to Wilmington to co-star in Tim Reid's independent film* Once Upon A Time ...When We Were Colored.

J. W. Brooks Building

10-18 South Water Street. The shops are open to the public; hours vary. The second and third floors are open only to residents.

James Van Der Beek ("Dawson's Creek") once owned an upstairs residence on the north end of the J. W. Brooks Building that was featured in a 1999 issue of *In Style* magazine. Retailers in the building include Poodle's Island Wear, one of the few shops that carry "Dawson's Creek" memorabilia. Decades earlier, the 1920 waterfront brick building with its pilings and stone base was home to J. W. Brooks Wholesale Grocer. Prior to the building's renovation in the late 1990s, productions such as "American Gothic" took advantage of its dark, eerie emptiness.

Circa 1922

8 North Front Street (910-762-1922). Circa 1922 is open from 5 P.M. to 10 P.M. Sunday through Thursday and from 5 P.M. to 11 P.M. Friday and Saturday.

Named for the year this Front Street building was erected, Circa 1922 quickly found favor with young professionals and visiting celebrities when it opened as a restaurant in 1999. Wood and mirrors lend a touch of class to the main dining room and bar. Most nights, Circa 1922 hums with energy, especially when stars such as John Travolta (*Domestic Disturbance*) are in. Famous customers upstairs in the private dining room have included Ashley Judd (*Divine Secrets of the Ya-Ya Sisterhood*), Darryl Hannah (*A Walk to Remember*), and Jenny McCarthy ("Going to California"). The independent film *Stateside*, starring Carrie Fisher and

Val Kilmer, shot a scene inside the dining room. The very next night, Ms. Fisher stopped in to enjoy the live music.

The gourmet tapas offer a taste of international cuisine. Order several, but make sure you save room for one of the standout desserts, which easily feed two.

A Slice of Life Pizzeria

122 Market Street (910-251-9444). The pizzeria is open daily from 11:30 A.M. to 3 A.M.

Who doesn't occasionally crave a good pizza? A Slice of Life Pizzeria tempts the stars' West Coast taste buds with California-style wood-fired pizzas, burritos, and enchiladas. This cozy pizzeria and sports bar is usually packed with professionals, students, and crew members. Celebrity sightings have included John Travolta and Vince Vaughn (*Domestic Disturbance*) and "Dawson's Creek" cast members Joshua Jackson (Pacey) and Katie Holmes (Joey), who was there with her boyfriend, *American Pie* star Chris Klein.

Downtown Coffeehouses

Wilmington's java joints are among the best bets for a chance celebrity encounter. Late-night shoots, long days, after-hours socializing, and a demand for high energy make caffeine a mainstay in showbiz. Stars typically prefer gourmet coffee to the craft-service variety.

Port City Java—Downtown I is located at 21 North Front Street. The star karma begins with the structure itself, the Masonic Temple Building (see pages 18-19), previously owned by Dennis Hopper (*Blue Velvet*). Star sightings at this PCJ location have included Donald Sutherland (*Virus*), Paula Abdul of "American Idol" (who served as the choreographer for *Black Knight*), Anjelica Huston (director of "Bastard Out of Carolina"), the late John Ritter ("Gramps"; "Holy Joe"), Shirley MacLaine (director of *The Dress Code*), Katie Holmes ("Dawson's Creek"), and Jeremy Irons (*Lolita*). TV Superman Dean Cain ("The Runaway") spent much of his down time at PCJ with a cup o' joe and his laptop. Customers whispered, "Is that Superman?" Cain, overhearing them, smiled in response. The phone number for this location is 910-762-5282.

Port City Java—Downtown II is at 300 North Front Street. It made its screen debut as Karen's Café in the "One Tree Hill" pilot episode. In subsequent shows, the internet café owned by Lucas's (Chad Michael Murray's) mom was re-created across the street in the historic I. M. Bear & Co. building, located on the southeast corner of Grace and Front streets. The Bear building also appears in "Dawson's Creek" as the crisis-call center where Jen (Michelle Williams) and Jack (Kerr Smith) work, as Pacey's (Joshua Jackson's) investment firm, and as Boston Bay radio station WBCW. During filming on this corner, the cast and crew of "Dawson's Creek" and "One Tree Hill" were PCJ regulars. You can reach the Downtown II location by calling 910-254-4534.

General Assembly Coffee House is at 303 North Front Street. Students and shoppers at the Cotton Exchange (see pages 14-15) drop in for a café latte and the chance to sip it beside someone famous like Katie Holmes (whose autographed picture is on display) or fellow "Dawson's Creek" cast members. Imagine everyone's delight when Val Kilmer (*Stateside*) stopped in for a java jolt. For information, call 910-343-8890.

Wilmington Espresso Company is located at 24 South Front Street. Star-studded coffee drinkers here have included Shirley MacLaine (*The Dress Code*), Michelle Pfeiffer (*To Gillian on Her*

Port City Java–Downtown II dressed as
Karen's Café in The WB pilot for "One Tree Hill."
PHOTOGRAPH BY C. L. NELSON

37th Birthday), James Earl Jones ("What the Deaf Man Heard"),
Ally Sheedy ("Buried Alive II"), and the cast of "Dawson's Creek."
Call 910-343-1155.

Port City Java—Downtown III is at 402 Chestnut Street.
This one-story curved brick building with bay windows appears
in *Blue Velvet* as the diner where Jeffrey (Kyle McLachlan) and
Sandy (Laura Dern) discuss a scheme to invade singer Dorothy
Vallens's (Isabella Rossellini's) apartment. For information, call
910-796-6646.

★ ★ ★ ★ ★ ★ ★ ★ ★ ★ ★ ★

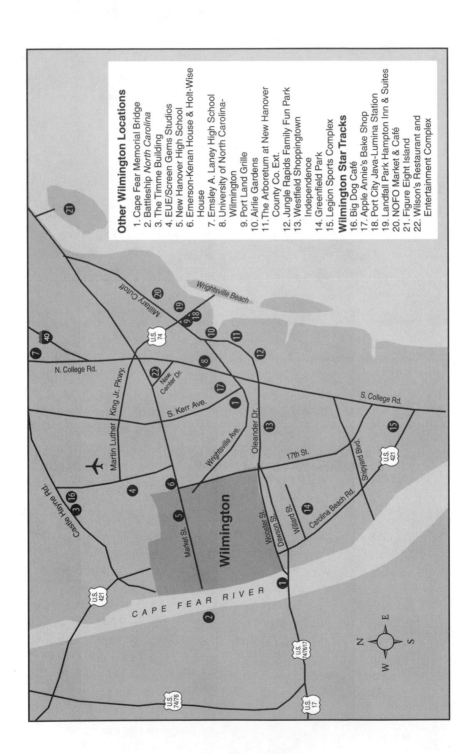

Other Wilmington Locations

Cape Fear Memorial Bridge

The U.S. 74 bridge spans the river between Eagle Island and Wilmington's Dawson and Wooster streets. The best view is from the Riverwalk downtown.

One of Wilmington's signature movie landmarks is the Cape Fear Memorial Bridge. Film junkies have seen the vertical-lift bridge on screens large and small. Constructed around 1967, the four-lane, 3,000-foot-long bridge is an establishing backdrop for countless "Dawson's Creek" scenes shot from Riverfront Park (see pages 7-8) and Chandler's Wharf (see pages 35-36). However, the unique bridge's most dramatic screen moment is in *Black Dog*, starring Patrick Swayze and Randy Travis, a native of Marshville, North Carolina. The bridge appears in a climactic nighttime shootout scene in which their 18-wheeler is pursued and captured by police in cars, boats, and helicopters.

Although few would call it beautiful, the bridge provides

an impressive photo opportunity with its lift span and twin steel elevator towers.

The bridge appears in the suicide scene in "Twilight Man" (Starz! 1996). You can also see it in "Dawson's Creek" (The WB, 1998-2003); *A Walk to Remember* (2002); *New Best Friend* (2002); *Black Dog* (1998); "A Mother's Instinct" (CBS, 1996); "A Step Toward Tomorrow" (CBS, 1996); "American Gothic" (CBS, 1995-96); *Empire Records* (1995); *Chasers* (1994); Stephen King's *Maximum Overdrive* (1986); and *Trick or Treat* (1986).

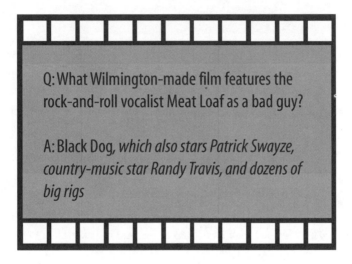

Q: What Wilmington-made film features the rock-and-roll vocalist Meat Loaf as a bad guy?

A: Black Dog, *which also stars Patrick Swayze, country-music star Randy Travis, and dozens of big rigs*

Battleship *North Carolina*

The battleship is located at the junction of U.S. 17/74/76/421 on the Cape Fear River across from downtown Wilmington. It is open daily from 8 A.M. to 8 P.M. from May 16 to September 15 and from 8 A.M. to 5 P.M. from September 16 to May 15. An admission fee is charged. For information, call 910-251-5797 or visit www.battleshipnc.com.

A truly great leading lady is a rare find. One such treasure, the Battleship *North Carolina*, began her first career in the sum-

"The Showboat," a.k.a. Battleship *North Carolina*, assumes command in films such as "James Cameron's Expedition Bismarck." Adjacent Battleship Park appears in "Dawson's Creek" and "One Tree Hill."
COURTESY OF BATTLESHIP *NORTH CAROLINA*

mer of 1942. In six years of active service, she played a role in every major naval offensive in the Pacific during World War II and earned 15 battle stars for distinguished service—much more impressive than 15 Oscars®!

In 1961, North Carolina schoolchildren collected nickels and dimes to bring her home to a permanent mooring in the Cape Fear River. Nicknamed "The Showboat" during the war, the battleship still lives up to the name as a popular TV and film location and World War II memorial.

Film junkies may want to view the battleship's orientation video, narrated by navy veteran, actor, and Carolina Beach resident Pat Hingle. Other stars who have filmed aboard The Showboat include Kris Kristofferson, Sir Edward Woodward, Rick Schroder, and Wilmington native and news journalist David Brinkley. Gean McAvoy, Cheryl Ladd's character in "Kiss and Tell," escapes danger by joining a tour group much like those that visit the battleship each day. Celebrity parent Jamie Lee Curtis was among the ship's visitors when she did a still shoot for *Virus*; she also brought her children to explore the *North Carolina*'s nine decks. On Friday nights in May and October, a 1940s film festival is presented on the ship's fantail.

Located adjacent to the ship is Battleship Park, which provided the setting for several "Dawson's Creek" scenes, including the Capeside Winter Arts Fair in season two. Other "DC" episodes also filmed here. However, the show's cameras carefully avoided the ship, lest they reveal Capeside's true location. Another production that filmed at Battleship Park was "One Tree Hill." The climactic basketball showdown during the pilot episode takes place here on a temporary outdoor basketball court, where Nathan (James Lafferty) challenges Lucas (Chad Michael Murray) as Tree Hill High School students watch the drama unfold. The court reappears in subsequent nighttime scenes with Wilmington's Riverfront Park (see pages 7-8) glowing from across the river in the background.

CREDITS

"One Tree Hill" (The WB, 2003-); "Dawson's Creek" (The WB, 1998-2003); "James Cameron's Expedition Bismarck" (Discovery Channel, 2002); "Battle Group: Spruance" (History Channel, 2001); "Battle Group: Halsey" (History Channel, 2001); "CI5: The New Professionals" (BBC, 1998); "Battleship" (Discovery Channel, 1997); "Love's Deadly Triangle: The Texas Cadet Murder" (NBC, 1997); "Kiss and Tell" (ABC, 1996); "In-

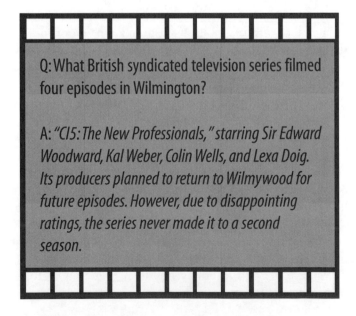

Q: What British syndicated television series filmed four episodes in Wilmington?

A: "CI5: The New Professionals," starring Sir Edward Woodward, Kal Weber, Colin Wells, and Lexa Doig. Its producers planned to return to Wilmywood for future episodes. However, due to disappointing ratings, the series never made it to a second season.

flammable" (CBS, 1995); "Spies" (Disney, 1992); "Too Young the Hero" (CBS, 1988)

Timme Building

1536 Castle Hayne Road. Visitors can get an exterior view during daylight hours.

A far cry from Hollywood glitz, this nondescript brick warehouse, just a stone's throw from a prison, once housed sets for more than a dozen major productions, including "American Gothic" and "Matlock." Its ample parking lot appears in the second season of "Dawson's Creek," when it hosts a Capeside carnival.

During the 1990s, this building donned the banner "Wilmington Film Studios," which consisted of 23,000 square feet of temporary production office space and two large studios. New tenants occupy the site today.

CREDITS

The building appears as a hospital set in *The Dress Code* (2000). You can also see it in the tunnel scene in "Ambushed" (HBO, 1998). Its other credits include "Dawson's Creek" (The WB, 1998-2003); *Black Dog* (1998); "What the Deaf Man Heard" (Hallmark/CBS, 1997); *Night Flier* (1997); "Miracle in the Woods" (CBS, 1997); *This World, Then the Fireworks* (1997); "The Ditchdigger's Daughters" (Family Channel, 1997); "Buried Alive II" (USA, 1997); "A Different

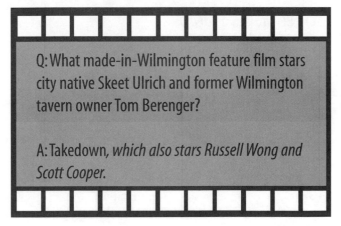

Q: What made-in-Wilmington feature film stars city native Skeet Ulrich and former Wilmington tavern owner Tom Berenger?

A: Takedown, *which also stars Russell Wong and Scott Cooper.*

Kind of Christmas" (Lifetime, 1996); "A Step Toward Tomorrow" (CBS, 1996); *The Grave* (1996); "The Summer of Ben Tyler" (Hallmark/CBS, 1996); "American Gothic" (CBS, 1995-96); "Search for Grace" (CBS, 1994); Truman Capote's "One Christmas" (CBS, 1994); *The Hudsucker Proxy* (1994); "A Burning Passion: The Margaret Mitchell Story" (NBC, 1994); "Matlock" (ABC, 1993-95); "The Young Indiana Jones Chronicles" (ABC, 1992-94); "Stompin' at the Savoy" (CBS, 1992); "Stephen King's The Golden Years" (CBS, 1991); and *Loose Cannons* (1990).

Home to Matlock, Dawson, and a cast of thousands, EUE/Screen Gems Studios offers weekend tours of the largest movie production facility east of Hollywood.
COURTESY OF CAPE FEAR COAST CONVENTION AND VISITORS BUREAU

EUE/Screen Gems Studios

1223 North 23rd Street (910-343-3433; www.screengemsstudios.com). Tours are available, weather permitting, from April to September on Saturday at varying times; during peak tourist season, they are sometimes offered on Sunday. Tours during other months vary. Call to confirm tours and demonstrations. An admission fee is charged. Advance reservations for groups are available. Set and backlot accessibility is not guaranteed.

Nine sound stages, casting offices, a hair and makeup studio, a screening room, a studio backlot. Sound like Hollywood? New York? Try Wilmington, home of EUE/Screen Gems Studios, the largest movie production facility east of California.

Much has transpired since 1983, when filmmakers Dino De Laurentiis and Frank Capra, Jr., brought *Firestarter* to Wilmington. One of the film's locations, a warehouse at 1223 North 23rd Street, is where Dino built DEG (De Laurentiis Entertainment Group) Studios and produced films such as *Year of the Dragon, Blue Velvet, King Kong Lives, Crimes of the Heart,* and *Raw Deal.* Four years later, without a major blockbuster, DEG closed.

The studio operated sporadically as a rental facility until 1989, when Carolco Pictures purchased it and hosted productions such as *The Crow* and "Matlock." In 1996, EUE/ Screen Gems Studios, Ltd., purchased it and hired as president Frank Capra, Jr., son of the legendary director. Under his direction, the 32-acre campus now offers technical and support services, tours, demonstrations, and a studio commissary/ coffee shop where film junkies can enjoy pastries, sandwiches, and snacks. A large mural of the "Dawson's Creek" original cast overlooks the commissary's outdoor deck.

On weekends from April to September, visitors can take guided walking tours of Screen Gems, a real working studio where tours change as productions change. Film junkies can experience an authentic screening room, a video orientation, a stroll around the complex, and up-close looks at movie props and sets, when available. Even without theme-park amusements, there's plenty to satisfy curious fans.

The "Dawson's Creek" sets on Stages 7, 8, and others were disassembled after the show wrapped. However, some sets have been re-created on Stage 1, which also showcases actual props from "Dawson's Creek," "Matlock," "American Gothic," *Black Knight, Muppets From Space, The Adventures of Elmo in Grouchland,* and *Year of the Dragon,* among other productions.

Thanks to blue-screen technology, memorable studio moments have included Tim Robbins's skyscraper fall in the Coen brothers' *The Hudsucker Proxy* and the sequence from George Lucas's *Radioland Murders* with actors dangling from skyscrapers. The turbulent tugboat close-ups in *Virus* used Stage 4's in-ground tank and electro-hydraulic gimbal. Over the years, the studio backlot has accommodated a Brooklyn streetscape in productions such as *Billy Bathgate* and a medieval castle in *Black Knight.*

★★★★★★★★★★★★★★
"Creek" Seekers: The "Dawson's Creek" Phenomenon

"Creek" seekers find a prime photo op at EUE/Screen Gems Studios'
landmark "Dawson's Creek" cast mural.
COURTESY OF CAPE FEAR COAST CONVENTION AND VISITORS BUREAU

By its second season, "Dawson's Creek" was more than just a television show; it was a phenomenon. The WB studio president Jordan Levin contends that the coming-of-age show defined The WB as a network for a generation of television viewers.

Although "Dawson's Creek" is set in New England, word spread quickly that Wilmington was the *real* Capeside, Massachusetts. Thus, the pilgrimage began. At first, dozens, then hundreds of Creekheads traveled to Wilmington to walk in the footsteps of Dawson (James Van Der Beek), Joey (Katie Holmes), Pacey (Joshua Jackson), Jen (Michelle Williams), Jack (Kerr Smith), and other principals. Fans arrived from Canada, Brazil, Europe, the U.K., and even Australia and Japan.

Your "Dawson's Creek" experience should begin with a guided weekend tour of EUE/Screen Gems Studios (see pages 58-61), where offices and sets were located. A larger-than-life mural of the cast is outside the commissary. Film junkies can find show locations in the Coast and Piedmont sections of this guide. Fans can request a "Dawson's Creek" FAQ sheet from the Cape Fear Coast Convention and Visitors Bureau; the sheet details a self-guided tour. Call 800-222-4757 or e-mail info@cape-fear.nc.us.

"One Tree Hill" (The WB, 2003), A Walk to Remember (2002);
Divine Secrets of the Ya-Ya Sisterhood (2002); *Dangerous Lives of Altar Boys* (2002); *Black Knight* (2001); *28 Days* (2000); *Muppets From Space* (1999); *The Adventures of Elmo in Grouchland* (1999); *Virus* (1999); "Dawson's Creek" (The WB, 1998-2003); *The Jackal* (1997); "American Gothic" (CBS, 1995-96); "The Twilight Zone: Rod Serling's Lost Classics" (CBS, 1994); "Matlock" (ABC, 1993-95); *The Road to Wellville* (1994); *The Crow* (1994); *The Hudsucker Proxy* (1994); *Radioland Murders* (1994); "The Young Indiana Jones Chronicles," (ABC, 1992-94); *Sleeping With the Enemy* (1991); *Rambling Rose* (1991); *Teenage Mutant Ninja Turtles* (1990); *Blue Velvet* (1986); *King Kong Lives* (1986); *Crimes of the Heart* (1986); *Raw Deal* (1986); *Year of the Dragon* (1985); and numerous others. Film, TV, and commercial credits number in the hundreds. For a complete list, visit www.screengemsstudios.com.

New Hanover High School

1307 Market Street. Visitors are limited to exterior viewing except during games.

Though many students past and present have complained of New Hanover High School's industrial, even prisonlike appearance, the school at 13th and Market Streets has certainly caught the eye of filmmakers—perhaps for that very reason. The school's dramatic sand-colored brick front entrance was the backdrop for the pilot of "Dawson's Creek," before Capeside High was moved to the UNC-Wilmington campus.

The striking pedestrian bridge that crosses Market Street is seen early in *Blue Velvet* behind the convertible of suave Jeffrey Beaumont (Kyle MacLachlan) as he picks up Sandy Williams (Laura Dern), who looks fetching in her pink, fuzzy sweater. Dern is seen earlier on the school's front lawn.

Interestingly, the back steps are where Channe Willis (Leelee Sobieski) and Billy Willis (Jesse Bradford) catch rides home in the Merchant Ivory feature *A Soldier's Daughter Never Cries*, based on Kaylie Jones's novel.

NHHS also appears in other teen-themed productions. Teenagers, rock-and-roll, and horror all come together in *Trick or Treat*, featuring rockers Gene Simmons and Ozzy Osbourne (long before "The Osbournes"). High-school life is also on display in *Dream a Little Dream*, a Corey Haim/Corey Feldman vehicle that features Piper Laurie, Harry Dean Stanton, and Jason Robards. More serious teen themes are addressed in "The Face on the Milk Carton," based on the novel by popular young-adult writer Carolyn B. Cooney; in that show, NHHS stands in as Carlington High.

The school's famous real-life students have included broadcast journalist David Brinkley, artist Claude Howell, writer Robert Ruark, and professional athletes Roman Gabriel, Trot Nixon, Clyde Simmons, and Kenny Gattison.

CREDITS

"Dawson's Creek" (The WB, 1998-2003); *A Walk to Remember* (2002); *A Soldier's Daughter Never Cries* (1998); "To Dance with Olivia" (CBS, 1997); "The Ditchdigger's Daughters" (Family Channel, 1997); "Blue River" (Fox, 1995); "The Face on the Milk Carton" (CBS, 1995); "Labor of Love: The Arlette Schweitzer Story" (CBS, 1993); *Dream a Little Dream* (1989); *Hiding Out* (1987); *Trick or Treat* (1986); *Blue Velvet* (1986)

Emerson-Kenan House and Holt-Wise House

Reminiscent of *Gone With the Wind*'s Tara are two of Wilmington's most grand and historic homes: the Emerson-Kenan House and the Holt-Wise House, both built around 1908. Sisters Sarah Graham Kenan and Jessie Kenan Wise once owned these magnificent homes, which were deeded by their heirs to the University of North Carolina-Wilmington. The sisters frequently entertained guests of great social status, but neither dreamed that their homes would become motion-picture locations. Although the houses are not open to the public, they make for great photo opportunities.

On location at the Emerson-Kenan House, a.k.a. the Atlanta
Coca-Cola mansion in *Divine Secrets of the Ya-Ya Sisterhood*
COURTESY OF E. MICHAEL HEWETT, LOCATIONS . . . +, INC.

Emerson-Kenan House
1705 Market Street

Lovely inside and out, the Emerson-Kenan House appears
as the Atlanta Coca-Cola mansion where the Ya-Yas visit
Teensy's relatives in *Divine Secrets of the Ya-Ya Sisterhood*. Its interiors appear in scenes of the foyer and the girls' bedrooms and
bathroom. The house also appears as a Tara-esque mansion in
"A Burning Passion: The Margaret Mitchell Story."

In 1923, Sarah Graham Kenan purchased and refurbished
the two-and-a-half-story brick house. Today it is the UNCW
chancellor's residence. It has been immortalized on film as Os-
car®-winning actress Nicole Kidman's hotel suite in *Billy Bathgate*
and as Miss Cornelia Beaumont's (Katharine Hepburn's) grand
house in Truman Capote's "One Christmas." It is also where
Dawson (James Van Der Beek) and Gail Leery (Mary-Margaret
Humes) pick out Dad's casket in season five of "Dawson's Creek."

CREDITS

The house appears in multiple episodes of "Dawson's Creek"
(The WB, 1998-2003). It serves as a fraternity house in "The
Locket" (Hallmark/CBS, 2002) and as a funeral parlor in "The
Lost Capone" (TNT, 1990). Its other credits include *Ball of Wax*
(2003); *Divine Secrets of the Ya-Ya Sisterhood* (2002); *The Dress Code*

(2000); 28 Days (2000); The Cutoff (1998); "Oprah Winfrey Presents: The Wedding" (ABC, 1998); "The Stepford Husbands" (CBS, 1996); "Timepiece" (CBS, 1996); "The Summer of Ben Tyler" (Hallmark/CBS, 1996); "Gramps" (NBC, 1995); "A Burning Passion: The Margaret Mitchell Story" (NBC, 1994); "One Christmas" (CBS, 1994); Rambling Rose (1991); Billy Bathgate (1991); and Betsy's Wedding (1990); Ordinary Heroes (1986).

Holt-Wise House
1713 Market Street

Imagine Miss Jessie Kenan Wise's delight if she knew that Sir Anthony Hopkins (portraying Dr. John Harvey Kellogg) spent hours filming in her formal dining room for a scene in *The Road to Wellville*. Imagine her horror if she knew that a bathtub fell through the second-story floor in "Black Magic."

The Holt-Wise House is a regal two-and-a-half-story frame structure that now serves as UNCW's alumni house. Musician Charlie Daniels held a press conference here in 2001 when he returned to his hometown to receive a star on the Celebrate Wilmington! Walk of Fame (see pages 14-15).

CREDITS

"Dawson's Creek" (The WB, 1998-2003); "The Sister-in-Law" (USA, 1995); *The Road to Wellville* (1994); "Simple Justice" (PBS, 1993); "The Young Indiana Jones Chronicles" (ABC, 1992-94); "Black Magic" (Showtime, 1992)

Emsley A. Laney High School
2700 North College Road. Visitors are limited to exterior viewing except during games.

At first glance, Laney High School looks like an ordinary public-school building. Even upon a second and third glance, one would never guess that basketball legend Michael Jordan scuffed the floors of Laney's gym. Jordan has also tried his hand

at acting; you can see him in such non-North Carolina productions as *Michael Jordan: To the Max* and *Space Jam*. Posters of the
1981 graduate are displayed in the school's Michael J. Jordan
Gymnasium. Although those posters don't appear in "One Tree
Hill," basketball scenes for the teen series were filmed in the
legendary gym.

Laney's film credits include documentaries tracing Jordan's
life. The most well-known piece of Laney lore is MJ's story of
not making the varsity on his first attempt. When he did, he
soon attracted the attention of coaches everywhere, including
UNC's Dean Smith. Michael led the Tar Heels to the national
title his freshman year. He went on to win six NBA titles with
the Chicago Bulls and Olympic gold medals in 1984 and 1992.

Wilmington hasn't forgotten Jordan. A stretch of I-40 is
dedicated to him, and memorabilia from his Laney days is on
permanent display at the Cape Fear Museum's Michael Jordan
Discovery Gallery (see pages 44-45).

Laney appears as Hanover High in the football stadium
scene featuring Leelee Sobieski and Kris Kristofferson in Mer-
chant-Ivory's *A Soldier's Daughter Never Cries*. Other school scenes
were filmed at rival New Hanover High (see pages 61-62).

Another Hollywood connection exists on the baseball field.
James Van Der Beek of "Dawson's Creek" trained with Laney
head coach Trent Mongero to prepare for a movie role. After
training, the actor accepted a position as assistant coach during
the Buccaneers' spring practice. He told a *Wilmington Star News*
reporter that his fondest memory was when the team, refusing
to pick a captain, made all members captain—that, and getting
caked in mud during a rainout drill.

CREDITS

The school appears in classroom scenes in "The Face on the
Milk Carton" (CBS, 1995). Its other credits include "One Tree
Hill" (The WB, 2003-) and *A Soldier's Daughter Never Cries* (1998).

Capeside High's most famous alumni film
outside UNCW's Alderman Hall
PHOTOGRAPH BY BILL RUSS
COURTESY OF N. C. DIVISION OF TOURISM, FILM, & SPORTS DEVELOPMENT

University of North Carolina-Wilmington

*601 South College Road (800-228-5571 or 910-962-3243;
www.uncw.edu). Guided tours of the campus depart from the
Trask Coliseum lobby at 10 A.M. and 2 P.M. Monday through
Friday.*

Featuring immaculate landscaping and Georgian architecture, the UNCW campus is always ready for a close-up. Its stately red-brick buildings lend an Ivy League look to Colby College in *New Best Friend*. Alderman Hall doubles as the entrance to Capeside High School in seasons one through four of "Dawson's Creek," except in the pilot episode, which was filmed at New Hanover High School (see pages 61-62). Look for the bench outside Alderman Hall with a plaque dedicated to the show. Kenan Auditorium doubles as the Capeside High auditorium in seasons one through four and as a New England university theatre lobby in seasons five and six.

Star sightings occur around campus even when the camera's not rolling. From 2000 to 2002, Michael Jordan brought the NBA's Washington Wizards to his hometown for preseason training at Trask Coliseum. Other celebs including Frank Sinatra, Liza Minnelli, Tony Bennett, and Edward James Olmos have appeared at Kenan Auditorium and Trask Coliseum.

Movie locations aside, UNCW consistently ranks among ~~U.S. News & World Report's top 10 universities in the South.~~

All right, Mr. DeMille, she's ready for her close-up!

CREDITS

Alderman Hall appears in "Dawson's Creek" (The WB, 1998-2003). The chancellor's office and the conference room can be seen in "Love's Deadly Triangle: The Texas Cadet Murder" (NBC, 1997); the chancellor's office is also in "What the Deaf Man Heard" (Hallmark/CBS, 1997). The building's south entrance is visible in "Murderous Intent" (CBS, 1995). The cannon located between Alderman Hall and James Hall makes several appearances in "Dawson's Creek."

Room 211 of Cameron Hall appears in "The Young Indiana Jones Chronicles" (ABC, 1992-94).

The Greene Track appears in "Dawson's Creek."

The Hanover Hall Gymnasium appears in "Dawson's Creek." The police-academy graduation in *29th Street* (1991) takes place in the outside courtyard.

Hoggard Hall was used in filming the first- and second-floor hospital hallways in *29th Street*. The building also appears in "Dawson's Creek."

Kenan Auditorium appears in "Dawson's Creek" and "Matlock" (ABC, 1993-95).

The main quad also appears in "Dawson's Creek" and "Matlock."

Morton Hall's commons and Bryan Auditorium may be seen in *New Best Friend* (2002).

The interior of Randall Library appears in "Dawson's Creek." The building's exterior appears in "Matlock."

The lobby and the exterior of Schwartz Hall may be seen in "The Perfect Crime" (USA, 1997).

Trask Coliseum appears in *New Best Friend* and "Never Give Up: The Jim Valvano Story" (CBS, 1996).

The Warwick Center appears in *Enchanted* (1998); "Dare to Love" (ABC/Lifetime,1995); "Matlock"; and "Twilight Man" (Starz! 1996).

The wooded area at Reynolds Drive and Cahill Drive appears in "Amy & Isabelle" (ABC, 2001).

Coastal Film Happenings

The North Carolina coast is a magnet for filmmakers and film-related events. Here's a sampling of film happenings.

Cine Noir: A Festival of Black Film, Wilmington

The Black Arts Alliance, Inc., hosts panel discussions and screenings of films in a variety of genres by African-American filmmakers at the Cape Fear Museum (see pages 53-54) and other venues during March. An admission fee is charged. For information, contact the Black Arts Alliance by calling 910-392-3725 or visiting http://blackartsalliance.org.

Cucalorus Film Festival, Wilmington

In 1995, Twinkle Doon filmmakers staged the first Cucalorus Film Festival, a one-night screening that's evolved into a five-day festival in downtown Wilmington in March. Hailed by *MovieMaker* magazine as the indie fest circuit's best-kept secret, it is the area's premier independent film festival. The films shown at this event span the globe in many genres. Screenings, filmmaker lectures, workshops, and question-and-answer sessions are offered. An admission fee is charged. For information, contact the Cucalorus Film Foundation by calling 910-343-5995 or visiting www.cucalorus.org.

EmeraldEye Short Film Festival and Screenwriting Competition, Greenville

Since 2002, independent shorts have been screened at this fall event. Prizes are given for filmmaking and screenwriting. For information, visit www.emeraldeye.org.

Fabulous Forties 50-cent Fantail Film Festival, Wilmington

For just 50 cents, film junkies can view wartime classics and musicals on a big screen from the fantail of the Battleship *North*

Carolina (see pages 54-55). Screenings are offered on Friday nights at 8:30 P.M. in May and at 7:30 P.M. in October. An admission fee is charged. For information, call 910-251-5797 or visit www.battleshipnc.com.

Fearless Cape Fear Film Festival, Wilmington

This event is a festival of films by gay and lesbian filmmakers. Screenings are offered at the City Stage Theater (see pages 18-19). For information, call 910-342-0272.

NCSA Student Film Festival, Manteo

Each February, the North Carolina School of the Arts screens award-winning student films at Roanoke Island Festival Park in Manteo. The event is free. NCSA also produced a documentary, *The Legend of Two-Path*, that is shown daily. For information, call 252-475-1500 or visit www.roanokeisland.com.

Sometime in October Film Festival and Regional Showcase, Wilmington

The Cape Fear Independent Film Network sponsors these two events. The Sometime in October Film Festival is a juried three-day event dedicated to independent films under 30 minutes in length; screenings are offered in downtown Wilmington. Held in February or March, the Regional Showcase features shorts by North Carolina and South Carolina filmmakers. An admission fee is charged. For information, visit www.cfifn.org.

UNCW Film-Related Events, Wilmington

The film school at UNCW (see pages 66-67) offers screenings, lectures, workshops, and seminars. Among them is Local Focus, a forum for "spirited creative and intellectual exchange" that kicks off the Cucalorus Film Festival in March. An admission fee is charged. For information, contact the UNCW Film Studies Department by calling 910-962-7502 or visiting www.uncw.edu/filmstudies/index1.html.

Port Land Grille

1908 Eastwood Road in Lumina Station (910-256-6056;
www.portlandgrille.com). The restaurant opens at 5:30 P.M.
Monday through Saturday. Call for reservations.

When the subject of fine dining in the Wilmington/
Wrightsville Beach area comes up, Port Land Grille is sure to
be mentioned. Executive chef and proprietor Shawn Wellersdick
crafts a new menu daily. An open window reveals the kitchen
"theatre" that appears in season four of "Dawson's Creek" when
Pacey (Joshua Jackson) and his rich girlfriend are waited on by
PLG's own Charlie Brookshire.

Celebrity diners have included Vanessa Redgrave ("The
Locket"), Sandra Bullock (*Divine Secrets of the Ya-Ya Sisterhood*),
Steve Buscemi and Teri Polo (*Domestic Disturbance*), Peter Coy-
ote and Mandy Moore (*A Walk to Remember*), and "Dawson's
Creek" cast members Katie Holmes (with actor Chris Klein),
Joshua Jackson, and James Van Der Beek, who returned several
times during the show's final week. Other patrons have included
Adam Shankman, who directed *A Walk to Remember;* Kevin
Williamson, creator and writer of "Dawson's Creek"; and the
late journalist and Wilmington native David Brinkley.

CREDITS
"Dawson's Creek" (The WB, 1998-2003)

Airlie Gardens

300 Airlie Road at Oleander Drive (910-798-7700;
www.airliegardens.org). From March to October, the gardens are
open from 9 A.M. to 5 P.M. Tuesday through Saturday and from
11 A.M. to 5 P.M. on Sunday. Hours are extended during April
and May. An admission fee is charged.

Enter the iron filigree gates of Airlie Gardens and you'll
behold 67 spectacular acres of post-Victorian European-style
gardens designed in the early 1900s. A sign and memorial garden at the gatehouse honor Airlie's beloved gatekeeper, vision-
ary artist Minnie Evans.

The 450-year-old Airlie Oak spreads her elegant limbs over a party scene in "Dare to Love," starring Josie Bissett and Jim Sikking. COURTESY OF E. MICHAEL HEWETT, LOCATIONS . . . +, INC.

Airlie provided settings for some of the most romantic and poignant scenes in "Dawson's Creek." Its signature 450-year-old Airlie Oak offered a sprawling, moss-covered canopy over a temporary graveyard for the episode in which Dawson (James Van Der Beek) visits his father's grave. Airlie's pergola appears in several "DC" love scenes. Rowboat sequences were filmed along Bradley Creek and Hewlett's Creek—the *real* Dawson's Creek. In the final episode, the Dawson-Joey dream wedding takes place on a creek-side lawn.

The lovely gardens' versatile charms have also been showcased in other productions. Sandra Bullock's horse-training therapy in 28 *Days* takes place at the stables. Airlie's lakes, forests, and natural botanical areas created a medieval mood for Martin Lawrence's *Black Knight*.

CREDITS

Black Knight (2001); 28 *Days* (2000); "Holy Joe" (CBS, 1999); "Dawson's Creek" (The WB, 1998-2003); "Dare to Love" (ABC/ Lifetime, 1995); *The Road to Wellville* (1994); "In the Best of Families: Marriage, Pride, Madness" (CBS, 1994); "Labor of Love: The Arlette Schweitzer Story" (CBS, 1993); *Betsy's Wedding* (1990); *King Kong Lives* (1986)

The Arboretum at New Hanover County Cooperative Extension

6206 Oleander Drive (910-452-6393; www.arboretumnhc.org).
The arboretum is open daily during daylight hours.

When location managers need a lush, flower-filled setting, they count on the Arboretum at New Hanover County Cooperative Extension and its 4,000-plus species of native and naturalized plants. Seven acres of picture-perfect gardens beckon with benches, gazebos, wide walkways, fabulous flowers, and a pond that provided the surreal setting for "Dawson's Creek: The Final Episode." This is where Dawson (James Van Der Beek) videotapes Jen's (Michelle Williams's) dying-wish message for her baby girl. Dawson and Joey (Katie Holmes) later ponder their lives on a nearby arboretum bench.

CREDITS
"Dawson's Creek: The Final Episode" (The WB, 2003)

Jungle Rapids Family Fun Park

5320 Oleander Drive (910-791-0666; www.junglerapids.com).
The park is open daily from 10 A.M. to 10 P.M. An admission fee
is charged.

On screen and off, Jungle Rapids Family Fun Park makes a splash. Famous father John Travolta (*Domestic Disturbance*) and son Jett had a great time here. James Van Der Beek (Dawson), Katie Holmes (Joey), and other cast members hung out when "Dawson's Creek" filmed in the arcade room and the Big Splash Café.

Among the attractions are a laser-tag arena, a climbing wall, and an indoor playground. Outdoors, there's a million-gallon wave pool, a 7,000-square-foot splash pool, a go-cart track, a miniature-golf course, and several action-packed water slides.

Westfield Shoppingtown Independence

*3000 Oleander Drive (910-392-1776). The mall is open from
10 A.M. to 9 P.M. Monday through Saturday and from
12:30 P.M. to 6 P.M. on Sunday.*

Westfield Shoppingtown Independence became an action/adventure set when Agent Kaminski (Arnold Schwarzenegger) was surprised by thugs during a shopping spree gone bad in *Raw Deal*. Not to worry. Ah-nold pitches the bad guys through the glass storefront across from Fleishman's Department Store. An equally intense scene—the lost-child sequence in the pilot of "Touched by an Angel"—was filmed at the interior Belk entrance.

American Eagle Outfitters, an official clothing provider for "Dawson's Creek," is among the 150-plus specialty shops. Celebrity mall shoppers have included Melanie Griffith (*Lolita*), and Katie Holmes, Michelle Williams, and Mary-Margaret Humes of "Dawson's Creek." During a brief layover in 2001, music superstars Britney Spears and Justin Timberlake shopped at Abercrombie & Fitch.

The Body Shop and the food court appear in "Going to California" (Showtime, 2001). The parking lot may be seen in Stephen King's "The Golden Years" (CBS, 1991). Other credits include "Touched by an Angel" (CBS, 1994) and *Raw Deal* (1986).

Greenfield Park

1702 Burnett Boulevard, off South Third Street (910-341-7855). The park is open year-round during daylight hours. Canoe and kayak rentals and guided canoe tours are available from May to September; call 910-762-5606 on weekdays or 910-341-7868 on weekends. Hours and fees for rentals and tours and for the skate park vary. Amphitheater events include the Shakespeare on the Green Festival in May and June.

Otherwise known as Burham Lake in "Dawson's Creek," Greenfield Lake is the star attraction of Greenfield Park, a city park with nature trails, 20 acres of gardens, and more than 200 acres of swamp, lakes, and moss-laden cypress trees.

The five-mile Lake Shore Drive, built by unemployed Wilmingtonians during the Great Depression, appears in driving scenes featuring the older Ya-Yas in *Divine Secrets of the Ya-Ya Sisterhood*. The park's wooden footbridges appear in other *Divine* scenes, including young Vivi's bicycle jaunt, which is interrupted by tragic news. Scenes in "Matlock" were filmed in the fragrance garden and by the arched bridge.

CREDITS

"Dawson's Creek" (The WB, 1998-2003); *Divine Secrets of the Ya-Ya Sisterhood* (2002); *The Dress Code* (2000); *What It Was Was Football* (1997); "What the Deaf Man Heard" (Hallmark/CBS, 1997); "Matlock" (ABC, 1993-95); "Against Her Will: The Carrie Buck Story" (Lifetime, 1994); Stephen King's *Maximum Overdrive* (1986); *Silver Bullet* (1985)

Legion Sports Complex

2131 Carolina Beach Road (910-341-7855; www.ci.wilmington.nc.us/prd/athletics.htm)

A mock football game was staged during the first season of "Dawson's Creek" for the Capeside High student film entitled "Helmets of Glory." A few dozen extras portrayed football players and fans while life-sized cardboard cutouts filled the empty stadium seats. The complex also appears in Capeside High football sequences featuring Coach Leery (John Wesley Shipp) and Jack McPhee (Kerr Smith) during season four. The long-running series "Matlock" used the stadium in a scene for the episode "The Conspiracy," in which a character dies from a push down the stairs.

Real-life sports drama unfolds when the Wilmington Hammerheads soccer team, the Wilmington Sharks baseball club, and the Port City Diesel football team take to the fields. The complex made international television when the Wilmington Hammerheads advanced to the 2002 and 2003 National United Soccer League finals.

CREDITS

"Holy Joe" (CBS, 1999); "Dawson's Creek" (The WB, 1998-2003); *What It Was Was Football* (1997); "Matlock" (ABC, 1993-95)

Other Wilmington Star Tracks

Big Dog Café

1632 Castle Hayne Road (910-762-1332). The café is open from 6 A.M. to 3 P.M. Monday through Friday.

Big Dog Café owner and chef Doug Meyer's reputation for tasty Southern-style breakfasts and lunches and the restaurant's proximity to the studios are big hits with celebs. Lining the walls are photos of stars from productions that have used Meyer's Big Dog Catering: Billy Zane (*This World, Then the Fireworks*), Dean Cain ("The Runaway"), Meat Loaf (*Black Dog*), Andie MacDowell (*Shadrach*), Randy Travis (*Black Dog*), John Travolta (*Domestic Disturbance*), and Teri Hatcher (*The Chester Story*). Big Dog also operates Studio Perk Café, the commissary at EUE/Screen Gems Studios (see pages 58-61).

Apple Annie's Bake Shop

837 South Kerr Avenue (910-799-9023). The bakery is open from 8 A.M. to 7 P.M. Monday through Thursday, from 8 A.M. to 6 P.M. Friday and Saturday, and from noon to 6 P.M. on Sunday.

Behind the doors of Apple Annie's Bake Shop, an array of confections and other sweet treats beckons. The photos lining the walls are proof that even Hollywood's A-list darlings give in to their sweet tooth. Isn't it comforting to know that the lovely (and thin) Ashley Judd (*Divine Secrets of the Ya-Ya Sisterhood*) just had to have the strawberry shortcake? Or that blond bombshell Melanie Griffith (*Lolita*), "designing woman" Annie Potts ("Her Deadly Rival"), and the cast of "Dawson's Creek" have succumbed to its sweet temptations? A picture of Jodie Foster's (*Dangerous Lives of Altar Boys*) custom Hannibal Lecter cake hangs alongside shots of the award-winning bakery's other celebrity customers, who have included Andy Griffith ("Matlock"), Richard Gere (*The Jackal*), basketball superstar Michael Jordan, and late NASCAR legend Dale Earnhardt.

Port City Java—Lumina Station

1900 Eastwood Road (910-256-0993). This location is open daily from 6 A.M. to 10 P.M.

Located just over the bridge from Wrightsville Beach, this java stop is convenient for celebrities opting for the beach scene. Celebrity Port City Javaheads have included Alec Baldwin, Kim Basinger (*No Mercy*), Michelle Williams and Katie Holmes of "Dawson's Creek," and Valerie Bertinelli ("In a Child's Name") and her former hubby, guitarist Eddie Van Halen.

★ ★ ★ ★ ★ ★ ★ ★ ★

Landfall Park Hampton Inn & Suites

1989 Eastwood Road (877-256-9600 or 910-256-9600;
www.landfallparkhotel.com)

Even before the Landfall Park Hampton Inn & Suites became headquarters for the Coastal Classic Celebrity Golf Tournament, Hollywood types enjoyed its hospitality and amenities. Guests can be at Wrightsville Beach in less than five minutes and at Screen Gems Studios in 10.

Celebrity guests have included Jim Sikking ("Dare to Love"), Leann Hunley ("Dawson's Creek"), Keith Carradine (*The Angel Doll*), and Mitchell Laurance ("Matlock"; "Dawson's Creek"). Others who have paid a visit include TV bionic wonder Lee Majors; Dan Cortese, best known for his role in "Veronica's Closet"; Dennis Franz of "NYPD Blue"; Matthew Laurance of "Beverly Hills 90210"; Barry Williams, who played Greg in "The Brady Bunch"; and Arte Johnson of "Laugh-In."

NOFO Market and Café

1125 Military Cutoff Road (910-256-5565; www
.NOFO.com). NOFO is open from 11 A.M. to 3 P.M. and from
5 P.M. to 9 P.M. Monday through Saturday and from 11 A.M. to
3 P.M. on Sunday.

NOFO, named for its former location on North Fourth Street, is a trendy gift shop, gourmet food market, and café. Light Southern fare dominates the menu; fresh soups, salads, daily specials, desserts, and creative sandwiches such as a grilled shrimp BLT on sourdough are among the favorites. Celebrity diners have included Kelly Preston, Elisabeth Shue ("Amy & Isabelle"), Michelle Williams and Katie Holmes ("Dawson's Creek"), Kim Basinger (*No Mercy*), David Andrews (*A Walk to Remember*), and TV and Broadway actress Linda Lavin ("Stolen Memories: Secrets from the Rose Garden").

★ ★ ★ ★ ★ ★ ★ ★ ★

Figure Eight Island

U.S. 17 between Wilmington and Hampstead. Visitors must be accompanied by a resident or an authorized realtor. The Figure Eight Realty office is located at 15 Bridge Road; call 800-279-6085 or 910-686-4400.

If you've got deep pockets—*really* deep pockets—you can rent a Figure Eight Island home, just like the stars. Houses on this private, gated island range from grand to grander. Most homes offer breathtaking views of the expansive beaches, the wild dunes, and the open sea.

Film junkies have seen Figure Eight Island in *Sleeping With the Enemy*. Celebrity guests have included former vice president Al Gore, Kim Basinger (*No Mercy*), Alec Baldwin, George C. Scott (*Firestarter*), Sissy Spacek (*Marie: A True Story*), Pierce Brosnan ("Noble House"), Richard Gere (*The Jackal*), Alan Alda (*Betsy's Wedding*), and Nicole Kidman and Dustin Hoffman (*Billy Bathgate*).

Figure Eight Realty can suggest a home that suits your preferences.

Wilson's Restaurant & Entertainment Complex

4925 New Centre Drive (910-793-0999). Wilson's is open daily from 11:00 A.M. to 2 A.M.

When the 1999 Coastal Classic Celebrity Golf Tournament was rained out, Lee Majors—best known for his title role in "The Six Million Dollar Man"—and other celebrity guests hung out in the sports bar and game rooms at Wilson's. There's also a jazz lounge, a tiki bar, a restaurant, and a dinner theatre. Celebrity sightings have included John Travolta (*Domestic Disturbance*), Sandra Bullock (*Divine Secrets of the Ya-Ya Sisterhood; 28 Days*), Vince Vaughn and Steve Buscemi (*Domestic Disturbance*), and Alec Baldwin.

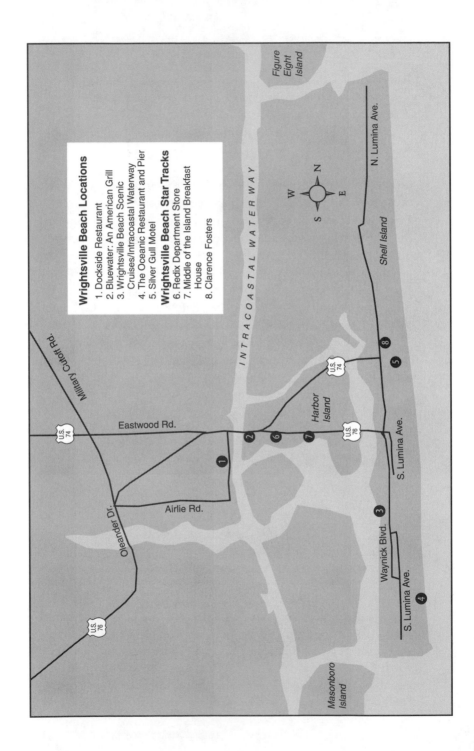

Wrightsville Beach Locations

1. Dockside Restaurant
2. Bluewater: An American Grill
3. Wrightsville Beach Scenic Cruises/Intracoastal Waterway
4. The Oceanic Restaurant and Pier
5. Silver Gull Motel

Wrightsville Beach Star Tracks

6. Redix Department Store
7. Middle of the Island Breakfast House
8. Clarence Fosters

Wrightsville Beach
PHOTOGRAPH BY JOHN NEWTON
COURTESY OF CAPE FEAR COAST CONVENTION AND VISITORS BUREAU

Wrightsville Beach Locations

Wrightsville Beach/Shell Island

Lighted dancing porpoises welcome film junkies to Wrightsville Beach, established in 1899. The five-mile-long island's celebrity visitors have included Atlanta native Margaret Mitchell, who penned the classic *Gone With the Wind*, and actor and president Ronald Reagan, who stayed here during the 1959 North Carolina Azalea Festival. Others who have opted for oceanfront accommodations include Sandra Bullock (*Divine Secrets of the Ya-Ya Sisterhood*), Jamie Lee Curtis (*Virus*), Shirley MacLaine

(*The Dress Code*), Barbra Streisand, and John Travolta (*Domestic Disturbance*). Celebrities such as LA-based radio deejay Rick Dees, a native of Greensboro, sometimes dock their yachts at local marinas. The island's restaurants, grocery stores, shops, and exercise trails are great places to star-gaze.

In the heyday of jazz during the 1920s and 1930s, Guy Lombardo, Woody Herman, Tommy Dorsey, Cab Calloway, and Paul Whiteman performed at the legendary Lumina Pavilion, once the coast's premier facility for dancing, music, and recreation. Sadly, the Lumina no longer exists. Fortunately, the Wrightsville Beach Museum of History preserves its memory with photographs, clippings, and memorabilia.

Another island structure preserved in film junkies' memories is the dreamy Cape Cod summer cottage in the psychological thriller *Sleeping With the Enemy*. Sorry to disappoint, but the beach home occupied by Laura (Julia Roberts) and Martin Burney (Patrick Bergin) was actually a 3,000-foot temporary structure on Shell Island, a man-made extension on the north end of Wrightsville Beach. The house overlooked Mason Inlet and nearby Figure Eight Island (see page 79). After wrapping, 20th Century Fox demolished the house and restored the dunes to their original condition, planting sea oats and beach grass.

The pristine shoreline along the island's southern tip provided *To Gillian on Her 37th Birthday* with ample beach for 20 sand sculptures that appear in the Nantucket sand castle contest scene. "Dawson's Creek" filmed along the island's beaches, waterways, and streets and in its shops, restaurants, homes, and yacht clubs. The cult classic *Blue Velvet* filmed on Borden Street.

For tourist information, contact the Cape Fear Coast Convention and Visitors Bureau by calling 800-222-4757 or visiting www.cape-fear.nc.us. You can contact the Wrightsville Beach Chamber of Commerce by calling 910-395-2965. The Wrightsville Beach Museum of History is located at 303 West Salisbury Street; call 910-256-2569.

CREDIT

"One Tree Hill" (The WB, 2003-); *Divine Secrets of the Ya-Ya Sisterhood* (2002); "Dawson's Creek" (The WB, 1998-2003); "Oprah Winfrey Presents: The Wedding" (ABC, 1998); *The Jackal* (1997); *To Gillian on Her 37th Birthday* (1996); *Empire Records* (1995);

"Matlock" (ABC, 1993-95); "The Young Indiana Jones Chronicles" (ABC, 1992-94); "T-Bone-N-Weasel" (TNT, 1992); *Sleeping With the Enemy* (1991); *Weekend at Bernie's* (1989); *Blue Velvet* (1986); *Manhunter* (1986)

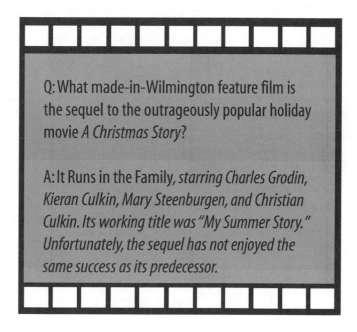

Q: What made-in-Wilmington feature film is the sequel to the outrageously popular holiday movie *A Christmas Story*?

A: It Runs in the Family, starring *Charles Grodin, Kieran Culkin, Mary Steenburgen, and Christian Culkin. Its working title was "My Summer Story." Unfortunately, the sequel has not enjoyed the same success as its predecessor.*

Dockside Restaurant

1308 Airlie Road (910-256-2752). The restaurant is open daily from 11 A.M. to 9 P.M.

Weekend afternoons are opportune times to catch film buzz on Dockside's outdoor deck. Overlooking the Intracoastal Waterway, it's a favorite hangout for actors and crew members, as well as a key "Dawson's Creek" location.

During the show's first and second seasons, Dockside doubled as The Icehouse—sort of. The real Icehouse, now closed, was located at 115 South Water Street in downtown Wilmington, but the script placed it along a channel. Scenes of The Icehouse from the outside looking in were filmed downtown, while scenes from the inside looking out were filmed at Dockside. For the final episode in 2003, a third Icehouse location at Chandler's Wharf (see pages 35-36) was introduced. In that

Wrightsville Beach Locations ★ 83

episode, Pacey (Joshua Jackson) rebuilds the restaurant, which is said to have burned down years before. Puzzling, eh? It kind of makes you feel for the editing professionals.

Dockside's menu offers fresh seafood and a range of salads, sandwiches, and desserts. Celebrity diners here have included Katie Holmes, Joshua Jackson, and Kerr Smith from "Dawson's Creek." Chris Klein, best known for his role in *American Pie*, has also paid a visit.

CREDITS

"Dawson's Creek" (The WB, 1998-2003)

Bluewater: An American Grill

4 Marina Street (910-256-8500; www.bluewaterdining.com). Bluewater is open daily from 11:30 A.M. to 10 P.M. From April through September, live entertainment is offered on Sunday from 4 P.M. to 8 P.M.

Film junkies will recognize this restaurant from the "Matlock" episode in which Atlanta attorney Ben Matlock (Andy Griffith) vacations in Wilmington and solves a crime. In an early "Dawson's Creek" episode, Joey (Katie Holmes) sings here in the Miss Windjammer Pageant talent competition and wins Dawson's heart.

There are few better places to while away an afternoon or evening than Bluewater's outdoor deck, which offers a panoramic view of the Intracoastal Waterway and three marinas. Before the sun sets, you'll observe enough characters and scenes to write your own screenplay.

Bluewater's menu features fresh seafood, along with chicken, beef, and pasta. The favorites of John Travolta (*Domestic Disturbance*) are the jumbo lump crab cakes and Bluewater's signature dessert, Caribbean Fudge Pie.

CREDITS

"Dawson's Creek" (The WB, 1998-2003); "Matlock" (ABC, 1993-95)

Wrightsville Beach Scenic Cruises/
Intracoastal Waterway

Wrightsville Beach Scenic Cruises is located on Banks Channel across from the Blockade Runner Resort; call 910-350-BOAT or visit www.cruiseinc.com. Hours vary according to the weather. Private charter boats are available.

Who needs the Skipper and Gilligan when there's Captain Bob and First Mate Marilyn? Wrightsville Beach Scenic Cruises invites visitors to board its 15-passenger pontoon boat and learn about pirates, island lore, and movie connections during a 90-minute tour of the Intracoastal Waterway (ICW). It also offers excursions to Masonboro Island, an uninhabited estuarine research reserve where *Manhunter* filmed. In a real-life drama, Joshua Jackson of "Dawson's Creek" rescued a troubled swimmer near Masonboro Island in 1999.

Winding its way from New Jersey to Florida, the ICW is a star in its own right. Spectacular homes, restaurants, and yachts line its banks. The ICW's credits include "Dawson's Creek," *Domestic Disturbance,* "Buried Alive II," "Matlock," *Sleeping With the Enemy,* and *Track 29.*

CREDITS

Domestic Disturbance (2001); "Dawson's Creek" (The WB, 1998-2003); "Buried Alive II" (USA, 1997); "Matlock" (ABC, 1993-95); *Sleeping With the Enemy* (1991); *Track 29* (1988); *Manhunter* (1986)

The Oceanic Restaurant and Pier

703 South Lumina Avenue (910-256-5551; www .oceanicrestaurant.com). The Oceanic is open daily from 11 A.M. to 10 P.M.

Reminiscent of the late, great Lumina Pavilion is The Oceanic Restaurant, which has three levels that offer breathtaking ocean vistas. Outside, the Oceanic Pier (also known as the Crystal Pier, formerly the Mira-mar) features umbrella-covered tables.

The Oceanic Pier, shown here during filming
of a commercial, is a popular beach location.
COURTESY OF E. MICHAEL HEWETT, LOCATIONS . . . +, INC.

Fans of "Dawson's Creek" will recognize the wooden pier
from the show's opening montage and various episodes.
Remember the beach party when Dawson comes to Joey's rescue?
The party takes place under and around the pier. The show's final
episode also features the pier and beach in flashback scenes.

Celebrity diners here have included Harvey Keitel
(*Shadrach*), William Baldwin (*Virus*), Jamie Lee Curtis (*Virus*),
Meredith Baxter Birney ("Holy Joe"), Mary-Margaret Humes
("Dawson's Creek"), and others at wrap parties on the private
third floor.

CREDITS

"Dawson's Creek" (The WB, 1998-2003); *Sleeping With the Enemy*
(1991)

Silver Gull Motel

*20 East Salisbury Street (800-842-8894 or 910-256-3728;
www.beachonline.com/slvrgull.htm). The Silver Gull is open
year-round.*

Film junkies who saw *Divine Secrets of the Ya-Ya Sisterhood* will
recall the Silver Gull Motel as young Vivi's (Ashley Judd's) Gulf
Coast hideout. The motel bedroom scenes were filmed in Room

327, and the mirror confrontation scene was filmed in another guest room.

This reputable, independently owned motel offers clean, no-frills oceanfront efficiency rooms.

CREDITS

Divine Secrets of the Ya-Ya Sisterhood (2002)

Wrightsville Beach Star Tracks

Middle of the Island Breakfast House

216 Causeway Drive (910-256-4277). The restaurant is open daily from 5:30 A.M. to 3 P.M. and from 5 P.M. to 10 P.M.

In June 2003, *American Way* magazine listed the 10 favorite restaurants of Mark Wahlberg (*Traveller*). Marky Mark's favorites spanned the globe from Paris, Tokyo, New York, and Boston to the Middle of the Island Breakfast House in Wrightsville Beach!

An island tradition since 1959, the Middle of the Island is known simply as "MOI" among the locals. Who doesn't love a hearty breakfast and a meat-and-three lunch or dinner? Proof that Hollywood types are no exception is found on the wall of fame behind the register. Bill Paxton (*Traveller*), Louis Gossett, Jr. ("To Dance with Olivia"), Brooke Shields ("The Almost Perfect Bank Robbery"), and Corbin Bernsen ("Murderous Intent") are among those who've dined here. Celebs who didn't provide a photo include Arnold Schwarzenegger (*Raw Deal*), Nick Nolte (*Weeds*), Julia Roberts (*Sleeping With the Enemy*), William Baldwin (*Virus*), Anthony Hopkins (*The Road to Wellville*), Mark Wahlberg, Jennifer Jason Leigh (*The Hudsucker Proxy*), Juliana Margulies (*Traveller*), Dennis Hopper (*Blue Velvet*), Sandra Bullock (*Divine Secrets of the Ya-Ya Sisterhood*), and Peter Gallagher (*To Gillian on Her 37th Birthday*).

Redix Department Store

120 Causeway Drive (910-256-2201). Redix is open from 9 A.M. to 7 P.M. Monday through Saturday and from 8 A.M. to 6 P.M. on Sunday.

Don't let the weather-worn exterior of this department store fool you. Inside, you'll find everything from fishing tackle and souvenirs to designer fashions and an excellent bathing-suit selection. Celebrities who've been able to transcend the notion that star-worthy shops must resemble flashy Rodeo Drive boutiques include Shirley MacLaine (*The Dress Code*). In spite of her dark glasses and floppy hat, shoppers and employees recognized the actress, director, and author. Among the many stars (incognito and otherwise) who have purchased clothing and beach supplies at Redix are Arnold Schwarzenegger (*Raw Deal*), Sissy Spacek (*Crimes of the Heart*), and Henry Winkler (Truman Capote's "One Christmas").

Clarence Fosters

22 North Lumina Avenue (910-256-0224). Clarence Fosters opens daily at 5:30 P.M. year-round.

Ask where to see and be seen in Wrightsville Beach and you'll hear about Clarence Fosters. On weekend nights, the lounge is packed with a bikini-to-black-tie crowd. The nightlife here is especially interesting when there's a celebrity in the house. Famous customers have included John Travolta (*Domestic Disturbance*), Martin Lawrence (*Black Knight*), Ashley Judd (*Divine Secrets of the Ya-Ya-Sisterhood*), William Baldwin (*Virus*), Dean Cain ("The Runaway"), Vince Vaughn and Steve Buscemi (*Domestic Disturbance*), Jason Gedrick and Christian Kane (*Summer Catch*), and basketball star Michael Jordan. Cast members of "Dawson's Creek" were on hand during filming here.

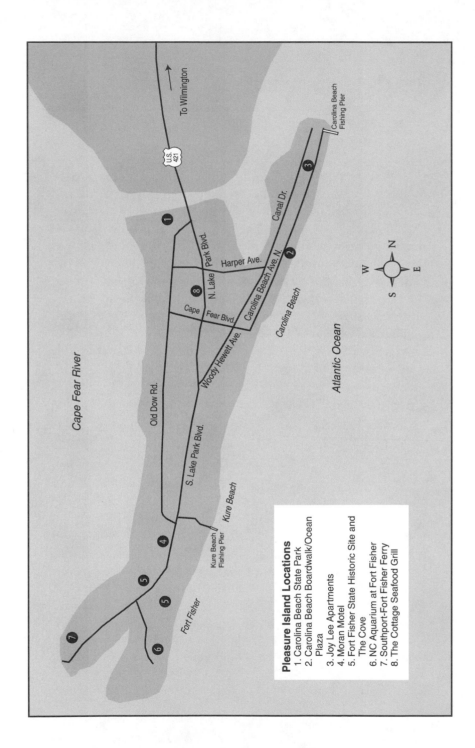

Pleasure Island Locations
1. Carolina Beach State Park
2. Carolina Beach Boardwalk/Ocean Plaza
3. Joy Lee Apartments
4. Moran Motel
5. Fort Fisher State Historic Site and The Cove
6. NC Aquarium at Fort Fisher
7. Southport-Fort Fisher Ferry
8. The Cottage Seafood Grill

To Wilmington

U.S. 421

Cape Fear River

Old Dow Rd.

S. Lake Park Blvd.

N. Lake Park Blvd.

Harper Ave.

Cape Fear Blvd.

Woody Hewett Ave.

Carolina Beach Ave. N.

Canal Dr.

Carolina Beach

Kure Beach

Kure Beach Fishing Pier

Fort Fisher

Carolina Beach Fishing Pier

Atlantic Ocean

N
W   E
S

Fort Fisher State Historic Site
COURTESY OF CAPE FEAR COAST CONVENTION AND VISITORS BUREAU

Pleasure Island Locations

Carolina Beach State Park

*1010 State Park Road, Carolina Beach (910-458-8206; http://
ils.unc.edu/parkproject/visit/cabe/home.html). The park is open
daily from 8 A.M. to 5 P.M. It is closed on Christmas Day.
Campground hours vary. Admission is free, though there is a fee
for camping and rentals.*

Filmmakers didn't discover Carolina Beach State Park until
the late 1980s. *Betsy's Wedding,* starring Alan Alda, Molly
Ringwald, and Madeline Kahn, was among the earliest
productions. A wedding tent and Alda's construction site

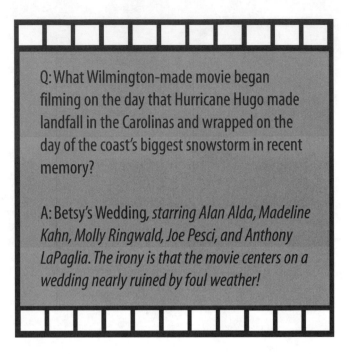

Q: What Wilmington-made movie began filming on the day that Hurricane Hugo made landfall in the Carolinas and wrapped on the day of the coast's biggest snowstorm in recent memory?

A: Betsy's Wedding, *starring Alan Alda, Madeline Kahn, Molly Ringwald, Joe Pesci, and Anthony LaPaglia. The irony is that the movie centers on a wedding nearly ruined by foul weather!*

overlooked the park's marshes. Tent interiors were filmed on a sound stage. Scenes for the first season of "Dawson's Creek" were shot along Snows Cut Trail. A drive along old Dow Road will take you to where the young Ya-Yas filmed their lingerie joy ride in *Divine Secrets of the Ya-Ya Sisterhood.*

The park's more than six miles of nature trails feature natural wonders like the Venus flytrap, a rare carnivorous plant that grows wild only within a radius of 75 to 100 miles of Wilmington. Another star attraction is the 50-foot sand dune known as Sugarloaf, where Civil War troops camped.

CREDITS

"Dawson's Creek" (The WB, 1998-2003); *Divine Secrets of the Ya-Ya Sisterhood* (2002); *Amos & Andrew* (1993); *Betsy's Wedding* (1990)

Carolina Beach Boardwalk/Ocean Plaza

The boardwalk is open year-round; merchant hours vary. The Plaza Pub is on Harper Avenue; call 910-458-8599. Club

Reminiscent of the famous boardwalks of Coney Island and Atlantic City, the Carolina Beach Boardwalk is a step back in time. Its tenants offer a nostalgic variety of souvenir and gift shops, eateries, arcades, and taverns.

Located at the north end is the 1946-vintage Ocean Plaza Building, distinguished by its stucco siding and frosted glass. From the 1940s to the 1960s, it hosted big bands and recording artists such as Chubby Checker, Jerry Lee Lewis, and Fats Domino.

The Plaza Pub (formerly called the Cilver Bullet and Bud & Joe's Lounge) at Ocean Plaza appears as the Big Ace during season four of "Dawson's Creek." The series returned during season five to film upstairs in Club Tropics, which claims to be the birthplace of the shag dance. Its roadhouse ambiance is seen in Alabama's 1996 music video "Shagging on the Boulevard." In "Day-o," starring Delta Burke, it's a pizza joint. When the pub was known as Bud & Joe's Lounge, *The Bedroom Window* shot the scene here in which Denise (Elizabeth McGovern) tries to seduce a serial killer; outside the bar, Terry (Steve Guttenberg) keeps watch. Bud & Joe's later changed its name to Cilver Bullet in honor of Stephen

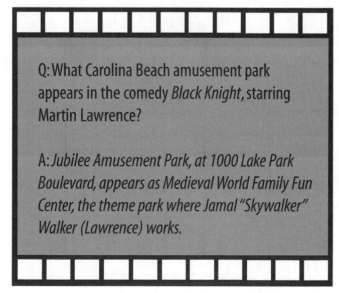

Q: What Carolina Beach amusement park appears in the comedy *Black Knight*, starring Martin Lawrence?

A: *Jubilee Amusement Park, at 1000 Lake Park Boulevard, appears as Medieval World Family Fun Center, the theme park where Jamal "Skywalker" Walker (Lawrence) works.*

King's *Silver Bullet*, the first movie to film there. *New Best Friend* chose the Plaza Pub for its Silver Bullet lounge scenes.

CREDITS
"Going to California" (Showtime, 2001) filmed at Ocean Plaza, *A Soldier's Daughter Never Cries* (1998) at a hot-dog stand, and "Matlock" (ABC, 1993-95) at Mama Mia's Pizza. The boardwalk's other credits include "Dawson's Creek" (The WB, 1998-2003); *New Best Friend* (2002); "CI5: The New Professionals" (BBC, 1998); "The Sister-in-Law" (USA, 1995); "Day-o" (NBC, 1992); *The Bedroom Window* (1987); and *Silver Bullet* (1985).

Joy Lee Apartments

317 Carolina Beach Avenue North, Carolina Beach (910-458-8361). Apartments are available year-round except during hard freezes.

A prime example of post-World War II architecture, the Joy Lee Apartments make a brief, yet memorable, appearance in Adrian Lyne's remake of *Lolita*. A scene with Lolita (Dominique Swain) and Professor Humbert Humbert (Jeremy Irons) was filmed inside Unit 4 of the Sea Horse Motel. Lyne moved the bathroom and kitchen and painted the room green. Sorry to disappoint, film junkies, but the vibrating bed was a prop, not a Joy Lee amenity.

The apartments were constructed between 1945 and 1948 by a Wilmington shipyard worker, who named the two-story building for his daughter.

CREDITS
Lolita (1997)

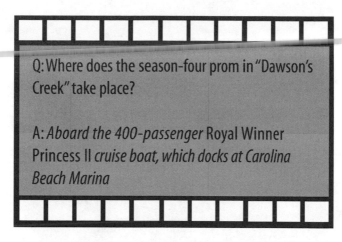

Q: Where does the season-four prom in "Dawson's Creek" take place?

A: *Aboard the 400-passenger* Royal Winner Princess II *cruise boat, which docks at Carolina Beach Marina*

Moran Motel's primary colors provide a striking location in *Traveller*, starring Bill Paxton and Mark Wahlberg.
PHOTOGRAPH BY C. L. NELSON

Moran Motel

118 Fort Fisher Boulevard South, Kure Beach (910-458-5395). The motel is open from April to Thanksgiving.

You can't miss the bold and sassy motif of the Moran Motel. This colorful, 25-room mom-and-pop motor lodge is the crooks' home base in *Traveller*, starring Bill Paxton (Bokky) and Mark Wahlberg (Pat). Rooms 2 and 10 appear in several scenes with Bokky, Pat, and Cousin Double D. Moran's parking lot is where the shifty travelers sell the RV. Other scenes feature the motel's bright green and fire-engine red siding.

Traveller (1997); "Love, Honor and Obey: The Last Mafia Marriage" (CBS, 1993)

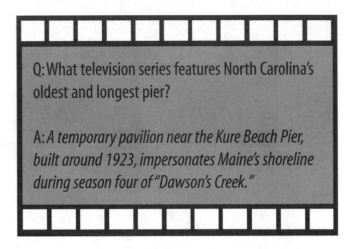

Q: What television series features North Carolina's oldest and longest pier?

A: *A temporary pavilion near the Kure Beach Pier, built around 1923, impersonates Maine's shoreline during season four of "Dawson's Creek."*

Fort Fisher State Historic Site and The Cove

1610 Fort Fisher Boulevard South, Kure Beach (910-458-5538; www.ah.dcr.state.nc.us/sections/hs/fisher/fisher.htm). From November to March, the site is open from 10 A.M. to 4 P.M. Tuesday through Saturday and from 1 P.M. to 4 P.M. on Sunday. From April to October, it is open from 9 A.M. to 5 P.M. Monday through Saturday and from 1 P.M. to 5 P.M. on Sunday. Admission is free; donations are welcome.

Fort Fisher was the largest of the Civil War earthen fortifications. When it fell in 1865, it marked the last gasp of the Confederacy. Today, approximately 10 percent of the earthworks remain.

Nearly a century and a half later, the curvy roads of Fort Fisher provided the setting for Vivi's (Ashley Judd's) Gulf Coast route in *Divine Secrets of the Ya-Ya Sisterhood*. It's also where the night bonfire scene in season four of "Dawson's Creek" was shot.

An area known as "The Cove" is located across the street from the fort. Windswept live oaks and rock jetties provided a New England look for the Nantucket beach-house facade that was constructed for *To Gillian on Her 37th Birthday*. This is also where Laura Burney (Julia Roberts) was supposedly buried in *Sleeping With the Enemy*.

The Cove's maritime forest provided the Cape Dune setting for the spaceship landing in *Muppets From Space*. A miniature set replica was created at EUE/Screen Gems Studios (see pages 58-61) using styrofoam rocks, sand, and a model lighthouse. Unless you know there's no lighthouse at Fort Fisher, it's virtually impossible to distinguish studio shots from Fort Fisher frames. The scenes at The Cove feature Andie MacDowell (the reporter), along with Katie Holmes (Joey) and Joshua Jackson (Pacey), who make tongue-in-cheek cameo appearances as their "Dawson's Creek" characters.

CREDITS

"Dawson's Creek" (The WB, 1998-2003); *Divine Secrets of the Ya-Ya Sisterhood* (2002); *New Best Friend* (2002); *Muppets From Space* (1999); *Black Dog* (1998); "CI5: The New Professionals" (BBC, 1998); "Buried Alive II" (USA, 1997); "The Crying Child" (USA, 1996); *To Gillian on Her 37th Birthday* (1996); "Inflammable" (CBS, 1995); "The Birds II: Land's End" (Showtime, 1994); *The Inkwell* (1994); "Linda" (USA, 1993); "Love, Honor and Obey: The Last Mafia Marriage" (CBS, 1993); "Spies" (Disney Channel, 1992); *Sleeping With the Enemy* (1991)

North Carolina Aquarium at Fort Fisher

900 Loggerhead Road, Fort Fisher/Kure Beach (910-458-8257; http://www.ncaquariums.com). The aquarium is open daily from 9 A.M. to 5 P.M.; call for holiday hours. An admission fee is charged.

The North Carolina Aquarium at Fort Fisher made its first silver-screen splash during the 1980s in *The Bedroom Window* scene in which Terry (Steve Guttenberg) meets his boss's wife, Sylvia (Isabelle Huppert), in front of the tanks to discuss a crime witnessed from his bedroom window.

Since that time, renovations have nearly tripled the aquarium's size. One of the main attractions today is a quarter-

"Dawson's Creek" films at the
North Carolina Aquarium at Fort Fisher.
PHOTOGRAPH BY BOB ROUSH
COURTESY OF NORTH CAROLINA AQUARIUM AT FORT FISHER

million-gallon saltwater tank labeled Cape Fear Shoals, which
was changed to read "Cape Cod Shoals" for a season-six episode
of "Dawson's Creek." In that episode, the sharks, stingrays, and
other reef fishes at the New England Aquarium provide
background for a scene between Pacey (Joshua Jackson) and
Emma (Megan Gray); an underwater camera captures the point of
view of the fish. The Cape Fear Shoals' fabricated sponges, coral
reef, rock formations, and plants were molded, attached, and

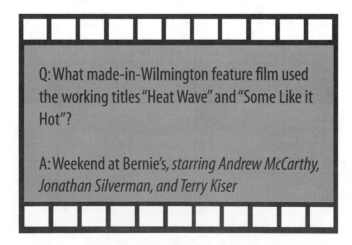

Q: What made-in-Wilmington feature film used
the working titles "Heat Wave" and "Some Like it
Hot"?

A: Weekend at Bernie's, *starring Andrew McCarthy,
Jonathan Silverman, and Terry Kiser*

hand-painted by a Wilmington-based movie set design firm.

Film junkies will recall the beach house in *Weekend at Bernie's*, which was a temporary structure built on the beach behind the aquarium. Filmmakers carefully replaced plants and rebuilt damaged dunes.

CREDITS

"Dawson's Creek" (The WB, 1998-2003); *Weekend at Bernie's* (1989); *The Bedroom Window* (1987)

Southport-Fort Fisher Ferry

Fort Fisher Boulevard/U.S. 421, Fort Fisher/Kure Beach (800-BY-FERRY; www.ncferry.org). The ferry operates between 6 A.M. and 8:30 P.M. in the summer; call for the off-season schedule. A fee is charged.

One of the Cape Fear River's most scenic stretches lies between Fort Fisher and Southport. A 30-minute ride aboard the ferry at Fort Fisher provides a backdrop of birds, plants, and maritime forests. Operated by the North Carolina Department of Transportation's Ferry Division, the ferry will transport you and your vehicle to Southport, a quaint town with its own movie credits (see pagess 103-10).

Demi Moore boarded the ferry for *The Butcher's Wife*. Several years later, box-office draw Bruce Willis boarded for a brief scene in *The Jackal*. In *The Inkwell*, the ferry transports actor Larenz Tate to Martha's Vineyard (Southport). For "Oprah Winfrey Presents: The Wedding," a period ferry was brought in for the Cape Cod ferry scenes.

CREDITS

"Dawson's Creek" (The WB, 1998-2003); *Takedown* (2000); "Oprah Winfrey Presents: The Wedding" (ABC, 1998); *I Know What You Did Last Summer* (1997); *The Jackal* (1997); "The Crying Child" (USA, 1996); *The Inkwell* (1994); *The Butcher's Wife* (1991)

Pleasure Island Star Tracks

The Cottage Seafood Grill

*1 Lake Park Boulevard North, Carolina Beach (910-458-4383;
www.dineatthecottage.com). The grill is open from 11:30 A.M. to
3 P.M. and from 5:30 P.M. to 9:30 P.M. Monday through
Saturday.*

Owner/manager Fred Crouch suggests that film junkies
watch Mae West in *Klondike Annie* to get a feel for his restaurant, which he describes as serving "occidental cuisine in an Oriental setting." The 1916 beach cottage's wraparound porch invites guests to sit a spell. The elegantly appointed rooms provide an intimate atmosphere. Inventive cuisine, divine desserts,
and an impressive selection of wine and microbrewed beers draw
locals, visitors, and celebrities. "Dawson's Creek" crew and actors are among the film types who have dined here. Others who
have graced the premises include Carolina Beach resident Pat
"Commissioner Gordon" Hingle (*Maximum Overdrive*; "The Member of the Wedding") and Wilmington resident Linda "Alice"
Lavin ("Stolen Memories: Secrets from the Rose Garden").

Old Baldy provides a historic backdrop in *Weekend at Bernie's,*
Sleeping With the Enemy, and other films.
PHOTOGRAPH BY BILL RUSS
COURTESY OF N. C. DIVISION OF TOURISM, FILM, & SPORTS DEVELOPMENT

Brunswick County
Locations

Bald Head Island

*The ferry departs from Indigo Plantation at West Ninth Street in
Southport; call 910-457-5003 for the schedule. For tour
information, call 800-795-7263 or visit www.ncbrunswick.com.*

The remote Bald Head Island is probably the perfect place
not to make a film. This beautiful barrier island, located at the
mouth of the Cape Fear River near Southport, is accessible only
by passenger ferry or private boat. There are no automobiles
anywhere on the island. While only a few projects have taken
on the daunting challenge of filming on Bald Head, the leisurely pace of an island boasting 14 miles of uncrowded beaches,

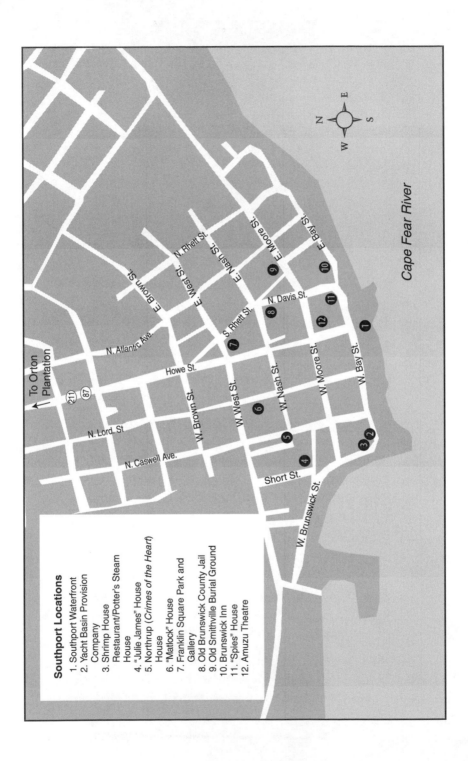

Southport Locations

1. Southport Waterfront
2. Yacht Basin Provision Company
3. Shrimp House Restaurant/Potter's Steam House
4. "Julie James" House
5. Northrup (*Crimes of the Heart*) House
6. "Matlock" House
7. Franklin Square Park and Gallery
8. Old Brunswick County Jail
9. Old Smithville Burial Ground
10. Brunswick Inn
11. "Spies" House
12. Amuzu Theatre

To Orton Plantation

21

87

N. Lord. St

N. Caswell Ave.

N. Atlantic Ave.

E. Brown St.

Howe St.

N. Rhett St.

E. West St.

E. Nash St.

E. Moore St.

E. Bay St.

N. Davis St.

S. Rhett St.

Short St.

W. Brunswick St.

W. Brown St.

W. West St.

W. Nash St.

W. Moore St.

W. Bay St.

Cape Fear River

no high-rise hotels, and 10,000 naturally preserved acres has attracted several Hollywood stars, including Bruce Willis and David Hartman. The island can be explored by regular folk, too. If you're interested, you can make a reservation for a historic tour.

The Pavilion, an independent feature from writer and director Grant Mitchell, was filmed exclusively on Bald Head. It won the Silver Award for Theatrical Feature Films (Drama) at Worldfest in Houston in 2000. This adaption of Robert Louis Stevenson's gothic suspense drama stars Patsy Kensit and veteran leading man Richard Chamberlain, who called the role of the swindling banker Huddelstone one of his favorites. The Demi Moore/Jeff Daniels comedy *The Butcher's Wife* did a five-day shoot on the island. The ferry landing was used for a scene in the Nicolas Cage/Samuel L. Jackson film *Amos & Andrew*. Bald Head has provided beach scenes for the cult favorite *Weekend at Bernie's* and Julia Roberts's *Sleeping With the Enemy*. Some episodes of "Matlock" and a few national commercials have also filmed here. The island has starred in several promotional films and documentaries dating back to 1916.

Film junkies should not miss Old Baldy, the 1817 lighthouse that is the island's most cherished symbol and historic landmark. The oldest lighthouse in the state, it is featured in the documentary *North Carolina Lighthouse Tour*. Old Baldy rewards visitors who climb to the top with a sweeping vista of the island's dramatic landscape.

CREDITS

The Pavilion (1999); "Matlock" (ABC, 1993-95); *North Carolina Lighthouse Tour* (1993); *Amos & Andrew* (1993); *The Butcher's Wife* (1991); *Sleeping With the Enemy* (1991); *Weekend at Bernie's* (1989); *Palmetto Island in Movie Film* (1916)

Southport Waterfront
Bay Street, downtown Southport

Perhaps the most picturesque spot in the charming town of Southport is the area around Waterfront Park, including the

Riverwalk, the Yacht Basin, and the marina. From the Riverwalk, you'll see boats and distant lighthouses and be within easy range of the town's quaint antique shops and craft dealers. It is an excellent place to sightsee and while away the day.

The area's timeless quality has led to many looks on film. It appears as a 1940s setting in the Billy Zane feature *This World, Then the Fireworks* and the Cloris Leachman TV film "Spies." It's dressed up as a 1950s setting in the Halle Berry TV mini-series "Oprah Winfrey Presents: The Wedding." Even in features such as *I Know What You Did Last Summer*, the waterfront harks back to a more peaceful era. On the other hand, there's quite a bit of action in the scene in "The Birds II: Land's End" in which a boat is blown up in the marina.

Film junkies will have to settle for more sedate pastimes, such as watching sailing vessels cruise up the Cape Fear River and pointing out Old Baldy and the Oak Island Lighthouse, which boasts the brightest lamp in the United States and the second-brightest in the world. And be sure to note historic Whittler's Bench, a local gathering spot under the ancient trees, perfect for whittling and spinning yarns.

CREDITS

"Dawson's Creek" (The WB, 1998-2003), "Oprah Winfrey Presents: The Wedding" (ABC, 1998); *This World, Then the Fireworks* (1997); *I Know What You Did Last Summer* (1997); "The Crying Child" (USA, 1996), "American Gothic" (CBS, 1995-96); "The Birds II: Land's End" (Showtime, 1994); "Matlock" (ABC, 1993-95); "Spies" (Disney Channel, 1992)

The Shrimp House Restaurant/ Potter's Steam House

106 Yacht Basin Drive, Southport (910-457-1881). The restaurant is open from 11 A.M. to 7 P.M. Monday through Saturday and from 11 A.M. to 3 P.M. on Sunday.

At The Shrimp House Restaurant on the Southport waterfront, the motto is "We break for sunsets." Diners and film junkies will certainly agree this is one of the most beautiful meetings of land and sea in town. The restaurant is quite popular with locals, tourists, visiting celebrities, and film industry professionals and has been featured a time or two on screen.

The Shrimp House Restaurant was purchased in the late 1990s by Southport native Donald Potter and his wife, Vickie. Diners enjoy the view along with their selection of grilled, fried, or broiled seafood and New England-style clam chowder. A variety of steamed shellfish is available from the adjacent Steam House, part of The Shrimp House.

Photos of celebrities—including North Carolina governor Mike Easley, Brian Dennehy and other cast members from *Summer Catch*, and the "Dawson's Creek" crew—dot the walls. The restaurant appeared in the latter show, and it's even rumored the owners had some influence over a certain character's last name.

Before opening as a restaurant in 1998, the building was used as the "Southport Muscle" gym in *I Know What You Did Last Summer*. The fishhook-wielding killer appears on top of the Potter's Steam House building during the parade.

CREDITS

"Dawson's Creek" (The WB, 1998-2003); *I Know What You Did Last Summer* (1997)

Southport Homes/Brunswick Inn

Southport is justly known for its beautiful historic homes. Film junkies need only walk a couple of blocks to see the screen homes of a favorite son, a spooked teen, Southern Gothic sisters, Oscar®-winning wedding participants, and spies.

The place that put Southport on the filmmaking map is the Northrup House. Located a few blocks from downtown at 229 North Caswell Avenue, it was built around 1910 but achieved worldwide fame 75 years later when it served as the Magrath home in Bruce Beresford's *Crimes of the Heart*. Both the interior and exterior were used for the fateful reunion of the Magrath sisters, played by Hollywood heavyweights Sissy Spacek, Diane

Keaton, and Jessica Lange. The angular two-story porch and round turret are unique features of this Victorian house. It has been reported that the place is haunted by the ghost of original owner Sam Northrup, who committed suicide in the home during the 1930s. Some crew members reported odd happenings while working on the set. *Crimes of the Heart*, based on Beth Henley's Pulitzer Prize-winning play, continues to be one of the most high-profile North Carolina films. It garnered three Academy Award® nominations—Spacek for Best Actress, Tess Harper for Best Supporting Actress, and Henley for Best Adapted Screenplay. Spacek *did* win the Golden Globe® and New York Film Critics Circle awards for her role.

"Matlock," of course, stars North Carolina favorite son Andy Griffith as a laid-back Atlanta lawyer. The last few years of the series were filmed in and around Wilmington. Home for Ben Matlock was a house on Lord Street in Southport, the next street up from the Magraths'. A little less fancy and more straightforward (a bit like Ben himself) than the Northrup House, the two-story structure has a nice, inviting front porch that fits in well with easygoing Southport. In fact, Andy was known for relaxing and hanging out around town during breaks in filming. Just another good ol' Carolina boy.

It's rare for a screen town to take on the name of its actual location, but the teen fave *I Know What You Did Last Summer* goes it one better. The actual street name of Julie James's (Jennifer Love Hewitt's) home is given when she returns from college (Duke, though it's never called that) and receives the first ominous letter letting her and her friends know their deeds from last summer didn't stay drowned. The home is on the aptly named Short Street, a block from those occupied by Matlock and the Magraths.

"Spies," a Disney Channel feature starring Oscar® winner Cloris Leachman, features a house on Bay Street across from the City Pier.

Another Oscar® winner, Halle Berry, is seen in "Oprah Winfrey Presents: The Wedding," which filmed several scenes at the Brunswick Inn, located at 301 East Bay Street. Dating from 1896, the inn has original heart-pine floors and nine working fireplaces.

Please note that the private homes discussed here are available for exterior viewing and pictures only.

The Brunswick Inn appears in "Oprah Winfrey Presents: The Wedding" (ABC, 1998). The Short Street house appears in *I Know What You Did Last Summer* (1997). The Lord Street house appears in "Matlock" (ABC, 1993-95). The Bay Street House appears in "Spies" (Disney Channel, 1992). The Northrup House appears in *Crimes of the Heart* (1986).

Franklin Square Park and Art Gallery

Franklin Square Park is on West Street in Southport. The gallery is located behind the park. It is open from 10 A.M. to 5 P.M. Monday through Saturday from March 1 to mid-December. Admission is free. For information, call 910-457-5450.

It's hard to know what will impress first-time visitors to Southport more, the stunning natural beauty and ambiance or the surprising concentration of art galleries and antique shops. All of the above are in store for those who visit Franklin Square Park and Art Gallery, which has been used as a location for several productions.

Franklin Square Park was planned by town founders Joshua Potts (an ancestor of actress Annie Potts) and Benjamin Smith in 1792 and redefined as a WPA project in the 1930s. The park's huge anchor was featured in episodes of "Dawson's Creek."

The gallery was built in 1904 as a public school. Its second-floor Blue Room was used as a ballroom in the 1930s. Forty years later, the city made the building available to the Associated Artists of Southport, a group of professional and aspiring artists. The gallery was used as the classroom of sexy schoolteacher Selena Coombs (Brenda Bakke) in episodes of "American Gothic."

CREDITS
"Dawson's Creek" (The WB, 1998-2003); "Holy Joe" (CBS,

1999); "The Crying Child" (USA, 1996); "American Gothic" (CBS, 1995-96); "Sweet Justice" (NBC, 1994); *The Inkwell* (1993)

Old Brunswick County Jail

320 East Nash Street, Southport. Visitors are limited to exterior viewing.

Though it dates from 1904, the building known in Southport as the "Old Jail" is actually relatively new. The first jail, complete with stocks and pillory, was built in the 1820s. Destroyed by fire in 1849, it was replaced by a structure complete with a garret! The present "Old Jail" housed prisoners until 1971. Its original iron window bars are still present.

The Old Jail's best-known inmate, however, wasn't incarcerated until 15 years after the facility closed. In *Crimes of the Heart*, Babe Magrath (Sissy Spacek) is housed here temporarily after shooting husband Zack (Beeson Carroll). The oppressive building is seen quite clearly as the handcuffed Spacek is led inside. The jail is spookily illuminated for episodes of "American Gothic."

If you're a hardcore film junkie, you'll be able to gaze into the abandoned lot catty-corner to the jail and envision a lush green field, bright lights, and bleachers full of fans. This was where most of the baseball scenes in *Summer Catch* were filmed. Don't see it? Many locations require you to use your imagination to recall how they appear in particular scenes, and this spot requires more than most. Though there was talk of keeping the field for local use, the stadium was torn down. Today, you'll just have to imagine Freddie Prinze, Jr., Jason Gedrick, Brian Dennehy, Brittany Murphy, and ex-big leaguers Hank Aaron and Carlton Fisk in action.

CREDITS

Summer Catch (2001); "American Gothic" (CBS, 1995-96); *Crimes of the Heart* (1986)

Old Smithville Burial Ground

East Moore and South Rhett streets, Southport. The cemetery is
open during daylight hours.

The serene, moss-laden, and, yes, somewhat creepy Old
Smithville Burial Ground dates from the 1700s. It contains a
number of small stones that poignantly mark the graves of
children lost in a diphtheria epidemic in 1873. A solemn
obelisk in the southeast corner honors pilots drowned in two
storms in the 1870s. Film junkies will also find that the place
has a rich cinematic history featuring the usual graveyard emotions: nostalgia and terror.

In *Crimes of the Heart*, Meg and Babe Magrath (Jessica Lange
and Sissy Spacek) walk through the richly filtered sunlight of
the cemetery as they visit the graves of their mother and the
recently departed Old Granddaddy (Hurd Hatfield). The tele-
scope scene in *A Walk to Remember*, featuring Mandy Moore as
Jamie, is also sweet and touching.

Of course, cemeteries lend themselves to horror and suspense, as seen in the eerie TV film "The Crying Child," in which
star Mariel Hemingway continues to hear the crying of her dead
baby. The title of "Buried Alive II" probably gives away the plot.
And "Matlock" used the location many times during its run in
the mid-1990s.

CREDITS

A Walk to Remember (2002); "Holy Joe" (CBS, 1999); "Buried Alive
II" (USA, 1997); "The Crying Child" (USA, 1996); "Matlock"
(ABC, 1993-95); *Crimes of the Heart* (1986)

Amuzu Theatre

Corner of Moore and Howe streets, Southport. Visitors are limited
to exterior viewing.

Appropriately enough, the name is pronounced "amuse you."
This venerable theatre in downtown Southport did just that for
over half a century.

But things get a bit more frightening in the cult teen hit *I Know What You Did Last Summer*, in which the Amuzu doubles as the Southport Community Theatre. Helen Shivers (Sarah Michelle Gellar) is crowned Croaker Queen in the early stages of the film. One year later, while sitting onstage as the reigning queen, she witnesses something horrible in the balcony involving Barry (Ryan Phillippe)—or does she? Sharp eyes will note North Carolina actress Lynda Clark as the female pageant official in both scenes. The theatre's other credits include a background shot in *Crimes of the Heart*.

Although it's commonly believed that this is the facade for the Rialto Theater in "Dawson's Creek," it's actually not. An office building nearby was dressed to *look* like a theatre. The interiors were shot in Wilmington at Thalian Hall (see pages 23-25).

The Amuzu Theatre has been in the same Southport family since Price Furpless built it in 1918. Price's son Bill ran it from 1945 until 1962, after which *his* son Bill (whose middle name is Price) and his mother ran it until 1980. Bill Price Furpless still owns the building. His dream is to renovate and reopen it someday.

CREDITS

I Know What You Did Last Summer (1997); *Crimes of the Heart* (1986)

Orton Plantation

9149 Orton Road, off N.C. 133, Winnabow (910-371-6851; www.ortongardens.com). Winnabow is 18 miles south of Wilmington and 10 miles north of Southport. The gardens are open daily from 8 A.M. to 6 P.M. from March to August and from 10 A.M. to 5 P.M. from September to November. They are closed from December through February and Thanksgiving Day. An admission fee is charged. Self-guided walking tours are available. The plantation house is privately owned and is not open to visitors, though it may be viewed from the garden paths.

Film junkies, history buffs, and nature lovers are all in for a treat at Orton Plantation, which offers breathtaking scenery,

Orton Plantation sparked Dino De Laurentiis to bring *Firestarter* to North Carolina. Orton, pictured here in *Divine Secrets of the Ya-Ya Sisterhood*, continues to be one of the state's hottest locations.
COURTESY OF E. MICHAEL HEWETT, LOCATIONS . . . +, INC.

lush gardens, and a house dating to the early 18th century. Orton's first screen credit was the seminal North Carolina production *Firestarter*. Since then, more than 40 film and television projects have used its 1,200 acres of varied terrain for virtually every time period and setting.

Orton Plantation was built around 1725 as the home of Roger Moore, one of the founders of the historic Brunswick Town. Prior to the Civil War, Orton became one of the leading rice plantations in the lower Cape Fear. It was used by Union troops as a hospital following the fall of Fort Fisher in 1865. Though hard for many Rebels to swallow, this action by the "Northern aggressors" actually saved Orton from the fate suffered by many old Southern manses. And don't worry—even though the house burned down in *Firestarter*, it was actually just a replica built on the grounds. Spared again!

Visitors and filmmakers are impressed by how both the formal and natural gardens take advantage of impressive oaks and other native trees, constructed lawns, water, and walkways. The gardens even stand in for the Vatican in the final scene of *The Dress Code*, Shirley MacLaine's directorial debut.

Dozens of major stars have filmed here over the years. Orton appears in *Crimes of the Heart* as the home where Babe Magrath (Sissy Spacek) shoots husband Zack (Beeson Carroll). The young Ya-Yas direct a food fight at their snobby, nouveau riche cousin in Orton's dining room in *Divine Secrets of the Ya-Ya Sisterhood*; sharp eyes will note that this is Martin Sheen's office in *Firestarter*. "Oprah Winfrey Presents: The Wedding" also shot interior scenes here.

The grounds have also appeared on screen. Ya-Yas' Cajun party scene took place on the front lawn. The plantation served as the assisted-living home of Esther Huish (Vanessa Redgrave) in "The Locket"; the house and gardens were widely used in this Christmas-themed production. Loula's Chapel, located on the grounds, was used for the poignant wedding in *A Walk to Remember* and by Will Walker (Danny Glover) in "Freedom Song." It was also used in the "Blair Witch" episode of "Dawson's Creek." The entrance is seen in the terrifying cougar scene in *The Dangerous Lives of Altar Boys*.

Q: What controversial television movie was Anjelica Huston's directorial debut?

A: *"Bastard Out of Carolina,"* starring Jennifer Jason Leigh, Lyle Lovett, and Kelsey Boulware and based on Dorothy Allison's novel of the same title. In the production's working title, the word bastard was conveniently dropped. It thus became " ... Out of Carolina," which was supposed to make it more digestible for Bible Belt Southerners. Furthermore, due to the sexually explicit and controversial content of the story, TNT shelved the project after filming was completed. However, the movie found an audience with Showtime in 1996. It aired with the full title.

"Dawson's Creek" (The WB, 1998-2003); Divine Secrets of the Ya-
Ya Sisterhood (2002); A Walk to Remember (2002); The Dangerous Lives
of Altar Boys (2002); "The Locket" (Hallmark/CBS, 2002); "The
Runaway" (Hallmark/CBS, 2000); The Dress Code (2000); "Freedom Song" (TNT, 2000); "Oprah Winfrey Presents: The Wedding" (ABC, 1998); Lolita (1997); "The Crying Child" (USA,
1996); "Stolen Memories: Secrets from the Rose Garden" (Family Channel, 1996); The Grave (1996); "Dead Giveaway" (USA,
1995); The Road to Wellville (1994); "The Road Home" (CBS,
1994); "Against Her Will: The Carrie Buck Story" (Lifetime,
1994); "The Young Indiana Jones Chronicles" (ABC, 1992-94);
Tune in Tomorrow (1990); Date with an Angel (1987); Raw Deal
(1986); Crimes of the Heart (1986); Firestarter (1984). For complete
credits, visit www.ortongardens.com.

★★★★★★★★★★★★★★ Discovering Columbus

The Green Swamp Byway begins on N.C. 211 a half-mile north of Supply and ends at N.C. 242; for information, visit www.byways.org. The Green Swamp Preserve is located 5.5 miles north of Supply on N.C. 211; for information, call 910-762-6277. Lake Waccamaw State Park, located at 1866 State Park Drive in Lake Waccamaw, is open daylight hours; for information, call 910-646-4748. For tourist information, contact the Columbus County Tourism Bureau by calling 800-845-8419 or visiting www.discovercolumbus.org.

Located just a county line away from its movie-star sisters, Brunswick and Pender, Columbus County features small towns, rural landscapes, and lush natural settings. From Whiteville's Courthouse Square and historic Chadbourn's Railroad Avenue to the natural beauty of the Green Swamp, Columbus County is poised for a blockbuster.

The county's film credits date to the 1970s, when prolific high-school filmmaker Fuller Royal made more than 30 science-fiction shorts and spoofs. Recent film production has been sporadic, however. One credit is Anjelica Huston's directorial debut, "Bastard Out of Carolina." The Classical Revival-style Columbus County Courthouse, built around 1914, appears in scenes in which Anney (Jennifer Jason Leigh) unsuccessfully attempts to change her daughter's birth certificate. The courthouse burns in the movie; the real-life structure is fireproof.

Stretching into two counties, the Green Swamp is a National Natural Landmark that is home to many exotic and insectivorous plants. Visitors can take a 52-mile scenic drive on the Green Swamp Byway or trek the preserve's designated trails. The ever-compelling Venus flytrap lured David Attenborough here to film the Emmy Award®-winning documentary "The Private Life of Plants."

Don't miss Lake Waccamaw State Park's 8,900-acre lake, the largest of the mysterious Carolina bays—oval depressions that some scientists believe resulted from meteor showers. Some even link the Venus flytrap to the bays. Sounds like a plot that might bring "X-Files" agents Mulder and Scully to the North Carolina coast!

CREDITS

Stateside (2004) filmed at the Columbus County Health Department in Whiteville. Portions of *Divine Secrets of the Ya-Ya Sisterhood* (2002) were shot in Chadbourn. Scenes in *Traveller* (1997) were filmed at the Holiday Motel on U.S. 701 in Whiteville. "Linda" (USA, 1993) made use of Whiteville's jail/courthouse. "Black Magic" (Showtime, 1992) includes a parade scene shot near the depot in downtown Chadbourn. Columbus County's other credits include "Funny Valentines" (BET/STARZ! 1999); "Bastard Out of Carolina" (Showtime, 1996); and "The Private Life of Plants" (BBC, 1995).

Brunswick County Star Tracks

Yacht Basin Provision Company

130 Yacht Basin Drive, Southport (910-457-0654). The restaurant is open daily for lunch and dinner from mid-March through mid- to late November.

Laid-back Southport's unique character contains a bit of Margaritaville, thanks in part to the Yacht Basin Provision Company. This is a perfect spot to relax on the covered deck, enjoy a beer and a bite, and watch boats, people, and sunsets. *Coastal Living* magazine has rightly placed this among America's "Top 25 Seafood Dives." The specialties of the house include shrimp and crab cakes, conch fritters, and grouper salad. Burgers and salads are also available. Not arriving by land? Don't worry. Boat slips are provided; depths run to six feet at low tide. If you're lucky, you may spot a celebrity or two, though the "Dawson's Creek" gang preferred to come here incognito. "Veronica's Closet" star Dan Cortese has been known to stop by when in town. Other star sightings have included Harvey Keitel, Robert Conrad, and the late Charles Bronson.

Q: What African-American Broadway, TV, and film star grew up in Chadbourn, North Carolina?

A: *Actor and dancer Ben Vereen, who occasionally returns for the annual North Carolina Strawberry Festival*

Filming the scene at Burgaw Antiqueplace in which actor Cody Newton spots his terminally ill sister's gift in *The Angel Doll*.
PHOTOGRAPH BY JAMES BRIDGES ©ANGEL DOLL PRODUCTIONS, 2000

Pender County Locations

Burgaw Antiqueplace

101 South Wright Street, Burgaw (910-259-7070). The Antiqueplace is open from 9:30 A.M. to 5:30 P.M. Monday through Saturday.

Burgaw Antiqueplace, housed in a historic building on the corner of Wright and Wilmington streets, has appeared in several films. Owner Johnny Westbrook will be glad to share stories, show pictures, and point out props and pieces that Hollywood left behind. This all goes down nice with a hunk or two of the Antiqueplace's homemade fudge while exploring two floors and over 7,500 square feet of antiques.

Although "Freedom Song" is set in a fictional town in Mississippi, the lunch-counter scene filmed in the Antiqueplace harkens memories of the Greensboro sit-ins of the early civil-rights movement. In fact, the counter built for "Freedom Song" is a replica of the famous Greensboro lunch counter, accurate in detail right down to the menu holders. And the seats used in the scene are from the actual Woolworth's, loaned to the production from permanent display at the Greensboro Historical Museum. The display cases and the wooden Woolworth's sign are also still on hand and are used by Westbrook and his wife in day-to-day business.

In another Triad connection, the Antiqueplace appears as the bakery where the angel cookie is found in the film adaptation of Asheboro author Jerry Bledsoe's *The Angel Doll*. Tar Heel influences are felt throughout this award-winning family drama, directed by Hickory native Sandy Johnston, who sadly passed away shortly after the film's completion. *The Angel Doll* was co-produced by Carolina Beach resident Pat Hingle, who stars along with Diana Scarwid and Keith Carradine.

CREDITS

The Angel Doll (2003); "The Runaway" (Hallmark/CBS, 2000); "Freedom Song" (TNT, 2000); "The Summer of Ben Tyler" (Hallmark/CBS, 1996)

Harrell's Department Store

107 South Wright Street, Burgaw (910-259-2112). Harrell's is open from 9 A.M. to 6 P.M. Monday, Tuesday, Thursday, and Friday; from 9 P.M. to 1 P.M. on Wednesday; and from 9 A.M. to 5:30 P.M. on Saturday.

When *I Know What You Did Last Summer* director Jim Gillespie saw the old-fashioned manual elevator in Harrell's Department Store in downtown Burgaw, he knew he had to feature it in the film. Many times, location moviemaking includes such found art, which can alter the script in often inspired ways. The rope-pulled lift, located in the rear of the century-old building, is utilized in Helen's (Sarah Michelle Gellar's) final chase scene, getting her up to the second floor, from which she jumps into

In search of an angel doll, actor Cody Newton and friends negotiate with a clerk (Wilmington actress Nina Repeta) at Harrell's Department Store in *The Angel Doll*.
PHOTOGRAPH BY JAMES BRIDGES ©ANGEL DOLL PRODUCTIONS, 2000

the alley. Most of *I Know* was shot in Southport, but Harrell's—called Shiver's Department Store in the film, pun obviously intended—was apparently too good to pass up. By movie magic, Gellar jumps out the window in Burgaw and lands in an alley in Southport. Safe, for at least a little while.

Harrell's takes you back to postwar, pre-mall America. The store celebrated its 100th anniversary in 2003. Harrell's is uncrowded and unrushed. There are no glaring lights or gaudy ads, just sturdy, old-fashioned wood-and-glass display cases.

The exterior of Harrell's can be seen in the pawnshop scene in *Divine Secrets of the Ya-Ya Sisterhood*. Owner Charles Harrell, a former mayor of Burgaw, will gladly tell you about this and other brushes with fame and, of course, sell you anything from a Burgaw T-shirt to a major appliance. The recently added coffee shop allows customers to relax and watch small-town life go by. Just look out for fish hooks.

CREDITS

The Angel Doll (2003); *Divine Secrets of the Ya-Ya Sisterhood* (2002); "The Runaway" (Hallmark/CBS, 2000); "Freedom Song" (TNT, 2000); *I Know What You Did Last Summer* (1997); "A Mother's Instinct" (CBS, 1996); "The Summer of Ben Tyler" (Hallmark/CBS, 1996)

The Angel Doll author/executive producer Jerry Bledsoe chats
with Nat Walker and Jim "Santa" Jenkins outside Dee's Drug Store.
PHOTOGRAPH BY JAMES BRIDGES ©ANGEL DOLL PRODUCTIONS, 2000

Dee's Drug Store

*111 South Wright Street, Burgaw (910-259-2116). Dee's is
open from 9 A.M. to 6 P.M. Monday through Friday and from
9 A.M. to 1 P.M. on Saturday.*

Dee's, an old-fashioned family-owned pharmacy, has been
around since 1916. Stepping inside takes you into the past. The
lunch counter serves real milk shakes and sundaes, sandwiches,
and orangeades, lemonades, and cherry smashes. In the back,
busy pharmacists fill prescriptions for Pender County residents,
as they have for generations. Most, however, are not quite as
well known as Vivi Walker (Ashley Judd), who picks up her
meds here in *Divine Secrets of the Ya-Ya Sisterhood.* Interestingly,
the exterior is seen in the pawnshop scene, in which Vivi hocks
the prized ring her daddy gave her.

Dee's storefront, complete with period lettering, is clearly
seen in the background during the scene in which Ben (Charles
Matthews) follows Temple Rayburn (James Woods) to become
his office assistant in "The Summer of Ben Tyler." In fact,
Woods's law office is located right above the drugstore; the Dee's
sign glows like an Edward Hopper painting as he peers out on
Courthouse Square late in the film. Meredith Baxter Birney's
real-estate office in "Miracle in the Woods" is also located
upstairs.

By the way, the Rayburn home in "The Summer of Ben Tyler" is the M. M. Moore House, located just down the road from Dee's at Cowan and Wilmington streets. The tiny house built for Ben was a temporary structure. The crew also put up a temporary stand of pine trees to obscure the modern Pender County Public Library across the street. Please note that the M. M. Moore House is private.

Stars and film crews have been known to drop by Dee's. The hot dogs are a particularly popular on-location snack. Dean Cain came in for a treat during filming of "The Runaway," as did Danny Glover while making "Freedom Song."

CREDITS

The Angel Doll (2003); *Divine Secrets of the Ya-Ya Sisterhood* (2002); "Miracle in the Woods" (CBS, 1997); "The Summer of Ben Tyler" (Hallmark/CBS, 1996);

Q: What Burgaw native has made a splash on stage, screen, and television?

A: *Samm-Art Williams, whose play* Home *put him on the map. He's gone on to write and produce such television programs as "The Fresh Prince of Bel Air." He also acts, perhaps most notably as Meurice in the Coen brothers'* Blood Simple.

Pender County Courthouse/Courthouse Square

The square is flanked by Walker, Wright, Wilmington, and Fremont streets in downtown Burgaw. Visitors are limited to exterior viewing of the courthouse.

For almost a century and a quarter, Burgaw's Pender County Courthouse Square has hosted numerous rallies, gatherings, and picnics. And the Pender County Courthouse has seen its share of courtroom drama. No wonder it looks so natural on film! The current courthouse, dedicated in 1937 on the site of a previous structure dating from 1885, is a three-story Greek Revival building with arched windows and a distinctive two-stage wooden cupola.

A Civil War monument honoring William Dorsey Pender, the man for whom the county is named, is clearly seen behind Sheriff Richards (Dean Cain) and Luke (Cody Newton) in "The Runaway." Patty Winston (Phoebe Cates) sits in a gazebo built specially for *Date with an Angel*; the gazebo makes a cameo background appearance in *I Know What You Did Last Summer* as Helen (Sarah Michelle Gellar) runs for her life. Film junkies can take pictures in this leftover movie prop. In "Freedom Song," 300 extras join star and executive producer Danny Glover for a protest march set in the early 1960s. The late 1940s is the time period for attorney Temple Rayburn's (James Woods's) campaign rally early in "The Summer of Ben Tyler," based on a novel by Charlotte's Robert Inman.

The Pender County Courthouse has one of the few courtrooms to feature a balcony, a painful reminder of the days when African-Americans had to sit upstairs. The balcony has been utilized for scenes set in segregated times. James Woods fights for the truth at the expense of his political future in "The Summer of Ben Tyler." Scenes from "In a Child's Name," featuring Valerie Bertinelli, were filmed here. And Pender County stands in for Topeka, Kansas, in one of future Supreme Court justice Thurgood Marshall's (Peter Francis James's) landmark cases in "Simple Justice."

CREDITS

"Freedom Song" (TNT, 2000); "The Runaway" (Hallmark/CBS,

2000); *I Know What You Did Last Summer* (1997); "The Summer of Ben Tyler" (Hallmark/CBS, 1996); "Simple Justice" (PBS, 1993); "In a Child's Name" (CBS, 1991); *Date with an Angel* (1987); *Cat's Eye* (1985); *Silver Bullet* (1985)

Stag Air Park

95 Aviator Lane, Burgaw (910-675-3927). Call for hours and special events.

The touching airplane scenes in *Divine Secrets of the Ya-Ya Sisterhood* were filmed at Stag Air Park in Pender County, affectionately known as "Burgaw International Airport" by locals and industry insiders. These scenes feature the young versions of Vivi (Ashley Judd) and Sidda (Caitlin Wachs) flying over beautiful countryside, including their home, Pecan Grove (see Buckner Hill Plantation, pages 128-30). Sharp eyes will note location manager E. Michael Hewett in the pivotal cameo role as the kind man assisting the ladies onto the bright red plane.

Located six miles east of Burgaw, Stag Air Park is a favorite of local small-airplane enthusiasts. It hosts a number of flight clubs, which frequently have air shows, open houses, and flying lessons. You may even get to take a flight like Vivi and Sidda.

CREDITS

Divine Secrets of the Ya-Ya Sisterhood (2002)

In *Divine Secrets of the Ya-Ya Sisterhood*, location manager E. Michael Hewett, a.k.a. "The Airplane Man," readies for take-off at Stag Air Park, affectionately called Burgaw International Airport.
COURTESY OF E. MICHAEL HEWETT, LOCATIONS . . . +, INC.

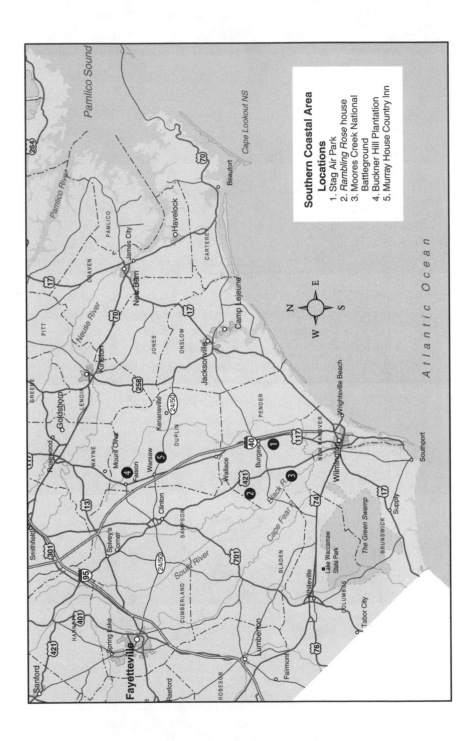

Southern Coastal Area

Locations
1. Stag Air Park
2. *Rambling Rose* house
3. Moores Creek National Battleground
4. Buckner Hill Plantation
5. Murray House Country Inn

Moores Creek National Battlefield

N.C. 210 near Currie (910-283-5591; www.nps.gov/mocr). *The battlefield is open daily from* 9 A.M. *to* 5 P.M. *Labor Day through Memorial Day and from* 9 A.M. *to* 6 P.M. *Memorial Day through Labor Day. Admission is free.*

Part of the story of Moores Creek National Battlefield, scene of one of the first decisive American victories in the Revolutionary War, is told in the documentary *North Carolina in the American Revolution*. The Battle of Moores Creek Bridge, fought on February 27, 1776, saw 1,000 Patriots defeat 1,600 Loyalists, raising morale for Americans throughout the colonies. Following the victory at Moores Creek, North Carolina voted to declare independence from the British on April 12, 1776, a date emblazoned on the state flag.

Moores Creek National Battlefield, established in 1926, is among the best historic and recreational attractions in the state. Its annual commemoration of the battle, held on the last weekend of February, features a living-history encampment, tactical demonstrations, folk singing, and a candlelight tour. Guided tours are available, or you can explore on your own.

Moores Creek's only other movie credit is an obscure but interesting independent feature based on an obscure but interesting event. *The Setting Sun* is an ultra-low-budget film concerning a real-life incident in Goldsboro, North Carolina, in 1961, in which two nuclear bombs were accidentally dropped during the crash of a B-52! The dark comedy also filmed in Goldsboro and Wilmington.

CREDITS

North Carolina in the American Revolution (1992); *The Setting Sun* (1987)

Rambling Rose House

Beatty's Bridge Road, on the Black River at the Pender County
line near Ivanhoe. Visitors are limited to exterior viewing.
Trespassing is forbidden.

Although most film locations in Pender County don't call much attention to themselves, a house on the Black River likes to boast of its claim to fame. Signs on the property indicate that this is the *Rambling Rose* house. Indeed, this is the home of the Hillyer family—Daddy (Robert Duvall), Mother (Diane Ladd), and son Buddy (Lukas Haas), who narrates the story. *Rambling Rose* is the last screenplay from noted Southern author Calder Willingham, co-writer of *The Graduate*. In it, the family's peaceful Depression-era life is turned upside down by the arrival of Rose (Laura Dern), an innocent, yet sexy, time bomb who certainly leaves her mark.

Interiors and exteriors of the house and grounds are used extensively in the film, which has the distinction of producing the only Academy Award® nominations for a mother and daughter in the same film. Dern was nominated for Best Actress and mother Ladd for Best Supporting Actress. Laura Dern's father, Bruce Dern, is also an Oscar® nominee.

CREDITS

Rambling Rose (1991)

★★★★★★★★★★★★★

Hallmark Hall of Fame Movies Made in North Carolina

For more than 50 years, Hallmark Entertainment has made quality motion pictures suitable for family viewing. The company earned a Lifetime Achievement Award for contributions to family programming at the third annual Family Television Awards, held in 2001. Hallmark Hall of Fame movies can be seen on the Hallmark

Channel and are available for purchase at select Hallmark stores and online at www.hallmark.com.

North Carolina's cinematic landscapes and period locations have made it a favored destination for Hallmark productions. Below is a list of North Carolina-made Hallmark Hall of Fame movies.

"The Runaway" (Hallmark/CBS, 2001) was shot in Burgaw and Wilmington.

"The Locket" (Hallmark/CBS, 2000) was shot in Wilmington and Winnabow.

"Saint Maybe" (Hallmark/CBS, 1998) was shot in the Charlotte region.

"What the Deaf Man Heard" (Hallmark/CBS, 1997) was shot in Wilmington, Winnabow, and Burgaw.

"The Summer of Ben Tyler" (Hallmark/CBS, 1996) was shot in Wilmington and Burgaw.

"Foxfire" (Hallmark/CBS, 1987) was shot in the Blue Ridge mountains.

Buckner Hill Plantation was Pecan Grove
in *Divine Secrets of the Ya-Ya Sisterhood*. The photograph
shows the sunflowers that wouldn't bloom on cue during filming.
COURTESY OF BRAD CHAPPELL AND TERRY GRIMES, BUCKNER HILL PLANTATION

Duplin County Locations

Buckner Hill Plantation

*522 Taylor Town Road, Faison (910-293-7860; www
.carolinaplantation.com). Tours are offered by appointment only.
The home is closed on major holidays. An admission fee is
charged. The home is available for private tours, parties,
meetings, weddings, and Ya-Ya reunions.*

If Buckner Hill Plantation looks vaguely familiar, that's because you've probably seen it on the silver screen. The handsome mansion, constructed around 1855, stars in *Divine Secrets of
the Ya-Ya Sisterhood*—based on Rebecca Wells's bestseller—as the
Walker family's beloved Louisiana plantation, Pecan Grove.
Thanks to the film and its devoted fans, the two-story frame
house, its lawn, and the town of Faison have become star
locations—a virtual Ya-Ya Land. Film junkies can tour the "di-

vine" house and photograph the pecan tree under which Vivi (Ellen Burstyn) performs goddess rituals and where her 60th birthday bash occurs. Owners Brad Chappell and Terry Grimes joined a Dixieland band and 125 extras for the all-night party scene.

Constructed of centuries-old heart pine, the Greek Revival/Italianate house was built by skilled African-Americans for Dr. Buckner L. Hill. Among the largest antebellum plantation homes in the state, it includes some period furnishings original to the house. Note the cruciform floor plan, a style more prevalent in the Deep South that allows for maximum ventilation.

A guided tour reveals fascinating details about the house's architecture and history, its former tenants, and its foray into the movies. The hallway staircase as you enter is where young Vivi falters and where the older Vivi yanks down family portraits. Vivi continues on a rampage to rid the house of Sidda's (Sandra Bullock's) photographs, entering the den (really the library) and removing pictures from the mantel. This is also where the young Vivi (Ashley Judd) lies unconscious on a red 1960s sofa. Notice the antique gold wallpaper in the library, which came courtesy of Bette Midler's All-Girl Productions, as did the wallpaper and the marbleized mantel in the adjacent dining room. Underneath the dining-room mantel mirror is where Vivi admits to Connor (Angus MacFadyen) that motherhood didn't always go smoothly.

The kitchen underwent several period transformations. In a flashback, Shep (James Garner) finds Vivi cooking (and drinking), after which she launches into a rage. The kitchen is also the site where the present-day Vivi reads the *Time* magazine article, telephones Sidda, slams the phone, and hurls a coffee mug in a fit of fury. And it's where Shep and the Ya-Yas (Maggie Smith as Caro, Fionnula Flanagan as Teensy, Shirley Knight as Necie) console Vivi afterward.

You can peek out the back door to see where a belt-hurling Vivi beats her children in a dramatic breakdown scene.

When you venture up the back staircase, notice the first door on the left, which is Shep's bedroom. The bedroom across the hall overlooking the pecan tree is Vivi's. Its window is the one from which Shep witnesses Vivi's sparkler ritual. The back bedroom/bath is the Walker children's room.

Upstairs, a Ya-Ya shrine includes a director's chair, memorabilia, autographed head shots, and a prized snapshot of a field of early-blooming sunflowers behind the barn. When they didn't bloom on cue, 3,000 silk sunflowers were wired up. The irony? The makeshift sunflowers never appear on film, and the real ones bloomed brilliantly *after* production wrapped!

The generous and inviting front porch is where present-day Sidda and Connor surprise Vivi on her birthday. It's also where mother and daughter make amends and where the men wait during the ending Ya-Ya ceremony.

Buckner Hill Plantation's owners delight in sharing its architecture, history, and movie connections. Winner of a Carraway Award of Merit in 2000, the house is listed on the National Register of Historic Places and is featured in the book *North Carolina Architecture* by Catherine W. Bishir.

Film junkie tip: Just a stone's throw from Buckner Hill Plantation is Bowden's Road, where the older Ya-Yas travel to and from Pecan Grove. It's along this stretch that Teensy sets up a roadblock with her yellow Rolls-Royce. The two-lane bridge is prominently featured in several scenes. From Buckner Hill, turn left on Taylor Town Road, then right on Herman Taylor Road, which intersects Bowden's Road.

CREDITS
Divine Secrets of the Ya-Ya Sisterhood (2002)

★★★★★★★★★★★★

Spivey's Corner's Hollerin' Contest

U.S. 13 and U.S. 421. The contest field is on Hollerin' Road behind Midway High School. For information about the contest, call 910-567-2600 or visit www.hollerincontest.com. For tourist information, call the Clinton-Sampson Chamber of Commerce at 910-592-6177.

Just across the line from Duplin County is Sampson County, the home of Spivey's Corner, otherwise known as the "Hollerin' Capital of the World," where the National Hollerin' Contest is held each June. Two documentaries—*Welcome to Spivey's Corner* and *Hollerin'* —have been based on the festival.

For 30-plus years, the contest has paid homage to the custom of high-pitched hollering, a communication system once used by farmers in eastern North Carolina. Each yodel has a signature style; some can be heard for up to two miles.

Late-night talk shows and morning news programs vie to book the hollerin' heroes. The winners have appeared on "The Tonight Show" with Johnny Carson and Jay Leno, "Late Night with David Letterman," and "Good Morning America," among other programs. The late Jim McCawley, former talent coordinator for "The Tonight Show," was intrigued enough to journey from Los Angeles for the 1995 competition.

Another Sampson County credit is the independent feature *Stateside*, filmed at the Sampson Regional Medical Center in nearby Clinton. The medical center appears as St. Anthony's Hospital. The movie stars Rachael Leigh Cook, Carrie Fisher, Ed Begley, Jr., Jonathan Tucker, and Val Kilmer.

Duplin County Star Tracks

Murray House Country Inn

201 N.C. 24/50, Kenansville (910-296-1000; www.murrayhouseinn.com).
The inn is available for weddings, meetings, and Ya-Ya reunions.

During filming of *Divine Secrets of the Ya-Ya Sisterhood*, director Callie Khouri and the Ya-Yas took over the Murray House Country Inn, a quaint bed-and-breakfast in Kenansville. Listed on the National Register of Historic Places, the two-story Needham Whitfield Herring House, built around 1853, is a fine example of Greek Revival architecture. When Lynn Dail Davis purchased it in 1990, carefully restored it, and opened it as a B&B in 1994, she never dreamed she'd host some of Hollywood's most famous actresses.

Framed by shade trees, boxwoods, and gardens, the carriage house offers eight comfortable guest rooms decorated with antiques and reproductions. Ellen Burstyn (Vivi) preferred the Hunter's Suite, where she could cook fresh vegetables in the kitchenette. Maggie Smith (Caro) stayed in the Lady's Retreat. Fionnula Flanagan (Teensy) slept in the Coachman's Suite. Shirley Knight (Necie) bunked in the Garden Room. Khouri chose the Gentleman's (or Honeymoon) Suite. Another famous guest was Martin Luther King III, who visited in April 2002.

Cape Lookout lighthouse

Road to the Outer Banks Locations

Beaufort

Nicknamed "the Crystal Coast," Carteret County's beaches, barrier islands, waterfront towns, and rural landscapes make a lovely backdrop. Celebrities who have arrived by yacht to explore its charms include news journalist Geraldo Rivera and *Terminator* heroine Linda Hamilton, whose North Carolina credits include *King Kong Lives* and *Mr. Destiny*.

While Carteret County claims a handful of independent films and movie-of-the-week credits, the town of Beaufort has hosted a studio feature. Cast and crew of *A Walk to Remember* trekked to Beaufort, established in 1723, for a day of filming. Film junkies who pay close attention will notice the "Welcome to Beaufort" road sign, the Front Street merchants, and the North Carolina Maritime Museum, located at 315 Front Street. Watch for Front Street when Jamie (Mandy Moore) gives Landon (Shane West) a ride home.

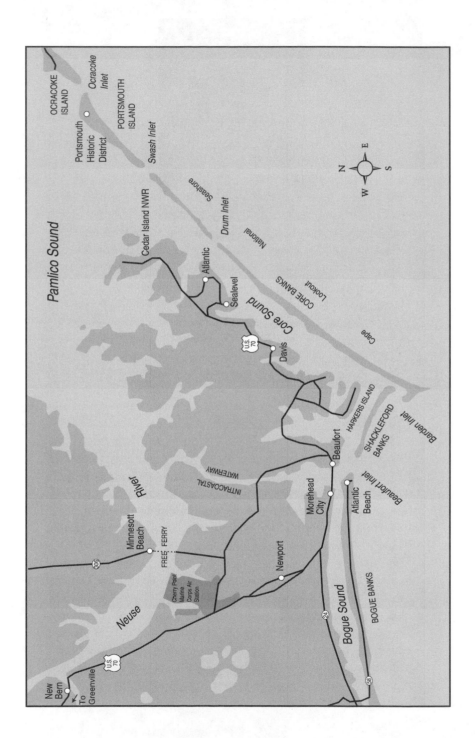

Beckoning from the nearby Cape Lookout National Seashore is the 163-foot Cape Lookout Lighthouse, constructed around 1859. You'll recognize its distinctive black-diamond design in *The North Carolina Lighthouse Tour* and *The Light in the Graveyard*. The discovery and recovery of the *Queen Anne's Revenge*, Blackbeard's flagship, off Beaufort has also inspired documentaries.

For tourist information, contact North Carolina's Crystal Coast by calling 800-SUNNYNC or visiting www.sunnync.com.

CREDITS

A Walk to Remember (2002); *The North Carolina Lighthouse Tour* (1993); *The Light in the Graveyard* (1982)

★★★★★★★★★★★★★★★

Famous East Carolina University Students

East Carolina University, established in Greenville in 1907, ranks among the South's top 10 public regional universities. Its celebrity connections are many.

Actress Sandra Bullock left ECU in 1985 to pursue acting. Her North Carolina productions include *Divine Secrets of the Ya-Ya Sisterhood, Forces of Nature*, and *28 Days*. Among her other credits are *Exactly 3:30, Two Weeks Notice, Murder by Numbers, Speed, A Time to Kill*, and *The Net*.

Screenwriter, director, and producer Kevin Williamson graduated in 1987. The Oriental, North Carolina, native studied theatre and film at ECU. By 1996, he had a hit screenplay for *Scream*. His North Carolina productions are *I Know What You Did Last Summer* and "Dawson's Creek." Among his other credits are *Cursed; Scream 2; Scream 3; Halloween: H20; The Faculty; Teaching Mrs. Tingle*; and "Glory Days."

Actress and Shelby, North Carolina, native Nina Repeta moved to Wilmington after college, then to L.A. to pursue acting. The role of Bessie in "Dawson's Creek" brought her back to Wilmington for six seasons. Her North Carolina productions include *Divine Secrets of the*

Ya-Ya Sisterhood, "Matlock," *The Angel Doll, Radioland Murders*, and "A Step Toward Tomorrow."

Other ECU film and TV personalities and their non-North Carolina credits are Beth Grant (*Pearl Harbor, Speed,* "Maximum Bob"); 1969 graduate Cullen O. Johnson ("General Hospital"); Stuart Ward (*Sleepless in Seattle*); 1991 graduate Emily Procter ("The West Wing," *Jerry Maguire*); and Maureen O'Boyle ("EXTRA," "A Current Affair").

Composer and jazz artist Loonis McGlohon (see pages 347-48) was a member of the class of 1942.

Other Pitt County celebs include Emmy Award®-winning jazz pianist Billy Taylor, rap music artist Petey Pablo, and novelist Sue Ellen Bridgers.

Q: What eastern North Carolina-made feature film stars Michelle Pfeiffer as a Jackie Kennedy-obsessed Dallas housewife on her way to JFK's funeral?

A: Love Field, *which filmed in Greenville, Fountain, Wilson, Rocky Mount, Red Oak, Elm City, and Raleigh. Most of Greenville's and Pitt County's other film credits are documentaries.*

Road to the Outer Banks
Star Tracks

Sanitary Fish Market

*501 Evans Street, Morehead City (252-247-3111;
www.sanitaryfishmarket.com). The Sanitary is open daily from
11 A.M. to 8 P.M. February through November.*

The Sanitary Fish Market, founded in 1938, may be the most famous restaurant on North Carolina's coast. Anybody who's anybody has been to the landmark restaurant in Morehead City. Photos of presidents, vice presidents, governors, beauty queens, musicians, writers, and actors grace the restaurant's wall of fame, among them Clint Eastwood, Linda Hamilton, Don Johnson, and author/screenwriters Nicholas Sparks, Mickey Spillane, and Charles Kuralt "North Carolina Is My Home."

Menu selections range from fried and broiled seafood to Alaskan snow crab, Maine lobster, and "Treasures of the Deep," a daily offshore game-fish special. The Sanitary's signature soups include clam chowder, she-crab soup, and conch chowder.

The spacious dining rooms offer spectacular views of the Intracoastal Waterway and are nearly always full. Though the restaurant seats 600, there's often a line during the summer.

★ ★ ★ ★ ★ ★ ★ ★ ★ ★

Langdon House Bed & Breakfast

135 Craven Street, Beaufort (252-728-5499). The inn is open year-round.

Guests at the Langdon House don't have to be stars to receive royal treatment. Innkeeper Jim Prest has welcomed guests since 1989, earning a reputation for excellent accommodations, great service, and Southern hospitality. Located near quaint waterfront shops, restaurants, and museums, the Langdon House, built around 1733, is the oldest home in Beaufort that operates as a bed-and-breakfast. The three-story white frame house with heart-pine floors is decorated with antiques. Rocking chairs on the first- and second-floor porches overlook a landscaped fern garden.

Tucked away in a quiet residential neighborhood, the Langdon House proved ideal for an incognito getaway by actress Michelle Pfeiffer.

Front Street Grill at Stillwater Café

300 Front Street, Beaufort (252-728-4956). The grill is open from 11:30 A.M. to 2:30 P.M. and from 5:30 P.M. to 9:30 P.M. Tuesday through Saturday. It is open from 5:30 P.M. to 9:30 P.M. on Sunday.

Creative "New World" cuisine places Front Street Grill at Stillwater Café in the upper echelon of coastal restaurants. Refined palates from around the globe have discovered Beaufort's waterfront culinary gem. Among them is Kevin Costner, who dined here while scouting for *Message in a Bottle*, which ultimately shot in Maine.

One of the grill's most memorable occasions was when it hosted a party for former president George H. W. Bush while

★ ★ ★ ★ ★ ★ ★ ★ ★ ★

he was on a fly-fishing vacation. Not only has Bush eaten at the restaurant, he has also ordered delivery meals for dining on his boat.

Other celebrity diners have included news journalist Geraldo Rivera and *The Terminator*'s buff and tough darling, Linda Hamilton, also known for her roles in the North Carolina-made films *King Kong Lives* and *Mr. Destiny*.

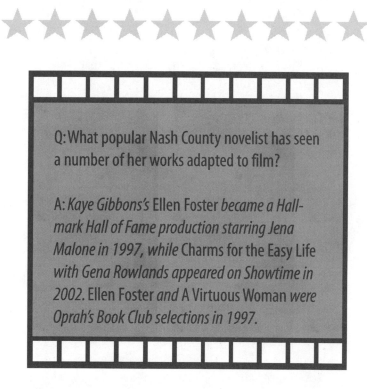

Q: What popular Nash County novelist has seen a number of her works adapted to film?

A: *Kaye Gibbons's* Ellen Foster *became a Hall-mark Hall of Fame production starring Jena Malone in 1997, while* Charms for the Easy Life *with Gena Rowlands appeared on Showtime in 2002.* Ellen Foster *and* A Virtuous Woman *were Oprah's Book Club selections in 1997.*

Nicholas Sparks

Author, screenwriter, and producer Nicholas Sparks has a deep and abiding love for what is now his home state. To date, each of his novels has been set in a town in eastern North Carolina. Film junkies may wonder what it is about North Carolina that compels this California native to base his stories and his family here. Sparks cites the relaxed way of life in eastern North Carolina and the culture of its small, yet progressive, towns.

Sparks has been praised as a master at generating authentic emotional power. His first best-selling novel, *The Notebook*, published in 1996, is set in his new hometown of New Bern. Hollywood took notice when his 1998 novel, *Message in a Bottle*, set mainly in Wrightsville Beach, also became a domestic and international bestseller. The Warner Brothers movie of *Message in a Bottle*, starring Paul Newman (*The Hudsucker Proxy*), Robin Wright Penn, and Kevin Costner (*Bull Durham*), reported box-office sales exceeding $120 million worldwide. His next book, the 1999 release *A Walk to Remember*, spent almost six months atop the hardcover bestseller list. It is set in Beaufort and Morehead City in the 1950s. Filmed around Southport, Wilmington, and Beaufort and released in 2002, *A Walk to Remember* stars pop diva Mandy Moore.

Sparks continued the bestseller trend with *The Rescue* in 2000, *A Bend in the Road* in 2001, and *Nights in Rodanthe* in 2002. Set in Edenton, New Bern, and the Outer Banks, respectively, all three books were optioned for film or television. In 2003 came the novels *The Guardian* and *The Wedding* (a sequel to *The Notebook*). *The Rescue* is being adapted as a television series.

A movie based on *The Notebook* filmed in Charleston, South Carolina, in 2003.

Manteo waterfront with *Elizabeth II*
COURTESY OF N. C. DIVISION OF TOURISM, FILM, & SPORTS DEVELOPMENT

Outer Banks Locations

Downtown Manteo

U.S. 64/264 runs directly through Manteo on Roanoke Island.

Downtown Manteo provided the idyllic waterfront setting for an early episode of "Matlock," starring local resident Andy Griffith. "Matlock" locations included the Manteo waterfront and the Green Dolphin Restaurant & Pub, located at 201 Sir Walter Raleigh Street. The 1904-vintage Dare County Courthouse, at 300 Queen Elizabeth Street, was the setting for the climactic courtroom scene in which attorney Ben Matlock defended his client. Subsequent episodes were filmed in Los Angeles, Atlanta, and Wilmington. The successful series ran from 1986 to 1995 and lives on in syndication heaven.

Brimming with 16th-century charm, Manteo is located on Roanoke Island. One of the town's principal attractions is Roanoke Island Festival Park, where you can find the 69-foot *Elizabeth II*, a replica of a 16th-century wooden sailing vessel. She makes a stunning appearance in *The Legend of Two-Path*, a poignant

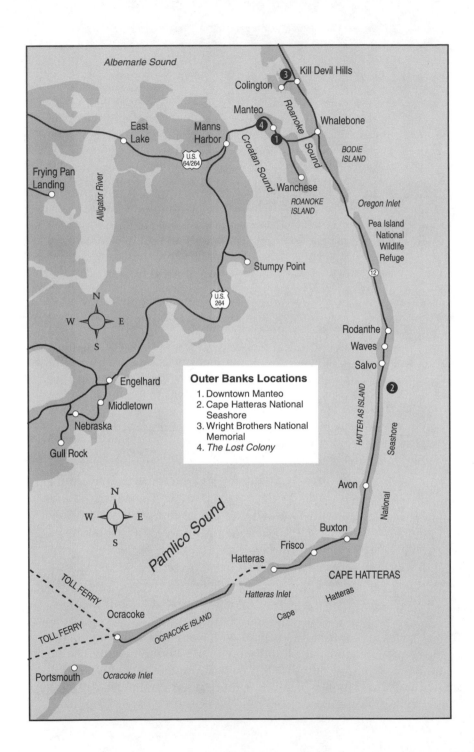

documentary produced by North Carolina School of the Arts students that tells of the 1584 arrival of English colonists from a young Algonquin Indian's point of view. Film junkies can view the film in the park's auditorium daily. In February, NCSA students bring their annual Student Film Festival to Festival Park.

Famous actors, playwrights, and directors have been associated with the outdoor drama *The Lost Colony* (see pages 147-48), staged at nearby Fort Raleigh. It traces the lives of the early colonists, including Virginia Dare, the first English child born in the New World.

For tourist information, contact the Outer Banks Visitors Bureau by calling 800-446-6262 or visiting www.outerbanks.org.

CREDITS

Manteo has appeared in numerous documentaries, including *Graveyard of the Atlantic* (1997); "Highway 64: A Passing View" (UNC-TV, 1996); *Treasure Coast* (1995); "North Carolina People" (UNC-TV, 1994); and Charles Kuralt's "North Carolina Is My Home" (UNC-TV, 1991). The town's other credits include *The Legend of Two-Path* (1998) and "Matlock" (NBC/ABC, 1986-92/93-95).

Cape Hatteras National Seashore

The headquarters for the national seashore are located at 1401 National Park Drive in Manteo; for information, call 252-473-2111 or visit www.nps.gov/caha. The seashore opens daily year-round at 9 A.M. It closes at 6 P.M. from June through August and at 5 P.M. the rest of the year. A fee is charged for camping and for climbing the Cape Hatteras Lighthouse. Call for lighthouse hours.

The beautiful and dangerous waters off Cape Hatteras are called "the Graveyard of the Atlantic." Many are the tales of shipwrecks, lighthouses, wicked storms, treacherous currents, dangerous shoals, pirates, ghost ships, wild ponies, and dramatic rescues.

The 70-mile-long Cape Hatteras National Seashore, established in 1953, was America's first national seashore. Its shining stars include the 156-foot Bodie Island Lighthouse; the 1823 Ocracoke Lighthouse, the state's oldest beacon still in operation; the 208-foot spiral-striped Cape Hatteras Lighthouse, the tallest brick beacon in the United States; and the Chicamacomico Lifesaving Station.

The Ocracoke Lighthouse makes a striking appearance in *Brainstorm* as the beacon illuminating Mike (Christopher Walken) in the shadows of Wright Brothers National Memorial (see below). Since the lighthouse is located 80 or 90 miles from the memorial, it took some clever editing to place the beacon in the park.

In 1999, the Cape Hatteras Lighthouse made international headlines when it was moved inland, away from the encroaching ocean. The process was painstakingly documented in *Cape Light: Away from the Edge*, among other documentaries.

The Chicamacomico Lifesaving Station's compelling story is interpreted in the film *Chicamacomico*.

CREDITS

Cape Light: Away from the Edge (1999); *Chicamacomico* (1997); *North Carolina Lighthouse Tour* (1993); *Brainstorm* (1983); *The Light in the Graveyard* (1982)

Wright Brothers National Memorial

800 Colington Road, Kill Devil Hills (252-441-7430; www.nps.gov/wrbr). The memorial is open daily from 9 A.M. to 6 P.M. June through August and from 9 A.M. to 5 P.M. the rest of the year. An admission fee is charged.

Little did brothers Wilbur and Orville Wright know that one of their old takeoff dunes would later be among the world's most photographed sites. The stunning 60-foot Wright Brothers National Memorial honors the Dayton, Ohio, residents and marks the spot where they conducted hundreds of glider flights. Their famous powered flights took place on the flat ground below the dune.

One Hollywood project, *Brainstorm*, filmed here. It includes

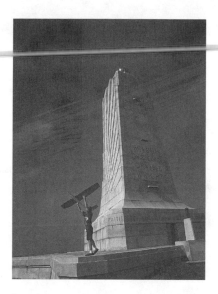

Wright Brothers National Memorial is seen in documentaries
and the Christopher Walken/Natalie Wood feature *Brainstorm*.
PHOTOGRAPH BY BILL RUSS
COURTESY OF N. C. DIVISION OF TOURISM, FILM, & SPORTS DEVELOPMENT

honeymoon flashback memories of Mike (Christopher Walken)
and Karen (Natalie Wood) riding bikes at sunrise, frolicking
around the base of the monument, and posing for pictures.
During the climactic nighttime ending, Mike races from Research
Triangle Park to the Outer Banks in under five minutes—only in
the movies! They're actually several hours apart. Outside at the
pay phone, Mike has a near-death experience as Project
Brainstorm goes awry. Movie magic places the Ocracoke
Lighthouse (see page 144) across from the memorial.

The memorial commanded international media attention
during the 2003 centennial celebration of Wilbur and Orville's
powered flights. Hollywood A-lister John Travolta (*Domestic
Disturbance*) served as master of ceremonies on centennial day and
flew his own Boeing 707 over Wright Brothers National
Memorial. President George W. Bush also made a special
appearance.

The PBS documentary "Kitty Hawk: The Wright Brothers'
Journey of Invention" premiered in 2003. The 12-second flight
on December 17, 1903, has also been recounted in *First Flight of the*

Wright Brothers, The Winds of Kitty Hawk, and *Wilbur and Orville: Dreams of Flying,* among other films.

"Kitty Hawk: The Wright Brothers' Journey of Invention" (PBS, 2003); *Wilbur and Orville: Dreams of Flying* (1994); *South Atlantic: A Coast of Contrasts* (1991); Charles Kuralt's "North Carolina Is My Home" (UNC-TV,1991); *Brainstorm* (1983); *The Winds of Kitty Hawk* (1978); *Land of Beginnings* (1965); *From Kitty Hawk to Calabash* (1961); *First Flight of the Wright Brothers* (1955)

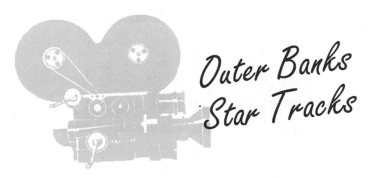

Outer Banks Star Tracks

The Lost Colony

1409 National Park Drive, Fort Raleigh National Historic Site, Roanoke Island (800-488-5012 or 252-473-3414; www.thelostcolony.org). The drama begins nightly at 8:30 except on Sundays from Memorial Day through late August. The shows are never canceled before 9 P.M. The box office is open from 9 A.M. to 5 P.M. An admission fee is charged.

An Outer Banks tradition since 1937, *The Lost Colony* is the nation's longest-running outdoor drama.

The celebrity connections begin with its Pulitzer Prize-winning playwright, Paul Green (1894-1981), a Harnett County native and UNC graduate who was commissioned to write a play about America's 16th-century colonists who mysteriously disappeared. Designed specifically for this production, the 2,000-seat Waterside Theater was built at Fort Raleigh, the very site where the script's events took place.

Many famous actors and directors have graced the Waterside Theater's stage. In 1937, President Franklin D. Roosevelt saw British actress Katherine Cale portray Eleanor Dare. Character actor

Andy Griffith as Sir Walter Raleigh in a production of "The Lost Colony," the nation's first and longest-running outdoor drama. Griffith performed in the production from 1947 until 1953.
PHOTO BY HUGH MORTON
COURTESY OF GRANDFATHER MOUNTAIN

R. G. "Bob" Armstrong has appeared, as has Chris Elliott, best known for his work in *Cabin Boy* and on "The Late Show with David Letterman." Soap-opera diva Eileen Fulton, an Asheville native who has played Lisa on "As the World Turns" since 1960, made her professional debut in *The Lost Colony*. Broadway actor and North Carolina School of the Arts alumnus Terrence Mann, a *TLC* dancer during the 1970s, played Old Tom during the 1977 season. He returns often to direct.

In 2003, *The Lost Colony* dedicated its 66th season to Cindi and Andy Griffith, both alums of the production. Andy, most beloved for his roles on "The Andy Griffith Show" and "Matlock," performed from 1947 to 1953, leaving the production as Sir Walter Raleigh. Cindi appeared from 1976 to 1979, playing the role of Eleanor Dare her final year.

DOCUMENTARY CREDITS
Roanoke (1997); "Highway 64: A Passing View" (UNC-TV,1996); *Genesis of Nationhood* (1984); *Land of Beginnings* (1965); *First Pageant of The Lost Colony* (1934)

SCENE: *The Piedmont*

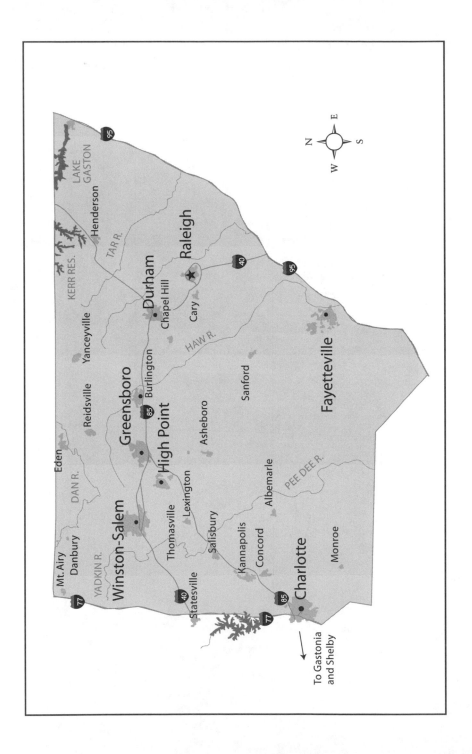

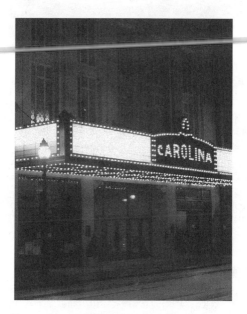

Greensboro's Carolina Theatre is known as
"the Showplace of the Carolinas."
PHOTOGRAPH © NYGHTFALCON

*F*ew places can mimic the Piedmont, yet the Piedmont can mimic many places. Stretching from North Carolina's mountains to its coastal plain, it contains virtually every landscape imaginable, except for the desert and ocean. Thus, talented location managers, set designers, and art directors can make anything happen—and they do. *Snake Eyes* created a tidal wave at Greensboro's Wet 'N Wild Emerald Pointe Water Park. Need a desert? Import sand and create it in a Piedmont rock quarry or full-service movie studio. From the rolling foothills at the base of the Blue Ridge Mountains to the metropolises of Charlotte, the Triad, and the Triangle to the farms, the Sandhills region, and the plains in the eastern part of the state, the North Carolina Piedmont is a vast and versatile location.

The production of documentaries and films here dates back to the dawn of filmmaking. A boom came in the 1980s and 1990s with titles such as *Brainstorm, Once Around, The Color Purple, Patch Adams, Nell, Days of Thunder, George Washington, The Bedroom*

Window, and *Kiss the Girls* and continues into the new millennium with *Cabin Fever*, "Dawson's Creek," *Shallow Hal*, and other film, television, and commercial productions.

The North Carolina Film Office in Raleigh facilitated production for the entire state until the early 1990s, when regional film commissions were formed. The Charlotte Regional Film Office, part of the Charlotte Regional Partnership, serves a 16-county area encompassing portions of North and South Carolina. The Piedmont Triad Film Commission, part of the Piedmont Triad Partnership, serves a 12-county area. The Triangle is served by the North Carolina Film Commission, while individual chambers of commerce in cities such as Durham support their efforts. State and regional film offices and community support are critical to the success of local film industries.

Each of the Piedmont's three film regions—the Triangle, the Triad, and the Charlotte area—offers variety. Each has a mix of urban and rural landscapes. Filmmakers make use of the skyscrapers, monuments, industrial buildings, restaurants, nightlife, international airports, and varied neighborhoods. Perhaps the greatest hook is that within minutes in just about any direction, you'll find quaint small towns, fields of cotton or corn, livestock farms, forests, country back roads, and lakes and rivers. Piedmont architecture stretches all the way back to Winston-Salem's Old Salem, an authentic 18th-century Moravian village, and Charlotte's Latta Plantation, which demonstrates life on an early-19th-century farm. The Piedmont is home to dozens of colleges and universities and is the state's hub for arts, culture, and college sports. The world-renowned Research Triangle Park gives the area a high-tech image.

Even film junkies intimately familiar with the Piedmont will be amazed when exploring the region through the camera lens. Locations included in this section more than prove the Piedmont's star quality.

For visitor information, contact the North Carolina Division of Tourism, Film and Sports Development by calling 800-VISITNC or visiting www.visitnc.com.

Raleigh skyline
PHOTOGRAPH BY BILL RUSS
COURTESY OF N. C. DIVISION OF TOURISM, FILM, & SPORTS DEVELOPMENT

The Triangle

*R*aleigh, Durham, and Chapel Hill—collectively known as the Triangle—are diverse cities boasting an international reputation as centers of government, higher education, college and professional sports, and culture. The cultural profile was raised in the early 1980s with the development of the North Carolina Film Office. While the film office is located in the Capital City, Raleigh has been a rather low-key film location, though a number of the city's landmarks and neighborhoods have turned up in major motion pictures and on television.

The city of Durham got name recognition that money can't buy courtesy of *Bull Durham*. This classic sports film explores baseball and romance through a fresh script and vibrant performances by Kevin Costner, Susan Sarandon, and Tim Robbins. Thanks to a wonderful convergence of producer Thom Mount (a Durham native and part owner of the Durham Bulls at the time), director and screenwriter Ron Shelton (a former minor-league baseball player), three principals poised for breakout performances, and a sharp eye for detail and nuance, *Bull Durham*

★ 153

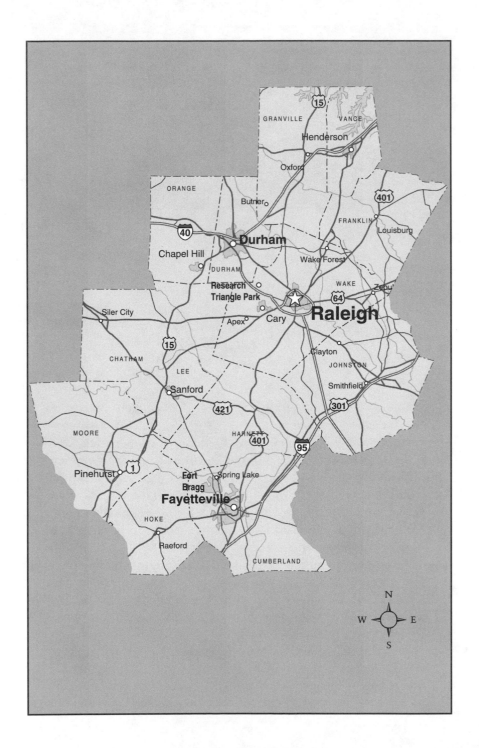

richly deserves its acknowledgment as one of the top sports films of all time. It was filmed at several ballparks throughout the state, including the historic Durham Athletic Park. That's not all for Durham, though. The Neo-Gothic campus of Duke University has made several appearances on film, most recently in "Dawson's Creek."

In recent years, Chapel Hill has welcomed the arrival of an independent filmmaking scene. Author James Patterson got the idea for his novel *Kiss the Girls* in Chapel Hill, and the subsequent film caused a bit of controversy when filmed in the Triangle. More recently, the UNC campus was seen in Robin Williams's maligned but sweet *Patch Adams*.

The Triangle is also home to a number of film festivals and film societies.

Dig in.

For visitor information, contact the Greater Raleigh Convention and Visitors Bureau (800-849-8499; www.visitraleigh.com); the Durham Convention and Visitors Bureau (800-446-8604; www.durham-nc.com); or the Chapel Hill/Orange County Convention and Visitors Bureau (888-968-2060; www.chocvb.org).

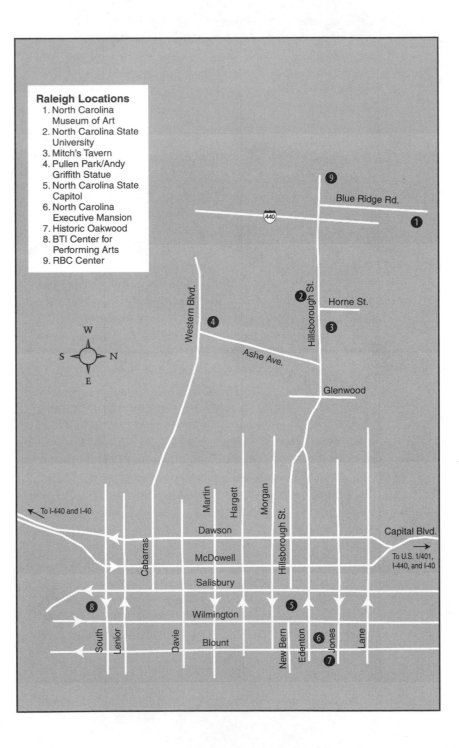

Raleigh Locations

North Carolina Museum of Art

2110 Blue Ridge Road (919-839-6262; www.ncartmuseum.org). The museum is open from 9 A.M. to 5 P.M. Wednesday through Saturday and from 10 A.M. to 5 P.M. on Sunday. It is closed on major holidays. Admission to the museum's permanent collection is free, though visitors must pay to see special exhibitions and to attend the film series.

Marking 20 years in its Blue Ridge Road location in 2003, the North Carolina Museum of Art is a cultural hub for the state. The museum houses a collection encompassing paintings and sculpture from ancient Egypt to the present. Among the favorites here are Renaissance and Baroque works by Van Dyck, Jan Breughel, and Raphael, works of Monet and other Impressionists, and works by American painters such as John Singleton Copley, Winslow Homer, and Georgia O'Keeffe. Collections of African, Oceanic, Egyptian, Greek, Roman, 20th-century, and Jewish ceremonial art are also on display.

NCMA offers several film events, including its popular Summer Film Series, held at the Museum Park Outdoor Cinema. Triangle area film junkies bring blankets, chairs, picnic baskets, and bottles of wine and settle down to watch a film often introduced by a live concert that represents the film's theme. Katherine Whalen's & Jazz Squad performed before the showing of *Chicago*, for example. The amphitheater was christened in 1997 when noted director Sidney Lumet premiered his 40th film, *Night Falls on Manhattan*, for 1,600 guests. The screening marked the first time a film not made in North Carolina had premiered in the state. The evening also featured a book signing by Lumet.

The museum itself appears on-screen in *Foresight*, an independent feature filmed entirely in Raleigh. Artwork depicting death or the afterlife—including an exhibition by North Carolina painter McKendree Robbins Long—is used by writer and director Jon Lance Bacon in a scene in which Detective Josephine Griggs copes with the pressure of investigating a series of murders.

CREDITS

Foresight (2004)

North Carolina State University

The campus is on Hillsborough Street. Tours leave from the Tally Student Center at 12:20 P.M. on Monday, Wednesday, and Friday and at 2:30 P.M. on Tuesday and Thursday; to contact the student center, call 919-515-2434. The university's website is www.ncsu.edu.

North Carolina State University, one of the nation's largest land-grant universities, offers film junkies the chance to see cutting-edge independent and experimental films and to visit the locations of an award-winning indie film and a TV movie about one of the university's biggest stars.

The Southern Circuit Film Series has featured noncommercial films by independent filmmakers since 1984. Documentaries are the mainstay of the Southern Circuit, with a few feature films thrown in. Oftentimes, the filmmakers are present for a Q & A session.

Andy Griffith Statue
Pullen Park, 520 Ashe Avenue, Raleigh

Andy Griffith may be the most popular actor North Carolina has produced.

Andy has gotten around in the Tar Heel State. Born and raised in Mount Airy, he went to college in Chapel Hill, spent several years filming "Matlock" in Wilmington, and is a longtime resident of the Outer Banks. So, naturally, the folks at the TV Land network unveiled a statue of him in Raleigh in October 2003. Of course, that's not really far-fetched. Andy's connection to the Capital City is pretty tight. About a dozen episodes of "The Andy Griffith Show" (affectionately known as "TAGS") were either set in Raleigh or featured state officials or other visitors from the Capital City.

Of course, this didn't quell the controversy. Those who argued that the statue should be in Mount Airy, the model for Mayberry, pointed out that Sheriff Taylor's forays to Raleigh weren't always successful, as he looked a little uncomfortable out of uniform and having to deal with the snobs and sophisticates of the big city. Others said the real honoree should have been the man whose name became synonymous with Raleigh as a vacation spot (the infamous corner room at the Y) and later served as a detective with the RPD: Barney Fife.

Despite these quibbles, everyone was pleased with the overall plan. The statue features Sheriff Taylor and son Opie on their way to the fishing hole, just like at the beginning of every episode. Hardcore film junkies probably know that "The Fishing Hole" is the title of the show's whistled theme song. And even casual junkies know that Opie grew up to be Academy Award®-winning director and producer Ron Howard. Howard has cited the training and discipline he learned on "TAGS" as the bedrock of his career.

Andy Griffith is the third classic TV star to be immortalized by TV Land. Mary Tyler Moore (Mary Richards) was honored in Minneapolis in 2002, and Jackie Gleason (Ralph Kramden) was immortalized in New York in 2000.

Oddly enough, an award-winning indie feature, *The Delicate Art of the Rifle*, was shot atop the building that is home to the Southern Circuit. Several N.C. State alums appear in this feature-length production by CLC Films. A pivotal sequence was filmed on the roof of the D. H. Hill Library, the tallest building on campus. The winner of the Best Feature awards at the 1996 Chicago Underground Film Festival and the 1996 North Carolina Film Festival is based loosely on the shootings at the University of Texas in the mid-1960s. Watch for Nebula Award-winning author and N.C. State English professor John Kessel in his acting debut.

The William Neal Reynolds Coliseum, for over 50 years the home of the Wolfpack men's two-time NCAA basketball champions, appears in "Never Give Up: The Jim Valvano Story," a television film based on the life of the late basketball coach. Sports fans will not soon forget when Valvano shocked the world by leading N.C. State to the 1983 national title. Many more remember his brave battle with cancer, a fight that continues through the V Foundation and the annual Jimmy V. Celebrity Golf Classic (see pages 171-72).

(see pages 171-72)

CREDITS

The Delicate Art of the Rifle (1996); "Never Give Up: The Jim Valvano Story" (CBS, 1996)

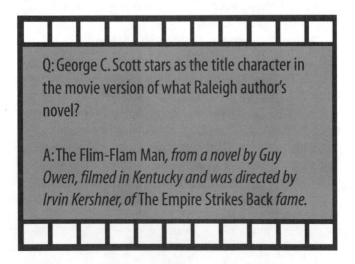

Q: George C. Scott stars as the title character in the movie version of what Raleigh author's novel?

A: The Flim-Flam Man, *from a novel by Guy Owen, filmed in Kentucky and was directed by Irvin Kershner, of* The Empire Strikes Back *fame.*

The window from Mitch's bar, featured in the
bar brawl scene in *Bull Durham*
PHOTOGRAPH BY BOB STUART, SACRED SHOTS

Mitch's Tavern

2426 Hillsborough Street (919-821-7771; www.mitchs.com).
Mitch's is open from 11 A.M. to 2 A.M. Monday through
Saturday and from 5 P.M. to 2 A.M. on Sunday.

Bull Durham revolves around a love triangle among Crash
Davis (Kevin Costner), Annie Savoy (Susan Sarandon), and Ebby
Calvin "Nuke" LaLoosh (Tim Robbins). The three meet for the
first time in the movie at Mitch's, a Hillsborough Street hangout
for generations of N.C. State students, in a scene in which sparks
fly and fists get thrown. As things open, Annie sits with Max
Patkin, "the Clown Prince of Baseball," as Crash sends over a
drink from a nearby booth. Nuke, meanwhile, is tearing it up on
the dance floor to the Smithereens' "Only a Memory" and George
Thorogood's "Born to be Bad." Robbins asked the costumer to
outfit him like John Travolta in *Saturday Night Fever*, and he indeed
has the look, if not the moves, in his ice-cream suit. The dance
scene, incidentally, was choreographed by Paula Abdul of
"American Idol." Of course, when Crash and Nuke meet, they

start acting like "guys" and have to go outside to settle the score. The fight scene was not filmed at Mitch's, though the glass window over Crash's shoulder clearly says "Mitch's Bar"—that is, until it's smashed with a baseball by Nuke, showing off his "million-dollar arm and five-cent head." A replica of the window (intact) is now proudly on display at Mitch's, as are photographs of Costner and other cast and crew members.

Today, Mitch's looks pretty much like it does on film. A classic college bar, it's located right across the street from N.C. State. Mitch gave up a career as a high-school teacher for the tavern business over 25 years ago. If he's there, he'll gladly share his brush with Hollywood fame. Film junkies can relive the *Bull Durham* scene while enjoying a cold beer or glass of wine with a sandwich or one of the lunch or dinner specials.

CREDITS

Bull Durham (1988)

North Carolina State Capitol

1 East Edenton Street, Union Square (919-733-4994). The State Capitol is open from 8 A.M. to 5 P.M. Monday through Friday, from 10 A.M. to 4 P.M. on Saturday, and from 1 P.M. to 4 P.M. on Sunday. It is closed Thanksgiving, Christmas, and New Year's. Admission is free.

Yes, the State Capitol is one of the finest examples of civic Greek Revival architecture in the country and was once the seat of North Carolina government. But it's also the location of a film portrayal of a favorite son's least favorite moment and of a favorite fictional film student's final scene in his first student film. And it's a place to see the father of our country in perhaps his least-flattering get-up. And the place where an American idol met the governor. Lot of firsts. Lot of favorites. Heady stuff for film junkies.

The State Capitol, a National Historic Landmark, was completed in 1840. It is the second such building to sit on Union Square. Until 1888, all of state government was housed in this

Celebrity sightings at the North Carolina State Capitol Building
include presidents, stars, and American idols.
PHOTOGRAPH BY BILL RUSS.
COURTESY OF N. C. DIVISION OF TOURISM, FILM, & SPORTS DEVELOPMENT

building. The governor and lieutenant governor still maintain offices on the first floor.

The legislative chamber was the setting for *The Impeachment of Andrew Johnson*, a 1974 documentary on what until recently was the only impeachment trial of an American president. The building stood in for the Capitol in Washington, D.C., where the actual trial took place in the 1860s. This is ironic, as Johnson, who assumed the presidency on the death of Abraham Lincoln, was born in Raleigh and is featured (along with the two other North Carolina presidents, Andrew Jackson and James K. Polk) in a statue on the State Capitol grounds. The stirring statue, featuring Jackson on horseback, is a favorite photo spot for visitors.

The State Capitol grounds provide the backdrop for the final scene of Dawson Leery's (James Van Der Beek's) student film in the season-five episode of "Dawson's Creek" entitled "Guerrilla Filmmaking." The snow for the night shoot was both fake and real. The episode features Charlie (Chad Michael Murray) and Audrey (Busy Philipps) working out their romantic issues, while Audrey, of course, is all mixed up over Pacey (Joshua Jackson). Ah, love!

Looking rather thespianish in the State Capitol's lobby is a marble statue of George Washington wearing a toga and sandals and holding a stylus and tablet. Another American idol, Raleigh native Clay Aiken, runner-up on the popular Fox series' second edition, appeared with Governor Mike Easley in the rotunda on Clay Aiken Day in May 2003. Aiken sang for the large gathering. Easley presented him with a signed photograph of another well-known Tar Heel singer, James Taylor.

CREDITS

"Dawson's Creek" (The WB, 1998-2003); *The Impeachment of Andrew Johnson* (1974)

North Carolina Executive Mansion

200 North Blount Street (919-733-3456). Hours vary; call for tour times. Admission is free.

The home of the biggest star in state government has shown up on the big screen as the site of a splashy wedding reception for a couple of Academy Award® winners.

Designed by architects Samuel Sloan and A. G. Bauer and constructed by prison labor during the Reconstruction era, the Executive Mansion, the fourth official North Carolina governor's residence, is one of the finest examples of Victorian and Queen Anne architecture in the state. The steeply pitched roofs, cupola, porches, pavilions, spacious halls, reception rooms, massive stairway, and 16-foot ceilings caught the eye of the makers of

The North Carolina Executive Mansion, where Sam (Richard Dreyfuss) married Renata (Holly Hunter) in *Once Around*.
PHOTOGRAPH BY BILL RUSS
COURTESY OF N. C. DIVISION OF TOURISM, FILM, & SPORTS DEVELOPMENT

Once Around, who used the mansion's gold-trimmed ballroom for the wedding reception of the aptly named Sam Sharpe (Richard Dreyfuss) and his naive Italian-American princess, Renata Bella (Holly Hunter). The scene is made memorable when Papa (Danny Aiello) croons "Fly Me to the Moon," backed by a small band of local musicians. During an exterior scene on a porch, Hunter overhears Aiello's *real* feelings about the nuptials; you'll note the mansion's distinctively patterned brickwork and woodwork. Between takes, kids in formal attire flocked around Aiello, calling out for Sal, a nod to his recent Oscar® nomination for Spike Lee's *Do the Right Thing*. "Sal" happily posed for photographs.

The cast of *Once Around* appeared at a reception that included the governor and then-first lady Barbara Bush, who tacitly approved of Dreyfuss's "Domestic Desert Storm" button.

The Executive Mansion has starred in a few documentaries, most notably "Mansion at 200 North Blount," a 28-minute program telling the home's colorful history.

CREDITS

Once Around (1991); "Mansion at 200 North Blount" (UNC-TV, 1988)

Historic Oakwood

Monroe, Madison, and State streets in downtown Raleigh. Visitors may take a self-guided tour of the neighborhood; daylight hours are recommended. Christmas tours are offered in mid-December. Tour brochures are available at the Capital Area Visitor Center. For information on Oakwood, call 919-733-3456.

Walking from downtown Raleigh's government and museum district into Historic Oakwood is a bit like happening onto a movie set from the Victorian era. In "The Portrait," an adaptation of the award-winning play *Painting Churches*, Oakwood appears as a tony Boston neighborhood perfect for college professor Gardner Church (Gregory Peck) and wife Fanny (fellow legend Lauren Bacall). Also featured in "The Portrait" is Peck's daughter

Cecilia, who earned a Golden Globe® nomination as his screen daughter, Margaret. A third legend working on "The Portrait" was director Arthur Penn, whose credits include *Bonnie and Clyde* and *Little Big Man*. Peck's classroom scenes were shot at Duke University (see pages 179-81). The Oakwood house used in the production is a private home whose owners do not wish to have identified.

Film junkies can enjoy a self-guided walking tour of the only intact 19th-century neighborhood in Raleigh. The walking tour is especially popular at Christmas. Oakwood is listed on the National Register of Historic Places.

CREDITS

"The Portrait" (TNT, 1993)

BTI Center for the Performing Arts
South Street between Salisbury and Wilmington streets in downtown Raleigh. For tickets, call Ticketmaster at 919-834-4000.

Shooting the exterior Washington, D.C., scenes in downtown Raleigh for her directorial debut, *The Dress Code*, must have felt a little like coming full circle for Shirley MacLaine. It seems Raleigh provided a memorable moment in one of her first breaks in show business. According to her 1970 autobiography, *Don't Fall Off the Mountain*, the teenage Shirley Beatty got her first big dancing gig after auditioning in New York for a tour of Southern cities promoting the Servel Ice Box Company. The tour's director persuaded her to use her middle name for the stage. The newly christened Shirley MacLaine embarked on the tour with instructions to keep on dancing around the company's ice maker even if the machine got stuck. It was during a performance in Raleigh that it did indeed get stuck. Thus, Shirley danced "until nearly turning into whipped cream" before a befuddled audience of salesmen.

MacLaine doesn't mention if the performance took place in Raleigh's Memorial Auditorium, but it is entirely possible, as the classically styled building has hosted everything from basketball games to beauty pageants since its completion in 1932. Today, the auditorium is part of the expanded BTI Center for the Performing Arts. Three new theatres—the Fletcher Opera Theater, the Meymandi Concert Hall, and the Kennedy Theater—join Memorial Auditorium to offer almost 5,000 seats for Triangle arts lovers.

In *The Dress Code*, MacLaine and her dress-wearing grandson, Bruno (Alex D. Linz), wear matching cowboy outfits as they make their way through a group of protesters into Washington's Shrine Auditorium for the finals of the National Catholic Spelling Championships. Memorial Auditorium's distinctive

Q: What Raleigh native served as an ambassador for the Greater Raleigh Convention and Visitors Bureau after his meteoric rise to superstardom in 2003?

A: Popular runner-up vocalist Clay Aiken was featured on a promotional page of the official Raleigh visitor's site (www.visitraleigh.org) inviting visitors to experience his hometown. In its first week, the page received several thousand hits! Aiken, who now lives in Los Angeles, was born and raised in Raleigh and studied special education at UNC-Charlotte before he was discovered on Fox TV's "American Idol." In November 2003, he took the Fan's Choice Award, presented by the American Music Awards. His 2003 album, Measure of a Man, debuted as double platinum.

Doric columns are clearly seen in the background as the demonstrators march through Lichtin Plaza, the two-acre pavilion fronting the BTI Center.

Home to the North Carolina Theater, Memorial has featured some of the world's most celebrated artists, including Mikhail Baryshnikov, Itzhak Perlman, Frank Sinatra, Tony Bennett, Dizzy Gillespie, Ray Charles, Dionne Warwick, Natalie Cole, Amy Grant, and Prince. The North Carolina Theater has presented Broadway musicals such as *Cats, Les Misérables, Miss Saigon,* and *Rent* using a combination of local casts and crews with Broadway, film, and television talent such as longtime artistic director Terrence Mann. Memorial Auditorium and the Fletcher Opera Theater host the Broadway Series South.

CREDITS

The Dress Code (2000)

RBC Center

1400 Edwards Mill Road (919-861-2300; www.rbccenter.com). The offices are open from 9 A.M. to 5 P.M. Monday through Friday.

The national sport of Canada, "American Idol," and the "Dawson's Creek" cast—both on-screen and off—all have a connection to Raleigh's RBC Center.

Many doubted NHL hockey would make it in ACC basketball-mad North Carolina, but the Carolina Hurricanes and their improbable run to the Stanley Cup finals in 2002 proved that wrong. The Hurricanes' home ice was a perfect stand-in for a New England hockey arena in the final season of "Dawson's Creek." When the series filmed in the Triangle, cast and crew became regulars at Hurricanes games. The RBC Center also hosted almost 9,000 rabid "American Idol" fans for the second edition's final episode—featuring hometown hero Clay Aiken— in May 2003. The arena was on the "American Idol Live!" tour that summer.

In its brief history, the RBC Center has hosted many top

names in music, including Jimmy Buffett, Bruce Springsteen, Luciano Pavarotti, Cher, the Judds, Tim McGraw, and the Boston Pops.

CREDITS

"American Idol" (Fox, 2002-); "Dawson's Creek" (The WB, 1998-2003)

Raleigh Star Tracks

Angus Barn

*9401 Glenwood Avenue (919-787-3505; www.angusbarn.com).
The restaurant is open from 4 P.M. to 11 P.M. Monday through
Saturday and from 4 P.M. to 10 P.M. on Sunday.*

The Angus Barn is *the* place in the Triangle, with a reputation
second to none. One of the area's oldest and most famous
restaurants, it has been a favorite of locals and stars for decades.
The trademark big red barn specializes in Black Angus beef and
mouth-watering homemade desserts. The Wild Turkey Bar is a
popular watering hole for relaxing, seeing, and being seen.

Diners here over the years have included a who's who of
show business, politics, sports, and entertainment. Pictures of
many famous people are on display. Who, you ask? Well, a partial
list includes wrestler and budding actor The Rock, actor turned
president Ronald Reagan, Claude Akins, June Lockhart, George
Peppard, Dave Matthews, Wynonna Judd, Judge Joe Brown,
Gerald Ford, Barbara Bush, and Don King, just to name a very
few.

This is a spot you won't soon forget.

Jimmy V. Celebrity Classic /
Prestonwood Country Club

Prestonwood Country Club is located at 300 Prestonwood Parkway in Cary. It is open to members year-round. For information, call 919-467-2566. The Jimmy V. Celebrity Golf Classic is headquartered at 1201 Walnut Street, Suite 203, in Cary. For information, call 919-319-0441.

"Don't give up. Don't ever give up."

Jim Valvano's big-time college basketball coaching career was highlighted by N.C. State's 1983 NCAA basketball championship, still one of the biggest upsets and most exciting title games in the history of sports. Valvano's spirit was put to an even greater test a few years later during a heroic battle with cancer. Coach V. handled his fate with characteristic candor and style, setting in motion a legacy of public awareness and research through The V Foundation for Cancer Research, established in 1993. The Jimmy V. Celebrity Classic, held each August in the coach's adopted hometown of Cary (with other related events at various locations in the Triangle), brings together one of the largest gatherings of celebrities from film, television, broadcasting, and sports for an informal weekend of golf, tennis, music, fun, and fund-raising.

For celebrity sightings, film junkies will want to attend the golf tournament, held at Cary's Prestonwood Country Club. Among the film and TV stars who have shown off their swings for a good cause are Kevin Costner, Gary Busey, Kevin Sorbo, Sharon Lawrence, Jamie Farr, Gregory Harrison, Susan Anton, Dennis Haskins, and James McDaniel. The host of supportive television and sports broadcasters has included Dick Vitale, Stone Phillips, John Saunders, Stuart Scott, and Rush Limbaugh. Music fans can check out the V. Jam concert. Musician/golfers have included Meat Loaf, Mike Mills of REM, Darius Rucker of Hootie and the Blowfish, and Edwin McCain. Of course, sports stars always turn out, among them Valvano's former Wolfpack players Thurl Bailey, Vinny Del Negro, Sidney Lowe, Dereck Whittenburg, and Terry Gannon, along with former basketball coaching rivals Dean Smith, Bill Guthridge, Matt Doherty, and Mike Krzyzewski. Other sports stars at the event have included Charles Barkley, Muggsey Bogues, Rod Brind'Amour, Vince Carter, Todd Eldredge, Ric Flair, and Meadowlark Lemon.

The private Prestonwood Country Club features 54 holes of golf, as well as opportunities for tennis, fitness training, swimming, and dining. Most events connected to the golf tournament are held at the club. Among them are a raffle, the Celebrity Tennis Challenge, clinics, a silent auction, and dinner.

Triangle Celebrities

Sharon Lawrence's role on "NYPD Blue" made her a household name, a position she seemed groomed for. After growing up in Raleigh and graduating from UNC, she moved to New York City, where she eventually won the role of District Attorney Sylvia Costas Sipowicz, which garnered her a Screen Actor's Guild Award® and three Emmy® nominations. Lawrence didn't stay too long from her childhood home, though. She appeared in the North Carolina Theatre production of *1776* and hosted the Special Olympics World Games in Raleigh in 1999. Sharon's father, Tom, was a longtime reporter for Raleigh's WRAL-TV.

Journalist Charles Kuralt was born in Wilmington, grew up in Hampstead and Charlotte, and found his calling as editor of the

Daily Tar Heel at UNC. During his 40-year career with CBS News, Kuralt left an indelible mark with his "On the Road" segments and as host of "Sunday Morning." He also authored *On the Road with Charles Kuralt* and *North Carolina Is My Home*, which became a documentary. Kuralt is buried in Chapel Hill, where his late brother Wallace operated The Intimate Bookshop, a much-loved independent bookstore.

Young Evan Rachel Wood is one of Hollywood's up-and-coming actresses. Acting is in her blood. Evan is the daughter of Ira David Wood III, the founder of Raleigh's Theatre in the Park, and actress Sara Elins, who appeared in a number of television shows, including the cult favorite "American Gothic." Evan played Jessica on ABC's "Once and Again." Her other credits include *Simone* (with Al Pacino), *Practical Magic* (with Sandra Bullock and Nicole Kidman), *Thirteen* (with Holly Hunter), and *The Missing* (with Tommy Lee Jones). She received a Golden Globe® nomination for Best Actress for *Thirteen*.

In the category of adopted North Carolinians, there's actor Dan Cortese, who attended UNC. Plus, he gets bonus points for marrying native North Carolinian Dee Dee Hemby of Wilmington. Cortese hosted sports for MTV, then moved on to "Melrose Place," "Veronica's Closet," *After Sex* (with Brooke Shields), and "A Weekend in the Country" (with Jack Lemmon and Dudley Moore).

Louise Fletcher, another UNC grad, will always be remembered for her Oscar®-winning role as Nurse Ratchet in *One Flew over the Cuckoo's Nest*, which made the top five on the American Film Institute's list of all-time screen villains. Fletcher has appeared in several North Carolina-made films, including *Brainstorm*, *Firestarter*, and "In a Child's Name." She's also well known as Kai Winn in "Star Trek: Deep Space Nine."

Fans of the cult HBO hit "Six Feet Under" know Raleigh

native Michael C. Hall as David in the offbeat Fisher family. A graduate of New York University's Master of Fine Arts program in acting, Hall has also starred in *Paycheck*, a sci-fi thriller with Uma Thurman and Ben Affleck.

One of the hottest directors in Hollywood is Raleigh native Peyton Reed, another UNC grad, who directed the surprise hit *Bring It On*, starring Kirsten Dunst, and the 1960s homage *Down with Love*, starring Renée Zellweger and Ewan McGregor.

Author and illustrator Daniel Wallace of Chapel Hill wrote the novel *Big Fish*, the basis for the Golden Globe®-nominated film directed by Tim Burton.

Q: What Henderson-born television journalist has interviewed almost every major news, sports, and entertainment figure of the past several decades?

A: *Charlie Rose, who according to* Esquire *magazine "brings a Southern civility to the most intelligent tête-à-têtes on TV," hosts an Emmy®-winning PBS interview show nightly and is also a correspondent on "60 Minutes II." Rose holds degrees in history and law from Duke and is a recipient of the George Peabody Broadcasting Award and the Cable ACE Award. He likes to unwind on his farm near Oxford, North Carolina.*

Ava Gardner Museum

325 East Market Street, Smithfield (919-934-5830; www.avagardner.org). The museum is approximately one mile from I-95, off U.S. 70. It is open from 9 A.M. to 5 P.M. Monday through Saturday and from 2 P.M. to 5 P.M. on Sunday. An admission fee is charged.

Hollywood glamour from the Golden Age can be seen at Johnston County's Ava Gardner Museum. This photograph shows Ava in *The Killers*.
COURTESY OF AVA GARDNER MUSEUM

At the height of Hollywood's studio era of the 1940s and 1950s, a small-town girl from rural Johnston County, North Carolina, was in the top ranks of movie stars and international sex symbols.

Though she lived the epitome of Hollywood rags-to-riches success, from B movies to A-list marriages, Ava Gardner never forgot the small community she came from. And thanks to the

Ava Gardner Museum, the community will never forget her. Located near Gardner's birthplace and final resting place, the museum in downtown Smithfield contains one of the most extensive collections on a movie star anywhere in America. Among the holdings are artifacts from her film career and her private life.

Ava Lavinia Gardner was born on Christmas Eve 1922 in rural Grabtown, just east of Smithfield. She was the youngest of Jonas and Mary Elizabeth Gardner's seven children. Her parents raised cotton and tobacco and ran boardinghouses for teachers at the rural Brodgen School and later in the Rock Ridge community in Wilson County. Ava graduated from high school in Rock Ridge in 1939 and attended Atlantic Christian College in Wilson for a year. A well-known showbiz story tells of her discovery. During Ava's trip to visit her older sister Bappie in New York City, Bappie's professional photographer husband, Larry Tarr, displayed in his studio window a photo he'd taken of Ava. That photo led to an MGM screen test and a movie contract.

Thus, the whirlwind years of movies, stardom, and marriages began. Shortly after arriving in Hollywood, Ava met and married Mickey Rooney, then one of the biggest stars in town. The marriage lasted just over a year. Her second short-lived marriage was to one of the kings of Swing, band leader Artie Shaw. Then came the great love of her life, the legendary Frank Sinatra. Their love was dubbed one of the "Romances of the Century" by *People* magazine. They were married for five pressure-cooker years. Ava remained friends with Sinatra, as with all her ex-husbands. She had no children but doted on her North Carolina nieces and nephews.

Of course, there were also the movies—over 60 in all. Her films were always popular, if not particularly memorable. She managed to appear opposite almost all of the leading men of the day, including Clark Gable, Burt Lancaster, Gregory Peck, and Richard Burton. She starred with the latter in the film version of Tennessee Williams's *The Night of the Iguana*, for which she was nominated for a Golden Globe®. She appeared sporadically in films following a move to Europe in the late 1950s. Her later years saw television roles, most notably in the nighttime soap "Knott's Landing."

During her years abroad, she continued to visit family and friends in North Carolina. Her last public appearance in the state came in 1978 at a Rock Ridge High School reunion. Her last visit to Smithfield was in May 1985. The following year, she suffered a stroke. She died of pneumonia on January 25, 1990, and is buried in Sunset Memorial Park, located on U.S. 70 in Smithfield.

The Ava Gardner Museum came about mostly through the ministrations of Smithfield native Tom Banks, who at 12 years of age was kissed on the cheek by Ava, then attending secretarial school in Wilson. Banks grew up to be a doctor. He and his wife devoted much of their lives to following Ava's career and assembling memorabilia from every imaginable source. In the early 1980s, Dr. Banks purchased the house where Ava lived as a child. He operated the first Ava Gardner Museum for nine years during the summers. Dr. Banks suffered a stroke at the museum in August 1989 and died a few days later. In the summer of 1990, Mrs. Banks donated the collection to the town of Smithfield, having been assured that a permanent museum would be maintained in Johnston County.

Ex-hubby Mickey Rooney paid a visit to the new museum and to Ava's grave when he traveled to Smithfield during the late 1990s to perform at Johnston Community College.

The museum contains photos, costumes, newspaper clippings, portraits, and a gift shop.

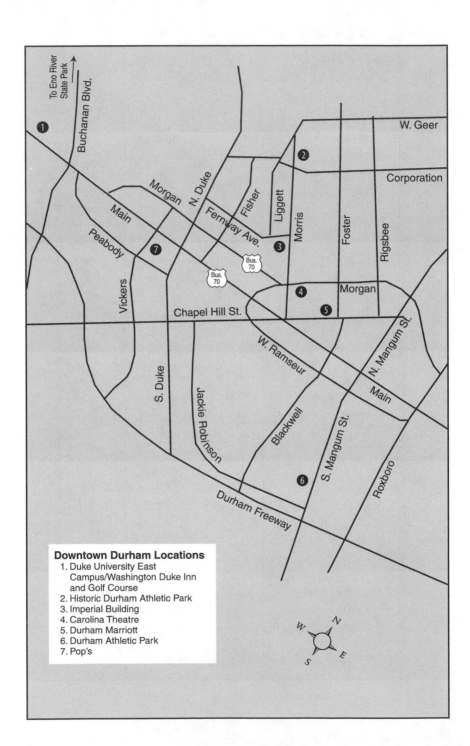

Downtown Durham Locations
1. Duke University East Campus/Washington Duke Inn and Golf Course
2. Historic Durham Athletic Park
3. Imperial Building
4. Carolina Theatre
5. Durham Marriott
6. Durham Athletic Park
7. Pop's

Filming at Duke University, which is frequently used for campus settings. It served as Worthington College in "Dawson's Creek."
COURTESY OF DURHAM CONVENTION AND VISITORS BUREAU

Durham Locations

Duke University

For information about the university, call 919-684-3214 or visit www.duke.edu. Tours are offered during daylight hours; call for times. Duke Chapel is located on Chapel Drive, West Campus.

Duke University has attained international prominence in fields ranging from medicine to basketball. It is one of America's most beautiful universities, especially the castle-like West Campus. *Bright Leaf*, a Michael Curtiz film starring Lauren Bacall and Gary Cooper, is a fictionalized account of a family much like the Dukes, founders of the college. The film shot and premiered in Durham back in the early 1950s. Recently, Duke has gotten maximum exposure as Worthington College, home to roommates Joey

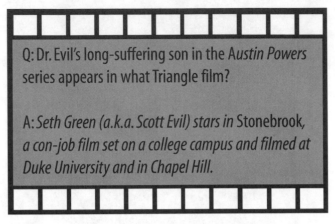

Q: Dr. Evil's long-suffering son in the *Austin Powers* series appears in what Triangle film?

A: *Seth Green (a.k.a. Scott Evil) stars in* Stonebrook, *a con-job film set on a college campus and filmed at Duke University and in Chapel Hill.*

(Katie Holmes) and Audrey (Busy Philipps) and epicenter for the "Dawson's Creek" gang. The gray stone exteriors of West Campus appear in the opening shots of the fifth and sixth seasons, and the girls' dorm room features Duke's trademark arched windows. Duke even made an appearance in two shows at once when Jack Osbourne had a cameo in a season-six episode. Behind-the-scenes segments from the filming (heavily bleeped, of course) appeared on "The Osbournes."

The centerpiece of West Campus is the signature Duke Chapel, dedicated in 1935 and one of the most impressive structures on any college campus. The architect of the chapel was Horace Trumbauer of Philadelphia, and his chief designer was Julian Abele, America's first black architect of note. The Reverend Billy Graham and Archbishop Desmond Tutu are just two of the noted clergymen who have led services here. The view is most impressive driving up Chapel Drive, scene of some well-known NCAA Tournament spots featuring Duke basketball coach Mike Krzyzewski as a chauffeur. The chapel is available for weddings, though one ceremony was almost indefinitely delayed for a rather stirring film shoot. It seems that *The Handmaid's Tale*'s director, Volker Schlondorff, kept insisting on one more take of a scene shot in front of the chapel—a public hanging featuring Victoria Tennant! All the while, a real-life wedding party was slowly coming in.

Most shoots are not as dramatic. A favorite site for filming is the quad between Chapel Circle and Duke Hospital. In *Getting In*, a film most notable for some unknowns named Matthew

Perry and Calista Flockhart in the supporting cast, Perkins Library was used as a dorm. The library's interior appears in *The Program* in a scene with Coach Winters (James Caan) and star recruit Darnell Jefferson (Omar Epps). Duke's campus appears in *Stonebrook* and in *I Know What You Did Last Summer*, most memorably when the ominous words appear on a fogged locker-room mirror before stunned Julie James (Jennifer Love Hewitt). The indoor pool was used for a scene in *Billy Bathgate*. And since Duke is known for excellence in both men's and women's basketball, it is ironic that a football movie, *The Program*, filmed interiors and a few exteriors here. Despite some controversy over *Kiss the Girls*, Duke is mostly film-friendly, with several commercials, made-for-TV movies, "Good Morning America," and even the soap opera "One Life to Live" to its credit.

Film junkies may also want to check out the American Dance Festival, held each summer at Duke. Madonna was an ADF dancer back in the 1970s.

CREDITS

"The Osbornes" (MTV, 2002-3); *Stonebrook* (1999); "Dawson's Creek" (The WB, 1998-2003); *Kiss the Girls* (1997); *I Know What You Did Last Summer* (1997); *Getting In* (1994); "A Burning Passion: The Margaret Mitchell Story" (NBC, 1994); *The Program* (1993); *Billy Bathgate* (1991); *The Handmaid's Tale* (1990); *Weeds* (1987); *Brainstorm* (1983)

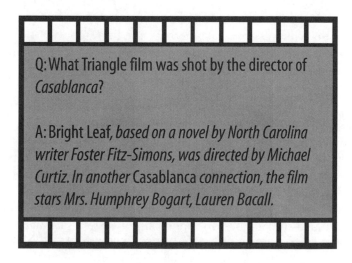

Q: What Triangle film was shot by the director of *Casablanca*?

A: Bright Leaf, *based on a novel by North Carolina writer Foster Fitz-Simons, was directed by Michael Curtiz. In another* Casablanca *connection, the film stars Mrs. Humphrey Bogart, Lauren Bacall.*

Play ball! A spiffier version of the ballpark where Crash, Nuke, and
Annie spent a memorable baseball season in *Bull Durham*
COURTESY OF DURHAM CONVENTION AND VISITORS BUREAU

Durham Athletic Park/Durham Bulls Athletic Park

*Durham Bulls Athletic Park (DBAP) is located at 409
Blackwell Street; call 919-687-6500. Durham Athletic Park
(DAP) is located at Washington and Corporation streets; call
919-560-4355. Visitors are limited to exterior viewing except
during games and events. For more information, visit
www.durhambulls.com.*

Fans of *Bull Durham* have perhaps the best opportunity of all
film junkies to re-create a movie experience. They can celebrate
minor-league baseball on the original set of the movie or on a
spiffier version thereof.

Bull Durham is justly celebrated as a film that got it right.
This is due in no small part to the attention to detail by the
filmmakers, including writer and director Ron Shelton's well-
documented stint as a minor leaguer. The multilayered story—
by turns an eccentric comedy and a bittersweet romance based
on second chances—has rightly become a classic. It has been
ranked the number-one baseball movie of all time by *Baseball
America* and the number-one sports film by *Sports Illustrated*.

As most movie and baseball fans know, the Durham Bulls

are a real team, so where better to experience the movie than the ballpark?

First off, the new park where you can catch a Bulls game isn't the park in the film. The makers of *Bull Durham* wanted to show the seedier side of minor-league ball—the patchy outfields, the hard seats, the small-town fans. To experience the site where the movie filmed, you need to visit Durham Athletic Park, the home of the Bulls beginning in 1939. Historic Durham Athletic Park (or "the DAP," as it's affectionately known) still hosts ball games, only now of teams even *deeper* in the bush leagues, such as the Durham Americans and the Durham Dragons women's professional softball team. Those unable to visit the DAP can experience its bygone charm through an award-winning video called *Ghosts in the Ballpark*, narrated by the real Crash Davis and featuring Shelton, Robert Wuhl, producer Thom Mount, and ex-big leaguers Willie Stargell, Joe Morgan, and the late Jim "Catfish" Hunter.

There's no denying that the movie's popularity has elevated the Durham Bulls into one of America's most recognized minor-league teams. And the Bulls have grown as well, moving from the Carolina League to the Triple-A International League, where they were champions in 2002 and 2003. They now play in the new Durham Bulls Athletic Park—known, of course, as "the DBAP" (*DEE-bap*). The team's uniforms remain pretty much unchanged, and fans at the new park will notice some nods to Bulls history and *Bull Durham*. There's a hand-operated scoreboard in left field on the 32-foot-high Blue Monster. And the giant bull above the wall in the left-field corner is a larger version of the one from the DAP, which was a touch put in for the film. Yes, it snorts steam whenever the Bulls hit a home run. That original bull from the movie is on display in the main concourse. Concession stands carry the ever-popular Durham Bulls souvenirs. Clay Aiken of "American Idol" fame was here to sing the national anthem in May 2003.

As Annie Savoy (Susan Sarandon) says in *Bull Durham*, the ballpark is where you come to worship. Film junkies, worship away!

CREDITS

Ghosts in the Ballpark (1995); *Bull Durham* (1988)

Imperial Building

215 Morris Street. Visitors are limited to exterior viewing.

Hardcore film junkies know that the working title for the baseball classic *Bull Durham* was "The Player to Be Named Later." When the movie gods conspired with producer Thom Mount to set the film in his hometown of Durham, a new title was born, and the working title was relegated to Crash Davis's (Kevin Costner's) opening line in the film.

This self-deprecating introduction and the other locker-room scenes were filmed at the Imperial Building in downtown Durham. *Bull Durham* has been rightly praised for director Ron Shelton's locker-room realism, such as rookie pitcher Ebby Calvin LaLoosh's (Tim Robbins's) banal interviews and "pregame warmups" with Millie (Jenny Robertson). Another example is the way that old veterans like Davis, skipper Joe Riggins (Trey Wilson), and assistant manager Larry Hockett (Robert Wuhl) hash out the realities of minor-league ball. A minor-league locker room hardly has the spacious, carpeted comforts of "The Show."

The Imperial Building, dating from the second decade of the 20th century, was the perfect spot for this weathered realism. The handsome building is part of the traditional red-brick tobacco industry architecture of downtown Durham. Not much remains from the 1987 *Bull Durham* shoot. The lockers, the showers, and Skipper Riggins's office have long been dismantled. However, the sign bearing the Bulls' movie motto—"The Greatest Show on Dirt"—seen several times in the film, still remains.

The building was also used in the Gregory Peck/Lauren Bacall television film "The Portrait."

CREDITS

"The Portrait" (TNT, 1993); *Bull Durham* (1988)

Carolina Theatre

309 West Morgan Street (919-560-3030; www.carolinatheatre.org).
Call for show times.

The historic Carolina Theatre has gone through many

changes, seen many stars, and become familiar to television viewers as—what else?—a theatre during the fifth and sixth seasons of "Dawson's Creek." The interior was used for auditorium shots. The exterior appears in an episode in which Jack (Kerr Smith) meets his modern cultures teacher—and has designs on more than history.

The Carolina is one of the best places to catch a film festival, a foreign or indie film, or an offbeat performance. The ornate setting is unforgettable. The theatre opened in the pre-talkie days of the mid-1920s. During the first heyday of the Durham Auditorium (as it was first called), patrons enjoyed silent films and vaudeville shows and witnessed performers such as opera star Marian Anderson, who appeared before a racially mixed audience in 1927; the Carolina was the only theatre in town to admit African-Americans, though it had separate entrances and separate seating. Other stars who performed here have included Will Rogers, Katharine Hepburn in the stage version of *The Philadelphia Story*, Tullulah Bankhead in *The Little Foxes*, and the original cast tour of *Oklahoma*.

The theatre was slated for the wrecking ball in the mid-1970s, but a volunteer group saved it and reopened it as the Triangle's first art house. The nonprofit Carolina Cinema Corporation ran it from 1977 to 1987 and brought in daring, obscure, and offbeat performers and films.

The Carolina Theatre and its newly named Fletcher Hall reopened with a week-long celebration in February 1994. The new theatre is truly amazing. Its architecture incorporates the Neoclassical and Beaux-Arts styles.

Featuring first-run art films and hosting such events as the North Carolina Gay and Lesbian Film Festival (see page 186), the North Carolina Jewish Film Festival (see page 187), and the Nevermore Horror, Gothic, and Fantasy Film Festival, the Carolina is truly a film junkie's heaven.

CREDITS

"Dawson's Creek" (The WB, 1998-2003)

Triangle Film Fests

Flicker Film Festival, Chapel Hill

Limited to Super 8 and 16 mm films, the Flicker Film Festival started in Athens, Georgia, in the late 1980s. A Chapel Hill locale was established in 1994 by filmmaker Norwood Cheek, who reveres "the graininess of this medium." Flicker is a grass-roots, noncommercial festival that screens films of less than 15 minutes. There is no entry fee for submissions. Held every few months in Chapel Hill, Flicker has branched out with chapters nationwide from L.A. and New York to Asheville. For information, visit www.chapel-hill.nc.us/flicker or www.ibiblio.org/flickerfilms.

North Carolina Gay and Lesbian Film Festival, Durham

Since 1996, the annual North Carolina Gay and Lesbian Film Festival has garnered a great deal of local and statewide support. Attendees are treated to a dizzying array of more than a hundred features, shorts, documentaries, and experimental films that address life as a homosexual man or woman. Film junkies usually can catch the world premieres of several movies, especially ones filmed around the Triangle or elsewhere in the state. This event is usually held in August. For information, visit www.carolinatheatre.org/ncglff/index.html.

Hi Mom! Film Festival, Chapel Hill

An intriguing mix of films, bands, and pancake batter, Hi Mom's recipe for success sounds like something only a bunch of college students could plan. In 1997, UNC's students staged the first film festival. Having vowed to accept submissions from filmmakers with "deep thoughts and shallow pockets," the event's organizers don't discriminate, no matter what the genre or format. The festival has expanded each year, from one day of screenings to three days in the spring. Between screenings, bands play and audience members buy pancakes. Why settle for something as ordinary as popcorn for your movie snack? For information, visit www.himomfilmfestival.org.

Full Frame Documentary Film Festival, Durham

The Full Frame Documentary Film Festival (FFDFF), formerly the DoubleTake Documentary Film Festival, has earned a prestigious reputation in a short time. The Academy of Motion Picture Arts and Sciences recently declared that films winning Best Documentary Short at Full Frame are eligible for an Oscar® nomination, an honor shared by only four American and nine foreign festivals. Festival attendance now runs close to 15,000. Both the *New York Times* and indieWIRE (an online community of independent filmmakers and aficionados) recognize FFDFF as the premier documentary film festival in the United States. For information, visit www.fullframefest.org.

North Carolina Jewish Film Festival, Durham

Organized as an all-encompassing family activity, the North Carolina Jewish Film Festival (NCJFF) offers movies, lectures, information booths, and children's amusements that celebrate Jewish history and culture. Since 1999, NCJFF has used popular media to express everything from historical events to everyday life in ways that promote learning by people of all faiths. NCJFF screens wide-release features, documentaries, and shorts. International films include movies direct from theatrical release in Israel. For information, visit www.carolinatheatre.org/ncjff.

Eno River State Park was the site for Casanova's lair in *Kiss the Girls*.
PHOTO BY BILL RUSS
COURTESY OF N. C. DIVISION OF TOURISM, FILM, & SPORTS DEVELOPMENT

Eno River State Park

*Eno River State Park is located at 5101 North Roxboro Road
(919-471-1623). It is open daily from 8 A.M. to sundown.
Admission is free.*

Few film locations are as different in real life from the way
they appear on screen as is Durham's Eno River. The outdoor
scenes of the lair of sadistic serial killer Casanova in *Kiss the Girls*
were filmed along the Eno's winding run through the Durham
County wilderness. Film junkies will remember the exciting scene
in which Dr. Kate McTiernand (Ashley Judd) makes her daring
escape from Casanova's hideout and plunges into the raging
river. Interestingly, Durham is called Durham in the film, as it
was in James Patterson's novel. But due to the supposed graphic
nature of the film (which actually isn't all that graphic), many
of the location shoots planned for the Triangle were moved to
L.A., including the filming of the interior of Casanova's creepy
dungeon.

Happily, there's nothing creepy or controversial about the
real Eno River. Around the Triangle, the very name conjures up
the essence of grass-roots conservation and ecology. The state
park, home to a reconstructed water-powered gristmill, features
hiking, canoeing, picnicking, and other outdoor activities.

Born in the 1960s, the nonprofit Eno River Association has proven to be a model for other conservation groups. Its crown jewel is the unique Festival for the Eno, held each Fourth of July holiday. Now in its third decade, the festival attracts over 30,000 people during its three-day celebration at the park. All proceeds from the festival go toward the protection of Eno River conservation lands.

CREDITS

Kiss the Girls (1997)

Manning House

911 North Mangum Street. Visitors are limited to exterior viewing and are cautioned against trespassing.

Annie Savoy, free-spirited part-time community-college English teacher and full-time baseball . . . well, *groupie* isn't exactly the best word, lived in a house just as colorful and whimsical as you'd expect. It's still drawing curious *Bull Durham* fans more than a decade and a half after the film's release.

Annie, made an icon by Susan Sarandon's Golden Globe®-nominated performance, is seen in her delightfully cluttered home in the opening credits, as she primps before her mirror and then heads off for a Durham Bulls baseball game. Both interiors and exteriors were shot at the two-story 19th-century Duke Park historical property.

Built in 1880, it was home to Durham lawyer James S. Manning until he moved to Raleigh to serve as North Carolina's attorney general from 1917 to 1925. The house was subsequently owned by one Durham family for over 40 years. It was vacant at the time of the *Bull Durham* shoot. Since 1996, it has been occupied by Jeff and Trudy Burdette, who have mostly enjoyed their movie connection. The film opens with framed pictures of baseball scenes hanging on Annie's wall. The Burdettes now display autographed photos of Tim Robbins and Susan Sarandon, who no doubt have fond memories of the shoot. However, the Burdettes are still waiting for the one they requested from Kevin Costner. They still have the cast-iron tub made memorable in a sweet, sexy scene between Costner and Sarandon. Guests enjoy getting their pictures made in it (clothed!) during parties. And though they're accustomed to seeing folks take pictures, they weren't quite ready for the group that showed up right before Thanksgiving dinner wanting to know about the tour. They've also found that everyone from the gas man to a cop investigating a stolen lawnmower has some connection to the film and enjoys telling them about it.

The Manning House, a National Historic Site, is a private home. No tours—on Thanksgiving or otherwise—are offered. But film junkies may respectfully gawk and take pictures.

CREDITS

Bull Durham (1988)

Durham Star Tracks

Durham Marriott
201 Foster Street (919-768-6000)

Going off to college means making some adjustments. When the "Dawson's Creek" gang made the rite of passage, cast and crew made the move as well. Duke University was chosen as Worthington College for the show's fifth and sixth seasons, and the downtown Durham Marriott housed the cast. Joshua Jackson even brought along his dog.

The Durham Marriott is part of a complex that includes the civic center and the Carolina Theatre (see pages 184-85). The "Dawson's" cast used the nearby Durham YMCA, a perk available to all guests at the Marriott.

Before "Dawson's," the Marriott was home base for *Bull Durham*. Actors and crew stayed here during the shoot. The Durham Bulls theme still permeates the lobby. The Bullpen Lounge features a baseball theme and a light menu and drinks. The Bull City Steakhouse offers casual dining for breakfast, lunch, and dinner.

The Marriott has also seen its share of real-life baseball teams and players, including big-league legends Cal Ripken, Jr., and Joe Morgan.

Pop's

*810 West Peabody Street (919-956-7677; www
.popsdurham.com). Pop's is open for lunch and dinner Monday
through Friday, for dinner on Saturday, and for brunch and
dinner on Sunday.*

Uptown chic meets Old Durham at Pop's, a trattoria featuring Italian cuisine in a funky atmosphere of exposed brick,
wrought iron, and hardwood. Combining the expertise of the
chefs from celebrated Durham restaurants Magnolia Grill and
Nana's, Pop's quickly became as trendy as its predecessors. Tom
Selleck certainly thought so. The popular "Magnum, P.I." star
ate at Pop's every other day for the week and a half he was in
town starring in the play *A Thousand Clowns*, which premiered at
Duke University before going on to Broadway. According to
Gonzalo Munoz of Pop's, Selleck just couldn't get enough of
the house specialty: a big bowl of mussels. He ordered them
every time he came in, along with a glass of wine. Munoz remembers Selleck as a gentleman who was friendly with recog-
nizing fans.

Film junkies may want to be a bit more selective and try
the brick-roasted chicken, the portabello pizza, the veal
saltimbocca, or any of the other gourmet dishes. Or just be like
Tom and stick with the mussels. You can't go wrong.

Washington Duke Inn and Golf Club

*3001 Cameron Boulevard (800-443-3853 or 919-490-0999;
www.washingtondukeinn.com)*

Southern hospitality, elegance, and a championship golf
course are just a few of the reasons that stars of screen, stage,
music, sports, and politics have stayed at the Washington Duke

Inn and Golf Club. Built in the style of an old English inn and located on the campus of Duke University, it has welcomed stars of the Broadway at Duke series, including Rex Harrison and playwright Neil Simon, who taught a class at the university during his stay at the inn. Film stars Faye Dunaway, Holly Hunter, Billy Crystal, Chevy Chase, Robert Duvall, Richard Dreyfuss, Tom Selleck, Jerry Lewis, and many others have enjoyed the inn while in town working on films and other projects. It is also a favorite of political figures and heads of state, including Elizabeth Dole and former presidents Jimmy Carter (who had a grandson at Duke) and George H. W. Bush.

The Washington Duke has 164 guest rooms, six junior suites, and a Presidential Suite, all overlooking the lush golf course or the wonderfully manicured front grounds. The inn is furnished with Duke family treasures. The Fairview Restaurant and the Bull Durham Lounge are on the premises.

The Duke University Golf Club's championship course is one of the best college facilities anywhere. It hosted the NCAA men's golf championship in 1962 and 2001. Famed golf-course architect Rees Jones recently renovated the course laid out by his legendary father, Robert Trent Jones. Each spring, the course hosts the annual Duke Children's Classic, which will probably always be associated with Perry Como, its first celebrity chairman. In the early days, the late crooner and movie star could be counted on to bring out celebrity pals such as Frank Sinatra. Having celebrated its 30th anniversary in 2003, the classic continues to benefit the Duke Children's Hospital and Health Center. Recent participants have included Jeff Foxworthy, Gary Collins, Vince Gill, Tim McGraw, Charles Barkley, Terry Bradshaw, Michael W. Smith, Amy Grant, and big-time pro golfers including Arnold Palmer, Lee Trevino, Michelle McGann, and Fred Couples. All weekend events are free.

Bullock's Barbecue

*3330 Quebec Drive (919-383-3211). Bullock's is open from
11:30 A.M. to 8 P.M. Tuesday through Saturday.*

Barbecue is "serious bidness" in North Carolina. The battle
lines are drawn between the east (where we're talking tangy,
slow-cooked shredded pork) and the west (pork smothered in a
red, tomatoey sauce). Bullock's, a member of the eastern Carolina camp, has been a great place for down-home eating since
1952. The decor is nothing fancy—booths and tables, polyes-
ter curtains—and the crowd is definitely a mix. But if you crave
hush puppies, Brunswick stew, turnip greens, pole beans, stewed
tomatoes, fried chicken, potatoes, liver, and, of course, barbecue, this is the place.

Bullock's has pictures of just about every star who's come
through Durham. Owner Tommy Bullock particularly remembers Robert Duvall, who was in town filming *The Handmaid's Tale*.
Duvall, who dined here several times, favored fried chicken liv-
ers, fried chicken, and vegetables. According to Bullock, Duvall
told him the last thing he wanted to do before leaving Durham
was to eat at Bullock's. He said he had traveled the world, and
that Bullock's served the best food he'd ever eaten. Tommy
seated Duvall in private spots so people wouldn't bother him.
In turn, Duvall introduced Bullock to Faye Dunaway.

Once Around stars Holly Hunter, Richard Dreyfuss, and
Danny Aiello all chowed down at Bullock's. And when eight
members of the "Dawson's Creek" film crew showed up after
closing one night, Bullock let them in. Tom Selleck ate here
several times with his staff when he was in Durham for the play
A Thousand Clowns. Music star John Tesh showed up in the late
1990s while filming a spot for the UNC-TV Festival. When
Patch Adams was filming in nearby Chapel Hill, Bullock's catered

a picnic and softball game for Robin Williams and other movie personnel. And during the 2002 holiday season, Bullock's sent food out to Los Angeles for Drew Carey's staff; one of the writers on Carey's TV show is from Durham. Bullock's also catered for Dom DeLuise, Joe Piscopo, Burt Reynolds, Kenny Rogers, and others at the Salute to Troops, held in Raleigh at Carter-Finley Stadium after the Gulf War in 1991. Other stars who have eaten at Bullock's include Jerry Lewis, Buddy Hackett, Ed Bradley, David Hartman, Connie Chung, Jeff Foxworthy, Jay Leno, Joe Namath, and Duke coach Mike Krzyzewski.

You can expect a wait of 30 to 45 minutes on some days. But it's worth it.

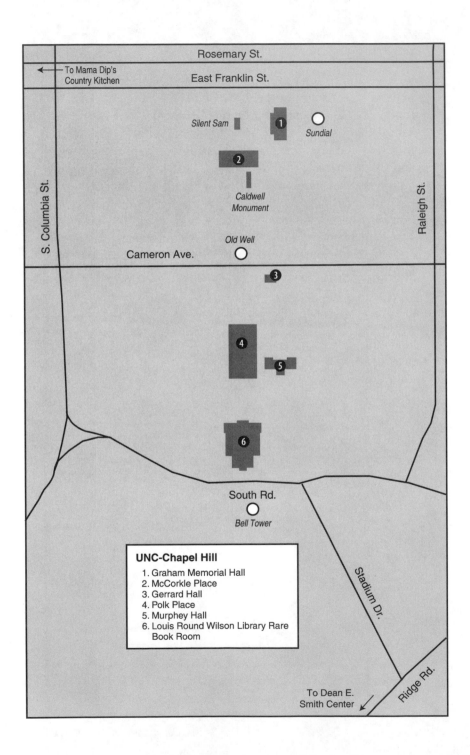

Rosemary St.

To Mama Dip's
Country Kitchen

East Franklin St.

Silent Sam

1

Sundial

2

*Caldwell
Monument*

Old Well

Cameron Ave.

3

4

5

6

South Rd.

Bell Tower

S. Columbia St.

Raleigh St.

Stadium Dr.

Ridge Rd.

To Dean E.
Smith Center

UNC-Chapel Hill
1. Graham Memorial Hall
2. McCorkle Place
3. Gerrard Hall
4. Polk Place
5. Murphey Hall
6. Louis Round Wilson Library Rare
   Book Room

The Old Well at the University of North Carolina at Chapel Hill, where Patch Adams shares his idea for the free medical clinic
PHOTOGRAPH BY BILL RUSS
COURTESY OF N. C. DIVISION OF TOURISM, FILM, & SPORTS DEVELOPMENT

Chapel Hill Locations

University of North Carolina-Chapel Hill

UNC is the heart of Chapel Hill. The locations mentioned here are available for exterior viewing and limited interior visits. The Rare Book Room is open to the general public. Hours vary according to the academic calendar. For more information, visit www.unc.edu.

The University of North Carolina-Chapel Hill has rarely been seen in films. The obscure comedy *Three in the Attic* filmed on campus during the swingin' '60s. But despite overtures, Hollywood didn't get the go-ahead again until *Patch Adams*. Exterior shots used in dramatizing the medical-school career of

Hunter "Patch" Adams (Robin Williams) include several well-known campus landmarks. Most *Patch* locations are within walking distance of Franklin Street. A handful of independent films have shot on campus, and ABC's "Good Morning America" has broadcast from UNC several times.

Graham Memorial Hall

Sets, costumes, lights, and other moviemaking staples are not unfamiliar around Graham Memorial Hall, once the home of the offices of Carolina's famous PlayMakers Repertory Company and the Department of Dramatic Art. Famous Carolina acting alums include Andy Griffith, Sharon Lawrence, and Dan Cortese. One of the first PlayMakers productions was *The Return of Buck Gavin*, written by 18-year-old Thomas Wolfe, who also acted the title role.

For *Patch Adams*, two stages were built for the offices of the dean and assistant dean of the medical school. These appear in the scenes when the unconventional Patch is called on the carpet to face his nemesis, Dean Walcott (Bob Gunton), who doesn't take to Patch's clowning and wants nothing more than to expel him. Patch's somewhat begrudging supporter is Dean Anderson (Harve Presnell).

Gerrard Hall

While the climactic medical-board scene in *Patch* may be a bit over-the-top, its location, Gerrard Hall, certainly needs no hype. Presidents, poets, and politicians have all orated here. Used as a chapel throughout the 1800s, the building became known for its "bull pen," an area for dignitaries in front of the stage. You'll notice that this is reversed in *Patch*, as the panel sits on the stage. This area is surrounded by rows and a gallery, which are clearly seen as Patch defends his unorthodox medical practices.

Gerrard has been the setting for addresses by Presidents Polk (a UNC graduate), Buchanan, and Wilson and for readings by famous writers like noted African-American poet Langston Hughes.

Murphey Hall

Murphey Hall is the home of UNC's Department of Classics. While it's a stretch to call the "legs" scene in *Patch* a classic, it is certainly inspired. For the scene in which Patch's medical school hosts a gynecological conference, he constructs huge papier-mâché legs at the front door, putting them in a position the doctors are, um, used to. Patch is also hilarious as he enters the building, his voice echoing. He even gets a bit of a chuckle from the rather stunned physicians.

McCorkle Place

McCorkle Place, the stately, wooded mall between Cameron and Franklin streets, is the oldest portion of the campus. The Old Well, the traditional symbol of the university, is clearly seen in the background when Patch walks with Carin (Monica Potter) after the balloon-filled birthday party. It's more noticeable when an exuberant Patch tells Carin about plans for his clinic.

McCorkle is also the location of the lighthearted scene in which 12,000 pounds of spaghetti are added to a swimming pool so a patient can fulfill a lifelong wish of swimming in pasta. Production staff and extras remember being kept in stitches as Robin Williams shot this scene.

UNC students still take a drink from the Old Well on the first day of classes for good luck.

Polk Place

Patch Adams director Tom Shadyac chose Carolina for the beauty of the campus. He was particularly impressed by the symmetry of the architecture, especially on Polk Place. Shadyac felt the campus offered a classic Ivy League look that was perfect for an academy of medicine. During shooting, the true-life Patch Adams remarked that if his real medical school had been so beautiful, he might not have been so rebellious.

Polk Place is also the location for Patch's final salvo upon graduation, in which an unexpected moonrise accompanies his diploma.

"Good Morning America," featuring Charles Gibson, Diane Sawyer, and Tony Perkins, broadcast its entire show from Polk Place in April 2002. It marked the fourth time "GMA" broadcast live from Chapel Hill.

Louis Round Wilson Library Rare Book Room

In a scene reminiscent of the classic film and television series *The Paper Chase*, Patch, Mitch (Philip Seymour Hoffman), Truman (Daniel London), and Adeline (Daniella Kuhn) lead their study group, joined by Carin (Monica Potter). The scene establishes the medical school's no-nonsense attitude, meant to intimidate Patch—and anyone else, for that matter. The Rare Book Room provides the perfect cloistered, serious, bookish location for the scene.

When the real Patch Adams met the man playing him on film, one topic of conversation was books. No doubt, both were impressed by the library's Second Folio of Shakespeare and the over 4,000 pieces included in the George Bernard Shaw Collection.

"Good Morning America" broadcast a segment from the Rare Book Room during a visit to campus in April 2002.

CREDITS

"Good Morning America" (ABC, 2002 et al.); *Patch Adams* (1998); *Three in the Attic* (1968)

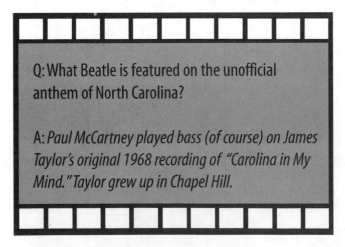

Q: What Beatle is featured on the unofficial anthem of North Carolina?

A: *Paul McCartney played bass (of course) on James Taylor's original 1968 recording of "Carolina in My Mind." Taylor grew up in Chapel Hill.*

James Taylor Bridge / James Taylor Theatre

The bridge is on U.S. 15/501 South in Chapel Hill. The museum is located at 523 East Franklin Street in Chapel Hill; for information, call 919-967-1400 or visit www.chapelhillmuseum.org.

James Taylor's song "Copperline" makes mention of Morgan Creek, a stream that flows through Orange, Durham, and Chatham counties. Fittingly enough, on April 26, 2003, the North Carolina Department of Transportation dedicated the bridge on U.S. 15/501 over Morgan Creek in Chapel Hill as the James Taylor Bridge to honor "his contributions to the music industry and for using his words and music to promote his home state of North Carolina."

Taylor was reared in Chapel Hill, moving there at the age of three. His father was dean of the UNC School of Medicine. Taylor is of course best known as one of the most popular singer/songwriters ever, and as the man who wrote the state's unofficial anthem, "Carolina in My Mind." He's also been in several films as himself, such as *No Nukes* and a 1994 episode of "The Simpsons." His one appearance as an actor was as "The Driver" in *Two-Lane Blacktop*, a 1971 feature that filmed partly in North Carolina.

The Chapel Hill Museum was instrumental in honoring Taylor with the bridge. It took the occasion of the dedication to announce the establishment of the James Taylor Theatre, a media center where visitors may enjoy special movie nights and view presentations on museum exhibits, Southern culture, and local and regional history. The theatre also shows a video about the life of James Taylor.

Interestingly, "Copperline" was co-written by noted North Carolina author and Duke University professor Reynolds Price, winner of the National Book Award in 1987.

Q: In what Triangle film can you see the rather eclectic collection of Robert Blake, Marilyn Manson, Richard Pryor, Henry Rollins, Giovanni Ribisi, Patricia Arquette, and Gary Busey?

A: *These and many others appear in* Lost Highway, *which filmed partly in Chapel Hill and was written and directed by (who else?) David Lynch.*

Mama Dip's Country Kitchen

*408 West Rosemary Street (919-942-5837). Mama Dip's is
open from 8 A.M. to 3 P.M. and from 4 P.M. to 10 P.M. Monday
through Friday; from 8 A.M. to 10 P.M. on Saturday; and from
8 A.M. to 9 P.M. on Sunday.*

They're fond of saying, "Put a taste of the South in your
mouth," at Mama Dip's Country Kitchen in Chapel Hill. Crowds
have been doing so for over 25 years. Mildred Edna Cotton
Council, better known as "Mama Dip," was born in nearby
Chatham County and started "dump cooking" (i.e., cooking
without recipes) at an early age. After serving as a family cook
in Chapel Hill, she had stints at the Carolina Coffee Shop, the
Kappa Sigma fraternity, and St. Andrews Hall. In 1976, Mama
Dip opened her own restaurant with $64. It's been a Chapel
Hill institution ever since. The nightly crowds include hungry
students, townies, and occasional celebrities.

Mama Dip has become a national celebrity, appearing on
the Food Network and ABC's "Good Morning America," where
she made her famous pecan pie. Well-known fans include former
Tar Heels basketball coach Dean Smith and his most famous
player, Michael Jordan. Articles on the restaurant have appeared

in the *New York Times*, the *Washington Post*, and *Southern Living*. The popular cookbook *Mama Dip's Kitchen* features over 250 Southern favorites, a running biography, and bits of philosophy. Autographed copies are on sale at the restaurant, as are T-shirts, aprons, caps, mugs, and a variety of sauces, pickles, preserves, and peppers.

Q: What Tar Heel novelist won an Emmy® as head writer for the soap opera "One Life to Live"?

A: UNC graduate Michael Malone won in 1984. He lives in Hillsborough. His novels include Handling Sin, Uncivil Seasons *and* First Lady.

Dean E. Smith Center

Off Bowles Drive (919-962-7777; www.unc.edu). The center is open from 9 A.M. to 5 P.M. Monday through Friday. It is not open to the public during practice and events preparation.

No sports fan's trip to Chapel Hill is complete without a visit to the Dean E. Smith Center, home of the three-time national champion Tar Heels men's basketball team. As every hoops fan knows, ACC basketball is the best soap opera/reality TV show going in the winter. The "barns" around the conference attract rabid fans, and millions more watch on the tube.

The "Dean Dome," as the Smith Center is nicknamed, was the setting for a memorable ESPN promo shoot in 1997 that ended up being a classic spoof of March Madness. Dean Smith, the all-time winningest coach in NCAA history, kept putting off shooting the spot because of an important announcement. When it turned out the big mystery was Smith's retirement, he wanted to back out of the filming. But Smith was finally talked into going ahead with the shoot—only as a fan, instead of a coach. Thus, the Tar Heel faithful witnessed the rather staid Smith as a cheering fan with a basketball on his head!

Fans are treated to seeing the jerseys of former Carolina stars Michael Jordan, James Worthy, and others hanging from the rafters. They may take a free, self-guided tour during visiting hours and enjoy the second-floor Memorabilia Room.

Q: What UNC basketball great appears in a critically acclaimed North Carolina indie film?

A: All-American backcourt star Phil Ford, later an NBA player and a UNC assistant coach, appears in a small role as a museum guard (of course) in Immortal, a spoof featuring vampires and Chapel Hill music legends Squirrel Nut Zippers and Archers of Loaf, among others. Immortal filmed in Chapel Hill, Raleigh, and Durham.

Research Triangle Park Locations

GlaxoSmithKline South Campus

5 Moore Drive. Visitors are limited to exterior viewing.

Research Triangle Park, a kind of Silicon Valley East, is home to a proliferation of high-tech companies. The park began as a government and industry project in the 1960s. A futuristic vision is evident in the sci-fi architecture of the GlaxoSmithKline building, which was picked as a location for *Brainstorm*. The angular, Jetsons-like structure is unique, heralding a future that hasn't quite arrived.

When filmmakers established a beachhead in the Triangle in the early 1980s, *Brainstorm* was a film of firsts. It was one of the first films in the new wave of projects actively recruited by the North Carolina Film Office. It was also one of the first directing efforts of Douglas Trumbull, renowned for his special effects on A-list sci-fi classics like Stanley Kubrick's *2001: A*

Space Odyssey, Steven Spielberg's *Close Encounters of the Third Kind*, *Star Trek: The Motion Picture*, and *Blade Runner*. Each of those films rightly earned him Oscar® nominations.

In *Brainstorm*, married scientists Michael and Karen Brace (Christopher Walken and Natalie Wood) develop a virtual-reality system that sends sensory input into the brain and records sights, sounds, feelings, and even dreams. As always happens in the movies with such projects, the military attempts to take over, after a senior worker begins to die of a heart attack and uses the system to tape the experience. All of the lab shots were done at RTP and feature Trumbull's Showscan, an ambitious technical process that aimed for super clarity, which would have required special theatres. It never came to pass.

Despite such firsts, *Brainstorm* will probably be remembered for being the last film of Natalie Wood, the beloved star who died in a boating accident before filming was completed. Wood's death altered the final product. Though the film boasted Trumbull's trademark special effects and a top-rate cast that also included Oscar® winners Cliff Robertson and Louise Fletcher, *Brainstorm* was not the hit everyone hoped for.

But the lab locations still look cool.

CREDITS

Brainstorm (1983)

"N.C. Visions"

UNC-TV provides an innovative way for independent Tar Heel filmmakers to reach film junkies across the state. Since the mid-1990s, it has produced "N.C. Visions," a showcase for film and video artists. In each of its six- to eight-week seasons, "N.C. Visions" has fulfilled public television's goal of educating, enriching, and informing all North Carolinians.

Each season, Tar Heel auteurs submit their work to a panel of peer filmmakers, film and video teachers, and UNC-TV personnel. As is typical in the competitive film world, the panel receives a wide variety of documentaries, narratives, animated shorts, and experimental pieces. The tight schedule accommodates only a fraction of the entries. But whittling down the number of features shown hasn't restricted the subject matter. Past selections have included documentaries about race relations and a film about an artisan practicing a rapidly dwindling craft. Next week's broadcast could showcase a fictional drama or a film highlighting North Carolina history. The following week may feature a cartoon.

Over the lifetime of the series, more than 160 films by North Carolina filmmakers have been shown. Film junkies may even catch a future award winner. The 2002 season included *The Elements* by Christoph Baaden and Jane Fields, which went on to win an Academy of Television Arts and Sciences national collegiate Emmy® for best musical.

"N.C. Visions" is a benefit to everyone who tunes in. Not only does it expose viewers to new cinematic talent, it brings Tar Heel locales and native actors and performers to audiences eager to enjoy the flavor of home-grown talent.

"N.C. Visions" airs on UNC-TV at 11 P.M. on Saturday. For information, visit www.unctv.org/ncvisions.

Fayetteville Area Locations

Fayetteville is on I-95 south of Raleigh. For information, call 888-NC-CHARM or visit www.visitfayettevillenc.com.

United States Army soldiers stationed at Fort Bragg in 1942 were in for a treat when actress and pin-up girl Betty Grable arrived to film the documentary *Betty Grable at Army Camp*. The rare footage is archived at the U.S.C. News Film Library. Another legend, Bob Hope, filmed a "Bob Hope Special" at Pope Air Force Base, in 1987.

Actors Bill Fichtner, Eric Bana, and Nikolaj Waldau trained at Fort Bragg for battle scenes in Ridley Scott's *Black Hawk Down*, which was filmed in Africa. John F. Kennedy, Ronald Reagan, and George W. Bush are among the presidents who have visited Fort Bragg/Pope Air Force Base, the world's largest airborne facility.

Fayetteville's movie locations include the historic Cumberland County Courthouse, built around 1900, where *Billy*

Bathgate filmed courtroom scenes featuring mob boss Dutch Schultz (Dustin Hoffman).

Soap-opera diva turned A-list film star Julianne Moore—noted for her roles in the North Carolina-made films *Hannibal* and *The Fugitive* and the New York-based "As the World Turns," among other productions—was born in Fayetteville, where her father worked as an army judge.

Credits: *Clowns* (1999); "The Exiles" (BBC, 1998); "James Banks" (BBC, 1998); *Billy Bathgate* (1991); "Unsolved Mysteries" (NBC, 1990); "Bob Hope Special" (1987); *Betty Grable at Army Camp* (1942); numerous military documentaries

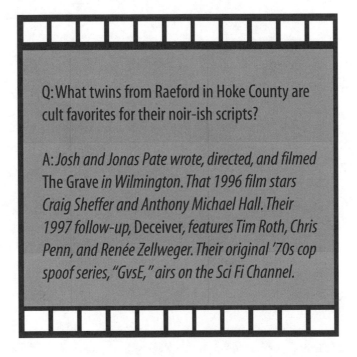

Q: What twins from Raeford in Hoke County are cult favorites for their noir-ish scripts?

A: *Josh and Jonas Pate wrote, directed, and filmed* The Grave *in Wilmington. That 1996 film stars Craig Sheffer and Anthony Michael Hall. Their 1997 follow-up,* Deceiver, *features Tim Roth, Chris Penn, and Renée Zellweger. Their original '70s cop spoof series, "GvsE," airs on the Sci Fi Channel.*

Pinehurst No. 2

Pinehurst Locations

Pinehurst is about 20 miles west of Fayetteville. For information, call 910-692-3330 or visit www.homeofgolf.com.

Golf is the game in Pinehurst. Hollywood came knocking—sorta—with *Tin Cup*, the reteaming of *Bull Durham* writer and director Ron Shelton and star Kevin Costner. In *Cup*, the fictionalized U.S. Open is held in Pinehurst, and Roy (Costner) provides the ultimate anti-heroic ending. However, only a few seconds of the film (including the "Welcome to North Carolina" sign) were actually shot in Pinehurst.

Real life proved even more dramatic a few years later, when the Open was held at Pinehurst's famed Number 2 course and the dashing Payne Stewart won the championship with a 15-foot putt on the last hole. Sadly, the story had a tragic ending, as Stewart was killed in a plane crash a few months after his stirring victory. Golf fans will want to visit the life-sized statue of Stewart near the 18th green. The U.S. Open returns to Pinehurst in 2005.

Golf is the subject of a couple of documentaries shot in the area. *Golf-Town USA* features President Dwight D. Eisenhower, while *Pinehurst: Good Times and Great Golf*, narrated by native son Charles Kuralt, features 1905 footage believed to be the oldest shot in North Carolina.

Golf and the area's other popular sports—fox hunting, archery, polo, and other horse sports—were the subject of a number of short films in the early days of movies, many featuring Glenna Collett, the most popular woman golfer of the early 20th century. One early feature, *Her Own Way*, a black-and-white silent film from 1915, was filmed in Pinehurst.

Many years later, *Brainstorm* filmed a few scenes at Yellowframe Farm in nearby Southern Pines.

The stars certainly know Pinehurst. They've been coming to this charming Sandhills village and the surrounding area since 1895. Lining the main hall on the first floor of The Carolina hotel are photographs of Fred MacMurray, Bing Crosby, Will Rogers, Howard Cosell, Presidents Nixon and Ford, First Ladies Mamie Eisenhower and Nancy Reagan, and, of course, bigtime golfers including Jack Nicklaus, Arnold Palmer, and Tom Watson. The quaint shops in the village are known for a star sighting or two, including Ron Howard and family.

CREDITS

Tin Cup (1996); "Pinehurst: Good Times and Great Golf" (UNC-TV, 1995); *Brainstorm* (1983); *Golf-Town USA* (1960); *Her Own Way* (1915)

The Triad

*T*ucked away in the center of the North Carolina Piedmont is the Triad region, the most diverse, yet underutilized, movie location in the state. The January 24, 2002, issue of *MovieMaker* magazine gave it an honorable mention as one of the Best Places in North America for Moviemakers. Up-and-coming independent filmmakers such as *Cabin Fever* director Eli Roth (a protégé of David Lynch) and *George Washington* director David Gordon Green and cinematographer Tim Orr—both of them North Carolina School of the Arts alumni—are casting a spotlight on the Triad. These and other talented renegade filmmakers aren't using magic lenses, they're using real Triad locations that happen to look magical.

The Triad encompasses 12 counties. Its core includes the cities of Greensboro, High Point, and Winston-Salem.

Greensboro, in Guilford County, embraces its Revolutionary War and civil-rights history with streets, parks, landmarks, and attractions named for events and heroes. Old Greensborough retains much of its turn-of-the-20th-century architecture and charm. Among the city's film-worthy attributes are its resorts, convention centers, shopping complexes, golf courses, upscale neighborhoods, restaurants, and universities and colleges.

High Point, also in Guilford County, is dominated by the

Triad Area

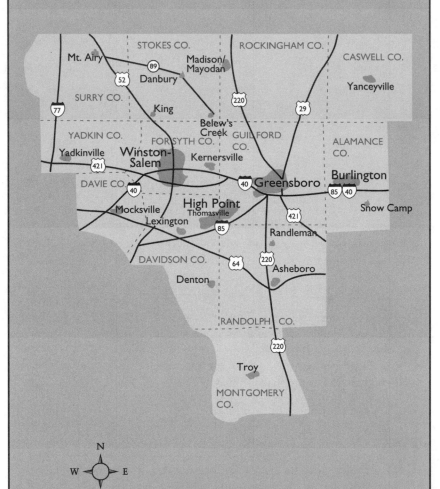

furniture industry. Nicknamed "the Home Furnishings Capital of the World," it hosts hundreds of thousands of national and international furniture buyers, sellers, and suppliers biannually. Just a stone's throw away are lush forests, farms, and parks. High Point boasts its own film studio, Carolina Atlantic Studios (see pages 233-34), and one of the state's only indigenous movie production companies, Down Home Entertainment.

Winston-Salem, in Forsyth County, is known as "the City of the Arts." It boasts museums, performing-arts venues, theatre and dance companies, and a world-renowned arts conservatory, the North Carolina School of the Arts (see pages 241-43). At first glance, Winston-Salem's skyline belies its artistic bent. Standing in the shadows of smokestacks and tobacco warehouses is a vibrant arts community. Many of its supporters earn their money working for the nation's second-largest tobacco company (R. J. Reynolds Tobacco Company) or one of the South's largest banking institutions (Wachovia). An overwhelming sense of pride in heritage and history prevails here. Nowhere is this more evident than at Old Salem (see pages 243-45), a restored 18th-century Moravian village.

The outlying counties that complete the Triad are Surry, Stokes, Rockingham, Caswell, Alamance, Yadkin, Davie, Davidson, Randolph, and Montgomery. Here, filmmakers have found farms, nature preserves, battlefields, barns, state parks, lakes, speedways, rolling foothills, and small-town Americana. The real Mayberry exists in Andy Griffith's hometown of Mount Airy (see pages 274-83) in Surry County. There's even a full-service movie studio and a film school in Yanceyville in Caswell County. Read on and discover some of the Triad's other film-worthy surprises.

For visitor information, contact the Greensboro Convention and Visitors Bureau (800-344-2282; www.visitgreensboro.com), the Winston-Salem Convention and Visitors Bureau (800-331-7018; www.visitwinstonsalem.com), the High Point Convention and Visitors Bureau (800-720-5255; www.highpoint.org), the Mount Airy Chamber of Commerce/Visitors Center (800-948-0949; www.visitmayberry.com), or the North Carolina Division of Tourism, Film and Sports Development (800-VISITNC; www.visitnc.com).

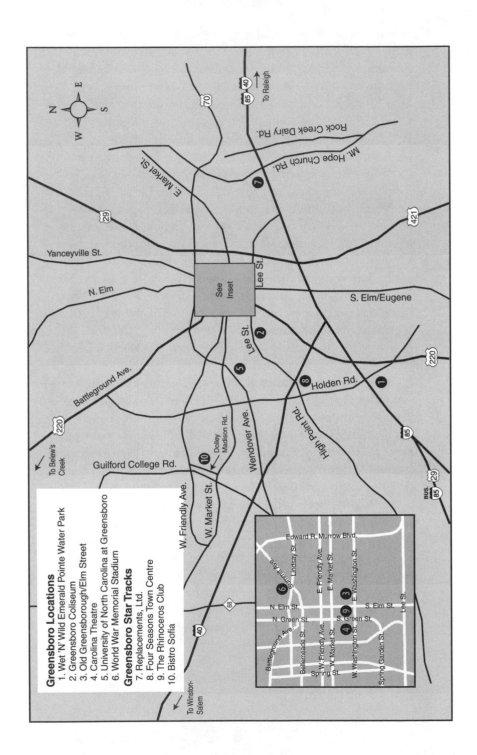

Greensboro skyline

Greensboro Locations

Wet 'N Wild Emerald Pointe Water Park

3910 South Holden Road (800-555-5900 or 336-852-9721; www.emeraldpointe.com). The park is open daily from 10 A.M. to 8 P.M. from Memorial Day to mid-August, plus Labor Day weekend. An admission fee is charged.

Remember the terrifying tsunami scene in the Nicolas Cage blockbuster *Snake Eyes*? No? That's because the original tidal-wave ending was cut by director Brian De Palma. The deleted scenes actually filmed more than 200 miles inland at Wet 'N Wild Emerald Pointe Water Park, where a miniature amusement park and pier were constructed in the middle of the park's Thunder Bay wave pool. When the park's 84-foot-wide waves were activated, the effect was one of tidal-wave magnitude. Apparently, test audiences didn't like it.

A miniature set for the deleted tsunami scenes in *Snake Eyes*, starring Nicolas Cage, was constructed at Wet 'N Wild Emerald Pointe Water Park.
COURTESY OF PIEDMONT-TRIAD FILM COMMISSION

Emerald Pointe, the Carolinas' largest water park, offers 34 rides and attractions. Watery thrills await at every turn—hydro roller coasters, water slides, raft rides, swimming pools, lagoons, waterfalls, cyclones, shipwrecks, and, of course, the almost-famous wave pool.

CREDITS

Snake Eyes (1998)

Greensboro Coliseum

1921 West Lee Street (336-373-7400; www.greensborocoliseum.com). The box office is open from 11 A.M. to 6 P.M. Monday through Saturday and two hours prior to events.

The Greensboro Coliseum appears ever so briefly in the Disney basketball film *Eddie*. This multiuse sports and entertainment facility seats up to 23,000. The coliseum hosts professional minor-league hockey and NCAA basketball. Since 1959, it has seen performances by some of music's brightest stars, including Elvis Presley, Cher, Ozzy Osbourne, Tina Turner, Elton John, the Osmond Brothers, Bruce Springsteen, Jimmy Buffett, Billy Joel, Aretha Franklin, the Backstreet Boys, the Dixie Chicks,

Shania Twain, and Aerosmith. Film and TV stars who have made recent appearances in Broadway touring productions at the 2,376-seat War Memorial Auditorium include Ann-Margret in *Best Little Whorehouse in Texas* and Richard Chamberlain in *The Sound of Music*.

CREDITS

Eddie (1996)

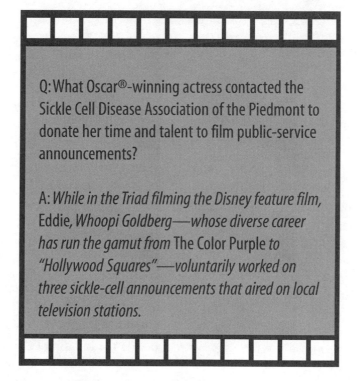

Q: What Oscar®-winning actress contacted the Sickle Cell Disease Association of the Piedmont to donate her time and talent to film public-service announcements?

A: *While in the Triad filming the Disney feature film,* Eddie, *Whoopi Goldberg—whose diverse career has run the gamut from* The Color Purple *to "Hollywood Squares"—voluntarily worked on three sickle-cell announcements that aired on local television stations.*

Old Greensborough/Elm Street

South Elm between Market and Lee streets (800-344-2282 or 336-274-2282; *www.visitgreensboro.com*)

Old Greensborough's character is exemplified by South Elm Street's turn-of-the-20th-century charm. Located in the heart of downtown, this commercial and residential area is listed on the National Register of Historic Places.

"Secrets" films on Elm Street in Old Greensborough.
COURTESY OF PIEDMONT-TRIAD FILM COMMISSION

For the TV movie "Secrets," the crew used period costumes, horse-drawn buggies, and mulched streets to create an antebellum look. "Secrets" stars Jessica Bowman and the always wonderful Julie Harris, whose five Tony® Awards and 10 nominations make her the most honored performer in Tony® history. Old Greensborough also provided locations for *Morning*, Ami Canaan Mann's directorial debut. Ami's dad, director Michael Mann, made *The Last of the Mohicans* in North Carolina's mountains.

Among the landmark buildings on Elm Street is the former Woolworth's store where, on February 1, 1960, four African-American students from North Carolina A&T State University staged a nonviolent protest at the whites-only lunch counter. A plaque and bronzed footprints of the protest leaders commemorate this monumental event, which inspired the civil-rights movement. The city renamed the street beside the building February One Place in honor of the Greensboro Four. Scheduled to open in 2005 is the International Civil Rights Center and Museum, which will showcase period artifacts, photographs, and memorabilia in the very building where the sit-ins took place. Photos and stools from the storied lunch counter are on display at the Smithsonian Institution and the Greensboro Historical Museum. They were also loaned to the TNT production "Freedom Song" for a scene filmed at Burgaw Antiqueplace (see pages 117-18) in Burgaw, North Carolina.

CREDITS

"Special Day" (Showtime, 2001); *Morning* (2000); *Passing* (1996); "Secrets" (ABC, 1995); "Jesse Jackson: Genesis of a Journey" (UNC TV, 1991)

Carolina Theatre

310 South Greene Street (336-333-2605 or 336-333-2601; www.carolinatheatre.com). The theatre's offices are open from 9 A.M. to 5 P.M. Monday through Friday.

Known as "the Showplace of the Carolinas," the Carolina Theatre is still among the grandest theatres in the South. Dating back to 1927, it exudes the glamour and glitz of Hollywood's golden era. Pictured on the cover of this book, it is listed on the National Register of Historic Places. An inviting marquis-style facade lures audiences into an elegant lobby with winding staircases that lead to the balcony. From every vantage point, the house is splendid. Its palatial decor includes a crystal chandelier, an elaborate proscenium arch, and red velvet curtains.

The Carolina appears as the 1950s Apollo Theater in the

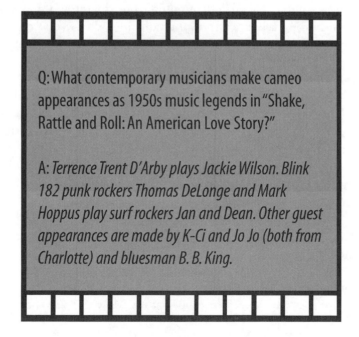

Q: What contemporary musicians make cameo appearances as 1950s music legends in "Shake, Rattle and Roll: An American Love Story?"

A: *Terrence Trent D'Arby plays Jackie Wilson. Blink 182 punk rockers Thomas DeLonge and Mark Hoppus play surf rockers Jan and Dean. Other guest appearances are made by K-Ci and Jo Jo (both from Charlotte) and bluesman B. B. King.*

miniseries "Shake, Rattle and Roll: An American Love Story." Brad Hawkins stars as the Elvis-like Tyler Hart and Bonnie Somerville as vocalist and love interest Lyne Danner.

In September 2003, the theatre hosted the East Coast premiere of *Cabin Fever*, which was filmed in the Triad in 2001. Actress Cerina Vincent was among the 700 people who attended the benefit premiere for the Piedmont Triad Film Commission.

Celebrities who have performed at the Carolina Theatre include actor and dancer Ben Vereen (a native of Chadbourn, North Carolina), crooner Tony Bennett, and jazz musicians Miles Davis and Chuck Mangione.

CREDITS

"Shake, Rattle and Roll: An American Love Story" (CBS, 1999)

University of North Carolina-Greensboro
Tate and Spring Garden streets (336-334-5360; *www.uncg.edu/bcn*)

A refuge for theatre, broadcast, and film students, the UNCG campus is located minutes from downtown and Old Greensborough. Its feature-film credits include the observation scenes in *House of Cards*, starring Kathleen Turner and Tommy Lee Jones, as well as scenes in *The Dark Power* and *'Til There Were None*, based on Agatha Christie's novel *Ten Little Indians*.

The university's fee-free-location status attracts independent, student, and shoestring productions. Its outstanding broadcasting and cinema school offers students undergraduate and master's programs in film and video production. The campus and its stalwart buildings have appeared in documentaries and student films such as "Teach Me To," written and directed by UNCG film-school alumnus Ellen Walters.

Each February since 1978, the university has hosted the juried Carolina Film & Video Festival, the state's oldest film festival.

Accomplished theatre and communications/broadcast alumni include radio host and actress Bernice Goodwin O'Crotty (class of 1939); broadcaster Virginia Tatum Mewis (1938); actress

Anne Pitoniak (1943); actor and director Barry Bell (1975); actress Beth Leavel (1980); actor, director, and theatre owner Stephen Gee (1980); special-effects makeup artists and producers Dean Jones (1984) and Starr Jones (1987); Jim Henson puppeteer Paul Hartis (1985); actor and director Eric Traynor (1989); special-effects artist Jeff Goodwin—and Connie Nelson (1994), coauthor of this guide!

CREDITS

Teach Me To (1997); *'Til There Were None* (1995); *House of Cards* (1993); *The Dark Power* (1985)

★★★★★★★★★★★★

Triad Film Happenings

RiverRun International Film Festival

The RiverRun International Film Festival was founded in 1998 by Gennaro "Gene" D'Onofrio and his adult children Vincent and Elizabeth through the Bella Visione Film Society. All three have North Carolina credits, Gene for *Dear Angry*, Vincent for *Dangerous Lives of Altar Boys*, and Elizabeth for *Household Saints*. Initially located in Brevard, North Carolina, RiverRun moved to Winston-Salem in 2003. It's now presented by the North Carolina School of the Arts' School of Filmmaking. The festival focuses on feature-length fictional and documentary films, along with live-action, documentary, animated, experimental, and student short films. Held in April, the three-day festival includes panels, workshops, screenings, and special events. Asheville resident and actress Andie MacDowell attended the 2003 RiverRun Southern premiere of *A Mighty Wind*. Festival venues include NCSA's ACE Exhibition Complex and the Stevens Center for the Performing Arts (see page 247). The festival office is at 305 West Fourth Street, Suite 1-B, in Winston-Salem; call 336-831-1914 or visit www.riverrunfilm.com. An admission fee is charged.

North Carolina School of the Arts Student Film Festival

NCSA's School of Filmmaking screens films by third- and fourth-year students during late May in the ACE Exhibition Complex. The NCSA campus is located at 1533 South Main Street in Winston-Salem; call 336-770-1330 or visit www.ncarts.edu. An admission fee is charged.

Elon Film Festival

Each spring, Elon University screens fictional independent feature films produced in the Southeast. One block is devoted to student and short films and videos. For information, call Elon University's School of Communications at 336-278-5675.

University of North Carolina-Greensboro's Carolina Film & Video Festival

Dubbed the "First and Feisty Film Festival," this event, begun in 1978, is the longest continuously operating film festival in the Carolinas. Held in February, it is a major regional showcase of independent and student creative film and video. First films and videos compete against each other. Other categories include scriptwriting, independent films, and college and high-school films. The festival is headquartered in Room 205 of the Brown Building at UNCG; call 336-334-4197 or visit www.carolinafilmandvideofestival.org.

Piedmont Community College Film Celebration

PCC student films and class projects are showcased in Yanceyville. For more information, call 336-694-5707 or visit www.pccfilm.com

Films on Fourth

The North Carolina School of the Arts and the Winston-Salem Cinema Society present first-run independent and foreign-language films at the Stevens Center. An admission fee is charged. For information, visit www.cinemasociety.org.

World War Memorial Stadium

Corner of Yanceyville and Lindsay roads (336-333-BATS). The season runs from May through September; call for the schedule.

Hoping for a closeup (or a close encounter with Kevin Costner), more than 100 volunteer extras donned sun dresses, shorts, and T-shirts and shivered in the grandstand of World War Memorial Stadium during a frigid October afternoon in 1987. The cold snap was untimely for *Bull Durham's* midsummer scenes. Between takes, extras wrapped themselves in blankets, but when director Ron Shelton screamed "Action!" wraps were shed and breathing was suspended, lest the oral fog spoil the take. But somebody must have breathed, because the spectator scenes got cut.

Built in 1926 as a memorial to the city's casualties during World War I, the stadium is believed to be the fourth-oldest minor-league ballpark in use. Film junkies will recognize its ornate facade when the Durham Bulls arrive by bus for a stand against the Greensboro Hornets. Scenes from the venerable playing field also made it onto the screen.

Since *Bull Durham*, the vintage 7,500-seat ballpark has been updated. It now has a canopied sky bar at the end of left field, where fans who choose to forgo the local soft-drink favorite, Cheerwine, can order beer. In 1994, the Hornets of the South Atlantic League changed their name to the Greensboro Bats. This class-A affiliate of the Florida Marlins would, no doubt, welcome a sequel to the now-classic sports film that immortalizes the stadium on celluloid. By 2005, the Bats hope to be in their new stadium on the corner of Eugene and Bellemeade streets.

CREDITS

Bull Durham (1988)

★★★★★★★★★★★★★★★

Guilford County's Celebrity Ties

Author Jerry Bledsoe's true-crime books *Before He Wakes, Bitter Blood*, and *Blood Games* have been made into TV movies; *Blood Games* was retitled "Honor Thy Mother." However, the former Guilford County resident admits to being soured on Hollywood for taking unthinkable liberties with his stories. In the case of *Bitter Blood*—retitled "In the Best of Families: Marriage, Pride and Madness"—the ending was changed, defying the book's very genre: *true* crime. Bledsoe's precious holiday novelette *The Angel Doll* was accurately adapted into a screenplay by Wilmington independent filmmaker Sandy Johnston. Bledsoe executive-produced the North Carolina-made *The Angel Doll*, a 2003 film that insiders believe will become a holiday classic. Born in Danville, Virginia, Bledsoe grew up in Thomasville and worked as a reporter and columnist for the *Greensboro News & Record* and the *Charlotte Observer*. He currently runs Down Home Press in Randolph County, where he resides.

Film junkies will find Greensboro native Rick Dees's star on the Hollywood Walk of Fame. According to *Billboard* magazine, Dees—the former host of *Rick Dees in the Morning* at KIIS-FM—is the "Number One Radio Personality in America." His wacky humor has entertained millions during L.A.'s morning drive, and his syndicated weekly radio program, *Rick Dees Weekly Top 40*, reaches 30 million people worldwide. Back in the 1970s, his runaway number-one hit, "Disco Duck," sold 4 million copies and garnered a People's Choice® Award and an appearance on "American Bandstand." His TV and movie credits include *La Bamba*; *Jetsons: The Movie*; "Roseanne"; "Married . . . With Children"; and "Burke's Law." Dees has served as host of "Into the Night" and "Solid Gold."

The winner of nine Emmy® Awards, Guilford County native Edward R. Murrow (1908-65) gained international fame with his live World War II broadcasts for CBS radio. His "See It Now" television news program is credited with bringing Senator Joseph McCarthy's radical theories under public scrutiny in 1954. He's been called the most famous man in broadcasting. His broadcasts were simple, direct, honest, and accurate. Murrow's war correspondent's uniform is on display in the Greensboro Historical Museum, located at 130 Summit Avenue; for information, call 336-373-2043 or visit www.greensborohistory.org. UNCG's School of Broadcast and Cinema has honored Murrow by naming a building after him. In 1986, Daniel J. Travanti portrayed the legendary newsman in the HBO movie "Murrow."

Born and raised near Greensboro, William Sidney Porter (1862-1910), better known as prolific short-story writer O. Henry, was a master at surprise endings. The website imdb.com credits his work with inspiring more than 150 television, feature, and short films. Among them is *Ruthless People*, a 1986 comedy starring Danny DeVito and Bette Midler, based on the story "The Ransom of Red Chief." The 1931 feature film *The Cisco Kid* and the 1950s television series "The Cisco Kid" were based on O. Henry's Western stories. A half-hour weekly television series called "The O. Henry Playhouse" aired in 1957. O. Henry's life and work are interpreted at the Greensboro Historical Museum.

Greensboro Star Tracks

Replacements, Ltd.

I-85/I-40 at Exit 132 (800-REPLACE or 336-697-3000;
www.replacements.com). Replacements, Ltd., is open daily. The
showroom is open from 9 A.M. to 8 P.M. Tours are offered from
9:30 A.M. to 7 P.M. Phone orders are accepted from 8 A.M. to
midnight.

It's 3 A.M. and an exhausted soap-opera crew member shatters a dozen rare china coffee cups. What's a New York City prop master or mistress to do? Call Replacements, Ltd., in Greensboro, North Carolina, of course! That's exactly what "The Guiding Light" did during taping of its Thanksgiving 2002 episode. Fortunately, Replacements stocks more than 10 million hard-to-find china, silver, crystal, and collectible items in more than 180,000 patterns, some of which are over 100 years old.

When the CBS sitcom "Everybody Loves Raymond" needed to replace eight discontinued Pfaltzgraff plates, Replacements promptly shipped them to Burbank, California. When North Carolina-made *Divine Secrets of the Ya-Ya Sisterhood* sought 1930s-style fine china, silver, crystal, tea service, and table accents,

Replacements was happy to oblige. Oprah even called to secure a discontinued Corningware "Spring Blossom" bowl for a guest with a seemingly insoluble household problem. "The Oprah Winfrey Show" later featured the unique retailer on a separate segment. Replacements has also appeared on CNN's "Business Unusual" and on Animal Planet's "Pet Story" for allowing employees to bring their pets to work.

Four Seasons Town Centre

*High Point Road at I-40 (336-292-0171;
www.fourseasonstowncentre.com). Four Seasons is open from
10 A.M. to 9 P.M. Monday through Saturday and from 12:30
P.M. to 6 P.M. on Sunday.*

Boasting over a million square feet of retail space, Four Seasons Town Centre is among the Southeast's largest malls. Many of the musicians and athletes who play at the nearby Greensboro Coliseum stay at the Sheraton Four Seasons Hotel and Convention Center, just steps away from the mall. A partial list of celebrities who've shopped at Four Seasons includes Tom Cruise, Whitney Houston, Michael Jordan, and WWE wrestlers. Other star tracks have been left by Ludacris, Lil' Bow Wow, Buddy Jewell, Colin Powell, Deniece Williams, and Grant Hill.

The Rhinoceros Club

*315 South Greene Street (336-272-9305; www.rhinoclub.com).
The club is open 365 days a year from 4 P.M. to 2 A.M.*

You never know who might walk through the doors of North Carolina's original Rhinoceros Club, a private club for

members and guests. Charter members still talk about the time Bruce Springsteen dropped by for a beer after a sold-out concert during his *Born in the U.S.A.* tour in January 1985. Bruce ended up center stage with a local band, performing memorable renditions of "Hang on Sloopy" and "Stand by Me."

Just like its sister club in Wilmington, the Rhino's decor includes elaborate mirrors, sculptures, classic books, turn-of-the-20th-century fans, original flooring, wooden booths, and an antique wooden bar. A trademark rhinoceros head greets patrons upon entry. On weekdays, the well-stocked jukebox offers a variety of tunes from the 1980s to the present. Live bands or deejays entertain on weekends.

Bistro Sofia

616 Dolley Madison Road (336-855-1313; www.bistrosofia.com). The bistro is open from 5 P.M. to 10 P.M. Tuesday through Sunday.

Bistro Sofia delivers the ultimate Triad dining experience. Occupying the former location of the Madison Park Restaurant, which burned and was rebuilt in 1999, the new, upscale, relaxed bistro carries on MP's celebrated tradition of fine dining. Its hallmarks include a casually elegant atmosphere, a wine list that has received an award from *Wine Spectator*, and an innovative Eastern European- and Asian-inspired menu that pleases even the most refined palates. The fresh herbs grown on the premises attest to the restaurant's commitment to organic, sustainable farming.

Adorning the plum and gold walls are vintage menus from restaurants around the world and plates dating back to the 19th century. Large windows overlook an outdoor patio. Private dining rooms are available upstairs.

While in town filming *Mr. Destiny*, actors Jim Belushi and Michael Caine were frequent diners at Madison Park. Should they return, they'll be equally or more impressed by Bistro Sofia, which is poised to build its own list of celebrity diners.

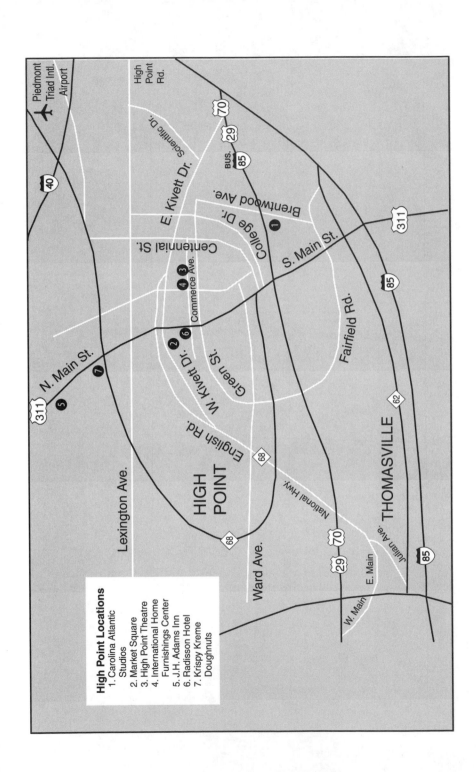

High Point Locations
1. Carolina Atlantic Studios
2. Market Square
3. High Point Theatre
4. International Home Furnishings Center
5. J.H. Adams Inn
6. Radisson Hotel
7. Krispy Kreme Doughnuts

High Point Locations

Carolina Atlantic Studios

2000 *Brentwood Street. For information, contact the North Carolina School of the Arts at* 336-770-3290. *Visitors are limited to exterior viewing.*

While High Point might not jump to mind when you think of movie production, the Home Furnishings Capital of the World does have its own studio and several film credits. The economic impact of Richard Pryor's feature film *Critical Condition* inspired investors to build Carolina Atlantic Studios in 1988. Situated on eight acres, the studio offers a 14,000-square-foot sound stage, nine catwalks, a lighting grid, offices, and an interior water tank. Post-production facilities include computerized editing bays and a state-of-the-art screening room.

In 1999, business partners donated the $2.35 million film complex to the North Carolina School of the Arts (see pages 241-43). Today, it's used by NCSA students and rented by local and visiting productions.

CREDITS

Interiors for *Doomsday Man* (1999) were shot at Carolina Atlantic. Other credits include *Cabin Fever* (2003); *Briar Patch* (2001); *Morning* (2000); "Above Suspicion" (USA, 2000); "Target Earth" (ABC, 1998); *House of Cards* (1993); *The Music of Chance* (1993); *Children of the Corn II: Final Sacrifice* (1993); *Hellraiser III: Hell on Earth* (1992); *Mr. Destiny* (1990); *Escape* (1990); and *Critical Condition* (1987).

Market Square

305 *West High Street* (336-339-2277). *The Boiler Room Bar and Grill is located on the ground and mezzanine floors of the Market Square building. It is open only during the International Home Furnishings Market and for special events and private parties. Select showrooms and businesses are open year-round. Others are open only during the market.*

Market Square's furniture showrooms often provide the setting for commercial photography. They became a movie set during the filming of *Hellraiser III: Hell on Earth*.

A former furniture factory listed on the National Register of Historic Places, Market Square was built around 1900. It is now a home-shopping mecca with permanent and temporary exhibitors of fabric, decorative accessories, and furnishings. Restaurants such as the rustic Boiler Room Bar and Grill occupy the ground floor and the mezzanine, where *Hellraiser III* filmed.

CREDITS

Hellraiser III: Hell on Earth (1992)

High Point Theatre/
North Carolina Shakespeare Festival

The theatre is located at 200 East Commerce Avenue. The box office is open from noon to 5 P.M. Monday through Friday; call 336-887-3001. To contact the North Carolina Shakespeare Festival, call 336-841-2273 or visit www.ncshakes.org.

Kathleen Turner caused quite a buzz when she came to the High Point Theatre for a screening of *House of Cards*, in which she plays the determined mother of an autistic daughter. Filmed at Wheatmore Dairy Farm in Trinity and Carolina Atlantic Studios in 1991, *House of Cards* won favor at the Sundance Film Festival but was panned by mainstream critics.

Though movie premieres are rare in High Point, a sneak preview of *Hellraiser III: Hell on Earth* had been held here just months before *House of Cards*. More often, residents enjoy world-class performances when the North Carolina Shakespeare Festival (NCSF) opens its season at the High Point Theatre. Since 1977, NCSF has staged quality professional theatre productions

★ ★ ★ ★ ★ ★ ★ ★ ★

featuring actors, directors, designers, and technicians from across the state and nation. Actor Terrence Mann, who originated the Broadway roles of Rum Tum Tugger in *Cats*, Javert in *Les Misérables*, and Beast in *Beauty and the Beast*, performed in NCSF's 1978 and 1979 seasons. He also performed several roles for NCSF's second-stage Festival Stage Company. Mann's film and television credits include *A Chorus Line, Big Top Pee Wee, Critters*, "One Life to Live" and "Law and Order."

Actor Earle Hyman was a guest artist with NCSF in 1993, playing the role of King Lear. Born in North Carolina, Hyman has performed on Broadway and international stages and in film and television. Nominated for an Emmy® and a Tony®, and the recipient of an ABC Arts Ace Award, he is best known for his role of Russell Huxtable, father to Bill Cosby's character on "The Cosby Show."

International Home Furnishings Center

210 East Commerce Avenue (336-888-3700; www.ihfc.com). Temporary and permanent showrooms are open to trade professionals; a pass is required. The furniture markets are held in April and October. Group tours are available year-round by appointment.

Celebrity sightings occur every day during the International Home Furnishings Market. Each April and October, approximately 80,000 manufacturers, exhibitors, sales reps, buyers, designers, suppliers, architects, news media, and, yes, even celebrities roam the city's 11.5 million square feet of furniture showrooms. What began in 1909 is now the largest and most important home furnishings trade show in the world. Of the 185 showroom buildings, the largest is the International

★ ★ ★ ★ ★ ★ ★ ★ ★ ★

Home Furnishings Center, where stars such as Kevin Sorbo of "Hercules" have made the market scene.

Manufacturers vie for buyer and media attention by staging guest appearances. Celebrity furniture endorsements are hot— a trend begun by fashion designers Oscar de la Renta, Alexander Julian, Martha Stewart, and others. When Thomasville Furniture unveiled its wildly successful Ernest Hemingway Collection, the novelist's granddaughter Mina introduced it. Other furniture companies were quick to jump on the celebrity bandwagon. Lenoir-based Bernhardt Furniture recruited Martha Stewart to promote her Signature Collection. Bedroom and dining-room importer Largo International added a line inspired, designed, and personally introduced in 2002 by Jaclyn Smith of "Charlie's Angels" fame. Fashion designer and former supermodel Kathy Ireland launched her Standard Furniture Home and Martin Furniture lines here. Television hosts Christopher Lowell of the Discovery Channel and Chris Madden of HGTV represent lines for Flexsteel and Bassett, respectively. And sports stars like Arnold Palmer have even gotten in on the star-studded furniture trend. Dead celebrities make their rounds posthumously at the market via licensing agreements. Actress Lauren Bacall, son Stephen Bogart, and Humphrey Bogart's 1951 Oscar® statuette for *The African Queen* took center stage to introduce Thomasville Furniture Industries' sophisticated Bogart Collection. Elvis Presley made a comeback with a line of retro furnishings by Vaughan-Bassett.

Since about 14 percent of home furnishings sales were attributed to celebrity licensees in 2002, you can count on seeing more stars at future markets.

J. H. Adams Inn

1108 North Main Street (888-256-1289 *or* 336-882-3267; *www.jhadamsinn.com*)

★★★★★★★★★★

This 1918 Italian Renaissance mansion was built as an exquisite private residence for John Hampton and Elizabeth Adams. Elegantly renovated into a bed-and-breakfast, the J. H. Adams Inn offers modern conveniences and historic charm. Located in downtown High Point and listed on the National Register of Historic Places, the inn quickly won favor with celebrities attending the International Home Furnishings Market. Since the inn opened in 2001, hostess incarnate Martha Stewart has checked in more than once. Supermodel and fashion designer Kathy Ireland and "Kudzu" cartoonist and North Carolina author Doug Marlette have attended soirees held at the inn during the furniture market. New York fashion designer and Chapel Hill native Alexander Julian has dined at the inn's restaurant. Another famous guest was Maury Povich.

No doubt, the inn's architectural majesty, amenities, and Southern hospitality will continue to lure both celebrities and film junkies.

Krispy Kreme Doughnuts

914 North Main Street (336-885-8081; www.krispykreme.com).
The store is open 24 hours per day except on major holidays.

While in town to promote her Signature Collection at the fall 2002 International Home Furnishings Market, renowned decorator and cookbook author Martha Stewart showed up at a local Krispy Kreme store to purchase a dozen original glazed and a dozen assorted yeast sweets. The home and kitchen diva sweetened her image in High Point when she bought customers a round of steaming coffee and "Hot. Fresh. Now." doughnuts. Martha can attest there's nothing like a hot-doughnut experience to soften the hearts of those who favor the glazed, sprinkled, or frosted treats.

The company, founded in 1937 and based in nearby Winston-Salem, makes more than 7.5 million doughnuts per day.

★★★★★★★★★★

Entertainment icon Dick Clark of "American Bandstand" fame was spotted at a Winston-Salem Krispy Kreme during a visit to seal a very . . . um . . . sweet deal. Clark is one of the investors of Chesire and Kent, Ltd., the company that partnered with Krispy Kreme and Donald Henshall to form Krispy Kreme U.K. Limited. Two dozen or so KK stores will open throughout the United Kingdom by 2008. Another celebrity, baseball Hall of Famer Hank Aaron, was awarded a Krispy Kreme franchise in Atlanta, Georgia, in 2002.

Radisson Hotel High Point

135 South Main Street (800-333-3333 *or* 336-889-8888; *www.radisson.com/highpointnc*)

Film junkies and furniture shoppers are sure to find the tastefully appointed suites and guest rooms at the Radisson Hotel High Point much to their liking. Centrally located along the "Home Furnishings Magic Mile" in downtown, the full-service hotel offers gracious hospitality and 252 spacious guest rooms and luxurious suites with lots of amenities, including an executive fitness center and an indoor heated pool.

High Point hosts its share of celebrities who endorse products at the International Home Furnishings Market. Others check in while filming on location or playing in celebrity golf tournaments. The Radisson's celebrity guests have included Johnny Cash, Richard Pryor, Randall "Tex" Cobb, Jaclyn Smith, Kathie Lee Gifford, Morris Day, Richard Petty, Bob Mackie, Alexander Julian, Julie Nixon Eisenhower, Kathy Ireland, Tommy Lee Jones, and Martha Stewart.

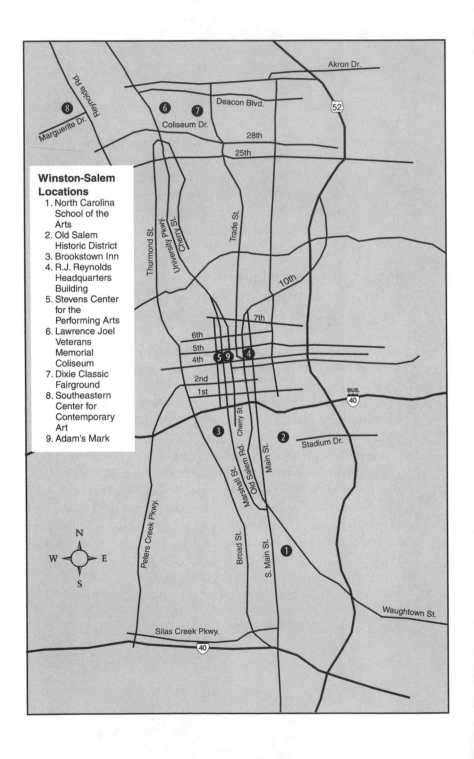

Winston-Salem Locations

1. North Carolina School of the Arts
2. Old Salem Historic District
3. Brookstown Inn
4. R.J. Reynolds Headquarters Building
5. Stevens Center for the Performing Arts
6. Lawrence Joel Veterans Memorial Coliseum
7. Dixie Classic Fairground
8. Southeastern Center for Contemporary Art
9. Adam's Mark

North Carolina School of Filmmaking's
studio village, where dreams begin
PHOTOGRAPH BY JOE LECHLEIDER
COURTESY OF NORTH CAROLINA SCHOOL OF THE ARTS

Winston-Salem Locations

North Carolina School of the Arts

*1533 South Main Street (336-770-3290; www.ncarts.edu). The
school is open to the public during film festivals. Prospective
students and their parents may take campus tours Tuesday
through Friday at 2 P.M. except during exams and breaks;
advance reservations are recommended.*

Established by the North Carolina General Assembly in
1963, the North Carolina School of the Arts (NCSA) became
the first state-supported residential school of its kind in the nation. It was absorbed into the University of North Carolina system in 1972. More than 1,000 students from high school through
graduate school train in five professional programs: dance, design and production, drama, filmmaking, and music.

Drama-school alumni whose names film junkies might recognize include actress Jada Pinkett Smith; author and screenwriter Peter Hedges, whose credits include *What's Eating Gilbert Grape* and *About a Boy;* and Tom Hulce, who won an Emmy® for "The Heidi Chronicles" and was nominated for an Academy Award® for *Amadeus.* NCSA's Broadway stars include Joe Mantello, who won a Tony® for Best Director for *Take Me Out;* Mary-Louise Parker, who won a Tony® for Best Actress for *Proof;* Gary Beach, who won a Tony® for Best Featured Actor for *The Producers;* Terrence Mann, a Tony® nominee for *Beauty and the Beast;* Jennifer Ehle, who won a Tony® for Best Actress for *The Real Thing;* and Celia Weston, a Tony® nominee for *The Last Night of Ballyhoo.*

Countless student films shoot on NCSA's sound stages and back lot. Award-winning film alumni include David Gordon Green (see pages 406-7); Tim Orr (*George Washington; All the Real Girls*); Randolph Benson ("Man and Dog" on Bravo!); Anna Dudley ("Special Day" and "Jacob's Sound" on Showtime); Nick Panagopulos (*Five Lines*); Jeff Fradley (*Ilyanovich Rasputin*); and David Rotan and Bob Jones (*Flowers & Freckle Cream*).

NCSA's School of Filmmaking was established in 1993. Students can earn a Bachelor of Fine Arts or a College Arts diploma in screenwriting, directing, editing and sound, producing, cinematography, or production design. The 62,036-square-foot studio village is home to all aspects of the school's professional conservatory program. The facilities include three sound stages, an indoor water tank, a recording stage, classrooms, offices, and three state-of-the-art motion-picture theatres. The village's backlot has period facades.

The School of Filmmaking houses the Moving Image Archives, a unique and rare collection of 25,000 original feature films on 35 mm, as well as thousands of trailers, short films, videocassettes, laserdiscs, and DVDs. Its noncommercial archives is second in size only to that of the Library of Congress. The ACE Exhibition Complex is a student screening facility and a primary venue for the RiverRun International Film Festival (see page 223), the National Black Theatre Festival (see pages 253-54), and the NCSA Student Film Festival. NCSA also owns and uses the Stevens Center (see page 247) and Carolina Atlantic Studios (see pages 233-34).

NCSA's faculty consists of accomplished working professionals. Faculty members boast a wide range of film, television, commercial, industrial, video, and documentary credits. Dean Dale Pollock is an award-winning journalist and producer of feature films who first came to the Triad as producer of *House of Cards*. Renowned guest artists have included directors John Landis, Spike Lee, and Kevin Reynolds; author and screenwriter John Ehle; and actors Kathy Bates, John Ritter, Emilio Estevez, and Andie MacDowell.

Q: What dancer and actress was rejected by the North Carolina School of the Arts but years later was awarded honorary doctorates by NCSA and also by her alma mater?

A: *Emmy*® winner Debbie Allen, whose credits include stints as actress and choreographer in "Fame," has honorary doctorates from NCSA and Howard University. Her famous relatives include hubby Norm Nixon (a former L. A. Laker) and sister Phylicia Rashad, best known for her role as Clair Huxtable on "The Cosby Show."

Old Salem

601 Old Salem Road (888-OLDSALEM or 336-721-7300; www.oldsalem.org). Visitors may wander Old Salem and enter some of the buildings for free. A fee is charged for guided tours, which are offered from 9 A.M. to 5 P.M. Monday through Saturday and from 12:30 P.M. to 5 P.M. on Sunday except on major holidays.

"Taking Liberty" films at Old Salem.
COURTESY OF PIEDMONT-TRIAD FILM COMMISSION

A period filmmaker's dream, Old Salem is among the most authentic 18th- and 19th-century restorations in the United States. Its pastoral setting reflects the influence of the German-speaking Moravians who settled here in 1766.

For "Tecumseh: The Last Warrior," Old Salem's streets were dirtied and signs changed for a scene of Native Americans passing through town; some scenes were shot in front of the Single Brothers House, constructed between 1768 and 1786. In "The Founding Fathers," the historic house provides the background for John Adams's stroll with his wife. Salem Square offers a New England-esque setting for some of the most dramatic sequences in "The Lottery."

Tickets, maps, and brochures for a self-guided tour of the 70-acre living-history village are available at the visitor center. You'll feel like a movie extra as you interact with costumed blacksmiths, gunsmiths, weavers, spinners, cobblers, brick makers, carpenters, gardeners, woodworkers, and soap, candle, and toy makers. Costumed servers offer Moravian-style chicken pie, meat loaf, and other favorites at the Salem Tavern, built around 1784. Moravian cookies and sugar cakes are baked daily in a brick beehive oven at the Winkler Bakery. Visitors can spend the night at the 1844-vintage Augustus T. Zevely Inn Bed & Breakfast, Old Salem's only lodging facility.

Old Salem encompasses museums, period gardens, and over a hundred buildings, including St. Philips Moravian Church, built around 1823, the state's oldest African-American church; Salem College; Home Moravian Church; and God's Acre, the Moravian cemetery.

CREDITS

"The Founding Fathers" (History Channel, 2000); "The Lottery" (NBC, 1996); "Tecumseh: The Last Warrior" (TNT, 1995); "Taking Liberty" (CBS pilot, 1993); "A Passion for Place" (UNC-TV, 1993); *Road to Carolina* (1961); numerous documentaries and NCSA student films

Downtown Winston-Salem

Filmmakers can't resist the many faces of downtown Winston-Salem. R. J. Reynolds Tobacco Company, the second-largest cigarette manufacturer in the nation, calls Winston-Salem home. Its influence is largely responsible for the very contrasts that define downtown. Smokestacks, warehouses, steam plants, and railroad tracks coexist with historic residential neighborhoods and uptown arts districts.

Several productions have captured downtown's industries. In "Target Earth," you can see the steam plants along Patterson Avenue. *The Lesser Evil* shows similar scenery along Trade Street. The independent film *George Washington* achieves a surreal feel by using the plants and railroad tracks near Seventh Street. Once-abandoned buildings are prominent in *Mr. Destiny* when Larry Burrows's (James Belushi's) station wagon breaks down in front of The Universal Joint, where bartender Mike (Michael Caine) prepares a life-altering "spilt-milk" drink. The television movie "Above Suspicion," starring Scott Bakula, filmed in the mayor's office at city hall. And "Patron Saint of Liars" shot at the Mr. Waffle restaurant on Peters Creek Parkway.

CREDITS

The Girls Room (2000); *George Washington* (2000); "Above Suspicion" (USA, 2000); *The Lesser Evil* (1998); "Target Earth" (ABC, 1998); "Patron Saint of Liars" (CBS, 1998); *Hellraiser III: Hell on Earth* (1992); *Mr. Destiny* (1990)

Q: What sold-out televised concert and best-selling soundtrack and DVD were recorded live for PBS at the 2,000-seat R. J. Reynolds Memorial Auditorium?

A: *"The Three Pickers: Legends of American Music" aired on PBS's "Great Performances" in 2003. The show was performed live at the R. J. Reynolds High School auditorium, at 301 North Hawthorne Road in Winston-Salem. The landmark concert features bluegrass great Doc Watson, banjo master Earl Scruggs, and mandolin player Ricky Skaggs, along with vocalist Alison Krauss. The concert marks the first time these musical legends performed together.*

R. J. Reynolds Building

401 North Main Street (www.rjrt.com). Visitors are limited to exterior viewing.

The larger-than-life Liberty Republic Sporting Goods skyscraper in *Mr. Destiny* may look like the Empire State Building, but it's not. Designed by architects Shreve and Lamb in 1929 as the prototype for the Empire State Building (which they also built), the Art Deco R. J. Reynolds Building was the South's first skyscraper. In 1982, Reynolds Tobacco opened the adjacent and connected RJR Plaza Building.

CREDITS

Mr. Destiny (1990)

Stevens Center for the Performing Arts

405 West Fourth Street (336-721-1945; www.ncarts.edu). Call for a schedule of events.

From silent-movie palace to movie location, the Stevens Center for the Performing Arts is a showcase. Film junkies will recognize the 1929 structure as the Townsend Theatre in the thriller *The Bedroom Window* when socialite Sylvia Wentworth (Isabelle Huppert) is murdered during a ballet performance and Terry (Steve Guttenberg) comes face to face with the killer. For *Mr. Destiny*, the lobby was transformed into the French restaurant where naïve millionaire Larry Burrows (Jim Belushi) woos union leader Ellen (Linda Hamilton).

Owned by the North Carolina School of the Arts, the elegantly restored 1,380-seat Neoclassical theatre is a venue for the RiverRun International Film Festival (see page 223), the Winston-Salem Symphony, the Piedmont Opera Theatre, the National Black Theatre Festival (see pages 253-54), and the North Carolina Shakespeare Festival. "Films on Fourth" is a series that screens first-run independent and foreign-language films at the Stevens Center; for information, visit www.cinemasociety.org.

CREDITS

Mr. Destiny (1990); "Doc Watson in Concert" (UNC-TV, 1990); *The Bedroom Window* (1987)

Lawrence Joel Veterans Memorial Coliseum Complex

The coliseum is located at 2825 University Parkway; call 336-725-5635 or visit www.ljvm.com. Ernie Shore Field is located at 401 Deacon Boulevard; call 336-759-2233 or visit www.ljvm.com/ernieshore.html. Call for a schedule of events.

More than 7,500 extras showed up at the 15,000-seat Lawrence Joel Veterans Memorial Coliseum on a Sunday in September 1995 for a chance to be in the feature film *Eddie*.

More likely, they came to see star Whoopi Goldberg. The movie, about a New York Knicks-loving cab driver (Goldberg) who becomes the team's head coach through an interesting twist of fate, includes cameo appearances by NBA stars. The scenes filmed at LJVMC are of an away game between the Knicks and the San Antonio Spurs, featuring NBA superstar Dennis Rodman. And *He Got Game*, directed by Spike Lee, filmed montage shots at LJVMC.

The coliseum and annex host games, concerts, rodeos, conventions, and other events. Wake Forest University basketball games dominate the winter and spring. Big-name performers who have appeared here include rocker Billy Joel and country-music stars Garth Brooks and Reba McIntire.

Ernie Shore Field is also part of the complex. Its red-brick arches, giant scoreboard, grandstand, carousel, and playground beckon fans and filmmakers. The playing field and locker room appear in *Mr. Destiny* in strike-out and home-run flashback sequences. Ernie Shore is the home of the Winston-Salem Warthogs, a class-A affiliate of the Chicago White Sox. Major leaguers like Wade Boggs once played here. Hall of Famer Hank Aaron reportedly played one of his first professional games here in an exhibition as a member of the Indianapolis Clowns.

CREDITS

He Got Game (1998); *Eddie* (1996); *Mr. Destiny* (1990)

Dixie Classic Fairgrounds

421 West 27th Street (336-727-2236; *www.dcfair.com*)

Tractor pulls, farmers' markets, motocross races, gun shows, livestock auctions, and the Dixie Classic Fair are the main events at the 97-acre Dixie Classic Fairgrounds complex. The early-American authenticity of the area called "Yesterday Village" has proven attractive to filmmakers, thanks to its general store, schoolhouse, church, tobacco barn, blacksmith shop, well, smokehouse, springhouse, outhouse, and other log structures that depict early rural life in the northwestern Piedmont. It proved ideal for settlement and barn exteriors and house interiors in "Tecumseh: The Last Warrior."

"Tecumseh: The Last Warrior" (TNT, 1995)

Q: What pair of women with Triad ties were the first mother and daughter to be nominated for the same Tony® Award for Leading Actress?

A: *In 2000, Winston-Salem's Rosemary Harris was nominated for* Waiting in the Wings, *and her daughter, NCSA alum Jennifer Ehle, was nominated for* The Real Thing. *Young Jennifer took home the shiny statue. This double nomination made husband, father, and novelist John Ehle very proud. (For more about this unique family, see pages 390-91.)*

★★★★★★★★★★★★★★

Forsyth County's Celebrity Ties

After overcoming a troubled childhood, Dr. Maya Angelou has spent her adult life empowering and inspiring others through her writing, acting, and teaching. She's currently a faculty member of Winston-Salem's Wake Forest University. Her first movie role was as a dancer in the film version of *Porgy and Bess*, followed by credits in "Roots" and a pair of North Carolina-based productions, "The Runaway" and *The Journey of August King*. Her directing credits include *Down in the Delta* and the TV series "Visions." Her writing credits include *Georgia, Georgia; I Know Why the Caged Bird Sings*; and "Sister, Sister," starring Diahann Carroll and Rosalind Cash. She is the subject of the documentary *Intimate Portrait: Maya Angelou*.

Born in Winston-Salem, Howard Cosell (1918-95) has been called the greatest sportscaster in history. His trademark rhythm, tell-it-like-it-is style, and love-him-or-hate-him persona elevated him to unprecedented status. Cosell reported sports for the series "Eyewitness News" from 1968 to 1970 and hosted "Monday Night Football" from 1970 to 1983. He became so recognizable to American audiences that he was cast as himself in television shows such as "The Odd Couple," "Saturday Night Live," and "Battle of the Network Stars" during the 1970s and 1980s, as well as in films like Woody Allen's *Broadway Danny Rose* and *Sleeper*, among others.

One of Winston-Salem's most remarkable families is author and screenwriter John Ehle; his wife, Emmy®-winning actress Rosemary Harris; and their daughter, Emmy®-winning actress and NCSA alumna Jennifer Ehle (see pages 390-91).

Film junkies will recognize Stuart Scott from ESPN's flagship show "Sports Center with Stuart Scott" and from the network's Wednesday-night NBA broadcasts. Known for his trademark expressions, Scott was born in Chicago and raised in Winston-Salem.

Born and raised in Winston-Salem and a 1942 graduate of Elon College, Kenneth Utt (1921-94) began his career on Broadway before segueing into television, where he produced programs such as "The Defenders" and Ed Sullivan's "Toast of the Town." His indelible mark, however, was as the producer of films such as *Midnight Cowboy, The French Connection, Something Wild*, and *Silence of the Lambs*, for which he won an Oscar® for Best Picture. He often cast himself in roles such as the sourpuss FBI man in *Married to the Mob* and a jury member in *Philadelphia*. Utt worked with another Winston-Salem-born Oscar® winner, screenwriter and playwright Ted Tally (1952-), who won an Academy Award® for his screen adaptation of *Silence of the Lambs*.

Emmy® nominee and Forsyth County native Rolonda Watts attended Salem Academy and Spelman College, where she developed a love for theatre and writing. One of her early jobs was as a reporter at WFMY-TV in Greensboro. She later worked in New York as a reporter and morning news anchor for NBC's "Today" and as an anchor, reporter, and moderator for WABC-TV's "Eyewitness News Conference." She followed her first talk show, "Attitudes," with a stint as a weekend anchor and producer for "Inside Edition." Her internationally syndicated talk show, "The Rolonda Show," ran for four seasons. Since then, she has played Vivica Shaw on ABC's "Sister, Sister." Her other credits include "Days of Our Lives" and "Live with Regis and Kelly." She now lives in Los Angeles, where she runs Watts Works Productions.

Winston-Salem Star Tracks

Brookstown Inn Bed & Breakfast
200 Brookstown Avenue (336-725-1120; www.brookstowninn.com)

By virtue of its location, history, and guest list, the elegant and historic Brookstown Inn is known as the "Hotel of the Arts." Constructed around 1837, it is located near Old Salem (see pages 243-45), downtown arts venues, and the North Carolina School of the Arts (see pages 241-43). The inn's celebrity guests have included actor and comedian Jerry Lewis, poet and actress Maya Angelou, rhythm-and-blues artist Freddie Jackson, bluegrass legend Doc Watson, and the late actor John Ritter, who was in town for a NCSA dedication. Ritter also filmed scenes for the TV movie "Holy Joe" in nearby Lewisville at Westbend Vineyards.

You'll find brick walls, high ceilings, and exposed beams in the cozy rooms decorated with European and American antiques and reproductions. Listed on the National Register of Historic Places, the 71-room inn was originally a textile mill. Its fourth floor served as a dormitory for female workers, who signed their names and drew on a "Graffiti Wall," which is preserved under glass. The guest rooms feature tin chandeliers, hand-stitched quilts, and handcrafted accessories. The lovely and comfortable surroundings, modern amenities, and Southern hospitality will make you feel like a celebrity.

Adam's Mark Winston-Salem

425 North Cherry Street (336-725-3500; www.adamsmark.com)

The Adam's Mark is the official headquarters hotel for the National Black Theatre Festival (see below). Celebrity sightings have included Denzel Washington, Sidney Poitier, Malcolm-Jamal Warner, Melba Moore, Ben Vereen, Kim Fields, Richard Roundtree, Lillias White, and Billy Dee Williams. Keri Russell of "Felicity" fame and UNC alumnus Dan Cortese, perhaps best known for his role on "Veronica's Closet," stayed here while making "The Lottery."

Located downtown, the Adam's Mark is a grand hotel that offers modern accommodations. Its event venues include the Forsyth and Mark 2 ballrooms and the adjoining Benton Convention Center, where the NBTF's opening-night red-carpet gala is held.

National Black Theatre Festival

Performances take place at various downtown Winston-Salem venues. For information, call 336-723-2266 or visit www.nbtf.org.

The best time for stargazing in Winston-Salem is every odd year during the first week of August, when red carpets are rolled out for an unparalleled theatrical event. Since 1989, the National Black Theatre Festival has attracted award-winning stage and screen actors.

★ ★ ★ ★ ★ ★ ★ ★ ★ ★

NBTF is the brainchild of Larry Leon Hamlin, founder of the North Carolina Black Repertory Company. Past festival chairs have included such luminaries as Academy Award® winners Sidney Poitier and Denzel Washington. The parade of stars with ties to North Carolina productions has included Ruby Dee ("Having Our Say: The Delany Sisters' First 100 Years"); poet, actress, and Winston-Salem resident Maya Angelou ("The Runaway"); Cicely Tyson (*The Color Purple*); Louis Gossett, Jr. (*To Dance with Olivia*); Al Freeman, Jr., and Richard Roundtree (*Once Upon A Time . . . When We Were Colored*); Danny Glover ("Freedom Song"); and Yolanda King (*Trick Dribble*). Other stars at the festival have included Della Reese ("Touched by an Angel"); Broadway and TV actress Melba Moore; Malcolm-Jamal Warner ("The Cosby Show"); Oprah Winfrey; Hattie Winston ("Becker"); Harry Belafonte; actress and vocalist Leslie Uggams; actress and dancer Debbie Allen-Nixon ("Fame"); actor, playwright, and Pender County native Samm-Art Williams ("Dance on Widow's Row"); Diahann Carroll ("Julia"); Kim Fields ("The Facts of Life"); Angela Bassett (*Waiting to Exhale*); and Tim Reid ("WKRP in Cincinnati"). Approximately 50,000 people attend the six-day festival.

NBTF includes theatrical productions, workshops, poetry readings, galas, and special events. The National Black Film Festival runs concurrently; it offers screenings of independent documentaries.

Southeastern Center for Contemporary Art

750 Marguerite Drive (336-725-1904; www.secca.org).
SECCA is open from 10 A.M. to 5 P.M. Tuesday through Saturday and from 2 P.M. to 5 P.M. on Sunday; the hours are extended to 8 P.M. on the first Thursday of each month. An admission fee is charged.

★ ★ ★ ★ ★ ★ ★ ★ ★ ★

A nonprofit visual-arts organization since 1956, the Southeastern Center for Contemporary Art (SECCA) is located in the elegant English hunt-style mansion once owned by James G. Hanes. Its spacious rooms showcase quarterly exhibitions of contemporary art by renowned national and regional artists.

Celebrities whose work has been shown in SECCA exhibitions include actor Billy Dee Williams (*Star Wars: Return of the Jedi*); photographer and director Gordon Parks (*Shaft*); artist and musician Yoko Ono; and artist, filmmaker, musician, and Talking Heads co-founder David Byrne (*True Stories*). Williams and Byrne have attended exhibition events.

Contemporary music, drama, dance, and film are showcased in the 300-seat McChesney Scott Dunn Auditorium, which also serves as a venue for the National Black Theatre Festival (see pages 253-54). Contemporary films are screened at a large outdoor theatre on the grounds.

Last Lives films in Yanceyville.
COURTESY OF PIEDMONT-TRIAD FILM COMMISSION

Caswell County Locations

Yanceyville/Carolina Pinnacle Studios

Carolina Pinnacle Studios is located at 336 West Main Street in Yanceyville. Visitors are limited to exterior viewing. For information, call 336-694-7785 or visit www.carolinapinnaclestudios.com. Piedmont Community College is located at 331 Piedmont Drive in Yanceyville. Its office is open from 8 A.M. to 5 P.M. Monday through Friday. For information, call 336-694-5707 or visit www.piedmont.cc.nc.us.

Yanceyville is a small Southern town with big Hollywood dreams.

The Caswell County seat since 1792, Yanceyville was the richest town in North Carolina before the Civil War. Evidence of this wealth can be seen in the exquisite antebellum architecture of the structures in the town's National Register Historic District.

The stunning Caswell County Courthouse, constructed around 1861, and other downtown buildings appear in "The Gardener's Son" and *Last Lives*, a favorite Sci-Fi Channel flick.

Last Lives, starring Judge Reinhold and C. Thomas Howell, was produced by Magder Entertainment Studios, a movie production company formerly located in Yanceyville. Today, the studio operates under new owners Blackwell & Associates, along with a new banner, Carolina Pinnacle Studios. The studio complex is situated on 315 acres near downtown. Its centerpiece is the two-story, 18th-century Dongola Plantation mansion, which is surrounded by a 15-acre lake, forests, and a former rest home retrofitted for offices and lodgings. Four sound stages provide 50,000 square feet of space. An additional 32,000 square feet are used for offices, shops, and equipment.

Faiger Blackwell, a Caswell County native, operates Carolina Pinnacle Studios, one of only a few minority-run movie studios in the United States. Its first feature-film credit was *Trick Dribble*, written by and starring former Harlem Globetrotter Tyrone "Hollywood" Brown. Yolanda King, the daughter of the Reverend Martin Luther King, Jr., stars as an ailing mother whose love inspires her son to enter a basketball tournament and use his winnings to pay for her kidney transplant. Scenes were also filmed at nearby Bartlett Yancey High School. In 2001, the studio began producing its own films, the first of which was *Mrs. President*, a story about a black woman appointed president by Congress.

Located just 40 miles from Greensboro and Durham and 60 miles from Raleigh, Yanceyville has positioned itself as a convenient, film-friendly community. Carolina Pinnacle Studios has partnered with Piedmont Community College's Caswell campus in providing internships and resources for students enrolled in the school's programs in film/video-production technology and digital effects/animation technology. Recent class projects have included *The Murder of John Stephens*, *Kickin' the Door In*, and *Some Words with a Mummy*.

CREDITS

Mrs. President (2001); *Trick Dribble* (1999); *Last Lives* (1997); "The Gardener's Son" (PBS, 1976)

Film Schools in North Carolina

Duke University in Durham offers programs in film, video, and digital production. For information, visit www.duke.edu/web/film.

The North Carolina School of the Arts (see pages 241-43) in Winston-Salem offers a BFA in filmmaking. For information, visit www.ncarts.edu.

St. Augustine's College in Raleigh offers a BA in film and a two-year advanced film program. For information, visit www.st-aug.edu/divs/lis/vpa.html.

UNC-Greensboro offers a BA in media studies and an MFA in film and video. For information, visit www.uncg.edu/bcn.

UNC-Wilmington (see pages 66-67) offers a BA in film studies. For information, visit www.uncw.edu/filmstudies.

Haywood Community College in Clyde offers an AAS degree in film and video production technology. For information, visit www.haywood.edu.

Piedmont Community College in Yanceyville offers an AAS degree in film and video production technology. For information, visit www.piedmont.cc.nc.us.

The School of Communication Arts in Raleigh offers programs in digital filmmaking, art and animation, media arts, animation production, and motion graphics. For information, visit www.higherdigital.com.

Cape Fear Community College in Wilmington offers a curriculum in film and video production technology. For information, visit www.cfcc.edu.

Alamance County Locations

Snow Camp Historic Site

Drama Road, Snow Camp (800-726-5115 or 336-376-6948; www.snowcampdrama.com). Outdoor theatrical productions are offered during the summer months. Ye Old Country Kitchen is open year-round. It serves lunch and dinner on Wednesday, Thursday, Friday, and Sunday and all three meals on Saturday.

Bring an appetite for history, theatre, and down-home cookin' when you visit Snow Camp. Located on the north bank of Cane Creek, Snow Camp is an 18th-century settlement named by hunters who camped here during the winter of 1748, when the camp was covered with two to three feet of snow.

Today, Snow Camp interprets colonial and antebellum life through living-history and theatrical productions. Its grounds include an indoor theatre and an outdoor amphitheater where scenes from Stephen King's *Children of the Corn II: Final Sacrifice* were filmed. Two historical dramas—*The Sword of Peace,* about the

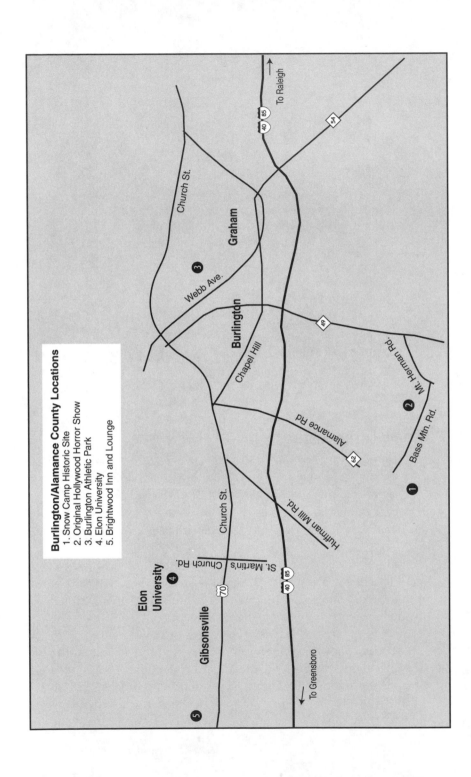

American Revolution, and *Pathway to Freedom*, about the Underground Railroad—are ~~performed during~~ the summer months.

Also on the grounds is Ye Old Country Kitchen, hailed as "one of North Carolina's best down-home restaurants" by UNC-TV. The homey restaurant appears in *Vampires Anonymous*, a comedy about a vampire who attends a 12-step program to overcome his forbidden appetite. Burlington natives Dean and Starr Jones executive-produced the independent film, which was a hit on the festival circuit. The Joneses are professional makeup and special-effects artists who also produce The Original Hollywood Horror Show (see below).

Credits

Vampires Anonymous (2003); *Children of the Corn II: Final Sacrifice* (1993)

The Original Hollywood Horror Show

Bass Mountain Road, Snow Camp (336-513-6938; www .originalhollywoodhorrorshow.com). From I-40/I-85, take Exit 147 and drive approximately five miles on N.C. 87 South to Mount Herman-Rock Road. After five miles on Mount Herman-Rock Road, bear right onto Mount Herman Church Road. Drive 0.2 mile and turn left on Bass Mountain Road. The Original Hollywood Horror Show will be on your right after five miles. It is open weekend nights in October and weekday nights during Halloween week. An admission fee is charged.

Dean and Starr Jones know how to tap into your darkest fears. The Burlington brothers prove their prowess each year when they produce The Original Hollywood Horror Show, perhaps the country's best haunted-house attraction. Each October since 1990, the special-effects artists have created unparalleled Halloween thrills. The sinister stage they set up on a rural Alamance County farm draws approximately 10,000 visitors.

Not surprisingly, the brothers grew up watching horror movies. But it wasn't until their parents took them to the set of *Killers Three* in nearby Ramseur that they became hooked on film.

The 1968 gangster movie inspired the boys to try a few special effects of their own, using makeup and prosthetics. Both studied at the film school at the University of North Carolina-Greensboro. They boast 75-plus credits, including the TV series "Star Trek: Deep Space Nine," for which Starr earned Emmy® Awards in 1992 and 1993.

The Original Hollywood Horror Show is a must-see. Its special effects rival any in the movies. Its indoor and outdoor sets appear in the comedy *Vampires Anonymous*, which the Joneses executive-produced. Film junkies can always count on a chilling performance by OHHS's live actors, who portray tortured souls, vampires, mummies, corpses, zombies, monsters, trolls, aliens, mad scientists, and psychos with chain saws! The outlandish sets, forbidding costumes, and creepy sound effects are sure to unnerve even the most experienced haunted-house buffs.

Film junkies should also visit the Hollywood Movie Makeup Museum and Frightmare Gift Shop.

Dean and Starr's North Carolina makeup and special-effects credits include *Vampires Anonymous* (2003); *Briar Patch* (2001); *Morning* (2000); "Above Suspicion" (USA, 2000); *Doomsday Man* (1999); "Patron Saint of Liars" (CBS, 1998); *Last Lives* (1997); *Chasers* (1994); "Black Magic" (Showtime, 1992); *Billy Bathgate* (1991); *Trapper County War* (1989); *Blue Velvet* (1986); *Alien Outlaw* (1985); *Order of the Black Eagle* (1985); and *The Dark Power* (1985). They were the executive producers of *Dead Inn* (1997).

Burlington Athletic Park

1450 Graham Street, Burlington (336-222-0223; www.btribebaseball.com). Games are scheduled from May through September.

Minorleagueballparks.com describes Burlington Athletic Park as a "cozy—almost cute—ballpark." This vintage stadium hosts home games of the Burlington Indians, whose affiliation with the Cleveland Indians dates back to 1958. Its small, no-frills grandstand stood in Danville, Virginia, until it was torn down and shipped to Burlington in 1960.

BAP provided the look sought by location managers for away games in Bull Durham. Crash Davis (Kevin Costner) and Nuke LaLoosh (Tim Robbins) aren't the only stars to appear here. Real-life local characters include "the Green Acres Lady," who, at the bottom of the sixth inning, belts out the theme from the 1960s TV show "Green Acres." Another sideshow at the park is Bingo, the team mascot, whose chants and antics personify the minor-league tradition—just like in the movies.

CREDITS

Bull Durham (1988)

Elon University

The university is located in the town of Elon in western Alamance County. The administrative offices are open from 8:30 A.M. to 5 P.M. Monday through Friday except on school holidays. For information, call 336-278-7415 or visit www.elon.edu.

Elon University's foray into the movies was as a Southern college in the Spike Lee basketball film *He Got Game*.

In reality, Elon boasts a strong athletics program and stands out academically as well, according to *U.S. News & World Report's Best Colleges* guide. Elon has also earned kudos from *Time, Harvard Schmarvard*, the *Princeton Review*, and the *Kaplan College Guide*. And Elon's campus is among the loveliest in the South. Perhaps that's why most of its one-day shoot for *He Got Game* took place outside in the courtyard.

Each spring, the Elon University School of Communications sponsors the Elon Film Festival, which showcases independent films by filmmakers in the Southeast. Notable alumni include producer Kenneth Utt (see pages 250-51) and 1998 graduate Jonathan Campbell, whose first film, *the big white wall*, received noteworthy reviews.

CREDITS

He Got Game (1998)

Brightwood Inn & Lounge

6501 Burlington Road (U.S. 70) at N.C. 61, Gibsonville (336-449-4737). The diner is open daily from 4:30 P.M. to 1 A.M.

Elvis left the building, but the good news is that he left his legacy when he departed. The King of Rock-and-Roll ate at this quaint roadside diner on his way to Greensboro after a 1955 concert at Williams High School in Burlington. The Brightwood Inn still looks much as it did back then. Even today, visitors can order a hamburger with lettuce and tomato and a glass of milk, just like Elvis did. On the day he stopped in, his band sat in Booth 1. Elvis dined with a Burlington beauty in Booth 4, where photos and memorabilia now immortalize the pop icon.

The King made 31 movies between 1956 and 1969, starring opposite Hollywood's brightest starlets. His 1968 movie *Speedway*, also starring Nancy Sinatra and Bill Bixby, filmed at the Charlotte Motor Speedway, now known as Lowe's Motor

Speedway (see pages 324-25). Elvis also appears post-mortem in *Forrest Gump*, which was filmed partly in North Carolina.

Film junkies, Elvis fans, and nostalgia buffs will appreciate the Brightwood Inn's authenticity. What began in 1936 as a truck stop along a farm-lined state highway now backs up to an upscale residential development. The contrast is delightfully conspicuous. Inside, check out the hats hanging behind the counter along the paneled wall; they were donated (or left behind) by Brightwood customers. The menu offers good, down-home food—steaks, fried chicken, burgers, sandwiches, onion rings, and choice desserts like homemade banana pudding. Be sure to ask for Lucille Little, the waitress who actually served Elvis.

To see this landmark for yourself and enjoy a brush with Elvis's past, follow old Burlington Road (U.S. 70). You'll find the Brightwood Inn straddling the Alamance County/Guilford County line.

Randolph County Locations

The Randolph County Tourism Development Authority is located at 919 South Cox Street in Asheboro. For information, call 800-626-2672; 336-626-0364; or visit www.visitrandolph.org.

Randolph County's claims to fame are pottery, exotic animals, racing, and a handful of movies.

Four generations of NASCAR's first family—the Petty family—hail from Level Cross, where Petty Enterprises and the Richard Petty Museum (see page 268) are based. Since they are central figures in the history of stock-car racing, their stories and talents are sought by filmmakers. The Petty drivers' Randolph County film credits include *The Petty Story*, based on Wilmington author Bill Neely's book *Stand on It*, and the documentary "Beyond the Glory," which filmed at the Richard Petty Museum.

Non-racecar productions have also been drawn to the rural charms of Randolph County. Thanks to the over 90 acclaimed potteries and the North Carolina Pottery Center in Seagrove, a slew of documentaries about noted potters has emerged in recent years. Among them is *Crawdad Slip*, which features fifth-generation potter Sid Luck. Located just minutes away, Asheboro is home to the world-class North Carolina Zoological Park, which boasts movie credits including "Healthy Pets, Healthy People."

Studio and independent productions, while few and far between, include the gangster movie *Killers Three*, which filmed in downtown Ramseur, Liberty, and Seagrove. The Dick Clark production stars Clark, Robert Walker, Jr., and Merle Haggard, who stayed at the Day's Inn (formerly the Holiday Inn) in Asheboro. Based on a Stephen King short story, *Children of the Corn II: Final Sacrifice* made use of rural locations in Randolph County, including the eerie cornfield that became the film's centerpiece.

House of Cards, starring Kathleen Turner and Tommy Lee Jones, found an idyllic farmhouse and land in Trinity on which to build its unusual spiral staircase to the moon. Ten years later, the surprise hit horror flick of 2003, *Cabin Fever*, filmed at the Terrell Farm in Trinity. The establishing shots in Spike Lee's *He Got Game* include aerial footage of rural Randolph County farms.

CREDITS

Vampires Anonymous (2003) filmed at the Rockingham County Jail. *Escape* (1990) filmed at Randolph Mills. The county's other credits are *Cabin Fever* (2003); "Beyond the Glory" (Fox, 2000); *Crawdad Slip* (1999); *He Got Game* (1998); "Highway 64: A Passing View" (UNC-TV, 1996); *House of Cards* (1993); "Healthy Pets, Healthy People" (WNET, 1993); *Children of the Corn II: Final Sacrifice* (1993); Charles Kuralt's "North Carolina Is My Home" (UNC-TV, 1991); "The Seagrove Potters" (UNC-TV, 1985); "The Gardener's Son" (PBS, 1976); *The Petty Story* (1972); *Killers Three* (1968); and *The American Farm* (1962).

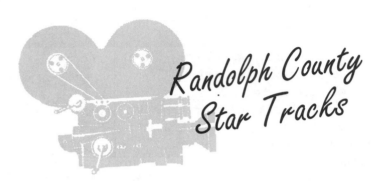

Randolph County Star Tracks

Richard Petty Museum

*142 West Academy Street, Randleman (336-495-1143; www
.pettyracing.com/www2/main/museum.html). The museum is open
from 9 A.M. to 5 P.M. Monday through Saturday. An admission
fee is charged.*

You can almost smell rubber burning and hear cars zoom-
ing at the Richard Petty Museum, a showcase of stock-car memorabilia that interprets the life and times of the NASCAR legend. RPM (pun intended!) features Petty's #43 stock cars and
engines, trophies, awards, mementos, photos, a gift shop, and a
video presentation.

Richard Petty, who lives nearby, has played himself in numerous North Carolina productions, including *Days of Thunder*
with Tom Cruise; *Stroker Ace* with Burt Reynolds; "43: The Richard Petty Story"; *Speedway* with Elvis Presley and Nancy Sinatra;
and "Beyond the Glory," which filmed at RPM.

"Tecumseh: The Last Warrior" films at Belew's Creek.
COURTESY OF PIEDMONT-TRIAD FILM COMMISSION

Stokes County Locations

Belew's Creek

N.C. 65, Walnut Cove. The "cool side" is open during daylight hours. The two public access areas are the Pine Hall Access and the Piney Bluff Access. You can contact Carolina Camp-In and Marina by calling 800-344-2628.

The word *creek* belies the significance of this body of water. Located near Walnut Cove north of Winston-Salem, Belew's Creek forms Belew's Lake, a 3,863-acre recreation destination. Also the site of Duke Power's largest coal-burning power plant, which generates over 50 million kilowatt hours of electricity each day, Belew's Creek has a "hot side" that's used as a cooling station and a "cool side" that's used for boating, camping, and other activities.

Location managers found a wooded area on the "hot side" ideal for the misty waterfront scenes in "Tecumseh: The Last Warrior." The North Carolina School of the Arts documentary *The Legend of Two-Path*, which traces the history of the Algonquin Indians through the eyes of an Algonquin youth, also shot at Belew's Lake. It shows daily at Roanoke Island Festival Park (see page 141) in Manteo. Some of *Cabin Fever's* water scenes featuring Jordan Ladd were filmed at Belew's Creek, but the cabin scenes were shot in Mount Airy at Camp Raven Knob.

CREDITS

Cabin Fever (2003); *The Legend of Two-Path* (1998); "Tecumseh: The Last Warrior" (TNT, 1995); *The Dark Power* (1985)

Cabin Fever films in Surry County.
COURTESY OF PIEDMONT-TRIAD FILM COMMISSION

Surry County Locations

Priddy's General Store

2121 Shepherd Mill Road, Danbury (336-593-8786). The store is open from 8:30 A.M. to 6 P.M. Monday through Saturday.

Tucked away in Danbury, a tiny hamlet near Hanging Rock State Park, is the century-old Priddy's General Store, where scenes were shot for the surprisingly successful horror flick *Cabin Fever*. First-time director Eli Roth hand-picked locations for the film. He found Priddy's to be the perfect country store, thanks in part to its light yellow exterior and aged pine floors. Film junkies will recognize it in scenes that feature old man Cadwell, the eccentric, gray-bearded storekeeper. The 70-something actor, Robert Harris, does not work at the store but is a Triad resident who impressed Roth with his first speaking role.

Cabin Fever revolves around five college friends who spend

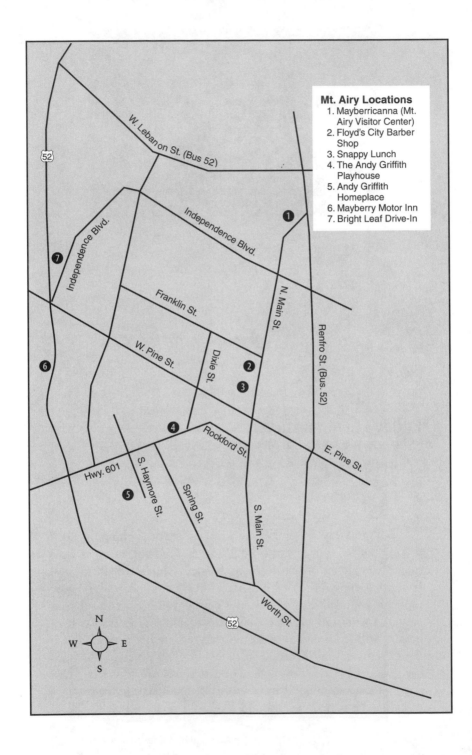

Mt. Airy Locations
1. Mayberricanna (Mt. Airy Visitor Center)
2. Floyd's City Barber Shop
3. Snappy Lunch
4. The Andy Griffith Playhouse
5. Andy Griffith Homeplace
6. Mayberry Motor Inn
7. Bright Leaf Drive-In

their vacation in a cabin deep in the woods. When one of them contracts a flesh-eating virus, their vacation takes a definite turn for the worse. The film stars James DeBello, Joey Kern, Jordan Ladd (daughter of Cheryl Ladd), and Cerina Vincent, who attended the East Coast premiere in Greensboro's Carolina Theatre (see pages 221-22).

CREDITS

Cabin Fever (2003)

Q: What movie, filmed partly in Surry County, originally boasted a David Lynch executive producer credit but dropped it before the film was distributed?

A: *Director Eli Roth's 2003 horror flick* Cabin Fever *created lots of buzz on the film-festival circuit and drew comparisons to cult classics like* The Evil Dead. *Offbeat director David Lynch of* Blue Velvet *fame originally put his name on the film as executive producer. However, he later had it removed because his name was drawing attention from up-and-coming protégé Roth. When the film was released, it simply recognized Lynch with a special thanks at the end of the credits. Lion's Gate Films bought the United States distribution rights (with a promise for a sequel) during the 2002 Toronto Film Festival.* Cabin Fever *filmed primarily in the Triad at locations in Mocksville, Ramseur, Trinity, High Point, Belew's Creek, Mount Airy, and Danbury. The campsite was at Raven Knob Boy Scout Camp, located at 266 Raven Knob Road, off Ledonia Church Road just west of Mount Airy. The hospital scenes were shot at the Davie County Hospital, located at 223 Hospital Street in Mocksville. The farmhouse, Terrell Farm, is in Trinity on Hoover Hill Road. Several water scenes were filmed at Belew's Creek (see pages 269-70).*

The Mount Airy Visitor Center, home of the Andy Griffith Museum
COURTESY OF GREATER MOUNT AIRY CHAMBER OF COMMERCE

Mayberricana: The Mayberry Experience

Mount Airy is on U.S. 52 about 30 miles northwest of Winston-Salem. For information, contact the Mount Airy Visitor Center by calling 800-576-0231 or 336-789-4636 or by visiting www.visitmayberry.com.

Film junkies seeking a Mayberry experience will find it in the foothills of the Blue Ridge Mountains in a town called Mount Airy. Actor Andy Griffith was born and spent most of his childhood here. In a 2002 ceremony dedicating a stretch of U.S. 52 Bypass as the Andy Griffith Parkway, Griffith publicly confirmed what had long been rumor: Mount Airy was indeed the inspiration for the idyllic TV town of Mayberry. Thus, Mount Airy finally staked its rightful claim in the annals of small-town Americana. Film junkies might call it "Mayberricana."

Your Mayberry experience should begin at the Mount Airy Visitor Center, at 615 North Main Street, where the Andy Griffith Museum houses the world's largest collection of memorabilia related to the actor. Props and mementos trace Griffith's television career from Mayberry to "Matlock." Predating his television days are school annuals, photographs, and posters from Broadway shows like *No Time for Sergeants* and films like *Angel in My Pocket* and *Onionhead.* The collection, owned by AG's lifelong friend Emmett Forrest, includes clippings, costumes, scripts, stills, and childhood furniture.

Just one block south is the business district, where you can get a sandwich at the Snappy Lunch (see pages 278-79); an ice-cream sundae at the Blue Bird Diner, located at 206 North Main Street; and a haircut at Floyd's City Barber Shop (see pages 277-78). You can even take pictures of a jail cell and a 1950s squad car at the local jail, located at 215 City Hall Street. At every turn are souvenir shops like Specialty Gifts, located at 140 North Main. Just a few blocks away at Mayberry Square are gems like Wally's Service, a restored 1937 service station where you can drink an RC Cola and munch on a Moon Pie. Film junkies can see a show at the Andy Griffith Playhouse (see pages 279-80) and spend the night at Andy's homeplace (see page 281) or at the Mayberry Motor Inn (see page 282).

Each year in late September, Mount Airy stages Mayberry Days, a three-day festival that celebrates the show and its legacy. The festival's parade features vintage cars, 1960s music, actors from "The Andy Griffith Show," and lookalike fans. During the festival, the downtown post office stamps mail with a "Mayberry, N.C.," postmark, and the Bright Leaf Drive-In Theatre on U.S. 52 North screens Andy Griffith movies.

★★★★★★★★★★★★★

North Carolina's Drive-In Theatres

Drive-in theatres recall days gone by. According to the National Organization of Theatre Owners, North Carolina boasted 209 drive-ins during the industry's peak in the late 1950s. Nostalgic film junkies should visit this shrinking list of North Carolina drive-ins still in operation.

Badin Road Drive-In, 2411 Badin Road, Albemarle (704-983-2900)

Belmont Drive-In, 314 McAdenville Road, Belmont (704-825-6044; www.belmontdrivein.us)

Bright Leaf Drive-In, Mount Airy
COURTESY OF GREATER MOUNT AIRY CHAMBER OF COMMERCE

Bessemer City/Kings Mountain Drive-In, Bessemer City Road, Kings Mountain (704-739-2150)

Bright Leaf Drive-In, U.S. 52 North, Mount Airy (336-786-5494)

Eden Drive-In Theatre, 106 Fireman Club Road, Eden (336-623-9669)

Raleigh Road Drive-In, 3336 Raleigh Road (U.S. 1), Henderson (252-438-6959)

Starlite Drive-In, 2523 East Club Boulevard, Durham (919-688-1037)

Sunset Drive-In, 3935 West Dixon Boulevard (U.S. 74), Shelby (704-434-7782)

George "Goober" Lindsey stops by Floyd's City Barber Shop for a trim.
COURTESY OF GREATER MOUNT AIRY CHAMBER OF COMMERCE

Surry County Star Tracks

Floyd's City Barber Shop

*129 North Main Street, Mount Airy (336-786-2346). The
shop is open from 7 A.M. to 5 P.M. on Monday, Tuesday,
Wednesday, and Friday and from 7 A.M. to 3 P.M. on Saturday.
Haircuts cost less than $10.*

Bearing a striking resemblance to Floyd on "The Andy
Griffith Show," Russell Hiatt is Mount Airy's star barber. He's
been cutting hair at his shop since 1948. Don't just peek, go
inside and behold an authentic Mayberry-style barbershop.
Adept at multitasking, Hiatt chats with clients and visitors, sells
souvenirs, poses for pictures, and waves at passersby—all the

★ ★ ★ ★ ★ ★ ★ ★ ★ ★

while smiling and cutting hair. Customers don't seem to mind the interruptions; the shop's two chairs are rarely empty. Don't be surprised if Hiatt asks to take your picture for his wall of fame, which now boasts over 20,000 images, including celebs Oprah Winfrey, Lou Ferrigno of "The Incredible Hulk" fame, and George Lindsey, who played Goober on "The Andy Griffith Show."

Snappy Lunch

125 North Main Street, Mount Airy (336-786-4931). Snappy Lunch is open from 5:45 A.M. to 1:45 P.M. on Monday, Tuesday, Wednesday, and Friday and from 5:45 A.M. to 1:15 P.M. on Thursday and Saturday.

For a taste of Mayberry, the Snappy Lunch is the place. An early episode of "The Andy Griffith Show" entitled "Andy the Matchmaker" refers to Mount Airy's oldest dining establishment, in business since 1923. Other references have followed in Andy's version of the song "Silhouettes" and more recently in a tune by bluegrass artists The VW Boys. But it's the show's reference that draws media attention and customers.

The Carolina blue exterior and 1950s sign beckon customers. Inside, the no-frills diner sports paneling, faux brick, booths, tables, a counter, and an old-fashioned grill. Lining the walls are stills from "The Andy Griffith Show," pen-and-ink drawings of Mayberry, and photos of Mount Airy landmarks.

Menu items include breakfast plates, burgers, hot dogs, and sandwiches at unbelievable prices. The house specialty—a generous fried porkchop sandwich served with mustard, chili, slaw, and onions—sells for less than three bucks. Sandwiches are prepared by owner Charles Dowell and served by friendly relatives and longtime employees.

Back in the 1940s, high-school students provided much of Snappy's lunch trade. Today, approximately 90 percent of lunch

★ ★ ★ ★ ★ ★ ★ ★ ★ ★

You can find a taste of
Mayberry in Charles Dowell's
famous porkchop sandwich at
the Snappy Lunch.
PHOTOGRAPH BY BILL RUSS.
COURTESY OF N. C. DIVISION
OF TOURISM, FILM, & SPORTS
DEVELOPMENT

patrons are visitors from across the United States and abroad. Celebrity customers have included Oprah Winfrey, Lou Ferrigno of "The Incredible Hulk," Mount Airy country-music diva Donna Fargo, Andy Griffith as a young boy, and George Lindsey (Goober) and Aneta Corsaut (Helen Crump) from "The Andy Griffith Show."

Snappy Lunch has been featured on the Travel Channel's "TV Road Trips," CNN, the Food Channel, TV Land, and UNC-TV.

The Andy Griffith Playhouse

218 Rockford Street, Mount Airy (800-286-6193 or 336-786-7998; www.surryarts.org). Call for a schedule of events. Guided tours are available by appointment. An admission fee is charged.

Andy Griffith's earliest performances came during the 1930s and 1940s at Rockford Street School, a 1920s structure that

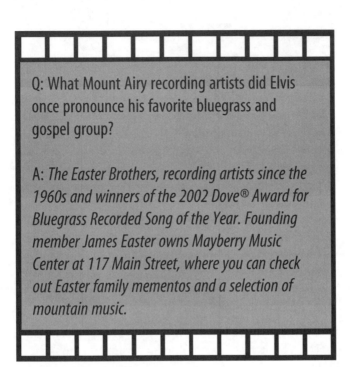

Q: What Mount Airy recording artists did Elvis once pronounce his favorite bluegrass and gospel group?

A: *The Easter Brothers, recording artists since the 1960s and winners of the 2002 Dove® Award for Bluegrass Recorded Song of the Year. Founding member James Easter owns Mayberry Music Center at 117 Main Street, where you can check out Easter family mementos and a selection of mountain music.*

now serves as the Andy Griffith Playhouse. The theatre retains its original stage floor. The lobby displays a photograph of Griffith with screenwriter Harvey Bullock of "The Andy Griffith Show" and another of him in his role as Sheriff Taylor.

The playhouse hosts theatrical and musical performances and is a venue for the Mayberry Days Festival each September. In 2002, actors Howard Morris (Ernest T. Bass) and Betty Lynn (Thelma Lou) of "The Andy Griffith Show" performed in the play *Love Letters.* On the third Saturday of each month, Barney Fife look-alike David Browning hosts talent competitions. On Thursdays, visitors can enjoy free bluegrass jam sessions.

Andy and Cindi Griffith visit Andy's homeplace,
now a bed-and-breakfast.
COURTESY OF GREATER MOUNT AIRY CHAMBER OF COMMERCE

Andy Griffith Homeplace

711 East Haymore Street, off U.S. 601, Mount Airy (800-565-5249 or 336-789-5999; www.andyshomeplace.com). Advance reservations are required. Check-in is at the Hampton Inn on U.S. 601.

Tucked away on a side street in a well-kept 1930s and 1940s neighborhood is the house where Andy Griffith spent much of his childhood. The modest frame home exemplifies the simple life with its two-bedroom, one-bath floor plan. Since it is now operated as a bed-and-breakfast, film junkies can spend the night in the pristine yellow cottage. Period antiques and Griffith memorabilia decorate the humble abode. Visitors here can kick back, let the world wind down, read a book under a generous shade tree out back, and admire the mountain vista from a covered swing on the front lawn. Neighbors even wave and tip their hats as they pass. Indeed, life is good in Mayberry.

★ ★ ★ ★ ★ ★ ★ ★ ★ ★

Mayberry Motor Inn

U.S. 52 Bypass, Mount Airy (336-786-4109; www .mayberrymotorinn.com)

The unassuming, one-story, red-brick-with-white-trim Mayberry Motor Inn beckons from U.S. 52 Bypass. A 1960s squad car and a vintage pickup truck parked out front are the first clues that there's something extraordinary about this place.

If you enter the nostalgic lobby filled with Mayberry memorabilia, you'll meet the world's friendliest innkeepers, Alma and Luther Venable, who take great pride in preserving the property's Mayberry qualities. Clean, comfy, and tastefully appointed rooms make an overnight stay here quite pleasant. There's even a room (Room 109) that's been designated "Aunt Bee's Room." It's lovingly decorated with furniture, clothes, trinkets, and accessories that Alma purchased from Frances Bavier's (Aunt Bee's) estate auction in 1990, which was held to benefit UNC-TV. The room is shown by appointment.

You just never know who might check into the Mayberry Motor Inn. Lookalikes for cast members of "The Andy Griffith Show" are frequent customers. Howard Sprague and Barney Fife lookalikes are regulars. In fact, David Browning of the Mount Airy Visitor Center is a dead ringer for Barney. He shows up at the inn at random moments to provide photo opportunities and write out autographed "citations" for guests.

Actual celebrity guests here have included country vocalist Donna Fargo, who hails from Mount Airy, and Hal Smith, who played Otis Campbell on "The Andy Griffith Show." Howard Morris (Ernest T. Bass) has also stopped by to give his regards.

Your best bet is to call ahead for reservations. The inn is booked a year or more in advance for Mayberry Days in September.

★ ★ ★ ★ ★ ★ ★ ★ ★ ★

Q: In what North Carolina town did Aunt Bee choose to live out her last years?

A: *When Emmy®-winning actress Frances Bavier retired from her role on "The Andy Griffith Show," she moved to Siler City, a town often discussed on the show. She lived as a recluse with more than a dozen cats in a house on West Elk Street until she died of heart failure in 1989 at age 86. Film junkies can travel to Oakwood Cemetery on North Chatham Avenue in Siler City to visit Aunt Bee's final resting place. Her eight-foot granite monument displays her birth and television names.*

Charlotte skyline
PHOTOGRAPH BY BILL RUSS
COURTESY OF N. C. DIVISION OF TOURISM, FILM & SPORTS DEVELOPMENT

The Charlotte Area

"So, what brings you to my town?"

*T*hus sayeth Shallow Hal (Jack Black) just before his fateful elevator ride with Tony Robbins. And it kind of sums up Charlotte's outlook on the world, and perhaps films in particular. The banking and business center has made bold bids for the big time in recent years, landing (then losing, then landing again) an NBA franchise and bringing in the Carolina Panthers of the NFL, who went all the way to the Super Bowl in 2004. Charlotte's stature and hip quotient have grown to the point that the Queen City is a hot spot among American cities. The film industry is certainly included. A healthy art/indie/film fest scene is found here, and Hollywood has come calling several times over the years. Unfortunately, as in the above quote, Charlotte often goes unnamed, or is a stand-in for New York or Boston (or someplace).

But there's plenty for film junkies to explore. Films shot in Charlotte have certainly featured the big stars. There's still lingering buzz over the *Shallow Hal* shoot that brought Black, Gwyneth Paltrow, Jason Alexander, and the Farrelly brothers to town. And even though Charlotte itself isn't identified, many of the locations retain their real-life names in the film.

Charlotte *is* named in *Nell,* in which it's sort of a big, bad city that frightens Jodie Foster's title character, a place filled with folks who want to exploit her. And *Juwanna Mann,* featuring Wilson, North Carolina, native Miguel A. Nunez, Jr., as a male pro basketball player for the Charlotte Beat *and* a female pro basketball player for the Charlotte Banshees, is based in the Queen City. Lowe's Motor Speedway appears in several films, including the Tom Cruise/Nicole Kidman vehicle *Days of Thunder, Born to Race,* and the Burt Reynolds/Loni Anderson race flick *Stroker Ace.*

Indigenous independent filmmakers have done a much better job revealing the city's true character. Ross McElwee's hilarious *Sherman's March* caused a big stir upon its release. And award-winning writer and director Dorne Pentes explored an underside of the Queen City in *The Closest Thing to Heaven.* Writers with Tar Heel ties have seen screen versions of their work filmed in the Charlotte area. In 1998, Hallmark Hall of Fame released "Saint Maybe," based on the novel of the same name by Raleigh's Anne Tyler. "The Price of Heaven," which aired in 1997, is an adaptation of *Blessed Assurance* by Nash County's Allan Gurganus.

The surrounding area also has a brief but impressive list of projects. Steven Spielberg's *The Color Purple* filmed in neighboring Anson and Union counties, as did the horror hit *Evil Dead II: Dead by Dawn.* Nearby Shelby, home to Earl Owensby Studios, provided locations for the Oscar®-nominated *Reuben, Reuben.*

For information, contact the Charlotte Convention and Visitors Bureau by calling 800-231-4636 or visiting www.visitcharlotte.org. You can contact the North Carolina Division of Tourism, Film and Sports Development by calling 800-VISITNC or by visiting www.visitnc.com.

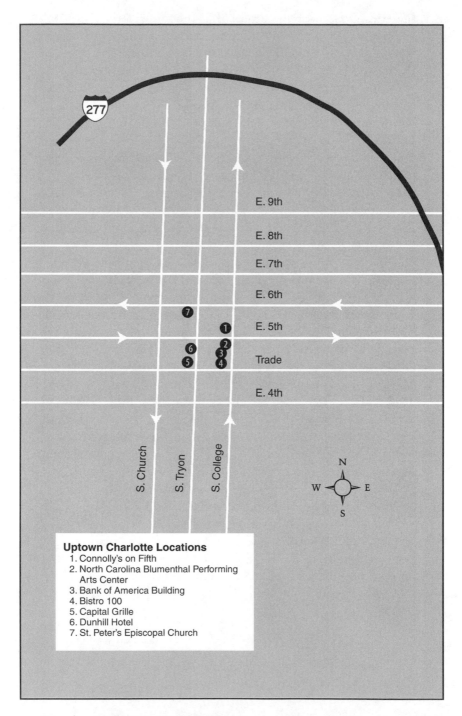

E. 9th

E. 8th

E. 7th

E. 6th

E. 5th

Trade

E. 4th

S. Church

S. Tryon

S. College

N
W—E
S

Uptown Charlotte Locations
1. Connolly's on Fifth
2. North Carolina Blumenthal Performing
   Arts Center
3. Bank of America Building
4. Bistro 100
5. Capital Grille
6. Dunhill Hotel
7. St. Peter's Episcopal Church

Stars perform and party at the North Carolina
Blumenthal Performing Arts Center.
PHOTOGRAPH BY FLOYD HARRIS

Uptown Charlotte Locations

North Carolina Blumenthal Performing Arts Center/Bank of America Building and Plaza

The Blumenthal Center is located at 130 North Tryon Street, adjacent to the Bank of America Corporate Center and Founders Hall. Spirit Square is located at 345 North College Street. Free walk-up tours are available the second and fourth Mondays of each month between 11 A.M. and 2 P.M. For information, call 704-372-1000 or visit www.blumenthalcenter.org.

The North Carolina Blumenthal Performing Arts Center is *the* place of excitement for the Uptown Charlotte arts district.

In *Shallow Hal*, the "JPS" Building is the Bank of America Building.
PHOTOGRAPH BY FLOYD HARRIS

Since the center opened in 1992, over 5 million people have seen or participated in its arts and educational programs. The Blumenthal's three performance spaces are the perfect places to catch stars like Bill Cosby, Hal Holbrook, Larry Gatlin, David Copperfield, and Russell Simmons; nationally touring Broadway productions; films; and performances by the Charlotte Symphony Orchestra, the Charlotte Repertory Theatre, Opera Carolina, the North Carolina Dance Theatre, Carolina Voices, the Charlotte Philharmonic Orchestra, Moving Poets Theater of Dance, and the Carolinas Concert Association.

The Blumenthal Center and the surrounding Bank of America Building and Plaza have a number of movie connections.

In August 2001, Andie MacDowell and co-stars Greg Kinnear and Dennis Quaid premiered their HBO film, "Dinner with Friends," at the Blumenthal as a benefit for Andie's Camp for Kids, which allows children with diabetes to visit the North Carolina mountains for a week.

The Blumenthal also includes the Spirit Square Center for Arts and Education, located in the former First Baptist Church. Spirit Square offers a Monday-night movie series and a Saturday-morning program of kids' flicks in the 720-seat McGlohon Theatre, named for Charlotte jazz pianist Loonis McGlohon, who collaborated with fellow Tar Heel Charles Kurault on a number of projects. The McGlohon stage was used as the Dallas stage location in the miniseries "Shake, Rattle and Roll: An American Love Story."

The Tryon Street entrance to the Blumenthal appears in *Juwanna Mann* in the arbitration scenes featuring Jamal (Miguel A. Nunez, Jr.) and Lorne (Kevin Pollack).

Juwanna also shot some interiors on the 29th floor of the Bank of America Building, once causing a small flood when a light set off the sprinkler system. In *Shallow Hal*, the BOA Building is the JPS Building, where Hal (Jack Black) works for Rosemary's father, Steve Shanahan (Joe Viterelli).

Exteriors of Spirit Square stand in for Boston in the David Caruso/Ving Rhames art-heist flick *Body Count*.

The shops and restaurants in the Bank of America Plaza are popular with visiting celebrities and with cast, crew, and patrons of Blumenthal performances.

CREDITS

Juwanna Mann (2002); *Shallow Hal* (2001); "Shake, Rattle and Roll: An American Love Story" (CBS, 1999); *Body Count* (1998)

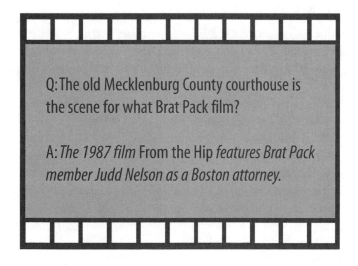

Q: The old Mecklenburg County courthouse is the scene for what Brat Pack film?

A: *The 1987 film* From the Hip *features Brat Pack member Judd Nelson as a Boston attorney.*

Capital Grille, featured in *Shallow Hal*, is a favorite of celebs.
PHOTOGRAPH BY FLOYD HARRIS

Capital Grille

201 North Tryon Street (704-348-1400; www.thecapitalgrille.com).
Lunch is served Monday through Friday and dinner daily.

The Capital Grille offers an elegant, traditional dining experience. It's almost a step back in time, with its white linen tablecloths, oil paintings, and rich oak paneling and wine racks. It's the perfect place for special family occasions and intimate dates.

Unfortunately, such events collide at just the wrong time in *Shallow Hal*. The Capital Grille is the setting for the dinner date of the slightly confused Hal (Jack Black) and the suddenly interested Jill (Susan Ward). It's also the night Rosemary (Gwyneth Paltrow) and her parents (Joe Viterelli and Jill Christine Fitzgerald) come to dine. That's Darius Rucker of Hootie and the Blowfish as the maître d' greeting the Shannahans. Hal and Rosemary have a scene at the pay telephones, then the distraught Rosemary talks to Hal on her cell phone just outside the grill, where the signature lions are visible in the background.

The Capital Grille offers upscale dining in 15 other cities besides Charlotte. It is known for its aged steaks, chops, seafood, and outstanding wine list. And while a rock star won't be there to seat you in real life, famous diners at the Charlotte restaurant have included the Eagles, in town just before their Farewell I Tour in 2003, and numerous NASCAR, sports, and entertainment stars.

CREDITS

Shallow Hal (2001)

The Dunhill Hotel has been used to depict a hotel in cities such as New York and Philadelphia.
PHOTOGRAPH BY FLOYD HARRIS

Dunhill Hotel

237 North Tryon Street (800-354-4141; 704-332-4141; www.dunhillhotel.com)

Though Charlotte occasionally gets to play itself on film, many times it's used as a stand-in for another (usually nameless or Northeastern) city. Though that's a little rough on civic pride, it's fortunate for filmmakers, as they get the perfect big-city feel at places like the historic Dunhill Hotel.

The elegant Dunhill serves as the Philadelphia hotel in the miniseries "Shake, Rattle and Roll: An American Love Story" and as the New York hotel in *Juwanna Mann*. Interiors of the Dunhill are used in the latter movie when members of the Charlotte Banshees gather in a room after knocking off the New

York team. Juwanna (Miguel A. Nunez, Jr.) finds out "she" is not as adept at girl talk as he thought in the funny scene, which includes Michelle (Vivica A. Fox) and Latisha (Kim Wayans).

The Dunhill, built around 1929, is in the heart of Charlotte's thriving Uptown arts and business district. Its distinctive architecture has made it a downtown landmark since its opening. It is Charlotte's only member of Historic Hotels of America.

CREDITS

Juwanna Mann (2002); "Shake, Rattle and Roll: An American Love Story" (CBS, 1999)

Jack Black gets the "hottie's" phone number in front of St. Peter's Episcopal Church in *Shallow Hal*.
PHOTOGRAPH BY FLOYD HARRIS

St. Peter's Episcopal Church

115 West Seventh Street at North Tryon (704-332-7746).
Visitors are limited to exterior viewing except during the various services scheduled throughout the week.

Is it symbolic that Shallow Hal (Jack Black) is standing before a church the first time he asks for the phone number of a girl he sees for her inner beauty? Probably not.

Indeed, it is in front of downtown Charlotte's historic St. Peter's Episcopal Church that Hal exchanges numbers with Katrina (Brooke Burns) after their cab ride. Or at least he tries to, not sure if the "Dog Eat Dog" host and former "Baywatch" babe is putting him on. St. Peter's is also seen in "Shake, Rattle and Roll: An American Love Story"; you'll notice the 1950s-era cars parked in front.

Founded in 1843 as the city's first Episcopal mission, St. Peter's is the mother church for Charlotte's Episcopal community. Famous visitors here have included Confederate president Jefferson Davis, who attended with members of his cabinet just after the assassination of his counterpart, Abraham Lincoln. The church was influential in beginning the city's first health-care facilities for minorities and the poor. It continues in a wide variety of ministries in its third century.

Nothing shallow about that at all.

CREDITS

Shallow Hal (2001); "Shake, Rattle and Roll: An American Love Story" (CBS, 1999)

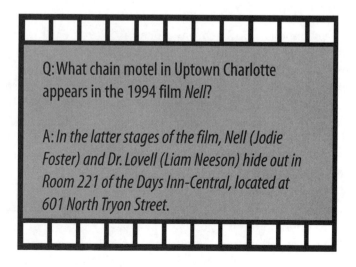

Q: What chain motel in Uptown Charlotte appears in the 1994 film *Nell*?

A: In the latter stages of the film, Nell (Jodie Foster) and Dr. Lovell (Liam Neeson) hide out in Room 221 of the Days Inn-Central, located at 601 North Tryon Street.

Uptown Charlotte Star Tracks

Connolly's on Fifth

115 East Fifth Street, between North Tryon and North College (704-358-9070). Connolly's is open nightly.

At Connolly's on Fifth, the slogan is "If you can't drop in, smile as you pass." Film junkies who pass this inviting Irish pub across from the North Carolina Blumenthal Performing Arts Center may miss the chance to hoist a pint or two next to a favorite personality—if they recognize the star in the discreetly dark interior. That was the case with veteran NBC anchorman Tom Brokaw, who sent an autographed picture to Connolly's with a note saying that he enjoyed his several moments of anonymity in the Queen City.

Pictures of classic Irish films abound at Connolly's, and there's even likely to be an authentic Irishman pouring your Guinness behind the bar.

The Farrelly brothers enjoyed the friendly, cozy confines of Connolly's during the filming of *Shallow Hal*. Andie MacDowell,

Dennis Quaid, and Greg Kinnear hosted an informal party after the premiere of the HBO film "Dinner with Friends" at the Blumenthal. MacDowell organized the Charlotte premiere to raise money for Andie's Camp for Kids in Asheville.

Be sure not to pass this place by!

Bistro 100

100 North Tryon Street (704-344-0515). Bistro 100 is open from 11:30 A.M. to 10 P.M. Monday through Thursday, from 11:30 A.M. to 11 P.M. on Friday and Saturday, and from 11 A.M. to 9 P.M. on Sunday.

The arty, cosmopolitan atmosphere, French/American cuisine, and prime location near the Bank of America Corporate Center and the North Carolina Blumenthal Performing Arts Center have made Bistro 100 a favorite of locals and visiting celebrities for the past decade. Upon entering the airy, upbeat

Q: What infamous Charlotte recording studio has hosted some of the biggest names in music and recorded numerous radio, TV, and film soundtracks, including *The Prince of Egypt?*

A: *Reflection Sound Studios. Its clients have included REM, the Dixie Chicks, Glen Frey, Whitney Houston, and Hootie and the Blowfish.*

restaurant and bar off the BOA Plaza, film junkies are met with a montage of posters (in English and French) signed by famous entertainment and sports figures. A random sampling includes Hilary Swank, Olympia Dukakis, Brooke Shields, Marla Gibbs, and Kevin Costner. Regis Philbin had to settle for having lunch from Bistro 100 delivered to his trailer while he was in Charlotte to promote "Who Wants to Be a Millionaire." Other famous showbiz diners have included actor turned president Ronald Reagan, William Shatner, Robert Goulet, Barbara Eden, Ralph Macchio, Justine Bateman, and Montel Williams. Andy Griffith, Don Knotts, and George "Goober" Lindsey could have held their own "Andy Griffith Show" reunion here. Sports stars like Tim Duncan, Jeff Gordon, and Dennis Conner have enjoyed the fine food and uptown atmosphere, as has Carolina Panthers honcho Jerry Richardson.

Other Charlotte Locations

Ovens Auditorium

*2700 East Independence Boulevard (704-335-3100; www
.ovensauditorium.com). The auditorium is open from 9* A.M. *to 5*
P.M. *Monday through Friday and on the weekends and evenings
when events are held.*

Ovens Auditorium is so alluring, with its outdoor fountains
and rose gardens, that location managers for "Shake, Rattle and
Roll: An American Love Story" used it to represent the Atlanta
Auditorium.

During the 1980s, Ovens hosted the world premiere of the
Burt Reynolds/Loni Anderson stock-car film *Stroker Ace,* which
filmed at Charlotte Motor Speedway (now Lowe's Motor
Speedway) and other locations. More than a thousand fans
waited outside to greet Burt and Loni and co-stars Jim Nabors and
former NFL player Bubba Smith. A black-and-white checkered

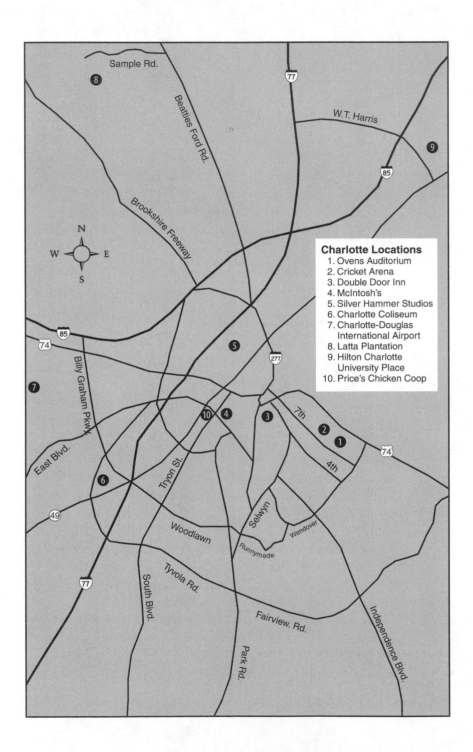

Charlotte Locations
1. Ovens Auditorium
2. Cricket Arena
3. Double Door Inn
4. McIntosh's
5. Silver Hammer Studios
6. Charlotte Coliseum
7. Charlotte-Douglas International Airport
8. Latta Plantation
9. Hilton Charlotte University Place
10. Price's Chicken Coop

carpet was rolled from the limousines to the entrance. The premiere benefit gala that followed included music by Wilmington native Charlie Daniels, who composed and sang the theme song "Stroker Ace."

Since Ovens opened in 1955, the world's biggest celebrities—among them evangelist and Charlotte native Billy Graham and comedian Bob Hope—have graced the stage of this 2,500-seat auditorium. Jazz songstress Ella Fitzgerald, blues great Ray Charles, pianist *extraordinaire* Liberace, Bruce Springsteen, Billy Joel, B. B. King, Tony Bennett, Melissa Etheridge, Willie Nelson, Jimmy Buffett, and Marilyn Manson have performed here. Mel Gibson, in town filming *The Patriot*, attended a 1999 Sting concert at Ovens Auditorium. Recent Broadway shows at Ovens have included *The Graduate*, starring Kelly McGillis as Mrs. Robinson, and *Seussical, the Musical*, starring Olympic gymnast Cathy Rigby as the Cat in the Hat.

CREDITS
"Shake, Rattle and Roll: An American Love Story" (CBS, 1999)

Q: What 1974 film starring Stephen Boyd of *Ben-Hur* fame, Cheryl Ladd of "Charlie's Angels," and Chuck Woolery of "Love Connection" held its world premiere at Charlotte's Park Terrace Theatre?

A: *Boyd arrived in 1974 for the world premiere of* The Treasure of Jamaica Reef, *a shark action movie partially financed by then-mayor John Belk of Charlotte. The film did poorly until it was re-released as* Evil in the Deep *in 1976, a year after* Jaws *came out.*

Cricket Arena

2700 East Independence Boulevard (704-335-3100; www .cricketarenacharlotte.com). From May through September, the ticket office is open from 10 A.M. to 5 P.M. Monday through Friday. From October through April, it is open from 10 A.M. to 5 P.M. Monday through Saturday.

Neon colors, checkerboard tile floors, and brightly lit concession stands welcome visitors to the Cricket Arena, formerly Independence Arena. Built in 1955, the distinctive dome was Charlotte's original coliseum. It served as the city's premier entertainment facility until the new coliseum opened in 1988.

In the early 1980s, the old coliseum was used as a location for *Stroker Ace*, based on Bill Neely's novel *Stand on It*. Director Spike Lee came here to shoot montage footage for *He Got Game*, starring Denzel Washington. Lee returned to shoot *The Original Kings of Comedy*, a performance documentary featuring four comedians: Cedric the Entertainer, Steve Harvey, D. L. Hughley, and Bernie Mac. Touted as the most successful American comedy tour in history, the show returned to end its North American run with a two-night stand in the same venue where it began in 1997—the old Charlotte Coliseum.

Home to the Charlotte Checkers of the East Coast Hockey League, Cricket Arena hosts a variety of sports and entertainment events.

CREDITS

The Original Kings of Comedy (2000); *He Got Game* (1998); *Stroker Ace* (1983)

Double Door Inn

218 East Independence Boulevard (704-376-1446). The club is open from 11 A.M. to 2 A.M. Monday through Friday and from 8:30 A.M. to 2 A.M. on Saturday and Sunday.

It's played both a ski lodge and a 1950s club in the movies. But

★★★★★★★★★★★★★★

Schizoid Locations

Hollywood is notorious for shooting in one region and passing it off as another.

"Dawson's Creek" filmed in North Carolina yet was set in Massachusetts. North Carolina locations often stand in for other states. To name only a few, Lake Lure stands in for the Catskill Mountains in *Dirty Dancing*; Lake James for Upstate New York in *The Last of the Mohicans* and for a New England inlet in *The Hunt for Red October*; Durham for Boston in *Once Around*; Chimney Rock for Upstate New York in *Firestarter*; Shelby for New England in *Reuben, Reuben*; Wilmington for Long Island in *Weekend at Bernie's*; Rocky Mount for Dallas in *Love Field*; and Marshville for rural Georgia in *The Color Purple*.

Contrary to popular belief, neither the original nor the remake of *Cape Fear* filmed along North Carolina's Cape Fear River. The original 1962 film lensed in Savannah, Georgia, and the 1991 remake in Fort Lauderdale and Miami, Florida. More recently, *Message in a Bottle* was set on North Carolina's Outer Banks but filmed along Maine's coast. The film adaptation of Nicholas Sparks's *The Notebook* was set in New Bern yet filmed in Charleston, South Carolina. The 2001 sleeper *Who Is Cletis Tout?* starring Christian Slater and Tim Allen, lensed in Canada, even though the story—which, ironically, is about mistaken identity—is set in North Carolina. That one *really* hurt, but not as much as losing Academy Award® nominee *Cold Mountain*. Based on the novel of the same name by Charles Frazier, a North Carolina writer, the script is set in the North Carolina mountains. So it filmed in North Carolina, right? Wrong. Romania was cast in that role, with only a few flyover shots of the Blue Ridge Mountains—home of the *real* Cold Mountain. Talk about schizoid!

in real life, it has hosted some of the all-time blues greats.

The Double Door Inn, Charlotte's oldest live-music establishment, appears in *Shallow Hal* as the mountain weekend destination for Hal (Jack Black), Rosemary (Gwyneth Paltrow), Walt (Rene Kirby), and Nurse Tanya (Nan Peeler, or Sascha Knopf, during the ride up). And it's the place where Hal's jealousy surfaces when they run into Rosemary's old Peace Corps flame, Pretty Boy Ralph (Zen Gesner), and his sidekick, Li'i Boy (Joshua Shintani/Ron Darling). The nationally renowned hot spot is also seen in "Shake, Rattle and Roll: An American Love Story" as the Chantilly Club.

Since 1973, the list of bluesmen at the Double Door has been a who's who. A sampling includes Eric Clapton, Stevie Ray Vaughan, Willie Dixon, Tinsley Ellis, Delbert McClinton, Buddy Guy, Leon Russell, and Elvin Bishop. Local and regional players are also featured, especially on Monday's "All-Star Night," when you never know who might show up.

CREDITS

Shallow Hal (2001); "Shake, Rattle and Roll: An American Love Story" (CBS, 1999)

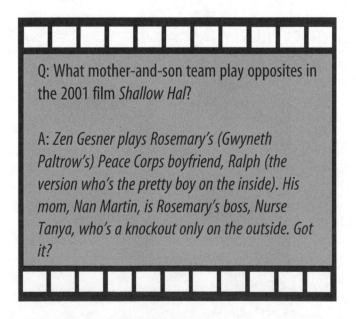

Q: What mother-and-son team play opposites in the 2001 film *Shallow Hal?*

A: *Zen Gesner plays Rosemary's (Gwyneth Paltrow's) Peace Corps boyfriend, Ralph (the version who's the pretty boy on the inside). His mom, Nan Martin, is Rosemary's boss, Nurse Tanya, who's a knockout only on the outside. Got it?*

McIntosh's

1812 South Boulevard (704-342-1088). McIntosh's is open from
5 P.M. to 10 P.M. Monday through Thursday and from 5 P.M. to
11 P.M. on Friday and Saturday.

Shallow Hal never indicates that it's set in Charlotte, but a
number of local spots are specifically named. Such is the case with
McIntosh's, a Queen City favorite known for serving prime rib,
steak, lobster, lamb dishes, and desserts such as Grand Marnier
soufflé in a casual, sophisticated atmosphere. McIntosh's also has
one of the city's best wine lists, a choice of 17 single-malt
scotches, and even an assortment of premium cigars.

McIntosh's is the place where Hal (Jack Black) finds out it's
not "cheap steel" that's causing Rosemary (Gwyneth Paltrow) to
keep breaking chairs. Look closely for Farrelly brothers regular
Rob Moran as Tiffany the hostess.

Credits

Shallow Hal (2001)

Silver Hammer Studios

817 Hamilton Street (704-377-4161; www.silverhammer.com).
Visitors are limited to exterior viewing.

Film junkies can't tour Silver Hammer Studios, probably
because it stays busy with commercial and industrial film
production. Though the filming of television shows and feature
films has been sporadic here, Silver Hammer does boast a number
of credits, including sets for *Shallow Hal; Juwanna Mann;* "Shake,
Rattle and Roll: An American Love Story"; and "Having Our Say:
The Delany Sisters' First 100 Years."

A full-service film and video production house, SHS offers
three sound stages of varying sizes and applications. There's also
a casting studio and production office space. The facility, located
on a 22-acre site in downtown Charlotte, is home to three post-
production and recording companies—Bridge Productions,
Silver Hammer Rentals, and Catwalk Digital—which collectively provide a full range of services; camera, lighting, and grip

rentals; and support personnel.

Juwanna Mann (2002); *Shallow Hal* (2001); "Shake, Rattle and Roll:
An American Love Story" (CBS, 1999); "Having Our Say: The
Delany Sisters' First 100 Years" (CBS, 1999)

Charlotte Coliseum
*100 Paul Buck Boulevard, off Tyvola Road (704-357-4738;
www.charlottecoliseum.com). The ticket office is open from
10 A.M. to 5 P.M. Monday through Friday; it is closed Saturday
and Sunday except on event days.*

Between concerts and athletic events, the new Charlotte
Coliseum is available as a movie location.

For *Juwanna Mann*, filmmakers scouted arenas nationwide and
found what they needed in Charlotte. Even before the coliseum
was selected, the script called for home and away games of the
fictitious UBA Charlotte Beat and WUBA Charlotte Banshees.
With only 15 days to create and shoot three different coliseums
in the same location, the crew worked diligently—overnight,
sometimes—to design three different floors to represent arenas in
New York, Phoenix, and Charlotte. That feat was nearly as
impressive as the dual role of Miguel A. Nunez, Jr., who portrays
Jamal Jeffries and his female alter-ego, Juwanna Mann. Nunez
was born in New York City and raised in Wilson, North Carolina.

In the feature film *Eddie*, starring Whoopi Goldberg, the
Charlotte Coliseum stands in as Madison Square Garden during
New York Knicks games. Hundreds of human extras showed up
as fans—as did cardboard stand-ins.

Since 1988, the 24,000-seat structure has also hosted the
NCAA men's Final Four, the NCAA women's Final Four, and
Charlotte Hornets games. Until a new $200 million arena opens
in 2005, the coliseum will serve as the home of the WNBA's
Charlotte Sting and the city's newest team, the NBA's Charlotte
Bobcats.

Stars from the entertainment world who have performed at

the coliseum include Janet Jackson, Tina Turner, Prince, Bruce Springsteen, Robert Plant, Garth Brooks, Kiss, the Rolling Stones, and the Grateful Dead.

CREDITS
Juwanna Mann (2002); *Eddie* (1996)

Carolinas Aviation Museum and Charlotte/Douglas International Airport

Charlotte/Douglas International Airport is located at 4108 Airport Drive (704-359-8442; www.chacweb.com). The Carolinas Aviation Museum is open from 10 A.M. to 4 P.M. Tuesday through Friday, from 10 A.M. to 5 P.M. on Saturday, and from 1 P.M. to 5 P.M. on Sunday.

Dozens of aircraft and thousands of artifacts and historical documents preserve and interpret aviation history at the Carolinas Aviation Museum, established in 1992. Located in an original hangar built in 1936 at what is now Charlotte/Douglas International Airport (CLT), the museum includes working aircraft and static exhibits. Docents provide guided tours of the exhibits, which include retired aircraft, models, a DC-3, an OV 1-D Mohawk reconnaissance plane, and a hall of fame that honors Carolina aviation heroes. Since 500-plus flights pass through the airport daily, you can bet that more than a few of CLT's passengers hold celebrity status.

For "Shake, Rattle and Roll: An American Love Story," production designers dressed a wing of the airport as a LaGuardia terminal from the 1950s. One of the museum's vintage DC5s can be seen taxiing in the background. In "Best Friends for Life," starring Gena Rowlands and Wilmington resident Linda Lavin, the airplane scenes take place at Charlotte/Douglas International Airport, the region's gateway to the world. *Juwanna Mann's* airport ticket counter is here, too.

CREDITS
Juwanna Mann (2002); "Shake, Rattle and Roll: An American Love Story" (CBS, 1999); "Best Friends for Life" (CBS, 1998)

Latta Plantation

5225 Sample Road, Huntersville (704-875-2312; www
.lattaplantation.org). From May through August, the plantation
is open daily from 10 A.M. to 5 P.M. From September through
April, it is open from 10 A.M. to 5 P.M. Tuesday through
Saturday and from noon to 5 P.M. on Sunday. An admission fee
is charged.

A scenic country road winds its way to historic Latta Plantation, built around 1800 in the Federal style for James and Jane Knox Latta. The home and its lush natural setting make a dramatic appearance during the final helicopter sequence in the thriller "Terror in the Night," starring Justine Bateman of "Family Ties" fame and Joe Penny of "Jake and the Fat Man."

Listed on the National Register of Historic Places, the plantation's restored two-story frame house is decorated with family heirlooms. Once a cotton plantation, it's now a living-history museum and a working farm. Costumed interpreters demonstrate life in the early 19th century. Adjoining is a nature preserve with hiking and horseback-riding trails; visitors also enjoy canoeing and fishing in Mountain Island Lake.

CREDITS
"Terror in the Night" (Lifetime, 1994)

Hilton Charlotte University Place

8629 J. M. Keynes Drive (704-547-7444; www.hilton.com)

As the official hotel of Lowe's Motor Speedway, the Hilton Charlotte University Place attracts NASCAR types. Minutes away from the speedway and Uptown Charlotte, it's located beside a picturesque lake surrounded by specialty shops and restaurants.

The hotel's exterior and parking lot appear in the Tom Cruise race movie *Days of Thunder*. Look for them in the scene in which Cole Trickle (Cruise) engages in an impulsive car chase that prompts his surgeon and love interest, Claire (Nicole Kidman), to pronounce him an "infantile egomaniac." Thus began a real-life courtship between Cruise and Kidman that eventually led to marriage, more name-calling, and divorce.

In recent years, the renovated Hilton has added another tower.

CREDITS

Days of Thunder (1990)

Dilworth

Latta Park is located at 601 East Park Avenue (704-336-3375; www.cmhpf.org/essays/dilworth.html). Visitors are limited to exterior viewing of private homes from the street. No trespassing is allowed.

Film junkies will enjoy a leisurely drive through Dilworth, Charlotte's first streetcar suburb, to see movie locations and homes with celebrity connections. Novelist Carson McCullers worked on her 1937 novel, *The Heart Is a Lonely Hunter*, in a Victorian cottage at 311 East Boulevard. Movie star Randolph Scott, who grew up in Charlotte, lived at 1301 Dilworth Road before heading west in 1928 to star in Westerns.

Begun in 1891, Dilworth offers fine examples of Victorian and Colonial Revival residences. Designed as a mixed-use New South neighborhood, it includes Latta Park, a premier recreational park that once hosted Buffalo Bill and his Wild West Show. Dilworth businesses shine on the sliver screen. Pike's Old-Fashioned Soda Shop (see page 309) appears in *Shallow Hal*. The Morehead Inn (see pages 309-10) shows up in "A Mother's Right: The Elizabeth Morgan Story."

CREDITS

Shallow Hal (2001); "A Mother's Right: The Elizabeth Morgan Story" (ABC, 1992); "She Says She's Innocent" (NBC, 1991); *A Dream of Dilworth* (1991)

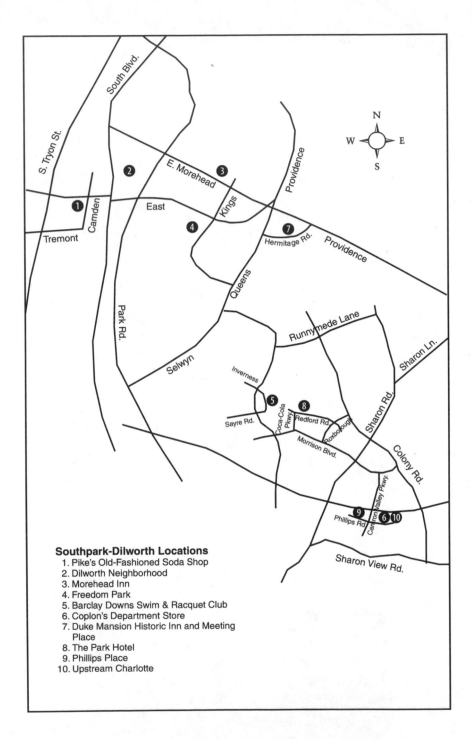

Southpark-Dilworth Locations
1. Pike's Old-Fashioned Soda Shop
2. Dilworth Neighborhood
3. Morehead Inn
4. Freedom Park
5. Barclay Downs Swim & Racquet Club
6. Coplon's Department Store
7. Duke Mansion Historic Inn and Meeting
   Place
8. The Park Hotel
9. Phillips Place
10. Upstream Charlotte

Pike's Old-Fashioned Soda Shop

Pike's Old-Fashioned Soda Shop is located at 1930 Camden Road (704-372-0092). It is open from 11 A.M. to 9 P.M. Monday through Friday, from 8 A.M. to 9 P.M. on Saturday, and from 8 A.M. to 2 P.M. on Sunday.

Known for its scrumptious milk shakes, cream sodas, floats, and sundaes, Pike's Old-Fashioned Soda Shop is a Dilworth favorite. It plays up the nostalgia with an authentic period soda-fountain counter. Fortunately, Pike's new owners have kept the name, the signature recipes, and the old-time atmosphere intact.

Film junkies can see the antique soda fountain used in *Shallow Hal* and order at the same counter where Hal (Jack Black) and Rosemary (Gwyneth Paltrow) share a . . . hmm . . . rather large milk shake. Other pharmacy artifacts used in the film were on loan from Pike's Pharmacy, located at 2133 Shamrock Drive, where they remain on display in the family-owned drugstore's renovated warehouse location.

The menu at Pike's Old-Fashioned Soda Shop includes such comfort foods as grilled cheese sandwiches, burgers, and the original owner's honey-dipped fried chicken.

CREDITS

Shallow Hal (2001)

Morehead Inn

1122 East Morehead Street (888-MOREHEAD or 704-376-3357; www.moreheadinn.com). Meeting and banquet rooms are available.

Built around 1917 for automobile mogul Charles Coddington, the elegant Morehead Inn was designed for entertaining. It remained a private residence until 1980, then became a country inn in 1984 and a movie location in 1992 for "A Mother's Right: The Elizabeth Morgan Story," starring Bonnie Bedelia. It serves as the London B&B where Dr. Elizabeth Morgan (Bedelia) hides out.

Overnight guests at this Select Registry property enjoy luxury accommodations with period furnishings and modern amenities. It is located in the prestigious Dilworth neighborhood (see page 307), minutes away from Uptown Charlotte.

CREDITS

"A Mother's Right: The Elizabeth Morgan Story" (ABC, 1992)

Freedom Park

1900 East Boulevard (704-336-2884). The park is open from dawn to dusk.

Charlotte's Freedom Park is a wonderful oasis amid the city's bustle, a favorite of kids, families, lovers, and amateur athletes. And you can add filmmakers to that list. *Shallow Hal* writers and directors Peter and Bobby Farrelly rave about Freedom Park in the movie's special-edition DVD. They must like the place, because it appears three times in the film! Freedom Park is where Hal (Jack Black) introduces Mauricio (Jason Alexander) to Rosemary (Gwyneth Paltrow). Of course, Mauricio thinks she must be behind the rhino. But then again, he's just turned down a date with Lindy (Manon von Gerkan) for the Beatles reunion concert . . . something about her toes. Anyway, the gorgeous stone bridge across the park's central pond is a recurring image in the film. Hal and Rosemary walk across it early in their relationship, and it appears in the background of other shots.

Freedom Park's amphitheater stands in for the Norfolk Amphitheater in the miniseries "Shake, Rattle and Roll: An American Love Story." The park is also seen in the Burt Reynolds race flick *Stroker Ace*.

In addition to being a favorite spot to hang out and feed the ducks, Freedom Park hosts special events and concerts throughout the year. Urban dwellers enjoy the 98 acres of walking paths (watch out for the BMX bikes and rollerbladers!), the athletic fields, the shelters, and the nature museum with its incredible butterfly pavilion.

Shallow Hal (2001); "Shake, Rattle and Roll: An American Love Story" (CBS, 1999); *Stroker Ace* (1983)

Barclay Downs Swim & Racquet Club, where Rosemary (Gwyneth Paltrow) makes a big splash in *Shallow Hal*.
PHOTOGRAPH BY FLOYD HARRIS

Barclay Downs Swim & Racquet Club

2800 Iverness Road. Visitors are limited to exterior viewing.

Tucked away in the middle of a sleepy residential area is Barclay Downs Swim & Racquet Club. *Shallow Hal's* cast and crew made quite a splash when they converged upon the small, private club. Peek over the fence and you'll see the infamous swimming pool where Rosemary (Gwyneth Paltrow) creates a splash so powerful that it ejects a young swimmer out of the water and into the trees. During filming, cannons were immersed and activated, causing massive amounts of water to explode upward when she dove in. You'll notice that the trees in the scene are long gone. Set designers placed them around the fence and pool to create a parklike appearance. Pool heaters were necessary to warm the water for the April filming. The diving board was temporarily swapped out for a trick board, allowing Gwyneth's stunt double maximum spring. No wonder crew members refer to the scene as "the swimming pool gag"!

CREDITS
Shallow Hal (2001)

Coplon's Department Store

6800C Phillips Place Court (704-643-1113). Coplon's is open from 10 A.M. to 6 P.M. Monday through Saturday.

To dress like a celebrity, you need not limit your shopping to Beverly Hills' Rodeo Drive and New York's Park Avenue. Coplon's at Phillips Place is an upscale department store where top designers frequently host trunk shows to introduce their new collections. Here, you'll find high-end clothing and footwear by designers such as Kate Spade, Chanel, Gucci, Armani, Prada, Gabbana, Dolce, and others that inhabit the fashion capitals. Serious shoppers will need lots of money. Sound intimidating? Well, at least peek inside to see where a memorable moment in the movie *Shallow Hal* takes place. Coplon's is where Hal (Jack Black) introduces himself to Rosemary (Gwyneth Paltrow) as she's shopping for rather large underwear—or, as he so rudely implies, a spinnaker for her sailboat. Film junkies will notice the strategically placed Coplon's shopping bag on the counter throughout the scene.

CREDITS
Shallow Hal (2001)

Charlotte Area Film Festivals and Events

Factory Films

The Light Factory, *the* place in Charlotte to explore contemporary visual art, presents Factory Films, a monthly event that includes screenings of provocative films; presentations by filmmakers, film historians, and critics; panels; and opportunities to network and socialize. The Light Factory also sponsors the Novel Concepts Film Festival, which highlights modern and classic literary adaptations. Prices vary per screening and event. The Light Factory is located at 345 North College Street. For information, visit www.lightfactory.org/factory_films.htm.

William Wilson Brown, Jr., Latin American Film and Video Festival

Held each November on the campuses of the University of North Carolina-Charlotte, Davidson College, Johnson C. Smith University, and Wingate University, this festival offers films exploring the richness and diversity of Latin American society. It aims to be educational as well as entertaining. The filmmakers are often on hand for lectures and question-and-answer sessions. Co-sponsored by UNCC and the Outreach Office of the Consortium in Latin American Studies at the University of North Carolina and Duke University, all screenings are free and open to the public. Most films are in their original language, with English subtitles.

Charlotte Film and Video Association Southern Exposure Film Forum

This series—featuring films from North and South Carolina, Tennessee, Georgia, Florida, Alabama, and Mississippi—offers cash prizes to outstanding work. Founded in 1987, the CFVA is a group of media-arts professionals in North and South Carolina dedicated to providing a solid filmmaking base to attract quality projects to the area. The film forum is held in November. For information, visit www.cfvonline.com.

Charlotte Film Society

For over 20 years, the Charlotte Film Society has brought foreign, classic, independent, and alternative films of all genres and origins to the Queen City. Expanded from its original subscription series of a dozen or so movies a year, the society now offers the "Second Week." It runs several films four times a day on the second week of each month (actually the second Friday to the next Thursday) at the Manor Theatre in Myers Park. During the following Friday-through-Thursday event, the films are screened at Movies at Birkdale in Huntersville. For information, visit www.charlottefilmsociety.com.

Real to Reel Film and Video Festival

During this festival, amateur and professional filmmakers screen their work at the beautiful Joy Performance Center in downtown Kings Mountain, North Carolina, 40 miles west of Charlotte. The festival is sponsored by the Cleveland County Arts Council, which holds a "Hollywood Past and Present" Premiere Party at the Arts Center in Shelby each year to kick things off. The festival will hit the five-year mark in 2004. For information, visit www.realtoreelfest.com.

Wild Wild South

Wild Wild South showcases the films of Charlotte's Dorne Pentes, one of the South's leading independent filmmakers. The UNC and New York University grad has written and directed *Confessions of a Southern Punk* (1991); *The Great Unpleasantness* (1993); *The Closest Thing to Heaven* (1996), which won Best Feature at the Atlanta Film Festival; and *Lullaby* (2003). Many of the Pentes films feature music from North Carolina's acclaimed alternative music scene, with maybe a little bluegrass thrown in. For information, visit www.wildwildsouth.com.

Other Charlotte Star Tracks

Price's Chicken Coop

1614 Camden Road (704-333-9866). Price's is open from 10 A.M. to 6 P.M. Tuesday through Saturday.

Although Charlotte is certainly a shining star of the New South, there's still some down-home to be found. That's certainly the case at Price's Chicken Coop, where you'll see a posted notice discouraging the use of cell phones and two-way radios while ordering. This South End hot spot, which is strictly takeout, is consistently voted by natives as serving the best fried chicken and soul food in Charlotte. For nearly 40 years, Price's has been offering up mouth-watering fare. On any day, you'll find several lines of folks and a motor pool of cars waiting.

The place was certainly a hit with the Farrelly brothers during the production of *Shallow Hal*. Filming came to a screeching halt for almost an hour one day as crew members munched Price's fried chicken at Freedom Park.

Presidents and movie stars have been
among the Duke Mansion's guests.
PHOTOGRAPH BY VAN MILLER
COURTESY OF THE DUKE MANSION INN AND MEETING PLACE

Duke Mansion Inn and Meeting Place

400 Hermitage Road (888-202-1009 *or* 704-714-4400;
www.dukemansion.org)

When the preeminent Myers Park suburb was developed,
Charlotte's wealthy bankers and retail, textile, and energy
executives were lured by its grandeur. Among them was James B.
Duke, the president of Southern Public Utilities Company (now
Duke Energy), who purchased and tripled the size of the Colonial
Revival-style Z. V. Taylor mansion, built around 1915. Today,
the 45-room, 12-bathroom Duke Mansion is listed on the
National Register of Historic Places. Since 1998, it has been
operated as a nonprofit bed-and-breakfast inn and meeting
venue.

A 150-foot fountain invites visitors to indulge in the
landscaped gardens and stay in one of the 20 luxurious guest
rooms. The mansion has welcomed national leaders like General
George Marshall, Eleanor Roosevelt, President John F. Kennedy,

and North Carolina governors. Celebrity guests have included Kevin Costner, Roger Daltrey, Lesley Stahl, Diane Rehm, Burt Reynolds, and Loni Anderson. Crooner and artist Tony Bennett used the mansion's kitchen garden as a painting subject during a visit in 2002. Literary guests have included Doug Marlette, Pat Conroy, and Nobel laureate Wole Soyinka.

The Park Hotel

2200 Rexford Road (800-334-0331 or 704-364-8220; www.theparkhotel.com)

European elegance, Southern charm, and coveted Four Star and Four Diamond ratings set The Park Hotel apart. The guest rooms and suites are tastefully appointed with classic furnishings and original artwork that lends a residential feel. This, combined with unsurpassed amenities, impeccable service, and proximity to upscale shopping and dining has appealed to movie stars Elizabeth Taylor, Whoopi Goldberg, and Cher; cast members from "Dawson's Creek"; and actor and comedians Jerry Seinfeld and Dennis Miller. Other famous guests have included recording artists Janet Jackson, Dave Matthews, Britney Spears, Christina Aguilera, Billy Joel, Elton John, New Kids on the Block, and the Red Hot Chili Peppers. Smoky's Grill at The Park is a favorite of NASCAR's Jeff Gordon.

Phillips Place

Fairview Road and Cameron Valley Parkway. To reserve accommodations, call 704-676-4886.

The place to see and be seen in Charlotte's popular South Park area is Phillips Place, where trendsetting boutiques, posh department stores, hip cafés and wine bars, a multiplex movie

theatre, and an organic food market coexist in an urban village setting.

Wait a minute. Is this really Charlotte, North Carolina? Even locals do double-takes when Hollywood types like Gwyneth Paltrow happen by. She caused quite a buzz when she shopped and dined at Phillips Place during the filming of *Shallow Hal*. Likewise, hearts were aflutter when Mel Gibson was out and about while filming *The Patriot*. He dined frequently at The Palm, a storied restaurant with Los Angeles origins. The Palm also hosted a benefit reception that preceded a preview screening of Golden Globe® and Academy Award® contender *Cold Mountain*, which filmed in Romania yet featured the North Carolina mountains. Two weeks prior to its theatrical release, *Cold Mountain* held a benefit screening at Phillips Place Cinemas. Actors Lucas Black and Winston-Salem's Kristen LaPrade were in attendance.

Phillips Place is a gated, pedestrian-friendly neighborhood. Condos are available for rent with a seven-day minimum. Celebrities feel right at home with upscale retailers such as Coplon's (see page 312), Restoration Hardware, Fore the Links, the Luna boutique, and Dean & DeLuca, all of which are located within walking distance. Restaurants like Upstream (see below) and The Palm make the grade with celebrity palates.

Upstream

6902 Phillips Place (704-556-7730; www.upstreamseafood.com).
The restaurant is open daily for lunch and dinner.

On warm, sunny afternoons and clear evenings, the sidewalk tables at Upstream hum with a decidedly Brentwood or Bel Air feel. Phillips Place Square, where this trendy restaurant is located, is much like the upscale West L.A. suburbs. No wonder Hollywood darling Gwyneth Paltrow returned several times

while filming *Shallow Hal*.

Enjoying a meal at Upstream is about as close as Charlotte gets to dining in West L.A. And it's everything you'd expect of a celebrity haunt, without being pretentious. At Upstream, you'll find exceptional cuisine, an extensive wine list, subtly elegant ambiance, and impeccable, friendly service. Upstream's famous guests have included Karen Allen of *Raiders of the Lost Ark* fame, Chris O'Donnell of *Batman Forever*, Andy Griffith, and NASCAR star Jeff Gordon. The champagne and oyster bar is a great place to mingle. There's even a banquet room where celebs like Michael Jordan have thrown parties attended by NBA stars and celebrity guests.

Renowned executive chef Tom Condron's genius is evident in the daily specials, the entrées, and the divine desserts. Dining at Upstream is a bit pricey, but for the ultimate film junkie dining experience, it's worth it.

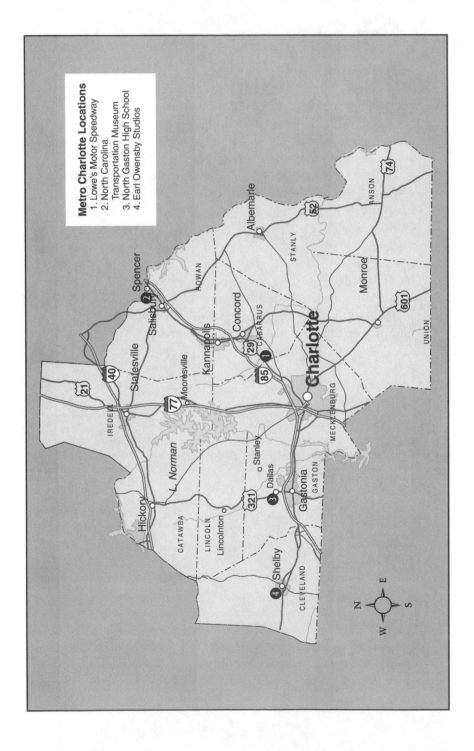

Metro Charlotte Locations
1. Lowe's Motor Speedway
2. North Carolina Transportation Museum
3. North Gaston High School
4. Earl Owensby Studios

Anson and Union County Locations

Anson and Union counties are due east of Charlotte on U.S. 74.
The rural filming locations are on private property.

Two wildly diverse films from the 1980s were made in the rural North Carolina counties of Anson and Union. They were directed by two of the top names in the business, one getting away from his trademark special effects, the other just starting out. Steven Spielberg's *The Color Purple* and Sam Raimi's *Evil Dead II: Dead by Dawn* are about as different as films can get. And yet parts of them were filmed at the same location.

The Color Purple was controversial for everything from its sexual and feminist themes to Spielberg's "audacity" in making a film about rural African-Americans in the early 1900s. Author Alice Walker won a Pulitzer Prize for her novel. She discusses the making of the film in her book *The Same River Twice: Honoring the Difficult*, which includes her original, unused version of the script. The lead role of Celie went to Whoopi Goldberg, a little-known standup comedian, while the supporting part of Sofia marked the film debut of Oprah Winfrey, whose talk show was just catching on in syndication. Both won Golden Globes® and were nominated for Academy Awards®. Goldberg and Winfrey have spoken of bonding while filming in rural North Carolina. Spielberg grew quite fond of Bojangles' chicken and biscuits.

The main house in the film is a vacant farmhouse off U.S. 74 and Lilesville-Morvan Road. The house is on private property and is not available to visitors. The church was moved here from another location in Anson County. The false front of Celie's house at the end of the film was built here. The town scenes were done in Marshville (the home of singer and actor Randy Travis), particularly along a two-block section of White Street between Main Street and U.S. 74. Mann Brothers Pharmacy is actually a produce store in real life. A livery stable, a storefront church, and the Blue Heaven Café were among the businesses created for the movie. Planks and dirt were put down to cover the sidewalks and pavement. A few remnants of the shooting are still around. Celie's dream of tossing golden chocolates to her sister was filmed on railroad tracks near Ansonville, and her trip to the immigration office was filmed at the Anson County Courthouse in Wadesboro.

Q: Four sequels to what popular 1977 movie filmed in Union County?

A: Smokey and the Bandit. *Writer and director Hal Needham kept many of the same characters for these "Bandit" TV movies, shot in 1994. Though Burt Reynolds, Sally Field, and Jackie Gleason weren't around, Brian Bloom starred as the Bandit. Guest stars included Tony Curtis, Elizabeth Berkley, Traci Lords, and Kathy Ireland.*

The Color Purple, nominated for a near-record 11 Oscars®, including Best Picture and Best Director, famously did not win any. But the good folks in Anson County honored the film at their Felix Awards in March 1986.

A year later, Raimi and crew showed up with a fraction of the budget but with their fear-wielding hearts in the right place and their tongues squarely in cheek. *Evil Dead II* didn't call for much in the way of locations: a cabin and some surrounding woods. Producer Bruce Campbell (who also stars as *EDII's* hero, Ash) found the same land off U.S. 74 used for *The Color Purple*, built the cabin and work shed from a couple of abandoned barns, and that was about it.

Evil Dead II is a high-concept satire disguised by gross-out gore and shock. Raimi's "shaky cam" technique and voice as the pervasive demon spirit make this a truly scary story that achieved cult status among horror fans.

Raimi has kept the offbeat vibe alive while producing the Wilmington-based TV series "American Gothic" and, of course, directing the *Spider-Man* series.

CREDITS

Evil Dead II: Dead by Dawn (1987); *The Color Purple* (1985)

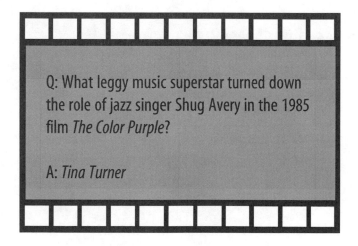

Q: What leggy music superstar turned down the role of jazz singer Shug Avery in the 1985 film *The Color Purple?*

A: *Tina Turner*

Dale Earnhardt, Jr., filming a commercial
on location at Lowe's Motor Speedway

Cabarrus County Locations

Lowe's Motor Speedway

5555 Concord Parkway South, Concord. To reach the box office, call 800-455-FANS or 704-455-3200. For tour information, call 704-455-3204. The speedway's website is www.lowesmotorspeedway.com. The box office is open from 9 A.M. to 5 P.M. Monday through Saturday and from 1 P.M. to 5 P.M. on Sunday. On nonevent days, tours are offered from 9:30 A.M. to 3:30 P.M. Monday through Saturday and from 12:30 P.M. to 3:30 P.M. on Sunday. An admission fee is charged.

Everyone's seen the 1.5-mile quad-oval Lowe's Motor Speedway on nationally televised races. Film junkies know it from the movies. Elvis Presley's *Speedway* was among the first full-length feature films to portray the exciting world of motorsports. The

King of Rock-'n'-Roll starred with Nancy Sinatra, Bill Bixby and Gale Gordon. The Charlotte Motor Speedway (as it was known back then) returned as the backdrop for the Burt Reynolds/Loni Anderson movie *Stroker Ace*, based on the novel *Stand on It* by Wilmington resident Bill Neely; another Neely book, *Grand National*, was adapted as *The Petty Story*. Later, the Tom Cruise vehicle *Days of Thunder* filmed here. Co-starring Nicole Kidman, Robert Duvall, and Randy Quaid, the film is among TNT's "New Classics" and airs regularly during NASCAR season.

The superspeedway stays busy year-round, especially in May and October during the major NASCAR races hosted here. The host of the longest race on the circuit, Lowe's Motor Speedway has been racing's premier facility since 1960. On nonevent days, visitors can tour the garage, Pit Row, and Victory Circle. After-ward, they can browse the gift shop's NASCAR memorabilia. When the speedway isn't hosting race teams or movie crews, there's still plenty of action like concerts, parties, fantasy camps, and tractor pulls.

CREDITS

Scenes from *Body Count* (1998) were shot along Speedway Bou-levard. The speedway's other credits include "Fast Women" (WTN/WE, 2001); *Don of the South* (2000); "Steel Chariots" (Fox, 1997); *Power Track* (1994); *Days of Thunder* (1990); *Born to Race* (1987); *Stroker Ace* (1983); *Stockcar!* (1977); *Speedway* (1968); *Red Line 7000: My Last Race for Coca-Cola* (1967); *Thunder in Carolina* (1960); numerous independent, industrial, and student films; and commercials.

Concord Hotel

14 Union Street North, Concord (800-848-3740; *www .concorddowntown.com*). *Visitors are limited to exterior viewing.*

There's a movement under way to list the historic Concord Hotel, built around 1926, on the National Register of Historic Places. The Classical Revival architecture, seen on the exterior of Hal's (Jack Black's) apartment in *Shallow Hal*, provides film junkies with a prime photo opportunity. The Concord Hotel also makes an appearance in *Black Rainbow*, a low-budget thriller starring Rosanna Arquette and Jason Robards.

Lovingly restored historic homes and buildings dominate downtown Concord's tree-lined streets. The city's most scenic streetscape is Union Street, where the Concord Hotel and other landmarks such as the Second Empire-style Cabarrus County Courthouse, built around 1876, capture the essence of a quaint Southern town. The Concord closed as a hotel in recent years and now serves as a residential building. Small suites occupy most floors, and a fabulous ballroom is near the lobby.

CREDITS

Shallow Hal (2001); *Black Rainbow* (1989)

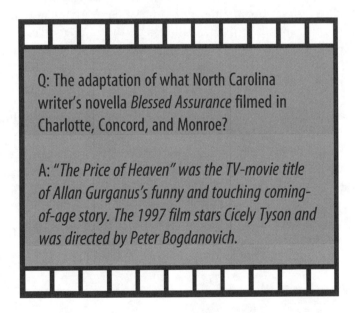

Q: The adaptation of what North Carolina writer's novella *Blessed Assurance* filmed in Charlotte, Concord, and Monroe?

A: *"The Price of Heaven"* was the TV-movie title of Allan Gurganus's funny and touching coming-of-age story. The 1997 film stars Cicely Tyson and was directed by Peter Bogdanovich.

North Carolina Transportation Museum
PHOTOGRAPH BY BILL RUSS
COURTESY OF N. C. DIVISION OF TOURISM, FILM, & SPORTS DEVELOPMENT

Rowan County Locations

North Carolina Transportation Museum/Spencer

U.S. 29 (Exit 79 off I-85), Spencer (704-636-2889;
www.ah.dcr.state.nc.us/sections/hs/spencer/Main.htm). From
April through October, the complex is open from 9 A.M. to 5 P.M.
Monday through Saturday and from 1 P.M. to 5 P.M. on
Sunday. From November through March, it is open from 10 A.M.
to 4 P.M. Tuesday through Saturday and from 1 P.M. to 4 P.M.
on Sunday. It is closed on holidays. Admission is free, though
there is a charge for the train ride.

Hoboes, stowaways, robbers, and villains are staples of the
Hollywood train picture. Filmmakers have found just the right
look for train movies at the North Carolina Transportation
Museum's authentic Southern Railway buildings and repair shops,

which date back to 1896. Known as "the Spencer Shops," these buildings have appeared in train-station scenes in "Having Our Say: The Delany Sisters' First 100 Years," a story about African-American sisters Sadie (Diahann Carroll) and Bessie (Ruby Dee) Delany, who were born in Raleigh at the turn of the 20th century. North Carolina filmmaker David Gordon Green (see pages 406-7) found railroad and other locations for his highly acclaimed *George Washington* at the museum and the Spencer National Register Historic District, the state's largest such contiguous district.

Now a state historic site, the museum interprets North Carolina's diverse transportation history. Exhibits include 19 locomotives, two planes, a Conestoga wagon, a vintage highway patrol car, a stock car, early automobiles, and thousands of artifacts. Barber Junction is a restored 1898 passenger station where film junkies can board trains that tour the 57-acre complex.

CREDITS

George Washington (2000); "Having Our Say: The Delany Sisters' First 100 Years" (CBS, 1999); "Shake, Rattle and Roll: An American Love Story" (CBS, 1999); *Lolita* (1997); "Secrets" (ABC, 1995); "Spies" (Disney Channel, 1992); railroad documentaries

Salisbury

The Rowan County Convention and Visitors Bureau is located at 204 East Innes Street, Suite120, in Salisbury; for information, call 800-332-2343 or visit www.visitsalisburync.com. It is open from 9 A.M. to 5 P.M. Monday through Friday, from 10 A.M. to 4 P.M. on Saturday, and from 1 P.M. to 4 P.M. on Sunday.

Of Rowan County's 11 historic districts, 10 are located in the county seat of Salisbury; the other is in Spencer (see above). Salisbury's 30-blocks of National Register Historic Districts include stately homes and commercial buildings. A 1.3-mile self-guided walking-tour brochure and audiotape of downtown

Salisbury and the West Square Historic District are available free of charge at the Rowan County Convention and Visitors Bureau. They're a great way to introduce film junkies to the county's 250-year history and to Salisbury's downtown streetscapes, which have appeared in "Having Our Say: The Delany Sisters' First 100 Years"; *Black Rainbow*, starring Rosanna Arquette and Jason Robards; Steven Spielberg's *The Color Purple*, based on Alice Walker's Pulitzer Prize-winning novel; and various documentaries.

CREDITS

"Having Our Say: The Delany Sisters' First 100 Years" (CBS, 1999); *Black Rainbow* (1989); *The Color Purple* (1985)

Q: What North Carolina-made model train movie did former Beatle George Harrison executive-produce?

A: Track 29, *a 1988 avant-garde cult film, lensed in Wrightsville Beach and in Wilmington at the Wilmington Railroad Museum and Coast Line Convention Center. John Lennon's song "Mother" is on* Track 29's *soundtrack. Harrison's production company, HandMade Films, backed more than two dozen movies.*

Iredell County Courthouse, where Theodore "Teddy" Johnson
(Brad Pitt) stood trial in "A Stoning in Fulham County."
PHOTOGRAPH BY C. L. NELSON

*Iredell County
Locations*

Mooresville

*Mooresville is just off I-77 north of Charlotte. To contact the
Mooresville Convention and Visitors Bureau, call 877-661-1234
or visit www.racecityusa.org. Another website of interest is
www.downtownmooresville.com.*

Mooresville's nickname, "Race City USA," belies the town's
historical significance. Long before the days of NASCAR, John
Franklin Moore brought the Atlantic, Tennessee and Ohio Railroad to town and built a depot for cotton exports. Incorporated
in 1873, Mooresville began as an agricultural community and
expanded into textiles. Now, it's also noted for health care,
motorsports, tourism, and, yes, film production.

Downtown Mooresville retains many of its original mid-

1800s buildings. A stroll along Main and Broad streets will bring film junkies up close and personal with locations used in "A Stoning in Fulham County," starring then-unknown Brad Pitt and veteran actors Ken Olin, Jill Eickenberry, and Ron Perlman. In one buggy scene, a horse rears excitedly along Main Street as it passes through town. In contrast, when the downtown area stands in for Hattiesburg, Mississippi, in "Shake, Rattle and Roll: An American Love Story," a violent civil-rights scene erupts in front of the 1899 D. E. Turner Hardware Store at 111-15 North Main Street.

Movies have also been shot outside downtown, among them "Vestige of Honor," which filmed its Vietnam scenes in a densely wooded area. "The Lookalike," starring Melissa Gilbert, Cheryl Ladd, and Diane Ladd, filmed at an old barn along N.C. 150. And scenic Lake Norman (see below) has had its share of credits.

Mooresville's Lakeside Business Park is the base for over 60 racing teams, so it's not uncommon to see NASCAR drivers like Rusty Wallace, Sterling Marlin, and Ricky Rudd in town or to see Junior hanging out at Dale Earnhardt Incorporated, located at 1675 Coddle Creek Road.

The local visitor center is located in the North Carolina Auto Racing Hall of Fame, at 119 Knob Hill Road. The hall of fame contains over 35 racecars, assorted displays, and a gift shop.

CREDITS

"Shake, Rattle and Roll: An American Love Story" (CBS, 1999); "Vestige of Honor" (CBS, 1990); "The Lookalike" (USA, 1990); "A Stoning in Fulham County" (NBC, 1988)

Lake Norman

The Catawba Queen riverboat is based at Queen's Landing, located at 1459 River Highway in Mooresville; for hours, call 704-663-2628. For information about the area, visit www.lakenorman.org or www.racecityusa.org., or call the Lake Norman Chamber of Commerce and Visitors Bureau at 800-305-2508.

Filmmakers have discovered the charms of Lake Norman,

the state's largest man-made lake. In *Days of Thunder*, Cole Trickle (Tom Cruise) and sexy surgeon Claire (Nicole Kidman) go for a boat ride on Lake Norman when they visit another couple at their lakefront home. In *Shallow Hal*, Lake Norman Regional Medical Center stands in as the hospital where Rosemary (Gwyneth Paltrow) works with burned children. And it's where Hal's dying father leads him astray with advice about women. Lake Norman Fire Equipment, Inc., poses as the exterior for Sun Records in "Shake, Rattle and Roll: An American Love Story."

World-class fishing, camping, boating, and hiking along six miles of nature trails are among the recreational opportunities at Lake Norman. You can even take a riverboat cruise or a hot-air balloon ride to see the elegant homes, charming bed-and-breakfasts, and fine hotels and restaurants that surround the camera-worthy lake.

CREDITS

"She Says She's Innocent" (NBC, 1991) stars Katey Sagal. Lake Norman's other credits include *Shallow Hal* (2001); "Shake, Rattle and Roll: An American Love Story" (CBS, 1999); and *Days of Thunder* (1990).

Statesville's "On Location" Walk of Fame
Statesville is located at the junction of I-40 and I-77 southwest of Winston-Salem and north of Charlotte.

Filmmakers will be hard-pressed to find a community more film-friendly than Statesville. Its picturesque historic district, residential communities, and rural areas willingly lend themselves to the camera, and its businesses welcome the economic impact. Eager to become a film mecca in the 1980s, local merchants partnered with the Statesville Film Committee, the Greater Statesville Chamber of Commerce, and the Downtown Statesville Development Corporation to purchase and install markers that memorialize several Statesville productions. The city has four "On Location" markers embedded in sidewalks in the downtown commercial district, which boasts 47 buildings on the National Register of Historic Places.

Marker 1 commemorates "A Stoning in Fulham County," which filmed in town between July 18 and August 6, 1988, and aired on NBC on October 24, 1988. The marker is located on the Center Street sidewalk outside the grand Historic Vance Hotel (see pages 335-36) and across from the red-brick, green-roofed, 1892-vintage city hall, a striking example of Richardsonian Romanesque-style architecture. Just a few steps away at 200 South Center Street is the stunning, 1900-vintage, Beaux Arts-style Iredell County Courthouse, where the movie's trial scene was filmed. It comes as a surprise even to most Statesville residents that the young Brad Pitt stars as a bad boy in this made-for-television movie about an Amish tragedy. The production also stars Ken Olin, Jill Eickenberry, and Ron Perlman.

Marker 2 commemorates "The Ryan White Story," which filmed between August 17 and September 9, 1988, and aired on ABC on January 16, 1989. The marker is located at 107½ East Broad Street in front of Olde Town Sweets. The school scenes were filmed at South Iredell High School, located at 299 Old Mountain Road. This television movie tells the true story of Ryan White, a 13-year-old hemophiliac who contracted AIDS from a blood transfusion. Ryan White actually appears as a friend of Lukas Haas, the actor who portrays Ryan. The impressive cast also includes Judith Light, George C. Scott, and, believe it or not, Sarah Jessica Parker, who appears as a nurse in the movie more than a decade before HBO's sizzling "Sex in the City" began airing.

Marker 3 commemorates *The Boneyard*, which filmed here between November 13 and December 16, 1989, and was re-leased in 1991. The marker is located at 122 West Broad Street in front of R. Gregory Jewelers (see pages 336-37). The cast includes Ed Nelson, Deborah Rose, Norman Fell, and Phyllis Diller as Miss Poopinplatz, the town coroner whose morgue is overtaken by zombie children. Filming took place downtown and at Davis Regional Medical Center, at 218 Old Mocksville Road.

Marker 4 commemorates *The Feud*, which filmed between October 10 and November 12, 1988, and was released in 1989. The marker is located at 240 West Broad Street, across from

Broad Street Methodist Church and in front of America's Grill and Totally Tan. This comedy, set in the 1950s, is based on a Thomas Berger novel about two feuding families. It stars Kathleen Doyle, Joe Grifasi, Stanley Tucci, and René Auberjonois, who is perhaps best known as Constable Odo in "Star Trek: Deep Space Nine." Filming took place at 110 West Broad Street at the former Lazenby Montgomery Hardware building, constructed around 1885. The bank scenes were shot at First Associate Reformed Presbyterian Church, at 123 East Broad Street.

In "The Lottery," starring Dan Cortese, Keri Russell, and Veronica Cartwright, Statesville's civic center appears as a bus station and apartment building, and its town hall appears as a courthouse. Other Statesville credits include *Weeds*, starring Nick Nolte, and "One of Her Own," starring Lori Loughlin and Martin Sheen.

CREDITS

"The Lottery" (NBC, 1996); "One of Her Own" (ABC, 1994); *The Boneyard* (1991); *The Feud* (1989); "The Ryan White Story" (ABC, 1989); "A Stoning in Fulham County" (NBC, 1988); *Weeds* (1987)

Iredell County Star Tracks

Historic Vance Hotel

226 South Center Street, Statesville (800-969-3688 or 704-873-3688)

More reminiscent of New York City than a small Southern town, the elegantly renovated Historic Vance Hotel welcomes dignitaries, celebrities, and discriminating visitors to Statesville. During the late 1980s and early 1990s, when Statesville hosted Hollywood film types, it was known as the Queen Ann Hotel. Production offices for "The Lottery" were set up at the hotel, and nearly every production that filmed in historic Statesville housed cast and top crew members here.

Listed on the National Register of Historic Places, the venerable hotel was built around 1922. Its celebrity guest list includes names like Ron Perlman ("A Stoning in Fulham County"), Phyllis Diller (*The Boneyard*), and Senator Elizabeth Dole, who, naturally, preferred the Presidential Suite. And these names are only the ones that current management could confirm.

★ ★ ★ ★ ★ ★ ★ ★ ★ ★

Locals recall other celebrity guests such as Ken Olin and Brad Pitt ("A Stoning in Fulham County"); Ed Nelson and Norman Fell (*The Boneyard*); René Auberjonois and Kathleen Doyle (*The Feud*); Judith Light, George C. Scott, and Sarah Jessica Parker ("The Ryan White Story"); and producer Alan Landsburg. The downstairs lounge was added so that cast and crew of "A Stoning in Fulham County" would have a place to hang out and throw a wrap party. The hotel's Library Restaurant is also popular with visiting celebs.

R. Gregory Jewelers

R. Gregory Jewelers is located at 122 West Broad Street in Statesville; call 704-872-8941 or visit www.rgregoryjewelers.com. The store is open from 10 A.M. to 5 P.M. Monday through Saturday. For information about the Hiddenite Gem Mine, call 828-632-3394.

Sure, visiting celebrities may shop at R. Gregory Jewelers, but the real stars hang out in the vault.

The world-famous Hiddenite emeralds first commanded attention in the 1880s, when Thomas Edison and mineralogist William Earl Hidden proclaimed the North Carolina fault line among the world's most complex. To date, one of the largest, finest, and most significant emeralds ever found on the North American continent is a 71-carat rough emerald unearthed in 1998 by miner James Hill in a dormant Hiddenite mine he owns. Hill's stone yielded America's royal family of emeralds: the Carolina Queen, an 18.88-carat dark green, pear-shaped beauty; and the Carolina Prince, a 7.85-carat oval-shaped emerald. Hill's discovery landed him on "The Oprah Winfrey Show," "Inside Edition," "Good Morning America," and CNN.

The Carolina Prince sold for $500,000. The Carolina Queen was still available at the time this book went to press; its retail value is $1 million! Photos of the emeralds are on

★ ★ ★ ★ ★ ★ ★ ★ ★ ★

display at R. Gregory Jewelers, the exclusive retailer of Hiddenite emeralds. Owner and jeweler Rick Gregory, a supporter of North Carolina films, is the man behind Statesville's Walk of Fame. His favorite celebrity customer? Phyllis Diller, with whom he posed for a picture in front of *The Boneyard*'s Statesville marker—just outside his jewelry salon.

Gaston County Locations

Gastonia

Gastonia is 22 miles west of Charlotte. The Carolina Speedway is on U.S. 274 (Union Road); for information, call 704-869-0313. Piedmont Community Charter School is located at 119 East Second Street; call 704-853-2428.

Gastonia, the second-largest city in the Charlotte area, has a nice history of hosting the filming of classy television, indie, and feature projects. "Saint Maybe," a Hallmark Hall of Fame adaptation of Raleigh native Anne Tyler's novel, filmed in the downtown area; South and Main streets are all made up for the holidays in the early scenes. A few of the set dressings remain on the buildings across from the Gaston County Courthouse. The CBS miniseries "Shake, Rattle and Roll: An American Love Story" used the historic Gastonia Central Elementary School for classroom scenes and the offices and studios of Sun Records. "The Last Brickmaker in America," starring Sidney Poitier in the title role, also filmed at the school, which is now Piedmont Community Charter School.

"Major Dad" star Gerald McRaney must really like the Gastonia area. Besides appearing in "Shake, Rattle and Roll: An American Love Story," the Mississippi-born actor starred (with Tyne Daly and Alicia Silverstone) in "Shattered Dreams," as well as in "Vestige of Honor." Randy Travis, a native of nearby Marshville, appears in "Steel Chariots," which filmed at the Carolina Speedway, where there's racing every Friday night. "Steel Chariots" features real-life NASCAR drivers Jeff Gordon, Mark Martin, Rusty Wallace, and Benny Parsons.

CREDITS

Shallow Hal (2001); "The Last Brickmaker in America" (CBS, 2001); *The Rage: Carrie II* (1999); "Shake, Rattle and Roll: An American Love Story" (CBS, 1999); *Body Count* (Showtime, 1998); "Saint Maybe" (Hallmark/CBS, 1998); "Steel Chariots" (Fox, 1997); "Shattered Dreams" (CBS, 1990); "Vestige of Honor" (CBS, 1990)

North Gaston High School
1133 Ratchford Road, Dallas (704-922-5285). Visitors are limited to exterior viewing.

Anyone who has seen the horror classic *Carrie*, released in 1976, certainly remembers the bloodbath at the prom and knows from the even scarier final graveyard scene that Carrie White won't stay buried. A sequel was probably inevitable, but the prospect of making one almost 25 years after the original—and without Stephen King and Brian De Palma behind the scenes and John Travolta and Sissy Spacek in front of the cameras (though Spacek does appear in a few flashbacks)—presented a few challenges. Nonetheless, *The Rage: Carrie II* was made.

A high school was needed so the tormenting of Carrie's half-sister, Rachel Lang (Emily Bergl), could proceed. Bergl appears with Jason London and sole survivor Amy Irving, who reprises the role of Sue Snell. Most of the shots of the subtly named Bates High School were filmed at North Gaston High

School in Dallas, North Carolina, just outside Charlotte. The main locations used were the cafeteria, the football field (along with the team and the cheerleaders), and the gym, where *American Beauty* star Mena Suvari makes a memorable jump from the top of the building into a car.

The Rage: Carrie II wasn't exactly a rage at the box office, but hey, the musical version didn't really work either.

CREDITS

The Rage: Carrie II (1999)

Gaston County Star Tracks

Schiele Museum of Natural History

*1500 East Garrison Boulevard, Gastonia (704-866-6900;
www.schielemuseum.org). The museum is open from 9 A.M. to
5 P.M. Monday through Saturday and from 1 P.M. to 5 P.M. on
Sunday. An admission fee is charged.*

To prepare for his Academy Award®-nominated role in *Cast
Away*, Tom Hanks famously halted production for a year while he
lost 50 pounds and grew out his hair and beard. Such attention to
detail in the hit movie, a re-teaming of Hanks and *Forrest Gump*
director Robert Zemeckis, extended even to the primitive tools
Chuck Noland (Hanks) uses while marooned on his Pacific
island. These tools were conceived by Steve Watts of Gastonia's
Schiele Museum of Natural History. Prototypes are on display at
the museum, along with a poster from the movie and international
articles written about it. Watts, an expert in primitive tools and
artifacts, was approached by scriptwriter Bill Broyles in 1995
about what sort of objects might be fashioned in Chuck Noland's

situation. They came up with such things as an ice-skate ax and a coconut canteen, which are among the items on display. Unfortunately, Wilson the volleyball is not.

The Schiele has been featured in an episode about early humans on the History Channel's "Extreme History" series, hosted by Roger Daltrey, actor and lead singer of The Who. Daltrey interviewed Watts at the museum in 2003.

Film junkies can see other "stars" at the Schiele's James H. Lynn Planetarium. They can also explore the nature trail, the 18th-century back-country farm, and the Catawba Indian village.

So You Want to Be an Extra?

"Are you sure?"

That's the question you need to answer when deciding to become a movie extra. The chance to hang out with a star and maybe land a few fleeting seconds in the background has its ups and downs. If you answer yes and land a job as an extra, you can't change it to a no. You're there for the duration, and film crews typically put in *long* days.

So your answer is no, right?

Of course not. You want a glimpse of that star up close and personal. Maybe you'll even share a "How's it goin'?" There's no heavy lifting involved, and the money's not bad. Plus, you usually get fed. You may indeed be in a scene with a star, anyone from an A-list celeb to a kid with only a couple of indies under her belt (but hey, you knew her back when . . .). And said star may or may not seem friendly that day. But remember, they are very busy and are there to do a job. Though some scenes can be physically demanding or unpleasant, that's generally not the case. As an extra, your "trailer" will be of the open-air variety—out in the sun, cold, or rain, that is. As for your big break, well, there's always hope, right?

The downside? Minor things, mostly, though they can add up. The phrase "hurry up and wait" was coined with film production in mind. So bring something to read, and get used to being told where to stand, what to do, what *not* to do—and to do it again and again. You'll also be told when to arrive and when you can leave. No questions. No excuses. You won't exactly get star treatment either. The artists and technicians (yes, there *are* a lot of them) are under a great deal of pressure in a very competitive field. Don't take it personally.

Okay, you *do* want to be an extra. You just want to know how. Below is a list of casting agents in North Carolina. Find them, fill out a form or two, send a picture, or pay them to take a Polaroid. Then you'll be in for a dose of "Don't call us, we'il call you." If there's a demand, and if you look right and are available, you may get called. If so, you'll be given a call time. It may be early in the morning. Be there on time. You may be asked (or told) to cut or color your hair. If you're unwilling, you probably won't be in the scene. Clear several days. You may be called back the next day or the rest of the week. Also, learn the movie term *continuity*. To preserve continuity, don't greatly alter your appearance during a multi-day shoot. This isn't the time to finally shave off that beard.

Being an extra can be fun. You'll make a friend or two, if only for the day. It's an experience you're not likely to forget, even if you swear you'll never do it again.

Casting Agents

Coast: Fincannon & Associates, 1235 North 23rd Street, Wilmington, N.C. 28405 (910-251-1500)

Piedmont: Corrigan & Johnston Casting, 3006 North Davidson Street, Charlotte, N.C. 28205 (704-374-9400; www.cjcasting.com)

Mountains: Marty Cherrix Casting, P.O. Box 216, Canton, N.C. 28716 (e-mail: locationcasting.@aol.com)

Other Helpful Numbers

North Carolina Film Office Hotline (800-232-9227; www.ncfilm.com and click on "Current Productions.")

First Friday Working Actors, Charlotte (704-561-2279; www.actors-hollywoodsouth.com)

Cleveland County Locations

Earl Owensby Studios

*1 Motion Picture Boulevard, Shelby (704-487-0500;
www.earlowensby.com). The studios are not open to the public.*

Some argue that Earl Owensby and his self-described
"billyflicks" of the '70s and '80s founded filmmaking in North
Carolina. True or not, this maverick *is* a legend in the state's
movie annals. He did things his way. Owensby was old-fashioned in his efficient, almost family-like approach, yet he was
also innovative in realizing the profitability of American action
movies in the overseas market. Not familiar with *Challenge?* Never
heard of *Chain Gang?* Didn't catch *Rottweiler?* You're probably in
the majority. But these hard-hitting titles were among the dozen
or so features Owensby produced, directed, and often starred
in from the mid-'70s to the mid-'80s. In a bottom-line business,
every one of them made money, often reaping a tenfold return

on investment. And you probably *have* heard of James Cameron, whose taut 1989 underwater thriller *The Abyss* shot at Owensby's South Carolina studio, converted from an unfinished nuclear power plant with a 7.5-million-gallon tank.

Earl Owensby Studios, outside Shelby, is a state-of-the-art 67-acre complex with eight sound stages, editing suites, screening rooms, and a 100,000-gallon film tank featuring underwater camera bays.

Owensby's story has been told in *GQ*, on "60 Minutes" (twice!), on "Late Night with David Letterman," and in the *Los Angeles Times* and the *New York Times*, among other places. A native of nearby Cliffside, North Carolina, Earl got fixated on films as a kid ushering at the Cliffside Theater. In fact, his admiration for John Wayne in *Sands of Iwo Jima* inspired him to join the Marines. After five years in the Corps, he returned to North Carolina and founded a number of successful companies, primarily in the industrial supply business. In 1973, he produced and starred in his first feature film, *Challenge*. He poured the profits into the construction of his film studios, which grew into the largest independent facility outside Hollywood. Over three dozen feature films and television and cable productions followed, featuring such stars as George Kennedy, Raul Julia, and Parker Stevenson. Owensby's acquisition of the uncompleted nuclear power plant in South Carolina led to his development of the world's largest underwater film tank. This attracted Cameron and no doubt contributed to *The Abyss*'s Academy Award® for visual effects.

The studios' other Oscar® connections include Tom Conti's nomination for Best Actor in *Reuben, Reuben* and the Best Documentary Short Subject award won by *The Johnstown Flood*.

CREDITS
The Johnstown Flood (1989); *Rottweiler* (1985); *Chain Gang* (1984); *Reuben, Reuben* (1983); *Challenge* (1974); and numerous others

Charlotte Area Celebrities

Concord's Skeet Ulrich overcame open heart surgery at age 10 to become one of Hollywood's hottest young hunks. The acting bug bit Skeet while he was doing work as an extra during his student days at UNC-Wilmington. Since then, he's been in a number of features, perhaps most notably the 1997 hit *As Good As It Gets*, in which he plays Vince, the street-tough artist's model. The film also stars Greg Kinnear, Jack Nicholson, and Helen Hunt.

Rich Hall of Waxhaw is a versatile actor and writer who's made a name for himself in TV, film, books, and CDs. Rich was in the 1984-85 cast of "Saturday Night Live." He wrote for that legendary series, as well as for "Late Night with David Letterman," where he won an Emmy®; ABC's "Fridays"; and HBO's "Not Necessarily the News," where he unleashed his first "sniglet" on the world. Hall has gone on to produce several best-selling volumes of these "words that don't appear in the dictionary—but should." He has also released several other humorous books and CDs.

Ben Browder, Neve Campbell's boyfriend Sam in the Fox hit "Party of Five," grew up in Charlotte, where his family owns and operates a NASCAR Busch Series racecar. Browder has also been seen as Commander John Crichton in the Sci Fi Channel's "Farscape" and in numerous other film and television roles. He has appeared on Broadway with Dustin Hoffman in *The Merchant of Venice*.

A musician, composer, and East Carolina grad from Ayden, Loonis McGlohon teamed with fellow Tar Heel Charles Kuralt for several projects, including music for "On the Road." The winner of a Peabody Award, McGlohon has been honored in his adopted hometown of Charlotte with the McGlohon Stage at the North Carolina Blumenthal Performing Arts Center (see pages 287-89).

"Whatever happened to Randolph Scott?" the Statler Brothers famously ask in one of their hit songs. Well, the handsome

Western star grew up in Charlotte and graduated from UNC. Scott went to Hollywood, starred in over a hundred cowboy films, and was a top box-office draw in the 1950s. He retired from the movies in 1962. He died in 1987 and is buried in Charlotte.

★★★★★★★★★★★★

Arthur Smith

Charlotte's Arthur Smith didn't invent TV in the Carolinas. He just conquered the medium, as he had radio, music, and the movies. His legend lives on well into its sixth decade.

It all began for Arthur back in the 1940s, when he and his band, the Carolina Crackerjacks, started on the radio at WBT in Charlotte. The 1950s saw television grab the foothold it's never released, and Arthur was right there, debuting a variety show that ran for 32 years and became the first nationally syndicated country-music show. Generations of Tar Heels remember Smith's Saturday-night TV family, whose guests included Andy Griffith, Johnny Cash, Loretta Lynn, and even future president Richard Nixon.

Smith opened the first major recording studio in the Carolinas. His 1948 composition "Guitar Boogie" became an early rock-'n'-roll classic. It's just one of his 500-plus country, rock, bluegrass, and gospel songs that have been recorded by artists such as Willie Nelson, George Beverly Shea, and Randy Travis. Smith's most famous song may be "Feuding Banjos," which gained notoriety in the film industry when it was used in the 1972 movie *Deliverance*— under the name "Dueling Banjos," and without Smith's credit or permission. He sued and won. The record went on to sell over

8 million copies. In all, Smith has scored more than a dozen films, many for fellow Carolinian Earl Owensby (see pages 345-46).

Arthur Smith has continued his career into the new millennium with UNC-TV's "Carolina Calling," which showcases budding talent from across North Carolina. The program also features guests such as Alison Krauss and Union Station, Earl Scruggs, and Maurice Williams and the Zodiacs, and it includes Smith's archival footage of Griffith, Cash, Ronnie Milsap, Chet Atkins, and other top stars.

Even his spare time makes for long-running TV! "The Arthur Smith Sportfishing Series," spotlighting his love of marine conservation, was an original ESPN show that ran for 12 years.

Q: What Shelby-born lawyer, legislator, and preacher wrote the controversial novel that was turned into what is considered the first classic film?

A: *Thomas Dixon's* The Clansman *was directed by his friend D. W. Griffith as the 1915 film* The Birth of a Nation. *Dixon died in Raleigh in 1946. A historical plaque commemorates on the site of his family home on Marion Street in Shelby.*

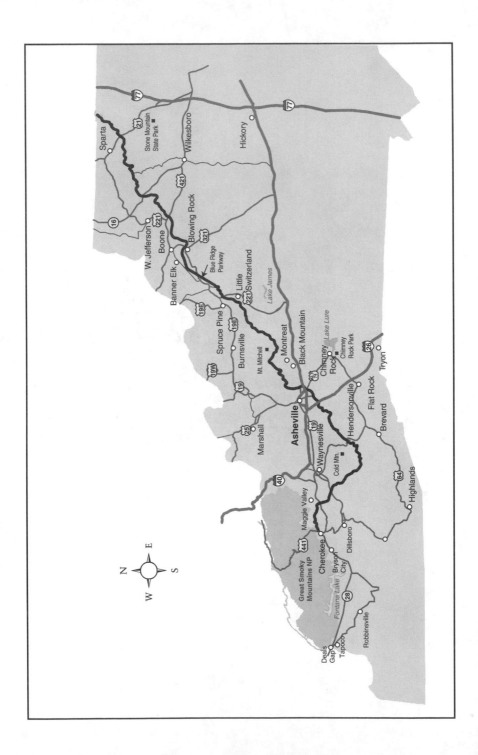

The Last of the Mohicans films in the North Carolina mountains.
COURTESY OF CHIMNEY ROCK PARK

*"The North Carolina mountains are the most beautiful place in the world,
and we want the world to see them."*
Mary Nell Webb,
former Western North Carolina
Film Commission director

*F*ew visitors would argue with the above statement. And filmmakers have certainly done their best to show the world this
enchanted region. The history of filmmaking here dates back
to the very roots, when Thomas Edison himself shot a few one-
reelers, and when a smattering of silents filmed in the crisp
mountain air. More recently, hits such as *Nell, Dirty Dancing,
Songcatcher,* and *The Last of the Mohicans* have shown off the natural beauty and color, as did *Cold Mountain* in brief aerial shots.

Western North Carolina has a rich historical and cultural
heritage, with Asheville a delightful focal point. You'll see why
the city has been called "the Paris of the South" when you visit
downtown's trendy bistros and hip bookstores and boutiques.
Film junkies will find a healthy blend of the arts (both folk and

fine) and dining (downtown and down-home), not to mention pristine spots nearby for hiking, camping, rafting, and other outdoor activities. You may even sight a star or two. They've been coming to Asheville for years. Recent projects including Robert Redford's *The Clearing*, *Patch Adams*, and *Hannibal* have continued the trend.

Not to be outdone, the northern mountains—Boone and environs—are familiar to film junkies worldwide, thanks to Academy Award®-winning films such as *Forrest Gump* and *The Green Mile*.

Western North Carolina is special. See for yourself. While several film locations are remote or not open for visitors, others have not only shown off their diversity by appearing in several movies but are top-notch attractions in their own right.

For tourism information, contact the Asheville Convention and Visitors Bureau (800-251-1300; www.exploreasheville.com), the Boone Convention and Visitors Bureau (800-852-9506; www.visitBoone.com), or the North Carolina Division of Tourism, Film and Sports Development (800-VISITNC; www.visitnc.com).

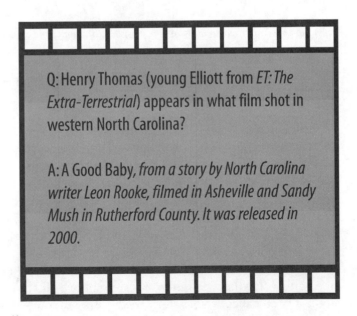

Q: Henry Thomas (young Elliott from *ET: The Extra-Terrestrial*) appears in what film shot in western North Carolina?

A: *A Good Baby*, from a story by North Carolina writer Leon Rooke, filmed in Asheville and Sandy Mush in Rutherford County. It was released in 2000.

Billy Graham preaches at "Singing on the Mountain"
on Grandfather Mountain in 1963.
PHOTOGRAPH BY HUGH MORTON
COURTESY OF GRANDFATHER MOUNTAIN

Northern Mountain Locations

Grandfather Mountain

*Grandfather Mountain is on U.S. 221 North one mile south of
the intersection with the Blue Ridge Parkway and two miles
north of Linville. It is open daily year-round except for
Christmas and Thanksgiving, weather permitting in winter. The
hours are 8 A.M. until dusk. An admission fee is charged. For
information, call 800-468-7325 or visit www.grandfather.com.*

Grandfather Mountain is "the face of all Heaven come to
earth," according to no less an authority than John Muir, the
noted conservationist and naturalist. Can't get much more cinematic than that! Many filmmakers have climbed the mountain
over the years to capture the beauty and traditions of the highest peak in the Blue Ridge, considered the most biologically

diverse mountain in eastern North America. Also, a certain Best Picture starring Tom Hanks did a brief "run-through" scene at Grandfather.

Visitors enjoy Grandfather Mountain's hiking, wildlife, and famous Mile High Swinging Bridge. Grandfather hosts the annual Highland Games and the "Singing on the Mountain" gospel gathering each summer. Over a hundred Scottish clans and societies celebrate their traditional dance, music, and athletics during the Highland Games, which are featured in *This Time Each Year*, a documentary narrated by celebrated Tar Heel singer/songwriter Mike Cross. Singing on the Mountain is a free, all-day gospel sing, church bazaar, and dinner held in MacRae Meadows. Almost every well-known preacher, gospel singer, and group has appeared, as have Johnny Cash, Roy Clark, and Doc Watson. People still talk about the 1963 message delivered by western North Carolina's own Billy Graham. A surprising number of non-gospel celebrities have also appeared over the years, including Bob Hope and Jerry Lewis. This event has also been featured in several documentaries.

At the park's Museum Theater, a life-sized statue of Mildred the Bear greets visitors. Mildred was named during a segment of Arthur Smith's popular regional television series (see pages 348-49). The theatre shows short films made primarily at Grandfather Mountain by the "Grandfather" of tourism Hugh Morton, the renowned photographer who created the attraction.

Film junkies will want to check out the summit parking lot at the beginning of the Bridge Trail. This was the location for the final scene with Natasha Richardson in *The Handmaid's Tale*. And of course, you'll want to see the "Forrest Gump Curve," where Forrest (Tom Hanks) runs across Grandfather's summit. This famed spot is three curves up from the nature museum. Interestingly, in this scene, Forrest is actually Tom Hanks's brother, used as a stand-in for the second-unit shot. But since Tom had that beautiful Saturday in October off, he decided to hang out on Grandfather Mountain with the crew.

CREDITS

Forrest Gump (1994); *The Handmaid's Tale* (1990); *This Time Each Year* (1986); numerous documentaries

★★★★★★★★★★★★★
Billy Graham

North Carolina native Billy Graham, one of the world's most admired leaders and confidant of presidents, has preached to over 200 million people in more than 185 countries. Millions more have seen him worldwide via television, video, and film.

Graham, one of the earliest and most enduring religious figures to use the media, is a longtime resident of Montreat, North Carolina. Born and raised on a dairy farm in Charlotte, he first gained national attention during a Los Angeles crusade in 1949; his early crusades are often shown on cable religious networks. His more recent crusades are still broadcast about six times a year in almost every market in the United States and Canada.

Graham's life has been profiled in several documentaries, including *Crusade: The Life of Billy Graham* and *Cry from the Mountain*, narrated by Walter Cronkite and featuring Barbara Bush, Patricia Cornwell, and Andie MacDowell. *Cry from the Mountain* has an original music score by Shelby, North Carolina, musician Richard Putnam.

Graham's ministerial organization includes World Wide Pictures, which has produced over 130 inspirational films and videos, including *The Climb*, with Dabney Coleman and Todd Bridges; *Road to Redemption*, starring Carolina Beach resident Pat Hingle; and *The Ride*. World Wide's films are available in over 40 languages and have been seen by more than 250 million people worldwide.

Billy Graham has received numerous national and international honors, including the Congressional Gold Medal and the Ronald Reagan Presidential Foundation Freedom Award. And he certainly hasn't been forgotten in his home state. There's a Billy Graham Expressway in Charlotte and another one in Asheville, the latter a section of I-240. The Billy Graham Training Center at The Cove near Asheville hosts adult and teen retreats. It is located near Exit 55 off Interstate 40. For information, call 800-950-2092 or 828-298-2092 or visit www.billygraham.org.

The Moses Cone Manor served as the
Georgia Pines nursing home in *The Green Mile*.
PHOTOGRAPH BY DAVID W. BEATTY

Moses Cone Manor

*Moses H. Cone Memorial Park is located at Milepost 294 on the
Blue Ridge Parkway near Blowing Rock. Between March 15
and November 30, the Parkway Craft Center is open daily from
9 A.M. to 5 P.M. For information, call 828-295-7938.*

The old man wakes from a very bad dream and heads down
the long green tile floor for breakfast at the nursing home where
it seems he's been living forever.

This opening shot is one of the poignant and ultimately
shocking framing scenes that Best Picture nominee *The Green Mile*
filmed at the Moses Cone Manor near Blowing Rock. The historic landmark, part of Moses H. Cone Memorial Park, serves
as the Georgia Pines nursing home of super senior Paul
Edgecomb and the equally ancient mouse, Mr. Jingles. Film junkies may be surprised to learn that it isn't Tom Hanks playing
Old Paul in these scenes. That was the original plan, but makeup
tests didn't make Hanks look credible enough as an elderly man.
The role went instead to veteran character actor Dabbs Greer,
whose Hollywood career dates back to the 1940s.

Film junkies can admire the magnificent house and furnishings, then browse the Parkway Craft Center for authentic moun-

tain folk art made by members of the Southern Highland Craft Guild. The home, named Flat Top Manor, was built at the turn of the 20th century by Moses Cone, one of the country's most successful textile manufacturers and philanthropists. The Cones had quite a connection to the European art world. Moses Cone's sisters, Claribel and Etta, were intimate friends of Gertrude Stein and artists like Pablo Picasso and Henri Matisse. They amassed a collection of over 3,000 paintings, which were featured in a BBC-Scotland documentary that filmed at the manor and was hosted by "Monty Python" member Michael Palin. The full story of the house and family is told in Philip Noblitt's book *A Mansion in the Mountains.*

CREDIT

The Green Mile (1999)

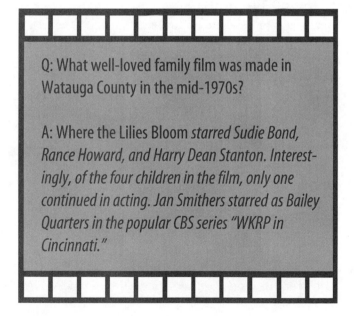

Q: What well-loved family film was made in Watauga County in the mid-1970s?

A: Where the Lilies Bloom *starred Sudie Bond, Rance Howard, and Harry Dean Stanton. Interestingly, of the four children in the film, only one continued in acting. Jan Smithers starred as Bailey Quarters in the popular CBS series "WKRP in Cincinnati."*

The 600-foot granite dome at Stone Mountain State Park
PHOTOGRAPH BY BILL RUSS
COURTESY OF N. C. DIVISION OF TOURISM, FILM, & SPORTS DEVELOPMENT

Stone Mountain State Park

3042 John P. Frank Parkway, Roaring Gap (336-957-8185; www.ils.unc.edu/parkproject/visit/stmo/home.html). The park is open daily year-round. From November through February, the hours are 8 A.M. to 6 P.M. Extended hours are in effect from March through October.

Mother Nature deserves a movie credit for creating the waterfall and forest sets seen in "Tecumseh: The Last Warrior." Based on the book *Panther in the Sky* by James Alexander Thom, "Tecumseh" tells the story of a Shawnee warrior who wants settlers to agree with his plan for an Indian state.

Stone Mountain State Park, a National Natural Landmark, offers spectacular views of the Blue Ridge Parkway. It encompasses 13,500 acres of forests, trails, lakes, rivers, waterfalls, and a spectacular, 600-foot granite dome. The park is renowned for its world-class trout fishing in 19 miles of well-stocked streams.

CREDITS
"Tecumseh: The Last Warrior" (TNT, 1995)

Lake James State Park

The park is located on N.C. 126 in Burke and McDowell counties near Morganton and Marion. It opens at 8 A.M. Fees are charged for various activities. For information, call 828-652-5047.

The list of film credits for Lake James State Park, located in the foothills near Morganton, is short but A-list all the way. Film junkies can explore the more than 150 miles of shoreline and visit the location of Fort William Henry, the centerpiece setting for *The Last of the Mohicans*. Though little remains of the set today, the beauty of the area is just as it was in the film. Numerous devotees of the movie still seek out the foundation markings. Besides being the British stronghold of Colonel Munro (Maurice Roëves), this site was also the location of the French camp. Other memorable scenes filmed here include the canoe escape led by Hawkeye (Daniel Day-Lewis) and the sequence when Duncan (Steven Waddington) falls during the Massacre Valley scene. All of the *Mohicans* locations are near the Haney's Island/White Creek area of the park. If you're lucky, members of the park staff will guide you to the spots used in the film.

Lake James also appears in the Sean Connery/Alec Baldwin thriller *The Hunt for Red October*, though just barely. It seems the executive producer was unhappy with the film's ending, and a location was needed for quick reshoots. Lake James had the right look, so a two-day shoot was done here between Christmas and New Year's Day.

The lake may have been a good-luck charm for the sound crews of both films. *Red October* picked up an Oscar® for Best Sound Effects, while *Mohicans* won for Best Sound.

CREDITS

The Last of the Mohicans (1992); *The Hunt for Red October* (1990)

The *Winter People* Cabin

The cabin is located along U.S. 19E in Plumtree. Please do not trespass on private property, but instead photograph the cabin from the roadside or from your automobile.

Folks in the high country still talk about the time in 1987 when Hollywood paid a five-month visit to Plumtree, a scenic mountain town that developed around mining. Traveling along U.S. 19E on the banks of the North Toe River, film junkies might recognize one of the cabins used in the film adaptation of John Ehle's novel *Winter People*. The late-18th- and early-19th-century cabin was occupied by Collie Wright (Kelly McGillis) and her baby.

Located adjacent to Plumtree's town square, or what's left of it, the sturdy cabin is the only structure from the movie that remains intact. The clock tower built by Wayland Jackson (Kurt Russell) has since been torn down, as has the cabin where he lives with his daughter, Paula (Amelia Burnette). Neither the storefronts nor the stable remain, but the cabin provides a wonderful photo opportunity, as does the Toe River, where many of the film's most memorable scenes take place.

Kay Wilkins, who taught high school and coached the girls' basketball team in nearby Cranberry for 35 years, is proud of the cabin's history and fame. And rightfully so; her family has owned it since the mid-1800s, when her grandfather purchased the one-room log structure and a store next door that no longer exists. Several families lived in the cabin during the 1900s, and a room was eventually added. In 1965, Kay and her late husband refurbished it as their own local retreat. She still opens it for close friends and family members and even decorates its exterior during the holidays, but it is not open to the public.

The structure provides film junkies an authentic encounter with one of the oldest log cabins in the country. It also happens to be a cool movie location. Mrs. Wilkins says that folks stop by to photograph the rustic log house nearly every day.

She doesn't seem to mind, as long as they keep a safe distance
and show respect for the historic cabin and its environs.

CREDITS

Winter People (1989)

Northern Mountain Star Tracks

Chetola Mountain Resort

*North Main Street, Blowing Rock (800-243-8652; www
.chetola.com)*

Chetola is a Cherokee word meaning "haven of rest." The posh Chetola Mountain Resort more than lives up to the name for film junkies, as it did for the production team of one of the most acclaimed films of recent years.

This gorgeous 87-acre Blue Ridge resort borders the spectacular Moses H. Cone Memorial Park. It has proven both a recreational and a therapeutic spot for visitors since before the turn of the 20th century. But it was work, not relaxation, that brought cast and crew of *The Green Mile* to Chetola, first to set up a temporary headquarters and then for lodging during a second visit for actual filming.

The film's present-day scenes featuring Old Paul Edgecomb (the Tom Hanks character) were shot at the Moses Cone Manor (see pages 358-59). The cemetery scene was also filmed in Blowing Rock. Among those enjoying Chetola's charms during the three and a half weeks of filming were director Frank Darabont, whose adaptation of Stephen King's serial novel earned an Academy Award® nomination, and veteran actor Dabbs Greer, who played Old Paul. The film was nominated for Best Picture.

Other celebrities spotted here over the years have included Lee Majors and Mickey Rooney.

Chetola offers adults and children a number of recreational opportunities, including boating and fishing on Chetola Lake. Guests can enjoy a choice of several massage therapy treatments and dine at either of the two restaurants, The Manor House and Snyder's Soda Shoppe.

MerleFest

Wilkes Community College, 1328 Collegiate Drive, Wilkesboro (800-343-7857; www.merlefest.org). An admission fee is charged.

MerleFest, a must event for bluegrass and Americana music lovers across the nation, has expanded its audience to television in the new millennium, offering a little better view than that enjoyed by most of the 75,000 who annually attend the four-day celebration in Wilkesboro. The 2003 fest was shot on location, to air later in national syndication. It's not the first time the event has spread to TV. North Carolina Public Television taped all four days of MerleFest in 1992 and produced the eight-part series "Pickin' for Merle," which was shown on public television stations nationwide. Segments have also appeared on National Public Radio's *E-Town* and have been broadcast live on satellite radio.

Held in late April, MerleFest honors the life and music of Merle Watson, son of the legendary Deep Gap picker Doc Watson. Merle, who along with his father won several Grammy Awards®, lost his life in an accident in the early 1980s. MerleFest began in 1988 at Wilkes Community College, drawing a crowd of about 4,000. Today, it takes 13 stages to accommodate all the musicians, who have included the likes of Dolly Parton, Willie Nelson, Ralph Stanley, Emmylou Harris, and Ricky Skaggs.

CREDITS

"Pickin' for Merle" (UNC-TV, 1992)

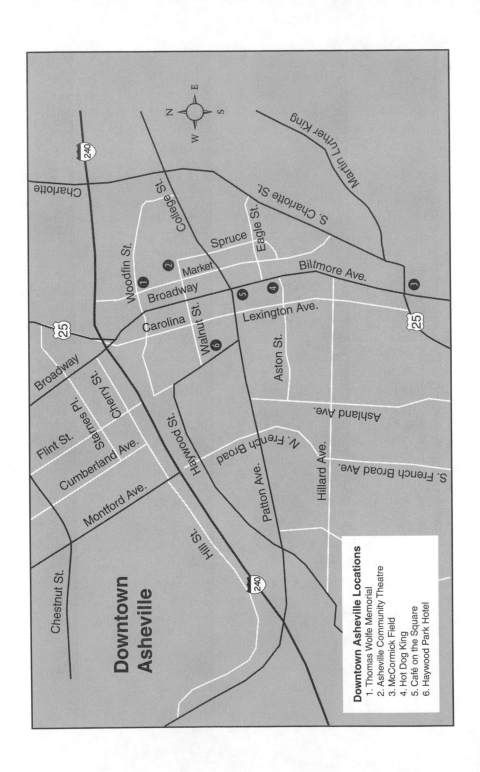

Downtown Asheville Locations
1. Thomas Wolfe Memorial
2. Asheville Community Theatre
3. McCormick Field
4. Hot Dog King
5. Café on the Square
6. Haywood Park Hotel

The Hot Dog King appears in *Hannibal*.
PHOTOGRAPH BY MEG CALLERY

Downtown Asheville Locations

McCormick Field

30 Buchanan Place (828-258-0428; www.theashevilletourists.com).
Visitors are limited to exterior viewing except during games and events.
Call for a schedule.

The baseball season winds down. The hotshot rookie goes
up to "The Show" in Atlanta, while the veteran catcher just wants
to finish out the season in Asheville. So it is in *Bull Durham* when
Crash Davis (Kevin Costner) is released by the Durham Bulls
and decides to chase the dubious minor-league home-run record
with the Asheville Tourists. As with the Bulls and their historic
stadium, the Tourists are indeed a real team with an equally
storied park. Scenes near the end of *Bull Durham* show Crash
driving up to historic McCormick Field and in the locker room
with the Asheville Tourists logo in the background. And it's in
a Tourists uniform that Crash does indeed hit his 247th home
run, before a sparse, only mildly interested crowd.

McCormick Field is a favorite destination for ballpark enthusiasts and baseball fans. Unlike Durham, the new version of Asheville's ballpark was constructed on the site of the old field. Built in 1924, it hosted legends such as Ty Cobb, Jackie Robinson, and Babe Ruth, who called McCormick "a damned delightful place."

Baseball has been around Asheville since 1866. If you're wondering about the name, the club was called by team names such as the Moonshiners and the Mountaineers before it became the Tourists. The new stadium seats 4,000 and is the perfect place to catch a ball game on a cool summer night in the mountains—and perhaps to recall a record-breaking cinematic performance.

CREDITS

Bull Durham (1988)

Q: Which country-music superstar was scheduled to play the baseball-player love interest of Sandra Bullock's character in the 2000 film *28 Days?*

A: *Garth Brooks, who actually gave big-league ball a shot with the San Diego Padres*

Hot Dog King

63 *Biltmore Avenue* (828-253-0448). *Hot Dog King is open from 9 A.M. to 8 P.M. Monday through Friday and from 9 A.M. to 6 P.M. on Saturday.*

For the past quarter-century or so, the unassuming Hot Dog King has been a fixture in downtown Asheville. It was recently immortalized on the silver screen, appearing under its own name in *Hannibal, the grisly sequel* to the Oscar®-winning 1991 film *Silence of the Lambs*. While more upscale and, yes, less caloric eateries have sprung up downtown, the King apparently has just the right cuisine for visitors from Sardinia. In a late scene, Carlo (Ivano Marescotti) carries a bag of dogs and drinks to the van after the call from Verger (Gary Oldman). Of course, the pork will have its revenge, but that's another scene. Look closely for Cynthia and Angie, who appear briefly as themselves and will be glad to tell you about their brush with fame—if they're not too busy serving up dogs and burgers all the way, with french fries and a cold drink.

CREDITS

Hannibal (2001)

Thomas Wolfe Memorial

52 North Market Street, Asheville (828-253-8304; www.wolfememorial.com). From April through October, the memorial is open from 9 A.M. to 5 P.M. Tuesday through Saturday. From November through March, it is open from 10 A.M. to 4 P.M. Tuesday through Saturday. An admission fee is charged.

Asheville's Thomas Wolfe wrote the novel *You Can't Go Home Again*, but film junkies with a literary bent can indeed visit the Thomas Wolfe Memorial in the author's hometown. The memorial includes the Old Kentucky Home, which was Wolfe's boyhood home and the model for the Dixieland boardinghouse in *Look Homeward, Angel*. The restored house was seriously damaged by fire in 1998 but is scheduled to reopen in 2004. The memorial offers a slide show, a tour that includes artifacts from Wolfe's New York City apartment and his father's stone-cutting shop, artwork, and books and pamphlets about Wolfe, his writings, and his connections to Asheville.

Although Wolfe is a world-renowned author (despite a brief

backlash from Asheville neighbors after his early fame), his dense, multilayered stories and novels have rarely been adapted for film. In the late 1970s, *You Can't Go Home Again* was made into a CBS movie starring Chris Sarandon as Wolfe alter-ego George Webber, Lee Grant as Esther Jack, and Tammy Grimes as Amy Carlton. A stage play of *Look Homeward, Angel* won the Pulitzer Prize® for playwright Ketti Frings and was presented on the "CBS Playhouse" series in 1972. A musical adaptation appeared later. Noted South Carolina author Pat Conroy—whose novels include *The Prince of Tides* and *The Great Santini*—has worked on a screenplay of *Look Homeward, Angel* that may emerge at some point. In the meantime, adventurous film junkies and Wolfe fans may want to seek out *Luke: A Tribute to Fred*, a 1979 documentary short about Fred Wolfe, the then-85-year-old brother of the author, who was the inspiration for Luke Gant in *Look Homeward, Angel*.

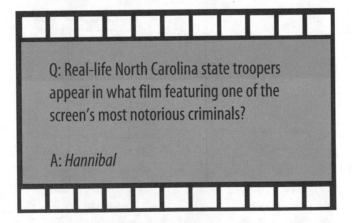

Q: Real-life North Carolina state troopers appear in what film featuring one of the screen's most notorious criminals?

A: *Hannibal*

Biltmore Estate
COURTESY OF N. C. DIVISION OF TOURISM, FILM, & SPORTS DEVELOPMENT

Other Asheville Area Locations

Blue Ridge Motion Pictures Studios

Old Charlotte Highway, off U.S. 74 West, Asheville (828-296-1499; www.blueridgemotionpictures.com). Tours are available every Saturday at 10:30 A.M. An admission fee is charged except for children under five.

They don't call them dream factories for nothing. The places where stories get turned to celluloid often don't look like much on the outside, but dreams are constructed within.

Blue Ridge Motion Pictures Studios, opened in Asheville in 2001, is the dream of executive producer Merwin Gross, a western North Carolina native who's made his career in independent films. This unassuming set of buildings just east of the city has served as a location and offices for *The Last of the Mohicans, My Fellow Americans, Patch Adams,* and *The Clearing.* BRMPS is now a full-production facility boasting five sound stages, a backlot, a recording studio, an animation division, and a

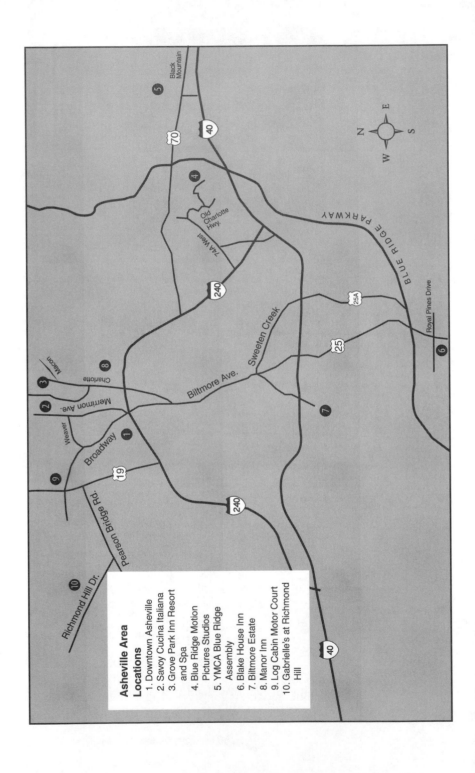

**Asheville Area
Locations**
1. Downtown Asheville
2. Savoy Cucina Italiana
3. Grove Park Inn Resort
   and Spa
4. Blue Ridge Motion
   Pictures Studios
5. YMCA Blue Ridge
   Assembly
6. Blake House Inn
7. Biltmore Estate
8. Manor Inn
9. Log Cabin Motor Court
10. Gabrielle's at Richmond
    Hill

wet stage—a tank that was once used for dyeing fabrics.

BRMPS is rapidly getting its feet wet in original productions, including "The Salsa Man," featuring renowned local chef Hector Diaz, who films episodes in Spanish and English for the Food Network and Telemundo. Other budding productions include Merwin Gross's *The Pond* and *Search* and Asheville writer Olson Huff's "The Window of Childhood." BRMPS actively provides advice and facilities to up-and-coming filmmakers. One day, future Spielbergs may return the favor.

CREDITS

The Clearing (2004); *Patch Adams* (1998); *My Fellow Americans* (1996); *The Last of the Mohicans* (1992)

YMCA Blue Ridge Assembly

84 Blue Ridge Circle, Black Mountain (828-669-8422; www. blueridgeassembly.org). The facilities are available for rent.

Film junkies can trace the plight of Gwen Cummings (East Carolina University's Sandra Bullock) from one end of North Carolina to the other as she reluctantly battles her alcohol addiction in the acclaimed feature *28 Days*. Things spin totally out of control when she crashes the limo into the house on the day of her sister's wedding. This scene was filmed in Wilmington's Forest Hills neighborhood. So the court orders her to a month in rehab at Serenity Glen, which in real life is part of the YMCA Blue Ridge Assembly in Black Mountain. The building where Gwen and the others try to get it together is part of a full-service conference center surrounded by 1,200 acres of streams, trails, and lakes, all of which were utilized during the filming.

Film junkies will remember Gwen's troubles and daring escapes as she comes to terms with her problems. Steve Buscemi plays counselor Cornell. Fellow rehabbers at Serenity Glen include Eddie (Viggo Mortensen) and Bobbie Jean (Diane Ladd). And yes, that's Chapel Hill native Loudon "Dead Skunk" Wainwright III as Guitar Guy.

The YMCA Blue Ridge Assembly will celebrate its 100th anniversary in 2006. Listed on the National Register of Historic

Places, it offers accommodations and meeting and dining facilities to over 20,000 guests a year. Recreational activities include swimming, hiking, tennis, volleyball, and instructional workshops.

CREDITS

28 Days (2000)

Biltmore Estate

1 Approach Road, off U.S. 25 in Asheville. Biltmore is open daily except for Thanksgiving and Christmas. The hours are 9 A.M. to 5 P.M. January though March and 8:30 A.M. to 5 P.M. April through December. An admission fee is charged. For information, call 800-624-1575 or 828-225-1333 or visit www.biltmore.com.

It is the largest private home in America and one of the most fabulous estates in the world. Is there a better one-sentence pitch? No. Thousands of photographs and numerous books and films have only added to the mystique of Biltmore, George Washington Vanderbilt's splendid palace. Quite simply, everyone—film junkie or otherwise—should experience Biltmore at least once.

Since the late 1940s, Biltmore has made sporadic appearances in films. The grounds and the house's glorious interiors and exteriors have served as backdrops for everything from Academy Award®-winning satire to kiddie pics, from horror flicks to farces. Though never called Biltmore in any film, the house is easily identified on posters for *Being There*, *Richie Rich*, *The Swan*, and others. Add the occasional travel special on television and you'll see that moviemakers can't get enough of the place.

First, a few facts. Biltmore Estate encompasses 8,000 acres of gardens, parks, and forests. Biltmore House contains 250 rooms, four acres of floor space, 34 master bedrooms, 43 bathrooms, three kitchens, a bowling alley, and an indoor swimming pool. Priceless furnishings and artwork by American and European masters adorn each room. The architect was Richard Morris Hunt, whose credits include the facade of the Metropolitan

The *Richie Rich* film crew sets up
an exterior shot at the Biltmore House.
COURTESY OF THE BILTMORE ESTATE, ASHEVILLE
© THE BILTMORE COMPANY

Museum of Art and the pedestal for the Statue of Liberty. The landscape architect was Frederick Law Olmsted, best known for designing New York's Central Park, the United States Capitol grounds, and Stanford University. Mr. Vanderbilt opened the house to family and friends on Christmas Eve 1895 but got to live in his dream house for only 20 years, dying unexpectedly at the age of 52. The home is still owned by descendants of the Vanderbilt family, though they do not live in the house at the present time.

The first film shot at Biltmore was *Tap Roots*, starring Van Heflin and Susan Hayward. Almost a decade later, *The Swan* featured the future princess of Monaco, Grace Kelly; Alec Guinness, playing a character named, ironically, Prince Albert; and Louis Jourdan. Biltmore staffers of that era were amused over a sequence in the movie in which a horse-drawn carriage pulls up and a bag is thrown into what is supposed to be a stable, but is actually a kitchen. Filming was dormant over the next couple of decades but came back strong with *Being There*, starring the brilliant Peter Sellers in the career-topping role of Chauncey.

Exterior shots lovingly show the grandeur of Biltmore House, which is supposed to be a mansion outside Washington. Melvyn Douglas won a Best Supporting Actor Oscar®, and Shirley MacLaine and Jack Warden also appear. And yes, that's the lagoon in Chance's famous final "divine" scene. The 1980s saw only the Don Knotts/Tim Conway vehicle *The Private Eyes* and the obscure *A Breed Apart* utilize the house and grounds, but the 1990s started a renaissance of first-rate productions, including the Michael Caine/Jim Belushi comedy *Mr. Destiny*, *Richie Rich*, Best Picture *Forrest Gump*, *My Fellow Americans*, *Patch Adams*, and *Hannibal*.

Most of the areas utilized in films are open to the public. Staff members will be glad to point out various locations, including the following highlights, starting with the grounds.

Film junkies will have to use their imaginations to re-create the mock-up of the White House built beside the lagoon for *My Fellow Americans*, starring Jack Lemmon and James Garner as ex-presidents on the run. The stone bridge over the bass pond on the way to the winery appears in Duncan's trip to Albany early in *The Last of the Mohicans*. Remote areas of the grounds appear briefly in the montage of Forrest Gump (Best Actor Tom Hanks) running across America. In *Patch Adams*, Robin Williams uses a run-down cabin on the estate as a medical clinic; this area is not accessible to the public.

Moving inside, the tapestry gallery was the setting for the opening shot of *Richie Rich*; observant film junkies will note the close-up of the portrait of George W. Vanderbilt hanging over the door to the library. Later, young Richie (Macaulay Culkin) rides his tricycle through the room. The opening scene in *Hannibal*, in which Verger (Gary Oldman) is offered Dr. Lecter's mask, takes place in the beautiful, wood-paneled library next door, which contains Mr. Vanderbilt's collection of 23,000 volumes. Other films using the library have included *Mr. Destiny*, *Richie Rich*, and *Being There*. The banquet hall, the largest room in the house, is where the Vanderbilts entertained and where their descendants continue to hold traditional Christmas parties. The room's long banquet table invites a *Citizen Kane* moment; *Richie Rich* supplied a satirical twist in the scene with the telephones. Another favorite is the music room, converted to a hospital in

Being There. The billiard room is seen in *The Private Eyes* and *Richie Rich.* And though it ~~sports a red color~~ scheme, Mr. Vanderbilt's bedroom *isn't* Richie's bedroom. The staff also points out that there is *not* a McDonald's on the site.

That's just a fraction of Biltmore's starring appearances on film. No doubt, film junkies will find more.

CREDITS

Hannibal (2001); *Patch Adams* (1998); *My Fellow Americans* (1996); *Forrest Gump* (1994); *Richie Rich* (1994); *The Last of the Mohicans* (1992); *Mr. Destiny* (1990); *A Breed Apart* (1984); *The Private Eyes* (1980); *Being There* (1979); *The Swan* (1956); *Tap Roots* (1948); and others

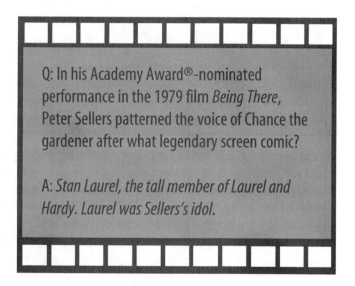

Q: In his Academy Award®-nominated performance in the 1979 film *Being There,* Peter Sellers patterned the voice of Chance the gardener after what legendary screen comic?

A: *Stan Laurel, the tall member of Laurel and Hardy. Laurel was Sellers's idol.*

Manor Inn

265 Charlotte Street, Asheville (828-253-1517). Visitors are limited to exterior viewing.

Asheville's stately Manor Inn, the centerpiece of the city's Albemarle Park-Manor Grounds Historic District, was transformed into 18th-century Albany, New York—complete with blacksmiths, villagers, and British militia—for *The Last of the*

Mohicans. The inn and the surrounding area are seen early on as Major Duncan Heyward (Steven Waddington) rides into town to meet with General Webb (Mac Andrews) and maybe catch up with Cora (Madeleine Stowe) while he's at it. Cora's picnic scenes with Duncan were filmed outside the Manor Inn and at Biltmore Estate (see previous entry), where Duncan is seen crossing the bridge. Interestingly, this was Stowe's second appearance in a film adaptation of James Fenimore Cooper's work. She was in a TV-movie version of *The Deerslayer* in the late 1970s.

Mohicans sparked a rehabilitation of the Manor Inn, the last of Asheville's famous 19th-century resorts. Now lovingly preserved and used as apartments, the inn was called home by Grace Kelly during the filming of *The Swan* in the mid-1950s.

CREDITS

The Last of the Mohicans (1992)

Log Cabin Motor Court

330 *Weaverville Highway, Asheville* (800-295-3392 or 828-645-6546; *www.cabinlodging.com*)

An unlikely film location is the Log Cabin Motor Court, located in the Reems Creek community between Asheville and Weaverville. An entire page of the company's website is devoted to *Thunder Road*, the 1958 mob-meets-moonshiner motion picture that was written, produced, and starred in by Robert Mitchum. The venturesome actor also wrote the movie's theme song, "Whippoorwill," and cast his teenage son, Jim, as his own brother.

Mitchum's action-packed film shot several scenes at the 1930s motor court, and it is said that the actor, preferring the quaint and cozy log cabins to more luxurious accommodations, spent several nights here. Even today, film junkies can choose from about 20 cabins ranging from 225 square feet to 1,800 square feet, each with beds, heat, indoor bathrooms with showers, cable television, and internet access. Some of the cabins even have air conditioning, microwaves, full kitchens, and fireplaces or gas-log stoves. There's also a coin laundromat and the Hunter's Lodge Restaurant on site. Sorry, no phones are provided, so bring your cell if you must.

Convenient to Asheville and area attractions, Log Cabin Motor Court offers a unique and affordable lodging experience that is family friendly, pet friendly, and film junkie friendly. Be sure to ask for directions to the famed Biltmore Avenue underpass, an old viaduct referred to by locals as the *"Thunder Road underpass."*

CREDITS

Thunder Road (1958)

Asheville Star Tracks

Savoy Cucina Italiana

641 Merrimon Avenue (828-253-1077 www.savoycusina.com).
Lunch is served Tuesday through Friday and dinner daily.

Eric Scheffer, the owner of Savoy Cucina Italiana, is no stranger to the film world, having been a motion-picture and television producer in L.A. for almost 20 years. Scheffer's film career has taken him all over the world, including an extended period in South America. But when L.A.'s earthquakes became a bit too intense, he and his wife, Heidi, relocated to Asheville in the mid-'90s. Since they took over Savoy in 2000 after the birth of their daughter, the restaurant has rapidly established itself as a favorite of locals and visiting celebrities.

Savoy Cucina Italiana offers modern Italian cuisine, with an emphasis on wine, seafood, and cosmopolitan fare. The menu changes weekly. Guests can also partake of monthly wine dinners, cooking classes, and wine tastings, including some featuring South American vintages.

Although Scheffer left Hollywood, that hasn't stopped Hollywood from finding his new digs. Famous diners at Savoy Cucina have included Robin Williams, Robert Redford, Andie

MacDowell, Kristin Davis, singer Bobby McFerrin, Kyle MacLachlan, and *Cold Mountain* author Charles Frazier.

The glorious Grove Park Inn Resort & Spa has been
a favorite of the stars for almost a century.
PHOTOGRAPH BY BILL RUSS
COURTESY OF N. C. DIVISION OF TOURISM, FILM, & SPORTS DEVELOPMENT

The Grove Park Inn Resort and Spa

290 Macon Avenue (800-438-5800; www.groveparkinn.com)

The venerable Grove Park Inn Resort and Spa features sweeping mountain vistas and elegant Old World interiors worthy of any film. But so far, the inn has resisted Hollywood overtures, most notably from *Dirty Dancing*.

Stars have been coming to the Grove Park Inn since the early 1900s to relax and unwind, either on vacation or while working on projects in the area. The new millennium finds the inn adding a state-of-the-art spa. Thus, the collection of eight-by-tens on the inn's walls of fame will continue to expand. There, you'll find the occasional president and Pulitzer Prize winner, as well as movie stars.

The doors of select rooms and suites at the inn feature plaques with the names of famous former occupants. Together, they add up to an all-time A-list. Actors? How about Anthony Hopkins, Daniel Day-Lewis, Danny Glover, Jack Lemmon, E. G. Marshall, Burt Reynolds, Gene Hackman, and Jason Robards, to name but a few? Presidents? Just Coolidge, Wilson, Hoover, Taft, FDR, Nixon, Eisenhower, and George H. W. Bush, as well as former first lady Lady Bird Johnson. Musicians? Well, that list includes Barbara Mandrell, Ellis Marsalis, Johnny Mathis, Peter Nero, Dave Brubeck, Pam Tillis, John Denver, and Judy Collins. Athletes? Okay, there's Reggie Jackson, Arnold Palmer, Dorothy Hamill, Bruce Jenner, Yogi Berra, Greg LeMond, Bobby Jones, and legendary coaches Tom Landry and Dean Smith. Authors? Only F. Scott Fitzgerald, Charles Frazier, Margaret Mitchell, Deepak Chopra, Alex Haley, and others. And this is just a fraction.

What draws such star power to this, one of the South's oldest and most famous grand resorts? Pretty much what attracted developer Edwin W. Grove back in the late 1800s. Remarkably, much of that unspoiled quality still exists today. Asheville and western North Carolina have long been known for the curative qualities of the fresh mountain air. Grove, a Midwestern businessman, spent summers in Asheville in the late 1800s as therapy for his bronchitis. He fell in love with Asheville and dreamed of building a resort hotel, for which he broke ground in 1912. The Grove Park Inn became—and still is—one of the most enduringly original and exciting resorts in America.

In 2001, the inn acquired another movie connection when it brought in Universal Studios to augment the natural rock used in building its first-class spa, which offers massages, facials, body wraps, and other pampering treats. Now, guests have another recreational option besides the Donald Ross golf course, the tennis courts, the swimming pool, the sports complex, and the fine dining and shopping.

Café on the Square

*One Biltmore Avenue (828-251-5565; www.cafeonthesquare.com).
Lunch is served Monday through Saturday and dinner daily. Call for
the winter schedule.*

Many restaurants in L.A. can't boast the star power that's
been seen in Asheville's Café on the Square. But that wasn't
always the case. In a better-than-Hollywood story, the restaurant struggled a bit before a little production called *The Last of
the Mohicans* came to town in the early '90s and set up shop on
Pack Square right above the café. Soon, this was the favorite
hangout of Daniel Day-Lewis and other actors and crew from
the film. Things took off from there. The café has become the
choice of the many stars who have worked or vacationed in
Asheville in recent years.

Featuring fine American cuisine, including seafood, beef,
pasta, and vegetarian dishes, the café with the big window overlooking historic Pack Square is *the* place to see and be seen.
Robert Redford became a big fan while in town filming *The Clearing* in late 2002. Other famous diners have included Robin Williams, who—shockingly!—is remembered as being funny; former
Asheville Community Theatre director Charlton Heston and
wife Lydia; Day-Lewis's *Mohicans* co-star Madeleine Stowe; Ben
Affleck; Isabelle Adjani; Dan Aykroyd; Sandra Bullock; Liam
Neeson; Natasha Richardson; and Justine Bateman. One celebrity who missed out, though, was John F. Kennedy, Jr., who
stopped by when the café was closed.

Of course, the famous aren't at the Café on the Square every night, but the staff will be glad to share stories with film
junkies enjoying the delicious fare.

Haywood Park Hotel

One Battery Park Avenue (800-228-2522 or 828-252-2522;
www.haywoodpark.com)

Adding to the chic contemporary atmosphere of downtown Asheville is the Haywood Park Hotel, whose 33 suites—each adorned with original artwork and decorations—have drawn an A-list collection of celebrity guests over the years, some of whom are featured on the lobby's wall of fame. The hotel hosted Robert Redford, Willem Dafoe, Helen Mirren, and the crew of *The Clearing*, who used several rooms for hair and makeup during the production. Daniel Day-Lewis and several other cast and crew members from *The Last of the Mohicans* stayed here and autographed photographs for the wall of fame. In keeping with the Academy Award® theme, Michael Caine (during *Mr. Destiny*) and Robin Williams (during *Patch Adams*) no doubt enjoyed the Haywood Park's signature turndown service. Anthony Hopkins and crew stayed here as he reprised his Oscar®-winning role as Hannibal Lecter in *Hannibal.*

Hopkins perhaps enjoyed a nice Chianti along with the French, German, and Indian cuisine at The Flying Frog Café and Wine Bar, located inside the Haywood Park. The hotel's atrium features antique and jewelry shops, galleries, restaurants, and other businesses for film junkies to enjoy.

The hotel appears on the silver screen during the Gay Pride Parade sequence of *My Fellow Americans*, starring Jack Lemmon and James Garner.

Blake House Inn

150 Royal Pines Drive (888-353-5227; www.blakehouse.com)

Andie MacDowell selected Asheville's Blake House Inn as the principal location for sit-down interviews for the Lifetime

network's "Intimate Portrait" of her life. The historic house, built around 1847, was the perfect choice. Andie spent many happy moments here as a child, when the house was in her family. She remembered the pretty spot when she moved to the Asheville area with her family. Interviews with Andie and family and friends took place in several of the rooms available to guests at the cozy bed-and-breakfast.

Rosalie Anderson MacDowell, still known as "Rose" to some, was born in Gaffney, South Carolina. She dropped out of Winthrop College to head for a wildly successful modeling career in New York. Her acting debut as Jane in the 1984 film *Greystoke: The Legend of Tarzan, Lord of the Apes* was not exactly memorable, but her portrayal of Ann in Steven Soderbergh's 1989 Palme d'Or-winning *sex, lies and videotape* really put her on the map. The performance earned Andie her first Golden Globe® nomination, which was followed by others for *Green Card* and *Four Weddings and a Funeral*. Her other memorable credits include *Groundhog Day, Unstrung Heroes, Michael,* and *Harrison's Flowers*. She's also done a couple of films in North Carolina—*Muppets From Space* and *Shadrach*. Since relocating to Asheville, she has worked on the pilot for a proposed television series, "Jo," which features Andie as a veterinarian in her adopted hometown. She continues to appear in films and commercials while enjoying her laid-back mountain home.

Film junkies visiting The Blake House can stay in "Andie's room"—the one she slept in as a child—and others where the Lifetime special was filmed. A fine example of Italianate architecture with Gothic influences, the house once served as a Confederate field hospital. Today, it is convenient to the city's many attractions.

★ ★ ★ ★ ★ ★ ★ ★ ★ ★

Asheville Film Festival

Debuting in the fall of 2003, the Asheville Film Festival quickly made its mark with big-name filmmakers Ang Lee and Rob Cohen, plus top-notch "locals" Andie MacDowell and Pat Hingle. The perfect place for a film festival if there ever was one, downtown Asheville offers a celebration of western North Carolina as a filmmaking mecca. The fest includes screenings, panel discussions, and student films. A North Carolina-made feature, *The Angel Doll*, won the Audience Favorite award at the 2003 festival. For more information, call 828-259-5800 or visit www.ashevillefilmfestival.com.

Gabrielle's at Richmond Hill

87 Richmond Hill Drive, Asheville (888-742-4536 or 828-252-7313; www.richmondhillinn.com). Richmond Hill Inn is open year-round. Gabrielle's Restaurant is open from mid-February until late December. Reservations are recommended.

One encounter with Gabrielle's tempting seasonal menus and award-winning wine list is enough to send even the most discriminating palates into overdrive. To dine here is to experience culinary perfection—well, as close as mere mortals, including celebrities, can expect. Needless to say, Gabrielle's AAA Four Diamond rating (ten years and counting) is well deserved.

Leading man Robert Redford, who was in western North

★ ★ ★ ★ ★ ★ ★ ★ ★ ★

Carolina to film *The Clearing*, is among Gabrielle's most recent celebrity diners. Actress Andie MacDowell, who is spotted frequently at Asheville's upscale eateries, is also fond of Gabrielle's creative continental cuisine. Fava beans frequently appear on the menu, which might prompt curious film junkies to wonder if they were favored by (or inspired by) a certain actor cast in the formidable title role of *Hannibal*, which filmed at nearby Biltmore Estate.

A local celebrity, house pianist Christopher Leonard, welcomes guests who enter Richmond Hill Inn's parlor Thursday through Monday evenings. Also on the ground floor are the handsome dining room and the glass-enclosed sun porch, which offers breathtaking views of the Blue Ridge Mountains and the French Broad River.

The noteworthy restaurant complements the highly acclaimed Richmond Hill Inn, a recipient of Mobil's coveted Four Star rating and a 2003 *Southern Living* Readers' Choice Award. Designed by James G. Hill and built in 1889 as the residence of Ambassador and Congressman Richmond Pearson and his wife, Gabrielle, the elegant Victorian mansion has enjoyed a long history of entertaining guests. Thanks to the local preservation society, the house was spared from destruction and moved 600 feet to its present location. During the 1980s, a couple from Greensboro purchased the property, restored the house to its original grandeur, and opened it as an inn. Offering 31 handsomely appointed guest rooms, the historic mansion serves as the centerpiece of a complex that includes the newer Croquet Cottages and Garden Pavilion guest rooms. At every turn, the estate's English cottage-style landscaping beckons with period gardens, a mountain brook, and a waterfall. What more could a film junkie or a celebrity want?

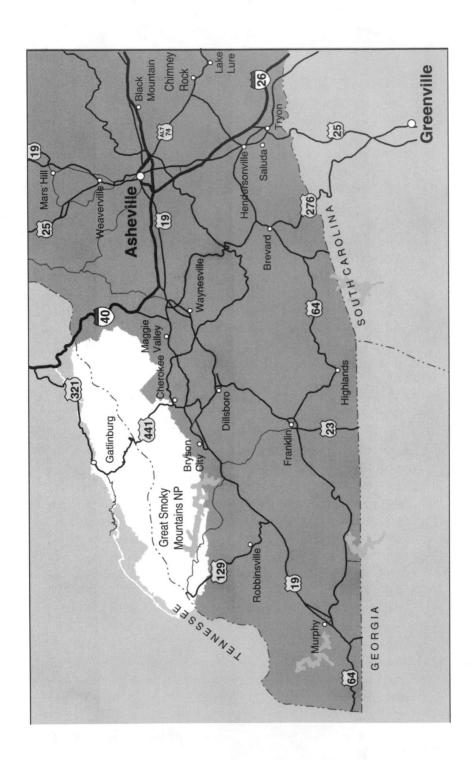

Filming on the Blue Ridge Parkway
COURTESY OF THE WESTERN NORTH CAROLINA FILM COMMISSION

Blue Ridge Parkway

Half of the Blue Ridge Parkway's 469 miles are in western North Carolina.

It's not nicknamed "America's favorite drive" for nothing. Its scenery, wildlife, recreational opportunities, folk history, and crafts make the Blue Ridge Parkway one of the most visited attractions in the National Park System. A WPA project from the 1930s, the parkway has drawn a number of documentary filmmakers over the years, and countless commercials have also filmed here. And the parkway's feature-film moments have been sparse but memorable.

The UNC-TV documentary "Blue Ridge Parkway: America's Grand Balcony" captures the mountain vistas, the farmsteads, the amazing varieties of flora and fauna, the music, the culture, and the oral history of the region. In Best Picture *Forrest Gump*, you'll notice the parkway during Forrest's (Tom Hanks's) run across America. These brief scenes were shot near Doughton Park in Alleghany County, between Milepost 339 and Milepost 341. The opening and closing scenes in *The Last of the Mohicans* were filmed at Greenknob Overlook in McDowell County. The scene after the battle of Fort William Henry was filmed at Linville Falls Recreation Area, located at Milepost 316.4. Aerial shots of the real Cold Mountain appear in the film version of Charles Frazier's bestseller, though most of it was shot in Romania.

The Blue Ridge Parkway Foundation sponsors the Banff Film Festival World Tour, held each spring at colleges in Boone, Brevard, High Point, and Winston-Salem.

CREDITS

"Blue Ridge Parkway: America's Grand Balcony" (UNC-TV, 1999); *Forrest Gump* (1994); *The Last of the Mohicans* (1992); documentaries

★★★★★★★★★★★★★

John Ehle / Rosemary Harris / Jennifer Ehle

Although John Ehle has written several nonfiction books on subjects as diverse as French wine and the civil-rights movement, he's rarely had to look beyond his native North Carolina mountains to find settings for his 11 acclaimed novels, two of which have been turned into movies that filmed in western North Carolina. The 1995 film *The Journey of August King*, set in the early 19th century, stars Jason Patric and Thandie Newton. The 1989 film *Winter People* features Kurt Russell, Kelly McGillis, and Lloyd Bridges.

Ehle, raised in Asheville, claims he inherited his storytelling gift from his mother, who comes from four generations of Appalachian people. Ehle wrote plays for NBC Radio while he was a

Filming John Ehle's *The Journey of August King*
COURTESY OF THE WESTERN NORTH CAROLINA FILM COMMISSION

student at UNC following his service in World War II. Later, he helped develop the North Carolina School of the Arts, the Governor's School, the North Carolina Film Board, and the North Carolina Institute of Outdoor Drama. He has won several national and statewide awards, including the Sir Walter Raleigh Award for fiction five times.

Ehle currently lives in Winston-Salem and Penland with his wife, the celebrated actress Rosemary Harris. Noted for her roles in film adaptations of Shakespeare, Harris played Desdemona in *Othello* (1955), Viola in *Twelfth Night* (1957), and the Player Queen in *Hamlet* (1996). The winner of Emmy® and Golden Globe® awards, she was nominated for a Best Supporting Actress Academy Award® for the 1995 film *Tom and Viv*. Of course, a whole new generation knows her more for *Spider-Man* than Shakespeare. Harris plays Peter Parker's (Tobey Maguire's) Aunt May in the action/adventure blockbuster and reprises the role in *Spider-Man II*.

Their daughter, Jennifer Ehle, is an actress and a graduate of the North Carolina School of the Arts. She has won a Tony® Award—in the same category as her mother, no less—and appeared as the younger version of her mother's character in the 1999 film *Sunshine*.

★★★★★★★★★★★★★

The Real Cold Mountain

Western North Carolina native Charles Frazier's first novel, *Cold Mountain*, came out of nowhere to win the National Book Award in 1997. And when the film version of the haunting, lyrical work appeared at Christmas 2003, film junkies from around the world sought out the real Cold Mountain in Haywood County. The highly praised film, starring Jude Law, Nicole Kidman, Renée Zellweger, and Winston-Salem youth Kristen LaPrade, came very close to being filmed in western North Carolina before the production settled on Romania.

Film junkies can visit the real Cold Mountain, part of Pisgah National Forest southwest of Asheville. One of the best places to begin exploration is near Milepost 411 on the Blue Ridge Parkway. A great photo opportunity exists here with the now-famous mountain in the background. Film junkies can trek part of Inman's journey home to Ada, but be forewarned that the hike is over ten miles one-way from the Daniel Boone Camp trailhead via the Art Loeb and Cold Mountain trails, and that Cold Mountain rises over 6,000 feet. For information about Pisgah National Forest, call 828-877-3265 or visit www.cs.unca.edu/nfsnc.

Deals Gap/The Dragon
U.S. 129 at the North Carolina/Tennessee line

Film junkies can get a cinematic rush by driving the 300-plus curves in just over ten miles on "The Dragon," a section of U.S. 129 at Deals Gap at the North Carolina/Tennessee line. The Dragon is considered one of the world's best motorcycling and sports-car roads, but those wanting a slower pace can visit the site of some exciting film scenes, many of which feature—what

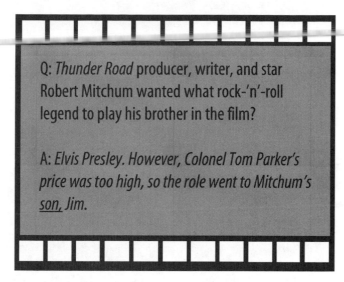

Q: *Thunder Road* producer, writer, and star Robert Mitchum wanted what rock-'n'-roll legend to play his brother in the film?

A: *Elvis Presley. However, Colonel Tom Parker's price was too high, so the role went to Mitchum's son, Jim.*

else?—fast cars and breakneck chases. Or you can see The Dragon in its own video, *Tail of the Dragon*.

The unofficial route of The Dragon begins on the North Carolina side at the aptly named Fugitive Bridge. Here, film junkies can get a marvelous view of Cheoah Dam (see next page), from which Dr. Richard Kimball (Harrison Ford) makes his memorable leap in *The Fugitive*. It ends 14 miles across the mountain at the Tabcat Creek Bridge in Tennessee.

The first feature made on U.S. 129 was *Thunder Road*. Robert Mitchum produced, wrote, and starred in this drive-in classic about backwoods moonshining. *Thunder Road* filmed several scenes on The Dragon, some featuring the old wooden safety posts, a few of which still remain. Another minor classic in the same vein is *Two-Lane Blacktop*, a muscle-car road movie starring North Carolina's James Taylor as "the Driver" in his only acting role to date, along with a fellow '60s music legend, Beach Boy Dennis Wilson. In *Two-Lane Blacktop*, which has standout performances by Warren Oates and Harry Dean Stanton, you'll see the state-line sign, some of the curves, and the original single-lane bridge at Tapoco Dam. Dragon historians will also note the original Deals Gap diner and Esso gas station, which appear at the end of the movie. In a bit of irony, one of the two '55 Chevys in the film turned up two years later in *American Graffiti*, driven by Dr. Richard Kimball himself, Harrison Ford.

CREDITS
The *Tail of the Dragon* video (2003) is available at www.tailofthedragon.com/shop. The Dragon's other credits include *In Dreams* (1999); *The Fugitive* (1993); *Two-Lane Blacktop* (1971); and *Thunder Road* (1958).

Cheoah Dam
U.S. 129 in northwestern Graham County on the Tennessee line. Visitors are limited to exterior viewing.

"I didn't kill my wife!"
"I don't care!"

Great dialogue, sure. And the scenery isn't bad either. This is, of course, the famous scene from *The Fugitive* when United States marshal Sam Gerard (Tommy Lee Jones) has Dr. Richard Kimball's (Harrison Ford's) back to the wall—or, in this case, to a long drop. Film junkies won't soon forget this scene, which probably went a long way toward winning Jones that Best Supporting Actor Oscar®.

Construction on Cheoah Dam—located where the Cheoah River meets the Little Tennessee—began in 1917. The dam is made of hand-cut stone and covered with a layer of concrete. At the time it was built, it was the highest outflow dam in the world and featured the world's largest turbines.

Though film junkies can't visit the actual pipe where the scene in *The Fugitive* was shot, a good view is available from the aptly named Fugitive Bridge on U.S. 129.

CREDITS
The Fugitive (1993)

Fontana Lake and Fontana Village
N.C. 28, Fontana Dam (800-849-2258; www.fontanavillage.com). A fee is charged for boat tours; call for hours.

Fontana Lake, in the extreme western "nose" of North

Carolina, due south of Knoxville, Tennessee, and just above where the Tar Heel State shares a brief border with Georgia, provided the perfect natural setting for the acclaimed feature *Nell*. Jodie Foster's Academy Award®-nominated performance was based on the true story of a backwoods woman, her idioglossia (a condition in which a person pronounces words so badly as to seem to speak a language all its own), and her introduction to society. It's hard to say what's more stunning in the film, Foster's performance or Fontana's beauty.

Foster lost almost 15 pounds for the role, mostly by eating what Nell would eat. Her use of Nell's speech and language (a kind of mountain English taught to the real-life Nell by her stroke-affected mother) is amazing. Interestingly, co-star Liam Neeson, who plays Dr. Lovell, was much taken by the local language, as it reminded him of his native Ireland. Foster, who also produced the film, spent part of her down time on the set exchanging faxes with her recent *Maverick* co-star, Mel Gibson, who was making *Braveheart* at the time.

But the true star of the film could be the beautiful lake and its surrounding area. For several years, visitors to Fontana Lake could take a "Nell Cabin Boat Tour." Unfortunately, the cabin now lies disassembled in a maintenance shed at Fontana Village, as the site was on land owned by the National Park Service. Film junkies can still visit the site on a three-hour round-trip "semi-guided" tour by boat. It's also possible to hike to the site.

Non-film activities at this historic resort include camping, hiking, boating, and fishing.

CREDITS

Nell (1994)

Robbinsville

Robbinsville is on U.S. 129 and N.C. 143 in extreme western North Carolina. All noted Nell locations are in the downtown area; most keep daytime business hours.

The theme song from composer Mark Isham's Golden Globe®-nominated score for *Nell* is called "Welcome to

Robbinsville," which is appropriate, as this beautiful Graham County town will forever be linked to the memorable Jodie Foster film. Robbinsville is civilization, in contrast to Nell's wild, untamed wilderness country. It is also home to the good doctor Jerry Lovell (Liam Neeson), who has Nell's best interest at heart, unlike the cold, hard city of Charlotte with its universities and news media and psychologist Paula Olsen (Natasha Richardson).

But *Nell* wasn't the first time the movies came calling. The silent feature *Stark Love* shot exclusively in the area. It was written, produced, and directed by Karl Brown, a protege of D. W. Griffith. Brown insisted on authenticity, using local, untrained "actors" (at $25 a week!) and shooting without makeup. This realism separated *Stark Love* from the usual silent-film melodrama and is one of the reasons it is held in high esteem by film historians of the pre-talkie era.

Of course, film junkies are more likely to remember *Nell*, which Foster produced as well as starred in, and for which she garnered a Best Actress nomination. A good starting point for a tour of Robbinsville's Main Street is Snyder's Department Store, where Jerry and Paula take Nell on her trip into town to acclimate her to society. In this memorable scene, Nell gets a little carried away with her shopping spree. Snyder's, a Robbinsville fixture for years, carries a little bit of everything; the folks here are happy to discuss their brush with fame. Of course, Nell escapes the little trip and ends up down at the Blue Beacon Pool & Pawn, where the coarser side of an exploitive society is on display. At the time of the filming, the restaurant where Sheriff Todd Peterson (Tar Heel Nick Searcy) comforts his wife, Mary (Robin Mullins), was called the Joyce Kilmer Restaurant, after the nearby national forest, which in turn was named for the author of the poem "Trees." Today, the place is called Lynn's, and it still serves up nice meals to hungry film junkies. The courtroom scenes were filmed at the Graham County Courthouse, a striking brown and tan quartzite structure built as a WPA project and first used in 1942.

CREDITS

Nell (1994); *Stark Love* (1927)

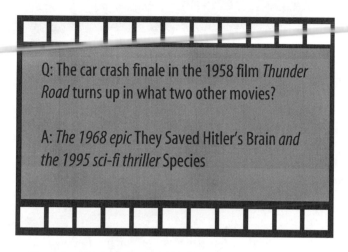

Q: The car crash finale in the 1958 film *Thunder Road* turns up in what two other movies?

A: *The 1968 epic* They Saved Hitler's Brain *and the 1995 sci-fi thriller* Species

Great Smoky Mountains Railroad

GSMR's depots are located in Dillsboro and Bryson City. Various packages and schedules are available at different prices. For information, call 800-872-4681 or visit www.gsmr.com.

Train wreck is a phrase most movies want to avoid, but Great Smoky Mountains Railroad is downright proud of having staged one of the most famous ones in contemporary film. Film junkies who visit GSMR can also ride in the same train cars as two "odd couples." And one of the railroad's locomotives is a star in its own right. Add in special programs that appeal to kids, gourmets, and murder-mystery buffs and you may feel like you're in a movie yourself during an exciting adventure through the trestles, tunnels, valleys, and gorges of the beautiful western North Carolina mountains.

GSMR took center stage in the early hours of a cold February morning in 1993, when one of the most stunning live-action train collisions in film history was set up and executed for a pivotal early sequence in *The Fugitive*. Even casual film junkies will remember the prison trip of wrongly accused and convicted Dr. Richard Kimball (Harrison Ford). A skirmish causes the bus on which he is riding to run off the road, down an embankment, and onto the tracks of an oncoming train.

After enduring several hours in the early-morning cold, as well as a snowstorm, the filmmakers got the shot on the first take. Afterwards, it was decided to leave the wreckage "as is" for a

The train wreck from *The Fugitive*,
staged at the Great Smoky Mountains Railroad
© LAVIDGE & ASSOCIATES
COURTESY OF GREAT SMOKY MOUNTAINS RAILROAD

tourist attraction. Today, visitors can see the site from the train out of Dillsboro or go down for their own close-up with this piece of Hollywood history.

But that's hardly all the moviemaking GSMR has experienced. The Ben Affleck/Sandra Bullock romantic comedy *Forces of Nature* features a daring scene on the train out of Bryson City. The free-spirited Sarah (Bullock) lures the uptight Ben (Affleck) to the top of the train car on an 800-foot-long trestle a hundred feet above Fontana Lake. The filmmakers wanted Ben and Sandy to be a bit *more* free during this scene, but GSMR insisted the actors be tethered for safety reasons. Though the film was less than a force at the box office, Affleck and Bullock, a former East Carolina University student, are remembered as friendly and flirtatious off-camera.

The popular James Garner was also a big hit off-camera, spending time between takes of *My Fellow Americans* talking NASCAR with GSMR conductors. The political comedy stars Garner and Jack Lemmon as former presidents on the lam. It filmed in a car on the Crescent Limited. While race fan and amateur driver Garner chatted with the conductors, Lemmon was content to spend his down time with his black poodle, often sharing ice cream with his pet.

Smaller features have also used GSMR cars and locations. *Digging to China* features Kevin Bacon and Raleigh native Evan

Rachel Wood. Fellow Tar Heels Sean Bridgers (the "Charlotte Tribune" reporter and photographer in Nell) and Nick Searcy (Sheriff Todd in that film) produced and starred in *Paradise Falls*, an independent feature set in the Depression that utilized Steam Engine 1702. *Paradise Falls*, co-written by Bridgers and his mother, noted young-adult author Sue Ellen Bridgers, won the Hollywood Discovery Award in 1998. It features music by North Carolina's legendary Red Clay Ramblers.

A star in its own right, 1702 is featured in *This Property Is Condemned*, the Robert Redford/Natalie Wood screen version of Tennessee Williams's play. *This Property Is Condemned* filmed in Louisiana. The steam engine was also used for *The Smoky Mountain Wilderness Adventure*, an interactive IMAX film starring Dolly Parton and playing—where else?—at Dollywood, the popular theme park down the road in Tennessee.

CREDITS

Forces of Nature (1999); *Digging to China* (1998); *Paradise Falls* (1997); *My Fellow Americans* (1996); *The Fugitive* (1993)

Cataloochee Ranch

119 Ranch Drive, Maggie Valley (800-868-1401 or 828-926-1401; www.cataloochee-ranch.com). The resort is open April through February.

Cataloochee, a Cherokee word meaning "wave after wave," refers to this ranch's view of range after mountain range. Tucked away in Maggie Valley at 5,000 feet in elevation, Cataloochee Ranch offers 1,000 acres that nestle up to Great Smoky Mountains National Park. Its extraordinary views were scouted heavily for the blockbuster *Cold Mountain*. While there's typically an abundance of snow in Maggie Valley during the winter months, there's no absolute guarantee of icy precipitation on a daily basis. Alas, director Anthony Minghella wanted snow, and lots of it! *Cold Mountain* ultimately filmed in Romania. Had the film lensed here, however, its scenery would have been equally beautiful.

One feature that did use Cataloochee is *Songcatcher*, which stars Janet McTeer as Professor Lily Penleric, Ph.D., a musicologist whose passion is collecting American ballads with British roots. She discovers these songs in their purest form in the Appalachians and sets out to scientifically document and record them. The film also stars Aidan Quinn as unlikely love interest Tom Bledsoe, a ruggedly handsome mountain man who plays a mean banjo. Rising starlet Emmy Rossum portrays Deladis Slocumb, a teenager whose hauntingly soothing vocals captivate the hearts of all, especially the unruly Fate Honeycutt (Greg Russell). Be on the lookout for Cataloochee Ranch when the two young sweethearts go into the woods and tie a "lover's knot" with tree branches. As the saying goes, if the knot remains, it's true love. You'll have to rent the movie to see if the knot holds. Even if love stories aren't your thing, the soundtrack alone is a remarkable piece of work. The original screenplay, breathtaking cinematography, and alluring mountain music combine to make *Songcatcher* a praiseworthy film. And if you're smitten by the amazing voice of Emmy Rossum, you can also catch her as Christine, the female lead in the 2004 film version of *Phantom of the Opera*.

Film junkies can visit Cataloochee Ranch, which has welcomed guests since 1961. It offers 12 cabins, six suites, and six guest rooms with fireplaces, antiques, and handmade quilts. The rustic resort includes a family-style restaurant, a lounge, a swimming pool, a Jacuzzi, and meeting facilities. Plenty of outdoor activities are available, too, such as horseback riding, skiing, tennis, fishing, hiking, and golf.

CREDITS

Songcatcher (2000)

Chimney Rock Park

The park is located on U.S. 66/74A in Chimney Rock. Weather permitting, it is open every day except Thanksgiving, Christmas, and New Year's. The ticket plaza is open from 8:30 A.M. to 5:30 P.M. during daylight saving time and from 8:30 A.M. to 4:30 P.M. the rest of the year. The park remains open an hour and a half after the ticket plaza closes. An admission fee is charged. For information, call 800-277-9611 or visit www. chimneyrockpark.com.

Spectacular natural beauty, including the unique Chimney Rock and one of the highest waterfalls on the East Coast, adds to film junkies' exploration of the locations for the final scenes of *The Last of the Mohicans.* The film won an Academy Award® for Best Sound, but it is the visuals that show off breathtaking western North Carolina at its finest.

The Chimney Rock area hosted quite a bit of movie activity back in the early days. Productions like *Blue Ridge Bandit* and *The Heart of the Blue Ridge* incorporated mountain scenery, while *The Masked Rider* was about a gang of moonshiners. But *Mohicans* director Michael Mann's film of James Fenimore Cooper's classic novel keeps Chimney Rock Park on the map. Film junkies with strong legs and sturdy hiking boots can relive some of their favorite moments at this privately owned park 25 miles southeast of Asheville. Chimney Rock Park takes great pride in its *Mohicans* connection, offering a location guide and map with the price of admission. And copies of the film are for sale here. This is a favorite gathering point for fans of the movie, so you may very well meet other film junkies along the

Filming the climactic scene in *The Last of the Mohicans.*

trail. Locations are accessed by both the Skyline Trail and the Cliff Trail.

The film features outstanding performances by Daniel Day-Lewis and Madeleine Stowe. One of the most memorable film sites is the top of Chimney Rock, where the Huron chief listens to the pleas of Hawkeye (Day-Lewis) and Magua (Wes Studi) before passing judgment on the unfortunate Duncan (Steven Waddington). The spectacular Hickory Nut Falls is seen over the chief's shoulder. This 404-foot waterfall is also where the climactic battle takes place. After Magua captures Cora (Stowe) and Alice (Jodhi May), and Hawkeye makes the film's signature "I will find you" speech, he, Chingachgook (Russell Means), and Uncas (Eric Schweig) pursue Magua up the steep slope of Groundhog Slide. The dramatic Nature's Showerbath is the backdrop for some of the more violent passages in the film. Magua brutally kills Uncas, prompting the shaken Alice to leap to her death. After witnessing these horrific events, Hawkeye and Cora share a brief embrace at the aptly named Inspiration Point just before Magua is killed by Chingachgook.

Chimney Rock Park is a treat for nature lovers, hikers, and picnickers, as well as film junkies. You won't forget it.

CREDITS

The Last of the Mohicans (1992); *The Masked Rider* (1916); *Blue Ridge Bandit* (1915); *The Heart of the Blue Ridge* (1915)

Lake Lure

The tour company is located at 2930 Memorial Highway in Lake Lure. During March, tours are offered hourly between noon and 3 P.M. on Friday, Saturday, and Sunday. From April through November, they are offered hourly from 10 A.M. until twilight daily. A fee is charged. For information, call 877-386-4255 or visit www.lakelure.com.

Johnny lifting Baby out of the water. Baby's bridge. The resort staff dancing to Motown and blue-eyed soul. All of these are memorable moments from *Dirty Dancing*. The gorgeous setting for this iconic film from the 1980s—homage to the

Recall the days of *Dirty Dancing* at Lake Lure.
PHOTOGRAPH BY BILL RUSS
COURTESY OF N. C. DIVISION OF TOURISM, FILM, & SPORTS DEVELOPMENT

1960s—is still attracting film junkies in the new millennium.

Beautiful Lake Lure has provided a backdrop for a few other films over the years, including *Firestarter* and *A Breed Apart*, but it will forever be viewed as Kellerman's, the Catskills resort where the aptly nicknamed Frances "Baby" Houseman (Jennifer Grey) comes of age, drawn by the swivel-hipped magnetism of Johnny Castle (Patrick Swayze).

Film junkies can relive it all thanks to Lake Lure Tours, which has hosted over 200,000 passengers since 1994. The tour will take you past several locations, point out shots, and share a few stories from the film. However, don't look for the Kellerman Hotel, which is actually the Mountain Lake Hotel in Pembroke, Virginia—but that's another book. All of the ballroom and dirty-dancing scenes with Johnny and the hotel staff were done in the gym of the old Camp Chimney Rock, which has unfortunately been claimed by fire. Part of the floor, however, was used in the lobby of the Esmeralda Inn (see pages 408-9).

But even though no buildings survive, the spirit of *Dirty Dancing* lives on.

Don't miss all the family-oriented attractions offered at Lake Lure. You'll have the time of your life.

CREDITS
Dirty Dancing (1987); *A Breed Apart* (1984); *Firestarter* (1984)

Western North Carolina Celebrities

Soap-opera diva Eileen Fulton was born in Asheville to a Methodist minister. After graduating from Greensboro College and performing in *The Lost Colony* (see pages 147-48), she headed for New York, where she originated the role of Lisa Miller in "As the World Turns" in 1960. Fulton briefly took the character to prime time in the 1960s and still pops up occasionally on the daytime drama. The multitalented entertainer also performs as a cabaret singer and has written six mystery novels.

The late Dr. Nina Simone was born Eunice Waymon in Tryon, North Carolina. A piano prodigy, she headed for New York's Juilliard School but was soon playing and singing in the city's jazz clubs. She took her new name from actress Simone Signoret. After recording a hit single of George Gershwin's "I Loves You, Porgy," Nina found herself a star. She went on to record and perform an eclectic blend of material and to contribute to numerous film soundtracks, including *The Thomas Crown Affair*, *Stealing Beauty*, and *The Crossing Guard*. She lived her later years in France and died in 2003.

Actress Andie MacDowell has relocated to Asheville, where her grandmother's house is now operated as the Blake House Inn (see pages 384-85), a cozy bed-and-breakfast inn.

Buffalo Bob Smith and Howdy Doody

Question: *"Hey, kids—What time is it?"*

With the dawn of television came a pioneer named Buffalo Bob Smith and his trusty sidekick, Howdy Doody, a freckle-faced marionette. Together, they created the wildly popular "Howdy Doody Show" and became pop-culture icons, ushering in several television firsts. "The Howdy Doody Show" was the first television variety show, the first children's show, the first show of the day on NBC-TV, the first show with live music, the first show to complete 1,000 and 2,000 broadcasts, and the first show to use split-screen images.

No one anticipated the impact television would have on pop culture. From 1947 to1960, "The Howdy Doody Show" produced 2,343 episodes and shaped the lives of today's "Howdy Doody alumni," a phrase Buffalo Bob coined for the generation otherwise known as baby boomers. In 1948, there was even a campaign to elect Howdy Doody president of the United States! Instead, he was proclaimed "president of all the kids."

In 1990, Buffalo Bob and wife Mildred retired to a golf community in Flat Rock. During his time in North Carolina, Buffalo Bob generously devoted his time and talents to charitable organizations, including Wilmington's Coastal Classic Celebrity Golf Tournament. In 1989, he was inducted into Disney World's Hall of Fame as one of the Ten Outstanding Legends of Television. He died in 1998.

In 2001, Howdy became part of the renowned Paul McPharlin Puppetry Collection at the Detroit Institute of Arts. Other permanent DIA residents include Punch and Judy and Jim Henson's Kermit the Frog.

Answer: *"It's Howdy Doody Time!"*

French Broad River

The French Broad River begins near Rosman in Transylvania County. A great way to experience it is via one of the outfitters that offer full-day and half-day rafting excursions. One of the most respected outfitters is the French Broad Rafting Company, located in Marshall; for information, call 800-570-RAFT or visit www.frenchbroadrafting.com.

Few waterways are more storied than the French Broad River. It's the third-oldest river in the world; only the Nile and New rivers are believed to be older. Named by English settlers because of its flow toward French-occupied land, the French Broad travels more than 200 miles northward from North Carolina into Tennessee. That's right—northward! And it's wider than the average mountain river, with low currents and gently sloping topography, all of which combine to create an ample flood plain. As the river flows northwest of Asheville through Pisgah National Forest toward Marshall, its waters become more intense, with steep gorges, narrow channels, and exciting rapids that are ideal for whitewater rafting.

Thanks to cinematographer Tim Orr, the David Gordon Green (see below) gem *All the Real Girls* boasts stunning footage of the mountains surrounding the ancient river near Marshall. In *A Good Baby*, there's a fight scene along the banks, and the bad guy, a sinister traveling salesman (David Strathairn), gets knocked into the river. Around Asheville, the French Broad flows a bit more serenely through Biltmore Estate. The replica of the White House in the James Garner/Jack Lemmon comedy *My Fellow Americans* was actually built along the river's edge.

CREDITS

All the Real Girls (2003); *My Fellow Americans* (1996); *A Good Baby* (2000)

David Gordon Green

The name David Gordon Green commands attention in the world of independent filmmaking. This 1998 graduate of the North Carolina School of the Arts first made headlines with his feature film *George Washington*. Filmed primarily in Winston-Salem and Spencer, North Carolina, the poignant film demonstrates the destructive nature of secrets, all told through the life and times of George, a special-needs youth. Though the film was not a major box-office draw, Roger Ebert named it one of his top ten picks for 2000, and critics across the board lauded its technical and artistic merits.

Skeptics thought Green's success was beginner's luck until he followed it with another North Carolina-made winner, *All the Real Girls*, which won a Special Jury Prize "for artistic merit and emotional truth" at the 2003 Sundance Film Festival. Fellow NCSA alum (class of '98) and Asheville native Paul Schneider stars in the film, which shot in Marshall, a mill town on the French Broad River north of Asheville. Green was drawn to Marshall's 1950s ambiance; there's nary a McDonald's or a Wal-Mart in sight. Adventurous film junkies can visit the diners, bowling alleys, and shops featured in *Girls* and maybe pick up a story from locals. Interestingly, Marshall also makes a brief appearance in *My Fellow Americans* as the small West Virginia mountain town where the characters played by Jack Lemmon and James Garner rent a vehicle.

Much of the credit for the look of Green's productions can be attributed to director of photography Tim Orr, another member of NCSA's illustrious class of '98.

Green appears to be on a track to stardom, thanks to his winning formula: Take a thought-provoking story, add simple dialogue, complex emotions, unusual locations, and a talented cinematographer and cast, and—voila!—you'll take home indie film awards. Stay tuned for Green's other projects, such as the film version of the Southern novel *A Confederacy of Dunces*, adapted by Steven Soderbergh.

Western Mountain Star Tracks

Harrah's Cherokee Casino and Hotel

777 Casino Drive, Cherokee (800-HARRAHS). Patrons must be age 21 or older.

Harrah's Cherokee Casino is not only *the* spot for gaming in western North Carolina, it's the best place around for catching a surprising number of major celebrities. Harrah's high-rise hotel features a Native American motif in its 250-plus rooms, five restaurants, conference center, and gift shop. There's also an indoor pool and, of course, all your favorite casino games. If the tables and machines aren't your thing (or you need a break), the 1,400-seat Cherokee Pavilion has state-of-the-art sound, lights, and projection screens and hosts such film, television, and music stars as Jay Leno, Bill Cosby, Charlie Daniels, Wayne Newton, Pat Boone, Wynonna, and many more.

Esmeralda Inn and Restaurant

U.S. 74A, Chimney Rock (828-625-9105; www. esmeraldainn.com). The inn is open from February through December.

The Esmeralda Inn is a charming historical landmark that started gathering its touch of Hollywood stardust in the earliest days. Built in 1890, the Esmeralda was a favorite of early film stars who liked to take in the clean mountain air and breathtaking scenery and to enjoy the slow pace of the charming community. Stars who visited the Esmeralda "back in the day" included Douglas Fairbanks, Clark Gable, and Mary Pickford. Lew Wallace finished the novel *Ben-Hur* at the Esmeralda in the 1890s. Film junkies may recall a movie or three made from that story. Several productions from the early days filmed at or near the inn, including *Heart of the Blue Ridge*, adapted from a novel by Tar Heel Waldron Baily.

The original inn was destroyed by fire in April 1997, but with the help of organizations and individuals, a detailed historic re-creation with thoroughly modern amenities was built in the same location. Film junkies should note the wooden floor in the lobby, taken from the gymnasium where parts of *Dirty Dancing* were filmed. Yes, Johnny Castle himself (Patrick Swayze) is rumored to have danced on this floor.

Q: Oscar®-winning actor Timothy Hutton made his directorial debut in what film shot in the North Carolina mountains?

A: *The 1998 film* Digging to China *features Kevin Bacon, Mary Stuart Masterson, and Raleigh native Evan Rachel Wood. It filmed several scenes at Mac's Indian Village in Cherokee.*

The Esmeralda has 14 rooms and spacious porches offering cool breezes and stunning mountain vistas. Its restaurant serves dinner Tuesday through Saturday; it also serves continental breakfast to guests of the inn.

CREDITS

Heart of the Blue Ridge (1915)

Community Theatres / Outdoor Dramas

Asheville Community Theatre

35 East Walnut Street, Asheville (828-254-1320; www.ashevilletheatre.org). Call for performance times.

One of Asheville's most enduring artistic endeavors has entertained audiences for over 50 years and has a unique connection to a legendary Hollywood star. In 1947, in only its second year of existence, the Asheville Community Theatre presented Tennessee Williams's *The Glass Menagerie* just after it closed its New York run. The production featured a young actor named Charlton Heston directing himself and his wife, Lydia Clarke. Heston served briefly as ACT's artistic director in the mid-'40s. He and Clarke rekindled the memories in August 1992, when they returned to ACT to star in *Love Letters*.

Future stars continue to perform in the beautiful downtown theatre.

Flat Rock Playhouse/ Carl Sandburg Home National Historic Site

The Flat Rock Playhouse is located at 2661 Greenville Highway in Flat Rock. For information, call 828-693-0403 or visit www.flatrockplayhouse.org. The Carl

Sandburg Home is located at 1928 Little River Road in Flat Rock. It is open daily from 9 A.M. to 5 P.M. except for Christmas. An admission fee is charged. For information, call 828-693-4178.

Flat Rock, just outside Asheville, has a rich theatrical history, as well as ties to one of the greatest American poets and writers.

The Flat Rock Playhouse is the State Theatre of North Carolina. Since the 1950s, it has presented professionally produced musicals, comedies, and dramas. The Vagabond Players, Flat Rock's resident company, includes performers with credits ranging from Broadway to feature films. Film junkies can catch performances from May through December.

Just across the street is the Carl Sandburg Home National Historic Site, the farm where the Pulitzer Prize-winning author lived for the last 22 years of his life. Free performances during the summer include *The World of Carl Sandburg, Rootabaga Stories*, and *Sandburg's Lincoln*. The latter was the basis for a memorable 1975 miniseries featuring an Emmy®-winning performance by Hal Holbrook in the title role. One of Sandburg's obscure writing ventures was as an uncredited screenwriter for the 1965 biblical epic *The Greatest Story Ever Told*, which featured . . . Charlton Heston as John the Baptist!

Horn in the West

The Daniel Boone Amphitheater is located just off U.S. 421, U.S. 321, and N.C. 105 in Boone. From June through August, performances are staged Tuesday through Sunday at 7:50 P.M. For information, call 888-825-6747 or visit www.horninthewest.com.

North Carolina is a hotbed of outdoor drama. Boone's *Horn in the West*, first staged in 1952, is the third-oldest such production in the country. This story of the nation's early settlers encompasses both fictional and historical characters, including Daniel Boone, the man for whom both the town and the amphitheater were named.

Several alumni of the play are familiar to film junkies, among them Barry Corbin, probably best known for his role on the CBS show "Northern Exposure" and more recently in The WB's "One Tree Hill," which films in Wilmington.

Unto These Hills

The theatre is located off N.C. 441 North in Cherokee. From June through August, performances are staged Monday through Saturday at 8:30 P.M. For information, call 866-554-4557 or visit www.untothesehills.com.

The proud and tragic story of the Cherokee Indians from 1540 to the Trail of Tears in 1838 is told in *Unto These Hills*, an outdoor drama performed in the town of Cherokee since 1950. Descendants of the historical characters in the play both perform and work behind the scenes at the 2,800-seat Mountainside Theatre.

Stars who got their feet wet in *Unto These Hills* include Academy Award® winner and UNC grad Louise Fletcher, Polly Holliday (Flo from the CBS series "Alice"), and Tarboro's Ben Jones (Cooter on the CBS series "The Dukes of Hazzard").

Tourism Contacts

State Tourism Contacts

North Carolina Association of Convention and Visitors Bureaus
(704-333-8445; http://visit.nc.org)

North Carolina Department of Transportation (919-733-2520;
www.ncdot.org)

North Carolina Division of Tourism, Film and Sports Development
(800-VISITNC; www.visitnc.com)

North Carolina Welcome Centers (www.nccommerce.com/tourism/
welcome)

Regional Tourism Contacts

Blue Ridge Mountain Host (800-807-3391; www.ncblueridge.com)

High Country Host (800-438-7500; www.highcountryhost.com)

North Carolina Coast Host (800-948-1099; www.coasthost-nc.com)

North Carolina's Northeast (888-872-8562; www.ncnortheast.com)

Partnership for the Sounds (252-796-1000; www.albemarle-nc.com/
pfs)

Piedmont Triad Visitor Center (800-388-9830)

Smoky Mountain Host (800-432-4678; www.visitsmokies.org)

Local Tourism Contacts
Coast

Cape Fear Coast Convention and Visitors Bureau (800-222-4757;
www.cape-fear.nc.us)

Clinton/Sampson County Chamber of Commerce (910-592-6177)

Columbus County Tourism Bureau (800-845-8419; www
.discovercolumbus.org)

Corolla/Currituck County Chamber of Commerce (252-453-9497;
www.currituckchamber.org)

Craven County Convention and Visitors Bureau (800-437-5767;
www.visitnewbern.com)

Crystal Coast Tourism Development Authority (800-786-6962;
www.sunnync.com)

Greater Topsail Chamber of Commerce (800-626-2780; www
.topsailcoc.com)

North Carolina's Brunswick Islands (800-795-7263; www
.ncbrunswick.com)
Onslow County Tourism (800-932-2144; www
.onslowcountytourism.com)
Outer Banks Convention and Visitors Bureau (800-446-6262;
www.outerbanks.org)
Pender County Tourism (888-576-4756; www.visitpender.com)
Southport/Oak Island Chamber of Commerce (910-457-6964)

Piedmont

Burlington/Alamance County Convention and Visitors Bureau (800-
637-3804; www.burlington-area-nc.org)
Cabarrus County Convention and Visitors Bureau (800-848-3740;
www.cabarruscvb.com)
Chapel Hill/Orange County Convention and Visitors Bureau (888-
968-2060; www.chocvb.org)
Charlotte Convention and Visitors Bureau (800-231-4636; www
.visitcharlotte.org)
Cleveland County Chamber of Commerce (800-480-8687; www
.clevelandcounty.com/tourism)
Durham Convention and Visitors Bureau (800-446-8604; www
.durham-nc.com)
Fayetteville Area Convention and Visitors Bureau (800-255-8217;
www.visitfayettevillenc.com)
Gaston County Department of Tourism (800-849-9994;
www.gastontourism.com)
Greater Mount Airy Chamber of Commerce (800-948-0949;
www.visitmayberry.com)
Greater Raleigh Convention and Visitors Bureau (800-849-8499;
www.visitraleigh.com)
Greensboro Area Convention and Visitors Bureau (800-344-2282;
www.visitgreensboro.com)
High Point Convention and Visitors Bureau (800-720-5255;
www.highpoint.org)
Johnston County Convention and Visitors Bureau (800-441-7829;
www.johnstonco-cvb.org)
Lake Norman Chamber of Commerce and Visitors Bureau (800-305-
2508; www.lakenorman.org)
Mooresville Convention and Visitors Bureau (877-661-1234;
www.racecityusa.org)
Pinehurst/Southern Pines/Aberdeen Area Convention and Visitors

Bureau (800-346-5362; www.homeofgolf.com)
Randolph County Tourism Development Authority (800-626-2672;
www.visitrandolph.org)
Rowan County Convention and Visitors Bureau (800-332-2343;
www.visitsalisburync.com)
Statesville Convention and Visitors Bureau (877-531-1819; www
.visitstatesville.org)
Union County Chamber of Commerce (704-289-4567; www
.unioncountycoc.com)
Winston-Salem Visitor Center and Convention and Visitors Bureau
(800-331-7018; www.visitwinstonsalem.com)

Mountains
Alleghany County Chamber of Commerce (800-372-5473;
www.sparta-nc.com)
Asheville Convention and Visitors Bureau (800-257-1300;
www.exploreasheville.com)
Avery County/Banner Elk Chamber of Commerce (800-972-2183;
www.banner-elk.com)
Black Mountain/Swannanoa Chamber of Commerce (800-669-2301;
www.exploreblackmountain.com)
Blowing Rock Chamber of Commerce (800-295-7851; www
.blowingrock.com)
Boone Convention and Visitors Bureau (800-852-9506; www
.visitboonenc.com)
Cherokee Welcome Center (800-438-1601; www.cherokee-nc.com)
Haywood County Tourism Development Authority (800-334-9036;
www.smokeymountains.net)
Jackson County Chamber of Commerce (800-962-1911; www
.mountainlovers.com)
Madison County Tourism Development Authority (877-262-3476;
www.madisoncounty-nc.com)
Rutherford County Tourism Development Authority (800-849-5998;
www.rutherfordtourism.com)

Appendix B
Film Commissions in North Carolina

State Film Commissions

North Carolina Film Commission
William Arnold, Director
301 North Wilmington Street
Mail Service Center 4317
Raleigh, N.C. 27699-4317
919-733-9900; www.ncfilm.com

Regional Film Offices

Charlotte Regional Film Office
Beth Petty, Director
1001 Morehead Square, Suite 200
Charlotte, N.C. 28203
704-347-8942; www.charlotteregion.com

Global Transpark
c/o North Carolina Film Commission
301 North Wilmington Street
Mail Service Center 4317
Raleigh, N.C. 27699-4317
919-733-9900; www.ncfilm.com

Northeast Regional Film Commission
Attention: Vann Rogerson
119 West Water Street
Edenton, N.C. 27932
252-482-4333; www.ncnortheast.com

Piedmont Triad Film Commission
Rebecca Clark, Director
7800 Airport Center Drive
Greensboro, N.C. 27409
336-393-0001; www.piedmonttriadnc.com

Research Triangle Partnership
c/o North Carolina Film Commission
301 North Wilmington Street
Mail Service Center 4317
Raleigh, N.C. 27699-4317
919-733-9900; www.ncfilm.com

Western North Carolina Regional Film Commission
c/o Advantage West
3 General Aviation Drive
Fletcher, N.C. 28732
828-687-7234; www.wncfilm.net

Wilmington Regional Film Commission
Johnny Griffin, Director
1223 North 23rd Street
Wilmington, N.C. 28405
910-343-3456; www.wilmington-film.com

Index